PLATONISM AND MYSTICAL THEOLOGY

The Spiritual Doctrine of St Gregory of Nyssa

Platonism and Mystical Theology

The Spiritual Doctrine of

St Gregory of Nyssa

JEAN DANIÉLOU

Edited by Rev. Ignatius Green

Translated by Anthony P. Gythiel and Michael Donley

ST VLADIMIR'S SEMINARY PRESS
YONKERS, NEW YORK
2022

Library of Congress Cataloging in Publication Data

Names: Daniélou, Jean, author. | Green, Ignatius, editor. | Gythiel, Anthony P., 1930-2014, translator. | Donley, Michael, 1940- translator. | Daniélou, Jean. Platonisme et théologie mystique.
Title: Platonism and mystical theology : the spiritual doctrine of St Gregory of Nyssa / Jean Daniélou ; edited by Rev. Ignatius Green ; translated by Anthony P. Gythiel and Michael Donley.
Other titles: Platonisme et théologie mystique. English
Description: Yonkers, New York : St Vladimir's Seminary Press, 2022. | Includes bibliographical references and index. | Summary: "In this seminal and classic work, Jean Daniélou examines the mystical theology of St Gregory of Nyssa and its relationship to non-Christian, especially Platonic, thought. He strikes a balanced view, asserting that Gregory's vision is fundamentally Christian, though he articulates himself in Platonic terminology and categories. In fact, Nyssen turns many classical Greek notions on their head, and posits a dynamic and inspiring vision of the spiritual life as an infinite pursuit of the infinite God. He articulates a vision of mystical theology that proved foundational for later thinkers and writers"-- Provided by publisher.
Identifiers: LCCN 2022051369 | ISBN 9780881417173 (paperback) | ISBN 9780881417180 (kindle edition)
Subjects: LCSH: Gregory, of Nyssa, Saint, approximately 335-approximately 394. | Mysticism--History--Early church, ca. 30-600.
Classification: LCC BR65.G76 D313 2022 | DDC 230/.14092--dc23/eng/20230124
LC record available at https://lccn.loc.gov/2022051369

COPYRIGHT © 2022 BY
ST VLADIMIR'S SEMINARY PRESS
575 Scarsdale Road, Yonkers, NY 10707
1-800-204-2665
www.svspress.com

ISBN 978-0-88141-717-3 (paper)
ISBN 978-0-88141-718-0 (electronic)

The views of the authors of St Vladimir's Seminary Press books do not necessarily reflect those of the seminary.

All Rights Reserved

In Memory of Anthony P. Gythiel

Translator translatus est

Αἰωνία σου ἡ μνήμη,
ἀξιομακάριστε καὶ ἀείμνηστε ἀδελφέ ἡμῶν

Table of Contents

Editor's Foreword ix

Introduction xv

PART ONE
The Light or Of Purification

1 Death and Resurrection 3
    The Three Ways 3
    The Mysticism of Baptism 11
    The Inner Man 26

2 The Structure of the Soul and the Passions 39
    The Image of God and the Garments of Skin 41
    The Winged Horses 57
    The Tyranny of the Passions 71

3 Paradise Regained 87
    The Struggle against Temptations 91
    The Life of Grace or *Apatheia* 97
    Familiarity with God or *Parrhēsia* 111

PART TWO
The Cloud or Of Contemplation

4 The Ladder of Love 129
    Contempt of the World 131
    Symbolic Theology 147

5 The City of Angels 161
    The Contemplation of Realities 164
    The Third Heaven 171
    The Vision of the Tabernacle 183

PART THREE
Darkness or On Love

6 The General Characteristics of the Third Way   201
    The Vocabulary of the Mysteries   205
    The Divine Darkness   221
    Eros and *Agapē*   232

7 Mystical Experience   245
    The Mirror of the Soul   247
    The Spiritual Senses   261
    The Indwelling of the Word   297

8 Ecstatic Love   307
    Going Out of Oneself   309
    Sober Drunkenness and Watchful Sleep   324
    The Wound of Love   336
    Epektasis   344

Conclusion   365

Abbreviations   373

Bibliography   375

Bibliography of St Gregory of Nyssa's Works in English   389

Indices   403
    General Index   403
    Index of Modern Authors   409
    Index of Greek Words   413

Editor's Foreword

Jean Daniélou, S. J. (1905–1974) was a world-renowned patristics scholar, theologian, and historian who proved profoundly influential in the movement to recover and study the Church Fathers in the mid-twentieth century. Along with other Catholic scholars like Henri de Lubac (under whom he studied) and Hans Urs von Balthasar, and their Orthodox contemporaries, Georges Florovsky, John Meyendorff, and Vladimir Lossky, this turn to the Fathers treated patristics not as a solely historical discipline in which the Fathers served as mere stepping stones to subsequent doctrinal development, but as important sources in their own right, able to help answer questions both timeless and timely.[1] This *ressourcement,* or "return to the sources," to the wellsprings of theology offered several promising opportunities, perhaps foremost a way to escape later theological dead ends or missteps (for Catholics, the narrowness of neo-Thomism; for the Orthodox, what Florovsky called "western captivity" and "pseudomorphosis"—the undue influence of western categories on Orthodox theology), along with the promise of a fundamental connection between faith and spiritual life that could speak persuasively to the existential ethos prevalent after the Second World War. Later scholars can and do question some of the specific conclusions of this earlier generation of patrologists. Attempting to approach the past with an eye to present concerns always entails the danger of distortion, of wresting texts from one context to another and seeking answers to questions that the Fathers were not posing, and of framing patristic arguments in ways their authors never would have (e.g., St Gregory would certainly have found it strange to regard *Contra Eunomium* as presenting a philosophy of language rather than a refutation of Eunomius' denial of the divinity of Christ). Though none of the scholars who participated in the return to the Fathers in the mid-twentieth century entirely avoided such tendencies, their writings remain influential and useful today.

[1] For a recent treatment of how and why three of these figures—Daniélou, von Balthasar, and Lossky—found St Gregory of Nyssa compelling in their particular context and useful for their theological projects, see Michel R. Barnes, "'Some Synchronic Moment': Gregory of Nyssa, *Théologie Mystique* and French *Ressourcement*," *Nova et Vetera* 18.2 (2020): 367–411.

This is a translation of Daniélou's first book. He defended his doctoral thesis in 1943 and published it in 1944 as *Platonisme et théologie mystique: doctrine spirituelle de Saint Grégoire de Nysse* (Paris: Aubier, 1944), releasing a slightly revised and expanded second edition in 1953. One year before Daniélou defended his thesis, von Balthasar wrote, "Only a very small number of initiates have read and are aware of Gregory of Nyssa, and they have jealously guarded their secrets. Scarcely a handful of studies ... have appeared on him.... [T]here are a few scattered references to him ... [but] from the critical point of view, the text of his works is the most neglected of the whole patristic era."[2] A very great deal has changed in the eight intervening decades. St Gregory of Nyssa is now one of the most studied Church Fathers. A vast proliferation of articles and monographs have been written by individual scholars, and several decades of conferences organized by the International Colloquium on Gregory of Nyssa resulted in a number of volumes focusing upon particular works and themes. Nearly all of Nyssen's works are available in English translation, and the pioneering work of Werner Jaeger has continued, producing fine critical editions of the original Greek in the Gregorii Nysseni Opera series.

Nevertheless, Daniélou's *Platonism and Mystical Theology* remains relevant.[3] Gregory can be hard to understand, with a large and complex body of writings. A selective reading of individual parts of that corpus can produce startlingly different conclusions, and this helps to explain the broad interest in his works: "Gregory can be read in many different ways ... he appeals to theologians of surprisingly diverse views from radical feminists to conservative evangelicals."[4] Caution must be urged. Reading a part at the expense of the whole distorts our perception of a text. Such a reading risks merely projecting the reader's values and concerns onto a very different pattern of thought, much like the nineteenth-century scholars who sought to discover the "historical Jesus," who ended up with

---

[2] Hans Urs von Balthasar, *Presence and Thought: An Essay on the Religious Philosophy of Gregory of Nyssa*, trans. Mark Sebanc (San Francisco: Ignatius Press, 1995 [French 1st ed. 1942]), 15.

[3] Orthodox readers will note some unfamiliar terminology and concepts, but this need not distract from the value of the text on the whole. While Daniélou and many of his contemporaries sought to return to the sources, he does still resort to certain ideas and expressions that are distinctively western and scholastic (e.g., prevenient grace, the state of grace, supernatural virtues, purgatory), and at times he refers to post-schism figures like Bernard of Clairvaux, Teresa of Avila, or John of the Cross. Nevertheless, Daniélou distinguishes St Gregory of Nyssa's views from later western ones (e.g., his articulation of the essence/energies distinction, his non-Augustinian view of the fall and of grace, his lack of a natural/supernatural dichotomy as it is understood in western theology).

[4] Morwenna Ludlow, *Gregory of Nyssa, Ancient and (Post)modern* (Oxford: Oxford University Press, 2007), 4.

a figure fashioned in their own image and likeness: "The Christ that Harnack sees, looking back through nineteen centuries of Catholic darkness, is only the reflection of a Liberal Protestant face, seen at the bottom of a deep well."[5] A broad reading can help to avoid such errors. For instance, we do well to remember that the same Gregory who makes certain observations about gender that might sound amenable to contemporary progressive trends is also the bishop who instituted canonical penances for sexual sins that are at times even stricter than his brother, St Basil (these cannot be dismissed as something inherited without further reflection; rather, in his letter to Letoius, Gregory articulates these penances within a nuanced vision of the soul's constitution, function, and healing); this makes him a poor patron saint for the sexual revolution of our confused and disordered age. Or, to take up the misreading Daniélou seeks to correct here, Gregory is a mystic but he is also, among other things, a polemicist, and if, in his spiritual writings, he sometimes echoes Plato or Plotinus, this cannot be marshalled as evidence that he was at heart a Platonist with a mere veneer of Christianity—this is hard to square with the large literary output and ecclesiastical activity that he devoted to articulating dogma and fighting heresy. Daniélou compellingly portrays a fuller and better-rounded picture of the bishop of Nyssa: Gregory is first and foremost a Christian, and his works, for all their borrowings and connections, cannot be properly understood apart from his fundamental commitment to faith and life in Christ. He does indeed use non-Christian authors and texts, or, as he put it, he does "plunder the Egyptians"—an image used in Origen's letter to St Gregory the Wonderworker over a century earlier—but he does so for a definite purpose: he plunders "the riches of reason ... for the adornment of the Church, the true tabernacle."[6] Gregory does (eclectically) use the concepts of Plato and other thinkers, but this cannot be misconstrued as a "Platonic deformation of Christianity"; Daniélou gives a rather striking example: Buddhist terminology could be substituted for the Platonist language in the Nyssene corpus without altering the foundation and the core, which is fully Christian: "With Gregory, the Platonic structure is incidental. The same basic ideas could be expressed by borrowing the framework, say, of Buddhist techniques. It would nonetheless be a Christian not a Buddhist mysticism" (pp. xx–xxi).

[5] George Tyrrell, *Christianity at the Crossroads* (New York: Longmans, Green and Co., 1909), 44.
[6] *De vita Moysis* 2.115–16; English translation: *Gregory of Nyssa: The Life of Moses*, trans. Abraham Malherbe and Everett Ferguson (Mahwah, NJ: Paulist Press, 1978), 81. For Origen's letter, see *St. Gregory Thaumaturgus: Life and Works*, trans. Michael Slusser, Fathers of the Church 98 (Washington, DC: The Catholic University of America Press, 1998), 189–92.

Once this crucial distinction is made, St Gregory's true contribution can be more clearly discerned. To take a single example, which Daniélou treats at the end of this study, the concept of *epektasis* demonstrates: 1) Gregory's use—and simultaneous transcendence—of Greek categories of thought by insisting upon the goodness of creaturely becoming; 2) a fundamental contribution to our understanding of God by asserting that God is infinite (again, a claim that Plato or Aristotle, or even earlier Christian thinkers like Origen, could not countenance—classical thought held that what was infinite, ἄπειρος [*apeiros*], was undefined and hence imperfect); 3) combining both of these notions, Gregory's dynamic and deeply scriptural vision of the spiritual life both here and in eternity as *epektasis*: an infinite and perpetual becoming—which constitutes creaturely perfection and beatitude—that ever more closely approaches and pursues the infinite God, ever reaching out, always being filled, and yet never being sated with the experience and the knowledge of God. It is a profound and beautiful vision, and Daniélou helps us to discern its outlines in the synthesis of Gregory's works that he presents here, and, in general, he helps the reader to appreciate both the uniqueness of Gregory's theological vision and spirituality while also stressing its continuity with the Christian past he inherited, and, if only briefly, to adumbrate its continuing influence on the later tradition.

A few words must be said about this edition. This is the last translation of Anthony Gythiel, of blessed memory, who began work on this project several years ago. He died before he was able to complete the editing process, and Michael Donley took up the mantle, preparing the text for publication, spending countless hours checking the manuscript against the French, and hunting through scores of books in the Bodleian Library to find both the original texts cited in several languages and English translations of them, when available.[7] I have added notes throughout the text to inform readers of more recent scholarship,[8] and I assembled a bibliography of English translations of the entire Nyssene

---

[7]Published English translations of texts were quoted whenever possible, especially for the Nyssene corpus. Citations use the standard abbreviated Latin titles of Nyssene texts, volume and column numbers from Migne's Patrologia Graeca, and the source of the English translation. PG numbers were retained (rather than updating references to correspond to the Gregorii Nysseni Opera) for several reasons: Daniélou used Migne, and if there is a difference between the PG and the GNO text, the former represents the text he is discussing here; PG column numbers remain a standard form of reference (though the GNO presents a better Greek text, many new translations still include both PG and GNO numbers); further, in the digital era, Migne's texts are universally available and free to access (especially online); finally, the GNO series includes the PG numbers in its margins, so the critical text can still be navigated using Migne references.

Editor's Foreword

corpus for those who are inspired to explore these texts further on their own (pp. 375–387). My hope is that in reading about St Gregory and in exploring his writings, the reader's goal will not be mere historical or theological knowledge, which is not an end in itself; rather, "knowledge becomes love,"[9] and love and desire for the Beloved know no end:

> This truly is the vision of God: never to be satisfied in the desire to see him. But one must always, by looking at what he can see, rekindle his desire to see more. Thus, no limit would interrupt growth in the ascent to God, since no limit to the Good can be found nor is the increasing of desire for the Good brought to an end because it is satisfied.[10]

—Rev. Ignatius Green
September 4, 2022
*Feast of Hieromartyr Babylas of Antioch
and the Holy Glorious Prophet and Godseer Moses*

---

[8] For those who want further information on Nyssene scholarship after Daniélou, though it is a little over a decade old, the most complete single source is *The Brill Dictionary of Gregory of Nyssa*, ed. Lucas Francisco Mateo-Seco and Giulio Maspero, trans. Seth Cherney, Supplements to Vigiliae Christianae 99 (Leiden: Brill, 2010). To get a sense of subsequent research and to examine the themes and concepts most closely related to the present book, the following entries are helpful: *Adyton*, Anthropology, *Apatheia*, *Aphtharsia*, *Apocatastasis*, *Apophatic Theology*, Aristotle, Baptism, Basil, *Beat*, Biography, Body, Darkness, Death, Desire, Divinization, *Cant*, Cavern, Christian Initiation, Confirmation, Contemporary Interpretations, Cross, *Eccl*, Energy, *Epektasis*, Eucharist, Evil, Glory, Good-Beauty, Gregory Palamas, Greek Mythology, Incorruptibility, Image, Infinity, Influence of Gregory, *Kinêsis*, Life, Light, Love, *Macr*, *Methorios*, *Metousia*, *Mimêsis* (the heading of the entry reads "Imitation," seemingly in error: the entry is found alphabetically in the M section, and the List of Entries [p. xvi] redirects "Imitation" to "*Mimêsis*"), Macarius, Monasticism, Mystery, Mysticism, Neo-Platonism, *Oikonomia*, *Op hom*, *Or cat*, *Or dom*, Origen, *Ousia*, Paradise, *Parrêsia*, Participation, Philo, *Phyrama*, *Physis*, Plato, Plotinus, Porphyry, Prayer, *Proairesis*, *Prof*, Psychology, Resurrection, Spiritual Theology, Sober Drunkenness, Stoicism, *Theologia*, *Theôria*, Tunics of Hide, Truth, *Virg*, Virginity, Virtue, *Vit Moys* (for narrower lists of thematic readings, see pp. 810–11).

[9] *De anima et resurrectione* (GNO 3/III:71.2; my translation).

[10] *Vit. Moys.* 2.238–39 (Malherbe, 116).

Introduction

The spiritual theology of Saint Gregory of Nyssa [c. 330–c. 395] has so far [1944] never been the subject of any overall, comprehensive study. Admittedly, there is no shortage of studies on specific themes. Among the most important, one might mention the pages devoted by Lewy to the doctrine of "sober inebriation";[1] those by Puech concerning darkness;[2] and those by Ziegler on the doctrine of the spiritual senses.[3] The problem of the immediate vision of the divine essence has, in particular, given rise to an entire literature.[4] Horn has made probing observations on the doctrine of mystical knowledge[5] and of mystical union.[6] Finally, Lieske has shown the importance of the theology of the Logos in Gregory's mysticism,[7] and Stiglmayr has studied the treatise entitled *On Virginity*.[8]

The existence of these various works of detail justifies us today in undertaking a comprehensive study, for only such an overall approach will enable us to clarify the meaning of the different parts. The pages that follow present no more than an outline of such a study. As this is a first exploration in an area that is often new, many of the suggested interpretations are presented as hypotheses, as a preliminary plan that might allow us to find our bearings in a work that is very

---

[1] H. Lewy, *Sobria ebrietas* (Giessen: Alfred Töppelmann, 1929), 132–39.
[2] H.-Ch. Puech, "La ténèbre mystique chez le Pseudo-Denys l'Aréopagite et dans la tradition patristique," *Études Carmélitaines* 23 (1938): 33–53, at 49–52.
[3] J. Ziegler, *Dulcedo Dei* (Münster: Aschendorff, 1937), 58–67.
[4] H. Koch, "Das mystische Schauen beim hl. Gregor von Nyssa," *Theologische Quartalschrift* 80 (1898): 397–420; F. Diekamp, *Die Gotteslehre des heiligen Gregor von Nyssa* (Münster: Aschendorff, 1896), 90–101; E. von Ivánka, "Vom Platonismus zur Theorie der Mystik (Zur Erkenntnislehre Gregors von Nyssa)," *Scholastik* 11 (1936): 163–95; J. Maréchal, *Étude sur la psychologie des mystiques*, tome II (Bruxelles/Paris: L'Édition universelle/Desclée de Brouwer, 1937), 101–115.
[5] G. Horn, "Le 'miroir' et la 'nuée,' deux manières de voir Dieu d'après Saint Grégoire de Nysse," *Revue d'Ascétique et de Mystique* 8 (1927): 113–31.
[6] G. Horn, "L'amour divin. Note sur le mot 'Eros' dans Saint Grégoire de Nysse," *Revue d'Ascétique et de Mystique* 6 (1925): 378–89.
[7] A. Lieske, "Zur Theologie der Christusmystik Gregors von Nyssa," *Scholastik* 14 (1939): 485–514.
[8] J. Stiglmayr, "Die Schrift des hl. Gregor von Nyssa 'Über die Jungfräulichkeit,'" *Zeitschrift für Ascese und Mystik* 2 (1927): 334–59.

rich but also very diffuse, and in which the literary notions of the author—who is more concerned with the aesthetics of composition than with logic—often make a precise definition of the subjects addressed more difficult. Analogous works by Völker on Origen[9] and on Philo[10] have been a help in this study, for they describe a type of spirituality on which our author is dependent. Nevertheless, in interpreting Gregory, I have also had to be wary of allowing myself to be overly influenced by his predecessors.

I

Two factors determined my choice of subject. First, there is the outstanding importance of the mystical works of the Bishop of Nyssa in themselves. To begin with, it is noteworthy that they reflect his personal experience and it is not without reason that George of Pisidia described him as being μυστικώτατος (*mystikōtatos*, the most mystical).[11] Gregory was born into an environment permeated by Christianity: his grandmother, Macrina the Elder; his mother, Emmelia; his older sister, Macrina the Younger; and two of his brothers, Basil and Peter of Sebaste [and, in Orthodox tradition, Naucratius—*Ed.*]; are all saints. After a pious youth, he underwent a serious crisis during which he abandoned the church career in which he had taken the first steps—he was a reader—got married and devoted himself to rhetoric. But under the influence of his older brother and Gregory of Nazianzus [see his Letter 11]—a friend of Basil and himself—he renounced the world. He may have led a monastic life for some time. In 372 he became bishop of Nyssa and played an important role from 381 to 385.

Yet it was to the contemplative life that he inclined, and his writings testify that he rose to great heights. In fact, we can follow this progression by consulting his texts chronologically, starting with the first—*On Virginity*, among others—which are earlier than 379, and then proceeding to *The Life of Moses* and the *Homilies on the Song of Songs*. Little by little, we see the love of God grow in his soul till at the end of his life it wrests from him cries similar to those of a St Teresa. Of all the Greek Fathers he is the greatest mystical theologian. If Dionysius the Pseudo-Areopagite has had greater influence, it is because his writings were, if not more readily understood, certainly less numerous and more

---

[9]W. Völker, *Das Vollkommenheitsideal des Origenes* (Tübingen: Mohr, 1931).
[10]W. Völker, *Fortschritt und Vollendung bei Philo von Alexandrien* (Leipzig: Hinrichs Verlag, 1938).
[11]PG 92:1649A. [Throughout the text, Greek words are given first in the Greek alphabet and then transliterated. English translations of these terms have been added after the transliterated Greek.—*Ed.*]

Introduction

available. But, as we have pointed out, Gregory's texts reflect an experience that is more authentic.[12]

Second, what makes Gregory more interesting and more important is that, by a rare stroke of fortune, this mystic is also a thinker—and one of the most eminent in Christian antiquity, though his philosophical works had not received the attention they deserve until von Balthasar's book, *Présence et pensée*, filled this gap.[13] Gregory's philosophical culture provided him, first of all, with a framework of thought that served him well in expressing his own mystical experience. Admittedly, it also created a very delicate problem of interpretation, one to which I shall return when dealing with the method followed in this work. On the other hand, his theological culture enabled him to link his mysticism to dogma—namely, to the concept that the Logos deifies the soul through sacramental life. It is a doctrine that will remain characteristic of the Greek East, one that we shall find again in Nicholas Cabasilas.[14]

Thus Gregory's writings are full of interest in themselves. Moreover, they have the advantage of having been written at a crossroads in the development of theological thought, thereby giving us an insight into mystical theology's historical development. Indeed, Gregory inherits an entire tradition that, through Clement of Alexandria and Origen, had begun to work out a theology that was mystical and at the same time dogmatic: the key terms ἀπάθεια (*apatheia*, dispassion),[15] θεωρία (*theōria*, contemplation) and ἔκστασις (*ekstasis*, ecstasy) are already found in these authors. Despite the divergent meanings to which these concepts give rise, Gregory managed to retain their richness while making the necessary clarifications. For this reason, he can be credited as being the founder of mystical theology.

The fourth century was a time when, after the warning sign of Arianism, Christian thought organized itself and became aware of its own structure. It

---

[12]Puech, "La ténèbre mystique," 53.

[13]Hans Urs von Balthasar, *Présence et pensée. Étude sur la philosophie religieuse de Grégoire de Nysse* (Paris: Beauchesne, 1942). [In English, *Presence and Thought: An Essay on the Religious Philosophy of Gregory of Nyssa*, Marc Sebanc, trans. (San Francisco, CA: Ignatius Press, 1995).—*Ed.*]

[14]On Gregory's life and work, see J. Daniélou, "Gregorio Nisseno," *Enciclopedia Cattolica* 6 (Vatican City, 1951): cols. 1096–111. [St Nicholas Cabasilas, a fourteenth century writer and a prominent figure in the hesychastic movement, expressed his vision of the spiritual life grounded in the sacraments in *The Life in Christ*. Nicholas Cabasilas, *The Life in Christ*, trans. Carmino J. De Catanzaro (Crestwood, NY: St Vladimir's Seminary Press, 1974).—*Ed.*]

[15][This is how the word will normally be translated, following the precedent set in the English version of *The Philokalia*. However, other renderings—e.g. impassibility—in quotations from published translations of Gregory will be retained.—*Trans.*]

was then that work was being done in dogmatic theology, with the dogmas of the Trinity, the incarnation, and the divinity of the Holy Spirit being defined in opposition to Arius, Apollinarius of Laodicea, and the Macedonians. In the field of mysticism, we witness a similar phenomenon. Eunomianism had pushed the intellectualism of Origen to extremes—as had Arianism with its own theory of the Logos—and had posited that knowledge of the divine οὐσία (*ousia*, essence) and the ἀγέννητος (*agennētos*, unbegotten), identified as the Father, was accessible to the intelligence. This endangered the whole of mystical theology. Gregory's achievement on the doctrinal level is to have established definitively that the divine οὐσία is inaccessible to speculative theology and that the knowledge we have of God, other than that gained by reason, is the fruit of his presence in us by grace. And it is this that is the proper domain of the mystical life.

Consequently, Gregory is a very important source. His influence on Pseudo-Dionysius, for example, is becoming increasingly evident. Without going so far as Pera,[16] who links Dionysius directly to the Cappadocian school, his reliance on Gregory does seem certain. Puech has demonstrated that this is the case for his interpretation of darkness. But the treatises *On the Divine Names* and the two *Hierarchies* also have their beginnings in the works of Gregory. Through Dionysius and St Maximus the Confessor, Gregory's influence in the East—but also in the West—would prove to be immense. Evagrius does not represent the same tradition and his intellectualism conflicts with Gregory's teaching concerning the primacy of ἀγάπη (*agapē*, love). Hausherr has shown that he intentionally brushes aside the Gregorian interpretation of darkness, which does, however, prove that he knew of it.[17]

To cite all the evidence the Eastern Church provides regarding the influence of Gregory in the field of mysticism would take too long. Of more interest to us is the effect he had in the West. We know that several treatises were translated by Scotus Eriugena. Later, he seems to have had a significant influence on the mystical renaissance of the twelfth century, especially on St Bernard. There is the same taste for things divine, the same disengagement from life here below. It is only the two cultures with their own specific flavor—that of the Byzantine

---

[16]C. Pera, "Denys le Mystique et la Theomachia," *Revue des Sciences Philosophiques et Théologiques* 25 (1936): 5–75. [For more recent research on the connection between the Corpus Dionysiacum and Gregory of Nyssa, see Michael Motia, "Dionysius and Gregory of Nyssa," *The Oxford Handbook of Dionysius the Areopagite*, ed. Mark Edwards, Dimitrios Pallis, and Georgios Steiris (Oxford University Press, 2022), 109–121.—*Ed.*]

[17]I. Hausherr, "Ignorance infinie," *Orientalia Christiana Periodica* 2 (1936): 351–62, at 359.

Introduction   xix

bishop of Cappadocia and that of the Burgundian monk—that are different. But the history of this influence remains to be written.[18] As things stand, we are able to discern certain common features, though not the details of the connections between the two men. However, research in this area would certainly yield considerable results.

II

Having explained the interest and importance of the subject matter of this book, it remains for us to specify the method we have followed. On first reading the works of Gregory of Nyssa, we were struck above all by the considerable number of terms borrowed from the language of Plato, Philo, and Plotinus. A more in-depth reading, however, led us to discover under this veneer an experience and a doctrine that are authentically Christian. Indeed, how could it have been otherwise with this monk who had left everything to follow Christ, with this bishop who was a champion of orthodoxy? This convinced us that it was important above all else to probe the depths of Gregory's thought, to become thoroughly familiar with it, and to reconstruct it from within. Indeed, for want of having done precisely this, many critics speak of the "Platonism" of the Fathers without taking the trouble of seeing beyond this literary veneer to the experience contained within.

The more we became acquainted with Gregory's writings, the more we realized that the terms he borrowed from the thought of antiquity all acquired a completely different meaning. For example, ἀπάθεια (*apatheia*, dispassion) is in no way related to the Stoic idea of detachment from what does not "depend" on us; it is supernatural life itself, which flows into the soul from God—the true ἀπαθής (*apathēs*, impassible one)—imparting divine life, which in turn protects the soul from sensory disturbances. Again, θεωρία (*theōria*) is not the contemplation of eternal ideas and a return to the intelligible world through internalization; it is a restoration wrought by Christ in the world of spiritual creatures and a contemplation of the mystery of salvation.

Two other examples related to the mystical life are of particular importance. The first concerns the knowledge of God gained by the soul that purifies itself

---

[18]See Étienne Gilson, *La théologie mystique de saint Bernard* (Paris: Vrin, 1934), 29–30. [*The Mystical Theology of Saint Bernard*, trans. A. H. C. Downes (London/New York: Sheed & Ward, 1940), 17f, and endnote 8 (p. 217). The note is an admirable page-long summary of Gregory's teaching that Daniélou must have found invaluable.—*Trans.*]. Jean-Marie Déchanet, *Aux sources de la spiritualité de Guillaume de Saint-Thierry* (Bruges: Beyaert, 1940), 25ff.

of all that is alien. Such κάθαρσις (*katharsis*, purification) allows the soul to find God within itself. In Platonic language this has a clearly defined meaning: the soul is divine by nature and it is only the bodily covering that prevents it from perceiving its true essence. Let the soul cleanse itself of this mud, and the divine beauty will shine in it once more. All these expressions are found in Gregory. Shall we then say that for him the mystical life consists in an effort of internalization through which the soul rediscovers its pure essence? This is what Plotinus, or Spinoza, would claim. However, while he uses the same words, Gregory's doctrine is nonetheless different. For him, the image of God is divine life, which is a gift of grace. To perceive God within itself, the soul must first rediscover his image, by detaching itself from sin and uniting itself to Christ. Only then will it be able to perceive this life of God within itself, which is not its own essence but a free gift from God.

The second example concerns darkness (γνόφος, *gnophos*). And here we shall refer not to Plato but Philo, for whom the entry of Moses into the darkness signifies the quest of the soul that is seeking the formless Being.[19] It is a quest that involves the relinquishing of all images. Yet this is an element of any mysticism, whether natural or divine, and does not go beyond the philosophical plane of wisdom. Gregory does sometimes use the word in this sense but, more especially, for him darkness signifies the positive reality of an excess of divine light. We must no longer think in terms of a material element that acts as a screen between God and the soul. God remains in darkness, even for the angels. What becomes apparent here is the absolute transcendence of God; and it is this that throws the soul that seeks him into ecstasy.

After examining all of Gregory's writings, we became convinced, then, that there was no need to investigate his thought with a view simply to detecting what the Platonic elements might be, but rather that we had to accustom ourselves to a way of thinking that was wholly Christian, though it had borrowed its forms of expression from the philosophical language of the time in which it was developed. This is also the conclusion Endre von Ivánka reaches at the end of his remarkable article, "From Platonism to the Theory of Mysticism,"[20] and our own study of Gregory has fully convinced us of the correctness of his opinion. With Gregory, the Platonic structure is incidental. The same basic ideas

---

[19] For more on the relationship between Gregory's *Life of Moses* and Philo's exegesis, see Albert C. Geljon, *Philonic Exegesis in Gregory of Nyssa's De Vita Moysis* (Providence, RI: Brown Judaic Studies, 2002).—Ed.

[20] Von Ivánka, "Vom Platonismus."

Introduction

could be expressed by borrowing the framework, say, of Buddhist techniques. It would nonetheless be a Christian not a Buddhist mysticism. In this respect, although the studies of Arnou[21] and Festugière[22] contain valuable information, the impression they create of a Platonic deformation of Christianity in the Fathers is altogether questionable in my view.

And so the approach we should adopt became clear. We have presented the thought of Gregory in its own right, in its original structure, such as we have understood it to be. We have also noted any similarities of expression with Greek authors, for these can contribute much to an understanding of the text. For example, the use of μετεωροπορεῖν (*meteōroporein*, to travel through the air, to levitate) in order to designate contemplation makes perfect sense if one refers to the myth of *Phaedrus*, even though the content is entirely different. One can say, in short, that Gregory has allegorized everything, even philosophy. Along with the Bible, Platonic language—especially that of the myths—offers him a wealth of telling turns of phrase that would speak to his audience and which enable him to describe the single mystery that preoccupies him: the transfiguration of the soul in Jesus Christ.

III

The order followed in our exposition is that of the various stages of the spiritual life. Since these are linked to each other and overlap, however, this has the disadvantage that we risk having to repeat ourselves. For example, the notion of a return to paradise may pertain either to Baptism,[23] ἀπάθεια (*apatheia*, dispassion),[24] θεωρία (*theōria*, contemplation),[25] or ἔκστασις (*ekstasis*, ecstasy), being "snatched away from this world."[26] Again, at each stage it is possible to say that the image of God has been restored, if one looks backwards, but that it has not been, if one considers the ground that remains to be covered. To counteract this difficulty, we decided to treat each theme thoroughly at that stage of the spiritual life where it is predominant. For example, it is clear that the process of

---

[21] R. Arnou, "Platonisme des Pères," *Dictionnaire de Théologie catholique* 12 (Paris: Letouzey et Ané, 1935): col. 2310ff.

[22] A.-J. Festugière, *L'enfant d'Agrigente* (Paris: Éditions du Cerf, 1941), 119–46.

[23] *Adversus eos qui differunt baptismum* (PG 46:417D).

[24] *In Canticum Canticorum* (Cant.), Homily 1 (PG 44:773A).

[25] *Cant.* 1 (PG 44:777A; Norris, 29).

[26] *De Virginitate* (*Virg.*) 13 (PG 46:376C). Translation from *St Gregory of Nyssa: Ascetical Works*, trans. Virginia Woods Callahan, Fathers of the Church 58 (Washington, DC: Catholic University of America Press, 1967), 47.

purification, even if continued to the summit of the mystical ascent, predominates above all in the first of what we have termed the "three ways." It is evident too that *contemplation*, although practiced until the end of the spiritual journey, is especially characteristic of the second way, where it makes its appearance. And *union*, while already granted at Baptism, corresponds above all to the mystical life proper, where it is consummated.

On the other hand, this method of proceeding has the advantage of enabling us to embrace the evolutionary movement of Gregory's thought—and this is especially important since its principal insight concerns movement itself, being entirely dominated as it is by the concept of progress. In order to describe these various stages, we have freed ourselves as much as possible from later systems in an attempt to identify Gregory's own thought. Several surprises were in store for us, but these had more to do with expression than substance. The most notable innovation—and it is a considerable one—is the importance attached to ecstatic love, above and beyond contemplation. And so we have made a special point of enlarging on this in the relevant part of our study, the final one.

The titles of the various parts are borrowed from Gregory himself. They correspond to the three major stages in the life of Moses, which is the prototype of the ascent to God. The first part—Light (Illumination)—corresponds to the scene of the Burning Bush and marks the entry into the spiritual life by knowledge of and esteem for spiritual goods. It has rightly been called the way of purification. The second part—the Cloud—corresponds to the crossing of the desert and describes disengagement from human things and a drawing closer to things divine. It corresponds in particular to the intellectual life and culminates in θεωρία (*theōria*, contemplation), as the first way had culminated in ἀπάθεια (*apatheia*, dispassion). The Darkness that Moses entered on Mt Sinai provides the title of the final part and represents the mystical way, the full flowering of the life of faith that began with θεωρία. This is properly the sequence of the mystical life.

If one compares this to the three ways of Origen—practice of the virtues, natural contemplation (i.e., of nature and creation), and theology (i.e., contemplation of God)—one notices that there is a considerable difference. For Gregory, natural contemplation and theology together form the second way. Moreover, his third way depicts a new category, where he introduces something we do not find in Origen: knowledge in darkness, which is the fruit of union. Now it is such knowledge that can properly be called mystical knowledge, a "sense of presence."

Introduction

It is not a question of knowing whether or not Origen experienced this himself. But what is certain is that, enlightened by the errors of Eunomius, Gregory has delineated more clearly mystical knowledge's proper domain, and it is for this reason that one can truly say that he is its founder. The *Mystical Theology* of Dionysius will be merely an exposition of Gregory's ideas.

IV

For this study, we have consulted all of Gregory's writings.[27] Nevertheless, we have made use above all of the treatises that specifically relate to questions of spirituality, especially *The Life of Moses* (whose subtitle is *Concerning Perfection in Virtue*).[28] It charts the stages of the spiritual life from its origins to the mystical life proper, and has as its central theme the thesis that perfection consists in progress itself. This is the only complete treatise Gregory has left us. Then there are the commentaries on the Wisdom books, of which Proverbs, Ecclesiastes, and the Song of Songs were together to have formed a complete treatise. Unfortunately, it seems that Gregory did not write a commentary on Proverbs. We can assume this to be the case, aside from the absence of any trace of such a text, from the rather long summary he gives of it in the Prologue to the *Homilies on the Song of Songs*, whereas, conversely, he makes only a passing allusion to Ecclesiastes, on which he did write homilies.

These *Homilies on Ecclesiastes*[29] relate to the second way—the Cloud—and is the main source for its study. In it, Gregory teaches a disdain for the things of this world, and an esteem of things eternal, which is the proper subject of this second way. The *Homilies on the Song of Songs* follow on from it and constitute the second of Gregory's two major works,[30] the other being *The Life of Moses*,

---

[27] In this section, the following information has been provided in footnotes to aid readers: the Latin titles of Nyssene works and their abbreviated forms by which they are commonly cited, their place in the Patrologia Graeca and Gregorii Nysseni Opera series, and the translation used in this volume. For more on the Nyssene corpus in English, see the bibliography on pages 389–402..—*Ed.*

[28] *De vita Moysis* (*Vit. Moys.*); Greek text: PG 44:297–429 and GNO VII/1; English translation: *Gregory of Nyssa: The Life of Moses*, trans. Abraham Malherbe and Everett Ferguson, Classics of Western Spirituality (Mahwah, NJ: Paulist Press, 1978).—*Ed.*

[29] *In Ecclesiasten homiliae* (*Eccl.*); Greek text: PG 44:616–753 and GNO V:277–442; English translation: *Gregory of Nyssa: Homilies on Ecclesiastes, An English Version with Supporting Studies, Proceedings of the Seventh International Colloquium on Gregory of Nyssa (St Andrews, 5–10 September 1990)*, ed. Stuart George Hall (Berlin: Walter de Gruyter, 1993).—*Ed.*

[30] *In Canticum canticorum* (*Cant.*); Greek text: PG 44:756–1120 and GNO VI; English translation: *Gregory of Nyssa: Homilies on the Song of Songs*, trans. R. A. Norris, Jr (Atlanta, GA: Society of Biblical Literature, 2012) (this is a bilingual edition; the English is always on odd-numbered pages).—*Ed.*

mentioned above. The influence of these homilies has been greater than that of Origen's commentary on the same book, to which it alludes expressly and which it intentionally completes. Here, Gregory expounds the way of union (ἀνάκρασις, *anakrasis*)[31] and describes the stages of the approach of the Word, who is perceived by the soul first as a light fragrance, then as a sound, and then savored as food. The concluding homilies describe the intense longing (ἔρως, *erōs*) that renders the soul impatient of everything that separates it from God.

We also have a commentary on the Psalms, in two books.[32] The first deals with the titles of the Psalms and contains much information about the spiritual life. The second shows how the order of the Psalms corresponds to the stages of the spiritual life, though it unfortunately ends with Psalm 58. Mainly it contains information relating to the Cloud, to the extent that this commentary should be grouped with the homilies on Ecclesiastes, as describing the second way. To this is also related an account of the itinerary of Abraham. It can be found in *Against Eunomius*,[33] and is of the greatest interest, since it describes the successive stages of the soul as it ascends to the life of pure faith.

To these biblical commentaries on the Old Testament, we should add two groups of homilies on passages from the New, since these are also relevant to our topic. They are the homilies on the Lord's Prayer—very important for the study of prayer itself and of the παρρησία (*parrhēsia*, boldness of speech) of which it is the expression—and the homilies on the Beatitudes, of which one should single out the sixth ("Blessed are the pure in heart"), as this is a key text for understanding Gregory's teaching concerning mystical knowledge.[34] It is here, developed

---

[31]The same term was used by St Gregory Palamas nearly a millennium later: "The term that is used to describe this union is ἀνάκρασις [in Palamas, *Against Acindynus* 2.9.28 and 5.4.11], a term not easily translatable into English—we might say *commixture*, if we take into account that the meaning of the Greek word is that the elements commixed remain unconfused, although they indwell in each other; Palamas understands the deifying participation precisely as ἀνάκρασις." Nikolaos Loudovikos, "Striving for Participation: Palamite Analogy as Dialogical Syn-energy and Thomist Analogy as Emanational Similitude," in *Divine Essence and Divine Energies: Ecumenical Reflections on the Presence of God in Eastern Orthodoxy*, ed. C. Athanasopoulos and Christoph Schneider (Cambridge: James Clarke & Co, 2013), 129.—Ed.

[32]*In inscriptiones Psalmorum* (*Inscr.*); Greek text: PG 44:432–608 and GNO V:24–175; English translation: Gregory of Nyssa, *On the Inscriptions of the Psalms*, trans. R. E. Heine (Oxford: Clarendon Press, 1995).—Ed.

[33]*Eun.* 2.88–89 (PG 45:940A–D; NPNF² 5:259).

[34]*De oratione dominica* (*Or. dom.*); Greek text: PG 44:1120–93 and GNO VII/2:1–74; *De beatitudinibus* (*Beat.*); Greek text: PG 46:788–817 and GNO VII/2:75–170; English translation: *St. Gregory of*

at length, that we find the idea of the soul as a "mirror" and the contention that he who enters into himself can have knowledge of the divinity—whose essence is nonetheless inaccessible—of which he can otherwise know only the attributes as they are manifested in the external world.

Finally, among the exegetical writings we find information relevant to our purpose in the group of commentaries relating to Genesis. This group includes the *Hexaemeron*,[35] which is intended to complete that of Basil, tackling the most difficult questions. Then there is the treatise *On the Making of Man*,[36] which is a continuation of Basil's *Hexaemeron* and contains important doctrinal details concerning the image of God in the soul. Then there are two homilies on the words, "Let us make man in our image and likeness."[37] Their authenticity has been questioned by Holl and Bardenhewer, who give as the main reason the distinction made between εἰκών (*eikōn*, image) and ὁμοίωσις (*homoiōsis*, likeness), which is not found elsewhere in Gregory, though it is frequent in other authors. But, Endre von Ivánka has recently taken up the question again with arguments that appear to strongly favor authenticity. In his opinion, both homilies constitute an oral supplement to Basil's *Hexaemeron* delivered to the community in Caesarea, whereas the text *On the Making of Man* is its sequel, in the form of a treatise.[38] Yet this line of argument has been authoritatively criticized by Giet and we must conclude that these two homilies are indeed inauthentic.[39]

Nyssa: *The Lord's Prayer; The Beatitudes*, trans. Hilda C. Graef, Ancient Christian Writers 18 (Mahwah, NJ: Paulist Press, 1954).—*Ed.*

[35] *Apologia in Hexaemeron* (*Hex.*); Greek text: PG 44:61–124 and GNO IV/1; English translation: *On the Six Days of Creation*, trans. Robin Orton, The Fathers of the Church: Shorter Works 1 (Washington, DC: The Catholic University of America Press, 2021).—*Ed.*

[36] *De hominis opificio* (*Op. hom.*); Greek text: PG 44:125–256 and GNO IV/2; English translation: NPNF² 5:387–427.—*Ed*

[37] *Sermones de creatione hominis* (*Creat. I, II*); Greek text: PG 44:257–77, 277–97 and GNO Suppl. I:2–40, 41–72; English translation: St Basil the Great, *On the Human Condition*, trans. Nonna Verna Harrison, Popular Patristics Series 30 (Crestwood, NY: St Vladimir's Seminary Press, 2005), 31–64.—*Ed.*

[38] E. von Ivánka, "Die Autorschaft der Homilien Εἰς τὸ Ποιήσωμεν ἄνθρωπον κατ' εἰκόνα ἡμετέραν καὶ ὁμοίωσιν," *Byzantinische Zeitschrift* 36.1 (January 1936): 46–57.

[39] S. Giet, "Saint Basile a-t-il donné une suite aux homélies de l'Hexaeméron?" *Recherches de Science Religieuse* 33 (1946): 317–359. [Scholars tend to attribute these two sermons to Basil the Great (as do most of the manuscripts), especially since they distinguish between the image and likeness, a distinction not found anywhere else in the Nyssene corpus; further, the sermons contain parallels with undoubted works of Basil (though their rough style is unlike either of the brothers' other works). The GNO supplement volume containing these texts is entitled: "of uncertain authors" (*auctorum incertorum*); for discussions of authorship see *Basile de Césarée: Sur l'origine de l'homme*, trans. and ed. Alexis Smets and Michel van Esbroeck, Sources chrétiennes 160 (Paris: Cerf, 1970), 13–126; Emmanuel Amand de Mendieta, "Les deux homélies sur la creation de l'homme que les manuscrits attribuent à Basile de Césarée ou à Grégoire

In addition to his exegetical writings, Gregory composed several ascetical treatises. The first in date as in importance is *On Virginity*.[40] This was intended for the monks gathered by Basil at Annesi and sings the praises of virginity as a return to man's true nature and a prerequisite for contemplation and the ascent toward God.[41] It is one of the texts where Plotinian influences are assimilated the least, which would seem to place it among his early works, as would the fact that negative mysticism nowhere features in it. Admittedly, this is also true of the *Sixth Homily on the Beatitudes*, which dates from the end of Gregory's life. Yet this was intended for a wider public. Gregory also wrote shorter works such as the treatises *On Perfection* and *On What It Means to Call Oneself a Christian*.[42] These are interesting because of the way they reveal the Christocentrism of Gregory's spirituality.

The authenticity of the *Hypotyposis*[43] has been contested and we shall refrain from using it, although Jaeger claims it afresh for Gregory in his new edition.

---

de Nysse: Le problème de leur redaction," in *Zetesis: Album amicorum*, Festschrift for E. de Strycker (Antwerp and Utrecht: Nederlandsche Boekhandel, 1973); PPS 30:14–15.—*Ed.*]

[40] *De virginitate* (*Virg.*); Greek text: PG 46:317–416 and GNO VIII/1:247–343; English translation: *On Virginity*, in *St. Gregory of Nyssa: Ascetical Works*, trans. Virginia Woods Callahan. Fathers of the Church 58 (Washington, DC: The Catholic University of America Press, 1967), 1–75.—*Ed.*

[41] This must be compared with Gregory's description of Moses as a married mystic, whom he compares to Gregory the Wonderworker, a virgin mystic. Both are capable of theophany: "Both left this agitated and beset life, Moses and Gregory each in his own time going off by himself, until to each the reward of the pure life was manifested by a theophany. But it is said that Moses had a wife along with philosophy, while Gregory made virtue his only consort." Nevertheless, the Wonderworker's virginity is portrayed as superior: "So although they both had the same aim, for each of them departed from the crowd with the purpose of penetrating the divine mysteries with the pure eye of the soul, someone who knows how to size up virtue is entitled to judge which of them was marked more by the passionless life: the one who stooped to the legitimate and permissible participation in pleasures, or the one who transcended even that and gave no opening into his life to material attachment." *De vita Gregorii Thaumaturgi* 25; translation in *St. Gregory Thaumaturgus: Life and Works*, trans. Michael Slusser, The Fathers of the Church 98 (Washington, DC: The Catholic University of America Press, 1998), 51.—*Ed.*

St Gregory's views on sexuality and gender have excited a great deal of research and speculation among contemporary scholars. Based on close re-readings and deconstructions of specific texts, Mark Hart, John Behr, and Rowan Williams argue that, contrary to appearances, Nyssen held marriage to be higher than virginity, while Elizabeth Clark and Virginia Burrus claim that St Gregory de-emphasized male/female sexual differentiation. All these claims have been contested and evaluated by other scholars, e.g., Hans Boersma, *Embodiment and Virtue in Gregory of Nyssa: An Anagogical Aproach* (Oxford: Oxford University Press, 2013), 85–145.—*Ed.*

[42] *De perfectione* (*Perf.*); Greek text: 46:252–85 and GNO VIII/1:173–214; English translation: *On Perfection*, in *St. Gregory of Nyssa: Ascetical Works*, trans. Virginia Woods Callahan, Fathers of the Church, Vol. 58 (Washington, DC: The Catholic University of America Press, 1967), 91–122. *De professione Christiana* (*Prof.*); Greek text: PG 46:237–49 and GNO VIII/1:129–42; English translation: *On What It Means to Call Oneself a Christian* (FC 58:77–89).—*Ed.*

[43] A. Wilmart, "La Tradition de l'Hypotypose (PG 46:287A–305C) ou traité de l'ascèse attribué à

Introduction

Finally, there is one more not insignificant group, consisting of hagiographies. These comprise two distinct literary genres: the eulogy or encomium (ἐγκώμια, enkōmia), and the biography. Of the eulogies, only one is of interest to us here—namely, that for Basil.[44] It is poor in biographical details, but does contain many of the themes discussed in the treatises on spirituality. The authenticity of the eulogy for St Ephraim has been called into question,[45] so we shall forbear from using it. On the other hand, Gregory has left us two very valuable biographies: that of Gregory the Wonderworker, Origen's disciple and the apostle of Cappadocia and Pontus;[46] and that of his own sister Macrina, in which one finds a number of invaluable details concerning the history of our saint as well as the customs and Christian manners of the time.[47] These two biographies also contain interesting spiritual developments.

A critical edition of the works of Gregory of Nyssa has been undertaken under the direction of W. Jaeger. To date, it comprises *Against Eunomius* in two volumes,[48] the *Letters*,[49] and the *Ascetical Works*.[50] A critical edition of *The Life of Moses* was undertaken by G. H. Forbes in 1861 for his Pitsligo Press, but it consisted of only one fascicule containing the first part of the work—the ἱστορία (historia)—which is simply a paraphrase of the biblical narrative and

---

Grégoire de Nysse," *Revue de l'Orient Chrétien* 21 (1918–1919): 412–21. [*Hypotyposis* = *De instituto Christiano* (*Inst.*); Greek text: PG 46:288–305 and GNO VIII/1:40–89; English translation: *On the Christian Mode of Life*, in *St. Gregory of Nyssa: Ascetical Works*, trans. Virginia Woods Callahan, Fathers of the Church 58 (Washington, DC: The Catholic University of America Press, 1967), 123–58. The text has obvious parallels with the Macarian *Great Letter*: one clearly depends upon the other, but scholars debate which text can claim priority. For a recent evaluation, see Marcus Plested, *The Macarian Legacy: The Place of Macarius-Symeon in the Eastern Christian Tradition* (Oxford University Press, 2004), 46–58, esp. 50–58. Plested concludes, "The evidence points firmly to the anteriority of the *Great Letter*. Gregory's reworking is subtle and concise, ironing out the inelegancies of Macarius' style and presenting in a more cultured and philosophical style all the essentials of Macarius' treatise" (p. 53).—*Ed.*]

[44] *In Basilium fratrem* (*Bas.*); Greek text: PG 46:788–817 and GNO X/1:109–134; English translation: the only readily-available English version is McCambley's unpublished translation, found online: http://www.lectio-divina.org/images/nyssa/Eulogy%20for%20Basil%20the%20Great.pdf.—*Ed.*

[45] Karl Holl, *Amphilochius von Ikonium in seinem Verhältnis zu den grossen Kappadoziern* (Tübingen: Mohr, 1969), 196. [Its authenticity is still doubted (see *Brill Dictionary*, xxii).—*Ed.*]

[46] *De vita Gregorii Thaumaturgi* (*Thaum.*); Greek text: PG 46:893–957 and GNO X/1:3–57; English translation: *Life of Gregory the Wonderworker*, in *St. Gregory Thaumaturgus: Life and Works*, trans. Michael Slusser, The Fathers of the Church 98 (Washington, DC: The Catholic University of America Press, 199), 39–87.—*Ed.*

[47] *Vita s. Macrinae* (*Macr.*); Greek text: 46:960–1000 and GNO VIII/1:370–414; English translation: *The Life of Saint Macrina* (FC 58:159–91)—*Ed.*

[48] *Gregorii Nysseni: Contra Eunomium*, W. Jaeger, ed. (Berlin: Weidmann, 1921).

[49] *Gregorii Nysseni: Epistulae*, G. Paschali, ed. (Berlin: Weidmann, 1925).

[50] *Gregorii Nysseni: Opera Ascetica*, W. Jaeger, et al., eds. (Leiden: E. J. Brill, 1952). [The list has of course now been greatly expanded.—*Trans.*]

is thus without interest for our own study. A comparative analysis of several manuscripts has enabled me to significantly correct the text given by Migne of this same *Life of Moses*,[51] which quite simply reproduces the 1586 Munich edition by Hoeschelius. This is based on a single manuscript, which I have consulted and which is faulty. As for the other works, except for partial revisions I have followed Migne's text.

March 1944

---

[51]Jean Daniélou, *Grégoire de Nysse: La Vie de Moïse*, Sources Chrétiennes 1 (Paris: Éditions du Cerf, 1942).

PART ONE

Light
or
Of Purification

1

Death and Resurrection

For Gregory of Nyssa spiritual life is entirely a mystery of death and resurrection. In this respect, it is nothing other than the fulfillment of the mystery of Baptism, which, according to the teaching of St Paul, makes us die with Christ in order to be resurrected with him [Rom 6.3–6]. Nevertheless, in the higher stages of the ascent to God the tone is set by other elements—namely, contemplation of the divine realities and intimate union with God. Without ever being totally accomplished, the resurrection already illumines the soul. By contrast, at the beginning of the spiritual life, this mystery of death and resurrection occupies the foreground. Dead to sin and resurrected with Christ in substance, the soul must work out this mystery concretely by a mortification of its sinful tendencies and a vivification of the divine energies implanted in it through Baptism.

Here, then, is the approach we will adopt. After an opening chapter in which we situate the first way in relation to the other two, and after justifying our overall plan, we will study this mystery of death and resurrection in its fundamental aspects: its sacramental source and its psychological reality. By "inner man" [Rom 7.22; Eph 3.16] will be meant both the new human being created by grace but also the inner life of the soul itself. We will then study how the spiritual life actualizes this initial momentum, dealing successively with the world of the passions—that is, with the "old man" [Rom 6.6; Eph 4.22], the one doomed to death—and that of the virtues; that is to say, the human being created in God's image and recreated in Christ, and whose triumph this first way ensures.

The Three Ways

As we know, Christian and pagan antiquity delighted in drawing up classifications of the various stages of the spiritual ascent. Among all such, it is the one by Origen in his *Commentary on the Song of Songs* that deserves to hold our attention, on account of the influence it had on our author. For Origen, "philosophy"[1] consisted of three major stages: ἐθική (*ethikē*, ethics, the practice of the virtues), φυσική (*physikē*, contemplation of nature), and θεωρική (*theōrikē*, mystical contemplation). The goal of the first is ἀπάθεια (*apatheia*, dispassion): "perfect purity and love by observing the commandments"; that of the second is "a good use of all things by means of a religious view of the world and a conviction of the vanity of everything visible"; and last, the objective of the third is "contemplation of the divine."[2] It is also with Origen that we associate the linking of these three ways to the three books attributed to Solomon—Proverbs corresponding to ἐθική, Ecclesiastes to φυσική, and the Song of Songs to θεωρική.[3] Gregory, at the beginning of his own *Homilies on the Song of Songs*, takes over Origen's division of the three books of Solomon, associating them with the three ages of the spiritual life. Proverbs corresponds to childhood, Ecclesiastes to youth, and the Song of Songs to maturity.[4] The first way consists above all in showing the value of spiritual goods in such a manner as to stimulate a desire for them; the second in making one understand the vanity of the world; and last, "having in this way purified the heart of its bent toward appearances, [the virtuous life] then, in the Song of Songs, initiates the mind into the innermost divine sanctuary [ἐντὸς τῶν θείων ἀδύτων μυσταγωγεῖ, *entos tōn theiōn adytōn mystagōgei*] [where occurs] the human soul's mingling [ἀνάκρασις, *anakrasis*] with the divine."[5]

It is interesting and worth noting that—in a manner typical of him—Gregory characterizes the first way more as a manifestation of the divine goods than as purification. This first way does inevitably involve a process of κάθαρσις (*katharsis*, purification), but it is also φωτισμός (*phōtismos*, illumination), and so we shall in due course point out that what we have here are precisely the twin aspects of Baptism. This will in turn lead us to important conclusions concerning the connections between the sacraments and the different stages of the spiritual life. The second way is defined by a disparaging of worldly values, as in

[1] [A common term used by the early Fathers for Christianity, the true wisdom.—*Trans.*]
[2] K. Rahner, "Le début d'une doctrine des cinq sens spirituels chez Origène," *Revue d'ascétique et de mystique* 13 (1932): 113–45, at 132.
[3] Origen, *Commentary on the Song of Songs*, Part I, Prologue, §3 (PG 13:73–76). English translation in Origen, *The Song of Songs: Commentary and Homilies*, trans. R. P. Lawson, Ancient Christian Writers 26 (Westminster, MD: The Newman Press, 1957), 39–41.
[4] *Cant.* 1 (PG 44:768A; Norris, 17). Basil the Great prefers to speak of childhood, maturity, and old age. See his *Homily 12: On the Beginning of Proverbs* [§13] (PG 31:412f.). English translation in St Basil the Great, *On Christian Doctrine and Practice*, trans. Mark DelCogliano, Popular Patristics Series 47 (Yonkers, NY: St Vladimir's Seminary Press, 2012), 71f.
[5] *Cant.* 1 (PG 44:772A; Norris, 23, 25).

Origen. As for the third, we notice on the one hand the use, in characterizing it, of a vocabulary borrowed from the pagan mystery religions—μυσταγωγεῖν (*mystagōgein*, to initiate into mysteries) and ἄδυτα (*adyta*, inner sanctuaries)—and, on the other hand, the fact that it is specified as resulting in a mingling or union (ἀνάκρασις, *anakrasis*) and not as contemplation (θεωρία, *theōria*). This is, in effect, the most important feature of Gregory's mysticism, and something that contrasts it with that of Origen and Evagrius.

The above divisions are taken up again by Gregory later in his *Homilies on the Song of Songs* as well as in other texts that are of the utmost importance for our study.[6] See, for example, the eleventh homily: "The revelation of God to the great Moses began with light as its medium [διὰ φωτός, *dia phōtos*], but afterwards God spoke to him through the medium of a cloud [διὰ νεφέλης, *dia nephelēs*], and when he had become more lifted up and more perfect, he saw God in darkness [ἐν γνόφῳ, *en gnophō*]."[7] Here we have a summary of the stages in the life of Moses as Gregory also describes them in the treatise that bears his name. Thus, this passage forms a link between the stages described in the *Homilies on the Song of Songs* and those in *The Life of Moses*, and allows us to move from one set of symbols to the other. In this respect it is central, which is why the divisions it contains are the ones we have used as titles for the three parts of the present work. Here is how Gregory comments on the above text:

> What we learn from this is something like the following: the first withdrawal [ἀναχώρησις, *anachōrēsis*] from false and erroneous notions about God takes the form of a transition from darkness [σκότος, *skotos*] to light. More attentive [προσεχεστέρα, *prosechestera*] apprehension of hidden realities, which leads the soul to the invisible realm by way of what appears, is like a cloud [νεφέλη, *nephelē*] that casts a shadow on everything that appears but yet induces and accustoms the soul to look upon what is hidden. But the soul that has made its way through these stages to higher things, having left behind whatever is accessible to human nature, enters within the innermost shrine of the knowledge of God [ἐντὸς τῶν ἀδύτων τῆς θεογνωσίας, *entos tōn adytōn tēs theognōsias*] and is entirely seized about by the divine darkness [γνόφος, *gnophos*].[8]

---

[6]See the comments of Puech, "La ténèbre mystique," 50–51.
[7]*Cant.* 11 (PG 44:1000C; Norris, 339).
[8]Ibid. (PG 44:1000C–D; Norris, 339, 341).

This is an important text from several points of view. In the first place, it explains—and this is its obvious meaning—why the spiritual life progresses from light to darkness. It is light to begin with in contrast to the darkness (σκότος, *skotos*) of sin and error. But this light is itself mere darkness (γνόφος, *gnophos*) when compared with the super-luminous divine reality. As already indicated, this teaching is also found in *The Life of Moses*.[9]

But in addition to this, the above passage gives us valuable information concerning the three different ways. First, there is the luminous aspect just noted. We will meet it again in *The Life of Moses* in the episode of the Burning Bush, which lies at the heart of this first way. Indeed, it is this luminous aspect that gives it its name. The passage also explains why, in the commentary on Proverbs—which corresponds to the first stage, ἠθική (*ethikē*, ethics), and which Gregory has inserted in the first of his *Homilies on the Song of Songs*—it is the manifestation of divine goods that is in the foreground. But this first way also involves separation or withdrawal (ἀναχώρησις, *anachōrēsis*). We find this concept, and even the word itself, in his commentary on the Psalms.[10] Nevertheless, here the idea is presented more on an intellectual than a moral level. But for Gregory, these are two parallel approaches: perfection consists in the union of εὐσέβεια (*eusebeia*, piety), the uprightness of faith, and of ἀπάθεια (*apatheia*, dispassion), purity of life.[11]

The second way is presented as an ascent of the mind through the great chain of being (διὰ φαινομένων, *dia phainomenōn*, through phenomena, i.e., things that are apparent to the senses), and consists in disengaging from all that is sensory and becoming habituated to invisible realities. Gregory explains this by means of the metaphor of "darkening," the word "cloud" (νεφέλη, *nephelē*) signifying this semi-darkness. It is a fitting symbol of this way,[12] yet we must not forget that it is also a figure of the Holy Spirit[13] and thereby, on a different level, links the second way no longer to Baptism, as does the first, nor to the Eucharist, like the third, but to confirmation.[14] Here—and we will return to this—we see a

---

[9]*De vita Moysis* 1.62–65 (PG 44:376D). English Translation in Gregory of Nyssa, *The Life of Moses*, trans. A. J. Malherbe and E. Ferguson (Mahwah, NJ: Paulist Press, 1978), 95.

[10]*In inscriptiones Psalmorum (Inscr.)* 1.9.120 (PG 44:485A). English translation in Gregory of Nyssa, *On the Inscriptions of the Psalms*, trans. R. E. Heine (Oxford: Clarendon Press, 1995), 122.

[11]*Cant.* 13 (PG 44:1041C–D; Norris, 397).

[12]In Pseudo-Dionysius, the νεφέλη (*nephelē*) corresponds to "symbolic theology"—that is, to the knowledge of God διὰ φαινομένων (*dia phainomenōn*). This is our second way.

[13]*Vit. Moys.* 2.121 (PG 44:361B; Malherbe, 82).

[14][Called Chrismation in the Orthodox Church.—*Trans.*]

parallel between the three ways and the three principal sacraments, which will in fact also be the framework of the treatise written ten centuries later by Nicholas Cabasilas, *The Life in Christ*. However, this sacramental aspect is not specifically mentioned in our passage. As for disparagement of the visible world, this will be the background of the *Homilies on Ecclesiastes*.

Finally, in connection with the third way, we again see here the vocabulary of the mystery religions that we met earlier. The characteristics of the third way are clearly identified: it lies entirely outside the sensible world (ἔξω τῶν φαινομένων, *exō tōn phainomenōn*; lit. outside [sensory] phenomena), because it has the invisible (τὸ ἀόρατον, *to aoraton*) as its objective. This transcendence is expressed by the metaphor of darkness (γνόφος, *gnophos*), to which we shall return at length. Even so, it is worth noting that the third way is here described as θεωρία (*theōria*, contemplation) and *not* as ἀνάκρασις (*anakrasis*, union). This is because in reality the duality of viewpoints noted earlier when discussing the first way—the intellectual and the moral—subsists in the mystical life. And throughout this passage it is the aspect of knowledge that Gregory is more concerned to present. The first way leads to separation from error, the third, to contemplation of the invisible.

As mentioned, this passage is of interest because it provides us with equivalencies between the symbols found in Exodus and those in the Song of Songs. Gregory himself makes the connection for, with the images used in the Song, he again takes up the division into three ways that he had presented in Exodus:

> But when she [the Bride] separated herself [ἀποστήσασα, *apostēsasa*] from any kinship with evil and sought, in that mystical kiss [μυστικοῦ φιλήματος, *mystikou philēmatos*], to bring her mouth to the fount of light [τῇ πηγῇ τοῦ φωτός, *tē pēgē tou phōtos*], then she became beautiful and good.... On this account, galloping [διαδραμοῦσα, *diadramousa*] like a horse and flying like a dove through everything that appears [τὸ φαινόμενον, *to phainomenon*] and is comprehended, she first rests, full of desire, in the shadow [τῇ σκιᾷ, *tē skia*] of the apple tree, calling that which shades her "apple tree" rather than "cloud." Now, however, she is already surrounded by the divine night [θείας νυκτός, *theias nyktos*], in which the Bridegroom draws near but is not manifest.[15]

---

[15]*Cant.* 11 (PG 44:1001B; Norris, 341, 343).

The parallelism between this passage and the preceding one is striking and provides us with a number of cross-references and interesting examples of equivalence. For the first way, we again find the twofold idea of separation and illumination, expressed by analogous words. The term ἀποστῆναι (*apostēnai*, to be absent from) is found elsewhere in Gregory.[16] Here, it is a question of separation from evil, which is clearly equivalent to separation from error. Moreover, our text itself speaks of the soul that has been "cleansed by water from the darkness of ignorance [τῆς ἀγνοίας, *tēs agnoias*]."[17] Thus we see emerging the link between this first way and Baptism, as is suggested by the threefold symbolism of "the fount of light," of "water" that washes away error, and of the "mystical kiss"—where the word μυστικοῦ (*mystikou*) may equally well be translated as "sacramental." Last, the first way has at its aim the restoration of beauty—that is, *apatheia*.

The passage also gives us valuable information concerning the second way. It consists essentially of a journey in which the soul crosses over from the visible world (φαινόμενον, *phainomenon*; lit. phenomenon) to the invisible. The vocabulary and images used specifically to characterize this second way are taken from the domain of racing—εὔδρομον (*eudromon*, swift of foot); διαδραμοῦσα, (*diadramousa*, galloping)—or flight (διαπτᾶσα, *diaptasa*). Also, we again find the visible world described as becoming darkened, though here this is not linked to a cloud but an apple tree (μῆλον, *mēlon*), the latter being a figure of the Word.[18] The soul is likened to a dove or a horse. The former comparison is found frequently in Gregory[19] and connotes both the lightness of a soul that has become disengaged from the sensible world through *apatheia*, which nothing slows down (τάχος, *tachos*, swiftness or speed) in its ascent, and also the grace of the Holy Spirit. In the preceding passage we saw the connection between the cloud and the Holy Spirit; here, we have a comparison with confirmation [i.e., Chrismation—*Ed.*], the sacrament of the Holy Spirit. As for the horse, it evokes an altogether different context: that of the central myth in *Phaedrus* with the team of winged horses that carry the soul off "to the rim of the heavenly vault."[20] We shall examine in due course the use Gregory makes of this symbolism for the second way.

[16]For example, *Inscr.* 2.12.157 (PG 44:552C; Heine, 170).
[17]*Cant.* 11 (PG 44:1001B; Norris, 341, 343).
[18]*Cant.* 4 (PG 44:844A–C; Norris, 139).
[19]For example, see *Virg.* 11 (PG 46:365C; FC 58:40).
[20]Plato, *Phaedrus* 247b. Translation from *Plato: Phaedrus*, trans. Robin Waterfield (Oxford: Oxford University Press, 2002).

Finally, for the third way—the mystical life proper—expressions borrowed from the mystery religions of classical antiquity reappear. Gregory writes, for example, "What is this initiatory process [μυσταγωγία, *mystagōgia*; lit. mystagogy], then, that this night causes the soul to undergo?"[21] Its essential characteristic is that it is in the realm of the divine (θεία νύξ, *theia nyx*, divine night), and is the equivalent of the darkness on Mount Sinai. There is also a new feature, which will prove to be very important in our study of the mystical life: the distinction between φαίνεται (*phainetai*, appears) and παραγίνεται (*paraginetai*, is near). God never appears (οὐ φαίνεται, *ou phainetai*); he does not manifest himself like a thing whose appearing (φαντασία, *phantasia*) the understanding could grasp (καταλαμβάνειν, *katalambanein*). He is a person—that is, a presence. The whole of the mystical life is contained in this idea of a night of the senses and concepts, in which God's presence draws ever closer (παραγίνεται, *paraginetai*). We are above and beyond natural knowledge in a person-to-person relationship between the soul and God.

One last passage from the *Homilies on the Song of Songs* is of interest to us in relation to the three ways. In it, we see how Gregory links them to three different dispositions: fear, hope, and love. These three degrees are presented in a context in which Gregory is discussing the three books of Solomon, which parenthetically assures us of their connection to the three ways: "In this work [the Song] the blessed and most perfect way of salvation [is manifested]—I mean that which comes through love [δι' ἀγαπῆς, *di' agapēs*]. . . . It may happen that salvation comes to some people even through fear. . . . And there are some who successfully practice virtue . . . not out of love for the Good but out of an expectation of recompense. The person who pursues perfection in the soul, however, drives out fear [cf. 1 Jn 4.18] . . . [and] despises the rewards themselves. . . . He loves [ἀγαπᾷ, *agapa*] with his whole heart . . ."[22] This passage is of particular interest because of the explicit link it establishes between the third way and love. For Evagrius, by contrast, *agapē* was included with *apatheia* in the first way, as part of the practice of the virtues. For the sequence πρᾶξις-θεωρία (*praxis-theōria*), Gregory substitutes a parallel structure: each of the three ways has its own "practical" and "contemplative" aspects. Furthermore, in the third way, it is the "practical" aspect—*agapē*—that is essential.

[21]*Cant.* 11 (PG 44:1001C; Norris, 343).
[22]Ibid., 17 (PG 44:765B). We find the same point of view on pages 489, 491 (PG 44:1112C-D) and *Vit. Moys.* 2.320 (PG 44:429C-D; Malherbe, 137). [For more on this threefold division of motivations in the spiritual life, see n. 136 on p. 232.—*Ed.*]

We now need to cross-check these classifications and to verify whether they are indeed found in Gregory's treatises. Things are clear enough as regards the commentaries on the books of Solomon: the *Homilies on Ecclesiastes* is about the second way, the *Homilies on the Song of Songs* about the third way. *On the Inscriptions of the Psalms*, however, can be classified with less certainty, a fact that might lead us to believe that it corresponds to a period in Gregory's life when his thought was not yet fully developed. But what of *The Life of Moses*? It is from Exodus that Gregory borrows the major symbol of three ways that he uses in his *Homilies on the Song of Songs*; but are we able to locate them in this commentary on Exodus—which is, in effect, what *The Life of Moses* is? It must be admitted that, though we may detect the outlines, no sharply delineated divisions are to be found. This should not surprise us, however, for Gregory is not a writer given to making rigid separations. Moreover, in conformity with the aesthetics of his time, his usual manner of composing reveals no particular concern to be systematic.

Nevertheless, many features help confirm what we have seen so far. The beginning of the spiritual life presents the twofold aspect of *separation* and *illumination*. Thus the link that we shall see established between "removing the shoes of skin" (symbolizing erroneous opinions) and the illumination of the soul by the Burning Bush—that is to say, the Incarnate Word—reminds us of what we saw earlier. The crossing of the desert, guided by the cloud, sets us on the second way; its aim is to cause the soul to lose its affection for earthly things (Egyptian foods) and to accustom it to live a life of faith. Finally, at the completion of the ascent of Mount Sinai, the entry into darkness leads us into the mystical life. But though lofty peaks emerge, transitions from one to the other are not clearly defined and are encumbered, moreover, by distracting developments. This will oblige us to conduct a thorough process of differentiation.

The above, then, are the principal texts that we should take into account in sketching out the various stages of the spiritual life according to our author. To establish things in this way on the threshold of this chapter has been useful in determining the context in which we will proceed. We have identified the three major ways that will correspond to the principal divisions of our study. Within the first way we have distinguished, as it were, three further stages: first, the entry into the spiritual life, which means renouncing evil, error, and the world, while at the same time being illumined by the Word; second, progress begins to be made, consisting essentially in purification from the passions; and third, there is the goal, which already constitutes a kind of perfection, though one that is relative—namely, *apatheia*, reacquired peace and spiritual freedom.

We will now broach the initial stage of this first way. In this manner, we shall be faithful to Gregory's own way of thinking since, for him, the spiritual life can be compared to a series of successive peaks from which, each time, new perspectives are discovered. This perpetual renewal of horizons enables one to avoid the potential monotony of an endless climb. Our plan will be to follow this approach as accurately as possible. Each of the three ways might easily seem to form a well finished whole. *Apatheia*, for example, is a form of perfection in its own class of virtues; θεωρία (*theōria*, contemplation) likewise. And yet when we arrive at these summits, new horizons open up before us, new realms that present their own peaks. Nor will our journey culminate in the ascent of one final summit, but on the contrary, with the enchanting realization that the countries already discovered are always only promises of lands more beautiful still.

The Mysticism of Baptism

As we have seen, the most common image chosen by Gregory when referring to entry into the spiritual life is that of *separation*; that is, from evil or error. Whether the word used be ἀπόστασις (*apostasis*, defection or distancing [the root of "apostasy" in English], ἀλλοτρίωσις (*allotriōsis*, estrangement), or ἀναχώρησις (*anachōrēsis*, withdrawal), the idea is always the same. It appears in the first lines of Book Two of *The Life of Moses* where reference is made to the putting to death of the daughters of the Hebrews, as symbolic of the sensuous life. Reading this passage, one is struck above all by the emphasis placed on the role of freedom in this initial step: "[Spiritual birth] occurs by choice. We are in some manner our own parents, giving birth to ourselves by our own free choice in accordance with whatever we wish to be."[23] One has the impression that conversion is above all a work of freedom in which grace plays no part. This emphasis on freedom was already typical of Origen, and Völker rightly observes that with him there is a hint of something that is not very Pauline.[24] This can be

---

[23] *Vit. Moys.* 2.3 (PG 44:328B; Malherbe, 55–56). See also *In Ecclesiasten homiliae*, Homily 6 (PG 44:701D); Hall, 104; *Oratio catechetica magna* 39.1 (PG 45:100A); English translation in Gregory of Nyssa, *Catechetical Discourse: A Handbook for Catechists*, trans. Ignatius Green, Popular Patristics Series 60 (Yonkers, NY: St Vladimir's Seminary Press, 2019), 150 [here specifically about the adult's ability to choose one's own Father in Baptism—*Ed.*].

[24] W. Völker, *Das Volkommenheitsideal*, 40.

explained by the reaction against gnostic determinism, and is something that takes us back to a pre-Pelagian world.

There is, however, an altogether different way of interpreting the passage from Gregory. This free act is possible only because the Word of God has first united himself to humanity and has deified it. Thus before freedom, there is already grace; and the role of freedom consists simply in opening oneself up to it. Gregory's mysticism is entirely structured, then, around a theology of the Logos and his union with humanity, as Lieske has correctly seen.[25] The union (ἀνάκρασις, *anakrasis*) of each soul with the Logos is but one aspect of the first and prior union of the Word with human nature as a whole (τὸ ἀνθρώπινον, *to anthrōpinon*) in the incarnation. Mystical theology describes the first relationship, dogmatic theology the second.

> In a figurative turn of speech the Bride uses the word *bed* to mean the mingling [ἀνάκρασις, *anakrasis*] of the human race with the Divine, just as the great apostle [Paul] has the virgin—us—"betrothed" to Christ (2 Cor 11.2) ... and declares that the joining of the two in the communion of one body is the great mystery of the union [ἕνωσις, *henōsis*] of Christ with the church (cf. Eph 5.32).... So it is in view of this mystery that the virgin soul gives the name *bed* to communion [κοινωνία, *koinonia*] with the Divine. But there was no way in which this communion could come to pass save by the Lord's manifestation to us by way of a shadow, by way of his body.[26]

Here the same words signify successively the (hypostatic) union of the Word and human nature, and the (mystical) union of the Word and the individual soul.

It is for this reason that, in the *Homilies on the Song of Songs*, the social (and theological) point of view of the union of the Word and the Church, and the individual (and mystical) viewpoint of the union of the Word and the soul perpetually interact. The Bride is sometimes the individual soul and sometimes the Church, which is the intermediary between the Word and the "young girls" who represent the souls.

> The following expression unveils in the Word the dispensation of the church [ἐκκλησιαστικὴ οἰκονομία, *ekklēsiastikē oikonomia*]. Those who were first made disciples by grace ... did not keep the Good to themselves. Rather did they work the same grace, by transmission, in those who were their

[25] Lieske, "Zur Theologie der Christusmystik."
[26] *Cant.* 4 (PG 44:836D–837A; Norris, 121).

companions. That is why the young women say to the Bride—who . . . was the first to be filled with good things and to be adjudged worthy of hidden mysteries—"Let us rejoice and be glad in you." . . . John, who rested on the Lord's bosom . . . having brought his own heart, as if it were a sponge, up to the fount of life, was filled, by an indescribable transmission, with the mysteries lodged in the Lord's heart. . . . He fills us up in turn with the things lodged in him by the fount of Goodness.[27]

Thus we see how Gregory imagines things. The spiritual life is, on the one hand, entirely dependent upon the divine life possessed by the Church, which communicates it through the sacraments.[28] The more we study Gregory, the more we see the importance this sacramental life has for him. In this, he is squarely in the tradition of the Eastern Church,[29] and foreshadows a Diadochus of Photiki and a Nicholas Cabasilas. On the other hand, the spiritual life is entirely free; not in the sense that man might procure divine benefits by his own means, but in the sense that it depends on him as to whether or not he turns to the Church, which can communicate them to him. As for the problem of individual grace, it had not yet arisen at this time. Prevenient grace is the collective grace given to humanity as a whole by the incarnation, and which secretly urges on every heart. But to this "prevenience" of grace, man is entirely free to respond or not.

This synergism is found throughout the spiritual life, which will always be a work of freedom. It is not only our initial conversion that Gregory attributes to it, but the various degrees of progress. He also strongly insists on the fact that Baptism is fruitful only when the soul actually renounces its vices.[30] Here we clearly see the need for the union of freedom and the sacraments. In this sense, our entire spiritual development is the work of our freedom: "In giving us the power to become like God, he let us be artisans [ἐργάτας, *ergatas*] of the likeness to God."[31] "For the Word wishes us, mutable as we are by nature . . . to make change cooperate [συνεργόν, *synergon*] in our ascent towards higher

---

[27]*Cant.* 1 (PG 44:785C; Norris, 43, 45).

[28]This dependency is highlighted in *Vit. Moys.* 2.12 (PG 44:330C; Malherbe, 57) and *Eun.* (PG 45:881B; NPNF² 5:239).

[29]This is a characteristic trait of Origen. See H. Rahner, "Taufe und geistliches Leben bei Origenes," *Zeitschrift für Aszese und Mystik* 7 (1932): 205–22.

[30]Cf. *Vit. Moys.* 2.128 (PG 44:364A; Malherbe, 84–85). See also *Or. cat.* 40 (PG 45:102B–105C; PPS 60:153–57).

[31]*Creat.* 1 (PG 44:273A–B); English translation from "On the Origin of Humanity, Discourse 1," *St Basil the Great: On the Human Condition*, trans. Nonna Verna Harrison (Crestwood, NY: St Vladimir's Seminary Press, 2005), 44.

things."[32] "For virtue has no master [ἀδέσποτον, adespoton];[33] it is voluntary and free of all compulsion."[34]

At the same time, the whole of spiritual life is represented as immersed in the sacramental life that feeds it. We have already noted the parallelism between the three ways and the three main sacraments. Thus, Baptism corresponds to the first way in its twofold aspect of purification (κάθαρσις, katharsis) and illumination (φωτισμός, phōtismos); confirmation corresponds to the second by its twofold aspect of an obscuring (νεφέλη, nephelē, cloud) of the visible world and an elevation (περιστερά, peristera, lit. dove) toward the invisible world; and finally, the Eucharist relates to the mystical life both as union (ἀνάκρασις, anakrasis) and as a going out from the world and from self (ἔκστασις, ekstasis; lit. ecstasy). The sacramental life is truly conceived as a "mystagogy," a progressive initiation that leads the soul to the summits of the mystical life, to "sober inebriation."[35]

The truth of this general fact is borne out from the very outset of the spiritual life. At the beginning of this section, for example, we stated that spiritual birth appeared at first sight to be a work of freedom. But a careful reading of the various texts will show that the baptismal mystery of death and resurrection is present everywhere at the core of this first stage, so much so that this stage can be said to be essentially an actualization of baptismal grace on the basis of freedom. As already noted, entry into the spiritual life can be thought of as a separation, a casting off, or a death; but at the same time it is also growth, illumination, and vivification. Therein resides the double aspect of the baptismal mystery of death and resurrection with Christ. Hence Gregory expressly links (voluntary) mortification with (sacramental) death. "I have risen up by being 'buried with him through baptism into his death,' (Rom 6.4) for the resurrection does not become actual if it is not preceded by voluntary death."[36] Death, accomplished

---

[32] *Cant.* 8 (PG 44:945C; Norris, 265).

[33] This phrase is found verbatim in Plato, *Republic* 617e.

[34] *Cant.* 5 (PG 44:877A; Norris, 173).

[35] Thus in Gregory's commentary on Psalm 22 [LXX]—in his *In ascensionem Christi Oratio* (*Ascens.*) (PG 46:A–B)—"the shadow of death" symbolizes Baptism; the "stick" and "the oil," confirmation; "the set table" and "the inebriating chalice," the Eucharist (English translation from *Homily on the Ascension*, trans. Richard McCambley, http://www.lectio-divina.org/index.php/reflections/reflections-on-the-writings-of-gregory-of-nyssa, p. 3). All this makes good sense if one recalls that this psalm was chanted (ψάλλειν, psallein) during the procession that led the newly baptized from the baptismal font to the communion table. See Didymus the Blind, *De Trinitate* (PG 39:708C). See also Ambrose, *On the Mysteries* 8 (NPNF² 10:719). The same psalm also symbolizes the three ways; see *Cant.* 12 (PG 44:1032B; Norris, 383).

[36] *Cant.* 12 (PG 44:1016D; Norris, 363). [Daniélou translates the final words as "voluntary mortification (νεκρότης, nekrotēs)."—*Trans.*]

in substance during Baptism, is prolonged by mortification throughout the spiritual life, from the first way's struggles against the passions to the passive purifications of the mystical life itself.

This baptismal symbolism is explicit in a certain number of passages. For example, in *The Life of Moses*—where the Egyptians, symbolizing the passions, are engulfed in the waters, whereas the Hebrews leave as freed men—the crossing of the Red Sea is expressly related to Baptism: "No one who hears this should be ignorant of the mystery of the water. He who has gone down into it with the army of the enemy emerges alone, leaving the enemy's army drowning in the water. For who does not know that the Egyptian army . . . are the various passions of the soul by which man is enslaved?"[37] This casting off of the passions is linked to the "mystery of the water"—that is to say, Baptism, which the crossing of the Red Sea clearly symbolizes.[38] And this same mystery (or sacrament) communicates life to the soul: "Then as the staff of faith leads on and the cloud provides light, the water gives life to those who find refuge in it."[39]

But the crossing of the Red Sea is not the only figure of Baptism in *The Life of Moses*. There is another, earlier, episode that also seems to have a baptismal meaning: that of the Burning Bush. It is composed of two parts: the removal of the shoes (the *discalceatio*), and the *illumination* (φωτισμός, *phōtismos*). This is how Gregory presents the first:

> That light teaches us what we must do to stand within the rays of the true light. Sandaled feet cannot ascend that height where the light of truth is seen, but the dead and earthly covering of skins [νεκρὰ . . . τῶν δερμάτων περιβολή, *nekra . . . tōn dermatōn peribolē*], which was placed around our nature at the beginning when we were found naked because of disobedience to the divine will, must be removed [περιλυθείη, *perilytheiē*] from the feet of the soul. When we do this, the knowledge of the truth will result and manifest itself. The full knowledge of being comes about by purifying [καθάρσιον, *katharsion*] our opinion concerning nonbeing.[40]

[37] *Vit. Moys.* 2.121–22 (PG 44:361C; Malherbe, 83).

[38] F.-J. Dölger, "Der Durchzug durch das Rote Meer als Sinnbild der christlichen Taufe," *Antike und Christentum* 2 (1930): 63–69; J. Daniélou, *Sacramentum futuri: Études sur les origines de la typologie biblique* (Paris: Beauchesne, 1950), 152–76. [In English, *From Shadows to Reality: Studies in the Biblical Typology of the Fathers*, trans. Dom Wulstan Hibberd (London : Burns and Oates, 1960), 175–201.—*Ed.*]

[39] *Vit. Moys.* 2.124 (PG 44:361D; Malherbe, 83).

[40] *Vit. Moys.* 2.22 (PG 44:332C–333A; Malherbe, 59–60). See also 2.201 (PG 44:392D; Malherbe, 106): "[The high priest] wears no sandals so he will not be encumbered in his race and hindered by the covering of dead skins."

Here, for the first time, we come across the symbolism of the "dead skins" that are to be cast off. As our text indicates, this is explicitly linked to the "garments of skin" (δερμάτινοι χιτῶνες, *dermatinoi chitōnes*), which, it is said in Genesis (3.21), were given to the first humans after the fall. These "garments of skin" are symbols, then, of our fallen human condition; the "sandals of skin" are a variant. This fallen condition includes various aspects that I do not wish to dwell on here, as I shall return to this at length. I shall simply note that its most obvious feature is the passions. Here, Gregory makes these a symbol of erroneous opinions (ὑπόληψις, *hypolēpsis*). Indeed, we know that for him virtue includes both ἀπάθεια (*apatheia*, dispassion), which is a casting off of the πάθη (*pathē*, passions), and εὐσέβια (*eusebeia*, piety), which is a casting off of those δόξαι, (*doxai*, opinions) that are also the results of the fall. We find this meaning in another passage, where Gregory is describing the first way as a "withdrawal [ἀναχώρησις, *anachōrēsis*] from false and erroneous notions [ὑπολήψεων, *hypolēpseōn*] about God."[41] The parallelism between the two passages is striking. Moreover, it is interesting to note that the interpretation of δόξαι as a garment to be cast off comes from Philo: "The high priest... [should] put off the robe of opinion [δόξης, *doxēs*] and vain fancy of the soul."[42]

Gregory adds that the casting off of "the garments of skin" is brought about by Baptism.[43] The very symbolism of the sacrament represents this, for before going down into the baptismal font, the catechumen took off his old clothes and on coming up again received garments that were white—φωτοειδής (*phōtoeidēs*, luminous), symbolic of regained incorruptibility: "You are outside paradise, O catechumen, sharing the exile of Adam, [our] first father. Now the door is opened to you.... Put off the old man, like a soiled garment.... Receive the clothing of incorruption, which Christ offers you."[44] This is still the case with the current ritual. The baptismal meaning of the casting off of the garments is therefore clear. But in our text, it is a question not of garments but sandals. Do we still have, then, an allusion to Baptism?

---

[41]*Cant.* 11 (PG 44:1000D; Norris, 341).

[42]Philo of Alexandria, *Allegorical Interpretation*, 2.15.56; English translation for all works of Philo found in *The Works of Philo: Complete and Unabridged, New Updated Version*, trans. C. D. Yonge (Peabody, MA: Hendrickson Publishers, 1993), 43. Cf. Plotinus, *The Enneads* 3.6.5; also *Poimandres* 7.2, where it is said, "But first thou must tear off from thee the cloak which thou dost wear—the web of ignorance." English translation from *Thrice Greatest Hermes: Studies in Hellenistic Theosophy and Gnosis*, trans. G. R. S. Mead (Boston: Weiser Books, 2001 [1st ed. 1905]), 2:77.

[43]See *Adversus eos qui differunt baptismum* (PG 46:417D, 420C; [trans. by Editor]).

[44]Ibid.

Death and Resurrection

It seems certain. Indeed, the existence of a ritual of *discalceatio* (the removal of shoes) in ancient baptismal ceremonies seems established today, ever since the research done by F.-J. Dölger.[45] According to him, the candidate had to present himself barefoot at the baptismal font and it was the baptizer who had to untie his shoes. In explaining this ritual symbolically, later church writers saw in the shoes a symbol of mortality. During the octave following Baptism, the neophytes had to wear new shoes, though leather ones seem to have been forbidden in favor of others, deemed more pure. What reinforces this hypothesis is that what we see here is the survival of a cultural usage earlier than Christianity. It is found already in Neopythagoreanism. All this gives a much more specific meaning to John's words to Christ—"I am not fit to undo the strap of your sandal" (Jn 1.27)—which would then mean, "I am not worthy to baptize you."

Dölger bases his argument on two texts. One is a passage from Peter of Laodicaea in his *Commentary on St Luke* (3.15), the other, a text by Clement of Alexandria: "It behooves those who purify others to free the soul from the body and its sins, as the foot from the thong."[46] But he does not mention a text that is more explicit still—and which, more importantly, is from Gregory of Nyssa. The reference is to the following verse from the Song of Songs: "I have put off my coat; how shall I put it on? I have washed my feet; how shall I defile them?" (5.3). What is remarkable is that the two themes—garment and shoes—are united in the same passage. Gregory comments on the first as follows:

> [The Bride] did what she heard. She put off that "tunic" of skin [δερματίνου χιτῶνος, *dermatinou chitōnos*] that she had put on after the sin . . . [and thus] opened a way into her soul for the Word, having rent the veil of her heart, that is, the flesh. When I say *flesh*, what I mean is "the old humanity" (Col 3.9), which the divine apostle commands to be stripped off and put aside by those who are going to wash off the filth of the soul's feet in the bath of the Word. . . . And when the Word has entered her, the soul makes him her garment in accordance with the instruction of the apostle; for he commands the person who has taken off the rags of the old humanity to "put on the new" tunic that "has been created after the likeness of God in holiness and righteousness" (Eph 4.24); and he says that this garment is Jesus (cf. Rom

---

[45] F.-J. Dölger, "Das Lösen der Schuhriemen in der Taufsymbolik des Klemens von Alexandrien"; "Das Schuh-Ausziehen in der altchristlichen Tauflìturgie"; "Das Verbot des Barfussgehens und der kultisch reine Schuh der Täuflinge in der Oktav nach der Taufe," *Antike und Christentum* 5 (1936): 87–115.

[46] Clement of Alexandria, *Miscellanies (The Stromata)* 5.8 (ANF 2:966).

13.14; Gal 3.27).... [Then the Bride affirms] that she will never again take up the tunic she has put off but will be content... with the one tunic that she put on when she was renewed through the rebirth from above.[47]

This text groups together all the variations on the theme of the garment, and shows conclusively that it has a baptismal meaning. The garment cast off at Baptism is explicitly related to the "garments of skin" of Genesis, on the one hand, and to the Pauline "old man," on the other. Thus, the parallelism between Baptism and asceticism is complete. Conversely, the new garment given to the neophyte is linked to the Pauline doctrine of "putting on Jesus Christ." The entire spiritual life, inasmuch as it is a "casting off of the old man" and a "putting on of Christ," is a development of the baptismal mystery. The baptismal meaning is revealed by yet more details, for example, that one should remove one's garments before washing the soul. In fact, this reflects the very order of the ritual, and the allusion to ablution is quite specific. Last, the advice to preserve the baptismal robe was followed symbolically by the wearing of the white garments throughout the Paschal octave.

Gregory continues as follows:

Nor does she whose feet have been washed ever again contract, in her walking, the defilement of things earthy.... Furthermore, it is related that Moses, after, at God's command, he had liberated his feet from their dead clothing of skins upon entering the holy and luminous ground (cf. Ex 3.5), did not put those shoes back on.... Hence too the Lord forbade his disciples to wear sandals when he ordered them not to travel "the way of the Gentiles" (Mt 10.9, 5) but to take the holy way.... Since, then, the Bride finds herself on this very road, on which the Lord washes with water the feet of those who walk it and dries them with the towel that girds his waist... she does not stray to the right or to the left, lest she step off the road on either hand and defile her foot with mud.

You perceive clearly, then, what these words convey: that she who has once and for all, through Baptism, taken off her sandals—for it is the proper business of the baptizer [ἴδιον τοῦ βαπτίζοντος, *idion tou baptizontos*] to loose the thongs of those who are wearing sandals, just as John testified that he was unable to do this in the case of the Lord...—has had her feet washed and has shed, with her sandals, all earthy filth.[48]

---

[47] *Cant.* 11 (PG 44:1004D–1005A; Norris, 347).
[48] *Cant.* 11 (PG 44:1005D–1008B; Norris, 349, 351).

The interest of this text is self-evident. First of all, it adds an important piece of information to Dölger's case for establishing the baptismal significance of the ritual of *discalceatio*, since untying sandals is clearly stated as the function of the one who baptizes. The reference to foot washing is not without interest either. The *mandatum* of Holy Thursday has been divested today of its sacramental character, but in the primitive liturgy it too was a baptismal ritual.[49] Now the washing of feet also necessarily entails a *discalceatio*. Nor is it the only vestige we have of the *discalceatio* as a preparatory ritual for Baptism, for the current Greek practice still includes a preliminary ceremony consisting of a blessing of the "barefoot" (ἀνυπόδητος, *anypodētos*) catechumen. And formerly a catechumen had to attend the exorcisms on Palm Sunday "barefoot." These two customs appeared in Syria in the fourth century.[50] This preparatory character of the *discalceatio*—a sort of prefiguration of the complete removal of one's garments—harmonizes nicely with the fact that, in *The Life of Moses*, the *discalceatio* at the Burning Bush precedes the crossing of the Red Sea. The faithful accustomed to the above baptismal liturgies must have found this concurrence entirely normal.

But for us the most interesting aspect is the *discalceatio* at the Burning Bush and we are brought back to the question we asked earlier: does the removal of sandals by Moses in the Exodus episode have a baptismal symbolism? First, we established that the removal of the sandals of skin had a baptismal meaning in general terms. That Moses' action should then itself have been viewed as a baptismal symbol seems entirely natural.[51] Moreover, its mention in a context that is a true mystagogy and where one senses that the allusions to Baptism lie just below the surface of the text leads us to think that a *discalceatio* was indeed a traditional figure of Baptism. Thus we may justifiably believe that it also has this meaning in *The Life of Moses*.

There is archaeological evidence that confirms this as well. In early Christian iconography the two most common scenes from the life of Moses are those of

---

[49]See Ambroise de Milan, *Des Sacrements, Des Mystères*, B. Botte, ed. (Paris: Éditions du Cerf, 1950), 3.4–7. [i.e., *De mysteriis* 6; in English, see *St. Ambrose: On the Mysteries and the Treatise On the Sacraments by An Unknown Author*, trans. T. Thompson, ed. J. H. Srawley (London: SPCK, 1919), 57–59.—*Ed.*]

The introduction of this rite into the sacrament of Baptism is perhaps linked to the institution of the sacrament by Christ at the washing of feet, as we find in Aphraates. See E. J. Duncan, *Baptism in the Demonstrations of Aphraates the Persian Sage* (Washington, DC: Catholic University of America Press, 1941), 70.

[50]See *Les Homélies catéchétiques de Théodore de Mopsueste*, R. Tonneau, tr., Studi e Testi 145 (Vatican City: Biblioteca Apostolica Vaticana, 1949), 323.

[51]See Justin Martyr, *Apology* 1.62.2 (ANF 1:490).

the Burning Bush and the Rock in the desert. Furthermore, we know that the Old Testament scenes of this period were never reproduced for themselves but in order to symbolize the realities of the New Law, particularly the sacraments. Might these two scenes, then, not be figures of Baptism and the Eucharist? The miniatures, mosaics, and frescoes of this period specifically depict Moses in the act of removing his sandals, or having done so. In one them, his large leather ὑπόδημα (*hypodēma*, sandals) are placed in the very center of the illustration.[52] It is very likely, then, that this scene evoked the baptismal ritual of the *discalceatio*, even being a symbolic representation of it. This is its meaning in our text as well.

We have not yet fully exhausted the symbolism of this scene. Indeed, the *discalceatio* constitutes only the first stage—the casting off of the old man, a participation in the mystery of the death of Christ. It is followed by the illumination of the soul by the Burning Bush. This represents the positive aspect—transfiguration through union with the risen Christ—and we can legitimately see here too a symbol of spiritual birth. In fact, in a text from which we have already quoted, Gregory explicitly interprets along these lines this illumination that takes place at the entry into the spiritual life: "But when [the Bride/the soul] separated herself from any kinship with evil"—(this is what the *discalceatio* symbolizes)—"and sought, in that mystical kiss [μυστικοῦ φιλήματος, *mystikou philēmatos*], to bring her mouth to the fount of light [τῇ πηγῇ τοῦ φωτός, *tē pēgē tou photos*], then she became beautiful and good, illumined by the light of truth [τῇ φωτὶ τῆς ἀληθείας, *tē phōti tēs alētheias*] and cleansed by water from the darkness of ignorance."[53]

This text is all the more interesting in that here it is the second part of the mystery—the φωτισμός (*phōtismos*, illumination)—whose sacramental aspect is emphasized. To begin with, the very word φῶς (*phōs*, light) evokes the term φωτισμός, the name by which Christian antiquity designated Baptism, the sacrament of regeneration [cf. Heb 6.4]. What is more, the illumination is accompanied by a cleansing by water. The sacramental symbolism of the latter becomes clear when we compare it with a passage such as the following, in which the same words are found: "Was it not a mystical [μυστικῷ, *mystikō*] cleansing which

---

[52]See F. Cabrol and H. Leclercq, *Dictionnaire d'Archéologie Chrétienne et de Liturgie*, vol. 11 (Paris: Letouzey et Ané, 1933), "Moïse," cols. 1655–56. The comparison between the Mosaic scene and Baptism was made by M. Lot-Borodine in "La grâce déifiante des sacrements d'après Nicolas Cabasilas," *Revue des Sciences Philosophiques et Théologiques* 25 (1936): 229–30, at 319.

[53]*Cant.* 11 (PG 44:1001B; Norris, 341, 343).

washed away [Paul's] ignorance [ἀγνοίας, *agnoias*] and filth of deception, having at once transported him to a more divine state?"[54] Here again we note that the sacrament is viewed above all as essentially a renunciation or abjuration of error. Last, the expression "mystical kiss" (μυστικὸν φίλημα, *mystikon philēma*) is also a direct allusion to Baptism. We shall return to this.

When Gregory describes this illumination in *The Life of Moses*, he *emphasizes* that its agent is the incarnate Word. This is crucial, since it places us squarely in the domain of the realistic and sacramental mysticism of which we spoke earlier. The purpose of the sacrament, of the mystical kiss, is to bring the soul into contact with the incarnate Word, from whom alone come light and grace: "And if the flame by which the soul of the prophet was illumined [καταφωτίζεται, *kataphōtizetai*] was from a thorny bush, even this fact will not be useless for our inquiry. If indeed the truth is God and truth is light [φῶς, *phōs*] ... such guidance of virtue leads us to know that light which has reached down even to human nature."[55] It is all the more important to emphasize that the incarnate Word is the source of the illumination, since its content runs the risk of appearing philosophical. And here we come across a problem frequently encountered—the expression in philosophical terms of a doctrine whose context shows that it must be understood quite differently. Gregory describes the content of the illumination in this way:

> It seems to me that at the time the great Moses was instructed in the theophany, he came to know that none of those things which are apprehended by sense perception really subsists, but that the transcendent essence and cause of the universe, on which everything depends, alone subsists. For even if the understanding looks upon any other existing things, reason observes in absolutely none of them the self-sufficiency by which they could exist without participation in true Being. On the other hand, that which is always the same [ὡσαύτως ἔχον ἀεί, *hōsautōs echon aei*], neither increasing nor diminishing [τὸ ἀναξὲς καὶ ἀμείωτον, *to anaxes kai ameiōton*] ... participated in [μετεχόμενον, *metechomenon*] by all but not lessened by their participation—this is truly real Being.[56]

---

[54] *In Basilium fratrem* (Bas.) (PG 46:793C–D); McCambly. 15.
[55] *Vit. Moys.* 1.20 (PG 44:332C; Malherbe, 59).
[56] *Vit. Moys.* 24–25 (PG 44:333B; Malherbe, 60).

This would seem to be pure Platonism; the expressions are the very ones used in Plato's *Symposium*.[57] And yet, it is a question of the illumination of the soul by the incarnate Word. In fact, the philosophical language is just as symbolic as the biblical language, the one and the other designating the same mystical reality of the Word living in the Church and communicating light through sacramental contact.

In the *Homilies on the Song of Songs*, it is the kiss that is the equivalent of the Burning Bush as a symbol of entry into the spiritual life. It appears in the very first verse of the biblical text: "Let him kiss me with the kisses of his mouth." This equivalence is made clear in the passage cited above where the soul, after separating itself from evil, brings her mouth to the fount of light in a sacramental (or mystical) kiss and finds herself cleansed by water from the darkness of ignorance. This passage is the exact parallel of the one in which, a few lines earlier, the same stage is described by using imagery from Exodus: "Withdrawal from false and erroneous notions about God takes the form of a transition from darkness to light."[58] Thus, these various images—illumination, ablution, and kiss—express in differing contexts the same baptismal mystery.

The symbol of the kiss, however, is not linked to baptismal rituals directly, at least not to our knowledge. Yet it nonetheless has liturgical echoes. These have been expounded at length by Dölger.[59] In particular, there is the ritual which consists in kissing the altar stone, as is still done in current liturgical practice. Here, the altar is a symbol of Christ, which brings us very close to our theme. But there is more to be said. The connection between the altar kiss and the verse from the *Song* was explicitly made by Innocent III: "Then the bishop coming near the altar, kisses it, signifying thereby that by his coming Christ is united to the Church according to the words of the Song: 'Let him kiss me with the kisses of his mouth.'"[60]

This kiss symbolizes first of all the union of the Word with humanity at the incarnation. We find this meaning in Gregory of Nyssa[61] and it will be found again in St Bernard.[62] We are reminded of what we said earlier, that the principle of any union of the individual soul with the Word is the prior union of the Word

---

[57]See Plato, *Symposium* 210e–211b. The same turns of phrase can also be found in *Virg.* 11 (PG 46:368C–D; FC 58:41–42).
[58]*Cant.* 11 (PG 44:1000D; Norris, 341).
[59]F.-J. Dölger, "Der Altarkuss," *Antike und Christentum* 2 (1930): 190–221.
[60]Innocent III, *De sacro altaris mysterio* 2.15 (PL 217:807).
[61]*Cant.* 1 (PG 44:777C; Norris, 29).
[62]Bernard of Clairvaux, *Sermons on the Song of Songs* 1.1.

with human nature as a whole. By his incarnation, the Word has sanctified the entire human mass, but this divine life—which is henceforth like leaven in mankind, conceived as a single body—must spread to each of its members. This is what is brought about by sacramental contact with Christ living in the Church. Consequently, the sacraments, Baptism in particular, are the one source of all illumination and of all virtue.

It is this contact of the individual soul with Christ through the sacraments that the kiss symbolizes in the second place. This is made clear in several texts. For example:

> [For since] everyone who is joined to the Spirit becomes spirit (1 Cor 6.17), while everyone who is attached to life "passes from death to life" (Jn 5.24) ... it follows that the virgin soul longs to approach the fount of the spiritual life. And that fount is the mouth of the Bridegroom. ... It follows that the soul, thirsty as she is, wills to bring her own mouth to the mouth that pours out life, saying "Let him kiss me with the kisses of his mouth."
>
> Moreover, he who is bursting with life for all and wills all to be saved [1 Tim 2.4] wants none of those who are being saved to be deprived of such a kiss, for this kiss cleanses [καθάρσιον, *katharsion*] away all filth.[63]

The last few words clearly show that it is not a question here of full mystical union but simply of contact with Christ, who purifies us from sins.[64] We have already pointed out this word καθάρσιον (*katharsion*) in connection with the Burning Bush. Here as there, we are only at the threshold of the spiritual life. It is important to note that purification is considered to be a consequence of contact with Christ, for this places us from the outset in a world of Christian mysticism, not one of natural purification.

This symbolism of the kiss in a baptismal context is found in another passage, one discussing the prodigal son: "[His] confession gave him easy access to the father who ran towards him and embraced him and kissed him. And this signifies the yoke of the Word. ... And he put on him the robe [χίτων, *chitōn*], not another one, but the first robe, of which he had been deprived by his disobedience. ... The ring on his hand, because of the carved stone, signifies the regaining of the Image [εἰκών, *eikōn*]. But he also protects his feet with shoes so that if he approaches the head of the serpent, it may not bite into his naked

---

[63] *Cant.* 1 (PG 44:777D; Norris, 33, 35).
[64] See also *Cant.* 1 (PG 44:785A; Norris, 43), where it is a case of a soul that is still imperfect.

heel."⁶⁵ The baptismal symbolism of this parable is found elsewhere among early Christian writers—for example, in Tertullian.⁶⁶

What is remarkable about this text is that all of the images have a baptismal symbolism. The robe symbolizes the restoration of original grace. The white garments of those who have been baptized appear again, along with their significance as a regaining of the original incorruptibility. The shoes appear, but in a new form—as new shoes given to the baptized. Now we know that this was indeed the case after Baptism, and that the newly baptized did not take back their old shoes. The recovery in the soul of the image of God—that is, as we shall see, supernatural life—is the very essence of Baptism. Finally, the kiss signifies the sacrament in its totality—that is, union with Christ.

These few examples, chosen from among many others precisely because they needed more explanation, have shown how the initial stages of the spiritual life are the expression of baptismal grace. Moreover, this is true not only of the early stages for, if each of the sacraments corresponds more particularly to one of the three ways, its effect extends to the others. This is preeminently the case with Baptism. As mentioned earlier, spiritual life in its entirety is simply the realization, through the mortification of the old man and the enlivening of the new man, of the initial grace of Baptism. And it is this initial grace that Gregory will find again in the supreme trials of the mystical life, the passive purification that strips the soul of the last vestiges of mortality. Commenting on the words from the *Song*, "myrrh dropped from my fingers" (5.5), Gregory links them to the Pauline theology of Baptism: "I have risen up by being buried with him through baptism into his death (Rom 6.4)."⁶⁷

He then describes the new mystical life in these admirable terms: "It is through death that the soul is raised up (for if it does not die, it remains for all time dead and incapable of life, but by dying it emerges into life once it has put off all its deadness)."⁶⁸ It is in similar terms that Bérulle describes the living death of Mary Magdalene, that symbol of the life of love: "Jesus is her life and, though she may seem alive, it is not she who lives; it is Jesus who lives in her [Gal 2.20]. And so she is living and not living, living and dying, all at the same time.... For Jesus who is her life is alive in her only to make her die.... O living death and

---

⁶⁵*De oratione dominica* (*Or. dom.*) 2 (PG 44:1144D). Translation in *St Gregory of Nyssa: The Lord's Prayer and The Beatitudes*, trans. Hilda C. Graef (Mahwah, NJ: Paulist Press, 1954), 41–42.
⁶⁶See Tertullian, *On Modesty* 9 (ANF 4:192f).
⁶⁷*Cant.* 12 (PG 44:1016D; Norris, 363).
⁶⁸Ibid. (PG 44:1020B; Norris, 367).

Death and Resurrection

dying life!"[69] Here we have the supreme effect of baptismal grace, of the mystery of death and resurrection with Christ.

It is important to note that this sacramental character of Gregory's mysticism is not peculiar to him. It is found—largely under his influence, incidentally—throughout Eastern Christian mysticism.[70] We pointed to the relationship in his writings between the baptismal φωτισμός, (*phōtismos*, illumination) and mystical illumination. In the words of the Orthodox theologian Myrrha Lot-Borodine, "The entire doctrine of mystical illumination is a reality beyond nature inherent in the grace of baptism. At the moment of baptism, Cabasilas says, a 'divine ray' invisibly touches the soul, which begins to know through direct intuition, with a transforming knowledge that already announces union. The theology of the sacraments, of which baptismal regeneration is the first initiation, accords with the theology of the mystical states and opens to Christian souls the path of ἕνωσις (*henōsis*, union) and θέωσις (*theōsis*, deification)."[71]

What is true of Baptism is true of the entire sacramental economy. This correspondence between the degrees of the spiritual life and the various sacraments that we see sketched out in our author, and which others besides ourselves have noted,[72] will become part and parcel of the structure of eastern mysticism. "One sees," writes Madame Lot-Borodine—and these words will provide a fitting conclusion to this section of our study—"how from the *ritual* level to the *mystical* level proper one finds the same stages of spiritual progress. For the contemplative ascetics—with their πρακτική (*praktikē*, ascetical practice), θεωρία (*theōria*, contemplation), and μυστική θεολογία (*mystikē theologia*, mysical theology)—continue for their own part these ideas of purification, illumination, and perfection-in-union that guide the Areopagite and his disciples on the path of the deifying sacraments."[73]

---

[69]P. de Bérulle, *Élévation sur Marie-Madeleine* (Saint Maximin: Éditions de la Vie spirituelle, 1922), 76–77.

[70]In St Basil a link is already made between the sacramental life and the degrees of the spiritual life, although he is concerned above all to describe the three ways in terms of three aspects of Baptism: the destruction of the passions, the putting on of Christ, and intimacy with the Father (*De baptismo* 21–25; PG 31:1561–68). Gregory, on the other hand, connects the three ways with the three main sacraments. Therein lies his originality.

[71]M. Lot-Borodine, "La grâce déifiante," 328.

[72]See Lewy, *Sobria ebrietas*, 136.

[73]M. Lot-Borodine, "Initiation à une mystique sacramentaire de l'Orient," *Revue des Sciences Philosophiques et Théologiques* 24 (1935): 664–75, at 672. [For a recent appraisal of the Dionysian corpus that emphasizes its organic place in the eastern monastic and ascetical tradition, see Abp Alexander Golitzin, *Mystagogy: A Monastic Reading of Dionysius Areopagita*, ed. Bogdan Bucur (Collegeville, MN: Liturgical Press, 2013).—*Ed.*]

The Inner Man

Together with this sacramental character, there is another feature of the spiritual life that is present from the beginning: namely, an inner dimension. For in addition to the separation from evil and error that is brought about by Baptism, there is also separation from the world. In the *Homilies on the Song of Songs*, the word ἀναχώρησις (*anachōrēsis*) is used for the first kind of separation,[74] but we come across it again, referring to the second kind, in connection with Moses.[75] And here, moreover, it has its technical meaning.[76] The two kinds of withdrawal are illustrated by two parallel scenes at the beginning of *The Life of Moses*: the *discalceatio* symbolizes separation from evil, the flight into the desert of Midian represents separation from the world. The two are complementary: the first marks the objective dependency of the spiritual life on Christ and the Mystical Body; the second indicates the inner dimension of this life. The "new man" of St Paul [Eph 4.24], which is a "covering" or "clothing" of the soul, is at the same time the "inner man" (ὁ ἔνδον ἄνθρωπος, *ho endon anthrōpos* [Rom 7.22]). We shall see the importance of this double aspect in the higher forms of the spiritual life, which are at one and the same time "instasis" and "ecstasis," "recollection" and a "going out from the self."

Thus external separation or withdrawal from the world—ἀναχώρησις (*anachōrēsis*) in the strict sense—is merely the prerequisite for a deeper reality: the return of the soul to itself. Here too, Moses is the great model. It is almost always in connection with him that the theme of withdrawal is developed. In Book One of *The Life of Moses*—the ἱστορία (*historia*) or literal account—we read: "Separating himself from association with the people, he thereafter lived alone [ἰδιάσαι, *idiasai*]. . . . Moses lived alone [ἰδιάζουσα, *idiazousa*] in the mountains away from all the turmoil of the marketplace [ἀπὸ ἀγοραίου τύρβης, *apo agoraiou tyrbēs*]; there in the wilderness [κατὰ τὴν ἔρημον, *kata tēn erēmon*] he cared for his sheep."[77] This "eremitical" life is discussed again as a symbol of inward recollection in Book Two—the θεωρία (*theōria*), the contemplation or interpretation that follows the literal account: "In the same way we shall live a solitary life [ἰδιάσομεν, *idiasomen*] . . . among those of like disposition and mind

---

[74]*Cant.* 11 (PG 44:1000D; Norris, 341).
[75]See Gregory, *Thaum*, 3.25 (PG 46:908D); Slusser, 51.
[76][Cf. the English term "anchorite."—*Trans.*]
[77]*Vit. Moys.* 1.19 (PG 44:305B; Malherbe, 34).

Death and Resurrection

who are fed by us while all the movements of our soul are shepherded, like sheep, by the will of guiding [ἡγεμονικόν, *hēgemonikon*] reason."[78]

Here, clearly indicated, we have both the outer solitude and the inner silence that is its goal and that facilitates the soul's contemplation. It is this twofold idea—once more in connection with Moses—that we find in *On the Inscriptions of the Psalms*: "[Moses] banished himself from human society for forty years and lived alone [μόνος μόνῳ συζῶν, *monos monō syzōn*], focusing steadfastly [ἐνατενίζων, *enatenizōn*] in undistracted solitude and in tranquillity [δι' ἡσυχίας, *di' hēsychias*] on the contemplation of invisible things [τῇ θεωρίᾳ τῶν ἀοράτων, *tē theōria tōn aoratōn*]."[79] The theme is the same as in the preceding passage, though the vocabulary is markedly more Plotinian. This can be explained by the fact that *On the Inscriptions of the Psalms* is one of Gregory's earliest works. What is evoked here is not just "eremitism" but "monachism" [i.e., monasticism] (μόνος μόνῳ, *monos monō*). We shall return to all these points.

Let us adduce two further passages that will confirm and complete what we have already found. They are from the eulogy for Basil and the biography of Gregory the Wonderworker. Gregory says of Basil that like Moses he "dwelt alone [ἐφ' ἑαυτοῦ ἰδιάζων, *eph' heautou idiazōn*] for a long time. He forsook the city's tumult and the clamor of material attractions and engaged in divine philosophy [προσφιλοσοφῶν τῷ θεῷ, *prosphilosophōn tō theō*] in solitude [ἐσχατιᾶς, *eschatiās*]."[80] At greater length, he compares Gregory the Wonderworker to the same Moses: "Both left this agitated and beset life, Moses and Gregory each in his own time going off by himself. . . . They both had the same aim, for each of them departed from the crowd with the purpose of penetrating the divine mysteries [τὰ θεῖα μυστήρια, *ta theia mystēria*] with the pure eye of the soul [τῷ καθαρῷ τῆς ψυχῆς ὀφθαλμῷ, *tō katharō tēs psychēs ophthalmō*]."[81]

As seen, this retreat far from the world is sometimes presented as a "flight" (φυγή, *phygē*). Thus, still commenting on the departure of Moses to the desert of Midian, Gregory writes: "If, therefore, we by ourselves are too weak [to live among the people] . . . we must flee as quickly as possible . . . from the conflict to the greater and higher teaching of the mysteries."[82] Similarly, the homilies on the Lord's Prayer, after describing our baptismal reconciliation, continue as follows:

---

[78] *Vit. Moys.* 2.18 (PG 44:332B–C; Malherbe, 59).
[79] *Inscr.* 1.7.52 (PG 44:456C; Heine, 101).
[80] *Bas.* (PG 46:809B; McCambley, 21).
[81] *Thaum.* 3.25 (PG 46:908D; FC 98:51).
[82] *Vit. Moys.* 2.16 (PG 44:332B; Malherbe, 58).

"In the same way it seems to me that if the Lord is teaching us to call upon the Father in Heaven, He means to remind us [μνήμην ποεῖσθαι, *mnēmēn poeisthai*] of our beautiful fatherland [πατρίδος, *patridos*].... Now the way which leads human nature back to Heaven is none other than that of avoiding the evils of the world by flight [φυγή, *phygē*]; on the other hand, the purpose of fleeing from evils seems to me precisely to achieve likeness with God [ὁμοίωσις πρὸς τὸν Θεόν, *homoiōsis pros ton theon*]."[83] It is interesting to see the themes of Baptism and withdrawal linked together once more, as being the two essential aspects of conversion.

But another observation needs to be made: namely, the Platonic, and above all Plotinian, character of all these passages. In them, we come across several expressions that are altogether characteristic. To begin with the last passage, the theme of flight and its connection with the idea of "likeness to God" is an obvious allusion to Plato's comment that "one ought to try to escape from here to there as quickly as one can. Now the way to escape is to become as nearly as possible like a god" (φυγὴ δὲ ὁμοίωσις θεῷ, *phygē de homoiōsis theō*).[84] The same theme is found almost word for word in Plotinus: "Since Evil is here ... and it is the Soul's design to escape from Evil, we must escape hence. But what is this escape? In attaining Likeness to God" (ὁμοιθῆναι θεῷ, *homoiōthēnai theō*).[85] As we saw above, this is the selfsame turn of phrase as that used by Gregory: "And the purpose of fleeing from evils seems to me precisely to achieve likeness with God." The very flow of the sentence suggests that Gregory had come across this Platonic phraseology in Plotinus. Elsewhere in Plotinus, the theme of flight is linked, as in Gregory, to that of a return to the beloved fatherland: "Let us flee then to the beloved Fatherland."[86]

Nor is this notion of a flight the only thing that evokes Plotinus. His famous definition of the summit of perfection as being a flight of "the alone towards the alone" (μόνους πρὸς μόνον, *monous pros monon*)[87] comes to mind. The expression μόνος πρὸς μόνον (*monos pros monon*) is found several times in his works.[88] It is also in Philo—and, more to the point, in his own *Life of Moses*

---

[83] *Or. dom.* 2 (PG 44:1145A; ACW 18:42). See also *Cant.* 9 (PG 44:961A; Norris, 287).

[84] Plato, *Theaetetus* 176b. Translation from *Plato: Theaetetus*, trans. John McDowell (Oxford: Oxford University Press, 1973, 2014).

[85] Plotinus, *Enneads* 1.2.1. Translation from *Plotinus: The Enneads*, trans. Stephen MacKenna, John Dillon, ed. (Harmondsworth: Penguin Books, 1991).

[86] Ibid. 1.6.8.

[87] Ibid. 5.1.6. E. Peterson has shown that this was an ancient Greek philosophical expression. See "Herkunft und Bedeutung der *Monos pros monon*-formel bei Plotin," *Philologus* 88 (1933): 40–41.

[88] See Plotinus, *Enneads* 1.6.7; 5.1.6; 6.7.34.

(2.163). The texts by Gregory that we have been examining contain expressions that are similar, as, for example, the phrase "lived alone" (μόνος μόνῳ, *monos monō*),[89] though here the second μόνος refers to the subject. Yet elsewhere in Gregory we find echoes of the same Plotinian expression in which the second term does refer to the object of contemplation. Take, for instance, the following verse from *The Song*: "Thou hast ravished my heart with one [μόνῳ, *monō*] of thine eyes" (4. 9). Gregory comments on this as follows:

> For the soul's work of seeing is twofold: there is one operation by which it sees the truth, and another that is led astray by attending to things that amount to nothing. And since the Bride's pure eye [καθαρὸς ὀφθαλμός, *katharos ophthalmos*] is open only to the nature of the good, while the other is inactive, the friends for this reason give praise to *one* of her eyes, by whose sole means she contemplates the only One [δι' οὗ μόνου θεωρεῖ τὸν μόνον, *di ou monou theōrei ton monon*], I mean [λέγω, *legō*], which is known in its immutable and eternal nature: the true Father, the Only Begotten Son, and the Holy Spirit.[90]

Here the allusion to Plotinus is certain. Not only does the resemblance between the two expressions allow us to suppose this, but we have more specific proof. Like other writers of the fourth century—and unlike those of the preceding century, such as Clement—Gregory never mentions his sources.[91] But his use of certain literary devices allows us to detect them. For example, when Gregory is conscious of using a secular expression—and thus one that is open to misunderstanding—he frequently repeats it, so as to specify the meaning, with the help of the formula "λέγω" (*legō*, I mean). Hence, when in another text he uses Philo's famous phrase, "sober inebriation" (μέθη νηφάλιος, *methē nēphalios*), he goes on to clarify things: "'Ἐκείνην λέγω τὴν μέθην, *Ekeinēn legō tēn methēn*" ("What I am referring to is the drunkenness . . .").[92] Now, this is precisely what we have in the above comments on the Song. Since his phraseology is potentially ambiguous, Gregory specifies that he in no way fails to recognize the Trinitarian reality of the one God.

[89] *Inscr.* 1.7.52 (PG 44:456C; Heine, 101).
[90] *Cant.* 8 (PG 44:949C–D; Norris, 271).
[91] See the translator's introduction to Sallustius, *Concerning the Gods and the Universe*, trans. A. D. Nock (Cambridge: Cambridge University Press, 1926), xxxviii.
[92] *Cant.* 5 (PG 44:873B; Norris, 169). [The quoted sentence continues: ". . . that occasion that self-transcendence [ἔκστασις, *ekstasis*] by which people move out of the material sphere toward what is more divine."—Ed.]

He continues as follows in a way that will provide us with the true meaning of the above phrase:

> For that is truly "only" [μόνος, *monos*] which is contemplated in a single nature, without the introduction of any division or estrangement on the ground that the hypostases are distinct. For there are people who, by making wrong use of different [διαφόροι, *diaphoroi*] eyes, have a clear vision of what is not real [τὸ ἀνύπαρκτον, *to anyparkton*] and divide the One [τὸ ἕν, *to hen*] into many natures because of the fantasies [φαντασίαις, *phantasias*] conjured by their perverse eyes. These are the so-called "many-seeing"; they see nothing because they perceive many things. . . . On the other hand, the person whose vision is keen solely [πρὸς μόνον, *pros monon*] where the Divine is concerned is blind in respect of all of those other things. . . . And so too the many-eyed person, who looks on empty things with a multitude of eyes, is blind, while the one who through one eye—that of the soul—looks upon the Good [δι' ἑνός . . . πρὸς μόνον, *di' henos . . . pros monon*] is sharp and clear of sight.[93]

This leads us to the heart of the topic we are examining. The return of the soul to itself entails the rejection of a multiplicity that is external in favor of spiritual unity within. Such unification is the prerequisite for gaining knowledge of him who is One, by virtue of the principle that only like knows like.[94] Thus, in this text the multiple (διάφορος, *diaphoros*) is identified with what has no consistency ([or "existence"—*Ed.*] ἀνύπαρκτος, *anyparktos*) and with what exists only in the imagination (φαντασία, *phantasia*). The multiple is unreal. (We shall come across this theme of the unreality of the external world again, when discussing the second way.) By contrast, what truly exists is that which is simple and single. Therefore, the soul should extricate itself from all multiplicity, should "collect itself." Then, having rediscovered a unified gaze,[95] it will be able to contemplate the One.

The texts discussed previously all become clearer in this light. In them it is always a question of "living as a solitary" (ἰδιάζειν, *idiazein*),[96] and the fruit of

---

[93]*Cant.* 8 (PG 44:949D–952A; Norris, 271, 273).

[94]Cf. *Virg.* 11 (PG 46:368C; FC 58:41). On this principle in Platonism, see A. J. Festugière, *Le Dieu cosmique* (Paris: Lecoffre, 1949), 217–18.

[95]Cf. "Your eye is one because it looks toward the One"; *Cant.* 8 (PG 44:952B; Norris, 273).

[96]*Vit. Moys.* 1.19, 2.18 (PG 44:305B, 332B; Malherbe, 34, 59); *Bas.* (PG 46:809B; McCambley, 21).

this solitude is that "all the movements of our soul are shepherded, like sheep, by the will of guiding reason [τοῦ λόγου, *tou logou*]."[97] It is by this means that the soul is able to arrive at "the contemplation of the invisible things."[98] To sensory knowledge—symbolized by the multiple eyes—which has as its object the world of appearances (the multiple), is opposed the eye of the soul, which is both single[99] and pure (καθαρός, *katharos*),[100] and through which the soul contemplates reality—that is to say, the One.

Moreover, this unification of the soul is a return to its true nature. Here again Gregory's mysticism is based on his ontology: "[H]uman life was originally uniform [μονοειδής, *monoeidēs*]; by uniform I mean [λέγω δέ, *legō de*] the life which exhibits the good only, unmixed with evil."[101] Μονοειδής is another Platonic term,[102] as we might have guessed from the interpolated clause beginning "λέγω δέ." It is also found in Plotinus.[103] This primal and fundamental unity of the spirit is symbolized in the story of creation by the prohibition against touching the tree of the knowledge of good and evil, a symbol of division: "This opinion is attested by God's first law, which gave to mankind unstinting participation in every one of the good things of paradise, excluding only that which had as its nature a mixture of opposites, evil combined with good."[104] For Gregory this means that only the first tree existed; the second simply symbolized the possibility of the fall. Moreover, he argues, the simultaneous existence of two trees in the center of the garden would have been an impossibility.[105]

This primal unity is what characterizes the natural state (κατά φύσιν, *kata physin*) of the human being; that is to say, "the image [εἰκών, *eikon*] of God," which, according to Gregory's doctrine, is alien to the sensory, animal world. Moreover, μονοειδής (*monoeidēs*, uniform) is equivalent to θεοειδής (*theoeidēs*,

---

[97] *Vit. Moys.* 2.18 (PG 44:332C; Malherbe, 59).
[98] *Inscr.* 1.7.52 (PG 44:456C; Heine, 101).
[99] *Cant.* 8 (PG 44:952A; Norris, 273).
[10] *Thaum.* 3.25 (PG 46:908D; FC 98:51). Gregory, *Cant.* 8 (PG 44:949C; Norris, 271).
[101] *De anima et resurrectione* (*An. et res.*) 5 (PG 46:81B). English translation from *On the Soul and the Resurrection*, trans. Catharine P. Roth, Popular Patristics Series 12 (Crestwood, NY: St Vladimir's Seminary Press, 1993), 70.
[102] Plato, *Phaedo* 78d.
[103] Plotinus, *Enneads* 6.9.3.
[104] Gregory, *An. et res.* 5 (PG 46:81B; PPS 12:70). See also *On the Making of Man* 20.3: "The very actual good is in its nature simple and uniform [μονοειδής, *monoeidēs*]" (PG 44:200C; NPNF² 5:410). Cf. Synesius of Cyrene, *De Regno* 6.1-2 (PG 66:1070); English translation: "On Imperial Rule" in *The Essays and Hymns of Synesius of Cyrene, including the Address to the Emperor Arcadius and the Political Speeches*, trans. Augustine Fitzgerald (London: Oxford University Press, 1930).
[105] See Gregory, *Cant.* Prol. (PG 44:761B; Norris, 9): "There can only be one midpoint in a circle."

godlike, deiform) as a way of characterizing the deiform state in which man was originally created and which constitutes his true nature: "So when the soul which has become simple [ἁπλῆ, *haplē*] and uniform [μονοειδής, *monoeidēs*] and an accurate image of God [θεοείκελος, *theoeikelos*] finds that truly simple [ἁπλοῦν, *haploun*] and immaterial good . . . it attaches itself to it. . . ."[106]

A particular aspect of the return of the soul to its original unity—but which corresponds to a higher stage of the spiritual life—is the disappearance of the multiple activity of the senses.[107] Gregory describes the first man as "not yet judging the beautiful by taste and sight, but only enjoying the Lord."[108] This doctrine will be taken to extremes by Diadochus of Photiki [c. 400–c. 486]. In his opinion the soul originally had only one sense, but following the disobedience of Adam it became divided between two tendencies: the one always leading him to the things of heaven, the other toward things here below, this latter tendency being further divided into the evil activities of the five senses.[109] Gregory does not go this far. On this point, we notice in him a curious hesitation. He is unwilling to identify as rigorously as Diadochus the opposition between good and evil, or between the one and the multiple. Although the soul must be unified, in the sense that all evil must disappear,[110] he is not certain that this implies the disappearance of all multiplicity. Thus he allows for the survival of a certain multiplicity in spiritual knowledge. We see this in his doctrine of the "spiritual senses," which we shall study later.

It is interesting to compare this interpretation of the multiplicity of the senses with another passage, one in which Gregory is discussing the incarnation. The order established by Christ is seen not as a simple return to some primal unity, but the creation of something distinctly new—a synthesis of unity and multiplicity. Here is this striking passage:

> For in truth it is through the church that the "multiform wisdom of God," which has worked its great marvels by the instrumentality of contraries, is made known to the powers above the cosmos: how life came through death

---

[106] *An. et res.* 6 (PG 46:93C; PPS 12:80). See also ibid. (PG 46:89B; PPS 12:77).

[107] See Philo, *On the Migration of Abraham* 28.153 (Yonge, 268); Clement of Alexandria, *Miscellanies* 4.23, 25 (ANF 2:923–28); Origen, *On Prayer* 21.2. English translation in Tertullian, Cyprian, and Origen, *On the Lord's Prayer*, trans. Alistair Stewart-Sykes, Popular Patristics Series 26 (Crestwood, NY: St Vladimir's Seminary Press, 2004), 158.

[108] *Virg.* 12 (PG 46:374C; NPNF² 5:46).

[109] Diadochos of Photiki, *On Spiritual Knowledge and Discrimination: One Hundred Texts* 25; in *The Philokalia*, vol. 1, G. E. H. Palmer, P. Sherrard and K. Ware, trans. (Faber and Faber: London, 1979), 259.

[110] *An. et res.* 5 (PG 46:81B; PPS 12:70).

Death and Resurrection

> ... and strength through weakness. In previous times, the powers above the cosmos knew only the simple and uniform [ἁπλῆ καὶ μονοειδής, *haplē kai monoeidēs*] wisdom of God ... and there was nothing "multiform" in the things that were to be seen. ... But they were brought to a clear knowledge of this manifoldness of wisdom, which consists in the knitting together of contraries, through the church: how the Word becomes flesh; how life is mingled with death; how by his own stripes our calamity is healed [cf. Is 53.5]; how by the weakness of the cross the power of the Adversary was overthrown.[111]

Later we shall again come across Gregory's hesitation between the Platonic opinion that diversity and unity are opposed to one another and an alternate point of view that envisages the possibility of their combination. This will be when we examine his theory of the passions, which parallels that of the senses. At times, he asserts that the passions, which are linked to man's animal condition, will disappear along with it. At others, more faithful to the Christian doctrine of the resurrection, he accepts that they will subsist, though in a transfigured form. The same holds true for the senses. Sometimes he thinks that all that will subsist is the unity of the νοῦς (*nous*, mind); sometimes he admits the survival of a certain multiplicity. On this point, the theology of the incarnation happens to collide with his Platonic tendencies and forces him to transcend them.

Flight and reintegration are not the only Plotinian themes encountered in the passages quoted above. Concerning Moses' retreat, for example, Gregory states that he spent it "focusing steadfastly [ἐνατενίζειν, *enatenizein*] in undistracted solitude [δι' ἡσυχίας, *di' hēsychias*] on the contemplation of invisible things."[112] The first word here is itself quite characteristic of Plotinus.[113] We find it elsewhere in Gregory too,[114] either in the physical sense of "staring" (for example, at the sun), or in the sense of prolonged contemplation. It clarifies what Gregory had said about the unification of the inner "gaze." As for ἡσυχία (*hēsychia*, [inner] stillness), this expresses the condition of a soul that is shielded from the agitations of the world. It is the fruit of separation from the world just as *apatheia* is the fruit of separation from evil. Consequently, we will study them together as a perfecting of the practice of the virtues.

[111] *Cant.* 8 (PG 44:948C–949A; Norris, 269).
[112] *nscr.* 1.7.52 (PG 44:456C; Heine, 101).
[113] Plotinus, *Enneads* 6.2.8; 4.7; 5.12.
[114] *Eccl.* 8 (PG 44:753C; Hall, 144). See also *Cant.* 1 (PG 44:773D; Norris, 29) and *Cant.* 4 (PG 44:833D; Norris, 117).

The above references are taken from *The Life of Moses*, but once again the *Homilies on the Song of Songs* offer a parallel theme, referring to the same fact: the return of the soul to itself at the beginning of the spiritual life. And this, too, is Platonic in nature. In the Song (1.8) we read: "If thou know [γνῷς, *gnōs*] not thyself, thou fair one among women, go thou forth by the footsteps of the flocks." Gregory comments on this as follows:

> So the most secure watch over the good things within us is not to be ignorant of ourselves and for each to know [γνῶναι, *gnōnai*] what he is and to distinguish clearly between himself and the things around his edges [περὶ αὐτόν, *peri auton*], so that he may not end up keeping guard over what is alien [τὸ ἀλλότριον, *to allotrion*] rather than over himself.
>
> Now the person who is concerned about the life of this world and who judges its honors worthy of being guarded does not know how to distinguish what is his own from what is alien, for none of the things that come and then go belongs to us. . . . [But] the person who takes account of what is proper [ἴδιον, *idiom*] to human nature—and that is reason [λόγος, *logos*]—will despise [καταφρονήσει, *kataphronēsei*] irrational [ἀλόγον, *alogon*] habit and will choose as good nothing that does not profit the soul.[115]

Here we have the Socratic and Platonic exhortation to "know thyself": γνῶθι σεαυτόν (*gnōthi seauton*).[116] It helps to clarify what the preceding texts have shown us: the soul must return to itself because that is where the true goods are, and for this it must learn to know them. Thus the return to self is based on a value judgment. The soul must understand that what is proper to it (τὸ ἴδιον, *to idion*) is of greater value than what surrounds it (τὰ περὶ αὐτόν, *ta peri auton*) and is alien (ἀλλότριον, *allotrion*) to it. This concept of the νοῦς, or the λόγος, as being unique to humans is entirely Platonic. So is the idea that the fault of the soul consists in losing a sense of its own value: "The souls . . . no longer discern either the divinity or their own nature; ignorance of their rank brings self-depreciation; they misplace their respect, honouring everything more than themselves."[117] The words—e.g., τιμῆσαι (*timēsai*, honor)—are the same in Plo-

---

[115] *Cant.* 2 (PG 44:804A–805A; Norris, 71, 73).

[116] The connection is made by Origen in his *Commentary on the Song of Songs* 2.8. The Christian transposition of the Socratic formula can already be found in Clement of Alexandria. See *The Instructor (Paedagogus)* 3.1 (ANF 2:578). See also Gregory, *De mortuis* (*Mort.*) 8 (PG 46:508D). English translation from *On Death and Eternal Life*, trans. Brian Daley, Popular Patristics Series 64 (Yonkers, NY: St Vladimir's Seminary Press, 2022), 11.

[117] Plotinus, *Enneads* 5.1.1.

tinus as in Gregory. So too is the idea that the first step of "philosophy" is for the soul to rediscover its value, which it had forgotten, having allowed itself to be seduced by the variety of external things. The soul should withdraw, regain full awareness of itself, and rediscover its unity—these same ideas are found time and again. It must first "know itself," know its own value, then retire in solitude (ἰδιάζουσα, *idiazousa*) far from what can distract it from itself. Then it will be able to rediscover its unity, to explore itself and its personal life (τὸ ἴδιον, *to idion*; what is proper to it).

This is a theme that is certainly central to Neoplatonism, to its initial approach. It is an idea that is found everywhere: in Plotinus, as in Gregory of Nyssa, and in St Augustine: "Withdraw into yourself and look," the first writes; "when you are self-gathered in the purity of your being, nothing now remaining that can shatter that inner unity [πρὸς τὸ εἷς οὕτω γενέσθαι, *pros to heis houtō genesthai*] nothing from without clinging to the authentic person . . . you are now become very vision. . . . Strain [ἀτενίσας, *atenisas*] and see. This is the only eye [μόνος ὁ ὀφθαλμός, *monos ho ophthalmos*] that sees the mighty Beauty."[118] Plotinus develops this idea by comparing it to a statue that must be chiseled, to an eye that must itself become luminous and clear so as to contemplate the light. All this is in Gregory, too. We have already encountered the unification of the soul, the single eye, and the gaze (ἀτενίσας, *atenisas*); but the image of the statue is also found.[119] Likewise the theme of the eye transformed into light,[120] which gazes upon (ἀτενίζει, *atenizei*) Beauty, if it is purified of the rheum (λήμη, *lēmē*)[121] of vice.

St Augustine writes in similar vein: "When, therefore, [the soul] is bidden to become acquainted with itself [*ut seipsam cognoscat*], let it not seek itself as though it were withdrawn from itself; but let it withdraw that which it has added to itself. For itself lies more deeply within, not only than those sensible things, which are clearly without, but also than the images of them."[122] This fits with Gregory's understanding of "self-knowledge" conceived as a return to self by the elimination of alien things. It is also the very essence of Neoplatonic purification, which is a restoring to the soul of its pure spiritual essence. As Gregory puts it,

---

[118]Ibid., 1.6.9.
[119]*Inscr.* 2.11.133 (PG 44:544A–C; Heine, 163–64).
[120]*Cant.* 4 (PG 44:833D; Norris, 117).
[121]See Plotinus, *Enneads* 1.6.9; Gregory, *Virg.* 10 (PG 46:360C; FC 58:36).
[122]Augustine, *On the Trinity* 10.8.11 (NPNF[1] 3:286).

"The rejection of what is alien means a return to what is proper and natural to oneself."[123]

Yet there is more. We said earlier that the unification (μονοειδής, *monoeidēs*) of the soul was the condition for it to know God, who is One. Generally speaking, the return of the soul to itself—which involves purification as well as unification—is, for Neoplatonism, the means to know God: "It is a fundamental theme common to Neoplatonism and Augustinianism," writes von Ivánka, "that the soul knows God not by concluding from external things, nor by a deduction on the basis of attributes, but by a return to its own inwardness, by a return to itself, which implies at the same time a separation from all things external. The true knowledge of self and the true knowledge of God are linked so intimately that the soul, if it is purified of all that is not itself, thereby knows God in itself and through itself."[124]

This is clear enough from the texts themselves. As Plotinus writes, "God ... is outside of none, present unperceived to all; we break away from Him, or rather from ourselves."[125] Likewise, St Augustine: "For they endeavor to find a path outwardly, and forsake their own inward things, within which is God."[126] The same idea is found in Gregory: "The person who has purified all the powers of his soul from every form of evil" will see "the only thing which is beautiful by nature."[127] "If the soul returns to herself [ἐπανελθοῦσα, *epanelthousa*], if she knows herself in her true nature, then she contemplates the model in her own beauty, as in a mirror and an image."[128] The same movement pervades all these texts: self-knowledge through purification of all that is external and knowledge of God in oneself.

But this equating of the two, if it is real, poses a serious problem: "How," asks von Ivánka, "does the purification of everything that is alien lead to knowledge of God? The answer to this question," he continues, "is easy for a Neoplatonist. For if the soul is divine by virtue of its simple and indivisible nature, it is certain that as soon as what is alien is removed, it can know God in itself. God and the unified soul are the same thing. . . . But, for a Christian, to claim that the soul and God are identical is inadmissible."[129] Here, then, is the specific problem we must

---

[123] *Virg.* 12 (PG 46:372C; FC 58:44).
[124] E. von Ivánka, "Die unmittelbare Gotteserkenntnis bei Augustin," *Scholastik* 13 (1938): 521–43, at 522.
[125] Plotinus, *Enneads* 6.9.7.
[126] Augustine, *On the Trinity* 8.7.11 (NPNF¹ 3:248).
[127] *Virg.* 11 (PG 46:368D; FC 58:42).
[128] *An. et res.* 6 (PG 46:89C; PPS 12:78).
[129] Von Ivánka, "Die unmittelbare Gotteserkenntnis bei Augustin," 523.

Death and Resurrection

examine: is the purified soul's knowledge of God the same in Neoplatonism as in Gregory of Nyssa?

But, we must first question the nature of the knowledge that the purified soul has of *itself*. We have noted all the Neoplatonic traits in Gregory's texts on this subject, but have they yielded their fullest meaning? On further examination, we notice that a number of the terms he uses have connotations that are quite different. For a start, the praise of the solitary life—in particular, the various expressions used to describe it (κατὰ τὴν ἔρημον; ἀναχώρησις; μόνος; *kata tēn erēmon; anachōrēsis; monos*)—brings to mind the historical world in which Gregory lived: that of the rise of monasticism. "Eremitism," "anchorite," "monk"—these are words with a very precise meaning and that place us squarely in the midst of a Christian world.

Gregory was familiar with this world, and not just by hearsay; he had been an intimate part of it. His brother Basil was the great lawgiver of the cenobitic life, the form of monasticism that was beginning to take over from ancient eremitism at this time.[130] Gregory himself had experienced this life. When he writes of Moses withdrawing "far from the busyness of cities" (ἀγοραίου τύρβης, *agoraiou turbēs*), he is thinking of Caesarea and the restless years of his own youth. The desert he describes that is situated at the end (ἐσχατιᾶς, *eschatias*) of the world is none other than the solitude of Annesi in the wild mountains on the banks of the river Iris, where he joined his brother Basil and where he spent many years in the contemplation of hidden realities.

This solitude allowed Gregory to withdraw into himself, to discover his soul. But here again we have to ask the same question: is the inner man for him the same thing as the Plotinian νοῦς (*nous*, mind)? Earlier, we saw a passage in which he affirmed that what is unique and proper to man is λόγος (*logos*, reason), but that does not exhaust all that Gregory has to say on the matter. He continues as follows:

> Know how much you have been honored by the Maker above the rest of creation. Heaven did not become the image of God [εἰκὼν τοῦ θεοῦ, *eikōn tou theou*], nor the moon, nor the sun, nor the beautiful stars.... Only you came into existence as a copy [ἀπεικόνισμα, *apeikonisma*] of the Nature that transcends every intellect, a likeness of the incorruptible beauty, an impress

---

[130]For a recent study of St Basil's role in the rise of monasticism in Asia Minor and a translation of his seminal rule, see *The Asketikon of St Basil the Great*, trans. Anna M. Silvas, Oxford Early Christian Studies (Oxford: Oxford University Press, 2005).—*Ed.*

of the true Deity—a model of that true Light in the contemplation of which you become what it is, imitating that which shines within you by the ray that shines forth in response from your purity [καθαρότητος, *katharotētos*].[131]

In this passage, two things are noteworthy. The first is that the inner man is the image of God. Here we have an expression that, in this sense, is not Plotinian. In due course, we shall see what this image of God is. We shall note that it is the divine (θεοειδής, *theoeidēs*) element of the soul—namely, sanctifying grace. Thus, what man discovers in himself is not merely his intellectual nature, his λόγος (*logos*); it is his spiritual life, the divine πνεῦμα (*pneuma*, spirit). Furthermore—and this is our second observation—this πνεῦμα is not discovered as something he possesses on his own account, but as something that is communicated to him, that is "reflected" in him if he turns toward it, as a "grace" in the full sense of the word.

We are beginning to see what the rest of our investigation will explore, and to realize that for Gregory the inner state is not that of Neoplatonism after all. What he finds when entering into himself is the communication God makes of his own supernatural life. And thus, the aspect of interiority, the immanence of the spiritual life, accords with the transcendence of the sacramental aspect. Christian interiority is a deepening of baptismal grace, not simply the mind's becoming self-aware. But what is striking is that this original experience is nonetheless expressed by Gregory in Neoplatonic terms. These provide him—when suitably modified—with a structure that enables him to give expression to an experience of a very different nature. We shall come across this feature at successive spiritual levels, above all when we come to the mystical life proper and the pressing question associated with it: what is the nature of the knowledge that a purified soul has of God within itself? But first we must survey the initial stages of purification (κάθαρσις, *katharsis*) and detachment from the world (καταφρόνησις, *kataphronēsis*; contempt, disdain).

---

[131]*Cant.* 2 (PG 44:805C–D; Norris, 75).

2

The Structure of the Soul and the Passions

We have seen that the aim of the first way was purification from the passions (τὰ πάθη, *ta pathē*) and the achieving of dispassion (ἀπάθεια, *apatheia*). But what, precisely, do these words mean?

In asking this question we come up against one of the most difficult problems in eastern spiritual theology, for all of these concepts are borrowed from pagan philosophy, where they are understood in different ways according to the various schools. Moreover, their use by Christian authors brings about new shades of meaning. In fact, the very concept of asceticism is entirely linked to one's understanding of what is meant by the passions and by dispassion. In Gregory, the problem is one of great complexity. Cherniss—who did no more than broach the subject—has demonstrated Gregory's dependence on Plato for his doctrine of the passions.[1] Yet Gregory's teaching remains to be studied in and for itself.

My own research into his use of the word πάθος (*pathos*) has shown that it has various meanings, depending on which level of reality or to which aspect of the spiritual life it is referring. Leaving aside secondary meanings—for example, when the context is that of a historical event[2] or an illness[3]—we find that there are two principal meanings. In the first place, the passions refer to everything in man that is linked to the animal life, whether in its external reality (birth, nutrition, generation, disease, death, and so on) or its psychological nature (sensory knowledge, desire, courage, and so forth). This animal nature, good in itself, nonetheless constitutes a degradation for man. As a rule, Gregory symbolizes this by using the image of the "garments of skin" in which, as Genesis tells us (3.21), Adam was clothed after the fall.

---

[1]See Harold Fredrik Cherniss, *The Platonism of Gregory of Nyssa* (Berkeley, CA: University of California Press, 1930), 12–25.
[2]*Inscr.* 2.2.12 (PG 44:489D; Heine, 126).
[3]*Inscr.* 2.6.66 (PG 44:512A; Heine, 140).

On the other hand, the term "passions" may also denote the totality of man's sinful proclivities. In this sense, they correspond exactly to what today we would call the "seven deadly sins." A perusal of any of the lists of sins given by Gregory is enough to convince one of this.[4] It is this second sense of the word that is properly that of Christian asceticism.[5] The struggle against the passions—which is the aim of the ascetic life—is a struggle against one's evil tendencies, not against corporeal life as such. It is here that Christian asceticism differs from the Platonic point of view, whose object is specifically to isolate the mind from the animal life.

But what renders the problem more complex still is that this latter consideration does exist in the Christian perspective, though at a different level. The struggle to become free from sin takes place on the level of asceticism and leads to a first degree of *apatheia*, as a culmination of the first way. But being freed altogether from the carnal mode of knowing and feeling that is part and parcel of human *miseria* ("misery")—to use St Bernard's term—is something that will take place fully only after death, when corporeal life enters into a state of glory. However, it does begin in part here below, and this is precisely what the mystical life proper brings to pass. To use the language of St Bernard again: "To be, while still living, delivered from the power of desires for things material is a degree of human virtue; but to be brought out of the sphere of material forms and ideas is a privilege of angelic purity."[6]

So, we find that Plotinus' concept of κάθαρσις (*katharsis*, purification) is used in mystical theology, though not without modification—which brings us to the problem of how Gregory transposes the entire framework of Plotinian thought so as to make it serve to express Christian mysticism. Hence we shall also need to examine the treatment that the concept of *apatheia* undergoes—for, as mentioned, it is central to the whole of spiritual life, which can in fact be seen as a process of achieving *apatheia* at different levels.

---

[4]For example, see *Beat.* 3 (PG 44:1228C; ACW 18:113).

[5]Gregory states this explicitly: "'[P]assion' is said at times in a proper sense, but at other times in a less correct sense. Therefore what is joined to the will and turns it from virtue to vice is truly passion; but whatever is seen in nature, which proceeds successively in its proper sequence, this would much more properly be called a 'work' than a passion, such as birth, growth, the continuance of the subject through the inflow and outflow of nourishment, the concourse of the elements of the body, the dissolution of the composition again, and [its] departure to kindred [elements]." *Or. cat.* 16.1 (PG 45:49B–C; PPS 60:99)

[6]Bernard of Clairvaux, *Sermons on The Song of Songs*, 52.5. Translation from *The Life and Works of Saint Bernard*, vol. 4, trans. Samuel J. Eales (London: John Hodges, 1896), 316.

The importance of this approach is that it reveals the close link that exists in Gregory between the spiritual life and the structure of the soul. By "nature"—and we shall specify the meaning of this word—the soul is an "image of God." As a result of sin, however, it has been clothed in various passions. The goal of the spiritual life is to divest it of these passions and restore it to its original state. This amounts to a "return to paradise," and the progressive stages of the spiritual life mark the stages of this return. As Gregory puts it, "This concern, then, for the finding of what is lost is the restoration [ἀποκατάστασις, *apokatastasis*] to the original state of the divine image [ἡ εἰκών, *hē eikon*] which is now covered by the filth of the flesh. Let us become what the first being was during the first period of his existence."[7]

With these words, Gregory outlines the very method we must follow. To understand what the spiritual life is one must first understand what man is, and what the constitution of his soul is. In particular, we must understand what the relationship is between his original state as the image of God and the passions in which he is presently arrayed. Such an analysis will enable us to arrive at a precise definition of *apatheia*, for it will provide the framework in which the various stages of the spiritual life are to be situated—from the mortification of the disordered tendencies to the passive purifications of the mystical life proper. It will also provide us with an anthropological foundation for spiritual theology as a whole.

The Image of God and the Garments of Skin

Gregory of Nyssa's entire anthropological doctrine is founded on the following verse from Genesis: "Let us make man in our image [εἰκόνα, *eikona*] and likeness [ὁμοίωσιν, *homoiōsin*]" (Gen 1.26). For him, these two terms are synonymous. He makes a distinction between them in a single treatise—*A Homily on the Words: Let us Make Man in Our Image and Likeness*.[8] Indeed, it is because of this that its authenticity has been questioned, for it would seem to be altogether contrary to Gregory's general outlook, in which the concept of "image" denotes the divine likeness in its fullness; that is, it signifies a natural likeness to God that comprises not merely the mind, but the entire supernatural life. The term

---

[7] *Virg.* 12 (PG 46:373C; FC 58:45).
[8] Partly because this distinction is found nowhere else in the Nyssene corpus, scholars now tend to assign this to Basil (as do most MSS, and Daniélou himself above; see p. xxv, esp. n. 39).—*Ed.*

ὁμοίωσις (*homoiōsis*), on the other hand, is normally used when referring to the effort involved in achieving the image.

To clearly understand the meaning of this word εἰκών (*eikōn*, image) as used by Gregory, it is instructive to look at its origins. In Plato, it refers to the relationship of the sensory world to the intelligible world. Thus he emphasizes both a certain analogy but also a deficiency. This pejorative connotation is sometimes present in Gregory's use of the term, as when he contrasts image with reality: "The ardent lover of beauty, although receiving what is always visible as an image of what he desires, yet longs to be filled with the very stamp of the archetype [ἀρχέτυπον, *archetypon*]."[9] We find an altogether different meaning in Philo[10] and in the hermetic writings. Here, by contrast, *eikōn* signifies the reality of participation. The term is applied to the *logos* [reason],[11] to the cosmos, and also to the human νοῦς (*nous*, mind).[12]

Gregory's use of the word resembles that of the latter group of writers; it denotes a genuine commonality of "nature." It includes, however, a certain number of distinctions that are absent in the non-Christian uses of the word. Applied to the *Logos*—as is already the case in St Paul (Col 1.15; cf. Wis 7.26)—it denotes not some deficient participation but an original relationship and an equality of nature. This is a new meaning, linked to the dogma of the Trinity.[13] Second, man's resemblance to God does not take place through the intermediary of his resemblance to the cosmos—as in Philo, for whom the cosmos is itself an image of God. On the contrary, it is man alone and not the cosmos that is the "image" of God: "Know how much you have been honored by the Maker. Heaven did not become the image of God, nor the moon, nor the sun . . . nor a single other one of the things that appear in the created order."[14]

In what, then, does man's likeness to God consist? For Gregory, it implies a real participation in all his attributes. He is quite explicit on this subject: "That which is made in the image of something else must keep in every [πάντως,

---

[9] *Vit. Moys.* 2.231 (PG 44:401D; Malherbe, 114).

[10] See H. Willms, *Eikōn: eine begriffsgeschichtliche Untersuchung zum Platonismus, I: Philon von Alexandreia* (Münster: Aschendorff, 1935).

[11] See *Corpus Hermeticum* 12.14.

[12] See Philo, *Allegorical Interpretation* 1.12.32 (Yonge, 28). See also H. Merki, ὉΜΟΙΩΣΙΣ ΘΕΩ: *von der platonischen Angleichung an Gott zur Gottähnlichkeit bei Gregor von Nyssa* (Freiburg in der Schweiz: Éditions universitaires, 1952).

[13] See Gregory, *Ref. Eun.* (PG 45:536B; NPNF² 5:123).

[14] Gregory, *Cant.* 2 (PG 44:805C; Norris, 75). See also *Op. hom.* 12.9 (PG 44:161C; NPNF² 5:398–99), *Op. hom.* 16.1 (PG 44:177D; NPNF² 5:404).

The Structure of the Soul and the Passions

pantōs] respect a similarity to its archetype [ἀρχέτυπον, *archetypon*]. The likeness of the intellectual [νοεράν, *noeran*] is intellectual. The likeness of the bodiless [ἀσώματον, *asōmaton*] is bodiless."[15] The soul is "as it were a living 'image' [ἔμψυχος εἰκών, *empsychos eikōn*], partaking [κοινωνοῦσα, *koinōnousa*] with the archetype both in rank and in name."[16] In his treatise *On the Making of Man*, Gregory describes the details of this likeness at length:

> The fact that it is the image of that Nature which rules over all means nothing else than this, that our nature was created to be royal [βασιλίδα, *basilida*] from the first. ... [But] not vested in purple, nor giving indication of its rank by sceptre and diadem ... but instead of the purple robe, clothed in virtue [ἀρετήν, *aretēn*], which is in truth the most royal of all raiment, and in place of the sceptre, leaning on the bliss of immortality [τῇ μακαριότητι τῆς ἀθανασίας, *tē makariotēti tēs athanasias*], and instead of the royal diadem, decked with the crown of righteousness [δικαιοσύνης, *diakosynēs*]."[17]

He specifies other traits, such as "purity [καθαρότης, *katharotēs*], freedom from passion, blessedness, alienation from all evil, and all those attributes of the like kind that help to form in men the likeness of God [ἡ πρὸς τὸ θεῖον ὁμοίωσις, *hē pros to theon homoiōsis*]."[18] Other traits still are added to these: "The Godhead is mind [νοῦς, *nous*] and word [λόγος, *logos*] ... humanity too is not far removed from these: you see in yourself word and understanding, an imitation [μίμημα, *mimēma*] of the very Mind and Word. Again, God is love [ἀγάπη, *agapē*] and the fount of love. ... [T]he Fashioner of our nature has made this to be our feature too."[19]

What is noteworthy and strikes one at once in this enumeration is that it places on the same level concepts between which western theology makes distinctions. Thus, grouped together are features that are characteristic of the mind (such as reason or freedom); others that are linked to a participation in the divine life that we call grace (for example, *apatheia* and love); and yet others that, to our way of thinking, relate to the final glorification (such as incorruptibility or the state of blessedness). For Gregory, no such distinctions exist. The soul, as

---

[15] *An. et res.* 2 (PG 46:41C; PPS 12:45).
[16] *Op. hom.* 4.1 (PG 44:136C; NPNF² 5:391).
[17] Ibid. (PG 44:136C–D; NPNF² 5:391).
[18] *Op. hom.* 5.1 (PG 44:137A–B; NPNF² 5:391).
[19] *Op. hom.* 5.2 (PG 44:137B–C; NPNF² 5:391).

he describes it, is the soul in the state in which God originally created it, which is its true reality, and which he calls its "nature."

We must clarify this point before proceeding further. For Gregory, man "in the image" is what man is by nature (φύσιν, *physin*). This image consists at the same time of what in western theology we call the intellectual life (the νοῦς, *nous*; mind or intellect) and the supernatural life (the πνεῦμα, *pneuma*; spirit). Together these constitute its nature, to which is contrasted the animal life (ψυχή, *psychē*; lit. soul) that was added later. As can be seen, this understanding of "nature" is totally different from what the word designates in western theology. For the latter, "nature" comprises the animal and the intellectual life, and is contrasted with the "supernatural" life that was added to it. For Gregory, by contrast, "nature" contains both the intellectual and the supernatural life, as mentioned, and what is added is the animal life. This explains how the Greeks can say that man is good by nature, without any reference to naturalism, and that he is united to God by nature, without any question of pantheism, as Myrrha Lot-Borodine has pointed out.[20]

Furthermore, all of the terms Gregory uses to denote the "image" of God are charged with a religious meaning and must be understood as referring to realities that are supernatural. He knows nothing of an autonomous natural order outside the world of grace and the world of sin. His entire system is precisely a transposition of Platonism in terms of sin and grace. Later, we shall see how—with the "garments of skin," the symbol of animal life—an order of reality appears that is nonetheless alien to the "image," but without being properly "sin." This is the equivalent of western theology's "natural" life. But first we must specify the meaning of certain terms that Gregory uses to describe man's participation in the divine life—that is, the image. We shall find once again that though many of these expressions may be Platonic, they must be read in context to understand the precise meaning that Gregory gives them.

Freedom, for example, is above all spiritual freedom (παρρησία, *parrhēsia*), one of the fruits of the first way. Understanding (νοῦς, *nous*—mind; λόγος, *logos*—reason, or διάνοια, *dianoia*—thought) refers to knowledge of realities (τὰ ὄντα, *ta onta*; lit. existing things), as Gregory himself says;[21] that is, the understanding that consists in a religious vision of the world. This is the objective of the second way. Virtue does not mean natural virtue but, as Gregory

---

[20]See M. Lot-Borodine, "Initiation à une mystique sacramentaire," 666, n. 1.
[21]See *Op. hom.* 5.2 (PG 44:137C; NPNF² 5:391).

puts it, it is an emanation (ἀπόρροια, *aporroia*) of the divine holiness; and the various examples of virtue—justice, for example—likewise. We shall see that ἀπάθεια (*apatheia*, dispassion) and καθαρότης (*katharotēs*, purity) are likewise descriptions of sanctifying grace, a participation in the life of God who alone is properly ἀπαθής (*apathēs*, dispassionate) and καθαρός, (*katharos*, pure). Finally, ἀγάπη (*agapē*, love) will be seen to be nothing less than the characteristic feature of the mystical life.

Leaving aside these aspects of the "image"—to which we shall return later, since their restoration is precisely the goal of the spiritual life—we shall consider for the moment only those aspects in Gregory that are particularly worthy of note. First, two traits characterize the divine state of the soul, as compared with its fallen condition: exemption from mortality and from sexuality. In fact, we shall see that it is above all these two things—mortality and sexuality—that constitute our "fallen" state, our "garments of skin." A few observations are called for.

Immortality is in the first place incorruptibility (ἀφθαρσία, *aphtharsia*). Properly speaking, it is the quality of that which is not subject to the corruption inherent in biological life. The word is frequently found in Gregory.[22] Among the Platonists it denotes the very quality of the mind, which is incorruptible in itself;[23] in Gregory, however, the perspective is theological, as always. Ἀφθαρσία (*aphtharsia*) is true, first of all, of God for, as he puts it, "God and incorruptibility are the same thing."[24] In man, on the other hand, it comes from partaking in the divine life. There is thus no natural state in which the mind is incorruptible, and to which the divine life is added. There is only the true state—that of deified man, who is ἄφθαρτος (*aphthartos*, incorruptible)—and the fallen (φθαρτός, *phthartos*; corruptible) state in which, although he is not physically corruptible, he is nevertheless plunged into corruptible realities. And it is this more positive understanding of corruption that matters. The related term ἀθανασία (*athanasia*, immortality), which Gregory uses alongside *aphtharsia* when referring to the image,[25] calls for the same observations. The contrast is not between exis-

---

[22] See *An. et res.* 10 (PG 46:156A; PPS 12:118); *Prof.* (PG 46:241D; FC 58:84); *Perf.* (PG 46:277D; FC 58:116 and PG 46:284C; FC 58:120); *Mort.* 15 (PG 46:521D; PPS 64:23) and 20 (PG 46:536B; PPS 64:33); *Beat.* 3 (PG 44:1225D; ACW 18:112).

[23] See Plotinus, *Enneads* 2.1.2; 3.6.10.

[24] Gregory, *Antirrheticus adversus Apollinarium* (*Antirrh.*) 28 (PG 45:1257A). English translation in in *St Gregory of Nyssa: Anti-Apollinarian Writings*, trans. Robin Orton, The Fathers of the Church 131 (Washington, DC: The Catholic University of America Press, 2015), 245.

[25] See *Op. hom.* 4.1 (PG 44:136D; NPNF² 5:391); *Cant.* 2 (PG 44:800C; Norris, 67)

tence and nothingness, but between the state of mortality—that is, the condition of man separated from God (which is true death) and as a result endowed with an animal nature subject to mortality—and the state of *athanasia*, which is both the life of the soul united to God and liberation from biological death.[26]

As for the second characteristic of the image of God—the absence of sexuality—Gregory returns to this point in several particularly important passages throughout his life: in *On Virginity*,[27] *On the Making of Man*,[28] and in the *Homilies on the Song of Songs*.[29] He interprets the story in Genesis 1.26–27 as being a double creation: first that of man "in the image," and then that of the human being, "male and female." "He devised [ἐπιτεχνᾶται, *epitechnatai*] for his image," he writes, "the distinction of male and female."[30] Here is how he presents this dual creation: "Thus the creation of our nature is in a sense twofold: one made like to God, one divided according to this distinction: for something like this the passage darkly conveys by its arrangement, where it first says, 'God created man, in the image of God created He him,' and then, adding to what has been said, 'male and female created He them,'—a thing which is alien [ἀλλότριον, *allotrion*] from our conceptions of God. I think that by these words Holy Scripture conveys to us a great and lofty doctrine."[31] What exactly are we to understand by this absence of sexuality? Not that all distinctions between man and woman were absent, since Gregory admits that in paradise God gave Adam a companion.[32] Nor is it the absence of fertility, but rather of the "animal" mode of propagation: "Since He saw beforehand by His all-seeing power the failure of their will to keep a direct course to what is good, and its consequent declension from the angelic life, in order that the multitude of human souls might not be cut short by its fall from that mode by which the angels were increased and multiplied—for this reason, I say, He formed for our nature that contrivance for increase which befits those who had fallen into sin, implanting in mankind, instead of the angelic majesty of nature, that animal and irrational mode by which they now succeed one another."[33] Thus the sexual life is not evil in itself; it is merely a degradation.

---

[26]The same concept is found in St Athanasius. See Louis Bouyer, *L'Incarnation et l'Église-Corps du Christ dans la théologie de saint Athanase* (Paris: Éditions du Cerf, 1943), 37.
[27]See *Virg.* 4 (PG 46:348A; FC 58:27).
[28]See *Op. hom.* 16.14 (PG 44:185A; NPNF² 5:406).
[29]See *Cant.* 7 (PG 44:916B; Norris, 225).
[30]*Op. hom.* 16.14 (PG 44:185A; NPNF² 5:406).
[31]*Op. hom.* 16.9 (PG 44:181B; NPNF² 5:405).
[32]See *Virg.* 12 (PG 46:373C; FC 58:46).
[33]*Op. hom.* 17.4 (PG 44:189C; NPNF² 5:407).

But it is nonetheless the source of passions that themselves lead to death: "For I think that from this beginning all our passions issue as from a spring, and pour their flood over man's life."[34]

It is worth noting that this doctrine of a double creation and of the absence of sexuality in man "in the image" are also found in Philo, who writes: "There is a vast difference between man as generated now, and the first man who was made according to the image of God. For man as formed now is perceptible to the external senses, partaking of qualities, consisting of body and soul, man or woman, by nature mortal. But man, made according to the image of God, was an idea, or a genus, or a seal, perceptible only by the intellect [νοητός, *noētos*], incorporeal, neither male nor female, imperishable by nature."[35] It is certain that Gregory is indebted to Philo, in whom we also find the notion of the immortality of man "in the image": "The leathern mass which covers us—namely, the body . . . plots against the soul [and] is at all times lifeless and dead."[36] However, Philo's conception of things is linked both to the Platonic idea of androgyny and to the doctrines of the gnostics. Gregory, for his part, here again transposes to a different, Christological standpoint these theories borrowed from secular thinking. Man as first created—man "in the image"—is for Gregory not a historical personage but a figure of the Christ to come. As he reminds us, St Paul says that in Jesus Christ "there is neither male nor female" (Gal 3.28). Thus Gregory's thought must be interpreted as applying to a spiritual life that transcends biological, sexual life, and to which man is called in Christ.

This doctrine is particularly important in that it gives an ontological foundation to virginity (παρθενία, *parthenia*), something to which Gregory attaches great importance. Indeed, he devoted an entire treatise to it. For him, virginity is the first stage on the road back to paradise, even as marriage has been the final stage in distancing us from it. Hence it is marriage that the Word exhorts all those who wish to live with Christ to forsake as a first step.[37] In his treatise, Gregory lists all the advantages of virginity, and it is worth reading the detailed study of them by Stiglmayer.[38] But all of these advantages stem from the fact that virginity is in essence man's return to his true nature and, at the same time as being a return to the paradisal state, it is thus also an anticipation of the

---

[34]*Op. hom.* 18.1 (PG 44:192A; NPNF² 5:407).
[35]Philo, *On the Creation* 46.134 (Yonge, 19).
[36]Philo, *Allegorical Interpretation* 3.22.69 (Yonge, 57).
[37]See Gregory, *Virg.* 12 (PG 46:376A; FC 58:46).
[38]See Stiglmayer, "Über die Jungfräulichkeit."

resurrection: "For if the life which is promised to the just by the Lord after the resurrection is similar to that of the angels—and release from marriage is a peculiar characteristic of the angelic nature—he has already received some of the beauties of the promise ... having imitated the purity of the incorporeal beings in the undefiled character of his life."[39] Virginity is not a necessary means of salvation,[40] but it is nonetheless a testimony to the true human condition and has prophetic value. It also creates better conditions for sanctification.

The first creation, then, denotes not only a humanity that is exempt from the biological condition, but also humanity as a whole. "For," as Gregory writes, "the image is not to be found in part of our nature, no more than grace [χάρις, *charis*] is located in one of its members, but it is human nature as a whole that is made in the image of God."[41] Nor is this first creation that of an abstract humanity, for in Gregory the word φύσις (*physis*, nature) always refers to a concrete, existing reality. But neither should it be understood as a historical reality. For the image of God in its fullness will exist only at the end of time, when God will be all in all [1 Cor 15.28].[42] This creation is of an intentional order. For God, who is outside time, the immediate purpose of creation is the total Christ, the εἰκών (*eikōn*). However, this creation unfolds in time according to an economy full of wisdom and in which, as we have seen, degeneracy itself has a providential meaning. Here too we find the Platonic idea of the primacy of the one over the many. But all is now transferred to the historic order; it is not a case of some ideal and lasting concept that is there to be reclaimed, but of a unity that must be realized throughout history. Now this is diametrically opposed to Platonic thinking as it is still expressed by a Julian [the Apostate] at the time of Gregory. Nothing is more alien to Julian's thought than the idea of the unity of mankind as the goal of the historic progress: "For him, the future can only be a matter of maintaining or restoring what has already been. . . . This disciple of Iamblichus associates the national idea with the conservative idea."[43]

This new way of understanding the *eikōn* will dominate an entire aspect of spiritual theology. For if the image exists only in the community, then the

---

[39] *Virg.* 14 (PG 46:384A; FC 58:51).

[40] See *Virg.* 33 (PG 46:353A).

[41] *Op. hom.* 16.17 (PG 44:185C; NPNF² 5:406). [Translation modified to match Daniélou's text.—*Trans.*]

[42] "Until that time when, since all have become one in desiring the same goal ... God may become all in all persons, in those who by their oneness are blended together with one another in the fellowship of the Good in our Lord Jesus Christ." Gregory, *Cant.* 15 (PG 44:1117D; Norris, 497–99).

[43] J. Bidez, *La Vie de l'Empereur Julien* (Paris: Les Belles Lettres, 1930), 308.

The Structure of the Soul and the Passions

spiritual life will be experienced in the community and will, moreover, be directed toward a more perfect development of the community. We are reminded at this point of the importance of the sacramental life in Gregory's mysticism, for the spiritual life can only be truly lived within the community of the Church. It is nourished by the sacraments and is subject to the church hierarchy. But this community also tends to expand the spiritual life in breadth as well as in depth, being motivated by an expansive love. Thus Gregory clearly combines the apostolic vision with personal sanctification. Moses, who flees into solitude only to better serve his brothers, personifies this type.[44] Finally, it is directed toward that ἀποκατάστασις (*apokatastasis*, restoration), that perfect realization of the image by the union of all things in Christ, which is the fundamental perspective of Gregory's thought: "Should love cast out fear completely . . . and should fear transformed become love, at that point that which is saved is discovered to be a unity, since on the basis of a perfection like that of the Dove all are united to one another in being joined to the life of the one Good."[45]

Little by little the divine goods are revealed that constitute God's image and which amount to a sharing in the very life of God since, according to Gregory's powerful way of putting it, the difference between God and man consists not in the ἐπιθεωρούμενα (*epitheōroumena*), the external traits, but only in the ὑποκείμενον (*hypokeimenon*), in what is underlying.[46] One word sums up all these paradisal goods, a word we have already encountered several times—beatitude (μακαριότης, *makariotēs*). In modern [Roman Catholic] theological language, it specifically denotes a soul that has entered its definitive state of perfection. For Gregory, however, it is "the summation and object of everything conceived in relation to the good."[47] Truly and properly (ἀληθῶς καὶ κυρίως, *alēthōs kai kyriōs*) it befits God alone. Hence we find it numbered among the divine perfections as listed by Gregory.[48] This is the meaning it has in St Paul: "[God is] the blessed and only Ruler, the King of kings and Lord of lords, who alone has immortality" (1 Tim 6.15).

Man's beatitude is a participation in that of God. This entire doctrine is explained at length in the first homily on the Beatitudes:

---

[44]See *Vit. Moys.*, 64 (PG 44:336D).

[45]*Cant.* 15 (PG 44:1116C–D; Norris, 495). See also *In illud: Tunc et ipse Filius* (*Tunc et ipse*) 9–16 (PG 44:1316–1321; PPS 64:75–82).

[46]See *Op. hom.* 16.13 (PG 44:184D; NPNF² 5:405).

[47]*Inscr.* 1.1.5 (PG 44:433B; Heine, 84).

[48]See *Op. hom.* 5.1 (PG 44:137A; NPNF² 5:391); *Beat.* 3 (PG 44:1225D; ACW 18:113).

Beatitude, in my opinion, is a possession of all things held to be good: now the opposite of beatitude is misery [ἀθλιότης, *athliotēs*]. The only thing truly blessed is the Divinity itself. In him, beatitude expresses incorruptibility [ἀκήρατος, *akēratos*; ἄφθαρτος, *aphthartos*], the ineffable good, inexpressible beauty, which is essential grace [αὐτοχάρις, *autocharis*], all-powerful, perpetual joy. But as he who fashioned man made him in the image of God; that which is called by this name should also be held blessed in the second degree [δευτέρως, *deuterōs*] the one who merits this name by participation of the essential beauty [μετουσία τῆς ὄντως μακαριότητος, *metousia tes ontōs makariotētos*].

The continuation of the passage is interesting in the way it applies the theology of the image to beatitude: "For as in the matter of physical beauty the original comeliness is in the actually living face, whereas the second place is held by its reflection shown in a picture; so also human nature, which is the image of the transcendent beatitude is itself marked by the beauty of goodness, when it reflects in itself the blessed features."[49]

This entire passage is noteworthy on account of the clarity with which it formulates the doctrine of participation. Here we are definitely at the core of the issue of the image, and Maréchal was right to point out that Gregory's entire mystical theology gravitates around this one concept.[50] Moreover, there are varying degrees of participation and so spiritual life as a whole may be portrayed as a process of increasing participation in the divine beatitude. "That nature which transcends everything is first and properly [κυρίως καὶ πρώτως, *kyriōs kai protos*] called blessed. Among humans, however, that beatitude which is the nature of the one participated in [μετέχοντος, *metechontos*], occurs to a certain extent, and is specified by participation [μέθεξις, *methexis*] in true being [τοῦ ὄντως ὄντος, *tou ontōs ontos*]. Likeness to God, therefore, is a definition of human blessedness."[51] Elsewhere, Gregory specifies what these degrees of blessedness are. The first (ἀρχή, *archē*; the beginning) is separation from evil. Then the soul gradually soars to the very limit of what it hoped for, and of what it can know. This is the second way. Beyond this is heavenly bliss, which surpasses all that the human mind may conceive and which constitutes the return of our nature to the choir of the angels.[52]

[49] *Beat.* 1 (PG 44:1197A–B; ACW 18:88).
[50] See Maréchal, *Psychologie des Mystiques*, 2:111ff.
[51] Gregory, *Inscr.* 1.1.6 (PG 44:433C; Heine, 84).
[52] See *Inscr.* 1.9.122 (PG 44:485C; Heine, 122).

The Structure of the Soul and the Passions 51

This bliss was man's in the beginning, and he still harbors a nostalgia for it: "When, therefore, we look to the East and recall to our memory how we were cast out from the bright regions of bliss [μακαριότητος, *makariotētos*] in the East, we shall have reason to utter such prayer. . . . 'Forgive us our debts.'"[53] Christ, the new Orient [Lk 1.78], brings human nature back to the paradise of old. "Did not He restore it to its former beauty? When I was exiled from paradise . . . submerged in the gulf of material things, was it not He who brought me back to man's first beatitude [ἐπὶ τὴν πρώτην μακαριότητα, *epi tēn prōtēn makariotēta*]?"[54] It is the aim of virtue to restore this beatitude: "The goal of the virtuous life is blessedness."[55] Thus we always find the same cluster of ideas: "image," "beatitude," "paradise"—all of which refer to the unique reality of man's original nature—darkened by sin, restored by Christ—and the culmination of the spiritual ascent.

Such, then, is human nature as originally created in the image of God, and possessing characteristics of the divine nature. But this is not how we experience humanity now. In the *Catechetical Discourse,* Gregory makes the point himself: "For where is the godlikeness of the soul? where is the impassibility of the body? where is the eternity of life?"[56] How can we explain this? It is because the humanity we see before us does not represent human "nature" as God had first willed it and such as it will exist ultimately. To the humanity created in the image of God, and which alone constitutes our true nature, is added, as we have seen, what Gregory calls the "garments of skin"; that is, biological existence, participation in the animal life. These "garments of skin" are the ones Scripture says that Adam was clad in as a consequence of sin [Gen 3.21]. But for Gregory, they denote the very condition in which Adam was created. We shall see why shortly.

What exactly does Gregory understand by these "garments of skin"? We know that for Origen they refer to the body itself.[57] As for Gregory, a few quotations will help us to clarify the distinctive, very interesting meaning he gives to them.

---

[53]*Or. dom.* 5 (PG 44:1184C; ACW 18:77).
[54]*Or. dom.* 1 (PG 44:1125C; ACW 18:26).
[55]*Inscr.* 1.1.5 (PG 44:433A; Heine, 84).
[56]*Or. cat.* 5.8 (PG 45:24B; PPS 60:75).
[57]This interpretation appears among the gnostics. See Tertullian, *Against the Valentinians* 24 (ANF 3:515). Methodius of Olympus explicitly attributes it to Origen. See *On the Resurrection* 1.27 in Bonwetsch's edition of his works: *Methodius,* ed. G. N. Bonwetsch (Leipzig: J. C. Hinrichs, 1917), 255.

> If a man wearing a ragged tunic [χιτών, *chitōn*] should be denuded of his garment, he would no longer see on himself the ugliness of what was discarded. Likewise, when we have put off that dead [νεκρόν, *nekron*] and ugly garment which was made for us from irrational skins (when I hear "skins" I interpret it as the form of the irrational nature [τῆς ἀλόγου φύσεως, *tēs alogou physeōs*] which we have put on from our association with passion) we throw off every part of our irrational skin [δέρμα, *derma*] along with the removal of the garment. These are the things which we have received from the irrational skin: sexual intercourse, conception, childbearing, dirt, lactation, nourishment, evacuation, gradual growth to maturity, the prime of life, old age, disease, and death.[58]

This text is important from several points of view. First, it clearly defines the "garments of skin" as comprising animal nature in its totality, all that we have in common with the animals. Hence it is not a question, properly speaking, of the body as such, nor of something simply moral, but of a certain bodily condition.[59] Now for Gregory, this bodily condition is alien to human "nature." It is a "dead" garment, "mortal," whereas the image of God possesses immortality. It is a condition that includes the sexual life. "He devised for His image the distinction of male and female," writes Gregory, "which has no reference to the Divine Archetype." [60] But having attributed to man what belongs to animal nature, God also attributed to our species this animal mode of propagation, which was not consistent with the excellence of his first creation: "For he says first that 'God created man in the image of God' (showing by these words, as the Apostle says, that in such a being there is no male or female): then he adds the peculiar attributes of human nature, 'male and female created He them.'"[61] Thus mortality, sexuality, and biological life as a whole are all alien to man's true nature.

Gregory sometimes compares it to the angelic nature.[62] This does not mean, however, that every type of "body" is alien to this true nature. For elsewhere we come across expressions that imply that he does acknowledge a bodily state that, although different from the present one, is just as real. Hence the "luminous" or "resplendent" (φωτοειδεῖς, *phōtoeideis*) garments of which he sometimes speaks:

---

[58] *An. et res.* 10 (PG 46:148C–149A; PPS 12:114).
[59] This is already the doctrine of Methodius. See *On the Resurrection*, 1.38–39 (Bonwetsch, 282–83).
[60] *Op. hom.* 16.14 (PG 44:185A; NPNF[2] 5:406).
[61] *Op. hom.* 16.9 (PG 44:181C; NPNF[2] 5:405).
[62] See *Op. hom.* 17.2 (PG 44:188D; NPNF[2] 5:407).

"We see each and all these garments of skin round our nature, and also the transitory fig leaves of this material life which we have badly sewn together for ourselves after being stripped of our resplendent garments."[63] When he speaks of the Father giving the prodigal son his robe, he specifies that it was "not another one, but the first robe, of which he had been deprived by his disobedience."[64] It is this "garment of incorruption, of immortality" (χιτὼν τῆς ἀφθαρσίας, *chitōn tēs aphtharsias*) that Christ gives to the newly baptized.[65] These expressions have a spiritual but also an eschatological meaning: Baptism is not only the resurrection of the soul, but a figure and principle of the resurrection of the body. And the symbolism of the garments applies to the incorruptibility of the body just as much as to that of the soul.

Other texts are more explicit still. In the *Funeral Oration for Meletius*, for example, Gregory speaks specifically about the vestments he will put on in glory: "He has taken off the 'garments of skin' (Gen 3.21), for there is no need of such clothing among those living in paradise. But he has clothing, which he wove by the purity of his life."[66] The parallelism with the "garments of skin"—whose material meaning is certain, as we shall see—allows us to interpret these pure "vestments" in the same sense. The "garments of skin" (nutrition, generation, sleep) were useful for life here below, but in paradise the functions they represented no longer apply. The same contrast is found in other passages. Thus, in the treatise *On the Soul and the Resurrection*, Gregory speaks of the "bodily covering [περιβόλαιον σωμάτικον, *peribolaion sōmatikon*] ... dissolved by death ... and woven again ... not indeed with its present coarse and heavy texture [παχυμερῆ, *pachymerē*], but with the thread respun into something subtler [ἀερῶδες, *aerōdes*] and lighter [λεπτότερον, *leptoteron*]."[67]

In this last quotation, the eschatological (and realistic) meaning is obvious. Sometimes this sense merges with the spiritual (and allegorical) meaning, as in this passage from *The Life of Moses* where we again find the same expressions as in the one we quoted above. It concerns the garment of the high priest, a traditional motif in allegorical treatments of Exodus. Dyed blue, for Philo it

---

[63] *Or. dom.* 5 (PG 44:1184A; ACW 18:76).
[64] *Or. dom.* 2 (PG 44:1144D; ACW 18:41).
[65] *Adversus eos qui differunt baptismum* (PG 44:420C).
[66] *Oratio funebris in Meletium episcopum* (*Melet.*) 8 (PG 46:861B; PPS 64:121).
[67] *An. et res.* 7 (PG 46:108A; PPS 12:88). The glorious body is described as being λεπτομερὲς καὶ ἀερῶδες (*leptomeres kai aerōdes*, fine and airy) by Methodius of Olympus. See *On the Resurrection*, 3.16 (Bonwetsch, 413). Bonwetsch rejects these expressions as being Origenistic.

is a symbol of the world,[68] likewise for Clement.[69] For Gregory of Nyssa, on the other hand, it represents the "heavenly" character of the purified life, in a mystical and at the same time a cosmological sense. By means of this symbol, the Word says of anyone who wishes to consecrate himself to the service of the Lord that he "should not inflict upon his soul a heavy and fleshy garment of life, but by the purity of his life, he should make all the pursuits of life as thin as the thread of a spider web. Reweaving this bodily nature, we should be close to what rises upwards and is light [λεπτότερον, *leptoteron*] and airy [ἀερῶδες, *aerōdes*], in order that when we hear the last trumpet we may be found weightless and light in responding to the voice of the One who calls us."[70]

Clearly, the subject here is virtue. The adjective "light" (λεπτότερον, *leptoteron*)—and references to spiders' webs or wings—occur frequently in Gregory when he wishes to express a disengagement from worldly things.[71] But, as already mentioned, the closing lines suggest a cosmological meaning and here again Gregory uses a vocabulary borrowed from Hellenistic philosophy. For the latter, garments do sometimes have a cosmological character. In Proclus, for example, it is a question of pneumatic bodies that the soul puts on like garments as it ascends through the planetary spheres while divesting itself of the coarser garments. He also explicitly makes the contrast between these spiritual "garments" and the "garments of skin" (δερμάτινοι, *dermatinoi*).[72] Elsewhere, in Philo[73] and Plotinus, the garments have an allegorical meaning and symbolize spiritual transformation. On the other hand, Gregory's thought moves on both planes, and the spiritual meaning does not exclude one that is realistic.

The "garments of skin," then, do not denote the body as such but merely the animal body, in contrast to the "light," "airy" garments that refer to the

---

[68]See Philo, *On the Life of Moses* 2.24.118 (Yonge, 501).

[69]See Clement of Alexandria, *Miscellanies* 5.6.32.

[70] *Vit. Moys.* 2.191 (PG 44:388D; Malherbe, 103–104).

[71]See *An. et res.* 7 (PG 46:108A; PPS 12:88); *Virg.* 11 (PG 46:365A–C; FC 58:40); *Beat.* 2 (PG 44:1209A; ACW 18:97).

[72]See Proclus: *The Elements of Theology*, E. R. Dodds, trans. and ed. (Oxford: Clarendon Press, 1933), 313ff. On this, see Franz Cumont, *Les Religions orientales dans le paganisme romain* (Paris: Leroux, 1906), 283, n. 69 [*The Oriental Religions in Roman Paganism*, trans. Grant Showerman (Chicago: Open Court Publishing, 1911), 270, n. 54]. Porphyry also speaks about garments of skin. See *De abstinentia* 1.31; Porphyry, *Select Works of Porphyry; Containing His Four Books on Abstinence from Animal Food; His Treatise on the Homeric Cave of the Nymphs; and His Auxiliaries to the Perception of the Intelligible Natures*, trans. Thomas Taylor (London: Thomas Rodd, 1823), 28. Origen shares this interpretation. For him, it is a matter of different bodies. For Gregory, by contrast, it is a matter of different states of the same body. Here he depends upon the criticism of Origen by Methodius. [See *Brill Dictionary*, "Tunics of Hide," pp. 768–70.—*Ed.*]

[73]See Philo, *Allegorical Interpretation* 2.15.56 (Yonge, 43).

The Structure of the Soul and the Passions

spiritual body. This animality—alien to man's true nature—creates in him a duality that Gregory strongly emphasizes: "For, as one may see in models those carved shapes which the artificers of such things contrive for the wonder of beholders, tracing out upon a single head two forms [διγλύφους, *diglyphous*] of faces; so man seems to me to bear a double likeness to opposite things—being moulded in the Divine element of his mind [τῷ θεοειδεῖ τῆς διανοίας, *tō theodei tēs dianoias*] to the Divine beauty, but bearing, in the passionate [κατὰ πάθος, *kata pathos*] impulses [ὁρμαῖς, *hormais*] that arise in him, a likeness to the brute nature."[74] Such indeed is man's present situation. He possesses at the same time a nature created in the image of God and also an animal nature. But these two natures are not on the same level: the one is his true nature, the other was added to it. Thus we arrive at a very particular concept of man, the opposite of that proposed by western theology, as we have said. In the latter, we are presented with a "natural" man to whom grace is added, with the associated danger of a closed humanism that excludes the supernatural. From Gregory's perspective, the opposite is true: what is original is "the image of God," and it is "natural" man that is added to this. It follows that the center of balance is not the same: it is present life that is affected by a very pronounced character of instability, since man has an inevitable longing to be restored to his true level, the paradisal level. From a standpoint such as Gregory's, the need for the spiritual life is consequently more obvious; it is a return to a true balance.

But the question arises as to why God gave man "the garments of skin." Gregory explains this in his *Catechetical Discourse*:

> For since [Moses] says the first human beings came to be amid forbidden things and were stripped naked of that blessedness [μακαριότητος], the Lord puts "garments of skin" [δερματίνους . . . χιτῶνας] on the first-formed ones. It does not seem to me that "skins" such as these bear the [literal] meaning of the word—for from what sort of slaughtered and skinned animals was the clothing contrived for them?—but, since every skin separated from the animal is dead, I certainly think that he who heals our vice, out of forethought, has clothed men after these [events] with the power to be dead, which was a special [characteristic] of irrational nature, [but] not to remain so forever. For a garment is one of the things put on us externally, handing over the use

[74]*Op. hom.* 18.3 (PG 44:192C; NPNF² 5:408).

of itself to the body for a time, not having grown together with [us] by nature [οὐ συμπεφυκὼς τῇ φύσει].⁷⁵

This passage is full of information. It makes clear that the garments of skin signify not the body itself, but man's mortal condition. It also explains that this mortal condition was given to man out of merciful foresight (ἐκ προμηθείας, *ek promētheias*), a fact that will help us to identify Gregory's thoughts on our mortal condition with more precision. To begin with, it is not bad in itself, for God has created nothing that is not good. In man, however, the condition is adventitious, and destined to be shed. But if it has been given to him, it is through a very wise economy. The treatise *A Discourse on the Dead* clarifies this:⁷⁶

> For if we were what we were made to be from the beginning, we surely would have had no need of this garment of skin, since our likeness to the Divine would be shining in us. And the divine form that appeared in us from the beginning was not some peculiar kind of shape or color, but the human person was made beautiful by those features in which the divine beauty could be contemplated, imitating the grace of the Archetype in his freedom from passion, his blessedness, his incorruptibility. But . . . through the deceit of the enemy of our life, the human person willingly took possession of his own urge toward what is bestial and irrational. . . . So when the human person preferred this material pleasure to the soul's happiness, [God] decided, one might say, to let him yield to the impulse that he felt through the garment of skin, which God had wrapped around him because of his impulse toward evil; through this, the characteristics of irrational nature, like those of the mute beasts, were made into a wrapping for his rationality, by the wisdom of him who brings about good things by their opposites. For that garment of skin, bearing in itself all the characteristics that it had acquired through being wrapped around an irrational nature—pleasure and anger and gluttony and greed and the like—opens up for human choice a way to be drawn in either direction, having become the raw material for both virtue and vice.⁷⁷

---

⁷⁵ *Or. cat.* 8.4 (PG 45:33C; PPS 60:84).

⁷⁶ In Gregory another interpretation is found, in which the garments of skin have as goal to make man mortal thereby preventing sin from remaining in him eternally (*Or. cat.* 8.4; PPS 60:84). See also Irenaeus, *Against Heresies* 3.23.6 (ANF 1:1149); Methodius, *On the Resurrection* 1.38–39; Athanasius, *On the Incarnation* 8—English translation in *On the Incarnation*, trans. John Behr, Popular Patristics Series 44a (Yonkers, NY: St Vladimir's Seminary Press, 2011), 67.

⁷⁷ *Mort.* 15 (PG 46:521D, 524D; PPS 64:22, 24–25).

The Structure of the Soul and the Passions 57

We see, then, the role of these "garments of skin." Had man been created as pure spirit, his choice in favor of evil would have been fixed in him forever. Foreseeing this, God endowed him with a biological condition that rendered him more fragile, in such a way that the sensory life outstrips the rational life and controls his habits before he has been able to reason with them.[78] Thus sin was inevitable. This is indeed what happened: shining on a nature that was still tender and unformed, the sun of temptation withered it from the beginning.[79] But this is also what makes it curable, for the biological condition is subject to time. Man can thus have the inevitable experience of sin and, having experienced its bitterness, can willingly return to the spiritual goods, "so that, having tasted the evil things he had yearned for, and having learned by experience what he had given up to gain them, he might turn again voluntarily, through his own desires, toward his first blessedness—shaking off everything passionate and irrational from his nature like some burden."[80]

In short, the carnal condition in which he is placed represents for man a temporary trial. It allows him to realize from experience (πειρᾷ, *peira*) the bitterness of the enjoyments toward which his freedom inclines him, and then to turn willingly toward the divine goods for which he is really made. Thus it is consistent both with man's freedom and God's goodness. With man's freedom, since God cannot compel or coerce him without destroying it, and instead he is led pedagogically to find his way freely toward his true nature. With the goodness of God, who did not wish to confine man to a single choice—which he foresaw would be bad—and who, by laying out choices before him throughout his biological life (less crucial ones to begin with), enables him to weary of evil and to turn to the good.

The Winged Horses

The above study of the "garments of skin" brings us directly to the problem that concerns us in this chapter: the passions. We have learned that, when "the garments of skin" were applied to man, they preserved all the properties they had when they were wrapped around unreasoning, animal creation: "pleasure

---

[78] See *Eccl.* 8 (PG 44:733C; Hall, 129). See also *Mort.* 13 (PG 46:517A; PPS 64:18).
[79] See *Cant.* 2 (PG 44:793B; Norris, 55–57).
[80] *Mort.* 23 (PG 46:524B). This "pedagogic" view of sin appears in Irenaeus, *Against Heresies* 4.38 (PG 5:1104–09) and was developed by Origen. See J. Daniélou, *Origène* (Paris: La Table Ronde, 1948), 272ff; 277–78. [*Origen*, trans. W. Mitchell (London and New York: Sheed and Ward, 1955), 277ff; 283–84]; Origen, *On Prayer* 29.13 (PPS 29:199).

[ἡδονή, *hēdonē*] and anger [θυμός, *thymos*] and gluttony and greed and the like."[81] Here we have a first list of passions. Similar ones can be found elsewhere in Gregory. In the treatise *On the Making of Man* he enumerates anger (θυμός, *thymos*), pleasure (ἡδονή, *hēdonē*), timidity (δειλία, *deilia*), audacity (θρασός, *thrasos*), cupidity (πλείονος ἔφεσις, *pleionos ephesis*), and ambition (μῖσος τοῦ ἐλαττοῦσθαι, *misos tou elattousthai*).[82] Then a few lines later, to anger, the taste for pleasure, and to cowardice he links fear (φόβος, *phobos*), gluttony (λαιμαργία, *laimargia*), and sadness or grief (λύπη, *lupē*).[83]

These various instincts and impulses, however, are merely the diversification of two fundamental tendencies that, since Plato's time, have been recognized as being the two preeminent passions: the desiring power (τὸ ἐπιθυμητικόν, to *epithymētikon*) and the incensive power (τὸ θυμικόν, *to thymikon*):

> Furthermore, whatever else appears around the soul, the qualities which appear in pairs of opposites, such as cowardice and boldness, misery and pleasure, fear and contempt, and the like, each of these seems indeed to be related to desire and anger, yet indicates its own nature by a particular definition. For boldness and contempt suggest a kind of manifestation of the angry impulse [θυμός, *thymos*], while the attitude of cowardice and fear suggests a diminution and reduction of this same impulse. Misery, however, has material from both impulses; for anger which is too weak to take vengeance on those who have previously troubled us becomes misery, and despair and deprivation of the things which we desire also create this condition in the mind.[84]

Gregory offers various definitions of these two fundamental tendencies, borrowed from the schools of philosophy: "Many people think that anger is a seething of the blood around the heart; others, that it is an appetite for retaliating upon one who has troubled you. But as I suppose, anger is an impulse to harm the one who provokes you.... And if we define desire [ἐπιθυμία, *epithymia*] in itself, we will say that it is a yearning for what we lack, or a longing for the enjoyment of pleasure, or a distress because what we want is not in our power, or an attachment to a pleasure which we may not enjoy."[85] All these things are

---

[81]*Mort.* 15 (PG 46:524D; PPS 64:25).
[82]*Op. hom.* 18.1 (PG 44:192B; NFNP² 5:408).
[83]*Op. hom.* 18.2 (PG 44:192C; NFNP² 5:408).
[84]*An. et res.* 3 (PG 46:56B; PPS 12:53).
[85]Ibid. (PG 46:56A; PPS 12:53).

πάθη (*pathē*) of nature, things that happen to it, not the essence (οὐσία, *ousia*) of nature itself.[86] "They are like warts [μυρμηκίαι, *myrmēkiai*]," he adds, "growing on the mental part of the soul which seem to be parts of it because they grow on it, but they are not what the soul is in its essence."[87]

From these last words, which are an echo of Plato,[88] we see that what was true of the "garments of skin" is also true for the passions: their character in man is accidental.[89] Gregory clarifies this in *On the Soul and the Resurrection*. "From the animals is anger, from them is fear, from them all the other qualities that conflict in us, except for the reasoning and thinking power [θεωρητική καὶ διακριτική καὶ ἐποπτική, *theōrētikē kai diakritikē kai epoptikē*], which indeed alone is distinctive of our nature [κατὰ φύσιν, *kata physin*], having in itself the imitation of the divine character."[90] "The rational power," he writes, "cannot enter into the bodily life otherwise than by entering through perception. Perception existed already in the nature of the irrational animals. Necessarily, therefore, through the faculty of perception our soul becomes associated also with the traits which are joined with perception. These are the traits which, when they occur in us, are called 'passions'."[91]

One could not be more explicit: the passions in us are the result of animal life. Indeed, they are part of it, as Gregory explains elsewhere: "These attributes, then, human nature took to itself from the side of the brutes; for those qualities with which brute life was armed for self-preservation, when transferred to human life, became passions; for the carnivorous animals are preserved by their anger [θυμός, *thymos*], and those which breed largely by their love of pleasure; cowardice [δειλία, *deilia*] preserves the weak, fear that which is easily taken by more powerful animals."[92] I do not propose to examine the origin of these concepts, which probably derive from Posidonius.[93] What is important is the coherence of Gregory's thought. On the one hand, he has established the nature of the passions, showing that they are a means of protection and

---

[86] [Here Daniélou is alluding to the first meaning of the word πάθος: "That which happens to a person or thing; an incident or accident."—*Trans.*]

[87] *An. et res.* 3 (PG 46:56C; PPS 12:54).

[88] See Plato, *Republic* 611d–612a.

[89] See also *Or. cat.* 8.5 (PG 45:33D; PPS 60:84–85).

[90] *An. et res.* 3 (PG 46:57B; PPS 12:56).

[91] Ibid. (PG 46:61A; PPS 12:56).

[92] *Op. hom.* 18.2 (PG 44:192B; NFNP² 5:408).

[93] See K. Gronau, *Poseidonius und die jüdisch-christliche Genesisexegese* (Leipzig: Teubner, 1914); E. von Ivánka, "Die Quelle von Ciceros *De natura deorum*, ii. 45–60. (Poseidonios bei Gregor von Nyssa)," *Archivum Philologicum* (1935): 1–62, at 1–12.

conservation for animal life. In addition, he has shown that man, to whom animal life was by nature alien, had been endowed with it by God. The conclusion is that man has been clad in the passions, which are alien to him by nature, by God' design. Thus, in us, they present the same characteristics as the "garments of skin," that is, of belonging to a lower order of reality, while not being evil in themselves.

Here is how Gregory explains things:

> [The passions] were not bequeathed to human life solely for evil (for the Creator would bear the blame for evil, if because of them the necessity of transgression had been built into our nature). Instead, by the particular use of our free choice [τῇ χρήσει προαιρέσεως, *tē chrēsei proaireseōs*] such impulses of the soul become instruments of virtue or wickedness, just as steel, forged according to the intention of the craftsman, is shaped toward whatever the smith desires, becoming either a sword or some agricultural implement. There if reason, which is the distinctive property of our nature, should gain dominion [ἡγεμονίαν, *hēgemonian*] over those traits which are added to us from outside (the word of the Scripture has also revealed this as in a riddle, bidding mankind to rule over all the irrational creatures), none of these impulses would work in us for servitude to evil, but fear would produce obedience in us, anger courage, cowardice caution, and the desiring impulse would mediate to us the divine and immortal pleasure.[94]

Here we come to the heart of our study of the passions. In man's present state they are part of his constitution. They are not evil; all depends on the use (χρῆσις, *chrēsis*) that is made of them. Consequently, we may envisage what *apatheia* will bring about. In the present life, it will not be the complete suppression of the passions, anymore than Baptism abolishes corporeal mortality; but it will be a "good use" of them. This teaching is also found in Platonism, which exhibits the same double approach: a condemnation of the passions as being foreign to the soul, combined with the doctrine of their good use in the present life. We are very close to Gregory's position, for example, in a passage such as the following from Proclus: "The vehicle [ὄχημα, *ochēma*] of every particular soul descends by the addition of vestures increasingly material; and ascends in company with the soul through divestment [ἀφαίρεσις, *aphaeresis*] of all that is material. . . . For the soul descends by the acquisition of irrational principles of life; and ascends

---

[94] *An. et res.* 3 (PG 46:61B; PPS 12:56–57).

The Structure of the Soul and the Passions

by putting off all those faculties tending to temporal process with which it was invested in its descent, and becoming clean and bare of all such faculties as serve the uses [χρείαν, *chreian*] of the process."[95] Here we have the same elements as in Gregory: a soul that has an ὄχημα (*ochēma*), a heavenly body; in its descent, it is clad in material garments, garments that are the biological life and all that accompanies it, and that are "useful" in the place where they are located.[96]

And so we come back to the distinction made at the beginning of this chapter between two forms of *apatheia*. One is eschatological in nature, consisting in the stripping off of mortality and sexuality—that is to say, of man's biological condition—and will be accomplished fully only after death. For the time being, virginity bears witness to it, and the purifications of the mystical life are a beginning of it. But this form is not primarily about asceticism. The second form of *apatheia*—which is the one we are dealing with in this chapter—is indeed concerned with this. Not with the destruction of the passions, but their good use. Its essential objective is to restore in the soul the order that has been disturbed, to subordinate anger (θυμός, *thymos*) and desire (ἐπιθυμία, *epithymia*) to the νοῦς (*nous*, mind). For although baptismal grace reconnects man's λόγος (*logos*, reason) to divine life and restores the image, the effects still need to permeate the human psyche—that is, the world of anger and desire.

This doctrine that order in the soul—and thus *apatheia* itself—entails the subordination of the passions will feature prominently in Gregory's ascetic theology. It dominates the beginning of *The Life of Moses*, which we shall discuss at length in due course. We have already seen how Gregory alludes to it in his description of man and the animals in paradise: the passions are the animals; man is made to be in charge of them.[97] In *The Life of Moses* the same idea reappears when the powers of the soul, unified under the command of the *logos*, are compared to sheep led by their shepherd.[98] This is another concept that had become classic in ancient philosophy. Here is how Synesius puts it: "man is not some simple [μονοειδής, *monoeidēs*] object nor is he cast in one [ἁπλοῦς, *haplous*] pattern, but God has made to dwell in the constitution of a single creature a host [ὄχλον, *ochlon*] of forces mingled together and with full-toned voices. We

---

[95]Proclus, *Elements of Theology*, Prop. 209 (Dodds, 182).

[96]For Gregory, however, the heavenly body is not different in its elements from the terrestrial body. Concerning this vehicle (ὄχημα, *ochēma*), see *An. et res.* 2 (PG 46:45B; PPS 12:47); *Virg.* 11 (PG 46:365C; FC 58:40).

[97]See *An. et res.* 3 (PG 46:61B; PPS 12:57).

[98]See *Vit. Moys.* 2.18 (PG 44:332C; Malherbe, 59). The image can be found in Philo, *On the Sacrifices of Abel and Cain* 10.45 (Yonge, 99–100).

are, I think, a monstrous animal more extraordinary than the hydra and still more many-headed.... There are in sooth all kinds of opposites within us and a certain medial force of nature runs through them which we call mind [νοῦς, *nous*]. It is this that I desire to reign in the king's soul, destroying the mob rule and democracy of the passions [δημοκρατία, *dēmokratia*]."[99]

This theory of the passions ultimately derives from Plato: the passions are alien to the mind, the true person, but are the necessary consequence of the temporary connection of the mind with the body. The first point is clearly expressed in the *Republic*:

> What we have to do, however, is try to see what the mind is really and truly like, when it's not deformed by its association with the body and with other evils (which is how we've been looking at it so far). We should try to see what it's like when it's untainted, and we'll have to rely on reason to get a clear enough view of that.... Our current ideas about the mind are true, in so far as they correspond to what we can see of it at the moment; but the condition in which we're observing it is like that of Glaucus the sea-deity. If people were to see Glaucus, it would be hard for them to discern his original state any more, because some of the original parts of his body have been knocked off, some have been worn away and generally deformed by the waves, and other things—shells, seaweed, and stones—have grown on him, so that his appearance is quite different from what it used to be, and he looks altogether more like a monster.[100]

The comparison is not unlike that of the warts (μυρμηκίαι, *myrmēkiai*) that Gregory uses to describe the passions.[101] He often uses other similar metaphors, as in the following passage: "This creature, man, therefore, did not have the elements of passion and mortality essentially and naturally in himself from the beginning. For it would not have been possible for the meaning of the word 'image' to be preserved if the copied beauty were different from the archetype. It was only later with the first fall that sin came upon man, and thus it crept in.

---

[99]Synesius, *On Imperial Rule* 6.2. English translation in *The Essays and Hymns of Synesius of Cyrene: Including the Address to the Emperor Arcadius and the Political Speeches*, vol. 1, trans. A. Fitzgerald (Oxford University Press, 1930), 118–19. Similar language can already be found in Chapter 17 of Maximus of Tyre, *The Dissertations*, vol. 1, trans. T. Taylor (London, 1804), 174–75.

[100]Plato, *Republic* 611b-d. Translation from *Plato: Republic*. Robin Waterfield, trans. (Oxford: Oxford University Press, 1993). [For "mind" in such classical quotations, Daniélou always prefers "soul."—*Trans.*]

[101]See *An. et res.* 3 (PG 46:56C; PPS 12:54).

The Structure of the Soul and the Passions

... And that godlike [θεοειδής, *theoeidēs*] beauty of the soul made in imitation of the prototype was darkened like some iron by the rust of evil."[102] The image of Glaucus covered by the stains and contamination of the sea stands for the "image" of God "darkened" by sin. As for the term "rust"—which we will come across again—it too is of Platonic origin.

Plato's first point, then, considers the true nature of the soul in itself, independently of the present state of affairs. But to this, he adds a second. From the moment the soul is joined to a body, the passions are the inevitable result. Thus the ideal is no longer to divest oneself of the passions, but to foster a good use of them, as is set out in *Phaedrus*.[103] This theme, too, occupies an important place in Gregory's thinking, as we have said, whether expressed in straightforward language or under various guises. There is a passage in *On the Soul and the Resurrection* that spells things out quite clearly: "If reason [λόγος, *logos*] ... should gain dominion [ἡγεμονίαν, *hēgemonian*] over those traits which are added to us from outside ... none of these impulses would work in us for servitude to evil. ... But if reason should let go of the reins [ἡνίας, *hēnias*] and like some charioteer entangled in the chariot should be dragged behind it, wherever the irrational [ἄλογος, *alogos*] motion of the yoke-animals carries it, then the impulses [ὁρμαί, *hormai*] are turned into passions, as indeed we can see also in the irrational animals."[104] This text is interesting from several points of view. As mentioned, in the background we recognize the central myth of *Phaedrus*. But, on the one hand, the reference to a rider who is carried away by the horses and falls off points to a biblical influence. The allusion is to the Egyptian horsemen who were thrown into the sea as they pursued the children of Israel (Ex 14.27f.). The influence is all the more plausible since Philo had already applied the same passage from Exodus to the *nous* and the passions: "We must comprehend that the horseman who has mounted upon the passions is the mind."[105]

On the other hand, Platonic thinking is influenced by Stoicism. In fact, the distinction between impulses and passions derives from it.[106] It is one that

---

[102] *Virg.* 12 (PG 46:369C; FC 58:42–43, 44).

[103] See Plato, *Phaedrus* 254 a–d.

[104] *An. et res.* 3 (PG 46:61B; PPS 12:57).

[105] Philo, *Allegorical Interpretation* 2.25.99 (Yonge, 48). The merging of the theme of the (Platonic) charioteer with that of the (biblical) horseman is already to be found in Philo's *On Husbandry* 16.73 (Yonge, 180); *On the Migration of Abraham* 11.62 (Yonge, 259); and *A Treatise on the Sacrifices of Abel and Cain* 10.45 (Yonge, 99–100). It is also found in Clement, *Miscellanies* 5.8, and in Origen, *Homilies on Exodus* 6.2; *Homilies on Joshua* 15.3.

[106] See *Stoicorum Veterum Fragmenta*, vol. 3, ed. H. von Arnim (Stuttgart: Teubner, 1964 [1st ed. 1903]), 228–36.

accords well with the distinction that Gregory himself often makes between those instinctual movements that are indifferent or good, if they are subjected to the reason—these are the impulses—and those that are left to themselves and become perverted. These are the passions in the strict sense of the term.

Yet, although Gregory sometimes makes this distinction,[107] he does not ordinarily do so. This is because, although it has its advantages, it also has the drawback of seeming to adopt the Stoic doctrine, according to which the passions form part of the soul's essence. The theory has been advanced that Gregory followed this Stoic teaching under the influence of Posidonius; but Cherniss has established that he always adhered to the Platonic theory of the passions, which sees them as alien to the soul, though susceptible of a good use in man's present state.[108]

In actual fact, one should move beyond both Stoicism and Platonism for, here again, Gregory is using philosophical language freely in order to express opinions that are his own. Moreover, he has made his position clear on this point:

> Everyone agrees that [desire and anger] appear in the soul; but what we should think about them reason has not yet discovered with accuracy, so that we may have a notion concerning them which is trustworthy. . . . For us, if the truth could be sufficiently demonstrated by the secular philosophy which has discoursed skillfully concerning these faculties, it would perhaps be superfluous to add a discussion of the soul to our investigation. But although some could theorize freely concerning the soul as the consequence of their reasoning led them, we have no part in this freedom (I mean the freedom to say whatever we want), since we always use the holy Scripture as the canon and rule of all our doctrine. . . . Therefore we shall abandon the Platonic chariot [τὸ πλατωνικὸν ἅρμα, *to platōnikon harma*] and the pair of horses yoked to it, which pulled unequally, and the charioteer controlling these horses, through all of which Plato presents symbolically a philosophy concerning these faculties in relation to the soul. We shall leave behind also whatever the philosopher who followed him [i.e., Aristotle] set forth, he who skillfully observed the phenomena and examined carefully the subject which concerns us now, inferring that the soul is mortal. We shall also set aside those who philosophized before these men and those afterwards.

---

[107] See *Beat.* 2 (PG 44:1216C; ACW 18:103); *Eccl.* 5 (PG 44:692C; Hall, 96).
[108] See Cherniss, *Platonism of Gregory*, 20–25.

... For our discussion we shall fix our eyes on the mark of the inspired Scripture.[109]

This text establishes the principle that one must never lose sight of when studying the Fathers—namely, their independence from all specific systems and—despite the clear allusions to Plato, Aristotle, and other philosophers—their final appeal to Scripture. If we examine Gregory's position on the passions, we find that, although he may be closer to Plato than anyone else, he nevertheless retains his independence. For instance, he places anger and desire on the same level, and we shall see shortly that he does not exclude the existence of passions even from man "in the image." He does use one or two Stoic terms, (e.g. ἡγεμονικόν, *hēgemonikon*—authoritative [part of the soul, reason]; ὁρμή, *hormē*—[irrational] impulse).[110] But, whatever Gronau may say, his overall theory is quite independent of Stoicism and can be adequately explained by reference to Plato. But, most importantly, all such philosophical terms are modified by the religious context in which they are found. Hence the issue of the structure of the soul is for Gregory merely an introductory problem. The real question is that of the two basic directions in which the soul can turn—toward God or vice. This is a question that no longer comes under the competence of philosophy. The philosophical foundations that we establish will simply help us to understand the problem better.

The myth of the steeds reappears elsewhere. Thus in the treatise *On Virginity*, Gregory notes that a charioteer whose team of horses do not advance at the same speed "guides them and stops them short and touches them with the whip until they go harmoniously along the race course; in the same way, our mind, which holds the reins of the body"[111] should do the same. Here too the allusion to the myth in *Phaedrus* is obvious, yet this time it is colored not by Stoicism but by the Aristotelian theory of virtue as the just mean.[112] The same image is also found in the homily on the second Beatitude: "Blessed are those who are not easily turned toward the passionate movements [ὁρμαί, *hormai*] of the soul, but who are steadied by reason. For the reasoning power restrains the desires

---

[109]*An. et res.* 3 (PG 46:49B–52A; PPS 12:50).

[110]These words had passed into the common vocabulary and are found in the Platonic philosophers. See Albinus, *Epitome* (*Disciplinarum Platonis epitome*), 31. [Cf. Ps 50.12 LXX: "a governing (ἡγεμονικῷ, *hēgemonikō*) spirit."—*Ed.*]

[111]*Virg.* 22 (PG 46:404D; FC 58:67–68).

[112]See Plato, *Phaedrus* 254b. [On Aristotle's theory of virtue as the mean between two extremes (excess and deficiency), see *Nicomachean Ethics* 1106a26–b28.—*Ed.*]

like a rein [χαλινῷ, *chalinō*] and does not suffer the soul to be carried away to unruliness."[113]

In *The Life of Moses* the same concept of the hegemony of the mind over the passions is expressed by a different symbol—a lintel and uprights:

> While in this way Scripture gives us through figures [the upper doorpost and the side posts] a scientific understanding of the nature of the soul, profane learning also places it before the mind, dividing the soul into the rational, the appetitive, and the spirited. Of these parts we are told that the spirit and the appetite are placed below, supporting on each side the intellectual part of the soul, while the rational aspect is joined to both so as to keep them together and to be held up by them, being trained for courage by the spirit and elevated to the participation in the Good by the appetite.
>
> As long, therefore, as the soul is kept safe in this manner, maintaining its firmness by virtuous thoughts as if by bolts, all the parts cooperate with one another for good. The rational for its part furnishes safety to its supports, and in its turn receives from them an equal benefit.
>
> But if this arrangement should be upset and the upper become the lower—so that if the rational falls from above, the appetitive and spirited disposition makes it the part trampled upon—then the destroyer slips inside.[114]

I have quoted this important passage at length, as it is essential for our purpose. First of all, one recognizes in it the Platonic theory of the tripartite division of the soul and of the hierarchy this entails. Moreover, Gregory himself indicates as much by his reference to "profane learning." We can go even further in studying the sources of this imagery, for the application to the Platonic theory of the passions of the symbol of a lintel and uprights is already found in Philo, from whom Gregory borrowed it—though with the differences that we shall see. "As for the deeper meaning" writes Philo, "... since our soul is threefold, the heart [θυμός, *thymos*] is likened to the lintel, desire [ἐπιθυμία, *epithymia*] to the house, and reason to the two doorposts."[115] This concept of subversion, of a soul in

---

[113] *Beat.* 1 (PG 44:1216C; ACW 18:103).
[114] *Vit. Moys.* 2.96–98 (PG 44:353C–D; Malherbe, 76–77).
[115] Philo, *Questions and Answers on Exodus* 1.12. Translation from *Philo: Supplement II. Questions on Exodus*, trans. Ralph Marcus, Loeb Classical Library, 401 (Cambridge, MA: Harvard University Press, 1953), 22.

which "the upper becomes the lower," when the passions dominate reason, is also from Plato.[116]

But what is most remarkable about the above passage is the explicit manner in which it explains the hierarchy of the parts of the soul. When the mind is trampled underfoot by the passions, this is a sign of vice; but, when the passions submit to the *nous*, they contribute to the acquisition of virtue. As Gregory says elsewhere, "If reason . . . should gain dominion over those traits . . . anger would produce courage . . . and the desiring impulse would mediate to us the divine and immortal pleasure."[117] What is proposed is that man should "construct, by the dynamism of his own self determination, a means of purging this present existence of the evil that is mingled with it, using reason to gain control of his irrationality" or "if he should be inclined toward diseased, mindless impulses, relying on the skin of the irrational beasts as his support for his passion, he will form other, better choices afterwards . . . having now come to know the difference of virtue from vice."[118] Let the order be respected and let the reason be in control of the passions and we have their good use, which is called virtue; let this order be violated and let the passions carry reason away, and we have vice (κακία, *kakia*) or simply passions in the pejorative sense of the word.

What is important to note here is not only that the passions should be mastered by reason in order not to be harmful, but that they then become allies in the ascent toward virtue. This too is a Platonic concept, as expressed in *Phaedrus*.[119] In another passage, taken from the *Treatise on the Inscriptions of the Psalms*, he presents it using the metaphor of the flocks, symbolic of the passions, which we have already come across. But ordinarily the submission of the flock to the mind simply indicates the hierarchy of the soul. Here Gregory goes much further and asserts that the flocks positively assist the *nous*. Among them, he writes, we find "anger, [which] is a good beast, whenever it becomes reason's beast of burden; and desire is another such beast, whenever, bearing the soul on its back, as it were, and carrying and lifting it up to the height, it is guided by the rein of the intellect [διάνοια, *dianoia*] to the things that are above."[120] Led by reason, then, the passions are useful servants.

---

[116]See Plato, *Republic* 424e, 442b.
[117]*An. et res.* 3 (PG 46:61B; PPS 12:57).
[118]*Mort.* 15 (PG 46:525A; PPS 64:25).
[119]See Origen, *Homilies on Genesis* 1.17; 2.6.
[120]*Inscr.* 1.8.103 (PG 44:477C; Heine, 116–17).

This idea is found in Plato elsewhere than in *Phaedrus*. Thus in the *Republic* we read: "[To say that] morality is profitable, is equivalent to saying that our words and behavior should be designed to maximize the control the inner man [ὁ ἔσω ἄνθρωπος, *ho esō anthrōpos*] has within us, and should enable him to secure the help of the leonine quality [σύμμαχον, *symmachon*; ally] and then tend to the many-headed beast as a farmer tends to his crops—by nurturing and cultivating its tame aspects, and by stopping the wild ones growing. Then he can ensure that they're all compatible with one another. And with himself, and can look after them all equally, without favouritism."[121] This is the source of the Synesius passage cited earlier—the one referring to the many-headed hydra, symbolic of the passions. The latter must be submitted to the "inner man." Then they will serve him as allies. Strangely, this passage brings to mind St Paul's words in Romans, concerning "the inner man" as contrasted with "the law that is in [his] members" (Rom 7.23). But in St Paul's text, which is of a religious nature, it is a question of two entirely opposing realities, ones that we will shortly find in Gregory. In the Platonic text it is simply a question of the structure of the soul, and it is this aspect that Gregory presents here. His thought moves now on the philosophic level (as in the dialogue *On the Soul and the Resurrection*), now on the religious level (as in *The Life of Moses*).

This involvement of desire and anger in the life of the image, when they submit to its hegemony, is found in Gregory a number of times. Thus, in his treatise *On Virginity* we read: "When the great image of the King which the Creator implanted in our hearts from the beginning is uncovered and brought to light, then, these faculties turn toward that divine joy and merriment, gazing upon the unspeakable beauty of what has been recovered. Reason and desire, and the faculty aroused by grief and anger, and whatever other faculties there are . . . do everything for the glory of God, for now they are no longer the instruments of sin."[122] Here the powers are imagined as the friends of the woman who had lost the drachma. In *The Life of Moses* they are the parents of the male children.[123] We note that the three powers are on the same level, as we shall see in the allegory of the Egyptian chariots. Consequently the passions are, as it were, "conformed" to the image of God, as Gregory puts it in *On the Making of Man*. "So, likewise, on the contrary, if reason [νοῦς, *nous*] instead assumes sway over such emotions, each of them is transmuted to a form of virtue; for anger

---

[121] Plato, *Republic* 589b.
[122] *Virg.* 12 (PG 46:373B; FC 58:45).
[123] *Vit. Moys.* 2.3 (PG 44:328B; Malherbe, 55–56).

The Structure of the Soul and the Passions

produces courage, terror caution ... and so we find that every such motion, when elevated by loftiness of mind, is conformed to the beauty of the Divine image [συσχηματίζεται τῷ κατὰ τὴν θείαν εἰκόνα κάλλει, *syschēmatizetai tō kata tēn theian eikona kallei*]."[124] Instead of the passions carrying away the image, it is the opposite that occurs. The life of the soul carries the passions with it and makes associates of them.

How far does this involvement of the passions in the virtuous life go? Does it correspond only to the lower stages? Do the passions have to be cast aside in eternal life, along with the garments of skin, after having proved useful? Or do they somehow subsist, just as the garments of skin are replaced not by mere nakedness of mind but the "luminous vestments" of the image? In other words, is the state that succeeds the virtuous life—which is a good use of the passions, and a negation of those passions that are perverted—a total absence of the passions or merely a stripping away of their animal form? It is true, of course, that this state no longer contains any animal nature strictly speaking. But is it pure spirituality? Does corporeality subsist in it? We have already seen that there is a "glorious form" of the body. Are there passions that correspond to this form?

This problem is tackled by Gregory in *On the Soul and the Resurrection*:

> "If such impulses of the soul," he says, "are considered to operate in us because of our relationship with the irrational animals, impulses which our discussion enumerated previously ... we said that the good use of these is virtue, but through their defective use evil comes about. Besides, we discussed the contribution of each of the other passions to the virtuous life and in particular to the fact that we are led to God by desire. We are drawn upwards toward Him as if by a rope [σειρά, *seira*]. The discussion seems somehow to be working against our purpose," I said ... "if every irrational impulse in us is quenched after our purification, not even the desiring impulse will exist at all. If this should not exist, there would not even be a yearning for the better."[125]

One sees the difficulty. If desire is a passion, then purification, in eliminating the passion, will also eliminate the desire. Gregory does not shrink from the conclusion. He has Macrina answer as follows:

---

[124]*Op. hom.* 18.5 (PG 44:193C; NFNP² 5:408).
[125]*An. et res.* 6 (PG 46:89A–B; PPS 12:77–78).

> To this we reply that the faculty of contemplation [θεωρητικόν, *theōrētikon*] and discernment is proper to the godlike part of the soul, since by these we comprehend even the divine. So, you see, if our soul should become free from its attachment to the irrational emotions . . . it will in no way be hindered from the contemplation of the beautiful. Therefore the soul will not receive any disadvantage in respect to participation in the good, if it should be freed from these impulses. It will go back to itself [ἐπανελθοῦσα εἰς ἑαυτήν, *epanelthousa eis heautēn*] and see clearly what it is in its nature, and through its own beauty it will look upon the archetype as if in a mirror and an image.[126]

It would seem that here there is a denial of any progress or desire in the purified soul. Yet we shall see that nothing is more contrary to Gregory's thought. What is eliminated from the purified soul is desire insofar as it is the painful attraction for an absent good. As soon as the soul possesses God—which is the case in the mystical life proper—it can no longer desire him in that sense, since he is present in it.

Is this then the denial of all progress? The analyses that follow are very interesting in this respect. They show us the soul continuing to make progress, no longer under the impulse of desire (it has all it wants, and there is no more desire), but through the attraction of God, who pulls it toward him "as if by a rope." We move to the order of passivity (which is precisely that of the mystical life)—a change that coincides precisely with the moment the soul is lifted above its animal nature and no longer merely above sin. Thus in one sense desire and anger have certainly disappeared, along with everything else that is linked to the "garments of skin." But that does not exclude a new and entirely divine principle of progress.

These views are confirmed by Gregory's spiritual writings. Thus in *The Life of Moses* we see that at a first stage, which corresponds to the ordinary virtuous life, the passions are submitted to the guidance of the spirit, "shepherded like sheep."[127] This corresponds to the first way—dispassion by means of virtue (ἀπάθεια κατ' ἀρετήν, *apatheia kat' aretēn*). It does not entail an elimination of the passions, but a perfect submission of them to the mind. Things are altogether different at the threshold of the mystical life, represented by the ascent of Mt Sinai. Here the "animals" must not only be submitted to the dominion of

---

[126] *An. et res.* 6 (PG 46:89B; PPS 12:77–78).
[127] *Vit. Moys.* 2.18 (PG 44:332C; Malherbe, 59).

The Structure of the Soul and the Passions

the mind, but must be completely removed.[128] Will the soul, for all that, cease to be animated by the "desire" for God or cease to be filled with "strength" to resist temptation? On the contrary. But henceforth it is a divine, supernatural force that raises it above itself and pulls it toward God. "If nothing comes from above to hinder its upward thrust (for the nature of the Good attracts to itself those who look to it), the soul rises ever higher and will always make its flight yet higher—by its desire of the heavenly things straining ahead for what is still to come, as the Apostle says [Phil 3.13]."[129] This is spiritual desire in the true sense and that can be defined as docility of the soul to divine attraction (ἑλκτική, helktikē).

The Tyranny of the Passions

We have now clarified how Gregory understands the structure of the soul in its present condition. We have seen that there is a dichotomy between "the image of God"—which includes the spirit (πνεῦμα, pneuma) and the mind (νοῦς, nous), and which constitutes man's true "nature"—and the "garments of skin" that go hand in hand with the passions. This is indicated clearly in a passage from the *Catechetical Discourse*: "Therefore mortality, [taken] from the nature of irrational [animals], economically enveloped [our] nature, [which was] created for immortality, enfolding the external [τὸ ἔξωθεν, to exōthen], not the internal [τὸ ἔσωθεν, to esōthen], embracing the sense perceptible part of man, but not fastening upon the divine image itself."[130] This passage clearly shows that the divine image is compatible with our mortal condition. Yet this is an unstable and ambiguous state of affairs: either the image will guide the sensory powers (the passions) or, conversely, the passions will carry away the image. And then it will no longer be a case of the chariot driver goading along his stubborn horses toward "the vault of heaven," but of the horses that have bolted and are dragging the mind into animality. From the spiritual point of view, what is of interest here is the domain of the passions in the pejorative sense of the word.

What complicates the question—and has necessitated this lengthy analysis—is the imprecision of Gregory's vocabulary on this point. A single word—πάθη (pathē, the passions)—serves to denote both the "natural" tendencies and weaknesses that derive from this animal nature and also the perversion of these

---

[128]See *Vit. Moys.* 2.156 (PG 44:373B; Malherbe, 93).
[129]*Vit. Moys.* 2.225 (PG 44:401A; Malherbe, 113).
[130]*Or. cat.* 8.5 (PG 45:33D; PPS 60:84).

tendencies. There was, however, one specific case in which he was obliged to clarify his meaning: that of the incarnation of the Word. Did the Word assume the passions? Here a distinction is in order:

> "Passion" is said at times in a proper sense [κυρίως, *kyrios*], but at other times in a less correct sense [ἐκ καταχρήσεως, *ek katachrēseōs*]. Therefore what is joined to the will and turns it from virtue to vice is truly passion [πάθος, *pathos*]; but whatever is seen in nature, which proceeds successively in its proper sequence, this would much more properly be called a "work" [ἔργον, *ergon*] than a passion, such as birth, growth, the continuance of the subject through the inflow and outflow of nourishment, the concourse of the elements of the body, the dissolution of the composition again, and [its] departure to kindred [elements].[131]

In this passage we again find listed those elements of the biological life that constitute the "garments of skin." Yet these are not passions in the strict sense; that is, evil inclinations. Thus here we have a text that is crucial for the topic we are investigating, one that will allow us to understand Gregory's thinking with greater precision. He continues as follows: "What then does our mystery say has been joined to the divine? 'Passion,' properly speaking, which is vice, or a movement in accordance with nature? . . . If birth itself in itself is not a passion, neither does anyone call life a passion; but pleasurable passion precedes human birth, and living things' impulse to vice—this is an infirmity of our nature—but indeed the mystery says he is pure of both."[132] Hence we can dismiss the objection of those who would see an incompatibility in the fact that the Word, who is essentially ἀπαθής (*apathēs*, without passion), assumed the πάθη (*pathē*, passions) of our nature. There is an order of *pathos* that the Word did not assume and that, since Augustine, we call "concupiscence"—that is, not nature itself, but the imbalance that sin has introduced into it.

Gregory repeatedly makes this important distinction. In the treatise *Against Eunomius*, he writes:

> Nothing is truly "passion" which does not tend to sin, nor would one strictly call by the name of "passion" the necessary routine of nature. . . . This then is rather a work than a passion of the nature. For we give the name of "passion" only to that which is opposed to the virtuous unimpassioned state and

[131] *Or. cat.* 16.1 (PG 45:49B–C; PPS 60:99).
[132] *Or. cat.* 16.2, 3 (PG 45:49C, D; PPS 60:99, 100).

of this we believe that He Who granted us salvation was at all times devoid, Who "was in all points tempted like as we are yet without sin" [Heb 4.15]. Of that, at least, which is truly passion, which is a diseased condition of the will, He was not a partaker.[133]

The valuable expression ἀπάθεια κατ' ἀρετήν (*apatheia kat' aretēn*, dispassion by means of virtue) has its exact counterpart in another that is common in Gregory—πάθη κατὰ κακίαν (*pathē kata kakian*, passions resulting from evil). It accurately identifies and describes the program of the Christian ascetic life. There is no Platonic doctrine of the condemnation of the flesh, which would be incompatible with the dogma of the incarnation.[134] This is something that Gregory insists on against Apollinarius, the forerunner of Monophysitism. Moreover, it is abundantly clear that there was no sin in Christ. Thus the special case of the incarnation obliges us to escape from the indeterminacy in which Greek thought remained, trapped between the concept of sin as something moral and the notion of matter as a stain.

We also find this distinction between the two types of passion in a passage from *The Life of Moses*, regarding the chariots of the Egyptians. The various passions to which the soul of man is enslaved are represented by the chariot and the horses, the riders, the archers, the slingers, and so forth. "For the undisciplined intellectual drives and the sensual impulses to pleasure, sorrow, and covetousness are indistinguishable from the aforementioned army.... The passion for pleasures is to be seen in the horses who themselves with irresistible drive pull the chariot. In the chariot there are three drivers whom the history calls 'viziers.' ... These three ... are completely carried along by the chariot, as the tripartite division of the soul, meaning the rational, the appetitive, and the spirited."[135] Some have used this text to argue that Gregory had abandoned the Platonic theory of the passions for that of the Stoics. And it is true that the contrast with the myth in *Phaedrus* is striking. Desire and courage, which in *Phaedrus* are symbolized by the horses, are here depicted as being installed on the chariots along with the mind. But in fact what Gregory envisages here is not the structure of the soul, but the two categories of passion. Insofar as they are functions of the soul, the passions are symbolized by the charioteers; insofar as they are evil

---

[133]*Eun.* 3.4.27–28 (PG 45:721C; NPNF² 5:186).
[134]See *Antirrh.* 19 (PG 45:1196A; FOX 131:172): *Eun.* 3.4.25 (PG 45:721A; NPNF² 5:185).
[135]*Vit. Moys.* 2.122–23 (PG 44:361C–D; Malherbe, 83).

passions, they are represented by the horses. It is this second category of passion that we must now consider, for it properly depicts that against which the soul should strive to arm itself so as to arrive at *apatheia*.

We shall now study the various symbols used by Gregory to describe this world of the passions, which is that of the deadly sins.

There are five main groups. First, they are symbolized by various animals—and we have just seen, for example, how the horses symbolize unbridled passion. Next, they are viewed as tyrants that keep the mind enslaved. Third, they are imagined as a stain, as mud, rust, and so on. Then they are portrayed as agitation and unrest, and, finally, as illusions. To each of these corresponds its opposite: to animality, *apatheia*; to tyranny, freedom (παρρησία, *parrhēsia*); to stain, purity (καθαρότης, *katharotēs*); to agitation, inner stillness (ἡσυχία, *hēsychia*); and to illusion, knowledge (γνῶσις, *gnōsis*). We have already looked at agitation and stillness when discussing the "inner man" and, when we come to consider the second way, most of our time will be taken up with an examination of illusion and *gnōsis*. Here, we need only retain for consideration the concepts of animality and tyranny.

In his symbolic vision Gregory ordinarily portrays sin in terms of being transformed into a beast. In this way of looking at things, there are two opposing realms: the angelic and the animal. People are divided into two races, depending on whether they choose to belong to the one or the other. The world of sin is contrasted with paradise, the former being represented by the West, which is the domain of evil: "Neglect of this duty [to guard the paradise] cast the human being out of the garden and made him a dweller in the place of the setting sun, having removed him from the sunrise."[136] But more specifically, it is represented by the forest,[137] the lair of wild animals: "As its custom is, the Holy Scripture assigns the name 'wood' to that material life of the human race that is bursting with the various sorts of passions, the wood in which the destroyer beasts lurk and hide, whose kind accomplishes nothing in the light of the sun but takes its strength from darkness. For after the sun has set, the prophet says, when night has come, 'the wild beasts of the wood' come out of their lairs (Ps 103.20)."[138]

This comparison of the passions to fierce creatures is very common with Gregory. Among them we find, of course, the serpent, symbol of sensual

---

[136] *Cant.* 2 (PG 44:797C; Norris, 63).
[137] See Philo, *Allegorical Interpretation* 3.1.1 (Yonge, 50).
[138] Gregory, *Cant.* 4 (PG 44:841C–D; Norris, 129). [See p. 235 n. 144.—Ed.]

The Structure of the Soul and the Passions 75

pleasure: "The passion of lust is but one animal; but the many various forms of lust . . . are the scales surrounding the serpent."[139] Then there is the lion: "Now sins were truly young lions for me formerly, or whelps of lions, which tore [me] in pieces with their fearful gaping mouths and their pointed claws."[140] We even find the figure of the tapeworm (ἕλμις, *elmis*): "Doctors say that tapeworms and some other similar parasites . . . are engendered in our intestines by some faulty humour. . . . There is an analogy between such physical conditions and diseases of the soul. When anger, sucking within, or enervating by resentment the vigour of the soul and the rational powers, generates the parasite of envy . . ."[141]

What we have here is a theme whose origins are very ancient and that is already to be found in Plato. From Book 9 of the *Republic* we are familiar with the myth of the many-headed monstrous beast, symbolic of the passions, that we have already referred to: "Licentiousness . . . allows that fiend, that huge and many-faceted creature, greater freedom than it should have. . . . And aren't obstinacy and bad temper considered bad because they distend and invigorate our leonine, serpentine side to a disproportionate extent?"[142] Here we no longer have the neutral powers of the soul, as with the horses of *Phaedrus*, but the unleashing of the raging forces of instinct that prevail over reason and transform man into a beast. In the passage from the *Republic* this is closely linked to another theme that we also find in Gregory of Nyssa—the passions as tyrants.

In Philo, this Platonic symbolism is linked to biblical imagery, which, here as elsewhere in his writings, plays an essential intermediary role. As Heinisch says, "animals, being unreasoning creatures, are with him symbols of the irrational part of the human soul, the instincts and the passions."[143] This is especially the teaching we find in Philo's *Allegorical Interpretation*, when he comments on the creation of the animals in paradise and their presentation to Adam: "You see here who are our assistants, the beasts [θηρία, *thēria*] of the soul, the passions. For after God had said, 'I will make him a helpmeet for him,' Moses adds subsequently, 'He made the beasts,' as if the beasts also were assistants to us. But these are not, properly [κυρίως, *kyriōs*] speaking, assistants, but are called so only in a catachrestic manner [καταχρηστικῶς, *katachrēstikōs*], by a kind of abuse of

---

[139]*Or. dom.* 4 (PG 44:1172B; ACW 18:65). Cf. *Eccl.* 2 (PG 44:648A; Hall); *Eccl.* 4 (PG 44:665D; Hall, 75); *Vit. Moys.* 2.275 (PG 44:416A; Malherbe, 124): the sinner assumes the nature of a serpent.
[140]*Inscr.* 2.14.236 (PG 44:588A; Heine, 197).
[141]*Eccl.* 6 (PG 44:705D; Hall, 106–107).
[142]Plato, *Republic* 590a–b.
[143]P. Heinisch, *Der Einfluss Philos auf die älteste christliche Exegese* (Münster: Aschendorff, 1908), 94.

language, for they are found in reality to be enemies to man."[144] It is interesting to note that Philo, before Gregory,[145] gives the pejorative sense of the term "passion" as being its proper (κυρίως, *kyriōs*) meaning.

We should note too the importance of the reference to the episode from Genesis. We often find a parallel drawn between the inner world of passions and the external world of animals. In fact, this is more than a mere symbol. It is a question of the link that exists between man and the universe, between the macrocosm and the microcosm, and their effect on each other. The inner disorder of man, the enslavement of the mind to the passions, has repercussions in the cosmos, where man really can become the prey of wild beasts. And, conversely, the return to the paradisal state in the case of the saints has the additional benefit of bringing about a miraculous dominion over the material world, especially over animals. In Hesiod [*Works and Days* ln. 109–121] and Isaiah [11.6–9], this dominion over the animal world is portrayed as one of the characteristics of the Golden Age and also of the future Jerusalem. Stolz writes as follows:

> The connection between man and the animals is thus very close. As microcosm, man includes the world within himself. The saintly doctors deduce from this that when man, by means of the gift of *apatheia*, controls and regulates his whole being, at the same time he controls and regulates the entire universe, as summarized and imaged within himself. Now the image, according to the old interpretation, implies the reality of what it represents. Hence it is entirely natural that the mastery that man has gained over himself should be manifested also in the macrocosm. From this idea of man's dominion over creation, St Paul's words (Rom 8.19–22), when he speaks of the entire creation waiting for man's redemption to be completed, acquire a new significance. And examples taken from the life of the mystics prove that God quite often reestablishes man's dominion over irrational creatures as evidence of his complete victory over himself.[146]

---

[144] Philo, *Allegorical Interpretation* 2.4.9–10 (Yonge, 39). See also Philo, *On Dreams* 2.7.50 (Yonge, 391). Likewise Origen, *Homilies on Genesis* 1.16.

[145] See Gregory, *Or. cat.* 16.1 (PG 45:49B; PPS 60:99).

[146] Anselm Stolz, *Théologie de la mystique* (Chevetogne: Bénédictins d'Amay, 1939), 103. [The English version, which is of the German original—*Theologie der Mystik* (Regensburg: Pustet, 1936)—was published prior to the French edition as *The Doctrine of Spiritual Perfection*, trans. Aidan Williams (St Louis, MO and London: Herder, 1938). But the translation of the above quotation (on page 95 of the English) differs in several important respects from the extract cited by Daniélou. This can no doubt be explained by the fact that the French edition was not a direct translation from the German, but was based on the

The Structure of the Soul and the Passions

But, this is not exactly the way Philo or Gregory see things. The Genesis episode is understood by them in a purely symbolic sense. The animals do represent the passions, but it is a question of gaining dominion only over these passions and not over the actual world of animals, all the more since, for Gregory, man's habitat in the animal world postdates his fall. As he himself says, "It does not seem to me that our hope is one for those things which are now subjected by God to man for the necessary uses of life, but one for another kingdom (βασιλεία, *basileia*), of a description that belongs to unspeakable mysteries [ἐν ἀπορρήτοις, *en apporrētois*]."[147] Hence it is a kingdom that is linked to the supernatural order. From this highly spiritual standpoint there is no room for thinking in terms of a regeneration of the actual universe, but rather for its replacement by a different order of reality. Let us not forget that Gregory never understands the Pauline expression "*exspectatio creaturae*" ([the expectation of creation] Rom 8.19) as referring to this world, but in the sense of the expectation of the angels, who for him are the true creation (κτίσις, *ktisis*).

For Philo, specific animals are symbols of specific passions.[148] Thus the horse, on account of its wildness, is symbolic of the passions in general.[149] For this reason, we came across it when discussing the "garments of skin." The same symbolism is found in Clement.[150] The tiger, on account of its savagery, symbolizes desire.[151] The serpent that crawls on the ground and induces man to vulgar pleasures symbolizes lust.[152] This is also found in Clement.[153] Thus we see how from Plato to Philo to Clement the bestiary of the deadly sins that Christianity would subsequently inherit was gradually put together.[154]

We saw that horses are a symbol of frenzied passion in the episode where the Pharaoh's chariots are carried away by them. And concerning this text, we noted how there is a clear distinction between the natural passions, symbolized by the people mounted on the chariot, and the guilty passions, symbolized

---

lectures Dom Stolz gave to the monks of Chevetogne. Accordingly, the above translation has been modified to agree with the French and with the point Daniélou is making.—*Trans.*]

[147] *Op. hom.* 21.4 (PG 44:204A; NFNP² 5:411).

[148] See also Clement of Alexandria, *Exhortation to the Heathen* (*Protrepticus*) 10.4.

[149] See Philo, *Allegorical Interpretation* 2.25.99 (Yonge, 48).

[150] See Clement of Alexandria, *Miscellanies* 5.8.52.

[151] See Philo, *Allegorical Interpretation* 1.21.69 (Yonge, 32).

[152] See ibid. 2.18.74 (Yonge, 45); *On the Creation* 56.157 (Yonge, 22); *Questions and Answers on Genesis* 1.48.

[153] See Clement of Alexandria, *The Instructor* 1.5.16; 3.2.5. On these various symbols, see Origen, *Homilies on Genesis* 1.8; Ambrose, *On Paradise* 11.51.

[154] See Pseudo-Melito, *De bestiis* in *Spicilegium Solesmense*, vol. 3. (Paris: F. Didot, 1855), 1.1–101.

by the horses. As for the serpent, symbol of lust, its role in the temptation scene in Genesis explains the considerable importance it has in Gregory's commentaries. Thus in *The Life of Moses*, concerning the bronze serpent, we read: "Every offspring of evil desire is a serpent."[155] More significantly, in his *Homilies on Ecclesiastes* Gregory explains how the temptation of lust, as soon as one lets it enter the soul, can no longer be removed, no more than a serpent—on account of its scales—can be withdrawn from a hole once it has entered it.[156]

The Life of Moses is particularly rich in animal metaphors. The plagues of Egypt, for example, provide Gregory with the image of the frog: "The breed of frogs is obviously the destructive offspring of the evil which is brought to life from the sordid heart of men as though from some slimy mire. These frogs overrun the houses of those who choose to live the Egyptian life, appearing on the tables, not even sparing the beds, and entering the very storerooms.... [Even so the licentious man] exhibits an amphibious form of life ambiguous in nature.... For such a man shows his profligacy in everything."[157] As for the flies, lice, and locusts, Gregory does not try to find a particular meaning in them. By contrast, in another passage of the same work, he develops an important parallel between envy and the vulture. "It is said that the vultures which devour corpses are destroyed by perfume.... Anyone who is in the power of this sickness [envy] is destroyed by the happiness of his neighbors as by some perfume; but if he should see any unfortunate experience he flies to it, sets his crooked beak to it, and draws forth the hidden misfortunes."[158] This image can already found in Basil.[159] Finally, there is the comparison with pigs, linked to the image of the Platonic mire.[160]

These comparisons of the guilty passions to animals is interesting, but it does not represent the most important aspect of Gregory's teaching on this point. What is most characteristic of his approach is the idea of the "metamorphosis"[161] of a man himself into a beast. It is this which properly constitutes a πάθος (*pathos*, passion) and makes man ἐμπαθής (*empathēs*, impassioned; κτηνώδης,

[155] *Vit. Moys.* 2.275 (PG 44:413D; Malherbe, 124).
[156] See *Eccl.* 4 (PG 44:676C; Hall, 82).
[157] *Vit. Moys.* 2.69–71 (PG 44:345B; Malherbe, 70).
[158] *Vit. Moys.* 2.258 (PG 44:409D; Malherbe, 121).
[159] See Basil the Great, *Homily 11: On Envy* 5 (PG 31:380D–385B).
[160] "... they wallowed, like pigs, in the slimy mire of uncleanness." *Vit. Moys.* 2.302 (PG 44:424C; Malherbe, 132).
[161] *Prof.* (PG 46:245B; FC 58:86).

The Structure of the Soul and the Passions

ktenōdēs—animalistic),[162] or θηριώδης (*thēriodēs*, bestial or savage), depending on the words Gregory chooses. Such is the consequence of sin, of the adhesion of the will to a guilty passion. The passion is in this way introduced to the higher part of the soul and thereby brings about its death: the image of God is replaced by the image of the beast. Thus humanity as depicted by Gregory is composed of two sorts of people: some with the faces of angels and others wearing the mask of the beast. As we explore the texts in which this idea appears, we shall see what the origins of this new theme might be.

To begin with, it must be said that this idea of the transformation of man into a beast by the passions is quite common in Gregory. In *The Life of Moses*, he writes: "Pleasure showed that she makes men beasts. The irrational [ἄλογον, *alogon*], animal [κτηνώδες, *ktēnōdes*] impulse to licentiousness made them forget their human nature."[163] Of the many other such examples, consider the following. After speaking of the teeth of lions that tear the soul to pieces, he adds: "The constitution of our nature does not know these perceptible arrows which lie in human mouths in place of teeth, but whenever one becomes like the passion and has been transformed [μεταμορφωθῇ, *metamorphōthē*] into the prevailing evil, he loses his natural form and becomes a beast."[164] "Whoever deserts to sin takes on the nature of the serpent."[165] "Changed into a beast by his own choice [he has] become a dog."[166] "If it has the look of some hateful thing, it is imitating that ugliness through a likeness, playing, in its own appearance, the part of a frog or toad or a millipede."[167] "For humanity, once it had put off its divine aspect, was brutalized and approached likeness to the irrational nature and through its evil habits became a leopard [πάρδαλις, *pardalis*] or a lion. For the person who is dragged off by the 'lion' that lurks 'in his den [μάνδρα, *mandra*],' as the prophet says, and is brought down 'in his snare' (Ps 10.9) is transformed [μεταμορφοῦται, *metamorphoutai*] into that nature.... In the same way, someone who has spotted [στιγματίσας, *stigmatisas*] his soul with life's blemishes becomes a leopard."[168]

Thus, for Gregory this is a matter of a genuine metamorphosis. He himself compares things to the metamorphoses we read about in the classic myths, in

---

[162] This word is also found in Philo, *Allegorical Interpretation* 3.36.111 (Yonge, 62–63).
[163] *Vit. Moys.* 2.302 (PG 44:424C; Malherbe, 132).
[164] *Inscr.* 2.14.237 (PG 44:588A; Heine, 197).
[165] *Vit. Moys.* 2.275 (PG 44:416A; Malherbe, 124).
[166] *Inscr.* 2.16.284 (PG 44:608A; Heine, 213).
[167] *Cant.* 4 (PG 44:833B; Norris, 115).
[168] *Cant.* 8 (PG 44:945A; Norris, 263–65).

particular to what happened to the companions of Odysseus—and this is all the more intriguing since he rarely makes such explicit references. "By 'magic' [the magic (γοητεία, *goēteia*) of Balaam] you will perceive the crafty deceit of this life through which men drugged as though by some philter of Circe are changed into the form of irrational animals."[169] This text is interesting in the way it links together two of the aspects of a given passion: it transforms men into beasts; and it is a spell (γοητεία, *goēteia*), an evil illusion. The use in the original of the word ἐκστάντες (*ekstantes,* displace) is also important, for the passions are a perverted form of "ecstasy" (ἔκστασις, *ekstasis*). They force man "out of" his nature—not for θέωσις, *theōsis* (deification) but for the opposite: θηρίωσις (*thēriōsis,* "bestialization").

The allusion to fables also appears in a passage from the second homily on the Beatitudes, where the transformation seems to be almost physical:

> When some word or deed or suspicion causing annoyance has roused this disease [wrath], then the blood boils round the heart, and the soul rises up for vengeance. As in pagan fables some drugged drink changes human nature into animal form, so a man is sometimes seen to be changed by wrath into a boar, or dog, or panther, or some other wild animal. His eyes become bloodshot; his hair stands on end and bristles; his voice becomes harsh and his words sharp. His tongue grows numb with passion and refuses to obey the desires of his mind. His lips grow stiff; and unable to articulate a word, they can no longer keep the spittle produced by passion inside the mouth, but dribble forth disgustingly when they try to speak.[170]

This portrayal of the physical effects of passion—a theme dear to Gregory—is not unlike a cynical diatribe in its realism, though the influence of mythical metamorphosis is still present in the background.

Although such a man as described above may call himself a Christian, in reality he belongs to the world of animals. "If someone is emotional [ἐμπαθής, *empathēs*] and brutal [θηριώδης, *thēriōdēs*], changing from one passion to another, and reflecting many forms of animals in his character (for it is easily possible to see how the changes in our nature correspond to animals) when such a one calls himself a Christian . . . then that person makes the divine . . . an object of blame among unbelievers."[171] Gregory illustrates this by the anecdote of the

---

[169] *Vit. Moys.* 2.316 (PG 44:428C; Malherbe, 135).
[170] *Beat.* 2 (PG 44:1216B; ACW 18:103–104).
[171] *Prof.* (PG 46:245B; FC 58:86).

monkey dressed up as a human being by a fairground showman in Alexandria. One of the spectators started to throw nuts in its direction and immediately, in its mad dash to get at the tidbits, the animal removed its mask, thereby showing its true nature.[172]

Even though the transformation into a beast may not be complete, one can still be partially affected. To describe this monstrous state—half-man, half-beast—Gregory again has recourse to mythology:

> There are men who fashion mythical creatures in their speeches and writings, constructing bull-headed horses or centaurs or serpent-footed monsters or other such things made up of different species. They do not achieve an imitation in keeping with a natural archetype, and, illogically overstepping nature, they fashion something other than man, fabricating the impossible. We would not say that what they have constructed in this strange synthesis is a man, even if some parts of the figure happen to resemble certain parts of the human body. In the same way, a person cannot accurately be called a Christian if he does not give assent to the faith with his mind, even if he conforms to it in other respects, or if his mind gives assent, but his body is not suited to his way of life, exhibiting the anger of dragons and the bestiality of serpents, or adding to his human character an equine madness for women. In such cases a man becomes double-natured, a centaur made up of reason and passion. It is possible to see many such people: either they resemble the Minotaur, being bull-headed in their belief in idolatry, although they appear to be leading a good life; or they make themselves centaurs and dragons by combining with a Christian façade a bestial body.[173]

These symbols take on their full meaning, if one remembers the role played by animal figures in ancient paganism. I will mention just one example, one that was discussed by Eisler precisely in connection with Gregory of Nyssa: the animal masks worn during the bacchanalia.[174] It seems certain that there is a similarity between this ritual and the Gregorian theme—Pauline in origin—of the metamorphosis of a human being into a wolf or a lion by passions. Likewise, the destruction of the vices are symbolized by the removal of the animal masks. Eisler names several monuments, both pagan and Christian, which support this

---

[172] See *Prof.* (PG 46:240C–241A; FC 58:82–83).
[173] *Perf.* (PG 46:256D–257A; FC 58:99).
[174] See R. Eisler, *Orphisch-Dionysische Mysteriengedanken in der christlichen Antike* (Leipzig: Teubner, 1925), 296ff.

idea. In their depictions, he detects a definite elaboration of opposites: angelic life versus bestial life, and a contrast between two types of garment, similar to the contrast we came across in the sacramental order, in the mystical order, and in the eschatological order.

In the portrayal of the passions, as mentioned above, the theme of wild animals is linked to that of tyranny. The world of sin is depicted as exercising tyrannical domination over man by means of these passions. Thus, at the beginning of *The Life of Moses,* the Pharaoh's tyranny over the Hebrews kept captive in Egypt symbolizes the tyranny of the passions over the man living in sin. Here, Egypt—like the forest earlier—is the habitat, the domain, of sin: "For uncontrolled passion is a fierce and raging master to the servile reasoning, tormenting it with pleasures as though they were scourges. Covetousness is another such master who provides no relief to the bondsman, but even if the one in bondage should slave in subservience to the commands of the master and acquire for him what he desires, the servant is always driven on to more. And all the other things which are performed by evil are so many tyrants and masters."[175]

Here, we encounter one of the essential aspects of the passions, and a standpoint from which the contrast between life in paradise and life in "Egypt" is most apparent. In fact, we should remember that, for Gregory, freedom is one of the main attributes of the image, not to say the most important one. By this he understands not the absence of external constraint, but the spiritual freedom of a soul that is not impeded by anything in realizing its goal, which is the love of God. It will be seen that "enslavement" to the passions—δουλεία (*douleia*) in the pejorative sense, for, like πάθος (*pathos*, passion), the word can be understood in two ways—is one of the essential features of a state of moral degeneration, one of the aspects of what will later be called original sin.

Moreover, the two theories are frequently drawn together:

> How should we not bewail our misfortune, when we contrast our former beatitude with our present misery? What was exalted has been brought low, and what was made in the image of Heaven has been reduced to earth. What was meant to rule has been enslaved, and what had been created for immortality has been destroyed by death. Man, who once lived in the delights Paradise, has been transplanted into this unhealthy and wearisome place, where his life, once accustomed to impassibility, became instead subject to passion and corruption.

[175] *Vit. Moys.* 2.129 (PG 44:364D; Malherbe, 85).

The Structure of the Soul and the Passions 83

> Thus the creature that had once been without a master and in full possession of his free will, is now dominated by so many great evils that we can hardly count all our tyrants. For as soon as any of our innate passions is allowed to dominate, it becomes the master of the person it has enslaved. It occupies the castle of the soul like a tyrant and afflicts the obedient lord through his own subjects. It uses our thoughts as its servants who carry out what seems good to it. For the whole army of passions, wrath and fear, cowardice and impudence, depression as well as pleasure, hatred, strife and merciless cruelty, envy as well as flattery, brutality together with brooding over injuries—they are all so many despotic masters who make the soul a slave in their territory as if it was a prisoner of war.[176]

As is often the case in Gregory, we have here the transposition to the moral level of a theme that elsewhere he discusses on the philosophical level. Indeed, in *On the Making of Man* while expounding various theories on the localization of thought in an organ, and after having spoken of the one that localizes it in the heart (and which derives from Chrysippus and Posidonius),[177] he recalls that others (the Platonists) place it in the brain: "Those, on the other hand, who consecrate the brain to reasoning [τῷ λογισμῷ, *tō logismō*], say that the head has been built by nature as a kind of citadel of the whole body, and that in it the mind dwells like a king, with a bodyguard [δορυφορούμενον, *doryphoroumenon*] of senses surrounding it like messengers and shield-bearers."[178] This same imagery is also found in Cicero: "*Sensus autem interpretes et nuntii rerum mirifice in capite, tamquam in arce (=akropolei) collocati sunt*" ("The senses, which act as intermediaries and reporters, have been marvellously created and placed for necessary service in the head, as though in a citadel").[179]

Gregory quotes this opinion only to discard it. However, he keeps the image, transposing it to the moral domain. The acropolis, or citadel, is the seat of the mind. When a passion seizes it, the (λογισμοί, *logismoi*; reasonings or thoughts) and the various passions, become tyrants to whom the soul is captive. This is

---

[176] *Beat.* 3 (PG 44:1228A–C; ACW 18:113–14).

[177] See I. Heinemann, *Posidonios' metaphysische schriften*, vol. 2 (Breslau: Markus, 1928), 309. See also Philo, *Allegorical Interpretation* 1.18.59 (Yonge, 31); Cicero, *Tusculan Disputations* 1.9.

[178] Gregory, *Op. hom.* 12.1 (PG 44:156D; NPNF² 5:397).

[179] Cicero, *On the Nature of the Gods* 2.56. Tullius Cicero, *De Natura Deorum*, trans. Francis Brooks (London: Methuen & Co., 1896), 146. This passage presents other striking parallels with Gregory's *On the Making of Man*, to the point that they obviously presuppose a common source, as Endre von Ivánka has established. See his "Die Quelle von Ciceros *De natura deorum*, 2.45–60: Poseidonius bei Gregor von Nyssa," *Archivum Philologicum* (1935): 1–12.

the theme of the hierarchy of the faculties, which we have already come across. Here, however, the door lintel and the charioteer are replaced by the citadel. But what becomes quite clear is that, once they have captured the mind, the passions become tyrannical. The loss of the image of God, which resides in the mind, brings in its wake the anarchy of the passions. It is into the will that evil must first gain entry.

This image of a citadel conquered by the passions can already be found in Plato's *Republic*, in a text whose importance for the theme of the tyrant is paramount. In it, we have a parallelism that is no longer cosmic–psychological but sociological–psychological. In fact, the entire book is based on this theme of the city as a reflection of the individual soul. "And in the end," Plato writes, "[the desires] seize the fortress [ἀκρόπολιν, *akropolin*] of the young man's mind and find it deserted: it holds no information of value, no sound habits and true ideas—none of the sentinels and guardians which best protect the minds of men who find favour in God's sight."[180]

But it is not just with the image of the citadel that the dependency on Plato can be detected.[181] The theme of tyranny, which is all important in Gregory, is equally so in Plato—as indeed in Greek thought in general, entirely permeated as it is by ideas of political freedom. It is important to note that the freedom spoken of here is not psychological freedom but, in essence, political freedom. The spiritual freedom that Plato and the other Greeks have in mind reflect this. Hence they think in terms of independence (ἀδέσποτος, *adespotos*) from domination; of παρρησία (*parrhēsia*, boldness or freedom of expression), the free speech of the free citizen that we would call freedom of opinion or freedom of the press; and of the absence of slavery (ἀδούλωτον, *adoulōton*). Only—and this is one of the major premises of Greek thought, one of its universally applicable achievements—let this freedom be internalized: if a tyrant is a slave of his passions, he is in reality not a free man; if a slave is free from passions, he possesses true freedom.

The whole of Book 9 of *The Republic* is devoted to a description of such a man: "Oppression and servitude must pervade [the] mind, with the truly good parts of it being oppressed, and an evil, crazed minority doing the oppressing. . . . Well, do you think a mind in this condition is free or enslaved?—Enslaved, I'd say—definitely."[182] A few pages later, the theme of the tyrant is compared to

---
[180] Plato, *Republic* 560b.
[181] The theme had become banal. See Marcus Aurelius, *The Meditations* 8.41.
[182] Plato, *Republic* 577d.

The Structure of the Soul and the Passions

the myth of the many-colored, many-headed beast. These are the same images that we find in Gregory, where the themes of tyranny and bestiality are likewise combined in his descriptions of sinful man. Plato's influence is clear. Of course, as mentioned, it is a theme that is widespread in Greek literature. Festugière cites examples from Herodotus, Sophocles, Thucydides, and Xenophon.[183]

This contrast between man's original freedom and his enslavement to the passions is often found in Gregory.[184] In a passage such as the following one, this can clearly be seen as constituting the character of fallen man:

> For virtue [ἀρετή, *aretē*] must be free from the fear of a taskmaster [ἀδέσποτος, *adespotos*], so as to choose the good by a voluntary act; since it is a principle that all that is good should be subject only to the power that gives life.
>
> Now since man's nature was deceitfully led astray from the discernment of the good, the inclination of his free will has been directed to the opposite and his life subjected to every base thing. . . . Since, then, we are hard pressed by such tyranny and become slaves to death through the assaults of the passions, which attack us like executioners and enemies in war, we rightly pray that the Kingdom of God may come to us. For we cannot escape the wicked dominion of corruption except the lifegiving power take over the government in its place.[185]

The richest of Gregory's texts on this theme is *The Life of Moses*. Its entire opening section is precisely an account of the way the passions—symbolized by the Egyptians—tyrannize the Hebrews: "For this demon who does men harm and corrupts them is intensely concerned that his subjects not look to heaven but that they stoop to earth and make bricks within themselves out of the clay. It is clear to everyone that whatever belongs to material pleasure consists assuredly of earth and water, whether one is concerned with the pleasures of the stomach and the table or with the pleasures of wealth. . . . Those who yearn after the pleasures of clay and keep on filling themselves with them never keep the space which receives them full; for although it is always being filled, it becomes empty again before the next pouring."[186] Moses is presented as a figure of the Word who

---

[183] See A.-J. Festugière, "La divinisation du Chrétien," *La Vie Spirituelle* 59, suppl. (1939): 90–99.
[184] See *Inscr.* 2.14.217 (PG 44:580B; Heine, 191); *Eccl.* 6 (PG 44:708D; Hall, 108).
[185] *Or. dom.* 3 (PG 44:1156C-D; ACW 18:51).
[186] *Vit. Moys.* 2.59–60 (PG 44:341D; Malherbe, 67–68).

frees men from this tyranny by drowning the tyrants in the Red Sea, a symbol of baptism.[187]

We shall encounter this theme of the tyranny of the passions again, on different levels. For it directly concerns the problem of Christian freedom, which we shall study in connection with the restoration of the divine image—tyranny being radical opposed to Christian emancipation. We shall then clarify how we may become freed from δουλεία (*douleia*) in the sense of "bondage" by entering, as Gregory reminded us, into divine *douleia*, which is the service of God and true freedom. We shall also examine how the struggle against the passions continues after Baptism: that is, the problem of temptation, which is all important in the psychological approach of the fourth-century Fathers. Finally, we shall need to pose the question of whether one can ever be totally free in this life from temptations associated with the passions. Can one can ever be immune from concupiscence and achieve dispassion?

---

[187]See *Vit. Moys.* 2.125 (PG 44:364D; Malherbe, 84).

3

Paradise Regained

The concept of asceticism, which is the main concern of the first way, is entirely determined, as we have seen, by how one interprets the notion of ἀπάθεια (*apatheia*, dispassion). Hence it seemed necessary first to clarify the corresponding concept of πάθος (*pathos*, passion). This enabled us to distinguish clearly between two different types of passion: the πάθη κατὰ κακίαν (*pathē kata kakian*, passions resulting from evil) and those that are merely part of what is meant by the "garments of skin," and, consequently, between two types of *apatheia*: the ἀπάθεια κατ' ἀρετήν (*apatheia kat' aretēn*, dispassion through virtue) and that which is a stripping away of mortality. Here we need only consider the former, which is of great importance since it enables us to specify the level of reality we are dealing with—not physical but spiritual. The goal is not, as in certain philosophical ascetic doctrines, simply to free the mind from the bodily passions. If we recall what was said about the true nature of the image, we will understand that *apatheia* for Gregory is about the supernatural life of the soul, as the investigation we shall shortly be making will enable us to verify. The purpose of asceticism, then, is to remove the passions, the capital sins, which prevent the blossoming of divine life in the soul. Beneath a philosophical vocabulary, we meet with realities that are entirely Christian.[1]

Through Baptism, the image of God is restored in the soul. Yet the passions remain present nonetheless as sources of sin, as evil dispositions. "Man is freed from sin through him who assumed the form and became like us who had turned into the form of the serpent. He keeps the bites from causing death, but the beasts themselves are not destroyed. By beasts I mean desires. For although the evil of death which follows sins does not prevail against those who look to the cross, the lust of flesh against spirit has not completely ceased to exist. In

---

[1]This is well seen by F. Hilt: "*Apatheia* sometimes signifies nothing other than the total absence of any disorderly inclination of the soul, of any defective activity of its energies." See his *Des hl. Gregor von Nyssa Lehre vom Menschen systematisch dargestellt* (Cologne, 1890), 89.

fact, the gnawings of desire are frequently active even in the faithful."[2] This is a problem to which Gregory frequently returns. In the *Catechetical Discourse*, he insists on the fact that Baptism requires an inner conversion: "Now if the washing is applied to the body, and the soul has not expunged the stains of the passions ... in these cases the water is water, since the gift of the Holy Spirit is nowhere manifest in what takes place."[3] Here the context is the scandal caused by Christians who continue to lead the same life as before.[4] The same concern is found in *The Life of Moses*: "Take for instance the one who became rich by robbery or injustice, or who acquired property through perjury. ... Does he think that even after his washing he may continue to enjoy those evil things which have become attached to him and yet be freed from the bondage of sin?"[5]

Thus, after Baptism, the new Christian must still fight against the evil inclinations that remain in him, in order that the new life he has received may triumph. This is precisely what is meant by the ascetic life. It is a continuation of Baptism in its double aspect of a stripping away and a resurrection, a restoration of the image of God, a "return to paradise." This is explained by Gregory in a striking passage in which the goal of asceticism—especially its connection with man's nature as described in the preceding chapter—is clarified. There we looked at the various stages of the fall: man originally made in God's image, then the adding of garments of skin, and finally the guilty passions. This constitutes the subject-matter of the theology of man—that is, religious anthropology. Here, however, we shall proceed in the reverse direction and trace the way in which Gregory gets back to the image by a shedding of all that has been added. For with him spiritual theology progresses in the reverse direction to dogmatic theology.

> This concern, then, for the finding of what is lost is the restoration [ἀποκατάστασις, *apokatastasis*] to the original state [εἰς τὸ ἀρχαῖον, *eis to archaion*] of the divine image which is now covered by the filth of the flesh. Let us become what the first being was during the first period of his existence. But what was he? Liberated from the threat of death, looking freely upon the face of God, not yet judging the beautiful by taste and sight, but only enjoying the Lord and using the helpmate given to him for this purpose. ... Through this sequence of events, we, together with our first father, were excluded from paradise, and now, through the same sequence it is possible

[2] *Vit. Moys.* 2.276–77 (PG 44:416A; Malherbe, 124–25).
[3] *Or. cat.* 40.3 (PG 45:101D; PPS 60:154).
[4] *Or. cat.* 40.4 (PG 45:104A–B; PPS 60:154–55).
[5] *Vit. Moys.* 2.128 (PG 44:364D; Malherbe, 84–85).

for us to retrace the steps and return to the original blessedness [μακαριότης, *makariotēs*]. What was the sequence? It was pleasure brought about through deceit which initiated the fall. Shame and fear followed upon the experience of pleasure and they no longer dared to be in the sight of God. They hid themselves in leaves and shadows and, after that, they covered themselves with skins. And in this way, they came as colonists to this place, which is full of disease and toil where marriage was contrived as a consolation for death.

If, then, we are going to return thence and be with Christ, we must begin at the point of deviation. . . . Since the point of departure from the life in paradise was the married state, reason suggests to those returning to Christ that they, first, give this up as a kind of early stage of the journey. Next, they must withdraw from the earthly wretchedness in which man became involved after his fall; in addition, they must put off the coverings of the flesh, the garments made of skin, that is, they must put aside the thought of the flesh, and, after they have rejected the concealments of their shame . . . and be once more under the eyes of the Creator; they must disdain the deceptions of taste and sight . . . partaking only of the pure and unmixed good. . . . And, if one may speak boldly, it is perhaps in this way that one could be snatched away from this world which lies in shame and restored to paradise where Paul saw and heard things unheard and unseen, which "It is not granted for man to utter."[6]

This passage conveniently groups all the ideas we have encountered thus far around the theme of paradise. What one notices first of all is that the return to paradise is understood not in an eschatological but a spiritual sense—we are on the level of ἀπάθεια κατ' ἀρετήν (*apatheia kat' aretēn*, dispassion through virtue)—and everything is interpreted figuratively. Gregory's texts in no way bear out the realistic and cosmic interpretation given by Stolz, who mixes up the spiritual level of inner regeneration with the eschatological level of the bodily resurrection.[7] We may add the above passage to all those others in which we have seen Gregory interpret the paradise of Genesis in a mystical sense.

Next, as mentioned, this passage gathers together the themes we have already encountered. Virginity, for example, is one of the aspects of a restoration of the image. There is also the reference to how the many different senses should make

[6] *Virg.* 12–13 (PG 46:373C–376C; FC 58:45–47).
[7] See Stolz, *Théologie de la mystique*, 27ff. [*Spiritual Perfection*, 17f.]

way for one, unified divine sense. But there are three other features that are of special interest. Before attaining the highest degrees of the spiritual life—a unified mind, a taste of God, ecstasy—that characterize the mystical life proper (and that we will discuss again in due course), we encounter various intermediate stages, which are precisely those that make up the ascetical life. Once one has chosen virginity—and let us not forget that the treatise *On Virginity* (from which the above passage is taken) is addressed to monks—man must divest himself of the garments of skin. Here these denote not mortality as in other passages but, as Gregory puts it, the thoughts of the flesh. They are our πάθη κατὰ κακίαν (*pathē kata kakian*), our evil passions, and the struggle against them will be the first element of an ascetic life that has *apatheia* as its goal. This identification of the passions with thoughts of the flesh is affirmed elsewhere in Gregory. However, the passions that trouble our flesh at the present time will no longer exist once we are united with God. Our life will enter a peaceful state where they will no longer fight against the soul.[8] The second fruit of the ascetic life will be the elimination of the shame (αἰσχύνη, *aischynē*) that took hold of Adam and Eve after the fall; man will again enjoy παρρησία (*parrhēsia*, boldness), filial confidence, and familiarity with God.

It is worth noting that *apatheia* and *parrhēsia* correspond exactly to the two main characteristics of the passions: on the one hand, as a clothing in animal life, and, on the other, as enslavement. With this in mind, we will be able to piece together the underlying structure of Gregory's thought from amid the maze of images he uses. The importance he attaches to *parrhēsia* deserves special mention. Indeed, its implications are more developed by him than anyone else, because of the emphasis placed on freedom throughout his doctrine—that freedom that is the essential feature of our likeness to God. It has been remarked that on this point Gregory is a forerunner.[9] The relevance of this stress placed on *parrhēsia*—the characteristic virtue of adoptive sonship—lies in the way it strongly emphasizes the specifically Christian character of *apatheia*, which is related to it and which would otherwise remain a more ambiguous concept.

---

[8]See *Cant*. 1 (PG 44:765A; Norris, 15).
[9]See Gilson, *Théologie mystique de saint Bernard*, 65–66, n. 1 [*Mystical Theology of Saint Bernard*, 48. In endnote 45 (on p. 225) we read: "The source common to Bernard, Bonaventure, and Descartes would be Gregory of Nyssa."—*Trans*.].

The Struggle against Temptation

Gregory of Nyssa's writings are situated at an interesting crossroads in the history of thought. On the one hand, through their speculative side, they are connected to an entire current of intellectual, contemplative mysticism, of which it is a remarkable example. But, on the other, Gregory is the brother of Basil, the lawgiver of monastic life. He is a contemporary of the emergence of monasticism. An entire facet of his work resembles the teaching of the Desert Fathers—that practical psychology of the spiritual life, of temptation and consolation, which they will develop to a rare degree of perfection.[10] It is even one of the disconcerting characteristics of a work such as *The Life of Moses* that considerations of elementary spiritual psychology constantly mingle with the highest of speculations. In fact, it is a work that is undoubtedly no stranger to a certain philosophical influence, for its practical moralism, its concrete, graphic portrayal of the vices, and its spiritual prescriptions are all related to that cynical trend whose influence can be detected in patristic thought.[11] It is this aspect that we must now examine.

The reality of temptation occupies an important place in Gregory's works, above all in *The Life of Moses*. From the beginning of the treatise, he shows us the demon creating difficulties for the soul that is starting out on the virtuous life: "For this demon who does men harm and corrupts them is intensely concerned that his subjects not look to heaven but that they stoop to earth and make bricks within themselves out of the clay."[12] As we have seen, this image symbolizes material pleasures. But it is above all toward the end of the book that Gregory gives us what amounts to an entire treatise on temptation. One is a little surprised to find it at this point in the text, coming as it does after a description of the highest states of the spiritual life. However, this is because here it is no longer a question of Moses himself, but of the people he has to lead and who are still exposed to demonic attack.

For Gregory, the primary and most important temptation is that of sensual pleasure, which explains why he often returns to it. In *The Life of Moses*, it is symbolized successively by the bricks made of clay, straw, and water; the frogs of the plagues of Egypt; the serpents in the desert; and the daughters of Moab.

---

[10]This double aspect is also found in Origen.
[11]See E. Bréhier, *Les idées philosophiques et religieuses de Philon d'Alexandrie*, 2nd ed., rev. (Paris: A. Picard, 1908; J. Vrin, 1925.), 261f. Sallustius, *Concerning the Gods*, xxvii (from Nock's introduction).
[12]*Vit. Moys.* 2.59 (PG 44:341D; Malherbe, 67).

"Pleasure is truly like evil's bait.... Especially through licentious pleasure is nature, when it is not on guard, drawn aside to evil."[13] But even if one escapes from this temptation, one should not imagine that one is beyond harm: pride then threatens the more advanced souls. Once the earth has ceased producing "the serpents of concupiscence," the disease of pride appears in its turn. "Judging that to keep to their assigned place was too lowly a thing, they thrust themselves into the honor of the priesthood and contentiously thrust out those who had obtained this ministry from God.... Overcoming one's pleasures does not mean being no longer liable to be seized by another kind of passion, for every passion is a fall as long as it is a passion."[14] This shows that for Gregory virginity is not the only virtue.

Gregory analyzes the various ruses the demon employs in order to make the soul stumble: "Since, as has been said, the assault of the Adversary accompanies the ascent of virtue and seeks out corresponding opportunities to subvert toward evil, as the people improve in the godly life, the Adversary launches another attack such as experts in warfare use. These latter, when they estimate that their adversary has superior power in open battle, lay their plans for an ambush."[15] We note the importance of the insight that temptations under various forms will continue to assail one throughout the spiritual life. Here below, man is never sinless. Nevertheless, the soul that has attained *apatheia* and has submitted to the action of grace becomes invulnerable to the passions. Thus Moses is not affected by the temptations to jealousy that wounded Aaron and Miriam: "He blunts the spears; the hardness of his armor deflects them."[16]

Asceticism proper, then, constitutes the struggle against the passions. It is at this stage that Gregory portrays the soul on its journey to God as a wrestler: "If [it] had been strengthened by the illumination of the light and had received such strength and power against [its] enemies, then, as one who has developed as an athlete by strenuous practice under his trainer, [it] would boldly and confidently strip for the contest with its opponents."[17] In other passages, he uses the image of a traveler who is well equipped against the dangers of the road: "So that

---

[13] *Vit. Moys.* 2.297 (PG 44:421A; Malherbe, 131).
[14] *Vit. Moys.* 2.280, 282 (PG 44:416A–417A; Malherbe, 126).
[15] *Vit. Moys.* 2.291 (PG 44:420C; Malherbe, 129).
[16] *Vit. Moys.* 2.262 (PG 44:412A; Malherbe, 122).
[17] *Vit. Moys.* 2.36 (PG 44:336D; Malherbe, 62). See also Gregory, *Inscr.* 2.2.16–17 (PG 44:492B–D; Heine, 127–28); *Vita s. Macrinae* (PG 46:968D); English translation from *The Life of Saint Macrina* in *St Gregory of Nyssa: Ascetical Works*, Virginia Woods Callahan, trans., Fathers of the Church 58 (Washington, DC: The Catholic University of America Press, 1967), 169–70.

the thorns of this life (the thorns would be sins) may not hurt our naked and unprotected feet, let us cover them with shoes. The shoes are the self-controlled and austere life which breaks and crushes the points of the thorns and prevents sin from slipping inside unnoticed."[18]

Gregory often describes the ascetic life as rough and austere, using words such as ἐγκρατής (*enkratēs*, self-control), αὐστηρός (*austēros*, austere, harsh, or bitter]),[19] κατεσκληκώς (*katesklēkōs*, parched, lean, or dry),[20] and κατεστυμμένος (*katestymmenos*, astringent, tough and dried in appearance).[21] The sweetness of the spiritual life is wrapped in a rough exterior. Gregory likes to present this concept by using the image of the pomegranate. It is one that we often find in his work.[22] Let us quote just one of these passages. It is from *The Life of Moses*, and occasioned by a description of the pomegranates that decorate the vestment of the high priest: "So let life imitate the nature of the pomegranate's fruit. Because it is covered with a hard and sour rind, its outside is inedible, but the inside is a pleasant sight with its many neatly ordered seeds and it becomes even sweeter when it is tasted. The philosophical life, although outwardly austere and unpleasant, is yet full of good hopes when it ripens. For when our Gardener opens the pomegranate of life at the proper time and manifests the hidden beauty, then those who partake of their own fruit will enjoy the sweetness."[23]

It is important to take note of this austere character of Gregory's spirituality, which we also find in Origen. He insists on the fact that the moral aspect, the practice of solid virtues, persists throughout the spiritual life and is its touchstone. This is a very realistic and demanding spirituality. Nonetheless, it is not asceticism. Mortification is first of all a partaking in the baptismal mystery of Christ's passion. "There is one antidote for these evil passions: the purification of our souls which takes place through the mystery of godliness. The chief act of faith in the 'mystery' is to look to him who suffered the passion for us. The cross is the passion, so that whoever looks at it . . . is not harmed by the poison of desire. To look at the cross is to render one's whole life dead and crucified to the world, unmoved by evil. Truly it is as the prophet says: 'They nail their own

---

[18] *Vit. Moys.* 2.107 (PG 44:357A; Malherbe, 79).
[19] *Cant.* 9 (PG 44:969B; Norris, 297).
[20] *Vit. Moys.* 2.193 (PG 44:389B; Malherbe, 104).
[21] *Vit. Moys.* 2.285 (PG 44:417C; Malherbe, 127).
[22] *Vit. Moys.* 2.193, 285, 316 (PG 44:389B, 417C, 427D; Malherbe, 104, 127, 136); *Cant.* 7, 9 (PG 44:929B, 969C; Norris, 241, 297).
[23] *Vit. Moys.* 2.193 (PG 44:389B; Malherbe, 104).

flesh with the fear of God' (cf. Ps 119.120). The nail would be the self-control that holds the flesh."[24]

How should the soul behave in this fight? Gregory gives us but few suggestions, yet they are full of wisdom. The most important—and one that he mentions frequently—is the need to stop the temptation from the very first impulse.[25] This is the meaning he attaches to symbols such as the following: the door marked with the blood of the Lamb, or the firstborn of the Egyptians that are put to death. "When through virtue one comes to grips with any evil, he must completely destroy the first beginnings of evil. For when he slays the beginning, he destroys at the same time what follows after it. The Lord teaches the same thing in the Gospel, all but explicitly calling on us to kill the firstborn of the Egyptian evils when he commands us to abolish lust and anger and to have no more fear of the stain of adultery or the guilt of murder. . . . Take for an example a snake: When one crushes his head he kills the rest of the body at the same time."[26]

It is especially significant that all such temptations are always attributed by Gregory to the Evil Angel. In *The Life of Moses* the demon occupies an important place, whether as the cause of original sin[27] or as the one who inspires all actual sins. Examples of this are countless. On the very first page of Book Two, it is symbolized by Pharaoh, who is portrayed as seeking to destroy the good movements of the soul. Throughout the text we encounter phrases such as the following: "When Moses had spoken these excellent words . . . the enemy was provoked";[28] "The one who schemes against our souls with many different deceits . . . knows how to introduce the devices of trickery against the divine law;"[29] "When the inventor of evil failed . . . he still did not stop completely conniving against those he was assaulting."[30] This is an important point, for it establishes a link between Gregory's teaching and that of Origen[31] and the

---

[24] *Vit. Moys.* 2.274 (PG 44:413D; Malherbe, 124).
[25] The idea is found in the Stoics. See Marcus Aurelius, *The Meditations* 10.7.
[26] *Vit. Moys.* 2.92–94 (PG 44:353A; Malherbe, 76). See also *Vit. Moys.* 2.304 (PG 44:424D; Malherbe, 132). [In two other works Gregory uses the image of crushing the serpent's head (Gen 3.15) in a different way, noting that while the snake dies at once when its head is crushed, the body continues to flail for a time. This illustrates that while Christ's victory over sin, death, and the devil is decisive and once-for-all, fallen realities endure until Christ's return. See *Or. cat.* 30.1 (GNO III/4:74; PPS 60:126–27); *Diem. nat.* (GNO X/2:243–44).—*Ed.*]
[27] *Vit. Moys.* 2.213 (PG 44:396D; Malherbe, 109–110).
[28] *Vit. Moys.* 2.56 (PG 44:341C; Malherbe, 67).
[29] *Vit. Moys.* 2.63 (PG 44:344B; Malherbe, 68).
[30] *Vit. Moys.* 2.297 (PG 44:421D; Malherbe, 131).
[31] See S. Bettencourt, *Doctrina ascetica Origenis* (Vatican City: Libreria Vaticana, 1945) 62ff.

Desert Fathers,[32] in which the demon also plays an important role. Consequently, temptation is seen as spiritual warfare "against the rulers of this world of darkness" (Eph 6.12), with the consequence that human life takes on a dramatic aspect—"man finds himself between these two [a good and a maleficent angel] who have contrary purposes for him."[33] This puts things into an entirely Christian perspective.

But in this struggle against the Adversary, man is not entirely alone. He has various forms of help at his disposal. On the simply human level, there is the significant place Gregory assigns to secular culture as a tool of education: "The ark, constructed out of various boards, would be education in the various disciplines, which holds what it carries above the waves of life."[34] The program of secular studies of his own day is symbolized by the education Moses receives in the household of the Pharaoh's daughter,[35] then through his marriage to the Midianite,[36] and especially through the Egyptian "spoils"—that is, the wealth of pagan learning—carried away by the Hebrews.[37] Gregory's position on this point is that of the other Church Fathers of his time—Basil,[38] say, or Augustine.[39] He acknowledges the usefulness of secular studies, but cautiously, insisting that they should be completely subordinated to one's religious development. For example, during the young Moses' stay with the Egyptian princess, he continued to be nursed by his natural mother's milk. Gregory interprets this as meaning that, even if we are involved with profane teachings during our education, "we should not separate ourselves from the nourishment of the Church's milk, which would be her laws and customs."[40]

---

[32] See J. Bremond, *Les Pères du désert*, vol. 1 (Paris: J. Gabalda, 1927), xxviii.
[33] *Vit. Moys.* 2.46 (PG 44:340A; Malherbe, 64).
[34] *Vit. Moys.* 2.7 (PG 44:329A; Malherbe, 56).
[35] See *Vit. Moys.* 2.10 (PG 44:329B; Malherbe, 57).
[36] See *Vit. Moys.* 2.37 (PG 44:336D; Malherbe, 62–63).
[37] See *Vit. Moys.* 2.115–16 (PG 44:360B; Malherbe, 81).
[38] See S. Giet, *Les idées et l'action sociales de saint Basile* (Paris: J. Gabalda, 1941), 216–32. [Basil and Gregory were following an established tradition: *The Philokalia*, an anthology of Origen's texts compiled by Basil and Gregory Nazianzen, includes Origen's letter to Gregory the Wonderworker, which uses the image of spoiling Egypt in the context of the Christian attitude toward secular learning and culture (FC 98:190–92; for questions regarding Origen as author, see pp. 36–37). Some scholars argue that Basil and Nazianzen owned and used *The Philokalia*, but did not compile it. See Susanna Elm, *Sons of Hellenism, Fathers of the Church: Emperor Julian, Gregory of Nazianzus, and the Vision of Rome* (Berkeley and Los Angeles: University of California Press, 2012), 22 n.23—*Ed.*]
[39] See H.-I. Marrou, *Saint Augustin et la fin de la culture antique*, vol. 1 (Paris: Boccard, 1938), 415ff.
[40] *Vit. Moys.* 2.12 (PG 44:329C; Malherbe, 57). [For "laws and customs," Daniélou's text reads "sacraments."—*Trans.*]

More crucially, it is indeed the sacraments that will be a source of strength in the struggle against temptations. In *The Life of Moses,* Gregory does speak of the Eucharist. But he views it above all as a source of joy, and thus related to the mystical life proper, rather than as a source of strength for those who have not yet reached this level. The sacrament that specifically corresponds to the ascetic life—related to Baptism as it is—is repentance, which is indeed nothing other than Baptism's extension. In *The Life of Moses,* it is symbolized by the water that gushes from the Rock:

> When it is perceived spiritually, this account teaches us what the mystery of repentance [τὸ μυστήριον τῆς μετανοίας, *to mystērion tēs metanoias*] is. Those who turn to the stomach, the flesh, and the Egyptian pleasures, after having once tasted the rock, are sentenced to be excluded from partaking in good things. But they can by repentance again find the rock which they abandoned and again open the spring of water for themselves and again take their fill. The rock gives forth water to Moses who believed that Joshua's spying is truer than his opponents, Moses who looked to the bunch of grapes which for our sake was suspended and shed blood, and Moses who by the wood prepared water to gush from the rock again for them.[41]

When we are confronted with the demon who sets traps for man, a third source of assistance comes from the angel who stands by the soul, ready to help. This is symbolized in *The Life of Moses* by Aaron, whom God sends ahead of his brother. Indeed, we already find in Gregory an entire doctrine of the guardian angel: "There is a doctrine (which derives its trustworthiness from the tradition of the fathers) which says that after our nature fell into sin God did not disregard our fall and withhold his providence. No . . . he appointed an angel with an incorporeal nature to help in the life of each person."[42]

What is more striking is that Gregory believes that there is also "a guardian demon," delegated by Satan: "Man finds himself between these two who have contrary purposes."[43] This doctrine of the guardian demon comes from Origen.[44] But what is even more important for our topic is that Gregory also has an

---

[41] *Vit. Moys.* 2.269–70 (PG 44:413B; Malherbe, 123–24).
[42] *Vit. Moys.* 2.45 (PG 44:337D; Malherbe, 64).
[43] *Vit. Moys.* 2.46 (PG 44:340A; Malherbe, 64).
[44] See Origen, *On First Principles* 3.2.4. An even earlier reference (to an "angel of wickedness") can be found in *The Shepherd of Hermas,* Mandate 6.2.4. It is undoubtedly related to the ancient concept of the good and evil genius. See G. Soury, *La démonologie de Plutarque* (Paris: Belles-Lettres, 1942), 130ff.

entire doctrine on the activity of the angels. It has two characteristic features. First, that of suggesting good thoughts to those who are advancing toward virtue.[45] Second, the fact that this activity ceases at a certain level of the spiritual life, when God begins to deal with the soul directly.[46] Thus, the role of the angels, in conformity with their nature, is above all one of preparation.

Such are the main features of Gregory's asceticism. His doctrine is not original. As already mentioned, it is related to that of Origen and to monastic teaching. We may nonetheless note that there is nothing purely voluntaristic about it. On the contrary, it seems firmly linked to the mystery of spiritual regeneration. The means used are not only penitence and mortification, but the sacraments. Mortification itself is a conforming of oneself to the mystery of the death of Christ. In other words, it is the continued bringing about of the death of the old man, destroyed mystically in Baptism. And, according to Gregory's synergistic approach, this death is the result both of the action of Christ through grace and the contribution of man's will. Its goal is to enable the growth in the soul of the life of grace. It is this life of grace that is the culmination of the first way and that Gregory describes by means of the terms *apatheia* and *parrhēsia*.

The Life of Grace or *Apatheia*

All those writers who have been influenced in one way or another by Platonism are agreed in making of *apatheia* (dispassion) the goal of virtue and in seeing in purification the means of arriving at it. Ἀρετή (*aretē*, virtue), *apatheia*, and καθαρότης (*katharotēs*, purity)—these three concepts are intimately linked in Plotinus, for example, as much as in Gregory of Nyssa. It is even one of the points where the similarity of the two authors is most obvious. Festugière views *apatheia* as the characteristic feature of this type of spirituality that developed alongside the Gospel, whose representatives he names as Clement, Origen, Gregory of Nyssa, Evagrius, and Dionysius the Pseudo-Areopagite.[47] However, it is a claim that calls for a fair amount of discrimination, for only a careful study of each of these authors would enable us to define what the word *apatheia* means to him. It is one of those words that one finds everywhere at a given period and, because of this, one that is open to a countless number of subtle differences in meaning.[48]

---

[45]See *Vit. Moys.* 2.46 (PG 44:340A; Malherbe, 64).
[46]See *Vit. Moys.* 2.119 (PG 44:361A; Malherbe, 82).
[47]See A.-J. Festugière, *L'enfant d'Agrigente*, 146.
[48]A first sketch for a comprehensive study of the use of the term *apatheia* in the Fathers can be found

To focus the debate, we need to see clearly the meaning the word has for philosophers, on the one hand, and for Christians, on the other. As Bréhier explains, "The Stoics wanted to suppress the passions altogether. Philo too saw in *apatheia* the ideal of Wisdom. Moses, his symbol of the perfect sage, does not stop at μετριοπάθεια (*metriopatheia*, restraint over the passions), but removes all violent emotions from his heart; likewise he is undefiled by desire and pleasure."[49] With Gregory, the perspective is altogether different. He writes as follows: "For in the human constitution there is a double pleasure, one that is in the soul and is activated by impassibility [ἀπάθεια, *apatheia*] and another that is occasioned in the body by passion."[50] Or again, in a paradoxical turn of phrase: "This passion [i.e., *erōs*], when directed to things incorporeal, is blameless and impassible [ἀπαθής, *apathēs*]."[51] From a Stoic standpoint, the notion of pleasure linked to *apatheia* would be simply unintelligible.

The writings of Plotinus confirm this impression: "In what sense can we call the virtues purifications, and how does purification issue in Likeness? As the soul is evil by being interfused with the body ... so it would be good, it would be possessed of virtue, if it threw off the body's moods ... [and] become thus intellective and immune to passion [ἀπαθής, *apathēs*]."[52] "Disengagement means simply that the soul withdraws to its own place. It will hold itself above all passions and affections."[53] These citations, to which one could add many others, clearly show what *apatheia* means for Plotinus: the removing of all contact between mind and body. This resembles what we have described as ἡσυχία (*hēsychia*, [inner] stillness). For Gregory, however, this constitutes only one aspect of true *apatheia*—and quite a negative one at that. It is what he calls ἀταραξία (*ataraxia*, calmness).[54] For him, cessation of turmoil and restlessness makes sense only if it allows the life of grace to develop.

It is not necessary to examine here what *apatheia* means for Christian authors other than Gregory. This too would require a careful study of each of them. However, we readily grant that Festugière is correct in suggesting that there is a certain Christian tradition that is not entirely free from being influenced by the

in the article "Apatheia" by G. Bardy in the *Dictionnaire de Spiritualité*. Reading this, one will readily appreciate the diversity of meanings the word has in Christian contexts.

[49]E. Bréhier, *Les idées philosophiques*, 254.
[50]*Cant.* 10 (PG 44:993C; Norris, 329).
[51]*Cant.* 1 (PG 44:772A; Norris, 25).
[52]Plotinus, *Enneads* 1.2.3.
[53]Ibid., 1.2.5.
[54]*Cant.* 4 (PG 44:833A; Norris, 115).

Neoplatonic understanding of the word. This would be partly true, for example, of Clement of Alexandria, who admits that the perfect man is entirely ἀπαθής (*apathēs*, impassible) already in this life. "What one should note carefully," writes de Faye, "is that, according to Clement, it is not merely a question of uprooting the guilty passions, but of suppressing all desires, whatever they might be. *Apatheia* results from the radical uprooting of the entire affective, sentimental, and passionate part of human nature."[55] And it is true that he identifies this with *ataraxia*.[56] This trend is also found in Evagrius, for whom *apatheia* is above all a prerequisite of gnosis and has a pronounced intellectual aspect.

The trend represented by Gregory of Nyssa is altogether different. It is related to the way the word is used by Ignatius of Antioch,[57] by Justin,[58] and by Athenagoras. It is used to describe the divine nature, whose characteristic property is "freedom from every passion."[59] "The Divine Nature is altogether impassible [ἀπαθής, *apathēs*]."[60] Like blessedness, this quality belongs to God πρώτως καὶ κυρίως (*prōtōs kai kyriōs*, primarily and properly). Furthermore, the two are linked to one another, as Gregory points out: "It is not doubted that blessedness exists in impassibility."[61] *Apatheia* is also related to the other divine attributes—incorruptibility in particular.[62] Hence it can be seen that what the word denotes above all is divine life, especially in those ways that contrast it with animal life. It also implies a certain indetermination in distinguishing between the *nous* and the *pneuma*, which is typical of Gregory's thought. But since the *nous* can only realize its full potential by means of the *pneuma*, it is clear that *apatheia* in the strong sense denotes the supernatural life of the soul as contrasted with the evil passions that typify its corporeal life. This is simply the Pauline opposition between σάρξ (*sarx*, flesh) and πνεῦμα (*pneuma*, spirit), transposed to a Platonic vocabulary.

So, *apatheia* is the word used by Gregory to denote the supernatural life, "habitual" grace—that is, participation of the soul in the divine life. It has a highly positive character. On the other hand, it coincides with the disappearance of the evil passions, which is its negative counterpart, the mortification that

---

[55] E. de Faye, *Clément d'Alexandrie* (Paris: E. Leroux, 1898), 295.
[56] See Clement of Alexandria, *Miscellanies* 4.7 (ANF 2:419).
[57] See Ignatius of Antioch, *Letter to the Ephesians* 7.2 (PPS 49:28–31).
[58] See Justin Martyr, *Dialogue with Trypho* 45.4 (ANF 1:217).
[59] Gregory, *Prof.* (PG 46:241D; FC 58:84).
[60] *Or. dom.* 1 (PG 44:1128D; ACW 18:31).
[61] *Or. cat.* 35.14 (PG 45:92B; PPS 60:143).
[62] See *Eccl.* 3 (PG 44:657B; Hall, 65).

goes hand in hand with the resurrection. Thus it is only secondarily that it is characterized by *ataraxia*, by calmness. This is indeed one of its characteristics, but not the most important one, as it is in Evagrius or the spiritual hesychasts. It has as synonym καθαρότης, (*katharotēs*, purity)—which is likewise essentially a "flowing" (ἀπόρροια, *aporroia*) of the divine life into the soul—and blossoms forth in the supernatural virtues that are, as it were, the tendrils, leaves, and flowers of the mystical vine of which it constitutes the root.

Let us look at *apatheia* in a little more detail. Its meaning may be clarified by certain clues. First, it is noticeable that it is always ranked among the good things of the paradisal state, the angelic life. Now we know that for Gregory these are two symbolic ways of denoting the state of the soul when it has become again "the image of God." Thus in the paradisal symbol of the vine, *apatheia* is named alongside likeness to God and immortality.[63] *Apatheia* is also described as the drink (πότον, *poton*) on which man lived in paradise.

The same observation holds true for comparisons with the angels. Here, however, the question is more delicate, for their world can signify two orders of reality. When one thinks of their nature, what then characterizes them is incorporeality. In that respect, *apatheia* would be the absence of all that accompanies the corporeal life. But the angels may also be viewed as representing the sphere of glory, the world on high as contrasted with the world below. As we shall discuss later, this is the usual way in which Gregory sees things. Consequently, comparisons with the angels ordinarily betoken entry into the life of grace that is theirs. In fact, we know that for Gregory humanity originally formed part of the angelic sphere, from which it fell. What separates it from the angels is its fall, not its nature. Hence it is a spiritual restoration, not a physical change, that will reinstate it.

There are a number of passages in which Gregory's thinking on this point is made clear. He refers, for example, to a soul that has "by impassibility become equal to the angels (ἰσάγγελος, *isangelos*)" [Lk 20.36][64] or that is "imitating the angelic purity by its impassibility."[65] This is also how he interprets the angels' choice of the term "sister," to describe the Bride in the Song of Songs: "For the mark of impassibility, which illuminates her just as it does the angels, brings the

---

[63] Again, it must be stated that these terms, which admittedly are also found in Plotinus, cannot be defined accurately except by taking into account the context in which they are used, which alone allows one to appreciate their true significance.

[64] *Cant.* 1 (PG 44:777A; Norris, 33).

[65] *Cant.* 4 (PG 44:857A; Norris, 147).

soul that has achieved impassibility in the flesh into a relationship of kinship [συγγένεια, *syngeneia*] and sisterhood with incorporeal beings."⁶⁶ We should note in passing that the term *syngeneia*—like φύσις (*physis*, nature)—points to a concrete reality. Thus, on the level of "nature," one may speak of a commonality between God and man or between human beings and angels, whereas one would not be able to speak of a commonality of "essence" (οὐσία, *ousia*).

Other clues enabling us to clarify the meaning of *apatheia* are the biblical sayings that are sometimes attired in Platonic garb. These equivalences are extremely valuable in that they provide the key to understanding expressions whose real content may be hidden under a seemingly philosophical vocabulary. Let us mention just one example. In his *Homilies on Ecclesiastes,* Gregory writes as follows: "The kingdom of God is not food and drink, but justice and freedom from passion [ἀπάθεια, *apatheia*] and blessedness [μακαριότης, *makariotēs*]."⁶⁷ What we have here is simply a variation on a verse from St Paul: "The kingdom of God is not eating and drinking, but righteousness and peace [εἰρήνη, *eirēnē*] and joy [χαρά, *chara*] in the Holy Spirit" (Rom 14.17). Here we are able to glimpse Gregory's method in action: for in the one word ἀπάθεια the Pauline εἰρήνη, the biblical χαρά, and the Greek μακαριότης are combined. Now it is quite clear that the Pauline εἰρήνη is not the simple νηνεμίη (*nēnemiē*), the "tranquility" of the sage, but rather the inner fulfilment of the saint. Hence this is also what is meant by *apatheia* in Gregory's use of the term. Yet what allows us to understand best the true nature of the concept is the frequently repeated assertion that *apatheia* is nothing other than a partaking of the divine life, a flowing of the divine *apatheia* into the creature, which is the very definition of grace. This idea is expressed in numerous passages, but perhaps nowhere more strikingly than in the following passage from *On Perfection*:

> What is free from every passionate inclination [καθαρεῦον πάσης ἐμπαθοῦς διαθέσεως, *kathareuon pasēs empathous diatheseōs*] looks to the source of dispassion [τὸν ἀρχηγόν τῆς ἀπαθείας, *ton archēgon tēs apatheias*], who is Christ. Drawing from Him as from a pure and uncorrupted stream, a person will show in his thoughts such a resemblance to his Prototype as exists between the water in the running water or stream and the water taken away from there in a jar. For the purity in Christ and the purity seen in the person

---

⁶⁶*Cant.* 8 (PG 44:948A; Norris, 267).
⁶⁷*Eccl.* 5 (PG 44:696B; Hall, 98).

who has a share in Him are the same, the One being the stream and the other drawn from it.[68]

Things could not be clearer. *Apatheia* is the divine life as it exists first in Christ, and then as he communicates it to the soul. This is diametrically opposed to mere moralism and to any purely natural asceticism. This understanding of *apatheia* as an emanation or "flowing forth" (ἀπόρροια, *apporoia*) of the divine life is what makes the soul an image of God and that thereby allows it to know God. We are reminded of what we have already said in connection with the image and what is admirably expressed by the following passage from the *Homilies on the Song of Songs*: "For the rays of that true and divine Virtue shine upon the purified life through the inward peace that flows from them [δι' ἀπορεούσης αὐτῶν ἀπαθείας, *di'aporeousēs autōn apatheias*], and they make the Invisible visible for us and the Incomprehensible comprehensible, because they portray the Sun in the mirror [κάτοπτρον, *katoptron*] that we are."[69] Here the themes of participation and exemplarism are linked together. *Apatheia*—a partaking of the very life of God—is what allows us to know God, whose essence remains nonetheless inaccessible. We will again encounter this form of knowledge that is gained from looking into the mirror of the purified soul when we come to examine the mystical life proper.

From man's perspective, then, *apatheia* is seen to be an imitation of God—and thus something that he strives for. It is quite clear that this effort consists essentially in developing the inner man—that is, developing the supernatural life that is created within us by grace. In no sense is it a negative asceticism. Throughout, then, Gregory presents *apatheia* as an imitation of the divine nature—in the strong sense of Greek exemplarism, as a real participation in this nature: "Just as the first fruit of the of the dough was assimilated through purity and innocence [ἀπάθεια, *apatheia*] to the true Father and God, so we, also, as dough in similar ways, will cleave to the Father of incorruptibility by imitating, as far as we can, the innocence and stability of the Meditator."[70] Once again, though now in the context of *apatheia*, we meet with the concept of the εἰκὼν εἰκόνος (*eikōn eikonos*, the image of the image): the Word become flesh realizing first in himself the state of deification, and then becoming the model toward which we must

---

[68]*Perf.* (PG 46:284D; ; FC 58:121).
[69]*Cant.* 3 (PG 44:824C; Norris, 101).
[70]*Perf.* (PG 46:280B; FC 58:117).

strive. Thus, there can be no question for Gregory of an *apatheia* whose content would be other than that of a specifically Christian holiness.[71]

As we have suggested, very similar to the concept of *apatheia* is that of purity (καθαρότης, *katharotēs*). It too is prone to being misinterpreted (for example, in a merely physical sense); it too forms part of pagan wisdom and asceticism and is even more closely related to Platonic thinking. Take, for instance, the well-known pages in *Phaedo* where Plato explains how, since the Divine is purity and since only like is able to partake of like, purification is the necessary condition for any communion with God. The same idea is also found in Plotinus.[72] Now for Gregory, as we have seen, purity (like *apatheia*) is in the first place a characteristic of the divine life. It is important to bear this in mind, lest we overlook the fact that for him purification is to be understood positively, as primarily the communication of divine grace, rather than negatively, as simply the result of eliminating earthly impurities. When describing God, Gregory frequently uses the concept of purity alongside *apatheia* and the absence of all evil—which only serves to emphasize the moral and religious character of the type of purity he has in mind. Thus we read in the *Homilies on the Beatitudes* that "the Godhead is purity, freedom from passion, and separation from all evil."[73] Again, in the *Sermons on the Lord's Prayer*: "The Divine Nature . . . is purity."[74] He often uses the phrase "God's purity," or "the purity of God," as in the following: "[The souls] have been joined together with God's purity by their desire for incorruption [τῷ πόθῳ τῆς ἀφθαρσίας, *tō pothō tēs aphtharsias*]."[75]

In this last example there is a clear link between purity and incorruptibility. They are often grouped together (along with *apatheia*) in the lists Gregory draws up of the attributes of the Godhead or of the image of God. For example, in the allegory of the vineyard, purity is the fruit: "That ripe and gleaming cluster whose appearance is a shining like the sun's and that pleases the soul's senses by its chaste simplicity."[76] Here we note the connection between the doctrine of the spiritual senses and purity, rather than *apatheia*. Should one wish to establish a

---

[71] See also Gregory, *Op. hom.* 5.1 (PG 44:137B; NPNF² 5:391): "Purity, freedom from passion, blessedness, alienation from all evil, and all those attributes of the like kind which help to form in men the likeness of God: with such hues as these did the Maker of His own image [τῆς ἰδίας εἰκόνος, *tēs idias eikonos*] mark our nature."

[72] See Plotinus, *Enneads* 1.6.6; 4.7.9; 6.9.3.

[73] *Beat.* 6 (PG 44:1272C; ACW 18:149).

[74] *Or. dom.* 2 (PG 44:1140C; ACW 18:38).

[75] *Cant.* 15 (PG 44:1122D; Norris, 491). See also *Eccl.* 6 (PG 44:708A; Hall, 107).

[76] *Cant.* 2 (PG 44:800C; Norris, 67).

relationship between all three of these concepts—incorruptibility, *apatheia*, and purity—one would have to say along with Gregory that it is through purity and dispassion (διὰ καθαρότητος καὶ ἀπαθείας, *dia katharotētos kai apatheias*) that one arrives at incorruptibility (ἀφθαρσία, *aphtharsia*). The latter term indicates a more ontological aspect of God's holiness.

Like *apatheia*, purity belongs to man qua image. It is evident from the important passage already quoted that it is a matter of participation in the divine nature, an aspect of deifying grace, not the mere absence of moral or physical stain, "For the purity in Christ and the purity seen in the person who has a share in Him are the same" (Μία τῇ φύσει ἡ καθαρότης, ἥ ἐν Χριστῷ καὶ ἡ ἐν τῷ μετέχοντι θεορουμένη, ἀλλ' ὁ μὲν πηγάζει, ὁ δὲ ἀρύεται; *Mia tē physei hē katharotēs, hē en Christō kai hē en tō metechonti theoroumenē, all' ho men pēgazei, ho de aruetai*).[77] Purity is also included as part of the description of the image in *On the Making of Man*,[78] constituting, along with *apatheia* and blessedness (μακαριότης, *makariotēs*), man's likeness to God (ὁμοίωσις πρὸς θεῖον, *homoiōsis pros theion*). In other texts, Gregory comments that it is a pure way of life (καθαρὰ πολιτεία, *kathara politeia*) that actualizes the image of God in the soul.

At this point one could repeat many of the observations that were made earlier in connection with *apatheia*. Let us simply mention the importance given to purity in the Beatitudes as a hallmark of the image of God: "Blessed are the pure in heart, for they shall see God." In his admirable homily on this verse, Gregory develops his favorite idea that the only knowledge we can have of God is the one we have by knowing the image of God that we ourselves are. And as we have seen, purity forms part of this image: "It is purity, sanctity, simplicity [ἁπλότης, *haplotēs*], and other such luminous reflections of the Divine Nature in which God is contemplated."[79] In a passage from the *Homilies on the Song of Songs*, Gregory expresses the same idea in other words, stating that purity combined with incorruptibility and holiness leads to a participation of the soul in the life of Christ, through which it comes to know Christ.[80]

Apatheia and purity denote the divine life of the soul, then, though in a general way—as sanctifying, deifying grace. It is a grace that blossoms in the ensemble of the virtues. But the word "virtue" presents problems similar to the ones encountered when discussing the related notions of *apatheia* and purity.

[77] *Perf.* (PG 46:284D; FC 58:121).
[78] *Op. hom.* 5.1 (PG 44:137B; NPNF² 5:391).
[79] *Beat.* 6 (PG 44:1272C; ACW 18:150).
[80] See *Cant.* 15 (PG 44:1096B; Norris, 469).

To our mind, it evokes the idea of moral perfection rather than a spiritual quality. But, in Hellenistic religious and philosophical language the meaning was richer, and the term should perhaps be translated as "value," or, in religious contexts, as "holiness." (On this topic, the pertinent comments made by Festugière are worth reading.)[81] We should note in particular that virtue (ἀρετή, *aretē*) makes man like God. As Plato wrote, in a famous passage from *Theaetetus* that is often referred to by Gregory of Nyssa: "[Evils] haunt our mortal nature, and this region here. That is why one ought to try to escape from here to there as quickly as one can. Now the way to escape is to become as nearly as possible like a god; and to become like a god is to become just and religious, with intelligence."[82] Likewise, Gregory writes that "man . . . through virtue, is likened to [ὁμοιούμενος, *homoioumenos*] God himself."[83]

More specifically still, Plotinus reflects on the manner in which virtue belongs preeminently to God: "For the Ideal-Form of justice [αὐτοδικαιοσύνη, *autodikaiosynē*] or of any other virtue is not itself a virtue, but, so to speak, an exemplar, the source of what in the soul becomes virtue: for virtue is dependent, seated in something not itself; the Ideal-Form is self-standing, independent."[84] It is difficult not to see the influence of this passage on the *Homilies on the Song of Songs*, where Gregory writes: "The spices we take to be virtues, such as wisdom, temperance, justice, courage, prudence, and the like, and each different individual assumes a different scent as he is dabbed with them in accord with his own power and choice. . . . Nevertheless, none of these can be compared with that absolute virtue of which the prophet Habbakuk asserts that it encloses the heavens when he says, 'His virtue veiled the heavens' (3.3). This is Wisdom herself [αὐτοσοφία, *autosophia*], and Justice itself [αὐτοδικαιοσύνη, *autodiakosynē*] and Truth herself . . . [αὐτοαλήθεια, *autoalētheia*]."[85]

These comparisons show that it was predictable that Gregory would give to "virtue" the connotation of participation in the divine life. He thinks of it, like *apatheia* and purity, as an "emanation" or "flowing forth" of the divine life: "For the rays of that true and divine Virtue shine upon the purified life through the inward peace [ἀπάθεια, *apatheia*] that flows from them. . . . Where this idea is concerned, it is one and the same thing to speak of rays of the sun or of

---

[81] See A.-J. Festugière, *La sainteté* (Paris: Presses Universitaires de France, 1942), 32f.
[82] Plato, *Theaetetus* 176b.
[83] *Or. dom.* 5 (PG 44:1177B; ACW 18:71).
[84] Plotinus, *Enneads* 1.2.6.
[85] *Cant.* 1 (PG 44:781B; Norris, 39).

emanations of virtue or of sweet aromatic scents."[86] (This text makes it quite clear that for Gregory "virtue" in the soul is a communication God makes of his own life.) The same idea can be found elsewhere, as in the following examples: "Virtues are the rays of the 'Sun of Justice' (Mal 4.2), streaming forth for our illumination";[87] "Every name and thought of virtue leads back to the Lord of virtues."[88]

It is because "virtue" is participation in the very life of God that it enables us to have knowledge of this life. This is a doctrine that we have encountered already in connection with purity. Later, we shall see that it forms the foundation of mystical knowledge, which is the awareness of grace in us. It is important, therefore, before proceeding further, to clarify the meaning of these words. This doctrine of the knowledge of God in the mirror of the virtues is affirmed by Gregory in several striking passages such as the following:

> That Reality, whatever it is in its essence [κατ'οὐσίαν, *kat' ousian*], which transcends the entire structure and order of Being, is unapproachable [ἀπρόσιτον, *aprositon*], impalpable [ἀναφές, *anaphes*], and incomprehensible [ἄληπτον, *alēpton*] but that, for us, the sweetness that is blended within us by the purity of the virtues takes its place because by its own purity it images that which is by nature the Undefiled—and by its goodness, the Good; and by its incorruptibility, the Incorruptible; and by its unchangeability, the Unchangeable; and by all the things within us that are rightly done in accordance with virtue, the true Virtue, concerning which the prophet Habbakuk says that it embraces all the heavens (3.3).[89]

This brings us to the threshold of mystical theology. However, I shall not enlarge here upon this doctrine of the incomprehensibility of the essence or of the knowledge gained in the mirror of the virtues, since all this will be treated in specific chapters in due course. I simply note that none of this makes sense, if virtue is not the life of God in us. Gregory continues: "If a person, having gathered every sweet-smelling flower or scent from the various blooms of virtue and having rendered his whole life a perfume by the fragrance of his daily doings, should become perfect in all respects, he does not have it in him to look intently [ἀτενῶς ἰδεῖν, *atenōs idein*] upon the divine Word itself any more than upon the

---

[86]*Cant.* 3 (PG 44:824C; Norris, 101).
[87]*Perf.* (PG 46:261C; FC 58:103).
[88]*Eccl.* 8 (PG 44:749B; Hall, 140).
[89]*Cant.* 3 (PG 44:824A; Norris, 99–101).

Paradise Regained

disc of the sun. Nevertheless, he sees the sun within himself as in a mirror [ἐν κατόπτρῳ, *en katoptrō*]."[90]

In Gregory's homilies on the psalms, we find the same doctrine and similar imagery. The passage below is occasioned by the following verse: *In umbram alarum tuarum sperabo*: "In the shadow of thy wings will I hope" (Ps 56.1).

> Now one will not err if he thinks that the virtues are the shadow of the divine wings. For, on the one hand, the divine itself, whatever it is in nature, remains unattainable and incomprehensible to human nature, flying ineffably somewhere above the thought of humanity. But, on the other hand, an impress [χαρακτήρ, *character*] of the ineffable nature through the shadow-outline of the virtues occurs in those who look to it, that is, all wisdom and prudence and knowledge and every approach of thought which conveys divine apprehension are not the divine wings, but are the shadow of the divine wings.
>
> Now this is a great benefit to us even if it is a shadow.... For "he saved me" through the Spirit which overshadowed (me) in the cloud.[91]

Things could not be more clearly expressed. First, the virtues are a participation in the divine life in that they are produced by the Spirit, whose symbols we recognize in "the wings" and "the cloud." They are the shadow of the Spirit—and "shadow" does not have the pejorative meaning here that it does when contrasted with "image."[92] On the contrary, like the image, it signifies commonality with the one whose shadow is cast. It is used in this sense in the hermetic writings, where σκία equals εἰκών (*skia* = *eikōn* [shadow = image])[93] and also in Plotinus.[94] Second, the text affirms that it is through this participation in the life of God that God can be known by us.

For Gregory, the supernatural character of "virtue" also results from the paradisal meaning of the word, as was the case with *apatheia*. "Virtue" in this sense represents the original good things, lost through sin, restored by Christ.

> The sense... is clear to anyone who pays close attention: how the human race flourished at the beginning, while it was lodged in the paradise, nurtured by the water of that spring. At that time, its nature was adorned not

---

[90] Gregory, *Cant.* 3 (PG 44:824B–C; Norris, 101).
[91] *Cant.* 6 (PG 44:585C; Norris, 196–97).
[92] See *Cant.* 5 (PG 44:877B; Norris, 173).
[93] See C. H. Dodd, *The Bible and The Greeks* (London: Hodder & Stoughton, 1935), 157.
[94] See Plotinus, *Enneads* 2.6.3.

> with leaves but with the blossom of immortality [ἀφθαρσία, *aphtharsia*]. But the winter of disobedience dried up the root. The blossom was shaken off and fell to earth; the human being was stripped of the beauty of immortality, and the green grass of the virtues was dried up....
>
> But then there came the One who works in us the springtime of souls.... Once again our nature began to flourish and to be adorned with its own blossoms. But the blossoms that are proper to our life are the virtues.[95]

Fruits of the presence of the Holy Spirit, the result of the incarnation of the Word—these features clearly show that the virtues are to be understood in a supernatural sense.[96]

Having clarified the meaning of ἀρετή (*aretē*, virtue) in Gregory and having seen that it is to be placed on the same supernatural level as *apatheia* and purity, we need now to consider in more detail its connection with these other concepts.

Sometimes "virtue" is a generic term that includes all the perfections of the "image." Thus, in his treatise *On the Making of Man*, Gregory tells us that God "paint[ed] the portrait to resemble His own beauty, by the addition of virtues, as it were with colours." Gregory goes on to list these as "purity, freedom from passion, blessedness, alienation from all evil, and all those attributes of the like kind which help to form in men the likeness of God."[97] But ordinarily the reverse is true and the virtues are represented as being the various supernatural activities connected with *apatheia*.

In describing this supernatural life of the virtues in the soul, Gregory makes use of a variety of symbols. Some of these we have already come across: the finery of the Bride, the colors that form the image, the threads of the vestment of glory,[98] the leaves of the mystical vine,[99] or the flowers that make up the "fragrance of Christ."[100] In the allegory of the vine, where purity is symbolized by the cluster of grapes and *apatheia* by the entire vine, the "exaltation" of the virtues is represented by the branches that climb up "to the height that belongs to the angels." The virtues themselves—the "adornment of the divine virtues"

---

[95]*Cant.* 5 (PG 44:869C; Norris, 165).
[96]See *Cant.* 9 (PG 44:972C; Norris, 301): "There is no virtue outside the Godhead." See also *Cant.* 15 (PG 44:1096C; Norris, 469).
[97]*Op. hom.* 5.1 (PG 44:137B; NPNF² 5:391). See also *Eccl.* 5 (PG 44:696A; Hall, 97–98).
[98]See *Cant.* 9 (PG 44:961A; Norris, 287).
[99]See *Cant.* 2 (PG 44:800C; Norris, 67).
[100]*Cant.* 3 (PG 44:824C; Norris, 101). Cf. 2 Cor 2.15.

(κόσμος τῶν θείων ἀρετῶν, *kosmos tōn theiōn aretōn*)—are the leaves, which open out and are lightly stirred by a gentle breeze (πνεύματι, *pneumati*).[101] Here we see that the origin of the virtues is the activity of the Holy Spirit (Πνεῦμα, *Pneuma*).

The relationship of the virtues to *apatheia* is indicated more clearly still in another passage:

> The goal of the life of virtue for human beings . . . is likeness to the Divine, and for the sake of this good both the soul's purity and its separation from any passionate disposition are in virtuous persons carefully realized, so that a certain impress [χαρακτήρ, *charactēr*] of the transcendent Nature comes to them also. . . .
>
> Now the virtuous manner of life is not uniform or marked by a single style, but just as in the making of a fabric the weaver's art creates the garment by using many threads, some of which are stretched vertically and others are carried horizontally, so too, in the case of the virtuous life, many things must twine together if a noble life is to be woven. Just so the divine apostle enumerates threads of this sort, threads by means of which pure works are woven together; he mentions love and joy and peace, patience and kindness (Gal 5.22) and all the sorts of things that adorn the person who is putting on the garment of heavenly incorruptibility in place of a corruptible and earthly life (1 Cor 15.53). This is why the Bridegroom acknowledges that the adornment of the bride's garment is, as far as its fragrance goes, like frankincense. . . . The meaning of the enigma is this: "In your case, O Bride, the garment of virtue imitates the divine blessedness [μακαριότης, *makariotēs*] because it has been made like [ὁμοιούμενος, *homoioumenos*] the unapproachable Nature by its purity and impassibility. For," he says, "the scent of your garments is such as to bear a resemblance to that fragrance that is dedicated to the honoring of God."[102]

In this passage all the expressions that we have been studying can be found. The virtues are the result of *apatheia*, its diversification, or, as Gregory put it, its "varied finery" (κόσμος πολυειδής, *kosmos polyeidēs*). The same idea is also found in one further symbol—that of the necklaces:

---

[101]Gregory, *Cant.* 2 (PG 44:800D; Norris, 67).
[102]*Cant.* 9 (PG 44:961A-C; Norris, 287). See also *Vit. Moys.* 2.196 (PG 44:392A; Malherbe, 106).

> She is rightly likened by our text to circlets. The plural form of the word denotes perfection in each kind of virtue....
>
> Now this is a piece of advice addressed by our text to the general membership of the church. It instructs us that we must not focus attention on one good thing and be careless of other righteous actions; but if self-control is your "circle" and adorns your neck with purity of life as with a string of pearls, wear another necklace too: that zeal that bears the precious stones of the commandments and increases the beauty of the throat by its presence. And have yet another adornment for your neck: that religious and healthful faith that girdles the throat of the soul.[103]

We note here the belief that it is necessary to possess *all* of the virtues. This is an important theme in Gregory, who devoted an entire chapter of *On Virginity* to it.[104] He is opposed to the contrary thesis of the Stoics.

One last question comes to mind. These virtues—the fruits of the action of the Holy Spirit and a manifestation of *apatheia*—which, exactly, are they? In answering this question, we shall find that there are a few surprises in store for us. Sometimes Gregory seems to confine himself to what are traditionally known as the four cardinal virtues—fortitude, justice, prudence, and temperance—which are sometimes called "the moral virtues," and which for him are just as supernatural as the others. For example, in the *Homilies on the Song of Songs*, he writes: "The spices we take to be virtues, such as wisdom, temperance, justice, courage, prudence, and the like."[105] Immediately we notice that wisdom is added, coming first in the list, and indeed that the list is open-ended. Elsewhere, by contrast, we find lists that are Pauline in nature: "love and joy and peace, patience and kindness" (cf. Gal 5.22).[106] Or lists that include more specifically Christian virtues, such as "meekness...humility...patience."[107] Yet nowhere is a distinction made between virtues that are "theological" and those that are "moral," between fruits of the Holy Spirit and gifts of the Holy Spirit. All of the above terms are used to denote the various aspects of the image; they

---

[103] *Cant.* 3 (PG 44:817A; Norris, 91–93).
[104] See *Virg.* 17 (PG 44:389A–396A; FC 58:54–55). [See Andrew Radde-Gallwitz, "Gregory of Nyssa on the Reciprocity of the Virtues," *Journal of Theological Studies* 58.2 (2007): 537–52. He argues that, unlike some philosophers (e.g., Socrates, in some scholars' opinion), Gregory does not hold the virtues to be identical. Rather, their unity is found in that they reciprocally entail one another.—*Ed.*]
[105] *Cant.* 1 (PG 44:781B; Norris, 39).
[106] *Cant.* 9 (PG 44:961B; Norris, 287).
[107] *Perf.* (PG 46:272C; FC 58:111).

describe the whole of the supernatural life. And in this respect, one should not be fooled by the use of terms borrowed from Greek morality. It is always a matter of imitating the divine nature.

In the course of this examination of *apatheia*, purity, and the virtues, the nature of the ascetic life has become clear. The soul must strip off the old man—the πάθη κατὰ κακίαν, (*pathē kata kakian*, the evil passions)—and put on the new—namely, Christ himself. And so we come back to the baptismal image discussed at the outset of this study of the first way: the removal of the soiled garment and the vesting in the white robe. "You who, in accordance with the counsel of Paul, have 'taken off' the old humanity with its deeds and lusts like a filthy garment (Col 3.9) and have clothed yourselves by purity of life in the lightsome raiment [ἱμάτια φωτεινά, *himatia phōteina*] of the Lord, raiment such as he revealed in his transfiguration on the mountain (cf. Mk 9.2–3), or, rather, you who have 'put on' our Lord Jesus Christ himself (Gal 3.27) together with his holy garb and with him have been transfigured for impassibility and the life divine: hear the mysteries of the Song of Songs."[108]

From this we clearly see yet again that for Gregory *apatheia* is nothing other than the life of Christ himself. Thus in the ascetic life as in Baptism, of which it is a prolongation, it is a question of participation in the mystery of Christ. Admittedly, the vocabulary used by Gregory—ἀπάθεια (*apatheia*, dispassion), καθαρότης (*katharotēs*, purity) and so on—is Plotinian; yet the thinking is purely Christian. It is Christ we must put on, with his love. More than any other part of our investigation so far, this section has initiated us into Gregory's spirituality, for nowhere is his vocabulary more philosophical yet nowhere is his thought more Christian. This will be seen to be even more the case when we turn to a new aspect of the ascetic life—namely, its development and fulfillment in the freedom that is enjoyed by the children of God. And this is something specifically Christian not only in its content, but in its very form.

Familiarity with God or *Parrhēsia*[109]

Among the good things that were part of the inheritance of the first Adam, and which the grace of Christ restores to man, a special place must be given to παρρησία (*parrhēsia*). In classical Greek, this denoted the right or freedom to

---

[108] *Cant.* 1 (PG 44:764D; Norris, 15).
[109] On the history of the word, see E. Peterson, "Zur Bedeutungsgeschichte von παρρησία" in Reinhold Seeberg Festschrift, vol. 2, W. Koepp, ed. (Leipzig: Scholl, 1929): 283–97.

speak in the people's assembly, the "outspokenness" that was the privilege of the free citizen as opposed to the slave. In Christian usage, it signifies man's confidence in his relationship with God, a confidence that results from his capacity as son. Thanks to this, he can speak to God on the same footing as it were, and not as a slave to his master.

In Gregory's descriptions of man's state in paradise, *parrhēsia* is associated with *apatheia*. Thus in the *Catechetical Discourse*, he writes: "For since man was exalted in dignity, empowered through the divine blessing—he was appointed to reign over the earth and all things on it . . . and [he had] an impassible [ἀπαθής; *apathēs*] nature, for he was a copy of the impassible one—he was full of confidence [παρρησία, *parrhēsia*], delighting in the presence of the divine manifestation itself."[110] Yet, this particular word is not found in Gregory's descriptions of man's creation, even though the character of freedom is itself strongly emphasized.[111] In fact, *parrhēsia* is a specifically Christian disposition, linked to the concept of the divine fatherhood. This may explain why it is that Gregory mostly deals with it in mature works such as *The Lord's Prayer*, or the *Homilies on the Song of Songs*, which date from the end of his life.

Parrhēsia (boldness, confidence) is, as it were, the crowning achievement or blossoming of *apatheia*. Hence this is the appropriate place in our investigation for us to study it. Purified by *apatheia*, the soul regains freedom in its relations with God. It dares to come before him again, is once again on terms of familiarity with him. The appearance of *parrhēsia* marks the end of the process of purification and the reinstatement of the soul in the paradise of divine friendship. It is noteworthy that, in an important passage, Gregory has placed its emergence exactly between the restoration of *apatheia* in the soul and the withdrawal from the world that is characteristic of the second way.

The passage in question—from the treatise *On Virginity*—describes the stages of the soul's return to paradise:

> This concern, then, for the finding of what is lost is the restoration to the original state of the divine image [ἡ ἀποκατάστασις εἰς τὸ ἀρχαῖον τῆς εἰκόνος, *hē apokatastasis eis to archaion tēs eikonos*]. . . . Let us become again

---

[110]*Or. cat.* 6.10 (PG 45:29B; PPS 60:80). In the *Homilies on Ecclesiastes*, boldness before God (παρρησία ἐπὶ θεῷ, parrhēsia epi theō) is likewise ranked among the good things of paradise, along with equality with the angels, likeness to God, and contemplation of supernatural goods. See *Eccl.* 6 (PG 44:708D; Hall, 108).

[111]See *Op. hom.* 4.1 (PG 44:136C; NPNF² 5:391).

what the first being was during the first period of his existence.... It is possible for us to retrace [our] steps [παλινδρομεῖν, *palindromein*] and return to the original blessedness. What was the sequence? It was pleasure ... which initiated the fall. Shame and fear followed ... and they no longer dared to be in the sight of God. They hid themselves in leaves and shadows....

If, then, we are going to return thence and be with Christ, we must begin at the point of deviation.... Since the point of departure from the life in paradise was the married state, reason suggests to those returning to Christ that they, first, give this up.... [I]n addition, they must put off the coverings of the flesh, the garments made of skin, that is, they must put aside the thought of the flesh, and, after they have rejected the concealments of their shame ... be once more under the eyes of the Creator; they must disdain the deceptions [ἀπάταις, *apatais*] of taste and sight ... partaking only of the pure and unmixed good which has no share in evil.[112]

Here Gregory mentions the garments of skin (which relate to *apatheia*) and the illusions of the senses (which relate to the "cloud"), but running through the entire passage is the theme of shame and the associated coverings of fig leaves. It is this theme that specifically relates to *parrhēsia*. For just as *apatheia* was explained by reference to the garments of skin (cf. Gen 3.21), so *parrhēsia* is explained in connection with that other passage in Genesis in which, after sinning, Adam and Eve hide from Yahweh and make for themselves coverings out of fig leaves (Gen 3.7–8). For Gregory, this symbolizes the loss of *parrhēsia*, of familiarity with God. There are numerous allusions to this episode in his writings as well as to the fact that in paradise Adam was filled with *parrhēsia* and enjoyed the vision of the divine countenance. (This relationship between *parrhēsia* and the vision of God is something we should take note of.) However, it is the above passage from *On Virginity* that contains one of the most important references. In it, Gregory tells us that Adam and Eve no longer dared to stand before God. This is surprising, since *parrhēsia* is the virtue that allows us to have access (προσαγωγή, *prosagōgē*) to God.[113] Moreover, the shame and fear that followed sin are precisely the two dispositions that are diametrically opposed to *parrhēsia*. "Shame [is opposed] to boldness [Ἀντίκειται ... τῇ παρρησίᾳ δὲ

---

[112]*Virg.* 12–13 (PG 46:376A–C; FC 58:45–47).

[113]St Paul establishes a connection between the two terms in the following verse: "In whom we have boldness [παρρησίαν, *parrēsian*] and access with confidence [πεποιθήσει, *pepoithēsei*] through faith in him" (Eph 3.12).

ἡ αἰσχύνη]";[114] it is also the opposite of fear. Hence a twofold restoration is needed: a restoration to the state of innocence, which is the opposite of shame; and to the state of friendship, which is the opposite of fear.

We find the same contrasts—although here there is no explicit mention of *parrhēsia*—in the following passage that describes the effect of Baptism: "Thou didst banish us from Paradise, and didst recall us; Thou didst strip off the fig-tree leaves, an unseemly covering, and put upon us a costly garment.... No longer shall Adam be confounded when called by Thee, nor hide himself, convicted by his conscience, cowering in the thicket of Paradise."[115] It is worth noting again the presence everywhere of Baptism in the background of this first way, which constitutes a return to paradise by means of *apatheia* and *parrhēsia*. It is Baptism that substantially brings about this restoration, which the practice of the spiritual life accomplishes.

Like the garments of skin, the coverings of fig leaves symbolize the state of degradation, though with a more specific relationship to the concept of lost *parrhēsia*—that is, to shame and dishonor. The following passage is typical: "Envy walled us off from the tree of life, divested us of holy garments [ἱερῶν ἐνδυμάτων, *hierōn endymatōn*], and in shame [δι' αἰσχύνης, *di'aischynēs*] led us away clothed with fig leaves."[116]

These two images are sometimes brought together, as in the following passage: "For since Adam is, as it were, living in us, we see each and all these garments of skin round our nature, and also the transitory fig leaves of this material life which we have badly sewn together for ourselves after being stripped of our own resplendent garments. For instead of the divine garments we have put on luxuries and reputation, transitory honours and the quickly passing satisfactions of the flesh."[117] However, here the specific meaning of the fig leaves is almost completely effaced. What remains is the more general idea of a fall from grace.

By contrast, Gregory explicitly contrasts *parrhēsia* and shame, in a paradisal context, in a passage such as the following: "Having been freed from death, then, and restored from the fall, he comes to be in the presence of God, whom he first forsook when he ate of the things forbidden by the commandment and hid himself from shame [ὑπ' αἰσχύνης, *hup' aischynēs*] in the shadow of the fig

---

[114]*Or. cat.* 6.11 (PG 45:29C; PPS 60:81).
[115]*Diem. lum.* (PG 46:600A; NPNF² 5:524).
[116]*Vit. Moys.* 2.256 (PG 44:409C; Malherbe, 120).
[117]*Or. dom.* 5 (PG 44:1184B; ACW 18:76).

Paradise Regained

tree. When, therefore, he has again received boldness [παρρησία, *parrhesia*], he is restored [ἀποκαθίσταται, *apokathistatai*] to the living light."[118] Note the connection between *parrhēsia* and restoration (ἀποκατάστασις, *apokatastasis*), the face of God, and light. By contrast, shame is linked to the darkness in which Adam tries to hide.

In all these texts, *parrhēsia* is defined in contrast to the shame that follows sin and that causes the soul to flee from the face of God, preventing it from approaching him with the simplicity of a child. This shame is the trace that sin leaves in the soul: "After the death of the frog-like emotions, the former manner of life of those who have been delivered from such an illness becomes to them a foul and odorous memory which disgusts the soul in shame."[119] "[I]t is as though those who love pleasure have grasped some deceptive phantom. Its splendor disappears immediately and it passes into non-existence. Shame is the one trace of such a phantom which remains after the departure. It stamps a deep and enduring impression of these activities on these people."[120] Gregory sometimes compares shame and remorse to a track (ἴχνος, *ichnos*) left in the soul by sin that allows one to recognize it.[121]

As long as this shame hangs over him, man avoids the gaze of God. In order to regain one's freedom and confidence, the conscience must first have recovered its serenity. Thus, *parrhēsia* is closely connected with purity of conscience and the absence of sin. As such, it can be said to be situated at the pinnacle of the purgative stage. Gregory often explicitly links it to the concept of conscience (συνείδησις, *syneidēsis*), as in the following: "What spirit a man must have to say this word [Father]—what confidence [*parrhēsia*], what purity of conscience!"[122] "Do you see how much preparation we need, and what kind of life we must lead? How ardent must be our zeal so that our conscience may achieve such purity as to have the courage [*parrhēsia*] to say 'Father' to God?"[123]

Although *parrhēsia* is connected with *apatheia*, from another point of view it is linked to a different aspect of the paradisal life—namely, freedom (ἐλευθερία, *eleutheria*). It is not a question of metaphysical freedom, of free will (προαίρεσις,

---

[118]*Inscr.* 2.14.222 (PG 44:581A; Heine, 192–93).

[119]*Vit. Moys.* 2.79 (PG 44:349A; Malherbe, 72). [An allusion to the plague of frogs in Exodus.—*Ed.*]

[120]*Inscr.* 1.4.32–33 (PG 44:448A; Heine, 93–94).

[121]*An. et res.* 6 (PG 46:92B; PPS 12:78). See also *Eccl.* 3 (PG 44:649D; Hall, 60) for the interesting contrast between the αἰδῶς (*aidōs*, modesty) that precedes the fault—and the αἰσχύνη (*aischynē*, shame) that follows.

[122]*Or. dom.* 2 (PG 44:1140C; ACW 18:38).

[123]Ibid. (PG 44:1141D; ACW 18:40).

proairesis; αὐτεξούσιον, *autexousion*), but of Christian freedom—though there is a connection between the two concepts. Yet, as we shall see when we come to consider the notions of ἔρως (*erōs*, intense desire) and ἀγάπη (*agape*, love)—and as we have already seen for *apatheia* and εἰρήνη (*eirēnē*, peace)—in Gregory of Nyssa there is an encounter between Platonic and Christian concepts and an endeavor to transpose ancient thought to the Christian level. But here, for the concept of freedom, Gregory refers to Stoicism more than Plato. Clarifying his thinking on this point will prove to be of interest.

But let us begin by attempting to pinpoint the exact relationship of *parrhēsia* to ἐλευθερία (*eleutheria*, freedom). Both words are borrowed from the vocabulary of politics. *Eleutheria* was what characterized the rank of citizen in the ancient Greek *polis*, or city-state, and was directly opposed to δουλεία (*douleia*, slavery). *Parrhēsia*, as we have said, was the privilege of the free citizen, the outspokenness based on equality with other citizens and on the sovereign (ἀδέσποτος, *adespotos*) character of the citizen in the democratic *polis*. These are all words that we find in Gregory's religious language. Since man is the image of God, he is in a certain sense his equal. He has a "dignity of royalty" (βασιλικὴ ἀξία, *basilikē axia*).[124] Consequently, he is "without a master." And with respect to God, he enjoys the free speech that is proper to a son, and that a slave does not have.

The linking together of these various notions is well reflected in the following passage from the dialogue *On the Soul and the Resurrection*: "When he has put away all that is alien [ἀλλότριον, *allotrion*] to him—which is sin—and taken off [ἀποδυσάμενος, *apodysamenos*] the shameful [αἰσχύνην, *aischynēn*] garment of his debts, he enters into freedom and confidence. Freedom consists in becoming like that which has no master [ἀδέσποτος, *adespotos*] and is under its own control [αὐτοκρατής, *autokratēs*]. This likeness was given to us by God at the beginning, but has been veiled by the shame of our debts."[125] All these words expressive of freedom—*eleutheria, adespotos, parrhēsia,* and *autokratēs*—are here grouped together, as descriptive of the royal state, the sovereign freedom given to the soul in the beginning by God.

As Gilson has correctly observed,[126] in strongly emphasizing freedom as a constituent part of human dignity, Gregory foreshadows St Bernard (whom

---

[124]*Op. hom.* 4.1 (PG 44:136C; NPNF² 5:391).
[125]*An. et res.* 7 (PG 46:101C; PPS 12:86).
[126]See Gilson, *Théologie mystique de saint Bernard*, 66. [*Mystical Theology of Saint Bernard*, 48.]

he influenced) and, later, Descartes and the modern philosophers of freedom: "For since the human person had been created like God [θεοειδής, *theoeidēs*; deiform], and had been made blessed by the ability to determine his own acts [αὐτεξουσίῳ, *autoexousiō*] (for being autonomous [αὐτοκρατής, *autokratēs*] and independent [ἀδέσποτος, *adespotos*] is what is proper to the divine blessedness), for him to be led forcefully, by constraint, would deprive him of his dignity."[127] "For to be self-determining is to be godlike [ἰσόθεον τὸ αὐτεξούσιον, *isotheon to autexousion*]."[128] The same ideas appear in Gregory's description of man "in the image," at the beginning of the treatise *On the Making of Man*:

> In saying that man was made "in the image of God": for this is the same as to say that He made human nature participant in all good; for if the Deity is the fullness of good, and this is His image, then the image finds its resemblance to the Archetype in being filled with all good. Thus there is in us the principle of all excellence, all virtue and wisdom, and every higher thing that we conceive: but preeminent among all is the fact that we are free from necessity [ἐλεύθερος τῆς ἀνάγκης, *eleutheros tēs anangkēs*].[129]

> The soul immediately shows its royal and exalted character, far removed as it is from the lowliness of private station, in that it owns no lord [ἀδέσποτος, *adespotos*], and is self-governed [αὐτεξούσιος, *autexousios*], swayed autocratically [αὐτοκρατορικῶς, *autokratorikōs*] by its own will; for to whom else does this belong than to a king? And further, besides these facts, the fact that it is the image of that Nature which rules over all means nothing else than this, that our nature was created to be royal from the first.[130]

These passages are extremely intriguing in the way they juxtapose, indeed blend, expressions pertaining to various types of freedom. On the one hand, there is the freedom linked to independence (ἀδέσποτον, *adespoton*) and *parrhēsia*, as defining the attitude of the soul that is freed from shame and that enjoys a certain equality with God—a type, as mentioned, that is similar to political freedom.[131] On the other hand, the same expressions are linked to the concept of free will (αὐτεξουσιότης, *autexousiotēs*), a psychological freedom that Gregory defines

---

[127] *Mort.* 15 (PG 46:524A; PPS 64:23).
[128] Ibid.
[129] *Op. hom.* 16.10–11 (PG 44:184B; NPNF² 5:405).
[130] *Op. hom.* 4.1 (PG 44:136B–C; NPNF² 5:391).
[131] See *Cant.* 5 (PG 44:877A; Norris, 173).

very precisely as "freedom from necessity." This is the inalienable freedom inherent in man's nature, constituting his natural resemblance to God.

It is significant that Gregory places on the same level—and thereby considers as together constituting man's likeness to God—both the supernatural, Christian freedom (which is the privilege of the sons of God and the opposite of the slavery of sin) and the metaphysical freedom that is common to all people, and that is the opposite of the slavery of necessity. St Bernard takes over this doctrine of freedom, but introduces distinctions. He distinguishes, for example, between *libertas a coactione* (freedom from coercion), which is metaphysical freedom, and *libertas a peccato* (freedom from sin), which is Christian freedom. It seems that Gregory, by contrast, endeavors to link the two, in a synthesis of Christian and metaphysical thought.

What is important is that this is related to a fundamental aspect of his anthropology that we have already come across in connection with the garments of skin, and that we will meet again in connection with mystical knowledge. Namely, human nature for him is constituted by what we identify as the soul and grace. The νοῦς (*nous*, mind)—whose attribute is αὐτεξούσιον (*autexousion*, free will)—and the πνεῦμα (*pneuma*, spirit)—which confers *parrhēsia*, since it is the spirit of adoption—are interdependent and indistinguishably constitute the image, with which the added garments of skin are contrasted. This should always be kept in mind in order not be surprised by comparisons that might seem shocking, viewed from another perspective.

Inasmuch as *parrhēsia* is linked to freedom, it is the direct opposite of slavery (δουλεία, *douleia*). But there are two aspects to this, connected with the two meanings the term *douleia* has in Greek Christian vocabulary. On the one hand, it is linked to the concept of slavery conceived as a violent condition. This is the meaning we find in passages dealing with man's enslavement to the passions, of which we spoke in the preceding chapter. In this understanding of the term, *douleia* brings about shame in a manner exactly parallel to the way in which *eleutheria*, linked to *apatheia*, leads to *parrhēsia*.

But *douleia* can also be used with respect to God. The word δοῦλος (*doulos*) is then the equivalent of the Hebrew *ebed*, in the sense not of slave, but servant. In this context, the relationship of the *doulos* to his master is not one of constraint, but merely reflects a difference of condition. The word is normally used by Gregory to designate the relationship of man to God insofar as he is a creature: "The creature's property is to serve [τὸ δουλεύειν τῆς κτίσεως, *to douleuein tēs ktiseōs]*";¹³² "[Everyone] knows clearly the difference which there is between the created and the uncreated—terms of which the divergence is marked by dominion [κυριότητος, *kyriotētos*] and service [δουλεία, *douleia*]."¹³³ Man's "service" (δουλεία, *douleia*) expresses this difference of condition, which alone justifies it. Had we not believed that the Word was God, we would not give him *douleia*.¹³⁴ God alone can demand such homage without violating our freedom, because it is simply the expression of an ontological dependency.

It follows from this that the "service of God" (δουλεία θεοῦ, *douleia theou*)—far from being degrading like the enslavement of one human being by another—reflects a high degree of perfection. It is in this sense that Philo uses the word: "To serve [God] [δουλεύειν θεῷ, *douleuein theō*] is not only better than all freedom, but even than royal authority [βασιλεία, *basileia*]."¹³⁵ Thus the title Servant of God, which the Old Testament confers on Moses, is the highest with which man can be honored: "When one has accomplished such noble actions, he is considered worthy of this sublime name, to be called 'servant of Yahweh,' which is the same as saying that he is better than all others. For one would not serve God unless he had become superior to everyone in the world."¹³⁶

Such service of God, then, signifies perfection of a very high order, one that is in a certain sense unsurpassable. Nevertheless, it also indicates the natural relationship that connects man to God as this is expressed in the Old Testament, and that involves the idea of reverential awe. The new supernatural relationship of adoptive filiation (which is the specific proposition of the Gospel) adds to it—without suppressing the difference between creature and Creator—a Father-son relationship that is not one of fear, but of a certain equality and love.

This difference is clearly indicated in the Gospel of St John, when Christ tells his Apostles: "No longer do I call you servants [δούλους, *doulous*] ... but I have called you friends [φίλους, *philous*]."¹³⁷ What is implied here is precisely the transition not merely from the world of sin to the world of grace, or from slavery to freedom, but from a world of fear to that of love, from the Old Testament to the New. It is the same nuance that Paul notes when he writes: "For you did not

---

¹³²*Or. dom.* 3 (PG 44:1157C; ACW 18:53); see *Eun.* 3.4.38 (PG 45:725D; NPNF² 5:187).
¹³³*Eun.* 3.3.54 (PG 45:701B; NPNF² 5:179, mod.).
¹³⁴See *Eun.* 1.5.25 (PG 45:413A; NPNF² 5:84).
¹³⁵Philo, *The Special Laws* 1.10.57 (Yonge, 539). See also *The Cherubim* 2.31.107 (Yonge, 91).
¹³⁶Gregory, *Vit. Moys.* 3.14 (PG 44:428A–B; Malherbe, 135).
¹³⁷And the reason Christ gives for this makes clear his thinking: "For a servant does not know what his master is doing ... [but] all things that I heard from my Father I have made known to you" (Jn 15.15). This friendship is related to the privileges of the Son, and to our adoptive sonship.

receive the spirit of bondage [πνεῦμα δουλείας, *pneuma douleias*] again to fear, but you received the Spirit of adoption by whom we cry out, 'Abba! Father'" (Rom 8.15). The order of *douleia* and fear—that is, the natural Law—gives way to the order of filiation and love that is brought about by Christ. The same distinction is made by Gregory. As seen, he contrasts *parrhēsia* with both shame and fear. The contrast with shame is similar to that between the Greek understanding of *douleia* and freedom; the contrast with fear[138] that between the biblical understanding of *douleia* and friendship.

The transition from fear to love is a mark of a higher stage in the spiritual life, which is why *parrhēsia*, the practice of divine familiarity, emerges at the end of the purgative life. In a sense, it already belongs to the highest degrees of the spiritual life through its relationship with φιλία (*philia*), divine friendship, which is one of the characteristics of the mystical life proper—the most elevated degree of all. *Parrhēsia* flourishes, then, at the pinnacle of the spiritual life; yet it is nevertheless present from its inception. For Baptism is at once both redemption and transformation, liberation and advancement, blotting out of sin and divine adoption. When contrasted with pagan *douleia*, *parrhēsia* denotes liberation from sin: this is the perspective of the Gentiles.

This will help us to understand those texts of Gregory in which fear is contrasted with freedom: "What can she accomplish who has never received within herself the independence and self-rule [τὸ ἀδέσποτον καὶ αὐτοκρατές, *to adespoton kai autokrates*] that belong to the virtuous mind, but keeps aloof from partnership in vice out of servile fear [δουλικῷ φόβῳ, *doulikō phobō*]?"[139] This is still in line with Scripture, for as St John says, "Perfect love drives out fear" (1 Jn 4.18). Thus Gregory writes: "What more trustworthy witness of the fact that Moses did attain the perfection that was possible would be found than the divine voice which said to him: 'I have known you more than all others'? [Ex 33.12, 17. LXX] It is also shown in the fact that he is named the 'friend of God' by God himself [Ex 33.11]. . . . This is true perfection: not to avoid a wicked life because like slaves [δουλοπρεπῶς, *douloprepōs*] we servilely fear punishment but [to become] God's friend."[140]

There is a special connection, then, between *parrhēsia* and *philia* (friendship), as with *apatheia* and *eleutheria*. This was already made clear by Philo,

---

[138] See Gregory, *In sanctum Stephanum I* (*Steph. I*) (PG 46:712D). English translation in Rowan A. Greer, *One Path for All: Gregory of Nyssa on the Christian Life and Human Destiny* (Eugene, OR: Cascade Books, 2015), 58–59.

[139] *Cant.* 15 (PG 44:1113A; Norris, 491).

[140] *Vit. Moys.* 2.319–20 (PG 44:430B–C; Malherbe, 136–37).

who writes: "And freedom of speech is nearly akin to friendship; since to whom would any one speak with more freedom than to his own friend? Very appropriately therefore is Moses spoken of in the scriptures as dear to God [φίλοι θεοῦ, *philoi theou*], when he goes through an account of all the dangers which he had incurred by reason of his boldness [παρρησία, *parrhēsia*], in such a way that they seem to deserve to be attributed to friendship [φιλία, *philia*] rather than to arrogance; for audacity belongs to the character of the arrogant man; but good confidence belongs to the friend."[141] The connection is also made by St John: "Herein is our love [ἀγάπη, *agapē*]"—the Johanine word for *philia*—"made perfect, that we may have *parrhēsia* [confidence] on the day of judgment" (1 Jn 4.17). We find the same connection between friendship and *parrhēsia* in Gregory: "They [Peter, James, and John] had a special place, as it were, compared with the other apostles, as well as a freedom of speech [παρρησία, *parrhēsia*] not acquired by human friendship, but by the divine determination of truth."[142] But what is noticeable, above all, is that *parrhēsia* is presented as a free and familiar way of dealing with God that presupposes an already purified soul, and, consequently, one that has already passed through the stages of purification and fear: "We should not venture upon thoughts about God before we have made ourselves worthy of much boldness."[143]

This explains the place *parrhēsia* has in the *Homilies on the Song of Songs*. To the extent that the soul grows in the life of love, it enjoys a greater familiarity with God: "[The soul] is not occasioned any suffering by the blow [it] receives but glories [ἐπικαυχᾶται, *epikauchatai*] in the freedom of access accorded [it] by the removal of the curtain, which is here called a veil."[144]

Another of the principal aspects of *parrhēsia* is its relationship to prayer (ἡ προσευχή, *hē proseuchē*).[145] In fact, Christian prayer is in essence "intimacy with God" (θεοῦ ὁμιλία, *theou homilia*).[146] Such intimate conversation presupposes a real connection, a commonality of life, which is precisely the adoptive sonship. It is this participation in the divine life that gives the soul the audacity to present itself before God and to speak with him familiarly. This link between prayer and *parrhēsia* appears clearly immediately prior to the recitation of the

---

[141] Philo, *Who is the Heir of Divine Things* 5.21 (Yonge, 277).
[142] *Steph. I* (PG 46:732A; Greer, 68).
[143] *Inscr.* 2.3.28 (PG 44:496B; Heine, 130).
[144] *Cant.* 12 (PG 44:1037A; 389).
[145] Cf. Gregory's phrase "that we may possess the boldness to pray" (τὴν τοῦ προσεύχεσθαι παρρησίαν, *tēn tou proseuchesthai parrhēsian*), *Inscr.* 2.3.35 (PG 44:497C; Heine, 132).
[146] *Or. dom.* 1 (PG 44:1124B; ACW 18:24).

Lord's Prayer in the Roman Mass. After the solemn conclusion of the anaphora, *"per ipsum et cum ipso et in ipso"* ("through him, and with him, and in him"), which confirms our union with Christ, the text continues, *audemus dicere: Pater noster* ("we dare to say: Our Father").[147] This audacity is precisely what is meant by *parrhēsia*, which has its foundation in this union with Christ that alone enables us to call God "Father." This connection between *parrhēsia and proseuchē* was clearly seen by Stolz:

> Christian prayer is based precisely on our divine sonship. The Christian speaks to God as to his Father. Hence the title "Father" stands at the head of the prayer which Christ Himself has taught us. "When then we confess with our own mouths that the God and Lord of the universe is our Father, we profess forthwith," as John Cassian puts it, "that we have been called from our condition as slaves to the adoption of sons." This filial relation gives us freedom of speech (*parrhēsia*) in regard to God: we now dare call him our Father.
>
> Both these properties of Christian prayer (its intrinsic relationship to mystical union and its filial attitude toward God) spring from the same root, the friendship and sonship granted us through Christ.[148]

Likewise, Marmion established the same relationship when he defined prayer as "the normal outcome, under the Holy Spirit's action, of the affections resulting from our divine adoption."[149]

In Gregory of Nyssa these ideas are developed quite explicitly.[150] Prayer is linked directly to *parrhēsia*, on the one hand, and to the filial relationship with God, on the other:

> Who will give me those wings, that my mind may wing its way up to the heights of these noble words? Then I would leave behind the earth altogether and traverse all the middle air; [I would] become a stranger to all that moves and changes, and apprehend the Stable Nature, the immovable Power which

---

[147] [Likewise, in the Orthodox Liturgy the priest exclaims: "And make us worthy, O Master, that with boldness [παρρησίας, *parrēsias*] and without condemnation we may dare to call upon thee, the heavenly God, as Father, and to say . . ." —*Trans.*]

[148] Stolz, *Théologie de la mystique*, 123. [*Spiritual Perfection*, 112–13.] John Cassian, *Conferences* 9.18.

[149] C. Marmion, *Le Christ, Idéal du moine* (Paris : Desclée de Brouwer, 1922), 491. [Translation from *Christ, The Ideal of the Monk*, trans. by a nun of Tyburn convent (London and Edinburgh: Sands & Company, 1926), 342].

[150] As they are by Origen in *On Prayer* 22.1–3 (PPS 26:159–61).

exists in its own right.... So first my mind must become detached from anything subject to flux and change and tranquilly rest in motionless spiritual repose, so as to be rendered akin to Him [οἰκειώσασθαι, *oikeiōsasthai*] who is perfectly unchangeable; and then it may address Him by this most familiar [οἰκειοτάτη, *oikeiotatē*] name and say: Father.[151]

A few lines later we read: "If we have now understood the meaning of the prayer [προσευχή, *proseuchē*], it may perhaps be time to prepare our souls so that we may pronounce the words with bold confidence: 'Our Father who art in heaven.'"[152] We have here an echo, as it were, of the liturgical formula referred to above. Elsewhere, *parrhēsia* is connected to the entry into the sanctuary, the *adyton* reserved for the High Priest, which also symbolizes communion with God: "He who has prepared himself so that he may boldly call God his Father is precisely he who is clad in such a robe as described in this sermon.... [H]e dwells in the supercelestial sanctuaries [ἄδυτα, *adyta*]."[153] This liturgical action has the same meaning as the above liturgical formula: entry into the sanctuary is symbolic of regained friendship with God.

Gregory speaks most often of *parrhēsia* in his sermons on the Lord's Prayer. Unsurprisingly so, since these deal specifically with what is properly Christian prayer, prayer that addresses God as Father. At the opening of the second homily, we read: "But when our Lawgiver the Lord Jesus Christ is bringing us to Divine grace, He does not present Mount Sinai covered with darkness.... But, first of all, He leads us not to a mountain but to Heaven itself, which He has rendered accessible to men by virtue. Secondly, He gives them not only the vision of, but a share in [κοινωνούς, *koinōnous*], the Divine power, bringing them as it were to kinship [συγγένειαν, *syngeneian*] with the Divine Nature."[154]

Thus Christian prayer is based first of all on a kinship, a relationship that places man on the same level as God and that justifies *parrhēsia*, freedom of speech, and that indeed presupposes a natural link. It is significant that here, in connection with prayer, we find again that transition from fear to friendship that we had pointed out as being a characteristic of *parrhēsia*, and of the progress in the spiritual life that it presupposes. The development of the life of prayer, understood as a familiar conversation with God—a prayer that is not yet mystical, but

---

[151] *Or. dom.* 2 (PG 44:1140B; ACW 18:37–38).
[152] Ibid. (PG 44:1145D; ACW 18:43).
[153] *Or. dom.* 3 (PG 44:1149D; ACW 18:47).
[154] *Or. dom.* 2 (PG 44:1137A-B; ACW 18:35). See *Cant.* 3 (PG 44:809A; Norris, 81) for the same contrast.

that is nonetheless specifically Christian—is thus linked to this purification of the conscience that we saw as being one of the characteristics of *apatheia*. Its exact place in the progress of the spiritual life is here, at the culmination of the purgative life.

Gregory often returns to the idea that the blossoming of a life of prayer presupposes a purification that only *parrhēsia* can bring about. Thus in the second homily on the Lord's Prayer, we read: "Since, therefore, we need confidence [παρρησία, *parrhēsia*] to approach God with the request for the things that are profitable for us, the performance of a vow [τὸ κατ' εὐχήν, *to kat' euchēn*] must necessarily come first. Then, when we have accomplished our part, we are confident [θαρσοῦντες, *tharsountes*] of being made worthy to receive in return the things that are God's to give."[155]

What is said here of the prayer of petition, Gregory says elsewhere concerning the prayer of praise. It too presupposes a pure conscience: "We must be eager that our life be in accord with [David's], that we may possess the boldness to pray."[156] And elsewhere: "What therefore does the prayer teach? ['Forgive us our debts.'] First, that we should be conscious of our likeness to God through the liberty of our life, then to be bold to call God our Father, and to ask that our sins should no more be remembered.... If we approach the Benefactor, we should ourselves be benefactors; if we go to Him who is good and just, we should ourselves be the same.... Thus a man should obtain the confidence presupposed by the prayer."[157] We note again, en passant, the connection that is made between *proseuchē* and *parrhēsia*.

But if one ought not to sin by presumption, daring to present oneself before God without being properly prepared, there is another fault that consists in not having enough confidence and not daring to approach God at all. It is this latter attitude that Gregory criticizes; "Do you realize to what height the Lord raises His hearers through the words of the prayer, by which He somehow transforms human nature into what is Divine? For He lays down that those who approach God should themselves become gods [θεοὺς γενέσθαι, *theous genesthai*]. Why, He says, do you go to God crouching with fear like a slave [δουλοπρεπῶς, *douloprepōs*] because your conscience pricks you? Why do you shut out holy audacity which is inherent in the freedom of the soul because it has been joined

---

[155] *Or. dom.* 2 (PG 44:1137D; ACW 18:36).
[156] *Inscr.* 2.3.35 (PG 44:497C; Heine, 132).
[157] *Or. dom.* 5 (PG 44:1177B–C; ACW 18:71–72).

Paradise Regained

to its very essence from the beginning?"[158] This text is of considerable interest, for all the ideas that we have encountered relative to *parrhēsia* are mentioned in it. As seen, this is grounded in the soul's free nature. But this *eleutheria* is a supernatural freedom—that is to say, it is the divine grace that enables us to partake of the life of God, and something that was part of man's original nature (συνουσιωμένην ἐξ ἀρχῆς φύσει, *synousiōmenēn ex archēs physei*).

This entire homily is an invitation to the Christian soul to rise above the slave mentality that corresponds to the ancient Law, the law of fear, and to take possession of the good things that participation in the life of God opens up for us in Christ. This is to be achieved through a life of prayer, which is a blossoming of the feelings that result from divine filiation. As we have also seen, however, two obstacles stand in the way of a life of familiarity with God, which is what prayer is: shame, which is the result of sin and requires purification, and fear, which is a consequence of lack of faith. It is significant that these two impediments to prayer are the same, as we discovered, with respect to *parrhēsia*. The relationship between the two—prayer and confident boldness—is abundantly clear.

---

[158] *Or. dom.* 5 (PG 44:1180A; ACW 18:72–73).

PART TWO

The Cloud
or
Of Contemplation

4

The Ladder of Love

In the correlation he drew up between the three books of Solomon and the three stages of the spiritual life, Origen linked Ecclesiastes to the second. Gregory of Nyssa, for his part, embraces this approach. Here, at the beginning of his *Homilies on the Song of Songs*, is how he defines the subject matter of Ecclesiastes: "In the latter work, [Wisdom] disparages the human tendency to dwell on the appearances [φαινόμενα, *phainomena*] of things and asserts that everything unstable and passing is vanity [μάταιον, *mataion*].... [S]he points out our soul's motion of desire toward the invisible Beauty that is beyond anything grasped by the senses [δι' αἰσθήσεως, *di' aisthēseōs*]."[1] The specific objective, then, of the second way is detachment from the world of appearances.

Later in the *Homilies*, in connection with this second way, Gregory writes as follows: "More attentive [προσεχής, *prosechēs*] apprehension of hidden realities, which leads the soul to the invisible realm by way of what appears [φαινόμενα, *phainomena*], is like a cloud [νεφέλη, *nephelē*] that casts a shadow on everything that appears but yet induces and accustoms the soul to look upon what is hidden [κρύφιον, *kryphion*]."[2] This passage clearly continues to develop the same subject, but its significance lies in how it connects the second way to the Mosaic motif of the cloud. The cloud that guides [χειραγωγοῦσα, *cheiragōgousa*] the soul is the one that leads the Hebrews across the Sinai desert. Thus, this stage in the spiritual life corresponds to that particular episode in Moses' journey. That the cloud is described as "casting a shadow" on appearances fits well with the negative character of the second way, which, as seen, consists in emptying the soul of sensory things by persuading it of their vanity and by purifying it of its attachment (σχέσις, *schesis*) to them. At the same time, it involves becoming accustomed to the invisible, which the image of a cloud also conveys. This deprivation of perceptible phenomena and this getting accustomed to living

---

[1]*Cant.* 1 (PG 44:769D; Norris, 23).
[2]*Cant.* 11 (PG 44:1000D; Norris, 341).

in the presence of God is precisely what characterizes Moses' experience as he crossed the desert.[3]

Renunciation of the world as perceived by the senses also figures as a characteristic of this second stage in the description Gregory gives—in *On Virginity*—of the return of the soul to paradise. He points out that, once it has regained *parrhēsia*—the crowning achievement of the *apatheia* that characterizes the first way—the soul "disdain[s] the deceptions [ἀπάτη, *apatē*] of taste and sight . . . fastening upon beauty alone."[4] The interesting word here is *apatē*, for it reminds us of the ματαιότης (*mataiotēs*, vanity) of Ecclesiastes and again emphasizes the illusory character of the sensible world from which one should detach oneself so as to adhere to reality.

This stage of the spiritual life is portrayed, then, as being a more attentive (προσεχεστέρα, *prosechestera*) scrutiny of hidden things—like a meditation, but of an intellectual order. It is no longer simply a matter of moral purification, such as characterized the first, or purgative, way. But it is not yet the union of love that defines the mystical life proper. The second way is the domain of the intellect and, as such, corresponds to what will come to be called "the illuminative way." With Origen, the third way too is a noetic activity—an activity of the νοῦς (*nous*, mind or intellect). For Gregory, by contrast, the third way is hypernoetic and specifically mystical, with the soul being thrust beyond and outside the ordinary ways of knowing. With him, the intellectual domain is entirely confined to the second way, the realm of θεωρία (*theōria*, contemplation).

The knowledge of hidden things that characterizes the second way consists of two stages. Disaffection with the sensible world leads, in the first instance, to a preliminary knowledge of God. This is knowledge of an intellectual nature—symbolic theology, "which leads the soul to the invisible realm by way of what appears."[5] Next, the soul must free itself from this form of knowledge and, entering the night of faith, be introduced to a higher knowledge of God, knowledge of a more mystical nature. These two stages correspond to Origen's φυσική

---

[3] See *Vit. Moys.* 117–18 (PG 44:360D; Malherbe, 81–82). Cf. 2.132 (PG 44:365B; Malherbe, 86): "For the one who has left behind the Egyptian pleasures . . . life removed from these pleasures seems at first difficult and disagreeable. But if the wood be thrown into the water, that is, if one receives the mystery of the resurrection which had its beginning with the wood [of the cross], then the virtuous life . . . becomes sweeter and more pleasant than all the sweetness that tickles the senses with pleasure." See also the metaphor of the pomegranate as a symbol of the ascetic life—harsh to begin with, then sweet. *Cant.* 9, 15 (PG 44:969C, 1108A–B; Norris, 293, 483).

[4] *Virg.* 13 (PG 46:376B–C; FC 58:47).

[5] *Cant.* 11 (PG 44:1000D; Norris, 341).

(*physikē*, contemplation of nature) and θεωρική (*theōrikē*, contemplation of things divine), although in Gregory they both belong to the second way.

Contempt of the World

The soul that has detached itself from sin and regained the *apatheia* and *parrhēsia* that were man's in the beginning must now disentangle itself from visible goods so as to become attached to invisible realities. To do so, it should understand their vanity, and that it has been the victim of an illusion, an error—that it has been duped by false appearances that have no consistency. Then it will safely attach itself to what is real. The soul must also begin to consider creatures in the light of God, and this will enable it to fathom their nothingness. This was also the goal of the second way in Origen: "Contemplation of nature ... will teach the good use of all things by means of a religious scrutiny of the world and will persuade us of the vanity and instability of all that is visible. It is to such a person that the doors of γνῶσις (*gnōsis*, knowledge) and θεωρία (*theōria*, contemplation) open."[6]

Gregory's insistence on the vanity of creatures and yet their significance as a means of helping us to come closer to God is the entire subject of his *Homilies on Ecclesiastes*. What we first notice is a diatribe (διαβολή, *diabolē*) in which the visible world is portrayed as a dream or illusion in a way that is similar to the disparagement of the sensible that we find in Plato or Buddhism. But then we are shown the significance that the visible world acquires once it is understood as being subordinate to God, thereby becoming a means of symbolic theology. The world then becomes one vast symbol, a means of leading us to him. Aside from this, it is nothing.

But first let us examine further this question of vanity. In his treatise *On the Inscriptions of the Psalms*, Gregory presents things as follows: "The capability of contemplating both the potentiality and the actuality of the things which exist [ἐποπτικὴ τῶν ὄντων δύναμις, *epoptikē tōn ontōn dynamis*] is the unique property of the deity. He, therefore, who has what he desired in himself also becomes capable himself of such contemplation and considers carefully the nature of the things which exist."[7] The word *epoptikē* comes from the vocabulary of the mystery religions, in which an "epopt" (an initiate or seer) was someone who had been admitted to the third and highest grade of initiation. In Gregory's the-

---

[6]Rahner, "Le début d'une doctrine," 132.
[7]*Inscr.* 1.6.42 (PG 44:452C; Heine, 98).

ology, on the other hand, it is love that is the highest degree. The term is clearly in keeping with the illuminative way, which affords us knowledge of what can be known. It consists in judging the things of this world according to the truth, and thereby dispelling the scandal of seeing the evil happy and the just unhappy in this life. Gregory compares the attitude of the "epopt" to that of a man who contemplates a landscape from a great height:

> He, therefore, who was lofty in mind, standing, as it were, on some prominent look-out point [σκοπιά, skopia],[8] and straining his vision to see those things which were far removed, saw wherein the difference between evil and virtue lies.
>
> The means of judging these matters is on the basis of their ends [ἔσχατα, eschata], not on the basis of what is currently to hand [παρόντα, paronta]. For by that eye of the soul which is capable of contemplation [ἐποπτικός, epoptikos] and discernment [κρίσις, krisis] he has understood what has been stored up for the good through hope as though it were present, and has passed over in his soul everything which appears to the senses. When he enters the heavenly shrines he upbraids the lack of judgement [ἀκρισία, akrisia] of those who basely pervert the discernment of what is good to our physical members capable of sense-perception. This is why he says, "For what do I have in heaven, and what do I desire on earth besides you?" (Ps 72.25)
>
> ... [H]e marvelously magnifies and exalts what is heavenly... and contemptuously and mockingly [καταφρονητικῶς, kataphronētikōs] disparages [ἐξευτελίζων, ezeutelizōn] and loathes [μυσαττόμενος, mysattomenos] that which the eyes of fools [ἀνοήτων, anoētōn] zealously pursue upon earth.[9]

The loftier perspective, the *skopia*, from which the contemplator examines earthly things is thus one that perceives their relationship to the last things, the *eschata*. In the context of death, Gregory points out, those who have attached themselves to earthly goods will understand their vanity.[10] Hence, the objective

---

[8]The same metaphor is used by Philo (*On Dreams* 2.25.170 [Yonge, 400]). It is also found in Origen (*Homilies on Numbers* 27.9) and Plotinus, who writes: "As one standing on some lofty height [ἐπί τινος ὑψηλῆς σκοπιᾶς, *epi tinos hypsēlēs skopias*] and lifting his eyes sees what to those that have not mounted with him is invisible" (*Enneads* 4.4.5). The reference is to knowledge of the intelligibles. The source is Plato, *Republic* 445b–c.

[9]*Inscr.* 1.6.44–46 (PG 44:453A-B; Heine, 98–99). Cf. "[He] spits on [διαπτύει, *diaptyei*] the worthlessness [τὸ οὐτιδανόν, *to outidanon*] and the vanity [τὸ μάταιον, *to mataion*] of that zealousness which is deceived [ἠπατημένης, *hēpatēmenēs*] about life" (*Inscr.* 1.6.47; PG 44:453C; Heine, 100).

[10]See *Eccl.* 1 (PG 44:629B; Hall, 41).

of the second, or illuminative, way is to rectify one's powers of discernment (κρίσις, *krisis*) to form a correct evaluation of things. In fact, the cause of evil is above all an error of judgment, a flawed scale of values that causes the soul to overestimate visible things and to underestimate what is real. It is this false appraisal that must be rectified. But for that one has to get to the root cause of the problem, which lies in the fact that man is totally immersed in the life of the senses and has difficulty in freeing himself. Though he is made for invisible things,[11] he has sunk so deep in the phenomenal world that his spiritual faculties have become dulled and he has lost all sense of his true nature. He can be compared, Gregory tells us, to a prisoner who considered as good the darkness in which he had been living, but who was then let out into daylight. He would surely denounce his previous opinion and say, "I used to prefer the darkness to which I was accustomed to such sights as the sun and the stars and every beauty in heaven because I was ignorant of that which is superior."[12] Here we have an echo of Plato's allegory of the cave. Elsewhere Gregory makes an even more precise allusion to it, when speaking of the difficulty that eyes grown accustomed to darkness have in getting used to a light that hurts them.[13] But the main point is the Platonic view that the source of one's attachment to creatures is above all ignorance and inexperience, and that one must dispel this illusion by seeing the things of this world in their true perspective.

The image of an "exalted height" (σκοπιά, *skopia*) is found elsewhere in Gregory,[14] as representing one of the stages of the soul's ascent. It marks the point where, having arrived at a certain height, the soul sees human life spread out before it and gets things into proportion:

> It is possible also, in respect to the greatness of the one who has progressively ascended [ἀναβεβηκότος, *anabebēkotos*] to the step [βαθμός, *bathmos*] of this psalm, to look down through the words themselves of the psalm on how much past greatness he has excelled. For he no longer complains that he is trodden on by enemies . . . but since he is now on high, he cries out these words critically, as from some lofty hilltop [σκοπιά, *skopia*], to

---

[11]See ibid. (PG 44:624B; Hall, 37).
[12]*Inscr.* 1.6.46 (PG 44:453B; Heine, 99).
[13]See *Mort.* 7 (PG 46:505D; PPS 64:9–10).
[14]See *Cant.* 7 (PG 44:916C; Norris, 225). Sometimes he uses the word περιωπή (*periōpē*, summit, look-out place)—e.g., *Beat.* 1 (PG 44:1193B; ACW 18:85). The same word is found in Maximus of Tyre, *Dissertations* 17.6.

those spending their lives in the valleys below at the foot of the mountain of human life, and says, Men, what are you saying and doing?[15]

Whoever has reached this degree of perfection sees the ordinary life of those below in its true perspective. It is the Preacher once again who proffers this "point of view":

> All the other things which are in sensual terms good, though they may seem good because of deluded thought [διὰ τῆς κατὰ τὴν οἴησιν ἀπάτης, *dia tēs kata tēn oiēsin apatēs*], have no real being or existence [οὔτε ἔστι οὔτε ὑφέστηκεν, *oute esti oute hyphestēken*]; although they are naturally subject to flux [ῥοώδους, *rhoōdous*] and transient [παροδικῆς, *parodikēs*], through some delusion [ἀπάτης, *apatēs*] and idle preoccupation [ματαίας προλήψεως, *mataias prolēpseōs*] they are regarded by the uninformed as truly existing. Those who cling to what is unstable [ἀστάτων, *astatōn*] do not reach out for what stands for ever.
>
> As if he were standing on a high watchtower [σκοπιά, *skopia*], the Ecclesiast seems to cry aloud to the human race through these words, *A moment for loving and a moment for hating*, that the truly good things are different, and they are good in themselves and make those who share in them good.[16]

Here we have the entire teaching of the Preacher: the vanity of human good things, which have no existence except through the idea we form of them, being an illusion created by our mind[17]—and, compared with them, true goods. The Preacher is someone who, having ascended half way up the mountain, turns to the people he sees occupied with a thousand vanities in the valleys of life and addresses to them one last appeal: "A time to love and a time to hate." It is an appeal for them to discern what is truly good, to discern what is worthy of love—and to extricate themselves from the illusion of false goods that deserve only hatred and contempt. The idea of a *skopia*, or observatory, provides an

---

[15]*Inscr.* 2.15.248 (PG 44:592C; Heine, 201).

[16]*Eccl.* 8 (PG 44:737C; Hall, 132).

[17]We find the same idea in Gregory's commentaries on the Psalms: "He says that they are 'dull of heart' who do not distinguish what is false and vain [μάταιον, *mataion*] from the truth, but love what is non-existent [ἀνύπαρκτον, *anyparkton*], and overlook what abides and is worthy of being loved. For he says that holiness alone is truly wonderful, and that all the other things which men eagerly pursue instead of those things which are good are conceits which have no existence in themselves, but seem to have being in the vain opinion [μάταια οἴησις, *mataia oiēsis*] of men." *Inscr.* 1.4.28 (PG 44:445B; Heine, 92–93).

accurate image of this stage of the ascent; yet, though it gives an overview of human life and allows one to appraise it judiciously, it is not yet the entry into the darkness at the summit nor into the vision of the heavenly wonders.

In the passage just quoted there is one further significant point. Namely, that the mistaken evaluation that falsifies our conduct in life seems almost inevitable. Its origin lies in the fact that the exercise of our reason is pre-empted by that of our sensibility, which becomes attached to perceptible things before we have been able to analyze their worth. It is again in his *Homilies on Ecclesiastes* that Gregory sets out this interesting doctrine, which has far-reaching consequences:

> Thus, since sense is part of our nature right from birth, but the mind waits for a proper age to be reached, to be able to reveal itself gradually in the person, the mind, which develops slowly, is for this reason dominated by the sense, which is complete, and by compulsion grows habituated to the perpetual superiority, so that it submits to sense, judging good or bad according to whatever sense selects or rejects.
>
> The reason why discernment of the true good is difficult, and hard for us to achieve, is that we are prejudiced by sensual criteria, and we define good as what is enjoyable and pleasant.[18]

Here we again see one of the characteristic aspects of Gregory's views on human nature and the divine plan. The divine pedagogy, he argues, consists in exposing man to error through the chronological primacy of sense perception over reason, so that, having an experience (πεῖρα, *peira*) of the bitterness of evil, he will pursue the good in an act of freedom and discover his fault for himself.

We now have all the elements that will enable us to contextualize Gregory's thoughts on this subject, and can now broach a more detailed account of his doctrine.

We have already met the principal expressions he uses to denote the unreality of the sensible world: "vain" (μάταιον, *mataion*), "illusion" (ἀπάτη, *apatē*), "a subjective evaluation, a false notion" (οἴησις, *oiēsis*), to which corresponds the "contempt" (καταφρόνησις, *kataphronēsis*) attached to worthless things.[19] But there are a number of other symbols that will help us to clarify this doctrine of "cosmic illusion." To begin with, there is the image of the spider's web, which is effective in getting us to understand the "insubstantiality" (ἀνυπόστατον,

---

[18]*Eccl.* 8 (PG 44:736B–C; Hall, 130).

[19]Cf. the phrase in the [pre-Vatican II] missal and breviary: *terrena despicere* ("to despise earthly things").

anypostaton) of the visible world, a world in which man lets himself be caught and devoured by the Enemy who has woven it:

> Life is unsubstantial [ἀνυπόστατον, *anypostaton*] and shadowy [σκιοειδής, *skioeidēs*], like the thread of a spider's web for the one over whom the power of wrath prevails. For just as that thread is visible so long as chance may preserve it, but if someone touch it with his hand it perishes immediately, wasted away by the touch of the fingers, so too that human life, which is always being woven from unsubstantial [ἀνύπαρκτον, *anyparkton*] ambitions, like so many ethereal threads, is weaving a non-existent web for itself. If someone assail this web with solid reasoning, the vain ambition escapes his grasp and disappears into nothing. For everything ambitiously pursued in this life is a conceit [ἐν τῇ οἰήσει, *en tē oiēsei*] and not reality [οὐκ ἐν ὑποστάσει, *ouk en hypostasei*]. Honour is a conceit, as is also rank, family, nobility, pride, pretention, wealth, and all those things in short which the spiders of life practise. ... Those who are soft and without vigour, and are greedy, like flies, for the sticky things of life, are entangled in their weak and feeble flight and bound up in the mantle of such threads as if they were nets. I am referring to those who are entangled in luxuries, honours, popular repute, and various desires, as if they were spider-webs, and who become the prey and food of that beast which hunts by such means.[20]

In this passage we have a summary of Gregory's thinking: pleasures, honors, and all the things that fill human life are insubstantial (ἀνύπαρκτον, *anyparkton*; ἀνυπόστατον, *anypostaton*). They are unreal, a pure mirage (οἴησις, *oiēsis*; or notion, conceit) that has no existence other the one that our own assessment attributes to it. This mirage is created by the enemy, the beast that is ever on the lookout. His ruse consists in tricking us into accepting as existing that which has no existence, diverting our gaze from real goods in the process. Man is a victim of a deception. He is deceived. His transgression is, as we have seen, above all an error, a mistake. Thus the goal of the second, or illuminative, way is to disabuse him, to make the illusion fade away, to awaken him from the sleep of appearances, and make him see reality.

This reference to sleep reminds us that comparisons with dreams are another way in which Gregory expresses the insubstantiality of the goods of this world. A

---

[20]*Inscr.* 1.7.67, 1.8.76 (PG 44:464A–465D; Heine, 106, 108–109). See also *Inscr.* 1.7.75 (PG 44:465C; Heine, 108): "The delusion [ἀπάτη, *apatē*] of the material life ... is unsubstantial [ἀνυπόστατος, *anypostatos*] and like a spider's web [ἀραχνιώδης, *arachniōdēs*]."

The Ladder of Love

notable example of this is found in an important passage of his *Homilies on the Song of Songs*—one of those digressions that are common in our author:

> One, and one of the weightiest, of the Lord's admonitions ... is this: that those who look to the life above must be stronger than sleep and ever wakeful in mind, fighting off the eyes' drowsiness as if it were some cheater of souls or plotter against the truth.
>
> I refer to that drowsiness and that sleep that manufacture, for those who are sunk deep in life's deceits [ἐν τῇ τοῦ βίου ἀπάτῃ, *en tē tou biou apatē*], dream images [τὰ ὀνειρώδη ταῦτα φανάσματα, *ta oneirōdē tauta phantasmata*] of high offices, treasures, lordship, self-conceit, bewitching [γοητεία, *goēteia*] pleasures, of lust for fame and luxury and vanity—and all things whatsoever that people without awareness chase after vainly in this life at the behest of some phantasy [διά τινος φαντασίας, *dia tinos phantasias*]. These things, which flow away with time as it passes [συμπαραρρέοντα, *sympararreonta*], have their being in seeming [ἐν τῷ δοκεῖν, *en tō dokein*]. They are not what they are esteemed to be. . . . In order, then, that our mind may be free of such fantasies [τῶν τοιούτων φασμάτων, *tōn toioutōn phasmatōn*], he orders that this heavy sleep be banished from the eyes of the soul, lest devotion to what is unreal [τὸ ἀνύπαρκτον, *to anyparkton*] cause us to bid farewell to true and substantive realities.[21]

The soul that is a stranger to sleep and illusion, Gregory goes on to say, "does not dally with any of these misleading dreams [οὐδενὶ τῶν ὀνείρων τούτων ἐμματαιάζουσα, *oudeni tōn oneirōn toutōn emmataiazousa*]."[22]

The role played by the imagination (φαντασία, *phantasia*) is understandably also frequently mentioned, as in the following examples: "Those who fatten their souls with the pure and sweet-scented nourishment have put away from themselves any shadowy and deceptive [ἀπατηλὴν καὶ σκιοειδῆ, *apatēlēn kai skioeidē*] imagining,[23] which belongs to people who are busied about this life. They will look toward the true ground [ὑπόστασις, *hypostasis*] of the being of things."[24]

---

[21]*Cant.* 11 (PG 44:996A–B; Norris, 333–35).

[22]Ibid. (PG 44:996D; Norris, 335).

[23]The expression σκιοειδῆ φαντασίαν (*skioeidē phantasian*)—"shadowy imagery"—is found applied to the Old Testament, which is the shadow (σκία, *skia*) or foreshadowing, the "type" (τύπος, *typos*), of the Gospel (*Cant.* 5; PG 44:868A; Norris, 161). This is a transposition to the historical order of the Platonic contrast between the intelligible world and the sensible world. [He also draws this characterization of the Old Covenant as a shadow of the New from the New Testament itself, e.g., Col 2.17; Heb 10.1.—*Ed.*]

[24]*Cant.* 5 (PG 44:884B; Norris, 181).

"Although such great things are freely theirs in heaven, nevertheless they consider to have come to be with God to be imaginary delusions in the category of a wish in relation to power or honour or wealth, or this wretched little glory for which human nature is mad."[25]

We are reminded by all this of one of the important themes of Hellenic mysticism. The soul is Psyche, asleep in the world of appearances, whom the divine Eros awakens. It is a theme developed by Plotinus, in terms that remind us of Gregory:

> Because representations [φάντασμα, *phantasma*] attack it at what we call the affective phase and cause a resulting experience, a disturbance [πάθημα, *pathēma*], to which disturbance is joined the image of threatened evil: this amounts to an affection [πάθος, *pathos* (or "passion")] and Reason seeks to extinguish it, to ban it as destructive to the well-being of the Soul . . . then Philosophy's task is like that of a man who wishes to throw off the shapes presented in dreams [τὰς τῶν ὀνειράτων φαντασίας, *tas tōn oneiratōn phantasias*] and to this end recalls to waking condition the mind that is breeding them.[26]

In Gregory's text, the awakening merely symbolizes the conversion of a heart that has been freed from the illusions of glory and pleasure. In Plotinus it already signifies the mode of being of a soul that is withdrawn from appearances. But, later—when we come to discuss the night of the senses—we shall see that this features in Gregory too.

To describe the above-mentioned cosmic illusion Gregory sometimes uses yet another image—and not the weakest. He compares it to an act of magic (γοητεία, *goēteia*) or a spell. "By magic [γοητεία, *goēteia*] you will perceive the crafty deceit of this life [ἡ τοῦ βίου ἀπάτη, *hē tou biou apatē*] through which men drugged as though by some philter of Circe are changed into the form of irrational animals and leave their proper nature."[27] Here we have the animal passions once again but also another image, one that is Platonic and Plotinian: "The souls," writes Plotinus, "are intent upon contriving for their charges and finally come to be pulled down by them; they are fettered in bonds of sorcery [γοητείας δεσμοῖς, *goēteias desmois*], gripped and held by their concern for the

---

[25]*Inscr.* 1.6.49 (PG 44:456A; Heine, 100). See *Inscr.* 1.7.67, 1.7.75 (PG 44:461D, 465B–C; Heine, 106, 108).
[26]Plotinus, *Enneads* 3.6.5.
[27]*Vit. Moys.* 2.316 (PG 44:428C; Malherbe, 135).

The Ladder of Love

realm of Nature."[28] "Judgment," writes Gregory, "flees everything that bewitches the senses [τὸ καταγοητεῦον, *to katagoēteuon*]."[29] Plotinus' thoughts on this matter are well explained by Puech:

> This non-being that matter is draws its appearance of being and splendor from the souls that are attached to it and take pleasure in it. It is a phantasm, a lie in action (*Enneads* 2.5.5); a thing of darkness illumined by borrowed reflections; a corpse adorned and dressed up in images that are merely forms sketched out by the mind (2.4.5). Born of a fool's bargain in which our "self" believes that it acquires being, whereas in fact it surrenders being to matter, the sensible world is but an illusion. And a *magic* illusion in the true sense of the word: it seduces and fascinates, and through its marvels engages the attention of the soul that then gazes at what it mistakenly believes to be its own reflection in the mirror of matter. It shackles the soul in the interdependence that links all things in the cosmos to one another. It is a web of sorcery into which man is embedded and kept in *dependency* (4.4.31–45).[30]

What is the true nature of this fantasy world, of this mirage of the senses? It is the world of becoming. It is essentially fleeting (ῥοώδης, *rhoōdēs*), ephemeral (παροδικός, *parodikos*), and unstable (ἄστατος, *astatos*). In this world of appearances (φαινόμενα, *phainomena*) everything is in a perpetual state of starting again: "What visible good lasts unchanged? The sun goes round its own course, bringing light and darkness in turn.... The sea is a receptacle for the confluence of waters from every direction, and neither does the confluence cease, nor does the sea increase."[31] We see from this that the law of nature is to conserve energy; everything always balances out. There is never any progress, or newness. By contrast, we shall in due course discover that it is precisely the concept of progress that underlies Gregory's understanding of the spiritual life.[32]

Thus he who becomes attached to appearances submits to their law and becomes the dupe of an everlasting mirage of desires that are continually reborn

---

[28]Plotinus, *Enneads* 4.3.17.

[29]*Cant.* 10 (PG 44:993C; Norris, 329). In Gregory, γοητεία (*goēteia*) always has an unfavorable meaning. See *Vit. Moys.* 68 (PG 44:344C); *Bas.* (PG 44:792C; McCambly, 14). We know that in his day—the century of Iamblichus and Julian the Apostate—magic and theurgy enjoyed a revival of favor. See also Methodius of Olympus, *Symposium* 6.5 (Bonwetsch, 70; ANF 6:330–31).

[30]H.-Ch. Puech, "Position spirituelle et signification de Plotin," *Bulletin de l'Asociation Guillaume Budé* 61 (Oct. 1938): 13–46, at 28.

[31]*Eccl.* 1 (PG 44:624D–625A; Hall, 38). It is a quotation from Ecclesiastes 1.5–7.

[32]See Vl. Jankélévitch, *La mauvaise conscience* (Paris: Alcan, 1933), 76.

and continually disappointed. Gregory describes this mirage by means of two striking images. The first, from *The Life of Moses*, is that of brick making:

> Those who yearn after the pleasures of clay and keep on filling themselves with them never keep the space which receives them full; for although it is always being filled, it becomes empty again before the next pouring. In the same way the brick maker keeps on throwing yet more clay into the mould while it is constantly being emptied. I think that anyone can easily perceive the meaning of this figure by looking at the appetitive part of the soul. For if he who fills his desire in one of the things which he pursues should then incline his desire to something else, he finds himself empty again in that regard. And if he should fill himself on this, he becomes empty and a vacant container once more for something else. And we never stop doing this until we depart from this material life.[33]

Equally striking is the image of a sand dune: "Those who toil endlessly as they climb uphill" find that "their footing in the sand always slips away downhill."[34] A sand dune is indeed an effective illustration of the endless movement of matter—a movement without progress, a perpetual dispersion, an unmitigated multiplicity. This metaphor of sand typifies the fundamental instability of material goods, and understandably Gregory takes it up again elsewhere: "Any interest which people have in worldly things is quite simply the same as children's toys of sand [νηπίων τὰ ἐπὶ ψάμμον ἀθύρματα, *nēpiōn ta epi psammon athyrmata*], in which the enjoyment of the products ends with the interest in their construction. As soon as they cease from their toil, the sand collapses, leaving behind no trace of what the children worked at."[35]

This fundamental instability of the sensible world—which is a manifestation of its unreality or, to be more precise, of its lack of reality—can be fully understood when compared with what really exists: namely, the order of grace. This is the reality that the Preacher contrasts with the illusion of the purely natural life:

> It is as if as a consequence of what we have been told we were to put an objection to him and say, "If everything is futility, it is clear that not even one of these things which do not exist [οὐχ ὑφέστηκεν, *ouch hyphestēken*]

---

[33] *Vit. Moys.* 2.60–61 (PG 44:344A; Malherbe, 68).
[34] *Vit. Moys.* 2.244 (PG 44:405C; Malherbe, 117).
[35] *Eccl.* 1 (PG 44:628C; Hall, 41).

The Ladder of Love

has come to be. For the futile is totally without reality [ἀνύπαρκτον, *anyparkton*], and one would not reckon the unreal among things that have come to be. If indeed these things do not exist, tell us, what is it that came to be and continues in existence?"

He has an immediate answer to the question: "Do you wish to know what it is that came to be? Think what it is that will be, and you will know what has been." That is: "Think, you human being," he says, "what you will become by elevating yourself through virtue.... If you carefully consider this with your mind, you have been taught what came to be in the beginning, which indeed will truly come to be, what is *in the image and likeness of God*."[36]

This important text teaches us that what is real in the human order is the world of the εἰκών, (*eikōn*, image [of God]); that is to say, the order of the supernatural life that existed in the beginning, which is man's true reality, and which the spiritual life aims to restore. "The resurrection [ἀνάστασις, *anastasis*] of the dead is nothing but the complete restoration of the original state [ἀποκατάστασις εἰς τὸ ἀρχαῖον, *apokatastasis eis to archaion*]."[37] Man's original state was abolished by sin, but can be recovered by grace. This is the subject matter of the fifth section of the Psalter: "For in the preceding section he investigated many things philosophically [φιλοσοφήσας, *philosophēsas*] concerning the changeable and the unchangeable by means of the voice of Moses. He considered how the one always continues to be what it is, but the other is always in the process of becoming what it is not.... He now reveals [ἀνακαλύπτει, *anakalyptei*] in many ways in his discourse all the grace [χάριν, *charin*] of God."[38] This contrast between philosophy and revelation—the revelation of reality—is significant. Philosophy can succeed in gaining knowledge of the nothingness of that which is—and for Gregory this is, in fact, its proper function—but it is unable by its own means to identify Being.

Clearly, Gregory's *Homilies on Ecclesiastes*—of which there are eight in all—is the treatise that corresponds exactly to this understanding of philosophy.[39] It

---

[36]Ibid. (PG 44:633A–B; Hall, 44–45).

[37]Ibid. (PG 44:633C; Hall, 45).

[38]*Inscr.* 1.8.77–78 (PG 44:468A; Heine, 109). [Gregory interprets the Psalter as being in five parts, corresponding to stages of the spiritual ascent. Part Five begins with Psalm 106.—*Trans.*]

[39]On the philosophical character of Ecclesiastes, see *Eccl.* 6 (PG 44:697C–D; Hall, 100). For observations concerning the ancient Greek philosophical concepts of "Nothing in excess" (μηδὲν ἄγαν, *mēden agan*), "fitting behavior" (καθῆκον, *kathēkon*), and virtue as the correct middle way, see *Eccl.* 7 (PG 44:724D; Hall, 120). Likewise, for the idea of "harmony" (συμφωνία, *symphōnia*), see ibid. (PG 44:725B; Hall, 121); for evil as non-being, *Eccl.* 6 (PG 44:708C; Hall, 108); for primitive communism, ibid. (PG

contains a series of diatribes (διαβολαί, *diabolai*), of accusations (κατηγορίαι, *katēgoriai*) brought against the various types of illusion (ἀπάται, *apatai*) by which people are taken in. The first is that of material goods and riches, which affords Gregory the opportunity to give a long, descriptive ekphrasis of villas and gardens. "What need of gardens has he who looks to the one Garden [παραδείσῳ, *paradeisō*]?"[40]

The next homily deals with arrogance (ὑπερηφανία, *hyperēphania*). It is a long, striking diatribe against man's self-conceited desire to prevail over others, and is especially critical of slavery. "How many obols did you reckon the equivalent of the [image] of God?"[41] With this very important point, we have the contrast that governs the entire treatise: namely, that between the futility and vanity of material goods and the reality of spiritual goods, summed up in the term "image." In this striking contrast between two orders of reality, the homily attains an impressive, unexpected eloquence.

The final two homilies are particularly noteworthy in this regard. They are a commentary on the following two verses: "A time to keep silence and a time to speak" [Eccl 3.7] and "There is a time to love and a time to hate" [Eccl 3.8]. In effect, this is a critique of the mind and the will, when they are dealing with apparent goods. The seventh homily is Gregory's most powerful account of the radical inability of the intelligence, enclosed as it is in its "aeon"—that is, within the categories of space and time—to attain to true reality, which is outside time and space. There is, however, a surprisingly tragic side to the homily. For, having shown that the world of appearances is unreal, he now demonstrates that it is with such a world that the human mind is commensurate. (This is the critique that Kant will make.) Yet, on the other hand, man is made for reality and cannot live without it. Hence the dizziness (ἴλιγγος, *ilingos*) that Gregory describes, and from which man will not be able to escape without going beyond the ways of intellection, to the way of love, ecstasy, and the mystical life.

> Because everything that is in creation looks toward what is naturally akin to it, and nothing that is, if it gets outside itself, remains in being.... How could

---

44:709; Hall, 108–109); and for a cynical portrait of the evils of life, *Eccl.* 7 (PG 44:724C–D; Hall, 120). The text also discusses the possibility of a return to God by means of the visible world. See too the diatribes against slavery and riches. The sources are varied—the Stoics, Aristotle, Plato, the Cynics, and Posidonius—presenting a clear example of Hellenistic eclecticism.

[40] *Eccl.* 3 (PG 44:661B; Hall, 69).

[41] *Eccl.* 4 (PG 44:665A; Hall, 74). For the influence of the cynic diatribe on the writers of Gregory's time, see Nock's introduction to Sallustius, *Concerning the Gods*, xxvii.

The Ladder of Love

our understanding, which moves about within extended space, comprehend what has no extension? ... It is like a person who finds himself on a mountain [ἀκρωρεία, akrōreia]—suppose it is a sheer precipitous rock face, which in its lower part stretches up with a vertical smooth surface for a vast distance, and high above rises that peak, which from its beetling crag plunges down to an immense depth—what he is likely to experience when with his toe he feels the ridge overhanging the drop and finds neither foothold nor handhold—that, I believe, is the experience of the soul when it goes beyond what is accessible to time-bound thoughts in search of what is before time and has no extension. Having nothing to catch hold of, neither place, nor time, nor space, nor anything else of the kind which offers a foothold to our intellect, but slipping in all directions from what it cannot grasp [ἰλιγγιᾷ τε καὶ ἀμηχανεῖ, ilingia te kai amēchanei].[42]

This striking passage demonstrates the clash that ensues when Gregory's theory of knowledge encounters his diatribe. On the one hand, his metaphysical standpoint is that the mind can know only the sensible;[43] on the other, his moral position is that the sensible is nothing, a mere illusion, a mirage. Hence the soul sees all its hopes dashed and finds itself without help. Yet it is from this very shock that mystical theology will emerge. For Gregory, as for Kierkegaard, the beginning of true philosophy is not curiosity but despair (ἀνελπιστία, anelpistia).[44] It is hopelessness that thrusts him outside the cyclical world of the "eternal return"—the world of sensible phenomena—to make him turn to the faith from which help will come.

To Gregory's critique of reason corresponds his critique of the will. He contrasts sensory love (φιλία, philia) with spiritual love (ἀγάπη, agapē), which focuses on God, and once again stresses the vanity of sensory things: "All the other things which are in sensual terms good ... seem good because of deluded thought [οἴησις, oiēsis]."[45] Now the distinctive feature of love is to bring about union. "Whatever may be the nature of what is shared, what shares in it must conform."[46] Thus, "love [ἡ ἀγαπητικὴ σχέσις, hē agapētikē schesis] works physical union [φυσικῶς τὴν ἀνάκρασιν, physikōs tēn anakrasin] with the beloved

[42] *Eccl.* 7 (PG 44:729A–732A; Hall, 125–26).
[43] On the Stoic sources of Gregory's theory of knowledge, see von Ivánka, "Vom Platonismus," 178–85.
[44] See *Cant.* 12 (PG 44:1037B; Norris, 389); *Vit. Moys.* 2.117 (PG 44:360D; Malherbe, 82).
[45] *Eccl.* 8 (PG 44:737B; Hall, 132).
[46] Ibid. (PG 44:737D; ibid.).

[τὸ ἀγαπώμενον, *to agapōmenon*]. That is why the one who always exists [ὁ ἀεὶ ὤν, *ho aei ōn*] offered himself to us as food so that, having received it in us, we become what he is. He says indeed 'My flesh is really food, and my blood is really drink'" (Jn 6.55).[47]

This passage is significant in the first place in showing how, for Gregory, the path of love (ἀγάπη, *agapē*) and of union (ἀνάκρασις, *anakrasis*) is open-ended, while that of *gnōsis* (knowledge) is closed. It is this primacy of love, and hence of the mystical life, that is the major characteristic feature of his doctrine. Second, it shows the similarity of his ontology and his Christology. Real being, which seemed abstract, is to be identified with the historical and mystical Christ. Finally, we note the link that is established between *agapē* and the Eucharist—which is itself the sacrament of union, of love. Thus, there is a special relationship between the Eucharist and the mystical life. These are ideas to which we shall return later.

The closing pages of the *Homilies on Ecclesiastes* bring us, then, to the threshold of the mystical life. In the *Homilies on the Song of Songs,* which are dedicated precisely to this, the journey continues: "Having in this way purified the heart of its bent toward appearances, [Wisdom] then, in the Song of Songs, initiates the mind into the innermost divine sanctuary."[48] However, before broaching this higher form of the spiritual life, there remain certain stages that we must first survey. But before we leave Gregory's critique of the sensible world, we need to raise the following important point. We have observed more than once that Gregory's diatribe against appearances resembles the Platonic disparagement of the sensible world. Indeed, everything we have seen up to now seems to entail an outright condemnation of it. Yet is this an accurate account of what he really thinks? Such Platonism was always the pitfall of Gregory's thought, as he himself realized. Here, at the beginning of his *Homilies on Ecclesiastes*, is how he responds to the objection:

> Let no one suppose that [my] words are an indictment [κατηγορία, *katēgoria*] of creation. For surely the charge would also implicate him who has made all things, if the one who constructed all things from nothing were manifested to us as a creator of this kind, if indeed all things were futility. But since man's nature is twofold, soul combining with body ... the words of the Ecclesiast point to this truth, that one ought not to look to this life of the senses, which

[47]*Eccl.* 8 (PG 44:737D–740A; ibid.).
[48]*Cant.* 1 (PG 44:769D; Norris, 23).

compared with the true life is unreal and unsubstantial [ἀνύπαρκτον καὶ ἀνυπόστατον, *anyparkton kai anypostaton*].

One might nevertheless say that even this argument is not without reproach to the Creator, since he is the source both of the soul and the body. . . . But surely these will be the words of one who has not yet escaped from the flesh. . . . For anyone trained in the divine mysteries is surely aware that the life conformed to the divine nature is proper and natural to mankind, while the life of sense-perception, lived through the activity of the senses, has been granted to that nature in order that the knowledge [γνῶσις, *gnōsis*] of the visible world might become a guide to the soul for knowledge [ἐπίγνωσις, *epignōsis*] of things unseen [ἀόρατα, *aorata*].[49]

Gregory does try to avoid the danger, then, but in a manner that may disconcert us. In fact, for him, the sensible does not form part of human nature. Man's true nature (φύσις, *physis*) is what it was in the beginning—the εἰκών (*eikōn*), the image of God. The sensory life was added, not as the result of the fall—hence it is not bad—but by a merciful plan (φιλανθρωπία, *philanthrōpia*; lit. love for man), in order that we might avoid greater evils. Indeed, it is this that enables man to ascend to knowledge of God and the invisible world. Sensory nature is alien, then, to real human nature, and is destined to be cast aside. But at the same time it has a temporary usefulness, and because of this God escapes condemnation (κατηγορία, *katēgoria*).

We discussed this interesting interpretation of original sin earlier, in connection with the garments of skin. It results in the belief that the sensory life is good and has meaning, not in itself but only as an instrument: it is a means of approaching God. What is certainly wrong is to stop short at the visible, as Gregory explains in the following passage from *On Virginity*: "Accordingly, in the seeking of the beautiful, the person who is superficial in his thought, when

[49]*Eccl.* 1 (PG 44:621D–624B; Hall, 36–37). [Similar language can be found in Plotinus, who claims in *Enneads* 4.8.7 that the soul, though it is better to be in the noetic realm (ἄμεινον μὲν ψυχῇ ἐν τῷ νοητῷ εἶναι, *ameinon men psyche en tō noētō einai*), is by necessity (ἀνάγκη, *anangkē*) a participant in the realm of the senses also, since it occupies the lowest or last place in the noetic realm (ἐν ἐσχάτῳ δὲ τοῦ νοητοῦ οὖσαν, *en eschatō de tou noētou ousan*), on the border of the sensory nature (ὅμορον οὖσαν τῇ αἰσθητῇ φύσει, *homoron ousan tē aisthētē physei*), a sort of intermediate rank (μέσην τάξιν, *mesēn taxin*) in the chain of being; nevertheless, this itself can be beneficial, and the soul can attain to clearer knowledge of the good (Γνῶσις . . . ἐναργεστέρα τἀγαθοῦ, *Gnōsis . . . enargestera tagathou*) through experience of evil (ἡ τοῦ κακοῦ πεῖρα, *hē tou kakou peira*) in the realm of the senses. Yet there is also a scriptural allusion here in the same sentence: "For from the creation of the world the invisible things [τὰ . . . ἀόρατα, *ta . . . aorata*] of him are clearly seen, being understood by the things that are made—his eternal power and divinity—so that they are without excuse" (Rom 1.20).—*Ed.*]

he sees something in which fantasy is mixed with some beauty, will think that the thing itself is beautiful. . . . But the man who has purified the eye of his soul is able to look at such things and forget the matter in which the beauty is encased, and he uses what he sees as a kind of basis [ὑποβάθρα, *hypobathra*] for his contemplation of intelligible beauty."[50]

This brings us to a new point of view. We have seen that the initial objective of the second or illuminative way was to detach the soul from the world of appearances by revealing their illusory and unreal character. Now the soul is taught how to use this information so as to ascend to knowledge of the real world. And so we arrive at a second stage, which is the beginning of contemplation: namely, symbolic theology, to which the conclusion of the book of Ecclesiastes invites us:

> In just the same way, he says, I know that each thing comes from God for all good, as long as use is made of it at the right moment for a proper purpose, but the perversion of right judgment about reality turns good things into the beginning of evils. What sort of thing do I mean? What is more pleasant than the activity of the eyes? Yet the sight becomes an agent of passion to such persons, what was made as a benefit is said to have become the cause of evil. . . . It is the same with everything else which nature gets from God—it depends on the choice of persons concerned whether it becomes the material for good or evil. Therefore, he says, all things which he made are good at his right moment.
>
> He also gave together time [τὸν αἰῶνα, *ton aiōna*; often "eternity," see Eccl 3.11] in their heart. Time, which is a dimensional idea [νόημα διαστηματικόν, *noēma diastēmatikon*], by itself signifies the whole creation which comes about in it. Because by referring to the container the sentence points to everything contained in it. Thus everything which exists in time God gave to the human heart for good, so that by the greatness and beauty of created things it may contemplate [ἀναθεωρεῖ, *anatheōrei*] thereby the Creator (Wis 3.5).[51]

---

[50] *Virg.* 11 (PG 46:364B-C; FC 58:38–39).

[51] *Eccl.* 8 (PG 44:752C-D; Hall, 142–43). The *Homilies on Ecclesiastes* end with this chapter, but it is continued in the *Catena Trium Patrum*. As this has not yet been published, we have been unable to consult it. See R. Devreesse, "Chaînes exégétiques grecques," *Dictionnaire de la Bible*, Supplément I (Paris : Letouzey et Ané, 1928), col. 1163. [Scholars now regard the eight homilies as a complete unit. The *Catena Trium Patrum* combines material from Gregory's eight homilies with commentary by Nilus of Ancyra and Maximus the Confessor. See *Anonymus in Ecclesiasten commentarius qui dicitur catena trium patrum*, ed. Santo Lucà, Corpus Christianorum, Series Graeca 11 (Turnhout : Brepols, 1983).—Ed]

Symbolic Theology

In his *Homilies on the Song of Songs*, Gregory identifies three major ways in the spiritual life by associating them, as we have seen, with three great Mosaic symbols. These are the light of the Burning Bush, representing separation from evil and error; darkness (γνόφος, *gnophos*), which denotes the mystical life proper; and, between the two, the cloud (νεφέλη, *nephelē*), which—in a sentence that we have already quoted—Gregory describes as follows: "More attentive apprehension [προσεχεστέρα κατανόησις, *prosechestera katanoēsis*] of hidden realities, which leads the soul to the invisible realm by way of what appears [φαινόμενα, *phainomena*], is like a cloud that casts a shadow on everything that appears but yet induces and accustoms the soul to look upon what is hidden."[52] The cloud, then, represents an intermediary stage between light and darkness. It has two aspects: an obscuring of the visible—this being the aspect we have just studied—but also, even at this stage, the acquiring of a certain amount of knowledge of God. To this we shall now turn.

If we refer to *The Life of Moses*, which develops this symbolism at greater length, we are initially somewhat disconcerted. For between the episode of the Bush and the darkness there seems to be an additional stage. The crossing of the desert, under the guidance of the cloud, accords well with part of the above description—the obscuring of what is sensible and a getting accustomed to the spiritual life. But before Moses finally enters the darkness, there is an important interruption—namely, the arrival at Mount Sinai. Does this arrival itself mark the beginning of the contemplative life? Yet we already know that access to it is symbolized by the darkness. Therefore we must conclude that what separates the beginning of the ascent of Sinai from entry into this darkness constitutes a distinct, specific realm.

It is one that falls well short of the mystical life proper. Still, bearing this in mind, we shall discuss it here, for it does fall within the scope of θεογνωσία (*theognōsia*, knowledge of God). Thus, what we have here is an intermediary stage and it is important to know what kind of contemplation this is. The texts cited above provide us with some information. It is a question of "a knowledge which leads the soul to the invisible realm by way of what appears [φαινόμενα, *phainomena*]." The important word here is *phainomena*. In the next line Gregory says that the darkness corresponds, on the contrary, to a knowledge of God that is *beyond* appearances (ἔξω τοῦ φαινομένου, *exō tou phainomenou*).

---

[52]*Cant.* 11 (PG 44:1000D; Norris, 341).

Referring once more to *The Life of Moses*, we find confirmation that this acquisition of the knowledge of God through phenomena takes place, according to Gregory, precisely between the beginning of the ascent of Sinai and entry into the darkness. It is expressed by the symbolism of the trumpets, whose sound becomes ever clearer:

> For it seems to me that in another sense the heavenly trumpet becomes a teacher to the one ascending. . . . For the wonderful harmony of the heavens proclaims the wisdom [σοφία, *sophia*] that shines forth in the creation and sets forth the great glory of God through the things which are seen, in keeping with the statement, *The heavens declare the glory of God* (Ps 19.1). It becomes the loud sounding trumpet of clear and melodious teaching, as one of the prophets says, *The heavens trumpeted from above* (Sir 46.17).[53]
>
> When he who has been purified and is sharp of hearing in his heart hears this sound—I am speaking of the knowledge of the divine power which comes from the contemplation of reality [θεωρία τῶν ὄντων, *theōria tōn ontōn*]—he is led by it to the place where his intelligence lets him slip in [διαδυῆ, *diadyē*] where God is. This is called *darkness* by the Scripture.[54]

This passage enables us to define exactly what kind of contemplation is meant. It is not a matter of dialectic knowledge, of a proof of God's existence from the order existing in the world. Besides, such reasoning is foreign to Gregory, and what Rahner says of Origen—"that all knowledge of God has a mystical coloring with him"[55]—is also true for Gregory. It is a matter of contemplation. In fact, to arrive at this stage, asceticism is first required. More precisely, it is necessary that "the ear of the soul be purified." Yet at the same time, this is not knowledge through faith—for that will only begin with the darkness—but a knowledge of God through visible things (διὰ φαινομένων, *dia phainomenōn*). It starts with contemplation of the visible world (θεωρία τῶν ὄντων, *theōria tōn ontōn*) and from this derives knowledge of the divine power (γνῶσις τῆς δυνάμεως, *gnōsis tes dynameōs*).

The objective of this contemplation is to extract from sensible objects knowledge of the divine attributes—δύναμις (*dynamis*, power), σοφία (*sophia*, wisdom)—that are revealed in them. It presupposes detachment from all that is

---

[53] [Lit., "The Lord thundered from heaven."—*Trans.*]
[54] *Vit. Moys.* 2.168–69 (PG 44:377D–380A; Malherbe, 96–97).
[55] Rahner, "Le début d'une doctrine," 135.

sensory—a "night of the senses"—but not from the intelligible, not a "night of the mind." Thus, it is clearly an intellectual form of knowledge. Later will come the explicit transcending of such intelligible notions as these, formed on the basis of phenomena, as the intellect is left behind for the place called "darkness."

This is of the greatest importance, for here we grasp the distinction between two kinds of theology: symbolic and apophatic. Of these, Dionysius will later give systematic expositions. His treatise *On the Divine Names* deals with symbolic knowledge, whereas his *Mystical Theology* focuses on the realm of darkness, the negation of all things, and the introduction to a supra-rational mode of knowing. Now this distinction is already made by Gregory:

> What the Deity is not, the signification of these names ["incorruptible," "infinite," "unbegotten"] does point out; but what that further thing, which is not these things, is essentially, remains undivulged. Moreover, even the rest of these names, the sense of which does indicate some position or some state [ἐνδεικτικὴ θέσεως, *endeiktikē theseōs*], do not afford that indication of the Divine nature itself, but only of the results of our reverent speculations about it [θεωρούμενα περὶ αὐτήν, *theōroumena peri autēn*].[56]

The above passage makes clear the proper subject of symbolic theology. It does not deal with God's essence (οὐσία, *ousia*)—for that is entirely unknowable—but with the ideas one can form of him by analogy with his creatures: namely, the positive, divine attributes of wisdom and power, which, as seen earlier, Gregory gives as the subject of *gnōsis*. It is not a case of pure imagination or of inventions (ἐπίνοιαι, *epinoiai*), as Eunomius had said, for these divine names are true. They teach us something about God. Thus, the domain of symbolic theology is clearly defined, both as to its method and its subject: it presupposes the night of the senses—an elevation above the sensible creation—and deals with the divine attributes. Apophatic theology, on the other hand, presupposes the night of the mind and has as object the divine *essence*.

Furthermore, these two stages are clearly indicated in *The Life of Moses*. At the foot of Mount Sinai, before beginning the ascent and before hearing the sound of the trumpets, the animals must be driven away from the mountain. This signifies, Gregory says, "that in the contemplation of the intelligibles [ἡ

---

[56] *Eun.* 2.582 (PG 45:1105C; NPNF² 5:308). On Pseudo-Dionysius, see Vladimir Lossky, "La théologie négative dans la doctrine de Denys l'Aréopagite," *Revue des Sciences Philosophiques et Théologiques* (April 1939): 204–221, at 207–208.

τῶν νοητῶν θεωρία, *hē tōn noetōn theōria*] we surpass the knowledge which originates with the senses. . . . He who would approach the knowledge of things sublime must first . . . withdraw himself from his customary intercourse with his own companion, that is, with his sense perceptions. . . . When he is so purified, then he assaults the mountain."[57] Here it is a question only of the night of the senses. The night of the mind will come later, after hearing the trumpets, with the entrance into the darkness: "For leaving behind everything that is observed, not only what sense comprehends but also what the intelligence thinks it sees, it keeps on penetrating deeper until . . . it gains access to the invisible and the incomprehensible, and there it sees God."[58]

This is a theme we frequently find in Gregory. The most explicit example is again to be found in *The Life of Moses*. It is of particular interest since it clearly contrasts the night of the senses with the night of the mind and links the former directly to a symbolic knowledge of God. It will enable us to give other texts their correct meaning.

After describing the ablutions and purifications that are necessary for the soul that wants "to have access to a contemplation of realities [ἡ τῶν ὄντων θεωρία, *hē tōn ontōn theōria*]," Gregory continues as follows:

> When this had been accomplished and the herd of irrational animals had been driven as far from the mountain as possible, Moses [the soul] then approached the ascent to lofty perceptions. That none of the irrational animals was allowed to appear on the mountain signifies, in my opinion, that in the contemplation of the intelligibles we surpass the knowledge which originates with the senses. For it is characteristic of the nature of irrational animals that they are governed by the senses alone, divorced from understanding. . . .
>
> The contemplation of God is not effected by sight and hearing, nor is it comprehended by any of the customary perceptions of the mind. . . . He who would approach the knowledge of things sublime must first purify his manner of life from all sensual and irrational emotion. He must first wash from his understanding every opinion [δόξα, *doxa*] derived from some preconception [πρόληψις, *prolepsis*] and withdraw himself from his customary intercourse with his own companion, that is, with his sense

---

[57] *Vit. Moys.* 2.156–57 (PG 44:373D; Malherbe, 93).
[58] *Vit. Moys.* 2.163 (PG 44:376D–377A; Malherbe, 95).

The Ladder of Love

perceptions [αἴσθησις, *aisthēsis*]. . . . When he is so purified, then he assaults the mountain.[59]

We note here the various words used to designate contemplation: contemplation of the realities (ὄντων, *ontōn*), of the intelligibles (νοητῶν, *noētōn*), and of God. Here we have the subject matter of *theologia*. Since it is of a spiritual order, it naturally eludes the grasp of the senses. Thus, the soul will have to progress beyond the knowledge that comes through the senses (τὴν γνῶσιν ἐξ αἰσθήσεως γενομένην, *tēn gnōsin ex aisthēseōs genomenēn*), which Gregory also calls opinions formed by induction (τὴν ἐκ προλήψεως δόξαν, *tēn ek prolēpseōs doxan*). For that, the soul must be separated from intimacy with the body, so that it operates in a purely spiritual fashion through the exercise of the reason.

It is interesting to compare this night of the senses with certain passages in Plato or Plotinus. Plato, too, requires that, in order to know the intelligible realities (νοητά, *noēta*), the mind should separate itself (χωρίζειν, *chōrizein*) from intimacy with the body: "We shall be closest to knowledge in this way—if we consort with the body as little as possible, and do not commune with it, except in so far as we must, and do not infect ourselves with its nature, but remain pure from it."[60] Plotinus develops the same concept: "The purification of the Soul is simply to allow it to be alone; it is pure when it keeps no company; when it looks to nothing without itself; when it entertains no alien thoughts [δόξαι, *doxai*]. . . . Separation [χωρισμός, *chōrismos*], in the same way, is the condition of a soul no longer entering into the body to lie at its mercy."[61] There is here a definite point of contact between Platonism and Gregory's theology, in the sense that the words used are the same—separation (χωρισμός, *chōrismos*), purification (κάθαρσις, *katharsis*)—and the things of which the soul must purify itself are in both cases the δόξαι (*doxai*, opinions) arising from the sensible world and with which they are bound up.

We find this night of the senses—a necessary preamble to *theologia*—in other passages. For example, although the *Homilies on the Song of Songs* focus primarily on the second part of *theologia*—namely, θεογνωσία (*theognōsia*), knowledge of a more mystical kind—nonetheless, in his preface, Gregory does describe the necessary preliminary purifications. They are the ablutions (περιρραντήρια,

---

[59]*Vit. Moys.* 2.156–57 (PG 44:373C–D; Malherbe, 93).
[60]Plato, *Phaedo* 67a. Translation from *Plato: Phaedo*, trans. David Gallop (Oxford: Oxford University Press, 1993), 13. See also 80c.
[61]Plotinus, *Enneads* 3.6.5.

perirrantēria) prescribed by Moses: "And just as Israel, at Mount Sinai, was prepared beforehand for two days by rites of purification and then, at dawn on the third day, was judged worthy of the theophany [θεοφάνεια, *theophaneia*] ... so now, in our own case, the insight into the prefatory parts of the Song of Songs that we achieved ... in our earlier homilies has been of profit to the extent that the sense contained in the words has been washed and scrubbed to remove the filth of the flesh."[62] Here it is principally a question of the spiritual meaning, but the thought is the same. A little earlier in the book, Gregory had written: "For every irrational idea that shows itself in the neighborhood of such a mountain will be done to death by more solid thoughts as by so many stones. Scarcely even in this way shall we be able to bear the voice of that trumpet."[63]

Similarly, in his description (in *Against Eunomius*) of the migration of Abraham, Gregory draws attention to the fact that his spiritual progress is characterized by successive stages:

> He, I say, went out by Divine command from his own country and kindred on a journey worthy of a prophet eager for the knowledge of God. For no local migration seems to me to satisfy the idea of the blessings which it is signified that he found. For going out from himself and from his country, by which I understand his earthly and carnal mind, and raising his thoughts as far as possible above the common boundaries of nature, and forsaking the soul's kinship [τὴν συγγένειαν, *tēn syngeneian*] with the senses [πρὸς τὰς αἰσθήσεις, *pros tas aisthēseis*]—so that untroubled by any of the objects of sense his eyes might be open to the things which are invisible, there being neither sight nor sound to distract the mind in its work—"walking," as saith the Apostle, "by faith, not by sight" [2 Cor 5.7], he was raised so high by the sublimity of his knowledge that he came to be regarded as the acme of human perfection, knowing as much of God as it was possible for finite human capacity at its full stretch to attain.[64]

As in *The Life of Moses*, it is a question of a night of the senses. "Let each depart [ἐκβάς, *ekbas*] from himself," writes Gregory elsewhere, "and get beyond the material cosmos."[65]

---

[62]*Cant.* 3 (PG 44:809A; Norris, 79–81).
[63]*Cant.* 1 (PG 44:773; Norris, 29).
[64]*Eun.* 2.84–96 (PG 45:940 B–C; NPNF² 5:259). On the spiritual interpretation of the migration of Abraham, see Philo, *On the Migration of Abraham* 32.177–81 (Yonge, 270); *On Abraham* 15.69–72 (Yonge, 417); *Who is the Heir of Divine Things* 20.97–99 (Yonge, 284). Also Origen, *Homilies on Genesis* 3.3.
[65]*Cant.* 1 (PG 44:772D; Norris, 27).

The Ladder of Love

As the spirit is purified, it rises above sensory appearances to a contemplation of the invisible realities they manifest—the ἐκβάς (*ekbas*, outgoing or departure), the *onta* [(truly) existing things—*Ed.*]. We will have to clarify their nature. At first glance it seemed that we were dealing with the divine attributes, the divine ἐνέργειαι (*energeiai*, energies) and δυνάμεις (*dynameis*, powers), which are seen in the visible creation. Purified of all that is sensory, the eye of the soul contemplates the divine attributes by extracting them from the contingent phenomena through which they appear. Gregory frequently describes this approach to contemplation that leads to symbolic theology, to knowledge of the divine names. We have seen that this was the meaning of the allegory of the trumpets that sounded in the ears of the purified soul, proclaiming divine wisdom and power. But other passages reveal the same approach.

In the sixth homily on the Beatitudes, Gregory expresses the amazement of the soul at Christ's promise that those who are pure in heart will see God, and he wonders whether such a vision is possible. He recognizes two modes of vision: the first being knowledge of God through the visible world; the second, that seen in the mirror of the pure soul. This corresponds to the two stages of the ascent of Sinai. The second type of knowledge is already of the order of mystical knowledge, as the descriptive terms Gregory uses indicate. But for the moment I do not wish to dwell on this parallelism. What is of importance at this juncture is what Gregory says concerning the knowledge of God gained through the visible world. "The Divine Nature, whatever It may be in Itself, surpasses every mental conception.... But it is possible to see Him who has 'made all things in wisdom' (Ps 103.24) by way of inference [στοχαστικῶς, *stochastikōs*] through the wisdom that appears in the universe [τῷ παντί, *tō panti*]."[66]

This text points to the contrast already noted between God's essence, on the one hand, and his attributes. It is the latter that belong to the domain of symbolic theology. Gregory compares the universe to a work that allows one to know not the nature but the art of the workman. And he adds:

> Thus also, when we look at the order of creation, we form in our mind an image not of the essence, but of the wisdom of Him who has made all things wisely. And if we consider the cause of our life, that He came to create man not from necessity, but from the free decision of His Goodness, we say that we have contemplated God by this way, that we have apprehended

[66] *Beat.* 6 (PG 44:1268B–C; ACW 18:146).

His Goodness—though again not His Essence, but His Goodness. It is the same with all the other things that raise the mind to transcendent Goodness, all these we can term apprehensions of God, since each one of these sublime meditations places God within our sight. For power, purity, constancy [ὡσαύτως ἔχειν, *hōsautōs echein*], freedom from contrariety—all these engrave on the soul the impress of a Divine and transcendent Mind. Hence it is clear through what has just been said that the Lord speaks the truth when He promises that God will be seen by those who have a pure heart; nor does Paul deceive when he asserts in his letters that no one has seen God nor can see Him [1 Tim 6.16]. For He is invisible by nature, but becomes visible in His energies, for he may be contemplated in the things that are referred to Him [τισι περὶ αὐτόν, *tisi peri auton*].[67]

The same vocabulary that we have already seen reappears: it is a question of a vision or contemplation of the divine energies—Goodness, Purity, and Constancy. These are realities that are not of God's essence, but that are περὶ αὐτόν (*peri auton*, around him). Eastern theology will later develop this distinction and will allow in God, alongside the unknowable essence, energies that are genuinely distinct and are the subject of symbolic knowledge.[68] We can see here how this doctrine has its first beginnings in Gregory of Nyssa.

In the *Homilies on the Song of Songs*—in another of the digressions with which he is lavish, especially in this work—Gregory analyzes this vision of God through the visible world at considerable length. He is commenting on the following text: "My beloved put forth his hand by the hole [of the door]" (Song 5.4) To Gregory's mind, this hand evokes creative activity:

> When, therefore, cleansed [ἐκκαθαρθεῖσα, *ekkatharteisa*] as soon as possible of her inclination toward a gross and earthly life, the soul looks up with the help of virtue toward what is akin to her [συγγενές, *syggenes*] and closer to the divine, she never stops searching and seeking after the Principle of the

---

[67]Gregory, *Beat.* 6 (PG 44:1268D–1269A; ACW 18:147).
[68]Thanks no doubt to his contacts with Myrrha Lot-Borodine and Vladimir Lossky and their work, Daniélou clearly has St Gregory Palamas in mind.—*Trans.* For a treatment of the history of the use of *energia* as a term and concept from pre-Christian philosophical roots, mediated through Philo and the Neoplatonists, continuing in the patristic era, and finally most fully articulated in the theology of St Gregory Palamas in the east, in contradistinction to Thomas Aquinas in the west, see David Bradshaw, *Aristotle East and West: Metaphysics and the Division of Christendom* (Cambridge: Cambridge University Press, 2004); for the Cappadocian contribution, see pp. 156–78; for the subsequent flowering of the eastern tradition, see pp. 179–220; for a comparative analysis of Palamas and Aquinas, see pp. 221–62.—*Ed.*

The Ladder of Love

things that are, after the Wellspring of their beauty, after the Source of the power that fills them, after whatever it is that pours forth the wisdom displayed in them.... When she stretches herself out from things below toward the knowledge of things on high, once she has grasped [καταλαβοῦσα, *katalabousa*] the marvels produced by God's working, she cannot for a while progress further by her busy search for knowledge, but is filled with wonder and worships the One who is known to exist only through the things that his activity brings about.

She sees the beauty of the heavens, the radiance of the lights, the precise revolution of the celestial sphere ... the earth adapting itself to what encompasses it and changing its own doings in accord with the variance in the motion of the heavens. She also sees, among living things, [their] multiform natures ... the plants in their unnumbered forms.... The soul, then, seeing these and other phenomena through which the working of God is signified, reckons [ἀναλογίζεται, *analogizetai*], on account of their marvelous character, that the One who is apprehended through his work in fact exists.[69]

This is entirely in line with the Stoic contemplation of God through the wonders of the world. It is also consistent with what was said earlier, when we discussed the night of the senses. It is a question of the kind of knowledge that is accessible to a purified soul: namely, an analogous (ἀναλογίζεται, *analogizetai*) type that achieves a certain understanding of the divine perfections by means of visible phenomena.[70] But there is an upper limit to such knowledge that the human mind, left to itself, can aspire. (Mystical knowledge, by contrast, is of a suprahuman order.) Gregory contrasts it with the kind of knowledge that will be given in another life: "In the age to come, when everything that is seen passes away ... then no longer shall we know ... as we do now, nor shall the transcendent be conceived by way of the workings of things that appear [τὰ φαινόμενα, *ta phainomena*]."[71]

---

[69] *Cant.* 11 (PG 44:1009B–D; Norris, 353–55).

[70] See also *Cant.* 13 (PG 44:1049D; Norris, 407): "Well, then, just as the person who looks upon the perceptible cosmos and has grasped the Wisdom that is displayed in the beauty of these beings infers [ἀναλογίζεται, *analogizetai*], on the basis of what the eye sees, the invisible Beauty and the wellspring of Wisdom [πηγὴ σοφίας, *pēgē sophias*], whose outflow [ἀπόρροια, *aporroia*] contrived the natural order of what is ..." [This also has a biblical foundation: "For from the greatness and beauty of created things their Maker is analogically contemplated [ἀναλόγως ὁ γενεσιουργὸς αὐτῶν θεωρεῖται]" (Wis 13.5; cf. Rom 1.20).—*Ed.*]

[71] *Cant.* 11 (PG 44:1012A; Norris, 355).

Gregory propounds the same teaching when commenting on another verse from the Song of Songs, though here he uses a different image. Not the hand, but fragrance:

> When [the Bride] says "Your name is a perfumed ointment emptied out," she makes it manifest that the divine power is inaccessible and incapable of being contained by human thought processes, for to me it seems that by this statement there is conveyed something like the following: that the Nature that has no boundaries cannot be accurately comprehended by means of the connotations of words [ῥημάτων, *rhēmatōn*]. On the contrary, all the power of concepts and all the significance of words and names, even if they seem to have about them something grand and worthy of the Divine, cannot attain the nature of the Real itself. On the contrary, it is as if by certain traces and hints that our reason guesses at the Invisible; by way of analogy [ἐξ ἀναλογίας, *ex analogias*], based on things it has comprehended, it forms a conjecture about the Incomprehensible. For whatever name we may think up to make the scent of the Godhead known, the meaning of the things we say does not refer to the perfume itself. Rather does our theological vocabulary [θεολογικοῖς ὀνόμασι, *theologikois onomasi*] refer to a slight remnant of the vapor of the divine fragrance.
>
> Here, then, is what we learn from the words: the perfumed ointment of the Godhead, whatever it may be in its own essence [κατ' οὐσίαν, *kat' ousian*], is beyond every name and every thought, but the marvels [θαύματα, *thaumata*] discerned in each name and thought provide matter [ἐνθεωρούμενα, *entheōroumena*] for our theological naming. By their help we name God wise, powerful, good, holy, blessed and eternal, and judge and savior and the like.[72]

The entire vocabulary of this passage—conjectures (στοχασμοί, *stochasmoi*), notions (ἐπίνοιαι, *epinoiai*), analogy, and so forth—is encountered again in Gregory's treatise *Against Eunomius*. In this work Gregory defends and provides a theological foundation for the validity of analogous knowledge of God. Eunomius had argued that all divine names were worthless, except one—the Unbegotten—and that this described the divine essence itself. Arguing against this view, at once rationalistic and fideistic, Gregory establishes both the fact of our ignorance concerning God's essence and also the value of the analogous

---

[72]*Cant.* 1 (PG 44:781C–784A; Norris, 39–41).

The Ladder of Love

names that we use to describe his energies.[73] We shall do no more than point this out, for a detailed examination of his arguments against Eunomius is not our prime concern here. We simply wish to note the significance of such analogous knowledge and its place in the development of the spiritual life.

One last passage will reveal even more clearly the nature of the spiritual approach we are analyzing, and at the same time show its exact place in relation to what precedes and what follows. In this passage Gregory is examining the migration of Abraham, and in so doing distinguishes two successive stages. (These are the same two stages that we have already noted in the *Homilies on the Beatitudes*, in the *Homilies on the Song of Songs*, and in *The Life of Moses*.) The first is the transition from the visible world of *phainomena* to that of the intelligibles (νοητά, *noēta*), which are the divine attributes. The second corresponds to the transition from the stage of the *noēta* to that of the *divine essence*—that is, as an introduction to the third way. Here is how the first transition is described: "His mind, unimpeded by any object of sense, was never hindered from its journeying in quest of what lies beyond all that is known, but having gone by reasoning far beyond the wisdom of his countrymen—I mean the philosophy of the Chaldees, limited as it was to the things which do appear—and soaring above the things which are cognizable by sense, from the beauty of the objects of contemplation, and the harmony of the heavenly wonders, he desired to behold the archetype of all beauty."[74] This is contemplation starting from the "heavenly wonders," by means of which the mind goes beyond appearances and beyond what can be known through the senses, and enters into knowledge of the *onta* [(truly) existing things].

But this is a theme we recognize. Moving beyond the contemplation of God in the universe in the Stoic manner, which is only a first step, we see the mind freeing itself from the senses and rising to intelligible beauty. It is, of course, the main theme of Plato's *Symposium*—the dialectic of Eros ascending from visible to invisible beauty. It is this same ascent that Gregory describes in *On Virginity*:

> Accordingly, in the seeking of the beautiful, the person who is superficial in his thought, when he sees something in which fantasy is mixed with some beauty, will think that the thing itself is beautiful because of its own nature, his attention being attracted to it because of pleasure, and he will

[73]*Eun.* 2.130–31 (PG 45:953B; NPNF² 5:287–88).
[74]*Eun.* 2.88–89 (PG 45:940D; NPNF² 5:259).

be concerned with nothing beyond this. But the man who has purified the eye of his soul [ὁ τῆς ψυχῆς ὀφθαλμός, *ho tēs psychēs ophthalmos*] is able to look at such things and forget the matter in which the beauty is encased, and he uses what he sees as a kind of basis [ὑποβάθρα, *hypobathra*] for his contemplation of intelligible beauty [τὸ νοητὸν κάλλος, *to noēton kallos*]. By participation [μετουσία, *metousia*] in this beauty, the other beautiful things come into being and are identified.[75]

This would seem to be pure Platonism. The entire vocabulary of the passage recalls the *Symposium*—participation, intelligible Beauty, contemplation, even the image of rungs of a ladder: "The proper way to go about or be guided through the ways of love is to start with beautiful things in this world.... You should use the things of this world as rungs [ἀναβαθμοῖς, *anabathmois*] in a ladder."[76] Plotinus, too, uses the same image, including the very word ἐπιβάθρα (*epibathra*, ladder or steps): "Using the beauty of bodies as a stepping-stone, we will arrive at a vision of other beautiful things."[77] The movement of Gregory's thought here is exactly that of the Platonic ascent toward absolute Beauty, through the beauty of the participants.

But Gregory's originality lies in the fact that he does not stop here. He goes much further than Plato, who identifies God with the sphere of the intelligibles. Just as he passed from the *phainomena* to the *noēta* [intelligibles, i.e., noetic things perceptible to the mind] through the night of the senses, so does he now pass from the *noēta* to the *ousia* through the night of the mind. Let us return to the text of *Against Eunomius*:

> And so, too, all the other things which in the course of his reasoning he was led to apprehend as he advanced, whether the power of God, or His goodness, or His being without beginning, or His infinity, or whatever else is conceivable in respect to the divine nature, using them all as supplies [ἐφόδια, *ephodia*] and appliances [ὑποβάθρας, *hypobathras*] for his onward journey, ever making one discovery a stepping-stone to another, ever reaching forth [ἐπεκτεινόμενος, *epekteinomenos*] unto those things which were before, and setting in his heart, as saith the Prophet, each fair stage of his

---

[75] *Virg.* 11 (PG 46:364B–C; Norris, 38–39).
[76] Plato, *Symposium* 211c. Translation from *Plato: Symposium*, trans. Robin Waterfield (Oxford: Oxford University Press, 1994), 55.
[77] Plotinus, *Enneads*, 1.6.1. [The above translation reflects Daniélou's French. MacKenna has: "If we possess ourselves of this, we have at once a standpoint for the wider survey."—*Trans.*]

The Ladder of Love 159

advance [Ps 83.5], and passing by all knowledge acquired by his own ability as falling short of that of which he was in quest, when he had gone beyond every conjecture [εἰκασία, *eikasia*] respecting the divine nature which is suggested by any name amongst all our conceptions of God, having purged his reason of all such fancies [καθαρὰν πάσης ἐννοίας, *katharan pasēs ennoias*], and arrived at a faith unalloyed and free from all prejudice, he made this a sure and manifest token of the knowledge [ἐπίγνωσις, *epignōsis*] of God, viz. the belief that He is greater and more sublime than any token by which He may be known.[78]

The contrast between the two nights is clear, and this enables us to identify their respective realms and accurately to situate the night of the senses. In fact, the night of the mind that follows on from it consists in going beyond the divine attributes, in purifying the mind of any concept whatsoever, and plunging into darkness. The realm of symbolic knowledge to which, as we have seen, the night of the senses introduces us is that of the divine attributes. These are in the first place an object of contemplation for the mind that has freed itself from the sensible world. They then become the starting point of further progress.

---

[78]*Eun.* 2.89 (PG 45:941A; NPNF² 5:259).

5

The City of Angels

In his sixth homily on the Beatitudes, Gregory differentiates between two ways of knowing God. First, there is the symbolic knowledge we have just discussed, which culminates in knowledge of God's attributes through his manifestations in the visible world. Then there is the knowledge called mystical, which is an experience of God's presence in the soul by grace. In our opinion, this homily contains Gregory's deepest and most original thinking, but in it there is no mention of intellectual knowledge of the divine essence (οὐσία, *ousia*). In fact, it completely rules out the entire realm of *gnōsis*—that is, knowledge in the sense of speculation about the divine essence—that we associate with Clement and Origen. For Gregory, it is not by way of a science restricted to a few that one has access to God, but by a double path: that of the visible world, accessible to every human being and which leads to contemplation, and that of love, which is accessible to every Christian and which, in the darkness of faith, unites one to the God who is present in the soul.

This mistrust of gnosis is frequently found in Gregory, as in the following passage:

> It is impossible to draw near to God, unless faith mediate, and bring the seeking soul into union with the incomprehensible nature of God. For leaving behind him the curiosity that arises from knowledge [ἡ ἐκ τῆς γνώσεως πολυπραγμοσύνη, *hē ek tēs gnoseōs polypragmosynē*], Abraham, says the Apostle, "believed God, and it was counted unto him for righteousness." "Now it was not written for his sake," the Apostle says, "but for us," that God counts to men for righteousness their faith [πίστις, *pistis*], not their knowledge [γνῶσις, *gnōsis*]. For knowledge acts, as it were, in a commercial spirit [ἐμπειρικὴ διάθεσις, *empeirikē diathesis*], dealing only with what is known. But the faith of Christians acts otherwise.... [This] faith makes our own that which we see not [κατανόησις, *katanoēsis*], assuring us by its own certainty

of that which does not appear. . . . Vain, therefore, is he who maintains that it is possible to take knowledge [ἐπιγνῶναι, *epignōnai*] of the divine essence, by the knowledge which puffeth up to no purpose.[1]

Numerous other texts could be cited that contrast πολυπραγμοσύνη (*polypragmosynē*), the useless agitation of curiosity, with the simplicity of the faith that alone leads to an understanding of the things of God. We have emphasized this important point since it is so typical of Gregory's thinking. It is why we shall study at length that other kind of knowledge, gained in "the mirror of the soul," and the "feeling of a presence" that characterizes the mystical life and that Gregory was the first to clearly discern.

Nevertheless, when we come to examine the concept of gnosis in greater detail, we find that the situation is more complex. If we take *The Life of Moses*, for example, we notice that after his crossing of the desert and after hearing the sound of the trumpets that symbolically "proclaim the glory of God"—but before the mystical experience in the cleft of the rock in which he has a vision of God's "back"—Moses is introduced in darkness to a vision of the tabernacle. It is a vision that is presented as affording gnosis, "true knowledge,"[2] "knowledge of things sublime," "contemplation of the intelligibles."[3] All these words come from Origen, who uses them precisely to denote gnosis.

How can these two points of view be reconciled? The explanation is that at this stage Gregory's thinking is still finding its way. On the one hand, he has clearly sensed the true character of the mystical life—and this will prove to be his definitive contribution—but on the other, he is following on from Origen. True, he goes beyond him, but he is nevertheless writing in his wake. To begin with, he depends on him literarily. Subsequently, certain of the master's elaborations are integrated by the disciple into his own work, although the thought is not always reflected exactly. As we have seen, this is also the case with Gregory's attitude to Plato; he sometimes reproduces his ideas, yet without appropriating them unmodified. But there is a more significant point. It is striking that it is in the polemical works and the homilies addressed to the faithful in general that Gregory omits all discussion of gnosis. By contrast, in texts such as *The Life of Moses* that were intended for candidates for the perfect life, for monks, he includes it.

[1] *Eun.* 2.91–93 (PG 45:941B–C; NPNF² 5:259–60).
[2] *Vit. Moys.* 2.163 (PG 44:376D; Malherbe, 95).
[3] *Vit. Moys.* 2.156 (PG 44:373C; Malherbe, 93).

Thus, it would seem that Gregory's position is not in fact a denial of the value of gnosis, of spiritual speculation. As we shall see, it is in fact something that he himself practiced, and he does give it a place in his work. But—and here is the main point—this place is not the first, nor is it indispensable. There is indeed a legitimate gnosis that can bring about a deepening of the faith, but it does not necessarily make for holiness. The perfect Christians are not gnostics, but those who display the most ardent love. The kind of knowledge of God that corresponds to this love is mystical, the fruit of union with him, and it is above all to this union that one should aspire. Gnosis is a good thing, but it is secondary.

It follows from this that, before embarking upon a study of mystical experience proper, we should reflect a little further upon what is meant by "gnostic knowledge." It is a somewhat ambiguous category since, on the one hand, it is heir to Origen's third way—his category of θεωρική (*theōrikē*). And with it we do indeed enter a new order—one of which mystical knowledge will also be a part. With symbolic knowledge we were still in the realm of natural knowledge; here we enter the domain of pure faith. We rise above the visible world, leaving appearances behind. It is no longer just a question of a night of the senses, but a night of the mind and concepts too. In this sense, *gnōsis* is already *gnophos*; entry into gnosis is entry into the divine "darkness."[4]

Given these traits, gnostic knowledge can be classed with mystical knowledge; together they form the third way, which is that of pure faith. Yet, on the other hand, it is the opposite of mystical knowledge in that it is a type of contemplation that is intellectual. As such, despite what was said above, it can be said to form a single group along with symbolic theology, representing its highest degree. It is knowledge and theology of a supernatural order. Thus symbolic and apophatic theology together form a group that is contrasted with mystical experience. For in the latter the soul abandons the paths not only of natural knowledge but of all speculative knowledge whatsoever. It sets out on the way of love and union and there discovers a superior knowledge of God. This is a new darkness, deeper than the other. It is true ecstasy, a going out not only from the world but from the self. It is this second darkness that defines entry into the mystical life. And it is this that characterizes Gregory's thought.

---

[4] *Vit. Moys.* 2.162–63 (PG 44:377A; Malherbe, 95).

The Contemplation of Realities

We have seen how the soul may acquire knowledge of God through a night of the senses. This symbolic theology is knowledge of an intellectual order, and corresponds to the first degree of gnosis. However, as the soul continues its ascent, it casts off the intellectual life—that is, the conceptual mode of knowing. This is the night of the mind, by means of which the soul passes to the order of pure faith, which is the beginning of the mystical life. The second way is entirely preoccupied with becoming purified and rediscovering *apatheia*, as the soul divests itself of successive layers of "tunics." Then, having found the wings it had lost, it returns to its homeland on high. At every stage in the ascent, from each *skopia*, each successive peak, it assesses the progress that has been made as it sees earth receding and heaven drawing near.

There is a fundamental passage in Gregory's *Against Eunomius*. We have already quoted from it, but we need to refer to it again at this point, for it describes with clarity the various stages of this ἀνάβασις (*anabasis*, ascent):

> [Abraham], having gone by reasoning far beyond the wisdom of his countrymen, (I mean the philosophy of the Chaldees, limited as it was to the things which do appear) and soaring above the things which are cognizable by sense,[5] from the beauty of the objects of contemplation, and the harmony of the heavenly wonders, he desired to behold the archetype of all beauty. And so, too, all the other things which in the course of his reasoning he was led to apprehend as he advanced, whether the power of God, or His goodness, or His being without beginning, or His infinity,[6] or whatever else is conceivable in respect to the divine nature, using them all as supplies and appliances for his onward journey, ever making one discovery a stepping-stone [ὑποβάθρας, *hypobathras*] to another, ever reaching forth unto those things which were before, and setting in his heart, as saith the Prophet, each fair stage of his advance, and passing by all knowledge acquired by his own ability as falling short of that of which he was in quest, when he had gone beyond every conjecture respecting the divine nature which is suggested by any name amongst all our conceptions of God, having purged his reason of all such fancies [εἰκασίαν, *eikasian*],[7] and arrived at a faith unalloyed and free from all prejudice [καθαρὰν πάσης ἐννοίας, *katharan pasēs ennoias*],

[5] This is the night of the senses.
[6] This is the aim of symbolic theology.
[7] This is the night of the mind.

he made this a sure and manifest token of the knowledge of God, viz. the belief that He is greater and more sublime than any token by which He may be known.[8]

Here we see the hierarchy of the three orders of knowledge: Chaldean philosophy, which focuses on appearances; symbolic philosophy, which deals with abstract truths; and apophatic philosophy, which is concerned with spiritual reality. To each of these corresponds a particular agent: sense perception (αἴσθησις, *aisthēsis*) for appearances; the φαντασία καταληπτική (*phantasia kataleptikē*) for abstractions; and faith (πίστις, *pistis*) for spiritual reality. It is worth noting that Gregory usually reserves the more general expressions, Platonic in origin—such as διάνοια or γνῶσις (*dianoia, gnōsis*)—for knowledge of the third order. This again shows that on the level of philosophy he uses Stoic language, whereas Platonic language is kept, and adapted, for the mystical level.

The domain of apophatic philosophy is specifically that of faith. That of symbolic theology, though for the Christian it is motivated by faith, belongs to the province of the intellect and corresponds to philosophy in the modern sense of the term. It does have a place in Gregory's teaching, as in Augustine's. In *The Life of Moses*, for instance, Gregory tells us that it corresponds to the "foreign wife" of the Lawgiver: "There are certain things derived from profane education which should not be rejected when we propose to give birth to virtue. Indeed, moral philosophy and natural philosophy may at certain times become a comrade, friend, and companion of life to the higher way."[9] He explicitly admits that knowledge of the divine attributes can be gained by means of philosophy and that pagans have attained this: "Perhaps the wise of this world, too, might gain some knowledge [κατανόησις, *katanoēsis*] of the divine Wisdom and Power from the harmony of the universe."[10] However, he contrasts this with the knowledge the Christian acquires through the indwelling of God by grace, which is inaccessible to philosophy, being the object of pure faith.

Thus the domain we surveyed in the last chapter and the one we are beginning to examine now are distinguished by this transition from the order of the intellect to that of faith. It is faith that introduces us to a new order of knowledge. As we determine its nature, we shall see that it enables us to know something about God, though not about his inaccessible essence. This stage is related to

[8] This is the aim of apophatic philosophy. *Eun.* 2.89 (PG 45:940D–941A; NPNF[2] 5:259).
[9] *Vit. Moys.* 2.37 (PG 44:337A; Malherbe, 62–63).
[10] *Beat.* 6 (PG 44:1269B; ACW 18:147).

the second way, inasmuch as it is part of the contemplative ascent, culminating in κατανόησις (*katanoēsis*) What still remains—and it is here that Gregory surpasses his predecessors—is to go beyond the order of contemplation to enter that of love. We will look first at the characteristics of the life of faith, and then see how it blossoms into contemplation.

This stripping away of the conceptual life and entry into pure faith introduce the soul into the world of realities (τὰ ὄντα, *ta onta*), which corresponds to the Platonic κόσμος νοητός (*kosmos noētos*, intelligible world). In *The Life of Moses*, Gregory demonstrates clearly the sequence of the different stages: "When he who has been purified and is sharp of hearing in his heart hears this sound (I am speaking of the knowledge of the divine power which comes from the contemplation of reality), he is led by it to the place where his intelligence lets him slip in where God is. This is called *darkness* by the Scripture, which signifies . . . the unknown and the unseen. When he arrives there, he sees that tabernacle not made with hands [Heb 9.11; cf. 2 Cor 5.1], which he shows to those below by means of a material likeness."[11] Thus the darkness—that is, the night of the mind—leads to a contemplation of the intelligible objects: namely, the two tabernacles, the heavenly and the earthly, which the Church is.

This stage corresponds to what, for the Alexandrians, constitutes gnosis. This denotes a form of knowledge whose characteristic feature is that it assimilates one to the realities that it makes known. Indeed, this constitutes the basis of Gnosticism: the revelation of certain secrets concerning the nature of things raises the initiate above the ordinary condition and introduces him into a higher sphere, the pleroma, even if he seemingly still belongs to the world here below.[12] In Clement of Alexandria and Origen, gnosis restores the human being to a condition equal to that of the angels and constitutes the very summit of the spiritual life. In Gregory, the notion of gnosis is still found—and he does use expressions that are from Origen—but for him it merely denotes one further stage in the ascent. It marks the return to the intelligible world, the entry of the soul into its heavenly homeland. There, the divine essence still remains inaccessible and in this luminous world of the intelligibles it discovers a new darkness. In vain, like the Bride in the Song of Songs, it seeks information concerning the whereabouts of its Beloved from all the guardians of the city—that is, the angels who inhabit

---

[11] *Vit. Moys.* 2.169 (PG 44:380A; Malherbe, 96–97).
[12] See H.-Ch. Puech, "Der Begriff der Erlösung im Manichäismus," *Eranos-Jahrbuch* (1936): 193ff.

the intelligible world. Despair then casts it onto the way of love and ecstasy where it will finally find God, though differently than it had believed.

In Gregory's usage, the term *theōria* has several meanings. However, we can discern three principal ones. First, it is contrasted with πρᾶξις (*praxis*, activity) to refer to the contemplative, as opposed to the practical, aspect of the spiritual life: "Practical philosophy should be joined to contemplative philosophy. So the heart becomes the symbol of contemplation, and the arms, of works."[13] This sense is the least common. Much more frequent is the term's use to denote the spiritual interpretation of Scripture, as opposed to the literal meaning. For example, *The Life of Moses* is divided into two distinct books or parts: the *historia* that records the events of his life; and the *theōria* that interprets them spiritually. Whenever Gregory is commenting on Scripture, this is the meaning the word has.[14] It is often used in conjunction with other words that clarify the sense, for instance, "anagogical interpretation" (θεωρία κατ' ἀναγωγήν, *theōria kat'anagōgēn*),[15] "noetic contemplation" (νοητὴ θεωρία, *noētē theōria*).[16] The raised arms of Moses, in the form of a cross, are a symbol of it: "Moses' holding his hands aloft signifies the contemplation [θεωρίαν, *theōrian*] of the Law with lofty insights; his letting them hang to earth signifies the mean and lowly literal [κατὰ τὸ γράμμα, *kata to gramma*] exposition and observance of the Law."[17]

This brings us to the third way in which Gregory uses the word. Here it denotes not merely the spiritual meaning of Scripture, but the contemplation of spiritual realities themselves. In this sense it is sometimes used alone, as in the following example: "As [the mind] approaches more nearly to contemplation [θεωρίᾳ, *theōria*], it sees more clearly what of the divine nature is uncontemplated [τὸ ... ἀθεώρητον, *to ... atheōrēton*]."[18] This is *theōria* in the technical sense of the term, the contemplation of intelligible realities. In this sense, it is at times also used in conjunction with other words. Thus on one and the same

---

[13] *Vit. Moys.* 2.200 (PG 44:392C; Malherbe, 106).

[14] On this meaning of θεωρία (*theōria*), see H. N. Bate, "Some Technical Terms of Greek Exegesis," *Journal of Theological Studies* (Oct. 1922): 59–66, at 61–63.

[15] *Vit. Moys.* 2.136 (PG 44:368A; Malherbe, 87). [The English version renders this as "*spiritual* contemplation."—*Trans.*] Cf. "contemplated spiritually," 2.162 (PG 44:376D; Malherbe, 95); "spiritual interpretation," 2.320 (PG 44:429C; Malherbe, 137).

[16] *Vit. Moys.* 2.269 (PG 44:413A; Malherbe, 123). [The English version renders this as "perceived spiritually."—*Ed.*] Cf. μυστικὴ θεωρία (*mystikē theōria*, mystical vision) (*Cant.* 1; PG 44:765B; Norris, 15) or πνευματικὴ θεωρία (*pneumatikē theōria*, spiritual comprehension) (*Cant.* 6; PG 44:900A; Norris, 203).

[17] *Vit. Moys.* 2.149 (PG 44:372B; Malherbe, 90–91).

[18] *Vit. Moys.* 2.162 (PG 44:376D; Malherbe, 95).

page, we find successively: "contemplation of the transcendent nature" (τῆς ὑπερκειμένης φύσεως θεωρία, *tēs hyperkeimenēs physeōs theōria*), "contemplation of Being" (τῶν ὄντων θεωρία, *tōn ontōn theōria*), "contemplation of the intelligibles" (τῶν νοητῶν θεωρία, *tōn noētōn theōria*), and "the contemplation of God" (τοῦ θεοῦ θεωρία, *tou theou theōria*).[19]

It is worth noting that these are all expressions that were traditionally used precisely to denote gnosis.[20] We find them in Clement of Alexandria: "Likeness to God consists first in the possession of a superior knowledge, or gnosis. . . . This gnosis has for its object τὰ νοητά (*ta noēta*), the world of ideas, or τὰ ὄντα (*ta onta*), the world of realities. . . . This perfect gnosis relates to what is above the cosmos, to things perceived only by the intellect."[21] We find the same expressions in Origen, too. He defines gnosis as knowledge of reality, of the things that really are (γνῶσις τῶν ὄντων, *gnōsis tōn ontōn*),[22] contemplation of intelligible, invisible things (θεωρία τῶν νοητῶν, *theōria tōn noētōn*),[23] or observation of intelligible things (κατανόησις τῶν νοητῶν, *katanoēsis tōn noētōn*).[24] As for its scope, we may gain some idea from *On First Principles*: it covers the entire sphere of the intelligible world—men, angels, and God, in as far as they are knowable to us.

Moreover, Origen himself tells us that gnosis "consists in knowledge of God, embracing knowledge of things divine and human, and their causes."[25] In particular, it deals with spiritual creatures, the angels, as Völker correctly observes: "The Pneumatics have, first of all, an insight into the world of the heavenly hierarchy; they know the angels and their opponents; they understand the ranks of the fallen angels."[26] He cites Origen himself to this effect: "*Agnoscet quoque quae et quantae quales qualesque virtutes sint bonae quaeque nihilominus contrariae.* 'He will come to know, moreover, about the good powers, what they are, their

---

[19] *Vit. Moys.* 2.153, 154, 156, 157 (PG 44:373B–D; Malherbe, 92–93).

[20] Maximus the Confessor demonstrates the stages in which the mind frees itself from the passions, as it makes its way to the θεωρία τῶν ὄντων (*theōria tōn ontōn*). See "First Century on Love" §§83–86, *Philokalia* 2:62–63 (PG 90:980A). Niketas Stethatos explains that *apatheia* enables one to progress from φιλοσοφία πρακτική (*philosophia praktikē*) to φιλοσοφία φυσική (*philosophia physikē*), which is equivalent to θεωρία τῶν ὄντων (*theōria tōn ontōn*). [Daniélou gives no reference here.—*Trans.*]

[21] De Faye, *Clément d'Alexandrie*, 286–89. Cf. Methodius of Olympus, who writes about γνῶσις τῶν ὄντως ὄντων (*gnōsis tōn ontōs ontōn*) in *On the Resurrection* 1.29 (Bonwetsch, 258) and 1.30 (Bonwetsch, 263).

[22] Origen, *Homilies on the Psalms*, Psalm 1 (PG 12:1084A).

[23] Origen, *Contra Celsum* 3.56.

[24] Origen, *Commentary on John* 10.40.

[25] Origen, *Commentary on Matthew* 17.2.

[26] Völker, *Das Volkommenheitsideal des Origenes*, 94.

greatness and qualities, and of those also of the opposite kind' . . ."[27] Finally, this knowledge also focuses on the origin—the causes (ἀιτίαι, *aitiai*)—and the end of man's destiny, the last things (ἔσχατα, *eschata*), which were also a prime concern for the gnostics.

All this enables us to see what this θεωρία τῶν ὄντων (*theōria tōn ontōn*) consists of. It is a contemplation of the world on high—and of human destiny in so far as it is connected with that world. This contemplation of humanity conceived as a heavenly creature that fell away from the angelic sphere and is to return to it—this aeonian superhistory of mankind, viewed as the lost sheep that must return to the heavenly flock so that the pleroma might again be realized—is constantly in the background of Gregory's thought. On the one hand, as we shall see in the final part of our investigation, he is the contemplative of the divine darkness that surpasses all gnosis. But he is also the contemplative of this intelligible world of angels, and of human existence conceived as an angelic adventure. This is indeed the cradle of his thought.

We shall see shortly the nature of the spiritual panorama that lies before us, but we must first clarify further this concept of gnosis. (Gregory prefers the word *theōria*). With respect to Clement, De Faye claims that his concept of gnosis is contradictory, because it contains, on the one hand, the world of ideas (νοητά, *noēta*), and on the other, "man, his nature, his morals, virtue, and the Supreme Good."[28] But the *noēta* for Clement—and for Gregory—resemble less the immutable ideas of Plato than the gnostic pleroma; that is to say, theirs is a dramatic universe that contains falls and restorations. Therefore what is specific about gnosis in their understanding is less the object than the point of view. Gnosis is about human realities, but seen in their heavenly perspective. It is neither the knowledge of God, who remains inaccessible, nor is it ordinary knowledge of human things. It is supernatural knowledge of God's "plan," his οἰκονομία (*oikonomia*, dispensation, lit. economy), the history of spiritual creatures. And its proper domain is indeed the sphere of the angels.

We are reminded of one of the major concepts of Hellenic thought as a whole; this contemplation of the ideas, which are the true realities, dates back to Plato.[29] For Gregory, the goal of the spiritual life is precisely to free oneself from cosmic illusion, to gain height and so enter the world of realities. Hence

---

[27] Origen, *On First Principles* 2.11.5. Translation from *Origen: On First Principles*, vol. 1, ed. and trans. John Behr (Oxford: Oxford University Press, 2017).

[28] De Faye, *Clément d'Alexandrie*, 27.

[29] See Plato, *Phaedrus* 250c; *Phaedo* 66c–d.

he writes of those "who devote their mind to the speculative and contemplative philosophy of reality [θεωρία τῶν ὄντων, *theōria tōn ontōn*]"³⁰ or who "are occupied in the contemplation of what really is [τῶν ὄντως ὄντων, *tōn ontōs ontōn*]."³¹ And the gnosis thereby gained includes knowledge of the last things, the ἔσχατα (*eschata*), as for Clement. "For if the apprehension of the truth of the things that are [τῶν ὄντων, *tōn ontōn*] is the peculiar power of wisdom, and prophecy includes the clear knowledge of the things that are about to be, one would not be possessed of the gift of wisdom in perfection, if he did not further include in his knowledge, by the aid of prophecy, the future likewise."³²

Such contemplation is the very essence of prayer. "Prayer," says Gregory, "is contemplation of the invisible."³³ This expression—θεωρία τῶν ἀοράτων (*theōria tōn aoratōn*), "the contemplation of invisible things"—is found in his writings quite frequently.³⁴ As we draw toward the end of the second way, this is a new aspect of prayer that we are discovering. At the end of the first way, prayer appeared as *parrhēsia*—the freedom of a child of God with his Father—restored by *apatheia*. *Theōria* signals the blossoming of this *parrhēsia*, the discovery of the realities of the divine life. From another point of view, we may also note that *theōria* affords knowledge of things divine, of the manifestation of God through the supernatural order inherent in the double cosmos of the heavenly hierarchy and the ecclesiastical hierarchy, to which the two tabernacles correspond. Symbolic theology, for its part, was limited to the human science of the manifestation of God in the natural order present throughout the cosmos of creation.

Finally, *theōria* is the return of man to his original state; it reintroduces him to the paradise that was lost. This brings us to an essential aspect of the question. Gregory ranks the θεωρία τῶν ὑπερκοσμίων (*theōria tōn hyperkosmiōn*, contemplation of the supramundane realities) among the goods of paradise, given back to the soul through grace, drawing a parallel between παρρησία ἐπὶ θεοῦ (*parrhēsia epi theou*, boldness before God) and equality with the angels (ὁμοτιμία πρὸς ἀγγέλους, *homotimia pros angelous*).³⁵ Thus we are once again brought back to the world of the angels.

---

³⁰*Inscr.* 2.3.26 (PG 44:496A; Heine, 130).
³¹*Eccl.* 5 (PG 44:684D; Hall, 90).
³²*Eun.* 3.1.43 (PG 45:580C; NPNF² 5:140).
³³*Or. dom.* 1 (PG 44:1124B; ACW 18:24).
³⁴See *Inscr.* 1.7.52 (PG 44:456C; Heine, 101).
³⁵See *Eccl.* 6 (PG 44:708D; Hall, 108).

The Third Heaven

When describing contemplation, Gregory typically uses the verb μετεωροπορεῖν (*meteōroporein*), to soar aloft. To his mind, this clearly indicates the comportment of a soul freed from the weight of the flesh and that, become light again, has re-ascended to the upper regions from which it had fallen, and now circulates there freely. Conversely, of sinners he writes, "They no longer soar mentally in freedom [ἐν ἐλευθερίᾳ μετεωροπορεῖν, *en eleutheria meteōroporein*] or look at the things on high."[36] This image of "celestial circulation" is found in several striking passages as a description of the heights of contemplation. In the *Homilies on the Song of Songs*, for example, we read that "[Humanity] was brought, by the Jordan [i.e., baptism] and the myrrh [i.e., *apatheia*] and the frankincense [i.e., ascent], to so great a height as already to be walking on high with God [συμμετεωροπορεῖν θεῷ, *symmeteōroporein theō*]."[37] Contemplation is seen, then, to be the pinnacle of the soul's ascent, its return to the spiritual world.[38]

We shall focus on two similar passages: one is from *The Life of Saint Macrina*, the other from the *Eulogy for Basil the Great*. In the first, Gregory is describing the heavenly life of his sister, after she had withdrawn from the world:

> What human word could bring this kind of life before your eyes? Their existence bordered [μεθόριος, *methorios*] on both the human and the incorporeal nature. On the one hand, a nature freed from human cares is more than human, whereas, to appear in the body and to be embraced by form and to live with the senses is to have a nature less than angelic [ἀγγελικῇ, *angelikē*] and incorporeal. Perhaps some daring person might say the difference was negligible because, although living in the flesh because of their affinity to the bodiless powers, they were not weighed down by the allurements of the body, but, borne upwards in midair [μετέωρος καὶ ἀνωφερής,

---

[36] *Virg.* 22 (PG 46:404A; FC 58:66).

[37] *Cant.* 8 (PG 44:945A; Norris, 265).

[38] To describe contemplative souls, Gregory forges the neologism μετεωροπόρος (*meteōroporos*)—literally, "traveling through the air." [Translated as "sublime," in Gregory, *Hexaemeron*, trans. R. McCambly, www.lectio-divina.org/index.php/reflections/reflections-on-the-writings-of-gregory-of-nyssa, p. 1 (PG 44:64A).—*Trans.*] Συμμετεωροπορεῖν (*symmeteōroporein*) is a similar neologism that Gregory was fond of. See L. Méridier, *L'influence de la seconde sophistique sur l'œuvre de Grégoire de Nysse* (Paris: Hachette, 1906), 94. Cf. *Virg.* 4 (PG 46:337D; FC 58:21): "[The one who] has his thoughts on high and is making his way up to God [συμμετεωροπορεῖ τῷ θεῷ, *symmeteōroporei tō theō*], being superior [to those who focus on this life], will have no common starting point for a discussion about the common cause of error regarding such matters—namely, marriage." We agree with this connection between contemplation and virginity, which Gregory goes on to develop in this text. See also *Mort.* 20 (PG 46:532C; PPS 64:30–31).

meteōros kai anōpherēs], they participated in the life of the celestial powers [συμμετεωροπορούσα ταῖς οὐρανίαις δυνάμεσιν, *symmeteōroporousa tais ouraniais dynamesin*].[39]

The interest of this text lies in the connection Gregory establishes in it between contemplation and the return to the intelligible world, identified here with the realm of the angels. The contemplative soul has an angelic nature, then, and circulates among the angels on high. There are two fundamental points here. First, contemplation (θεωρία, *theōria*) restores the soul to the angelic state, for what characterizes it is that it entails not merely the removal of passions, as is the case with *apatheia*, but the removal of images and concepts. It is purification of the mind, as Gregory makes clear: "In the contemplation of the intelligibles, we surpass the knowledge which originates with the senses."[40] This knowledge is equivalent to angelic knowledge. St Bernard will take this idea up again: *Corporum similitudinibus speculando non involvi angelicae puritatis est*; "to be brought out of the sphere of material forms and ideas is a privilege of angelic purity."[41] (Whatever Stolz may say,[42] this is a traditional theme of mystical theology.) Among the goods of the supernatural life, it is this "equality in honor with the angels" that Gregory associates with "the contemplation of the good things in the realms above."[43]

The second point is that *theōria* is not only a return to the nature of the angels, but to their company; the soul that is freed from the life of the flesh "circulates with the angelic powers." Here is how Gregory describes the existence of the first humans: "The first humans . . . used to sing in chorus with the angelic

[39]*Macr.* (PG 46:972A; FC 58:171).
[40]*Vit. Moys.* 2.156 (PG 44:373C; Malherbe, 93).
[41]Bernard, of Clairvaux, *Homilies on The Song of Songs*, 52.5.
[42]See Stolz, *Théologie de la mystique*, 112. [*Spiritual Perfection*, 103.]
[43] *Eccl.* 6 (PG 44:708D; Hall, 108). See also *Op. hom.* 17.2 (PG 44:188D; NPNF² 5:407); *Cant.* 4 (PG 44:857A; Norris, 147); *Bas.* (PG 46:813D; McCambley, 23). "For the mark of impassibility, which illuminates [the soul] just as it does the angels, brings the soul that has achieved impassibility in the flesh into a relationship of kinship . . . with incorporeal beings" (*Cant.* 8; PG 44:948A; Norris, 267). On Origen, see Völker, *Das Volkommenheitsideal*, 192.

[44]*Inscr.* 2.6.60 (PG 44:508C; Heine, 139). [Daniélou gives this as "dance," another possible translation of χορός (*choros*).—*Trans.*] The same idea is found in Gregory the Great: "After Adam, the father of the human race, was driven from the joys of paradise as a result of sin . . . he was no longer able to perceive the joys of heaven which had been the object of his contemplation before. In paradise he habitually enjoyed converse with God and in purity of heart and loftiness of vision mingled with holy, angelic spirits." *Dialogues* 4.1 (PL 77:317B). English translation from *Saint Gregory the Great: Dialogues*, trans. Odo John Zimmerman, Fathers of the Church 39 (Washington, DC: The Catholic University of America Press, 1959), 189.

The City of Angels

powers."[44] This life was lost through sin, with the following result: "Instead of living with the angels on the heights, we have been condemned to dwell with the beasts of the earth."[45] Nevertheless, Gregory believes that humanity is to take its place again in the pleroma of spiritual creatures. In fact, this has already been accomplished for us in substance by the incarnate Word at the Ascension. But for the time being, this return is realized by each contemplative soul individually; for humanity as a whole it will take place only at the end of time.[46]

In our second passage, from the *Eulogy for Basil the Great*, we also find a "soaring aloft":

> Having risen above the entire world and feeling constricted [στενοχω-ρούμενος, *stenochōroumenos*] in the visible cosmos, he could not even endure to have heaven above him. But he elevated himself in his soul into the beyond [ἐπέκεινα, *epekeina*], and raising his head above [ὑπερκύψας, *hyperkypsas*] the sensible sphere of the cosmos, he kept company with the intelligibles [τοῖς νοητοῖς, *tois noētois*] and traversed the heights together with the heavenly powers [συμμετεωροπορεῖν ταῖς οὐρανίαις δυνάμεσι, *symmeteōroporein tais ouraniais dynamesi*], without any fleshly weight preventing the journeying [πορείαν, *poreian*] of his mind.[47]

As can be seen, we find here the same way of presenting things as in the passage from *The Life of Saint Macrina*. It is in fact Gregory's customary way. Note as well the term στενοχωρούμενος (*stenochōroumenos*); this image of the world as a cramped or confined abode from which the wise man endeavors to escape belongs to the Cynic tradition.[48]

---

[45] *Beat.* 5 (PG 44:1275D; ACW 18:138).

[46] A symbol of this return to the angelic nature is "wakefulness, keeping awake" (ἐγρήγορσις, *egrēgorsis*): "The soul [of a person purified and illumined] abides untouched by sleep or by any deception and does not dally with any of these misleading dreams. And if this is accomplished under the guidance of the Word, a life of angelic quality accrues to us" (Gregory, *Cant.* 11; PG 44:996D; Norris, 335). This is because sleep, together with death, marriage, illness, and so on is one of the characteristics of biological life. Thus the absence of sleep, wakefulness, signifies figuratively that the soul is now removed from the biological order, from the world of illusion, and that it has entered the order of realities, the ὄντα (*onta*). As previously mentioned, the angelic life is the opposite of the biological life, not because of the lack of a body, but the lack of an animal body.

[47] *Bas.* (PG 46:813D). [McCambly's translation (p. 23) has not been used, being too different from Daniélou's French and the Greek.—*Trans.*]

[48] See Sallustius, *Concerning the Gods*, xxvii, where the editor (Nock) refers to Gregory of Nyssa. See also *Thaum.* 6.44 (PG 46:921A; FC 98:60) for a still more characteristically Cynical outlook: "Are you cramped [στενοχωρεῖτε, *stenochōreite*] by the vault of heaven and seek another lodging than this?"

But what is perhaps most striking is the close parallel with a Platonist view of things. More specifically, one thinks of the episode in *Phaedrus*—most dear to Gregory—where the return of the souls to the intelligible world is described, a world which is at the rim, the outer edge of the vault of heaven. Here is how Plato puts it:

> Souls patrol [περιπολεῖ, *peripolei*] the whole universe, taking on different forms at different times. A complete soul—which is to say, one that is winged [ἐπτερωμένη, *epterōmenē*]—journeys on high [μετεωροπορεῖ, *meteōroporei*] and controls the whole world, but one that has lost its wings [πτερορρυήσασα, *pterorryēsasa*] is carried along until it seizes upon something solid . . .[49]

> This is a recollection of the things which our souls once saw during their journey as companions to a god [συμπορευθεῖσα θεῷ, *symporeutheisa theō*], when they saw beyond [ὑπεριδοῦσα, *hyperidousa*] the things we now say and poked their heads up [ἀνακύψασα, *anakypsasa*] into true reality [τὸ ὂν ὄντως, *to on ontōs*].[50]

The similarity with Gregory's texts is striking. We cannot fail to notice such closely related, characteristic expressions as *meteōroporein* or *anakypsasa*. Other of the expressions and ideas are also found in Gregory. For example, the domain of *theōria* is that which is really real: τὸ ὄντως ὄν (*to ontōs on*), "real Being."[51] These are the *onta*. Moreover, the soul was able to circulate in this heavenly place because it had wings.[52] It has lost them through sin,[53] and must find them again to be able to look at earthly things from on high.

Phaedrus depicts souls "as they journey skyward to the rim of the heavenly vault [τὴν ὑπερουράνιον ἁψῖδα, *tēn hyperouranion apsida*] . . ." The passage continues as follows: "When the souls we call 'immortal' reach the rim, they make their way to the outside and stand on the outer edge of heaven [ἐπὶ τῷ τοῦ οὐρανοῦ νώτῳ, *epi tō tou ouranou nōtō*], and as they stand there the revolution carries them around, while they gaze [θεωροῦσι, *theōrousi*] outward from the

[49] Plato, *Phaedrus* 246c.
[50] Ibid., 249c.
[51] *Vit. Moys.* 2.25 (PG 44:333C; Malherbe, 60). [Cf. "true Being" (ἀληθῶς τὸ ὄν, *alēthōs to on*) earlier in the same passage. *Vit. Moys.* 2.23 PG 44:333A–B; Malherbe, 60)—*Ed.*]
[52] See *Cant.* 15 (PG 44:1101A; Norris, 475). Concerning the wings of the soul, see A. d'Alès, "Les ailes de l'âme," *Ephemerides Theologicae Lovanienses* 10 (1933): 63–72.
[53] See *Cant.* 15 (PG 44:1101C; Norris, 477).

heaven."⁵⁴ These forms of expression are found in Gregory, too. He criticizes them on the level of physics, in the *Hexaemeron*: "What pertains to water within the spherical shape of the heavens above [τῆς οὐρανίου ἁψῖδος, *tēs ouraniou apsidos*] cannot determine its flow. How can what is made of water be curved which by necessity always flows from the sphere above to lower parts?"⁵⁵ But he accepts their spiritual symbolism and so can write as follows: "But if the sermon [Homily 1] has given us wings [πτερωθείημεν, *pterōtheiēmen*] and we have been placed on the ridge of the heavenly ark [τά νῶτα τῆς οὐρανίου ἁψῖδος, *to nōta tēs ouraniou apsidos*], we shall then find the supercelestial earth."⁵⁶ This last adjective is a direct echo of the τόπος ὑπερουράνιος (*topos hyperouranios*, "the region beyond heaven") that in *Phaedrus* follows immediately after the passage about the heavenly vault.⁵⁷

What is especially interesting is the freedom with which Gregory uses this Platonic vocabulary. He never quotes literally but incorporates Platonic terms and expressions into his own syntax in a way that shows how imbued he was with this imagery but yet how little he was its slave. His is an encoded vocabulary, a system of symbols, analogous to that which Scripture provides, and whose value lies not in itself but only in the meanings he gives to it. With him, there is neither Platonic literalism nor Mosaic literalism, but two systems of symbols that serve to express reality, the true *onta*: namely, Christ and his mysteries.

We should emphasize that Gregory's Plato is the Plato of the myths. Now this Plato "is everywhere":⁵⁸ in Philo and Plotinus; in Clement and Origen. Philo, for example, connects contemplation with initiation into the divine mysteries: "For when the mind busies itself with sublime [μετεωροπολῇ, *meteōropolē*] contemplations, [it] becomes initiated into the mysteries of the Lord."⁵⁹ Elsewhere he writes of "the mind which has been purified and initiated in the divine mysteries [συμπεριπολοῦντα, *symperipolounta*] with the choirs [τοῖς χοροῖς, *tois chorois*] of the heavenly beings."⁶⁰ The "choirs" also derive from *Phaedrus*.⁶¹ They occupy

---

⁵⁴Plato, *Phaedrus* 247b–c.
⁵⁵*Hex.* (PG 44:65D; McCambley, 2).
⁵⁶*Beat.* 2 (PG 44:1209A; ACW 18:97).
⁵⁷Plato, *Phaedrus* 247c. See Cherniss, *Platonism of Gregory of Nyssa*, 45.
⁵⁸J. F. Denis, *De la philosophie d'Origène* (Paris: Thorin, 1884), 9.
⁵⁹Philo, *Allegorical Interpretation* 3.22.71 (Yonge, 58).
⁶⁰Philo, *On Rewards and Punishments* 20.121 (Yonge, 675). [Translation modified.—*Trans.*] See also Philo, *On Dreams* 1.6.34 (Yonge, 368), and Völker, *Fortschritt und Vollendung bei Philo von Alexandrien* (Leipzig, 1938), 181–88.
⁶¹See Plato, *Phaedrus* 250b.

a very important place in Gregory.[62] In Philo we see the same freedom in the use of Platonic terms as in Gregory; he uses περιπολεῖν (*peripolein*), for example, in place of μετεωροπορεῖν (*meteōroporein*).

Turning to Plotinus, we find that he not only uses the same vocabulary from *Phaedrus* but even quotes directly, as in the following examples: "Our soul, entering into association with that complete soul and itself thus made perfect, 'walks the lofty ranges [μετεωροπορεῖ, *meteōroporei*], administering the entire Cosmos'";[63] "'The perfect soul,' we read, that of the All, 'going its lofty journey' [μετεωροπορούσα, *meteōroporousa*], operates upon the Cosmos not by sinking into it, but, as it were, by brooding over it; and 'every perfect soul exercises this governance' [διοικεῖ, *dioikei*]; he distinguishes the other, the Soul in this sphere ... as 'the soul when its wing is broken' [πτερορρυήσα, *pterorruēsasa*]."[64] The same cluster of terms and expressions is found in both Philo and Gregory. We are without doubt at the heart of Greek thought.[65]

Yet it is precisely the use of this *lexis* by writers whose thought is very different that should help us to grasp its meaning. The borrowing of vocabulary from *Phaedrus* in particular confirms that we are in the realm of *theōria*. This provides us with an excellent point of reference, and in addition implies a certain common Platonic vision of the world; one in which the domain of the realities is that of the intelligibles. It involves a certain asceticism, through which the soul frees itself from the weight of the flesh and, having become light and nimble (κοῦφος, *kouphos*), can re-ascend to its heavenly homeland and walk with the powers on high. But there the likeness between the various authors—Plato, Philo, Gregory—ends. The common mental and cultural framework must not be allowed to conceal their fundamentally different real intentions.

Thus, we need to determine what "the region beyond heaven," the Platonic κόσμος νοητός (*kosmos noētos*), corresponds to in Gregory's system. In the *Hexaemeron*, he gives a description of three heavens: the first is ruled by the winds and clouds; the second, which is situated at the summit of the sensible world and at the boundary of the intelligible world (μεθόριον νοητῆς κτίσεως, *methorion noētēs ktiseōs*), is that of the stars. He then continues as follows: "Having shown us his desire as an example, Paul knows that every man lives in the

---

[62]E.g., *Inscr.* 2.6.60 (PG 44:508B–C; Heine, 138–39).
[63]Plotinus, *Enneads* 4.8.2. The quotation is from *Phaedrus* 246c.
[64]Ibid., 4.3.7. Cf. *Phaedrus* 246b–c.
[65]See Festugière, *Le Dieu cosmique*, 444–45. For Christian authors, see Methodius of Olympus, *Symposium* 1.1 (Bonwetsch, 7–8); 8.1–2 (Bonwetsch, 81–82).

perceptible world, and he has entered the inner sanctuary of the spirit. Since he is familiar from childhood with holy words, by his own written words he designates the third heaven that realm of these three divisions in which the world is located. Paul left the air, passed through the midst of the circling stars, transcended the limit of ether's bounds and having come to firm and intelligible nature, knows the beauties of paradise and has heard what human nature cannot utter."[66]

This text sets out Gregory's cosmology quite clearly. It distinguishes three heavens. First, there is the air, the domain of the wind, the clouds, and the birds—and that is delimited by a first firmament. Next is the ether, the sphere of the stars and the domain of fire, and a second firmament demarcates this. These two heavens together constitute the sensible heaven (αἰσθητόν, *aisthēton*). Beyond them lies the third heaven, which is the intelligible world. Gregory identifies it with the third heaven of St Paul. In this way, a parallel is established between the Platonic vision of a sensible and an intelligible world and the biblical vision of the three heavens. This enables us to identify the intelligible world with the *adyta*, the inner sanctuaries, the secret places into which faith alone can penetrate. Furthermore, a parallel is also drawn between this domain, to which we are reintroduced by *theōria*, and paradise, man's original state.

It is essential to be familiar with this way of representing things, if one is to understand those passages in which, to describe the ascent of the soul, Gregory makes use of the Platonic vocabulary of an ascent through various heavenly spheres, as in such passages as the following: "Who will give me those wings, that my mind may wing its way up to the heights of these noble words? Then I would leave behind the earth altogether and traverse all the middle air; I would reach the beautiful ether, come to the stars and behold all their orderly array. But not even there would I stop short, but, passing beyond them, would become a stranger to all that moves and changes, and apprehend the Stable Nature, the immovable Power which exists in its own right, guiding and keeping in being all things."[67] Thus the mystical ascent is portrayed as a crossing of all the sensible heavens and an entry into the immovable reality where God dwells.

Sometimes Gregory adopts a different symbolism. Instead of three heavens, he confines himself to the two heavens of ordinary cosmology. But in these cases, the first alone represents the sensible world; the second heaven, the ether,

[66]*Hex.* (PG 44:121C–D; McCambley, 21–22). Cf. ibid. (PG 44:85B; McCambley, 9) and Gregory, *Eun.* 1.272 (PG 45:1004A; NPNF[2] 5:278).
[67]*Or. dom.* 2 (PG 44:1140B; ACW 18:37).

is taken figuratively as symbolizing the intelligible world. Thus in the *Sermons on the Lord's Prayer*, the ether is designated as the habitat of the angels. To Gregory's mind, this can only have a figurative meaning.[68] This symbolism is explicit in a passage such as the following: "Just as this earthly air, when it is forced upwards by the wind, becomes light-like, being changed in the clarity of the aether, so the mind of man, when, after leaving this muddy and dusty life, it is purified through the power of the Spirit, becomes light-like, and it is mixed with the true and lofty purity, and it glows" (cf. Prov 4.18).[69]

The interest of these texts lies in the fact that they show us in what sense we should understand this concept of three heavens. In reality, it is above all a matter of imagery that Gregory makes use of freely and ingeniously. One should not be fooled by it. There is nothing here resembling the localization of paradise, such as Stolz claims to find in the Greek Fathers.[70] On the contrary, these cosmological expressions are simply symbols of the different stages of an inner ascent that—though it is profoundly real and takes the soul on a voyage across distinct, objective worlds—cannot be located in space. What we find in Gregory is the same interiorization of the concept of the soul's return through the cosmic spheres as in Plotinus or Augustine.

Plotinus writes as follows: "Admiring the world of sense as we look out upon its vastness and beauty . . . let us mount to its archetype, to the yet more authentic sphere: there we are to contemplate all things as members of the Intellectual—eternal in their own right, vested with a self-springing consciousness and life."[71] We note here the fundamental opposition between the sensible world and the world of the intelligibles, and "presiding over all these, the unsoiled Intelligence."[72]

As for Augustine, writing at almost the same period as Gregory, he too describes the ascent of the soul in comparable fashion. We shall single out two passages to illustrate the point. In the first, from the *Confessions*, he is describing the ecstasy at Ostia: "Our minds were lifted up by an ardent affection toward eternal being itself. Step by step we climbed beyond all corporeal objects and the

---

[68] See *Or. dom.* 4 (PG 44:1165C; ACW 18:60–61).
[69] *Virg.* 11 (PG 46:365D; FC 58:40–41). This is a spiritual transposition of the Pythagorean idea according to which the souls, during their ascent through the celestial spheres, ignite on contact with the ether. Cf. J. Carcopino, *Virgile et le mystère de la IVe Églogue* (Paris: L'Artisan du livre, 1930), 85. On the air that ignites on contact with the ether, see Pseudo-Aristotle, *De Mundo*, Chapter 2: The Elements of the Universe: Ether, Fire, and Air [391b9–392b12—*Ed.*].
[70] See Stolz, *Thélogie de la mystique*, 27f. [*Spiritual Perfection*, 22f.]
[71] Plotinus, *Enneads* 5.1.4.
[72] Ibid.

The City of Angels

heaven itself, where sun, moon, and stars shed light on the earth. We ascended even further by internal reflection and dialogue and wonder at your works, and we entered into our own minds. We moved up beyond them so as to attain to the region of inexhaustible abundance where you feed Israel eternally with truth for food."[73] In a much later work, the *Expositions of the Psalms*, we still find the same momentum:

> [Idithun] had leapt with the penetrating gaze of his mind, with his strong, bold, supremely confident keen-sightedness; he had leapt over the earth and all it contains, beyond the air and all the clouds from which God spoke. . . . He had leapt with the sharp gaze of his faith even beyond the angels, for this leaper was not content with earthly things, but like a soaring eagle was carried beyond all the cloud that enshrouds the entire earth. . . . So as he leapt beyond all created things, seeking God, he attained to a limpid reality; he poured out his soul above himself, he reached the very Beginning, the Word who is God-with-God.[74]

For Augustine, beyond the sensible world is the world of the soul, beyond which there is nothing but God. The angels are mentioned, but after the clouds and before the soul. It has been well said that for Augustine the νοητά (*noēta*) are above all the soul itself: "We entered into our own minds [and] we moved up beyond them."[75] Thus in Augustine, the emphasis is put strongly on the movement of interiorization. The intelligible world is above all the inner world, the *nous*, where the soul collects its thoughts far removed from the dispersion of the outer world and beyond which it flows into God.

With Gregory, the question is more complex. The aspect of interiorization does exist, as, for example, when he describes Macrina as being μεθόριος (*methorios*), "at the boundary" between the sensible and the intelligible world. This is the same adjective that he used in the *Hexaemeron* in his cosmological descriptions.

---

[73] St Augustine, *Confessions* 9.24. Translation from *Saint Augustine: Confessions*, trans. Henry Chadwick (Oxford: Oxford University Press, 1991), 171.

[74] St Augustine, *Expositions of the Psalms*, 61.18. Translation by Maria Boulding in *The Works of Saint Augustine, Part Three, vol. 17: Expositions of the Psalms, 51–72* ed. John E. Rotelle, (Hyde Park, NY: New City Press, 2001), 220.

[75] *Mentes* for νοητά (*noēta*), notes Paul Henry. See P. Henry, *La vision d'Ostie* (Paris: Vrin, 1938), 23. [In his *Soliloquies*, an early work, reason personified addresses Augustine inwardly and asks what he desires to know. He responds "God and the soul, that is what I desire to know"; when reason further prompts, "Nothing more?" he replies, "Nothing whatever." *Soliloquies* 1.7 (NPNF[1] 7:539). For a more recent study of Augustine's movement of interiorization, see Phillip Carey, *Augustine's Invention of the Inner Self: The Legacy of a Christian Platonist* (Oxford: Oxford University Press, 2003).—*Ed.*]

Again, the homily on the sixth Beatitude shows us that the way to find God lies in the return of the soul to itself: "Hence, if your thought is without any alloy of evil . . . the darkness caused by material entanglements has been removed from the eyes of your soul, and so you see the blessed vision [τὸ μακάριον θέαμα, *to makarion theama*] radiant in the pure [αἰθρίᾳ, *aithria*] heaven of your heart."[76]

Here we recognize the words used by Plato in the same passage from *Phaedrus* to describe the vision afforded the souls that circulate in the heavenly vault: "They saw a blessed vision and spectacle [μακάριον ὄψιν καὶ θέαν, *makarion opsin kai thean*]."[77] (In the technical language of Christian eschatology, this would refer to what is called the "beatific vision." I am not aware whether anyone has noticed that the phrase is literally Platonic in origin.) It is this same expression—μακάριον θέαμα (*makarion theama*)—that we find in Gregory, although the spectacle is now inside the soul, revealed to the contemplative in the infinite depths of his heart.

In Gregory, however, the Platonic *noēta* do not simply have a psychological aspect; they are also existing spiritual creatures that surround God, the pleroma of the angels of which humanity once formed part. In fact, it seems that in Gregory it is this aspect that is most decisive. The descent of the soul into itself will belong to a later stage, when it sets out in a blind search for the inaccessible divine essence. What is developed here—and this constitutes *theōria* properly speaking—is the realm of the angels, something to which Augustine alluded only to point out that he had passed beyond it.

Yet this level does not mark the pinnacle of the spiritual ascent for Gregory either. It simply indicates restoration to the angelic sphere. Beyond, God still remains the object of an infinite quest, hidden in the incomprehensibility of his essence (οὐσία, *ousia*). This aspect appears in a notable passage in which Gregory depicts the soul that has re-entered the world of the angels and seeks there for its Beloved without finding him:

> Hence she bestirs herself again and in her understanding moves about the intelligible [κόσμος νοητός, *kosmos noētos*] and supercosmic nature (which she calls *the city*), in which are the Rulers and Lordships and the Thrones set over the Powers and the assembly [πανήγυρις, *panēgyris*] of the heavenly

---

[76]*Beat.* 6 (PG 44:1272C; ACW 18:150–51). [For a recent study of the beatific vision in Gregory, see Hans Boersma, *Seeing God: The Beatific Vision in Christian Tradition* (Grand Rapids, MI: Eerdmans, 2018), Chapter 3.—*Ed.*]

[77]Plato, *Phaedrus* 250b (trans. modified—*Ed.*).

beings (which she calls *the square*) as well as the unnumbered multitude (which she denotes by the word *street*)—to see if she can find the Beloved among these. So she went about, searching every angelic order; and since she did not see the one she sought among the good beings she found, she mused thus within herself: "May it be that the one I love is known to them?" . . . But they fell silent in the face of this inquiry and by their silence showed that the One she sought was imperceptible even to them. As, then, she went, in the persistent curiosity of her understanding, through the whole of that super-cosmic city and even among intelligible and incorporeal beings did not see the object of her desire—at that point she left behind everything she had already found and in this way recognized the object of her search, whose existence is known only in incomprehension of what it is, in whose case every conceptual trait is an obstacle to its discovery for those who seek it.[78]

This key text enables us to situate *theōria* definitively. We saw first that it is contrasted with the sensible world, as the world of the intelligibles. But now we discover that, from another point of view, it is defined as an intelligible world compared with the unknowability of the essence. Thus, in the ascent of the soul, *theōria* represents as it were an intermediary domain. It is a summit in comparison with the world below, but it is only a beginning compared to the infinity of the divine essence. It determines the domain of the soul returned to its original state. It is truly its homeland, the place that is connatural to it, equally distinct from the inferior world of the senses and the higher world of the essence. It is this new dimension, this perspective without end opening up there where one had thought the term to be, that characterizes Gregory's vision.

One sees the complete reversal that the Platonic perspective undergoes here. In Plato, the κόσμος νοητός (*kosmos noētos*), the spiritual or intelligible world, is identified with the sphere of the divine, with which the sensible world is contrasted. Something of this idea persists in Philo, Plotinus, and Origen where, between the unknowable God and the soul, a domain subsists that is that of the *logos* or the *nous*. For his part, Gregory dispenses with this intermediary world altogether.[79] With him there remains only the creature and the Creator. The order of the creature is the *kosmos noētos*, which contains the totality of the spiritual creatures: therein is all of created reality, that which existed at the

---

[78]*Cant.* 6 (PG 44:893A–B; Norris, 195).
[79]See E. von Ivánka, "Vom Platonismus," 193–94.

beginning and will exist at the end when the mirage of the sensible or perceptible world (κόσμος αἰσθητός, *kosmos aisthētos*) has vanished. The divine order, on the other hand, is that of the unknowable essence. The separation between the two is real, being between Creator and creature. But at the same time the two worlds communicate through participation.

We can also cite other passages, in which Gregory points out the transcendence of God in relation to the angelic world: "Knowledge of the divine essence is unattainable not only by men but also by every intelligent creature."[80] Moreover, the return of the soul to the angelic state, the fact of "walking with the angels in the heights," does not imply a vision of God. Just now, we saw the Bride of the Song searching for God in the *kosmos noētos*, but in vain. Similarly, Paul does not name him in what he has seen in the third heaven: "He proceeds . . . to another most distinct division into the things that have been made in the way of creation, and the existence that is above creation. He mentions the several classes of these created intelligibles: 'thrones,' 'dominions,' 'principalities,' 'powers,' conveying his doctrine about these unseen influences in broadly comprehensive terms: but by his very silence he separates from his list of things created that which is above them."[81] This is an important text that shows us that the *theōria* of Paul, the prototype of all *theōria*, has as its object the *kosmos noētos*.

This *kosmos noētos* itself contains several aspects, as is well expressed by Hans Urs von Balthasar:

> What distinguishes Gregory at once from Philo and Plotinus is the radical opposition between the triune God and the creature, an opposition that is not mitigated by any kind of intermediary zone. . . . Personalized by Origen, who identifies it with the Logos, *nous* had retained an intermediary place between the Father (βύθος, *bythos*) and the soul in Christian metaphysics. But once the absolute transcendence of the divine essence was recognized, this place became untenable. Augustine will try to maintain it, but not without skirting the edges of contradiction. Gregory, who is more categorical, abandons it. This fundamental dogma of Platonism is completely absent from his philosophy. But what happens in such a case to universal and necessary being, to the spiritual realm? Christian metaphysics divides the elements of it into three regions of being. Its formally divine aspect is linked to its true proprietor, God himself. . . . Its psychological aspect returns to

[80] *Vit. Moys.* 2.163 (PG 44:377A; Malherbe, 95).
[81] *Eun.* 1.306–307 (PG 45:345B; NPNF² 5:64).

The City of Angels

> the soul ... whose very being, insofar as it is spiritual, keeps a mysterious character of concrete universality. Finally its existential aspect is absorbed into the realm of the angels, which Gregory readily calls the spiritual world (κόσμος νοητός, *kosmos noētos*). But in his eyes they are sheer creatures like souls, inasmuch as they are not an object of essential knowledge for the latter. ... Thus the impersonal domain of Ideas finds itself completely absorbed by three categories of personal beings.[82]

It remains the case that the three realities that constitute this domain, even though they are distinguished from each other, do together form a specific domain, one precisely in which the soul moves freely. Indeed, for Gregory to enter into the company of angels, to restore the image of God in oneself, and to know God through participation are one and the same thing. Though it is true that Gregory does not always maintain a distinction between God and the Logos, we see in him the emergence of another distinction, one that will become standard in Eastern theology: God incommunicable in his divine essence but participable in his energies. Now it is precisely the *kosmos noētos* that is the domain where this participation in God by deifying grace takes place, which is identical with the image of God in the soul, and which constitutes the angelic state. It remains for us to survey this world.

It has two clearly distinct aspects. The first concerns the restoration of the soul to the *kosmos noētos*—that is, to the pleroma of spiritual creatures. Thus we need to specify the nature of this angelic world to which the soul is restored through *theōria*, and then the nature of the blessed spectacle that is the proper object of *theōria*. This still belongs to the second way, of which it is the culmination. Further still, beyond contemplation, the quest of the soul's search for its Beloved begins. It passes beyond the sphere of the angels and immerses itself in the depths of participation in the divine life. This is the third way, the order of love, darkness in the strong sense. It will be the subject of the final part of our investigation.

The Vision of the Tabernacle

We have seen that, in its modus and its position in the spiritual life, *theōria* is a return to the world of the angels, which in Gregory takes the place of the Platonic κόσμος νοητός (*kosmos noētos*, the spiritual or intelligible world). This angelic world is still an object of contemplation, though not its essential term. Von

---

[82]Hans Urs von Balthasar, *Présence et pensée*, xvii–xix. [*Presence and Thought*, 18–20.]

Balthasar is correct in writing that, for the soul, the angels "are not an object of essential knowledge." The true object of *theōria* is the mystery of salvation, what St Paul means by οἰκονομία (*oikonomia*). However, with Gregory this mystery is understood from an angelic standpoint. Humanity is thought of as a single angel who fell from the intelligible world, and whom the Son of God comes to seek out and restore to the pleroma of spiritual creatures: τὸ τῶν νοητῶν δυνάμεων πλήρωμα, *to tōn noētōn dynameōn plērōma* (the fullness of the noetic powers).[83] The real world for Gregory is this pleroma, made up of a hundred angelic worlds. This is what for him takes the place of Plato's intelligible world, as constituting the real world in contrast to the cosmic illusion. But at the same time, it is a created world, radically other than God, which thereby ensures that his vision is authentically Christian.

Thus *theōria* has two objects: on the one hand, the angelic world (corresponding to the Platonic intelligible world), symbolized by the tabernacle on high; on the other hand, the ecclesiastical world, symbolized by the tabernacle here below. This double hierarchy is described in *The Life of Moses*. There would seem to be similarities with the two hierarchies of Dionysius—*On the Celestial Hierarchy* and *On the Ecclesiastical Hierarchy*. But there is an essential difference, in that for Dionysius the two hierarchies are conceived of as two immutable realities, whereas for Gregory they are in a historical relationship. In the beginning, only the tabernacle on high existed. The tabernacle below is linked to the drama of man's fall and redemption, and is to be restored to the tabernacle on high in the end, along with the return of humanity to the sphere of the angels. In short, for Gregory *theōria* is contemplation of the mystery in its timeless essence. And here we find ourselves very close to the liturgy, which is also a representation of the mystery. Liturgical *theōria*, scriptural *theōria*, and mystical *theōria* are ultimately various aspects of one and the same reality.[84]

[83] *Hex.* (PG 44:81C; McCambley, 7–8). This idea appears in a passage such as the following: "The noble prophet [David], having gone out [ἐκβάς, *ekbas*] of himself, as if unburdened by the weight of his body and having mingled with the hypercosmic powers [ὑπερκοσμίοις δυνάμεσιν, *hyperkosmiois dynamesin*], reports their words when, accompanying the Lord in his descent [ἐπὶ τὴν κάθοδον, *epi tēn kathodon*], these powers order the angels that surround the earth to lift up their gates [cf. Ps 23.7, 9]" (*Ascens.*; PG 46:693A). It is clear that this "departure" from the natural world is a return to be among the angelic powers and that, once there, the soul hears the words of the angels and begins to contemplate redemption from their point of view. Likewise, the *ekstasis* of St Paul is a return to "the third heaven," that is, to the world of the angels. [McCambly's translation—although used above—has not been used, being too far removed from Daniélou's French and from the Greek.—*Trans.*]

[84] Nicholas Cabasilas' *Explication de la divine liturgie*, Sources chrétiennes 4, trans. S. Salaville (Paris: Éditions du Cerf, 1943) includes a *historia* and a *theōria*, just as Gregory's book on Moses consists of the

To gain a clearer idea of what Gregory understands the content of *theōria* to be, we might think we need simply gather together the references to it scattered throughout his works. In reality, however, one would end up quoting the entire corpus, for it is altogether one long reflection upon this angelic proto-history of mankind. Being raised by *theōria* onto the rim of the heavenly vault, he contemplates the blessed spectacle. But this spectacle is no longer the procession of the Platonic divinities, nor the unchanging ideas. It is the choir of angels who surround the κορυφαῖος (*koryphaios,* the leader), the Word. Then there is the fall of the angel "humanity," the departure of the Word as he sets off in search of this lost sheep, the anticipation of the angels as they wait at the gates of heaven, the triumphal return of the King bringing back mankind (to which he has became united by the incarnation), and the new presence in the sphere of the angels—a presence now become perpetual—of the Lamb that was slain.

Gregory describes this by means of various symbols, the first being that of the heavenly tabernacle:

> For the power which encompasses the universe, in which "lives the fullness of divinity," (Col 2.9) the common protector of all, who encompasses everything within himself, is rightly called "tabernacle." . . . For [Paul] says somewhere with reference to the Only Begotten . . . that "in him were created all things, everything visible and everything invisible, Thrones, Dominations, Sovereignties, Powers," (Col 1.16) or forces. Then the pillars gleaming with silver and gold, the bearing poles and rings, and those cherubim who hide the ark with their wings, and all the other things which are contained in the description of the tabernacle's construction—all of these things, if one should turn his view to the things above, are the heavenly powers [ὑπερκόσμιοι δυνάμεις, *hyperkosmioi dynameis*] which are contemplated in the tabernacle.[85]

Thus, inasmuch as Christ is "the one in whom all things consist" (Col 1.17), the head of all the spiritual creatures, it is he ultimately who is the object of *theōria*.[86] The All, as always in Gregory, is not the visible universe but the pleroma of

story of the Life of Moses and a Contemplation [*Theōria*] on this Life. [Nicholas Cabasilas, *A Commentary on the Divine Liturgy*, trans. J. M. Hussey and P. A. McNulty (London: SPCK, 1960; repr. St Vladimir's Seminary Press, 2002)].

[85] *Vit. Moys.* 2.177, 179 (PG 44:381A–384A; Malherbe, 99–100). See *An. et res.* 10 (PG 46:133B–C; PPS 12:105–106).

[86] This idea of the Logos as a tabernacle can be found in Philo (*The Life of Moses* 2.15.74 [Yonge, 497]), but he interprets the Logos as containing the impersonal powers of the divinity. This is the world of ideas.

the angels.[87] The *dynameis*, that we saw just now circulating with the souls in heaven, are now seen as constituting this world on high. They form the sanctuary of God: "All creation is, as it were, a palace for the Lord of creation."[88] In this heavenly tabernacle the angels are considered from the point of view of their office of praise, or their participation in the work of salvation. "These are our true supports, sent to help ... those being saved (cf. Heb 1.14) ... [and to] raise to the height of virtue those lying upon the earth."[89]

Elsewhere, Gregory uses another image, one that we have already alluded to and that is borrowed from Plato: the chorus around its coryphaeus. In *Phaedrus*, Plato writes of the "happy company" (εὐδαίμονι χορῷ, *eudaimoni chorō*) to whom the souls were united before their fall.[90] Even more precisely, Plotinus describes the souls surrounding the One as follows: "We are always before it [the Supreme]: but we do not always look: thus a choir, singing set in due order about the conductor, may turn away from that centre to which all should attend: let it but face aright and it sings with beauty."[91] For his part, Gregory writes: "For there was a time when the dance of the rational nature was one, and looked to the one leader of the chorus, and, in its movement in relation to his command, interpreted the choral song in relation to the harmony exhibited thence."[92] The similarity of vocabulary—κορυφαῖον (*koryphaion*), βλέπειν (*blepein*, to look at), and ἔνθεος (*entheos*, full of God, inspired), which is found a few words later in both texts—leads us to suppose a direct influence.[93]

For Clement of Alexandria, on the other hand, the Logos contains in himself not the impersonal powers but the angelic creatures. Here Gregory depends on Clement.

[87]He speaks of "the power that encompasses existing things, the realities [τὰ ὄντα, *ta onta*]" (*Vit. Moys.* 2.177; PG 44:381D; Malherbe, 99). These ὄντα (*onta*) are the angels, personal forms of the ideas. [The English version—which gives "encompasses the universe"—has been modified to reflect the Greek and Daniélou's emphasis.—*Trans.*]

[88]Gregory, *In diem natalem* (*Diem. nat.*) (PG 46:1128C). English translation from *Oration on the Savior's Nativity*, trans Andrew Radde-Gallwitz, in *The Cambridge Edition of Early Christian Writings, Volume 3: Christ*, ed. Andrew Radde-Gallwitz and Mark DelCogliano (Cambridge University Press, 2022), 405.

[89]*Vit. Moys.* 2.180 (PG 44:384B; Malherbe, 100).

[90]Plato, *Phaedrus* 250b.

[91]Plotinus, *Enneads* 6.9.8.

[92]*Inscr.* 2.6.60 (PG 44:508B–C; Heine, 138–39). See also *Cant.* 12 (PG 44:1033A; Norris, 383).

[93]We should note, however, that the import of the metaphor is different. For Plotinus, it symbolizes the unity of creatures united to the One by means of contemplation in this life. For Gregory, on the other hand, it has an "archeological" [i.e., protological] and eschatological meaning. In fact, this unity only existed before sin, in the angelic preexistence of humanity (which, for Gregory, is not a historical preexistence, but intentional in the mind of God) and will not be restored except eschatologically, through

This image of a chorus has the advantage of placing the emphasis on the intelligible world's unity, for the choir of the spiritual creatures is one—which is why we can describe the totality of creation as the All, the pleroma. Of this pleroma humanity forms a part: "the first humans... used to sing in chorus with the angelic powers";[94] "when sin entered in, the mouths of those conquered by wickedness were closed, the sound of exultation was silenced, and the harmony of human nature was ripped from those who celebrate the festival, no longer keeping the festival with the hyper-cosmic nature."[95] Elsewhere Gregory speaks of "living with the angels on the heights"[96] as one of the goods of the paradise that was lost. These assertions give rise to two important questions: what of the community of nature between the angels and men, and what is meant by the angelic preexistence of humanity? Clearly, this line of thought sounds Origenistic. It is thus even more important to make clear Gregory's own thinking.

As regards the first question, we should above all note that for Gregory the world of the angels represents less an order of nature than an order of grace. By this I mean that for him the angelic world is the world of glory, which is identical with the real world in contrast to the fallen world. It includes the spiritual creatures of which humanity forms a part, though it is not, properly speaking, an actual angel. In fact, Gregory prefers to use the expression "equal to the angels" (ἰσάγγελος, *isangelos*),[97] which both indicates the commonality of belonging to the spiritual world and at the same time the difference in nature. Similarly, he writes that an angel can be called a brother because it "does share kinship with the soul in its intellectual and incorporeal aspects."[98]

Moreover, the picture Gregory forms of this world of spiritual creatures is quite distinctive. He does mention various angelic orders, but does not establish a definite hierarchy, as Pseudo-Dionysius will do.[99] Thus, in one place, he identifies the thrones with the cherubim and the seraphim with the powers.[100]

---

the initiative of the chorus-leader himself, who will abandon the ninety-nine sheep in order to seek the one that is lost, bringing it back on his shoulders. That is, taking on human nature by his incarnation (cf. Gregory, *Antirrh*. 11 [PG 45:1153A; FC 131:127]).

[94]*Inscr*. 2.6.60 (PG 44:508C; Heine, 139).
[95]*Diem. nat*. (PG 46:1129A; Radde-Gallwitz).
[96]*Beat*. 5 (PG 44:1257D; ACW 18:138).
[97]*Cant*. 1 (PG 44:777A; Norris, 33). [The term is not only biblical but dominical (Lk 20.36).—*Ed*.]
[98]*Vit. Moys*. 2.51 (PG 44:340D; Malherbe, 66).
[99]See F. Prat, *La Théologie de saint Paul*, vol. 2 (Paris : Beauchesne, 1912) 407ff. [*The Theology of Saint Paul*, vol.2, trans. John L. Stoddard (London: Burns, Oates and Washbourne, 1927), 408ff.]
[100]See *Eun*. 1.23.310 (PG 45:348B; NPNF² 5:64).

In *The Life of Moses*, he groups together the hierarchies listed in Colossians (1.16) and Ephesians (1.28),[101] and also speaks of the cherubim.[102] In the *Homilies on the Song of Songs*, describing the city on high that the soul traverses in its search for God, he refers to "the Rulers and Lordships and the Thrones set over [ἀποτεταγμένοι, *apotetagmenoi*] the Powers."[103] The only passage where the enumeration is more complete and where some sort of hierarchy is sketched out is to be found in the same work:

> For the serried ranks drawn up are in that pace where the Authorities are ever engaged in governing, where the Dominions are always exercising power, the Thrones stand firmly, the Principalities remain unsubdued, the Powers bless God without pause (Ps 102.21), the flight of the seraphim ceases not and their fixed station does not change (Is 6.2),[104] and the cherubim never stop upholding the high and exalted throne (cf. Ezek 10.1), and the ministering spirits do not stop doing their work and hearing the words (cf. Ps 102.20–21).[105]

In this passage eight choirs of angels are mentioned, but the first thing to note is that the "ministering spirits" (λειτουργοί, *leitourgoi*) and the "powers" (δυνάμεις, *dynameis*) do not figure in the enumeration that Pseudo-Dionysius will draw up. Second, among these eight there is no clear hierarchy. This is because Gregory's habitual way of seeing things is different. For him, it is not nine choirs ranked hierarchically that constitute the heavenly world but rather one hundred spiritual creations, of which humanity is one, and each of which contains legions of individuals. This is the Holy Hundred,[106] the pleroma of which he frequently speaks: "When that manifestation of the sons of God takes place which they look for and expect, and when the sheep is brought safe to the hundred

---

[101] See also *Diem. nat.* (PG 46:1129A).

[102] See *Vit. Moys.* 2.179–80 (PG 44:384A; Malherbe, 99–100).

[103] *Cant.* 6 (PG 44:893A; Norris, 195).

[104] This stable movement, this "progress [that is] a standing still" that characterizes the seraphim will also be typical of the soul that has become like the angels through virtue. See *Vit. Moys.* 2.243 (PG 44:405C; Malherbe, 117).

[105] *Cant.* 15 (PG 44:1100A; Norris, 473).

[106] On the number one hundred as a symbol of perfection, see the apocryphal Letter 180 (24) attributed to Julian in *Iuliani Imperatoris: Epistulae et Leges*, ed. J. Bidez and F. Cumont. (Paris: Les Belles Lettres, 1922), 235 (395D). [Apocryphal Letter 80, "To the most illustrious Serapion" in *The Works of the Emperor Julian*, Vol 3, ed. and trans. W. C. Wright (London: Heinemann, 1923), 281 (395B): "With the round number one hundred [Zeus] harmonizes the conception of the intelligible world as a whole" (τὸ ὅλον τῶν νοητῶν, *to holon tōn noētōn*).]

[ἑκατοντάς, *ekatontas*] above (and we surely—humanity that is to say—are that sheep which the Good Shepherd saved by becoming the first-begotten), then especially will they offer, in their intense thanksgiving on our behalf, their worship to God."[107] We notice how in this text, seen from the point of view of the angels, human history appears as that of a single reality. It is *theōria* that will enable us to see things from this angelic perspective. The spiritual creatures are the heavenly flock whose shepherd is the Word, and whom he leaves to look for the lost sheep: "He Who is the Shepherd of the whole rational Creation left in the heights of heaven His unsinning and supramundane flock and, moved by love [φιλανθρωπία, *philanthrōpia*], went after the sheep which had gone astray, even our human nature."[108]

But although humanity is related to the angels in so far as it forms part of the pleroma of spiritual creatures, it nonetheless has its own specific nature. In fact, for Gregory the composition of body and soul is not the result of a fall, but *is* human nature itself. What mankind has put on as a result of the fall are the "garments of skin" that constitute mortality. In this respect, he diverges from Origen. Human nature and angelic nature are regarded as being two spheres of the same spiritual creation, which sin alone has separated. Hence in *On the Inscriptions of the Psalms* the final restoration is portrayed as the reunion of the two natures as if they were two halves of a cymbal: "The beautiful concord of the cymbal[s] ... elevates our zeal to the divine choir [χοροστασία, *chorostasia*]. I take this to mean the union of our nature with the angels.... The supernatural nature of the angels is one cymbal; the rational creation [λογικὴ κτίσις, *logikē ktisis*] consisting of mankind is the other. But sin separated the one from the other. Whenever, then, the mercy of God [φιλανθρωπία, *philanthrōpia*] again unites the two with one another, then what comes about from the two with one another will cause that praise to resound."[109]

---

[107] *Eun.* 3.2.49 (PG 45:636B; NPNF² 5:158).

[108] *Eun.* 3.10.11 (PG 45:889A; NPNF² 5:241). See also *Antirrh.* 1 (PG 45:1154A; FC 131:127): "We human beings are that lost sheep, we who have strayed through sin from the flock of the one hundred rational sheep." See also *Eccl.* 2 (PG 44:641B; Hall, 52): "Our humanity too was once counted within the totality [τὸ πᾶν, *to pan*] of existence; for we too went to make up the sacred hundred [ἱερὰ ἑκατοντάς, *hiera ekatontas*] sheep, the rational beings." Cf. J. Daniélou, "Notes sur trois textes eschatologiques de saint Grégoire de Nysse," *Recherches de Science Religieuse* 30.3 (July 1940): 348–56, at 348. It is a traditional theme. See Irenaeus, *Against Heresies* 3.19.3; Origen, *Homilies on Numbers* 19.4; Methodius, *Symposium* 3.6; Cyril of Jerusalem, *Catechetical Lectures* 15.24.

[109] *Inscr.* 1.9.116–17 (PG 44:484B–C; Heine, 120–21).

There remains the difficulty that the two concepts—the unity of the spiritual creatures that constitute the world above (a more mystical idea) and the distinction between angelic and human nature (a more dogmatic notion)—sometimes overlap:

> The whole rational creation is divided into the incorporeal and the corporeal natures. The incorporeal species is the angelic creature, and the other one is we men. The spiritual creature, inasmuch as it is separated from the body that weighs down—I mean the earthly body that is solid and heavy—sojourns in the upper region. It dwells in the light and ethereal places and is of a nimble and agile nature. But the other nature has necessarily been allotted to the earthly life because the kinship of our nature, which is, as it were, a sediment of mud, with what is earthly.[110]

Here the difference in nature seems to be identified with the moral difference, and humanity seems to be excluded by nature from the intelligible world. As the passage continues, the confusion becomes greater still:

> Hence, whether the wisdom of God intend this or anything else besides, every rational nature is assigned to one of these two lives: the one, incorporeal, obtains the heavenly beatitude; whereas the other is turned toward the earth because of the affinity between it and the flesh. . . . Now the heavenly life is perfectly free from evil, and none of the powers known to be opposed to it has communion with it. On the other hand, every impulse or emotion connected with the passions resides [περιπολεῖ, *peripolei*] in the life below, where human nature is at home.[111]

Here there seems to be a connection between the fact that humanity has a body and the fact that it is sinful. This is the exact opposite of Gregory's usual thesis. Ordinarily with him, nature is absorbed by grace; here grace is separated from nature. This shows the indecisiveness of his thinking on this point.

However, there is one case in which Gregory insists on the commonality of nature between humans and angels—namely, that of integrated human nature, the case of virginity. He is quite explicit in teaching that humanity's present mode of propagation is the result of sin. It did not exist in man's original state; it will cease to exist after the resurrection. "Had there not come upon us . . .

---

[110] *Or. dom.* 4 (PG 44:1165B–C; ACW 18:60–61).
[111] Ibid. (PG 44:1168A; ACW 18:61–62).

removal from equality with the angels, neither should we have needed marriage that we might multiply."¹¹² "[T]he life which is promised to the just by the Lord after the resurrection is similar to that of the angels, according to the promise of the Lord—and release from marriage is a peculiar characteristic of the angelic nature."¹¹³ The ascetical consequences of this doctrine are considerable, because they justify virginity ontologically, seeing it as a return to the angelic state, beginning in this life: "The power of virginity is such that it . . . takes part in the chorus of the supramundane powers [χορεύειν μετὰ ὑπερκοσμίων δυνάμεων, *choreuein meta tōn hyperkosmiōn dynameōn*]."¹¹⁴ It is worth repeating that this does not mean that there is identity of nature between humans and angels, but simply that marriage belongs to the biological, animal sphere into which man was thrust by accident and which is alien to the celestial sphere. There it is not said that man will no longer have a body, but that he will have a transfigured body.

Turning now to our second question—the angelic preexistence of humanity—can we say that man really did possess a dignity equal to that of the angels? And did he indeed fall from the sphere of angels into the world of bodies? In short, is it the case that Gregory follows Origen's line of thought? The answer is no, and for two reasons. In the first place—and this is fundamental—for Gregory the preexistence of humanity was in the sphere of grace as opposed to that of the fall, not in the sphere of angelic nature in comparison with human nature. Second, Gregory holds that the prime object of creation was humanity as a totality, in a state of perfection, as the image. This places strong emphasis on human nature's unity which, taken as a whole, is one of the "aeons" of the pleroma of spiritual creatures. But he understands this preexistence to be an intentional preexistence in the divine thought. It will be actualized historically only at the end of time. What comes first chronologically is fallen humanity, clothed in garments of skin that symbolize in particular the sexual life.¹¹⁵ Such is the central doctrine of the treatise *On the Making of Man*.

As mentioned, this doctrine strongly emphasizes human unity. It is as a single creature that God wanted humanity, and in his plan this unity is prior to any fragmentation or division. The reunion of all things in Christ at the end of time will be the free ratification of what is an ontological reality. In this respect, the doctrine of the creation of man is an important part of *theōria*, because it

---

¹¹²*Op. hom.* 17.2 (PG 44:189A; NPNF² 5:407).
¹¹³*Virg.* 14 (PG 46:381A; NPNF² 5:51).
¹¹⁴*Virg.* 2 (PG 46:324B; NPNF² 5:11).
¹¹⁵*Op. hom.* 22.1–6 (PG 44:204B–205D; NPNF² 5:411–12).

touches upon eschatology, on the world of preexistence, and also because it considers humanity as a totality, as a unity that is a part of the pleroma of spiritual creatures from which it has been separated through sin and to which it is destined to be restored through Christ at the ἀποκατάστασις (*apokatastasis*), "the restoration of all things" (Acts 3.21).

Whatever the case may be with this interpretation of the fall, it is Gregory's normal practice to consider humanity as having belonged historically to the pleroma of the angels. Its fall from this pleroma constitutes the first act of the cosmic drama whose contemplation is the second object of *theōria*, after that of the company of the angels surrounding the Logos. Gregory frequently returns to this account of the fall, using the various symbols we have already encountered, as in the following examples. "But later, when sin occurred, it put an end to that divine concord of the chorus, when it poured the slipperiness of deceit at the feet of the first humans who used to sing in chorus with the angelic powers and caused the fall, wherefore man was separated from connection with the angels. Because the fall put an end to this conjunction."[116] Here it is the harmony of the dance that is interrupted; elsewhere it is that of the voices. We pass from the Platonic choirs to the Jerusalem liturgy: "But when sin entered in, the mouths of those conquered by wickedness were closed, the sound of exultation was silenced, and the harmony of human nature was ripped from those who celebrate the festival, no longer keeping the festival with the hyper-cosmic nature."[117]

Then there intervened the central peripeteia or turning-point. The choir leader is also the shepherd who leaves his flock to look for the lost sheep. Gregory portrays this descent (κατάβασις, *katabasis*) of the Word, endowed—and here we have the vestige of an Origenistic theme—with the natures of the different spheres of beings he encounters on the way, so much so that the angels appointed to guard the earth do not recognize him on his arrival and ask: "Who is this King of Glory?"[118] Gregory also depicts angels as either accompanying the Word in his descent,[119] or watching out for his return from the loggia of heaven: "For it is the angels who wait for the return of their Lord from the marriage feast and sit at the heavenly portals with sleepless eye."[120]

---

[116]*Inscr.* 2.6.60 (PG 44:508C; Heine, 139).
[117]*Diem. nat.* (PG 46:1128C–1129A; Radde-Gallwitz).
[118]See *Ascens.* (PG 46:693A; McCambley, 4).
[119]See ibid.
[120]*Cant.* 11 (PG 44:997A; Norris, 335).

However, meanwhile the Word has taken upon his shoulder the lost sheep, which symbolizes the incarnation: "Christ lays the whole sheep on his own shoulders. . . . The hide is not taken and the innards left behind, as Apolinarius would have it. Once the sheep is on the shepherd's shoulders, that is, in the divinity of the Lord, it becomes one with him through this taking up."[121] Gregory also compares the incarnation to a wedding between the Word and humanity: "Hence, as the hymn in the Psalms (Ps 18.6) would have it, the Bridegroom, having emerged as from the bridal chamber, espoused the virgin—that is to say, us—in the mystic rebirth, even though she had been prostituted to idols, and restored her nature to virginal incorruptibility."[122]

Having thus assumed humanity and having redeemed it through his passion (which, preexisting in the divine thought, is symbolized by "the skin dyed red"[123] that covers the tabernacle), the Word leads it back to the choir of angels by his ascent or ascension (ἀνάβασις, *anabasis*), which correlates with his κατάβασις (*katabasis*). This triumphal return of the Word bringing back the lost sheep is one of Gregory's favorite themes. (We know, too, that it was around this date that the feast of the Ascension was first celebrated—and in Cappadocia.)[124] Sometimes he stays with the image of sheep and portrays the heavenly flock greeting the return of its sister Humanity.[125] At other times, it is the Bridegroom bringing back the Church to which he is united, in the blessedness it possesses by nature.[126] Sometimes it is the women of Israel welcoming with dance and song the young David, conqueror of Goliath.[127]

Gregory depicts the victorious Lord climbing back up through the angelic spheres, but he is not recognized on his return either:

> Some voices say—the mystery of death had already been fulfilled, victory was achieved against the foe, the cross is raised as a trophy and "he who has made captivity captive is ascended on high" (Ps 67.19) . . . —that once

---

[121] *Antirrh.* 11 (PG 44:1154A; FC 131:127).

[122] *Cant.* 11 (PG 44:997A; Norris, 335).

[123] *Vit. Moys.* 2.187 (PG 44:384D; Malherbe, 102).

[124] For recent scholarship on the development of the feast of the Ascension, see Paul F. Bradshaw and Maxwell E. Johnson, *The Origins of Feasts, Fasts and Seasons in Early Christianity*, Alcuin Club Collections 86 (Collegeville, MN: Liturgical Press, 2011), 71 and esp. 74; for more detail, see Thomas J. Talley, *The Origins of the Liturgical Year* (New York: Pueblo Publishing Company, 1986), 66–70, esp. 67, which mentions Daniélou and St Gregory's Ascension sermon.—*Ed.*

[125] See *Eun.* 3.2.49 (PG 45:636B; NPNF² 5:158).

[126] See *Cant.* 11 (PG 44:997A; Norris, 335).

[127] See *Inscr.* 2.6.59 (PG 44:508B; Heine, 138).

again the transcendent gates are opened for him. Our guards[128] exchange the escort and ask that once again the transcendent gates are opened for him. ... But he who has girded himself with our life's dirty robe is not recognized because his garments were red from the wine vat of human evils (cf. Is 63.2). Therefore we have the voice of those attending him repeat: "Who is this King of Glory?"[129]

Thus the entire drama of the redemption is seen from a heavenly perspective, in its relation to the world of the angels. And for Gregory this is what properly constitutes *theōria*.

But the work of Christ does not consist only in restoring humanity to its original state in the world of the angels; it is also the creation of a new universe, that of the Church. This is what is symbolized by the lower tabernacle in the vision of Moses. In this tabernacle, the pillars are the apostles and the teachers. The incense of prayer offered morning and evening is a figure of the liturgical life. The lavers, or basins for washing, represent those who administer Baptism. The skin dyed red and the coverings made of woven hair are a symbol of the monastic life. Finally, the interconnecting courts "are fittingly understood as the harmony, love, and peace of believers."[130] Thus, the Church is as it were a reflection of the heavenly hierarchy, its own hierarchies replicating those of the angels.[131] This kind of reflection on the church hierarchy is something we often find in Gregory. At times he explicitly compares it to a new cosmos:

> The creation of the cosmos signifies the foundation of the Church, in which, according to the word of the prophet, both a new heaven is created (which is "the firmament of faith in Christ" [cf. Col 2.5], as Paul says) and a new earth is established (cf. Isa 65.17) which drinks "the rain that ... falls upon it" (cf. Heb 6.7), and another humanity, renewed by the birth from above "after the image of its Creator" (cf. Col 3.10) is fashioned, and a different race of heavenly lights comes to be, about which it says, "You are the light of the cosmos" (Mt 5.14), and "Among whom you shine as lights in the cosmos"

---

[128] The angels guarding the earth.
[129] *Ascens.* (PG 46:693B; McCambley, 4). It is a traditional theme. See Justin, *Dialogue with Trypho* 26.4–5; Irenaeus, *Demonstration of the Apostolic Preaching* 84; Origen, *Commentary on John* 6.56. See also J. Daniélou, *Bible et Liturgie* (Paris: Éditions du Cerf, 1951), 429–38. [In English: *The Bible and the Liturgy* (Notre Dame, IN: University of Notre Dame Press, 1956), 319–26].
[130] *Vit. Moys.* 2.186 (PG 44:385C; Malherbe, 102).
[131] See *Cant.* 7 (PG 44:917B; Norris, 227).

The City of Angels

(Phil 2.15), and many stars, which rise in the firmament of faith. Nor is it a matter for wonder if in this new cosmos there is "a multitude of stars" that are numbered and named by God (Ps 146.4), whose names, says the Creator of such stars, have been written in heaven (cf. Lk 10.20). . . . Well, then, just as the person who looks upon the perceptible cosmos and has grasped the Wisdom that is displayed in the beauty of these beings infers, on the basis of what the eye sees, the invisible beauty and the wellspring of Wisdom . . . so too the person who attends to this new cosmos that appears in the creation of the Church sees in it the One who is and is becoming "all in all" (cf. 1 Cor 15.28).[132]

Thus, according to an idea that we have already encountered, the earthly tabernacle is not simply a degraded version of the heavenly tabernacle. By virtue of the incarnation, God is made manifest in it—something that is a revelation even to the angels [cf. Eph 3.10—Ed.]. It is thus still always a matter of the incarnation as seen from the standpoint of the angels:

> For in truth it is through the Church that the multiform wisdom of God, which has worked its great marvels by the instrumentality of contraries, is made known to the powers above the cosmos [ταῖς ὑπερκοσμίοις δυνάμεσι, *tais hyperkosmiois dynamesi*]: how life came through death, and righteousness through sin. . . . In previous times, the powers above the cosmos knew only the simple and uniform [μονοειδής, *monoeidēs*] wisdom of God. . . . But they were brought to clear knowledge of this manifoldness of wisdom, which consists in the knitting together of contraries, through the Church.[133]

Thus Gregory's vision, this examination of *theōria* in his writings that has led us to survey the entire course of God's economy, ends with the last things, the restoration of all humanity to the world on high, the apokatastasis.[134] The unity of

---

[132] *Cant.* 13 (PG 44:1049B–D; Norris, 405–407).

[133] *Cant.* 8 (PG 44:948C–D; Norris, 269).

[134] On the interpretation of apokatastasis in Gregory, see Jean Daniélou, "L'Apocatastase chez saint Grégoire de Nysse," *Recherches de Science Religieuse* 30.3 (July 1940): 328–47. [Daniélou resisted simply identifying apokatastasis with universal salvation, and while his 1940 article (cited above) maintained that Gregory's thought was uncertain and fluctuating, tending toward universalism yet including clear affirmations of eternity of hell, in a 1970 article on apokatastasis he concluded, "One cannot say that he maintains the thesis of universal salvation." Jean Daniélou, "Apocatastase," in *L'Être et le Temps chez Grégoire de Nysse* (Leiden: Brill, 1970), 205–26 at 224. In contrast, other scholars, both then and now, have maintained that Gregory certainly affirmed universal salvation, e.g., Hans Urs von Balthasar, *Presence and Thought*, 85–87; Morwena Ludlow, *Universal Salvation: Eschatology in the Thought of Gregory of Nyssa*

the two tabernacles is restored: "So that . . . there might be a single harmonious feast as through the covering the tabernacle of the creation below joins in chorus with the preeminent powers appointed around the altar above. For the horns of the intelligible altar, the preeminent and appointed powers of the intellectual nature, are the 'princes, authorities, thrones, and dominions' to which human nature—covered in the renewal of bodies—is joined in the feast's communion through the tabernacling of the resurrection."[135] Restored too, then, is the unity of the intelligible, or spiritual, world. But this is not to be understood as simply a return to the original state. For the human adventure has given rise to the appearance of a new reality: that of the God-Man who introduces the paradox of the incarnation into the prior simplicity of his creation, mingling the purple of his passion with the white robes of the angels.

Such, then, is this realm of the angelic world that assumes such a large place in Gregory's thought, in that for him it constitutes the real world. From the point of view of his confident spiritualism, the *onta* are the *noēta*, except that the *noēta* are no longer the Platonic ideas, but spiritual persons. By nature, the soul belongs to this world. It is its present situation that is abnormal. Gregory's entire corpus is permeated by this profound feeling of the unreality of the world of sense perception and of nostalgia for the intelligible world of the angels, which is the homeland of his soul. With all his soul, this Christian Platonist yearns to circulate on high with the supra-mundane powers and to contemplate the splendors of the divine spectacles.

---

and Karl Rahner (Oxford: Oxford University Press, 2000), 1–111; and Ilaria L. E. Ramelli, *The Christian Doctrine of* Apokatastasis: *A Critical Assessement from the New Testament to Eriugena*, Supplements to Vigiliae Christianae 120 (Leiden: Brill, 2013), 372–440. In contrast, some scholars deny universalism in Gregory, e.g., Mario Baghos, "Reconsidering Apokatastasis in St Gregory of Nyssa's *On the Soul and Resurrection* and the *Catechetical Oration*," in *Cappadocian Legacy: A Critical Appraisal*, ed. Doru Costache and Philip Kariatlis (Sydney: St Andrew's Orthodox Press, 2013), 395–440; Michael Azkoul, *St. Gregory of Nyssa and the Tradition of the Fathers* (Lewiston, NY: The Edwin Mellen Press, 1995), 139–48. Giulio Maspero's article on apokatastasis in the *Brill Dictionary of Gregory of Nyssa* (pp. 55–64) is balanced and helpful. While many Nyssene passages and themes seem to lead to universal salvation, nevertheless, "The Nyssen's corpus contains explicit affirmations of the eternity of hell"; finally, regardless of the conclusion one draws regarding who Gregory thinks will be saved, he is always clear in affirming human freedom, and, as Mateo-Seco and Daniélou emphasize, in characterizing apokatastasis as an eschatological return to the protologically intended purpose of man (*Brill Dictionary*, 63–64). For a brief discussion of apokatastasis, its place and meaning in the Nyssene corpus, and the later patristic reception of such passages, see the introduction to Gregory of Nyssa, *Catechetical Discourse: A Handbook for Catechists*, trans. Ignatius Green, Popular Patristics Series 60 (Yonkers, NY: St Vladimir's Seminary Press, 2019), 38–58.—*Ed.*]

[135]*Diem. nat.* (PG 46:1129A–B; Radde-Gallwitz, 405).

But at the same time, God remains for him the one object of the soul's quest. The Bride of the Song inquires of all the watchmen of the city for her Beloved but, like Mary Magdalene at the sepulcher in her encounter with angels, finds no consolation, for it is her Beloved she needs. If Gregory sometimes pauses to describe the marvelous landscapes of the angelic world—"white rejoicing nations"[136]—he does not linger there, but prefers the vast divine night. Similarly, he shows us angels, friends of the Bridegroom, being more anxious to lead the Bride to him than to draw his attention to themselves. In *The Life of Moses* we see them assisting the soul at the beginning of its spiritual life,[137] then moving aside when it has reached a higher stage.[138] Such is always their role, one of preparation, which explains their special link with the Old Testament, with the life of children, and with the beginnings of the spiritual life. For Gregory, they are not necessary intermediaries between God and the soul as they are, for example, in Pseudo-Dionysius. Therefore the domain of *theōria* that is theirs is not the highest stage, but rather a point of departure.[139] But once it has reached this point, having found its true homeland, the soul will finally be able to set out on the way of love, in search of its Beloved.

---

[136][A quote from Rimbaud's prose poem *Adieu*, the final section of *Une Saison en Enfer*. The complete sentence is as follows: "*Quelquefois je vois au ciel des plages sans fin couvertes de blanches nations en joie*" (Sometimes I see in the sky endless shores covered with white nations rejoicing). There is a clear allusion to Revelation 7.9 and the multitude of nations standing before the throne, "clothed in white robes."—*Trans.*]

[137]See *Vit. Moys.* 2.45 (PG 44:337C; Malherbe, 64).

[138]See *Vit. Moys.* 2.119 (PG 44:361A; Malherbe, 82).

[139]See *Cant.* 6 (PG 44:893B–C; Norris, 195).

PART THREE

Darkness
or
On Love

6

The General Characteristics of the Third Way

In the second part of our study, we saw how, at the culmination of its ascent, the soul returns to the world of the supernatural powers, which is its own. Already in this life, it anticipates through contemplation its eschatological restoration to the world on high. But in our concluding pages we also saw that, having arrived at the third heaven and circulating among the angels, the *Soul-Church* sought for its Beloved in vain. Thus although there is a sense in which θεωρία (*theōria*, contemplation) is an accomplishment—just as ἀπάθεια (*apatheia*, dispassion) was, at the level of ethics—even so it is not a conclusion. And it is here that Gregory of Nyssa's originality becomes most clearly apparent, allowing one to see in him the true founder of mystical theology. Indeed, his key concept is that, even for the soul that has reached a state of contemplation, the divine essence still remains infinitely inaccessible.

With regard to this, no theme appears more frequently in his mystical writings than that of "disappointment." The soul always believes that it has arrived at the end, yet each time discovers that what it took to be the end is in reality nothing other than a new beginning. This is particularly true of *theōria*, and one may see here a criticism of the Platonic understanding of things. It is true that Plotinus had already shown that the One is situated beyond the *nous* (which corresponds to the world of ideas) and cannot be reached except through ecstasy, but this intuition is far more developed in our author. Moreover, in Gregory the transcendence of God's essence (οὐσία, *ousia*) is conceived of as infinitely greater than that of the Plotinian One, which does not in fact differ in nature from the soul. Here again, then, we find in Gregory a Plotinian theme, but whose significance is quite different in the two authors.

It is this quest for God's essence that the mystical life embodies. It corresponds to the highest levels of contemplation. Consistent with the perspective to which Gregory accustoms us, what had appeared first as a single reality unfolds in successive degrees. When we have managed to climb to what we think to be the highest rung, a new ladder always appears before us. Should the Gregorian soul even arrive at "the vault of heaven," it learns that it must ascend further still, differing in this respect from the Platonic soul. The stages of these new ascents are described in general terms in *The Life of Moses*—after the vision of the tabernacle, which is itself a symbol of *theōria*[1]—and in the *Homilies on the Song of Songs*. In the latter, which is entirely devoted to the mystical life, they correspond to an increasing awareness—symbolized by the different spiritual senses—of the presence of God, who little by little reveals himself.

In all this we see how Gregory heralds what at a later stage will become known as mystical theology. For him it essentially consists in the higher states of gnosis, which is itself a superior form of faith. Compared with Origen, his originality lies in the fact that he points to a third dimension beyond gnosis, which is precisely that of the mystical life. Yet although from one point of view this is indeed a continuation and extension of gnosis—and corresponds to the flowering of the life of faith produced in us by the gifts of the Holy Spirit—at the same time it displays new characteristics.

Thus our investigation will lead us to look again at certain themes, but to see them in a new light. In fact, one of the most pronounced characteristics of Gregory's approach to the spiritual life is precisely its holistic, comprehensive nature. By this I mean that the same facts and truths are taken up time and again, but at ever deeper levels. As pointed out at the beginning of our study, everything is already given in Baptism and Gregory will demonstrate that purification at the highest level, even purgatory itself, simply represents the full actualization of the sacrament. But this reality of our death and resurrection with Christ must come to fruition on the different levels of human nature. First is the death to sin and the passions—the night of the passions—that leads to dispassion. As seen, this is itself a process that is made up of many stages. Then there is the dying to the natural modes of knowing—both sensible and conceptual—that blossoms into *theōria*.

The mystical life encompasses a whole world of deaths and new resurrections. The latter are more difficult to discern with exactitude, although the mystics have described them. They are also as different from each other as are the deaths, or nights, of the senses and the understanding. It would appear that the human soul consists, as it were, of several layers of reality contained within each other, and that the successive removal of the superimposed outer garments

---

[1] *Vit. Moys.* 2.227–51 (PG 44:401B–408D; Malherbe, 113–19).

allows for progressive access to the inner man. Gradually one draws nearer to God, who inhabits the soul's center but who remains inaccessible, so much so that the spheres of interiority are of an infinite number. For Gregory, perfection consists, as we shall see, precisely in this perpetual movement toward the interior that constitutes a never-ending discovery of God.

Thus we see here a second characteristic that is common to spiritual life as a whole, and one that will play an important role in our study—namely, interiority. From the beginning of our investigation, we have seen that, together with the sacramental life that configures us to the death and Resurrection of Christ, two principal features of the spiritual life are withdrawal from the world and entering into the self—ἀναχώρησις (*anachōrēsis*) and monasticism. We then saw that this was also characteristic of the life of faith and in particular of *theōria* that, at the same time as being a "going out," an egress, from the world of nature, it is also an ingress, an "entering into" the inner world ever more deeply.

The essential characteristic of this concept of interiority is a progressive awareness of the presence of God in the soul, a theme that Gregory develops at length in his homily on the sixth Beatitude. It is an awareness that grows in proportion to the transformation of the soul in God—that is, in proportion to the restoration of the image of God in us. Here, too, we take up again a central theme: the image was restored at Baptism, but the *via purgativa* is entirely devoted to a concrete realization of this. Although this process leads, as seen, to dispassion, it does not cease there, despite what we might imagine. In fact, since it consists in partaking of the divine nature and since the divine nature is infinite, this participation is by definition always capable of further increase.

The restoration of the image is a process that can be envisaged, then, as consisting of different stages. Its starting point is Baptism; its first realization comes with *apatheia*. Then a return to angelic knowledge through the nights of the senses and all concepts is brought about by *theōria*. It is the higher stages of this process that lead to the mystical life proper. Progressively, through increased participation, the Participated One reveals himself; through the gift we begin to discover the Giver—so much so that an awareness of grace gradually becomes the experience of a Presence, a presence always veiled but always drawing closer, setting the heart on fire with a love that is ever more fervent. We shall see that what typifies the mystical life is those intense states where the soul is, as it were, wrested from itself through love, and which are described by means of such terms as wound, inebriation, or ecstasy.

On the one hand, then, a certain awareness of God is produced in the soul, which Gregory calls "a sense of presence," (αἴσθησις παρουσίας, *aisthēsis parousias*).[2] This presence, the result of grace itself, is perceived at first as a faint vestige of God. Then, through its effects, uncreated grace becomes more and more manifest. Moreover, the transformation of the soul results in a growing attraction to God, a love that is ever more ardent and that wrests the soul from itself. And here we have the second aspect of the mystical life proper: love, a going out from the self, ecstasy.

As can be seen, these two aspects follow on from one another. An awareness of grace and the sense of a presence come first. Then, as God reveals himself more and more, love grows stronger and gnosis is transformed into love. Thus after studying each of these two elements individually, as general characteristics of the mystical life, we shall consider their successive development. In so doing, we shall examine how the doctrine of the spiritual senses helps to express the progress made in this mystical perception of the presence of God. The "taste" for God typically leads to the idea of "sober inebriation." This in turn introduces us to the world of ecstasy, which is that of love. But this particular sequence of events should not be over-emphasized, for in reality mystical knowledge and mystical union are correlative. The one relates more to the intelligence, the other to the will. The first draws attention to the internality of God with regard to the soul, his indwelling in it; the second indicates the externality that at the same time he always maintains in relation to it. The difference is between that of a God partaken of, who has become immanent and is the object of experience, and that of a God not yet partaken of, who remains transcendent and is the object of love. It is precisely the uniting of these two elements that defines the mystical state, and thereby the very structure of the image: that is, of the soul in its essential depth as it was first created, since the mystical life is simply a return to this. This state is one of tension but progress, a perpetual deification. To refer to it, Gregory uses the symbol of the well of living waters, and such expressions as "stable movement" or "luminous darkness"—so many that point at the same time to the reality of deification and yet the distinction between God and man.

---

[2]*Cant.* 11 (PG 44:1001B; Norris, 343).

The Vocabulary of the Mysteries

The use of the vocabulary of the mystery religions is widespread in Hellenistic religious literature; it can be found in the writings of the gnostics, as in Philo and Plotinus. It seems that its introduction into the Christian liturgy was mainly due to Clement of Alexandria.[3] Koch's research has shown the important place it has in Pseudo-Dionysius.[4] As for Gregory of Nyssa, he represents a link in the tradition that extends from the one to the other. It is significant, too, that Gregory of Nazianzus also makes frequent use of this vocabulary. But only one point is of interest to us here. From the use of this particular vocabulary, can we gain any insights into the content of the texts in which it is found? A brief examination of the way our author uses the main terms is the only way to settle the question.

Mystērion

The first term to consider is the word μυστήριον (*mystērion*) itself.[5] In Gregory of Nyssa, it has four principal meanings. First, in many cases it simply denotes the "mystery" in the Pauline sense—that is, the "secret" hidden in God from all eternity and revealed in Christ of the economy or dispensation of salvation for humanity [Rom 16.25; Eph 3.9; Col 1.26; cf. 1 Cor 2.7—*Ed.*].[6] Thus we come across such phrases as "the mystery of the economy" (τὸ τῆς οἰκονομίας μυστήριον, *to tēs oikonomias mystērion*),[7] or "the mystery of godliness" (τὸ τῆς εὐσεβείας μυστήριον, *to tēs eusebeias mystērion*).[8] It can also refer to this or

---

[3]See A.-M. Festugière, "Εἰς ἄνθρωπον ὑποφέρεσθαι," *Revue des Sciences Philosophiques et Théologiques* 20 (1931): 476–82, at 478f.

[4]See Hugo Koch, *Pseudo-Dionysius Areopagita in seinen Beziehungen zum Neuplatonismus und Mysterienwesen* (Mainz: Kirchheim, 1900), 92f. [Such terminology continues in the later Byzantine Liturgy, e.g., the priest's prayer before the Great Entrance twice refers to the Divine Liturgy as an ἱερουργία (*hierourgia*, lit. sacred work; though this is an older word, cf. Plato, *Laws* 774e–775a); likewise, the pre-Communion prayers' verses before Communion call the Eucharist "Θεουργὸν Αἷμα" (*Theourgon Aima*, usually translated as "deifying Blood"), a reminder of the vocabulary of Neoplatonic theurgy (θεουργία, *theourgia*; lit. divine work, used by Neoplatonists to refer to magical rituals that were intended to achieve union with the divine, i.e., deification), associated especially with the Chaldean Oracles, Iamblichus, Julian, and Proclus.—*Ed.*]

[5]For a similar survey, concerning the use of this word by St Athanasius, see K. Prümm, "Mystērion bei Athanasius," *Zeitschrift für Katholische Theologie* 63 (1939): 350–59.

[6]This is in contrast to the Old Testament: "What do we learn from the mystery that is new [καινή, *kainē*]?" *Inscr.* 2.8.80 (PG 44:517D; Heine, 146).

[7]*Eun.* 3.1.46 (PG 45:581A; NPNF[2] 5:140). [The NPNF translation reads "the mystery of the Incarnation" but gives the Greek "τῆς οἰκονομίας" (*tēs oikonomias*) in a footnote.—*Ed.*]

[8]*Vit. Moys.* 2.273 (PG 44:413C; Malherbe, 124). [Gregory uses this Pauline phrase (taken from 1 Tim

that aspect of the total "mystery," in a way that is similar to the concept of the "mysteries of Christ" in the medieval sense. Accordingly, we find references to the "mystery of the Lord according to the flesh" (τὸ κατὰ τὴν σάρκα τοῦ Κυρίου μυστήριον, *to kata tēn sarka tou Kyriou mystērion*),[9] the "mystery of the cross,"[10] or the "mystery of the resurrection."[11]

Unlike the pagan mysteries, this mystery is meant to be promulgated. Thus Peter "manifestly reveals" (φανερῶς ἐγκαλύπτει, *phanerōs enkalyptei*) the "unspeakable [ἀπόρρητον, *aporrēton*] dispensation of this mystery."[12] "What evangelist," writes Gregory, "proclaims [ἐκβοᾷ, *ekboa*] the mystery so plainly [as the Psalmist]?"[13] Essentially, then, it is the mystery of the good news, the "mystery of the gospel,"[14] and the apostles are the "servants of the ... mystery" (οἱ ὑπηρέται τοῦ μυστηρίου, *hoi hypēretai tou mystēriou*).[15]

A second meaning, no longer Pauline, is the word's sacramental inference. Here we move from a Hebrew to a Hellenistic way of thinking,[16] and, as well as the noun *mystērion*, it is the entire vocabulary of the mystery religions that is used: μυεῖν (*myein*, to initiate), for example, or μυσταγωγία (*mystagōgia*, initiation into mysteries). It is no longer a question of revealing a secret but of initiating into reserved rites. In this sense, then, *mystērion* is used by Gregory to refer to the sacraments in general, to "the observance of the sacraments" (ἡ ἀκρίβεια τῶν μυστηρίων, *hē akribeia tōn mystēriōn*).[17] It is also used to denote the various sacraments individually. Thus the Eucharist is a "mystery."[18] Baptism is referred to as "the mystery of regeneration" (τὸ τῆς παλιγγενεσίας μυστήριον,

---

3.16) throughout his works, e.g., *Or. cat.* Prol. 1 (GNO III/4:5e.2; PPS 60:60); *Cant.* 13, 15 (GNO VI:387, 432; Norris, 409, 461); *Eun.* 1.30.438c, 3.3.9.54, 3.3.9.56 (GNO I:154, GNO II:284, 285; NPNF[2] 5:238; the penultimate instance is quoting Eunomius).—Ed.]

[9] *Eun.* 3.3.52 (PG 44:700D; NPNF[2] 5:179). Cf. *Vit. Moys.* 2.159 (PG 44:376A; Malherbe, 93).

[10] *Vit. Moys.* 2.151, 277 (PG 44:372C, 416B; Malherbe, 91, 125).

[11] *Vit. Moys.* 2.132 (PG 44:365C; Malherbe, 86)

[12] *Eun.* 3.3.44 (PG 45:697B; NPNF[2] 5:178).

[13] *Inscr.* 1.8.91 (PG 44:473B; Heine, 113).

[14] *Inscr.* 2.8.75 (PG 44:516B; Heine, 144).

[15] *Vit. Moys.* 2.184 (PG 44:385A; Malherbe, 101).

[16] One sometimes finds this vocabulary used in sense one. For example, see *Eun.* 3.5.13 (PG 45:744C; NPNF[2] 5:192): "παρὰ τοῦ ἀποστόλου μυσταγωγούμενοι [*para tou apostolou mystagōgoumenoi*, being led onward by the Apostle in the mysteries] ... μαθόντες παρὰ τοῦ μυηθέντος [*mathontes para tou myēthentos*, learning from him who was initiated into the unspeakable mysteries]." See also *Cant.* 15 (PG 44:1089A; Norris, 461): δᾳδουχήσας αὐτῷ τὸ τῆς εὐσεβείας μυστήριον [*dadouchēsas autō tēs eusebeias mystērion*, illuminating for him the mystery of true religion (1 Tim 3.16)].

[17] *Eccl.* 8 (PG 44:745D; Hall, 138).

[18] *Perf.* (PG 46:268B; FC 58:107); *Vit. Moys.* 2.139 (PG 44:369D; Malherbe, 88).

The General Characteristics of the Third Way 207

to tēs palingenesias mystērion)¹⁹ or the "mystic economy" (τῆς μυστικῆς ... οἰκονομίας, tēs mystikēs ... oikonomias).²⁰ Confession is "the mystery of repentance" (τὸ τῆς μετανοίας μυστήριον, to tēs metanoias mystērion).²¹

As indicated above, this use of *mystērion* is linked to that of other words of the same root. Μυεῖν (*myein*, to initiate), for instance, is used for baptismal initiation, as in "after initiation" (μετὰ τὴν μύησιν, *meta tēn myēsin*),²² or "the initiated" (τῶν μεμυημένων, *tōn memyēmenōn*).²³ Μυστικός (*mystikos*) must often be translated as "sacramental." Indeed, the sacraments are called the μυστικὰ σύμβολα (*mystika symbola*), literally the "mystic symbols."²⁴ Gregory refers to "participation in the mystical customs and tokens" (τῶν μυστικῶν ἐθῶν ... κοινωνίᾳ, *tōn mystikōn ethōn ... koinōnia*).²⁵ To give one last example, μυσταγωγία (*mystagōgia*) is used to mean "mystagogical instruction" with reference to the institution of the Eucharist.²⁶

The third way in which Gregory uses the term is to refer to "the hidden meaning" or "spiritual sense" of Scripture. Here it is a synonym for such words as αἴνιγμα (*ainigma*, a dark saying, a riddle) or ἀναγωγή (*anagōgē*, raising or leading up [the mind to higher things]). Thus the spiritual interpretation of Scripture is described as "knowledge of the mysteries" (γνῶσις τῶν μυστηρίων, *gnōsis tōn mystēriōn*).²⁷ This spiritual understanding comes from God; it is he who reveals the "hidden mysteries" (τὰ κεκρυμμένα μυστήρια, *ta kekrymmena mystēria*) of Scripture.²⁸ In line with this third use of the term, we come across such phrases as the following: "the mystery of the rock" (τὸ τῆς πέτρας μυστήριον, *to tēs petras mystērion*);²⁹ "the mystery of the Sabbath;"³⁰ or of the

---

¹⁹*Eun.* 3.2.51 (PG 45:877D; NPNF² 5:238). [Cf. "the mystery of the birth from above [τὸ τῆς ἄνωθεν γεννήσεως ... μυστήριον (*to tēs anōthen gennēseōs ... mystērion*)]." *Cant.* 8 (GNO VI:250; Norris, 263), alluding to John 3.3–8.—*Ed.*]
²⁰*Or. cat.* 34.4 (PG 45:85C; PPS 60:138).
²¹*Vit. Moys.* 2.269 (PG 44:413A; Malherbe, 123).
²²*Or. cat.* 40.3 (PG 45:101D; PPS 60:154).
²³*Eun.* 3.9.59 (PG 45:881A; NPNF2 5:238). Cf. "Τὸν τὰ θεῖα μεμυημένον μυστήρια" (*Ton ta theia memyēmenon mystēria*, a man who has been initiated into the Divine mysteries). Gregory, *Or. dom.* 3 (PG 44:1153B; ACW 18:49).
²⁴*Eun.* 3.9.59 (PG 45:881A; NPNF² 5:239). ["Sacramental tokens," in the translation referred to, which consistently replaces "mystery" with "sacrament." In the Orthodox Church, the sacraments are still habitually called "mysteries."—*Trans.*]
²⁵*Eun.* 3.9.56 (PG 45:880B; ibid.).
²⁶See *Cant.* 10 (PG 44:989B; Norris, 325).
²⁷*Cant.* Prol. (PG 44:757A; Norris, 5).
²⁸*Cant.* 12 (PG 44:1036C; Norris, 387).
²⁹*Vit. Moys.* 2.148 (PG 44:372A; Malherbe, 90).
³⁰*Inscr.* 2.9.89 (PG 44:524A; Heine, 149).

Shulamite.[31] In a more general manner, Gregory speaks of the "mysteries of the law"[32] or of the prophetic symbols.[33]

The fourth meaning is of special interest to us, for it is related more specifically to the spiritual life. The first thing to note is that, in this sense, the word is used in the plural: τὰ μυστήρια (*ta mystēria*). Thus Gregory writes of Benjamin that he is "instructed in the mysteries by means of ecstasy,"[34] or of Paul, to whom "the mysteries of Paradise were revealed ... by the Spirit,"[35] or of David, who "declared the heavenly mysteries."[36] We notice at once that in these examples the word is linked to the highest degree of the spiritual life—the "ecstasy" of Benjamin, the "rapture" of Paul into paradise, the "voyage to heaven" of David. Here the term "mysteries" specifically denotes the object of "mystical" knowledge.

It is noteworthy that Gregory uses the word to refer in particular to the two most distinctive cases of persons having such mystical knowledge—Paul and Moses. For Paul, we have already given two examples, since Benjamin is a figure of Paul [Phil 3.5]. In the famous passage from Paul's letter to the Corinthians (2 Cor 12.4) to which Gregory alludes, the term *mystērion* does not actually appear, although it is found in another verse to which he often refers—namely, "We speak the wisdom of God in a mystery" (1 Cor 2.7).[37] Here are examples from Gregory that are more specific still: "[Paul], lifted up as far as the third heaven (2 Cor 12.2) ... rejoiced [ἐναγαλλόμενος, *enagallomenos*] in the secret [ἀπορρήτοις, *aporrētois*] mysteries of paradise, and saw the invisible [ἀθέατα, *atheata*] things, and delighted [ἐντρυφῶν, *entryphōn*] in all those things which are beyond perception and sense."[38] We see how the concept of "mysteries" is related to the third heaven, to the invisible things, to the night of the senses and the intelligence, and to supernatural joy. Elsewhere, we find other terms that are equally characteristic: "Doubtless [Paul] himself had a vision [ὀπτασία, *optasia*] of the tabernacle when he entered the supercelestial sanctuary [ἐν

---

[31]See *Cant.* 7 (PG 44:909A; Norris, 217).
[32]*Cant.* 13 (PG 44:1037D; Norris, 391).
[33]See *Bas.* (PG 46:800B; McCambley, 17).
[34]*Inscr.* 2.14.212 (PG 44:577B; Heine, 190). [See Ps 67.27, which in the LXX reads: "There is Benjamin the younger in ecstasy" (ἐν ἐκστάσει, *en ekstasei*).—Ed.]
[35]*Vit. Moys.* 2.178 (PG 44:384A; Malherbe, 99).
[36]*Eun.* 3.5.14 (PG 45:744D; NPNF² 5:192).
[37]See, for example, *Eun.* 3.2.158 PG 45:676A; NPNF² 5:170) and *Vit. Moys.* 2.174 (PG 44:381A; Malherbe, 98).
[38]*Eccl.* 5 (PG 44:685A; Hall, 90–91).

The General Characteristics of the Third Way 209

ἀδύτοις, *en adytois*] where the mysteries of Paradise were revealed to him by the Spirit."[39]

As for Moses, the way Gregory uses the vocabulary of the mysteries during the episode at Sinai is even more distinctive. Moreover, mystical initiation is here presented in terms recalling that of Baptism:

> [After the episode of the cloud], Moses guided them in a most secret initiation [ἀπορρητοτέρας μυήσεως, *aporrētoteras myēseōs*]. The divine power itself by marvels beyond description [ὑπὲρ λόγον, *hyper logon*] initiated [μυσταγωγούσης, *mystagōgousēs*] all the people and their leader himself in the following manner. The people were ordered beforehand to keep themselves from defilements of all kinds ... [so that] they might approach the mountain to be initiated [μυηθησόμενον, *myēthēsomenon*], cleansed of every emotion and bodily concern.[40]

Gregory refers elsewhere to this historic episode as "the initiation on the mountain" (ἡ κατὰ τὸ ὄρος μυσταγωγία, *hē kata to oros mystagōgia*),[41] but throughout *The Life of Moses* he will use it symbolically to interpret the mystical life, using similar expressions.[42]

Consequently, it comes as no surprise to find vocabulary from the mystery religions being used frequently in what is Gregory's preeminent treatise on the mystical life, the *Homilies on the Song of Songs*: "Having ... purified the heart of its bent toward appearances, [Wisdom] then, in the Song of Songs initiates

---

[39] *Vit. Moys*. 2.178 (PG 44:384A; Malherbe, 99). See also *Perf*. (PG 46:264C; FC 58:105); *Cant*. 8 (PG 44:940D; Norris, 257);

[40] *Vit. Moys*.1.42 (PG 44:316A; Malherbe, 41–42). Cf. "πρὸς γὰρ τὸ ἄρρητον τῆς θείας μυσταγωγίας [*pros gar to arrēton tēs theias mystagōgias*, he entered the inner sanctuary of the divine mystical doctrine]" (ibid. 1.46; PG 44:317A; Malherbe, 43); "τούτοις τοῖς νόμοις προκαθαρθεὶς τὴν διάνοιαν ἐπὶ τὴν τελειοτέραν μυσταγωγίαν παράγεται [*toutois tois nomois prokathartheis tēn dianoian epi tēn teleioteran mystagōgian paragetai*, with his mind purified by these laws, he was led to the higher initiation]" (ibid. 1.49; PG 44:317C; Malherbe, 44); ἐν τῇ ἀπορρήτῳ τοῦ θεοῦ διδασκαλίᾳ ἐξεπαιδεύθη ... τῇ προσθήκῃ τῶν μυστικῶν μαθημάτων [*en tē aporrētō tou theou didascalia exepaideuthē ... tē prosthēke tōn mystikōn mathēmatōn*, After he was instructed ... by the ineffable teaching of God ... by the aid of the mystical doctrines]" (ibid. 1.56; PG 44:320D; Malherbe, 46); cf. also "that divine initiation" (ibid. 1.58; PG 44:321A; Malherbe, 46).

[41] *Or. dom*. 2 (PG 44:1136D; ACW 18:35). Philo had already presented the ascent of Sinai as a μυσταγωγία (*mystagōgia*, initiation into the mysteries): "And while [Moses] was still abiding in the mountain he was initiated [ἐμυσταγωγεῖτο, *emystagōgeito*] in the sacred will of God, being instructed in all the most important matters which relate to his priesthood [ἱερωσυνήν, *hierosynēn*]." *On the Life of Moses* 2.15.71 (Yonge, 497).

[42] See, for example, *Vit. Moys*. 2.162 (PG 44:376D; Malherbe, 94–95), 2.188 (PG 44:388A; Malherbe, 102), 2.315 (PG 44:428C; Malherbe, 136).

[μυσταγωγεῖ, *mystagōgei*] the mind into the innermost divine sanctuary [τῶν θείων ἀδύτων, *tōn theiōn adytōn*]."⁴³ Thus entry into the mystical life is the quintessential "mystagogy." Already in the *Homilies on Ecclesiastes*, the highest stage following purification (προκαθήρας, *prokathēras*) and detachment from vain desires (πάσης ἀποστήσας τῆς κατὰ τὸ μάταιον ἐπιθυμίας, *pasēs apostēsas tēs kata to mataion epithymias*) was presented as an "initiation."⁴⁴ Likewise, from the beginning of the first of the *Homilies on the Song of Songs* the entire treatise is presented as a "mystical vision" (μυστικὴ θεωρία, *mystikē theōria*).⁴⁵ The contents of the book are described as mysteries: "Let each depart from himself [ἐκβὰς ἑαυτοῦ, *ekbas heautou*] . . . and ascend somehow, by way of impassibility into paradise . . . [and] let him in this fashion journey to the inner shrine [τὸ ἄδυτον, *to adyton*] of the mysteries manifested to us in this book."⁴⁶ Candidates to the mystical life are "candidates for initiation" (μυσταγωγούμενοι, *mystagōgoumenoi*).⁴⁷ The very phrases that we find in the book are described as μυστικά (*mystika*).⁴⁸ And the teaching in it is qualified as μυστήρια μυστηρίων (*mystēria mystēriōn*, mysteries of mysteries)."⁴⁹

This all goes to demonstrate the technical character of the vocabulary of the mysteries when used to denote the third way and all that is linked to it. Moreover, this vocabulary is connected with the various features that characterize this third way, such as darkness: "What is the initiatory process [ἡ μυσταγωγία, *hē mystagōgia*], then, that this night causes the soul to undergo?"⁵⁰ Here darkness is clearly presented as typifying the third way, after separation from evil, after the sacramental (μυστικοῦ, *mystikou*) kiss,⁵¹ and the successful transcending of appearances. Likewise, the term "mysteries" is linked to the love that also characterizes the third way, the way of union: "Young maidens of this sort, then, who have made increase by the practice of the virtues and have already participated in the mysteries of the divine chamber [θεῖα μυστήρια, *theia mystēria*] . . . love

---

⁴³*Cant.* 1 (PG 44:772A; Norris, 23).
⁴⁴*Eccl.* 5 (PG 44:680B; Hall, 87).
⁴⁵*Cant.* 1 (PG 44:765A; Norris, 15). Here the word could also mean a "spiritual interpretation" of the biblical text. This would be sense three.
⁴⁶*Cant.* 1 (PG 44:773A; Norris, 27).
⁴⁷Ibid.
⁴⁸See *Cant.* 1 (PG 44:773D; Norris, 29).
⁴⁹*Cant.* 1 (PG 44:773C; Norris, 29). The mystical graces are κεκρυμμένα μυστήρια (*kekrymmena mystēria*, hidden mysteries) (*Cant.* 1; PG 44:785C; Norris, 45), St John is filled with the mysteries of Christ by "an indescribable [ἄρρητον, *arrēton*] transmission" (ibid.).
⁵⁰*Cant.* 11 (PG 44:1001C; Norris, 343).
⁵¹Here *mystērion* is used in the second sense.

Adyton

We have already encountered the word ἄδυτον (*adyton*) several times. It refers to the most secluded part of the Jerusalem temple, the part forbidden to the multitude, the Holy of Holies. As we have already seen, the third way was itself referred to as an entrance "into the innermost shrine of the knowledge of God" (ἐν τοῖς ἀδύτοις τῆς θεογνωσίας, *en tois adytois tēs theognōsias*).[53] The word was also used of Paul's "vision of the tabernacle when he entered the supercelestial sanctuary" (ἐν τοῖς ὑπερουρανίοις ἀδύτοις, *en tois hyperouraniois adytois*).[54]

Gregory included a lengthy study of this word in his third homily on the Lord's Prayer. I quote below the most important passages:

> The Law, having a shadow of the good things to come, prefigures the truth in types and allegories. When it introduces the priest into the Holy of Holies [τὸ ἄδυτον, *to adyton*] in order to pray to God, it purges him before entering by purifying aspersions. It then puts on him the priestly robe ... and thus brings him into the Holy of Holies to perform the sacred [ἀπορρήτους, *aporrētous*, lit. ineffable or unspeakable] rites [ἱερουργίας, *hierourgias*].
>
> But the spiritual Lawgiver, Our Lord Jesus Christ, strips the Law of its material veils and lays bare the types and allegories [τῶν τυπῶν, *tōn typōn*]. First of all, He does not give communion with God only to one whom He separates from everyone else, but He bestows this honour equally on all, offering the grace of the priesthood as common to those who desire it.[55]

Gregory then explains how the vestments of the high priest were symbolic of the inner dispositions of the soul: the vestment with the brilliant colors represents the beauty of the virtues; the golden plaque purity of conscience. And he continues:

---

[52]*Cant.* 1 (PG 44:784C; Norris, 41).
[53]*Cant.* 11 (PG 44:1000D; Norris, 341).
[54]*Vit. Moys.* 2.178 (PG 44:381D; Malherbe, 99). Cf. *Bas.* (PG 46:793B–D; McCambley, 15): "[Paul] then put off this crass, fleshly covering and was received into the heavenly chambers [ἄδυτα, *adyta*] ... where he underwent an unutterable initiation [τῇ ἀρρήτῳ μυσταγωγίᾳ, *tē arrētō mystagōgia*] by truth."
[55]*Or. dom.* 3 (PG 44:1148D–1149A; ACW 18:45).

> [Christ] leads him to the *adyton*, that is, to the innermost part [ἐνδότατον, *endotaton*] of the Temple. This *adyton* is not inanimate nor made by hands; but it is the hidden inner chamber [τὸ κρυπτὸν ταμιεῖον, *to krypton tameion*] of our heart, if it be truly impenetrable [ἄδυτον, *adyton*] to evil and inaccessible [ἀνεπίβατον, *anepibaton*] to vile thoughts.... Being thus led by the Lord to this sacrifice, he mortifies his fleshly mind with the sword of the spirit, which is the word of God, and thus appeases God.... He dwells in the supercelestial *adyta* (sanctuaries) which are *adyta* (forbidden) to all profane thought and truly inaccessible [ἀνεπίβατα, *anepibata*].... Now there remains to consider the petition itself which the person within the sanctuary has been ordered to offer to God.[56]

An initial observation is that the context is no longer one of mysteries but of the priesthood. In reality, however, it is both, for the two have been merged together. Gregory does not refer to the mysteries in a direct manner. Nor does Dionysius, despite the opinion of Koch.[57] Both writers are simply following in the footsteps of Philo in applying the vocabulary of the mystery religions to the Old Testament, in particular to the texts that relate to the tabernacle and the high priest. They do so in two ways: the one ritual—such as we encountered when discussing the sacraments—the other spiritual, as here, where the priestly realities of the Old Law are regarded as figures of spiritual realities.[58]

The role played by the tabernacle and the high priest in Philo's allegorical system is well known. It is this entire imagery—which is already highly developed—that Gregory takes over, after Clement. The passage we have translated is interesting in that it demonstrates Gregory's method, illustrating the typological foundation of his spiritual interpretation and showing how he effects a transition from the letter to the spirit. Thus he shows the way in which we are to understand the *adyton*. It does represent the interior (τὸ ἐνδότατον, *to endotaton*). Here, though, he has in mind not the most secluded part of the temple, but rather the innermost depths of the soul, the secret chamber. It is a holy place, forbidden to everything that is profane (βέβηλος, *bebēlos*); hence its name, *adyton*, which literally means "not to be entered." The reference, then, is to the mystical reality of the sanctuary of the soul, a place where God dwells

---

[56]Gregory, *Or. dom.* 3 (PG 44:1149D–1152A; ACW 18:46–47).
[57]See Koch, *Pseudo-Dionysius Areopagitica*.
[58]See J. Pascher, *Hē basilikē hodos: Der Königsweg zu Wiedergeburt und Vergottung bei Philon von Alexandreia* (Paderborn: Schöningh, 1931): 266–72.

and which one must enter (εἰσδύειν, *eisdyein*) to find him and live in intimacy (ὁμιλία, *homilia*) with him.[59]

In the above text it is a matter of the highest level of prayer, which presupposes that one has already become separated from the external world and withdrawn into this sanctuary of the soul. With this prayer we are already on the threshold of the mystical life, and it is the *adyton* that delimits this threshold. In an analogous allegorical context, the *adyton* denotes that which is properly supernatural, the grace of divine adoption:

> Moses the Lawgiver fashioned the sacred Tabernacle for the Israelites according to the pattern which God had shown him on the mountain. Whatever was contained within [κατὰ τὸ ἐντός, *kata to entos*] the sanctuary was pure and sacred; but its innermost part [τὸ ἐνδότατον, *to endotaton*] was forbidden (*adyton*) and inaccessible [ἄβατον, *abaton*] and was called the Holy of Holies. I think this more emphatic appellation shows that the sacredness of this part was not the same as that of the others; but inasmuch as something that has been duly consecrated differs from what is common and profane, the *adyton* is of purer holiness [ἱερώτερον, *hierōteron*] than the sacred places around it. But what we are now invited to contemplate is truly *adyton*, and the Holy of Holies. For if the blessedness of seeing God cannot be surpassed, to become a son of God transcends bliss altogether. . . . It is fulfilment that outstrips prayer, gift surpassing hope, grace transcending nature.[60]

I have quoted this text, although it is not directly related to the spiritual life, because more than any other it makes us appreciate the spiritual significance both of the *adyton* and the two features that characterize it: maximum interiority and total transcendence. The latter is expressed by a crystal-clear formula that is unique to Gregory and that sounds quite modern: "grace transcending nature" (ὑπὲρ φύσιν ἡ χάρις, *hyper physin hē charis*). Thus the *adyton* denotes

---

[59] This vocabulary is found in Plotinus: "Εἰς τὸ εἴσω τοῦ ἀδύτου εἴσδυς" (*Eis to eisō tou adytou eisdys*, having penetrated the inner sanctuary); *Enneads* 6.9.11.

[60] *Beat.* 7 (PG 44:1277A–C; ACW 18:154). We find a third allegorical interpretation of the tabernacle in *On the Soul and the Resurrection*, with similar vocabulary: "Τὸ ἀπόκρυφον καὶ ἄδυτον τοῦ ναοῦ . . . ἀπορρητοτέραν καὶ μυστικωτέραν προσάγων ἱερουργίαν ἐπὶ τὰ ἐντὸς παρεδύετο" (*To apokryphon kai adyton tou naou . . . aporrētoteran kai mystikōteran prosagōn hierourgian epi ta entos paredyeto*, The hidden and inaccessible part of the Temple . . . bringing a more secret and mystical sacrifice, [the high priest] entered alone into the interior room). *An. et res.* 10 (PG 46:133A; PPS 12:105). But here the allegory symbolizes the various classes of people. Those who have strayed to false beliefs are outside the divine enclosure.

that which is properly supernatural. Its allegorical use, then, could be applied to various contexts: to the grace of divine filiation as here, or to mystical graces elsewhere.

Normally the term *adyton* will feature when a text is dealing with the third way, as the place where the union of God and the soul is consummated, and where the soul contemplates God in the darkness. This is particularly the case in *The Life of Moses*, as is illustrated by the following passage: "First, [it] leaves behind the base of the mountain and is separated from all those too weak for the ascent. Then as [it] rises higher in [its] ascent [it] hears the sound of the trumpets. Thereupon, [it] slips into the inner sanctuary of divine knowledge" (εἰς τὸ ἀόρατον τῆς θεογνωσίας ἄδυτον, *eis to aoraton tēs theognōsias adyton*).[61] Here, the *adyton* is seen to be the proper domain of mystical knowledge. It is contrasted with the second way, for example, in the introduction to the *Homilies on the Song of Songs* or in *On the Inscriptions of the Psalms*: "[Having] passed over in his soul everything which appears to the senses. When he enters the heavenly shrines [ἐντὸς τῶν ὑπερουρανίων ἀδύτον, *entos tōn hyperouraniōn adytōn*] . . ."[62]

A comparison between the Holy of Holies, the *adyton*, and the sanctuary of the soul is clearly seen in the following:

> If the interior, which is called the Holy of Holies, is not accessible [ἀνεπίβατον, *anepibaton*] to the multitude, let us not think that this is at variance with the sequence of what has been perceived. For the truth of reality [ἡ τῶν ὄντων ἀλήθεια, *hē tōn ontōn alētheia*] is truly a holy thing, a holy of holies, and is incomprehensible and inaccessible [ἄληπτον καὶ ἀπρόσιτον, *alēpton kai aprositon*] to the multitude. Since it is set [καθιδρυμένη, *kathidrymenē*] in the secret and ineffable areas [ἐν ἀδύτοις καὶ ἀπορρήτοις, *en adytois kai aporrētois*] of the tabernacle of mystery, the apprehension of the realities above comprehension should not be meddled with. . . . [O]ne should rather believe . . . that it remains in the secret [ἐν τοῖς ἀδύτοις, *en tois adytois*] and ineffable areas of the intelligence.[63]

---

[61] *Vit. Moys.* 2.167 (PG 44:377C-D; Malherbe, 96). The same progression is evident in the following: "ἐντὸς τῶν ἀδύτων τῆς θεογνωσίας γίνεται, τῷ θείῳ γνόφῳ πανταχόθεν διαληφθεῖσα" (*entos tōn adytōn tēs theognōsias ginetai, tō theiō gnophō pantachothen dialēphtheisa*; But the soul that has made its way through these stages to higher things . . . enters within the innermost shrine of the knowledge of God and is entirely seized about by the divine darkness). *Cant.* 11 (PG 44:1000D; Norris, 341).

[62] *Inscr.* 1.6.45 (PG 44:453B; Heine, 99).

[63] *Vit. Moys.* 2.188 (PG 44:388A; Malherbe, 102–103).

The General Characteristics of the Third Way

The most noteworthy aspect of this passage is the accumulation of negative terms marking the inaccessibility of the sanctuary of the heart: aside from *adyton*, we have *aporrēton* (ineffable), *anepibaton* (inaccessible), and *alēpton* (incomprehensible). This helps us to grasp more fully the meaning of the term *adyton*. It clearly refers to a domain that is beyond the reach of the senses or reason, forbidden to the natural man, a place to which only God can gain admittance, and for which it is consequently necessary to be pure and free from all defilement. The domain of the mystical life and its strictly supernatural character could not be better defined.

This idea of prohibition is emphasized in the following passage: "Not all thrust themselves [εἰσωθεῖν, *eisōthein*] toward the apprehension of the mysteries, but, choosing from among themselves someone who is able to hear things divine, they give ear gratefully to him, considering trustworthy whatever they might hear from someone initiated [μυηθέντος, *myēthentos*] into the divine mysteries."[64] In fact, anyone who attempts to point the way without being purified and chosen will be stoned with stones from the mountain.[65] This passage also hints at the social character—charismatic, in the apostolic sense of the term—of the graces of contemplation, which are granted to some for the benefit of all, given precisely to those whose mission it is to lead others. We shall return to this essential point.

In connection with the use of *adyton* to indicate the transcendent quality of the mystical life, we may note the use of a certain number of other terms of similar meaning. The most important are ἀπόρρητον (*aporrēton*, ineffable, or forbidden, secret) and ἄρρητον (*arrēton*, inexpressible). The second is used by St Paul (2 Cor 12.4) when discussing his own experience and refers to the mystical silence associated with the highest levels of revelation.[66] *Aporrēton*, which is very similar to *adyton*, is used more frequently. Indeed, we have already encountered a unique expression formed from a combination of these two terms: "in the secret and ineffable areas" (ἐν τοῖς ἀδύτοις καὶ ἀπορρήτοις, *en tois adytois kai aporrētois*).[67] It too is also used to refer to the secret chamber of the soul, "the storeroom, that is to say the secret and unmentionable things of [the sinner's] life" (τὰ ταμιεῖα, τοῦτ' ἐστὶ τὰ κρυπτὰ τοῦ βίου καὶ ἀπόρρητα, *ta tamieia, tout' esti ta krypta tou biou kai aporrēta*).[68] We find it linked to other

---

[64] *Vit. Moys.* 2.160 (PG 44:376B; Malherbe, 94).
[65] See *Cant.* 1 (PG 44:773B; Norris, 29).
[66] See *Cant.* 15 (PG 44:1108C; Norris, 485).
[67] *Vit. Moys.* 2.188 (PG 44:388A; Malherbe, 102–103).
[68] *Vit. Moys.* 2.72 (PG 44:345D; Malherbe, 70).

words typical of the third way. For example, Moses is "led to the ineffable knowledge of God" (τῇ ἀπορρήτῳ θεογνωσίᾳ, tē aporrētō theognōsia).[69] He alone is allowed "to learn . . . the secrets" (γνῶναι τὰ ἀπόρρητα, gnōnai ta aporrēta).[70] Aporrēton is synonymous with mystēria, when it is said of David that he "was initiated into the mysteries in the same inner sanctuary" (ἐν ἀδύτῳ μυηθεὶς τὰ ἀπόρρητα, en adytō[71] myētheis ta aporrēta theōria).[72] Mystical contemplation is described as "contemplating the ineffable secrets" (ἡ τῶν ἀπορρήτων θεωρία, hē tōn aporrētōn theōria).[73] The word is sometimes used in conjunction with adyton and gnophos: "He entered the darkness [γνόφος, gnophos]. He slipped into [παραδύεται, paradyetai] the inner sanctuary [ἄδυτα, adyta] of the tabernacle not made with hands. He learned the secrets [τὰ ἀπόρρητα, ta aporrēta] of the divine priesthood."[74]

The examples so far cited are all from *The Life of Moses*, but the word is also found in other texts and contexts. Thus, it can refer to an inspiration of the Holy Spirit: "*Diapsalma* is a teaching from the Spirit which occurs in a mysterious manner [κατὰ τὸ ἀπόρρητον, kata to aporrēton] in the soul."[75] Elsewhere it is characteristic of what is beyond nature: "Whenever you go beyond [ὑπερβάς, hyperbas] the things which appear and approach the secret things [τοῖς ἀπορρήτοις] in the Word . . ."[76] It is always the same contrast between the realm of nature (the world of appearances, where the mind is at home) and that of the supernatural (the world of realities, which is forbidden to it). Finally, in the strict sense, the term denotes the mysteries that ecstasy leads to: "[Paul] rejoiced in the secret mysteries [ἐν τοῖς ἀπορρήτοις μυστηρίοις, en tois aporrētois mystēriois] of paradise."[77]

Transcendence is also indicated by Gregory's frequent use of other privative words, such as ἄληπτος (alēptos, hard to grasp, incomprehensible), ἀνεπίβατος

---

[69] *Vit. Moys.* 2.152 (PG 44:372D; Malherbe, 91).
[70] *Vit. Moys.* 2.160 (PG 44:376B; Malherbe, 94).
[71] I read ἀδύτῳ (*adytō*) with the Venetian manuscript. [The one that belonged to Cardinal Bessarion: *Venetus Marcianus 67, membr. saec. XIV.—Trans.*] Migne (PG 44:377B) has αὐτῷ (*autō*).
[72] *Vit. Moys.* 2.164 (PG 44:377B; Malherbe, 95).
[73] *Vit. Moys.* 2.181 (PG 44:384C; Malherbe, 100).
[74] *Vit. Moys.* 2.229 (PG 44:401C; Malherbe, 114).
[75] *Inscr.* 2.10.116 (PG 44:536B; Heine, 158). See also *Inscr.* 2.10.129 (PG 44:541A; Heine, 162–63).
[76] *Inscr.* 2.11.154 (PG 44:552A; Heine, 169).
[77] *Eccl.* 5 (PG 44:685A; Hall, 91). The meaning is more general and linked to the general sense of mystery in the following: "τὴν ἀπόρρητόν τε καὶ κεκρυμμένην . . . θεολογίαν" (*tēn apporrēton te kai kekrymmenēn theologian*, the esoteric teaching about God hidden in doctrines which are hard to understand). *Inscr.* 1.3.17 (PG 44:437D; Heine, 87). See also *Inscr.* 2.12.164 (PG 44:553C; Heine, 172).

The General Characteristics of the Third Way

(*anepibatos*, not to be climbed, inaccessible), ἄβατος (*abatos*, untrodden, inaccessible), ἀνέφικτος (*anephiktos*, out of reach, beyond understanding), and ἀχώρητος (*achōrētos*, uncontainable). Let us mention just one other example, differently formed but expressing the same idea: ὑπερουράνιος (*hyperouranios*, supercelestial). We have already come across it several times, in combination with *adyton*. Thus "when he enters the heavenly shrines,"[78] "he dwells in the supercelestial *adyta*" (ἐν τοῖς ὑπερουρανίοις ἀδύτοις, *en tois hyperouraniois adytois*).[79] Here we find the imagery of spheres superimposed on the imagery of the temple—which is all the easier to understand since the temple is itself a metaphor for the cosmos, so that there is a correspondence between "the third heaven"—which is above the natural heavens—and the *adyta* of the tabernacle.

But, as already pointed out, transcendence is but one aspect of the *adyton*; there is also the idea of interiority. It is the union between these two that more accurately characterizes the mystical life. At the beginning of his *Homilies on the Song of Songs*, Gregory underlines this characteristic of the return of the soul to itself. But this is only the beginning. The soul should progress further and enter into its innermost depths, into that realm of which all the mystics speak. St Teresa of Avila, for example: "[The mystic] perceives quite clearly, in the way I have described, that [the Three Persons] are in the interior of her heart—in the most interior place of all and in its greatest depths."[80] The *adyton* is this "most inward part"—τὸ ἐνδότατον (*to endotaton*), as Gregory calls it.

These last two words are frequently used in conjunction: "[Moses is led to] the *adyton*, that is, to the innermost part of the Temple [ἐπὶ τὸ ἄδυτον καὶ ἐνδότατον, *epi to adyton kai endotaton*]."[81] Thus, the progress the soul makes is by plunging ever more deeply into its own interiority: "For leaving behind everything that is observed, not only what sense comprehends but also what the intelligence thinks it sees, it keeps on penetrating deeper [ἐνδότερον, *endoteron*] until by the intelligence's yearning for understanding it gains access to [διαδυῇ, *diadyē*] the invisible and the incomprehensible, and there it sees God."[82] The

---

[78]*Inscr.* 1.6.45 (PG 44:453B; Heine, 99).
[79]*Or. dom.* 3 (PG 44:1152A; ACW 18:47).
[80]Teresa of Avila, *The Interior Castle*, Seventh Mansions, Chapter 1. English translation: Teresa of Avila, *The Interior Castle*, trans. and ed. E. Allison Peers (London: Sheed & Ward, 1974), 149.
[81]*Or. dom.* 3 (PG 44:1149C; ACW 18:46).
[82]*Vit. Moys.* 2.163 (PG 44:377A; Malherbe, 95).

culmination of this progress is the arrival at the innermost part, where God dwells in darkness.

One of the paradoxes of the mystical life—such as the concept of a "luminous cloud"—is this double characteristic of there being a place *beyond* the soul, which is nonetheless reached by leaving the external sensible world and entering *into* the soul's innermost part. Gregory conveys this paradox by bringing together the concepts of leaving and entering, ecstasy and enstasy: "What a happy exodus is this, which the soul makes that is following the Word! 'The Lord will preserve your exodus and your entrance' (Ps 120.8), says the prophet. This is truly at one and the same time the exodus [ἡ ἔξοδος, *hē exodos*] and the entrance [ἡ εἴσοδος, *hē eisodos*] that God keeps for those that are worthy, since the exodus from our present state becomes an entrance upon the good things that lie beyond."[83] Thus, such a soul "always 'strains forward [ἐπεκτεινόμενος, *epekteinomenos*] to what lies ahead' (Phil 3.13). She does not stop departing from where she is, or working her way inwards [εἰσδυόμενος ... εἰς τὸ ἐνδότερον, *eisdyomenos ... eis to endoteron*] where she has not yet been."[84]

The verb used to describe this entering into the depths is δύω (*dyō*, enter, make one's way into), together with various compounds. Used in combination with *adyton*, it forms another of Gregory's oxymoronic expressions—comparable to ἰδεῖν ἀόρατα (*idein aorata*, to see the invisible)—to convey the idea of penetrating the impenetrable. It also highlights the two aspects of interiority and transcendence. We have already come across this type of wording several times. The following examples are chosen at random: "When he enters [παραδύς, *paradys*] the heavenly shrines [*adyta*],"[85] "He slipped into [προσδύεται, *prosdyetai*] the inner sanctuary of the tabernacle [τὰ ἄδυτα τῆς σκηνῆς, *ta adyta tēs skēnēs*],"[86] "[The soul] gains access to [διαδυῇ, *diadyē*] the invisible ... and there she sees God,"[87] "... working her way inwards [εἰσδυόμενος ... εἰς τὸ ἐνδότερον, *eisdyomenos ... eis to endoteron*]."[88] These few examples give us four different compounds—παραδύεσθαι (*paradyesthai*), προσδύεσθαι (*prosdyesthai*), διαδύεσθαι (*diadyesthai*), and εἰσδύεσθαι (*eisdyesthai*)[89]—which illustrate all the possible nuances.

[83] *Cant.* 12 (PG 44:1024D; Norris, 373–75).
[84] Ibid. (PG 44:1036A; Norris, 385).
[85] *Inscr.* 1.6.45 (PG 44:453B; Heine, 99).
[86] *Vit. Moys.* 2.229 (PG 44:401C; Malherbe, 114).
[87] *Vit. Moys.* 2.163 (PG 44:377A; Malherbe, 95; mod).
[88] *Cant.* 12 (PG 44:1036A; Norris, 385).
[89] This particular compound will be borrowed from Gregory by Dionysius the Pseudo-Areopagite. (Puech, "La ténèbre mystique," 45.)

The General Characteristics of the Third Way 219

Many other examples could be adduced, but they are always in a similar context and are used in a technical sense to refer to the mystical life. "He slips into [παραδύεται, *paradyetai*] the inner sanctuary of divine knowledge [θεογνωσίας, *theognōsias*]."[90] "When he who has been purified and is sharp of hearing in his heart hears this sound—I am speaking of the knowledge of the divine power which comes from the contemplation of reality [ἡ τῶν ὄντων θεωρία, *hē tōn ontōn theōria*]—he is led by it to the place where his intelligence lets him slip into [διαδῦναι, *diadynai*] where God is. This is called 'darkness' by the scripture."[91] Here we have a clear reference to the three ways: purification, illumination, and finally union, symbolized by the entry (διαδυῇ, *diadyē*) into the darkness.

In the following passage there is a similar progression:

> [The] soul, empowered by her success in slipping through [διαδυεῖσα, *diadyeisa*] to the interior of what thought cannot articulate [ἀπορρήτων, *aporrētōn*], cries out her request that her running not be confined to the outer courts [προθύροις, *prothyrois*] of the Good but by the first fruits of the Spirit (cf. Rom 8.23)—of which she was made worthy by the first gift of grace, that is, by a kiss—she may come to the inner shrine [ἀδύτοις, *adytois*] of paradise and search "the depths of God" (1 Cor 2.10) and, like the great Paul, see (as he says) invisible things and hear unspeakable words (cf. 2 Cor 12.2–4).[92]

Here too the innermost place to which the soul penetrates is described in no uncertain terms as *aporrēton* and *adyton*, the first fruits of the Spirit, paradise. The "outer courts" (πρόθυρα, *prothyra*) represent the preliminary purification and illumination.

Theognōsia

Finally, of the words used to describe in a general way the domain of the mystical life, there is the term θεογνωσία (*theognōsia*, knowledge of God). It is this that Gregory chooses when specifically referring to the mystical life proper, the third way. Origen, by contrast, opted for θεολογία (*theologia*). Admittedly, Gregory does sometimes use this latter term, as in the following example: "The knowledge of God [θεολογία, *theologia*] is a mountain steep indeed and difficult to climb."[93]

---

[90] *Vit. Moys.* 2.167 (PG 44:377D; Malherbe, 96).
[91] *Vit. Moys.* 2.169 (PG 44:380A; Malherbe, 96–97).
[92] *Cant.* 1 (PG 44:785A; Norris, 43).
[93] *Vit. Moys.* 2.158 (PG 44:373D; Malherbe, 93).

But when he does so use it, it tends to have a more general meaning, as when he writes concerning "the esoteric teaching about God [θεολογίαν, *theologian*] hidden in doctrines which are hard to understand."[94] Here the vocabulary does resemble that of mystical theology, but it is really more a question of interpreting things spiritually.

Although the term *theognōsia* is found in Clement, and indeed in Origen, Gregory specifies its meaning by restricting it to knowledge of the mysteries in the *adyton*. In a sentence such as the following, it still has a fairly general meaning: "[Profane philosophies] miscarry before they come to the light of the knowledge of God [θεογνωσίας, *theognosias*]."[95] Even though the contrast between *theognōsia* and rational ways of knowing is common in theological works, it typically signifies knowledge of the Trinity. This is its meaning in the phrase "the [mystery] of knowing God" (τὸ τῆς θεογνωσίας μυστήριον, *to tēs theognōsias mystērion*).[96]

In Gregory's commentaries *On the Inscriptions of the Psalms*, the meaning is already much more specific and closer to the context of mystical knowledge: "The inscription, 'Concerning the Hidden Things,' (Ps 9) enjoins that we achieve accuracy concerning knowledge of God [θεογνωσίαν, *theognosian*] ... the inscription offers you, as it were a light, the word which investigates the hidden things of the knowledge of God, the source of which is faith in the Son. For how truly is that hidden which is incomprehensible, invisible, and which transcends every thought."[97] Here the two meanings of mystery—a hidden secret and essential incomprehensibility—are brought together, as is also the case in this passage found a little later in the book:

> He has revealed to you, O men, that it is possible for the human sense of hearing to receive the divine mysteries. But when you have been led by these things to the pious knowledge of God [θεογνωσίαν, *theognōsian*], exalt the glory of God to the extent that your mind is capable, knowing that your understanding has been strained to the uttermost, and has exceeded every imaginable exalted notion about God, then what you have discovered and worship is not the majesty itself of the one who is sought, but his footstool.[98]

---

[94]*Inscr.* 1.3.17 (PG 44:437D; Hiene, 87).

[95]*Vit. Moys.* 2.11 (PG 44:329B; Malherbe, 57).

[96]*Eun.* 1.314 (PG 45:349A; NPNF² 5:122). [The translation referred to reads "secret," not "mystery."—*Trans.*]

[97]*Inscr.* 2.5.49 (PG 44:504B; Heine, 135 [mod.]).

[98]*Inscr.* 2.9.112 (PG 44:533B; Heine, 156–57).

The General Characteristics of the Third Way

Yet in the above passages, the basic idea is that of the ordinary knowledge of the faith. In the more spiritual treatises, however, *theognōsia* signifies not only the orthodox faith, but the most exalted mode of this knowledge of God,[99] and it is linked to the themes we have just been examining. Thus of Moses we read that, after passing through various trials, "[he] is then led to the ineffable [ἀπορρήτῳ, *aporrētō*] knowledge of God. Scripture teaches us by these things the nature and the number of things one must accomplish in life before he would at sometime dare to approach in his understanding the mountain of the knowledge of God [θεογνωσίᾳ, *theognōsia*]."[100] Entering the darkness, Moses "slips into the inner sanctuary of divine knowledge" (παραδύεται εἰς τὸ ἀόρατον τῆς θεογνωσίας ἄδυτον, *paradyetai eis to aoraton tēs theognōsias adyton*).[101]

In the *Homilies on the Song of Songs* Gregory refers to "the spiritual mountain of the knowledge of God" (τῷ πνευματικῷ τῆς θεογνωσίας ὄρει, *tō pneumatikō tēs theognōsias orei*).[102] The Song itself offers "guidance in all matters having to do with philosophy and the knowledge of God [θεογνωσία καὶ φιλοσοφία, *theognōsia kai philosophia*]."[103] This knowledge—"the gold of undefiled knowledge of God"—is symbolized by the gold of the Bride's necklace.[104] Finally, and even more explicitly, after retracing the necessary preparatory stages of the soul's ascent, Gregory writes: "But the soul that has made its way through these stages to higher things, having left behind whatever is accessible to human nature, enters within the innermost shrine of the knowledge of God [ἐντὸς τῶν τῆς θεογνωσίας ἀδύτων, *entos tōn tēs theognōsias adytōn*] and is entirely seized about by the divine darkness."[105] Here the word is directly and specifically linked to the *adyton* and the darkness; that is, to the terms that characterize the third way.

The Divine Darkness

We have seen that—using the journeying of Moses as a symbol of the return of the soul to God—Gregory associated the first of the three ways with the Burning Bush, the second with the cloud, and the third with the darkness in which God

---

[99] It is thus contrasted with πίστις (*pistis*, faith) in, for example, *Bas.* (PG 46:817B; McCambley, 24), which recalls the Pauline contrast between faith and gnosis.
[100] *Vit. Moys.* 2.152 (PG 44:372D; Malherbe, 91).
[101] *Vit. Moys.* 2.167 (PG 44:377C; Malherbe, 96).
[102] *Cant.* 1 (PG 44:773C; Norris, 27).
[103] *Cant.* 2 (PG 44:788C; Norris, 49).
[104] *Cant.* 3 (PG 44:817B; Norris, 93).
[105] *Cant.* 11 (PG 44:1000D; Norris, 341).

appears on Sinai. This theme of darkness is part of an entire tradition that goes back to Philo, and it seems likely that on this point Gregory is directly dependent on him. The following two texts suggest as much. The first is from Philo's *On the Posterity of Cain*, the second from Gregory's *The Life of Moses*:

> [Moses] will now penetrate into "the darkness where God was" (Ex 20. 21). That is to say, into those unapproachable [ἀδύτους, *adytous*] and invisible [ἀειδεῖς, *aeideis*] conceptions which are formed of the living Being. ... When, therefore, the soul that loves God seeks to know what the one living God is according to his essence, it is entering upon an obscure and dark subject of investigation, from which the greatest benefit that arises to it is to comprehend that God, as to his essence, is utterly incomprehensible to any being, and also to be aware that he is invisible [ἀόρατος, *aoratos*].[106]
>
> What does it mean that Moses entered the darkness? ... Scripture teaches us by this that ... as the mind progresses and ... approaches more nearly to contemplation, it sees more clearly what of the divine nature is uncontemplated. ... This is the true knowledge of what is sought; this is the seeing that consists in not seeing.[107]

But what meaning does this darkness have for Philo? The above extract resembles a philosophical exposition dressed up in allegorical language rather than the expression of some personal mystical experience. As Puech says, "Philo's commentary on the cloud shows that his allegorism rests not on experience, but on dogmatic speculation governed by the very clear affirmation of the incomprehensibility of the divine essence, that remains forever transcendent to any finite and changing creature."[108]

Philo's interpretation is taken up by Clement of Alexandria,[109] but no author has devoted more space to it than Gregory of Nyssa. It is from him, as is proved by the instances of textual dependence, that Pseudo-Dionysius will inherit this theme. And through Pseudo-Dionysius all subsequent mysticism, up to St John of the Cross, will be enriched by it. It is thus one of the places where his influence on the creation of a mystical language is most evident. Although Gregory did not invent this theme, his own influence—as is the case with other symbols, such as "sober intoxication"—lies in the fact that he transposed it from

---

[106] Philo, *On the Posterity of Cain and his Exile* 5.14–15 (Yonge, 133).
[107] *Vit. Moys.* 2.162–63 (PG 44:376D–377A; Malherbe, 94–95).
[108] Puech, "La ténèbre mystique," 47. See also Völker, *Fortschritt und Vollendung*, 306ff.
[109] Cf. Clement of Alexandria, *Miscellanies* (*Stomata*) 2.2.

the realm of abstraction to being the expression of actual mystical experiences, and gave it a psychological meaning. "Should one wish to find something that is similar to the concrete content of the Dark Night of St John of the Cross," writes Puech, "one must look in the direction of a Gregory of Nyssa, in whom the loving and desperate pursuit of an object that is infinite is depicted with a degree of emphasis and emotion that gives the impression of something personally experienced."[110]

Here too, we shall proceed by making a careful study of the texts, for it is in this way that we shall be able to determine the significance of Gregory's doctrine with certainty. This will also allow us accurately to situate it within the overall context of his thought. But first, a preliminary remark: the theme of darkness is always linked to the allegory of the life of Moses.[111] The "darkness" is that of Sinai and so always refers to Moses' own experience, which is regarded as being the model of all mystical experience. It is not a question of some vague theme, but a definite allusion to a specific event. We shall first point out certain texts where *gnophos* appears without commentary, and then examine the texts where this darkness is explained.

The first thing to say is that darkness is the "place" of revelations: "As on Mt Sinai, strive to enter with the great Moses the darkness of unutterable contemplation [εἰς τὸν γνόφον τῆς τῶν ἀπορρήτων θεωρίας, *eis ton gnophon tēs tōn aporrētōn theōrias*], in which he beholds invisible, ineffable realities."[112] Here darkness is linked to the contemplation of the mysteries. This already places us on the level of the third way, which is a vision of invisible realities. It is this very paradox that it seeks to express: first, the affirmation of a vision, yet at the same time of a non-vision (namely, of the intellect). It is the contrast between these two affirmations that defines the "super-vision" that is characteristic of the mystical level.

This darkness reappears in the various references to Moses throughout the corpus. As in the following comment: "He had keen vision in the divine

[110]Puech, "La ténèbre mystique," 53. On this question, see Koch, "Das mystische Schauen," 397–420, at 416; J. Lebreton, "La nuit obscure, d'après Jean de la Croix: Les sources et le caractère de sa doctrine," *Revue d'ascétique et de mystique* 9 (1928): 2–24; G. Horn, "Le 'miroir' et la 'nuée.' "

[111]Similarly, when the term *eikōn* is used, the reference is always to Genesis. This explains why it appears only once in *The Life of Moses*, and why *gnophos* does not appear at all in the sixth homily on the Beatitudes (which belongs to the paradisal cycle). This does not mean that it is a question of different realities, as Horn claimed in the article cited above, but rather that Gregory has three cycles of images at his disposal—that of paradise (with *eikōn*), that of Exodus (with *gnophos*), and that of the Song (with *eros*)—to express the same reality.

[112]*Hex.* (PG 44:65C; McCambley, 2).

darkness [ἐν τῷ θείῳ γνόφῳ, *en tō theiō gnophō*], and beheld the One who is invisible in it."[113] He returns to it in the lives of the saintly people he compares to Moses. Thus of Basil he writes: "We know that he often entered the darkness where God resided. To other persons the mystagogy of the Spirit was made visible which was unseen and appeared within the darkness' embrace which concealed [ἐναποκρύπτεται, *enapokryptetai*] the word concerning God."[114] This direct testimony is interesting, for it defines the darkness as a supernatural mode of knowing, whose principle is the Spirit, and which is inaccessible "to other persons." It is important to take note of this positive, supernatural character.

The cloud also has a very positive character in the following passage from Gregory's biography of Gregory the Wonderworker:

> For just as the word says that Moses, having left the world of appearances and calmed his soul within the invisible shrines (for this is what "the darkness" stands for), learned the divine mysteries, and in person instructed the whole people in the knowledge of God, the same dispensation is to be seen in the case of this Great One. He had not some visible mountain of earth but the pinnacle of ardent desire for the true teachings; for darkness, the vision [θέαμα, *theama*] which others could not comprehend. . . .[115]

Here, grouped together, are all the themes and terms characteristic of the third way: transcending appearances, *adyton*, *theognōsia*, *mystēria*, and *gnophos*. But let us note above all that the cloud is described as a spectacle.[116] There is no question here of absolute obscurity, of total darkness, but of a spectacle that is forbidden to most and contemplated by only a few. Here we are far from the "formless" quest of Philo, or "the void" of Plotinus. It is not even a question of a negative asceticism that might enable one to grasp invisible things. Rather, it is a case of a radical invisibility that is beyond the scope of all asceticism, and yet at the same time a visibility whose principle is in the "new eyes" created by the Spirit.

We can now tackle the essential texts in which Gregory goes into more detailed explanation of this darkness. The first are taken from *The Life of*

---

[113] *Inscr.* 1.7.54 (PG 44:457A; Heine, 102). Cf. *Cant.* 12 (PG 44:1025C; Norris, 375). In *Ad Theophilum, Adversos Apollinaristas* (*Theoph.*) (PG 45:1272D; FC 131:262), Gregory distinguishes a series of manifestations: "in light, in darkness, in a pillar of cloud, in face-to-face encounter." See also *Inscr.* 2.9.107 (PG 44:532A; Heine, 154–55).

[114] *Bas.* (PG 46:812C; McCambley, 22).

[115] *Thaum.* 4.32 (PG 46:913B; FC 98:55).

[116] ["Spectacle" (θέαμα, *theama*)—translated as "vision" in the above citation.—*Trans.*]

The General Characteristics of the Third Way

Moses. Gregory has already mentioned the preparations necessary for anyone who wants to enter "the darkness where God is."[117] He then continues as follows:

> What does it mean that Moses entered the darkness and then saw God in it? What is now recounted seems somehow to be contrary to the first theophany, for then the Divine was beheld in light but now he is seen in darkness. . . . Scripture teaches by this that religious knowledge comes at first to those who receive it as light. Therefore what is perceived to be contrary to religion is darkness. . . . But as the mind progresses and, through an ever greater and more perfect diligence, comes to apprehend reality, as it approaches more nearly to contemplation, it sees more clearly what of the divine nature is uncontemplated [ἀθεώρητον, *atheōrēton*].
>
> For leaving behind everything that is observed, not only what sense comprehends but also what the intelligence thinks it sees, it keeps on penetrating deeper until by the intelligence's yearning for understanding it gains access to the invisible and the incomprehensible [τὸ ἀθέατον καὶ ἀκατάληπτον, *to atheaton kai akatalēpton*] and there it sees God.[118]

This passage should be compared with the following similar text from the *Homilies on the Song of Songs*: "The revelation of God to the great Moses began with light as its medium, but afterward God spoke to him through the medium of a cloud, and when he had become more lifted up and more perfect, he saw God in darkness." Gregory links these first two theophanies to the first two ways, and then continues: "The soul that has made its way through these stages to higher things, having left behind whatever is accessible to human nature, enters within the innermost shrine of the knowledge of God [ἐντὸς τῶν ἀδύτων τῆς θεογνωσίας, *entos tōn adytōn tēs theognōsias*] and is entirely seized about by the divine darkness [τῷ θείῳ γνόφῳ, *tō theiō gnophō*]; and in this darkness, since everything that appears and is comprehended has been left outside, only the invisible [τὸ ἀόρατον, *to aoraton*] and the incomprehensible [τὸ ἀκατάληπτον, *to akatalēpton*] remain for the soul's contemplation—and in them God is."[119]

Both these passages detail the same progression: separation from the ungodliness that corresponds to the purgative first way; attention (προσοχή, *prosochē*)

---

[117] *Vit. Moys.* 2.152 (PG 44:372D; Malherbe, 91).
[118] *Vit. Moys.* 2.162–63 (PG 44:376C–377A; Malherbe, 94–95).
[119] *Cant.* 11 (PG 44:1000D–1001A; Norris, 339–41).

to gaining knowledge of the realities that represents the illuminative or second way; and finally, at the end of the process, a transcending of all appearances, not only sensible but conceptual (καταλαμβανόμενον, *katalambanomenon*). This implies a transcending of all of the mind's natural activity. It is this, strictly speaking, that is the darkness: namely, the darkness of the mind when faced with the divine reality, which is invisible and incomprehensible. Although this state is formulated in negative terms, this is not because it is itself a negative entity—on the contrary, it is very positive—but because its reality, which surpasses nature, cannot be formulated in conceptual terms. Gregory clarifies this as follows:

> This is the true knowledge of what is sought; this is the seeing that consists in not seeing, because that which is sought transcends all knowledge, being separated on all sides by incomprehensibility as by a kind of darkness [τινι γνόφῳ τῇ ἀκαταληψίᾳ πανταχόθεν διειλεμμένον, *tini gnophō tē akatalēpsia pantachothen dieilemmenon*].[120] Wherefore John the sublime, who penetrated into the luminous darkness [λαμπρῷ γνόφῳ, *lamprō gnophō*], says, "No one has ever seen God," [Jn 1.18] thus asserting that knowledge of the divine essence is unattainable [ἀνέφικτον, *anephikton*] not only by men but also by every intelligent creature.
>
> When, therefore, Moses grew in knowledge, he declared that he had seen God in the darkness, that is, that he had then come to know that what is divine is beyond all knowledge and comprehension, for the text says, "Moses approached the dark cloud where God was." [Ex 20.21] What God? He who "made darkness his hiding place," [Ps 17.11] as David says, who also was initiated into the mysteries in the same inner sanctuary.[121]

This key passage enables us to understand the true meaning of this darkness. It is the radical transcendence of God with regard to all that is natural, and to all that the intellect is capable of. In this respect, God is truly surrounded by "incomprehensibility" (ἀκαταληψία, *akatalēpsia*) as if by darkness. But this darkness, according to a formula we find here for the first time and which Pseudo-Dionysius will take up, is nonetheless a "luminous darkness" (λαμπρὸς γνόφος, *lampros gnophos*). It is a supremely positive reality that natural man

---

[120]Cf. "the darkness of obscurity" (ὁ γνόφος τῆς ἀσαφείας, *ho gnophos tēs asapheias*). *Cant.* 1 (PG 44:773B; Norris, 29).

[121]*Vit. Moys.* 2.163–64 (PG 44:377A–B; Malherbe, 95). The link with Ps 17.12—"[God] made darkness his hiding place"—goes back to Origen (*Contra Celsum* 6.17).

The General Characteristics of the Third Way

has no experience of, since his eyes are not made for it, but to which God can introduce him mysteriously.

The texts describing this life "in darkness" should now be clearer. It is in the first place a life of pure faith, freed from any intellectual support whatsoever. That is the important lesson that the Bride (the soul), in her quest for God, receives from the angels:

> But they fell silent in the face of this inquiry and by their silence [σιωπῇ, *siōpē*] showed that the One she sought was imperceptible even to them. At this point ... she left behind everything she had already found and in this way recognized the object of her search, whose existence is known only in incomprehension of what it is. ... So she says, "No sooner had I passed them by, having departed from the whole created order and passed by everything in the creation that is intelligible and left behind every conceptual approach, than I found the Beloved by faith, and holding on by faith's grasp [τῇ λαβῇ, *tē labē*] to the one I have found, I will not let go until he is within my chamber." Now the chamber is surely the heart, which at that moment became receptive of his divine indwelling [ἐνοικήσεως, *enoikēseōs*]—at the moment, that is, when it returned to that condition in which it was at the beginning.[122]

This was also the lesson of the story of Abraham: "It is impossible to draw near to God, unless faith mediate, and bring the seeking soul into union with the incomprehensible nature of God."[123]

These texts clearly show that we are here in another order of reality. The "darkness" signifies a break with the ordinary domain of knowledge. Through faith we begin to glimpse the proper type of relationship that is established, in the dark, between God and the soul. There is no longer any intellectual grasping, but something entirely different: a relationship with an existing person. This is the meaning of that "indwelling" (ἐνοίκησις, *enoikēsis*) toward which faith aspires and which reminds us of the *adyta*, the *endotata*, the inner chamber of the heart. This is the mysterious domain where, beyond all concepts, in a union of love, contact is established between God and the soul. As we better understand the meaning of the darkness, we understand why it takes the soul so long to get used to it. For it is always wanting to return to its familiar ways of knowing,

---

[122]*Cant.* 6 (PG 44:893B–C; Norris, 195–97).
[123]*Eun.* 2.91 (PG 45:941B; NPNF² 5:259).

to its "gains" (τὰ εὑρισκόμενα, *ta euriskomena*; lit. the things that are found, or earned). The divine pedagogy lets it understand little by little that it must divest itself of all this, that it is only in pure faith that one is able mysteriously to contact the one who always remains "hidden in darkness."

Gregory expressed this experience of faith by a phrase that goes to the very heart of mysticism and that shows how well he had understood its essence: the "sense of presence," (αἴσθησις παρουσίας, *aisthēsis parousias*). "[After the soul has gone beyond all the sensory] she is already surrounded by the divine night [θείας νυκτός, *theias nyktos*], in which the Bridegroom draws near but is not manifest [παραγίνεται, οὐ φαίνεται, *paraginetai, ou phainetai*]. But how may that which is not seen appear in the night? It confers on the soul some perception of its presence [αἴσθησιν παρουσίας, *aisthēsin parousias*], but it escapes clear and distinct intellectual grasp in being concealed by the invisibility of its nature."[124] Here we have the very core of the mystical experience. All that we shall have to say is but a commentary on this sense of presence, which is something infinitely real and yet at the same time always veiled. This presence, perceived to begin with as a faraway fragrance, a distant sound, will become more clearly defined—as nourishment, touch, inebriation—but always in the night, that is, in an order different from that of ordinary experience, a supernatural, ineffable, reserved order. Although referring in particular to the intellectual order, the "darkness" is the same reality under another name as that which we saw described as "mystery" and "sanctuary."

The fact remains—and this is its second aspect—that it is not only darkness because it is in a domain that is inaccessible to ordinary knowledge, but because the experience is always infinitesimal compared with its object. This is the last aspect that Gregory develops: "'And when you have received me, and taken me into your home [ἐνοικήσασθαι, *enoikēsasthai*], your reward will be the dew from my head, of which I am full, and the drops of the night that flow from my locks.'... It is not possible, after all, for one who has entered the place of things beyond our grasp and vision [ἐντὸς τῶν ἀδύτων καὶ ἀθεάτων, *entos tōn adytōn kai atheatōn*] to take in some great torrent or deluge of knowledge, but it is enough if Truth drizzle down knowledge of them by way of thoughts that are subtle and only just discernible."[125]

---

[124] *Cant.* 11 (PG 44:1001B–C; Norris, 343).
[125] Ibid. (PG 44:1004A; Norris 345).

The General Characteristics of the Third Way

Compared to the immensity of the darkness, each of these drops of the divine night is minuscule. Even Paul, no matter how high he was raised, "is shown not truly to have seized [his] goal."[126] Even though raised to the third heaven, he showed that the words he uttered were only a drop of dew next to the reality of the Logos.[127] Yet compared with our own abilities, they seem "rivers, and seas and billows."[128] Thus if the smallest drop with which God deigns to quench the soul fills it with such an ocean of delight, what are we to think of what God is himself, of whom such graces represent only a minute participation? Thus, notwithstanding the minute amount of light he communicates to the soul, God always remains surrounded by the darkness of his vastness. The faith that gives us a certain knowledge of the unseen realities does not enlighten them entirely. Gregory's thinking on this point is very clear: for the soul, God will always remain a mystery. Here, then, we encounter a new darkness. It is no longer simply a symbol of natural man's radical inability, as he stands at the threshold of the mystical life, to understand God. For even to one who has already embarked upon this life, it remains a symbol—though now at a deeper level. Namely, a symbol of the superabundance of the divine Being in comparison to the knowledge the soul has of him. At the very heart of the mystical life, then, the "darkness"—or at least this new reality that bears the same name—persists.

This new aspect of darkness features clearly in the following passage from the *Homilies on the Song of Songs*:

> The Bride [soul] who in her own mind has attained the highest of her hopes and has already, in her own judgment, been united with [ἀνακεκρᾶσθαι, *anakekrasthai*] the One she desires should call her more perfect participation [μετουσίαν, *metousian*] in the Good a "bed" and should term the time of her going to bed "night." Now the word "night" points to contemplation of things unseen [θεωρία τῶν ἀοράτων, *theōria tōn aoratōn*], just like Moses, who entered into the darkness in which God was (cf. Ex 20.21)—God who, as the prophet says, "made darkness his hiding place round about him."[129] And once the soul was there, she learned that she was as far from arriving at

---

[126]*Cant.* 5 (PG 44:860B; Norris, 151). [See Phil 3.12–13 (NB: ἐπεκτεινόμενος, *epekteinomenos* in v.13 helps to inspire Gregory's concept of *epektasis*). See Daniélou's discussion below (pp. 344–63).—*Ed.*]

[127]See also *Cant.* 3 (PG 44:820B; Norris, 93–95).

[128]*Cant.* 11 (PG 44:1004C; Norris, 345).

[129]We find the same comparison between the "darkness" of Exodus and the "night" of the Song in a passage attributed by the catenae to St Athanasius (PG 27:1349A) but which, according to Puech, should be restored to Gregory of Nyssa.

perfection as those that had not yet made a beginning. For she says: "Even when, as one judged worthy of perfection, I am taking my rest as upon some bed of the comprehension of what I have known; when I have entered into the Invisible, with the world of sense left behind me; when surrounded by the divine night, I am seeking what is hidden in the darkness—that is when I have indeed laid hold on love for the one I desire, but the object of my love has flown from the net of my thoughts.[130]

The darkness here is, of course, also to be understood in the first sense of the word, that is, as a state that is beyond the sensible and intelligible life. The words used to describe it in the above passage—such as love and participation—show that this is a state of union. Even so, however, the soul does not necessarily apprehend all that it seeks. God still remains darkness. For Gregory, what this second connotation of darkness points to is the never-exhausted nature of our knowledge of God. We will never be able to comprehend him. The soul must therefore persist in a quest that is perpetual, since even if God does from now on begin to communicate something of himself, nevertheless—and this is the radical difference from the first type of darkness—he continues infinitely to outstrip its grasp. The soul is united to him by love; it does not apprehend him by its understanding of the faith.

This is of considerable importance, since it is an intrinsic feature of Gregory's approach to mystical knowledge and indeed defines an entire aspect of it. To identify this, we shall use a word that he himself sometimes resorts to: *epektasis*. In fact, it is this that constitutes what is most original in his thinking on darkness. That God's essence exceeds the capacity of the natural intellect is something that has been asserted by all Christian writers. But that his essence will always remains a "luminous darkness" for the faith, even in the beatific vision, is something that only mystical experience could make us fully understand.[131] Let us note that this in no way detracts from mystical knowledge's positive character, but simply clarifies its permanently and radically unfinished nature.

Several writers have noticed this characteristic of the second darkness. Lossky, for example, rightly distinguishes between the two aspects of the apophatic principle. "Apophatic theology is the essential principle of Christian thought from very early on. Thus we read in Clement of Alexandria that God . . . is inaccessible by his very nature. . . . However, another conception of the apophatic principle

[130] *Cant.* 6 (PG 44:892C–D; Norris, 193).
[131] The same idea is to be found in St John of the Cross.

also appears early on, introduced into Christian theology by Origen ... and which is related to Neoplatonic philosophy. God is inaccessible, it is argued, not because of his nature, but only because of the weakness of our reason, obscured as it is by the flesh.... Steeped though he is in Origen's works, Gregory of Nyssa expresses his opinion on the subject no less forcefully than Clement."[132]

I am not convinced that the contrast is as pronounced as Lossky suggests or that we have here two conceptions, the one Neoplatonic, the other Christian. In fact, I believe that, at least in Gregory's case, darkness as a symbol of the night of the senses and the mind is a Christian transposition of the Philonic "night," indicating the radically inaccessible character of the knowledge of God for mere reason. The second darkness, however, expresses another reality, which is properly mystical—namely, the absolutely inexhaustible nature of the vision of God. Thus, both aspects can perfectly well co-exist in Christian thought, yet the fact remains that the contrast noted by Lossky is well founded, even though his interpretation of it is questionable. It is the first aspect that is influenced by Neoplatonism—though a transposed Neoplatonism—whereas the second pertains solely to the actual experience of Gregory himself.

Puech distinguishes things admirably:

> The appearance of the cloud only occurs at the intersection of two radical inadequacies (and this is what explains it): 1) the pronounced inadequacy of unknowing, compared with the mind's ordinary ways of knowing; 2) the inadequacy—in this case by deprivation—of this same unknowing, compared with the unattainable nature of the goal. Thus the relative light that is granted to the soul in the union appears as gloom, "a ray of darkness," in two respects: 1) in that it negates gnosis; 2) in being deficient by comparison with the absolute light. The cloud represents the floating passage of a symbolic knowledge that ἀγνωσία [*agnōsia*, ignorance or unknowing] transcends to a form of knowledge that is decidedly mystical, whose ideal content *agnōsia* (unknowing) is far from exhausting.[133]

Of these two darknesses the first is relative and transitory, and will cease with the beatific vision. But this vision will not put an end to the second, which is on the contrary absolute and permanent. This point is well articulated by Maréchal:

---

[132]Lossky, "La théologie négative," 204–205.
[133]Puech, "La ténèbre mystique," 42.

To this twofold incompleteness of the mystical vision of God correspond the two layers of meaning contained in Gregory of Nyssa's doctrine of the divine inaccessibility, as symbolized by darkness. In fact, as long as the soul is not freed from the bonds of the body, the total elimination of sensible images and concepts as we approach the threshold of the divine mystery thwarts the native aptitude of our faculties. This privation of our customary ways of knowing may, in a relative sense, be called darkness. At this level, darkness is but the blinding effect of a superior brightness. To the extent that the intellect, uplifted beyond itself, adapts to this new luminosity—that is to say, penetrates more deeply into the divine cloud—to the same extent does the vastness of the latter seem insuperable and its darkness thicker. The darkness is then no longer measured in terms of the relative powerlessness of our faculties but in terms of the unfathomable depths of the divine essence.[134]

Eros and *Agapē*

Darkness refers, then, to the "negative" character of the mystical life, its transcendence beyond thought. But there is a corresponding positive reality, for the mystical life is the realm of union and love. It is Gregory of Nyssa's great achievement to have clearly determined this, whereas Origen placed contemplation (*theōria*) and knowledge (*gnōsis*) at the summit of the spiritual ascent. Gregory thereby opened a path along which other great mystics would subsequently follow in his wake. St Bernard's commentary on the Song of Songs, for example, is a direct echo of his.

Gregory explains things quite clearly, particularly at the beginning of his own *Homilies on the Song of Songs*. He contrasts three methods of salvation: one caused by fear, another by hope;[135] but "the blessed and most perfect . . . comes through love [διὰ τῆς ἀγάπης, *dia tēs agapēs*]."[136] The same idea reappears later

---

[134]Maréchal, *Études sur la psychologie des mystiques*, vol. 2, 110–11. See also Diekamp, *Die Gotteslehre des heiligen G. von N.*, 94–101.

[135]Hope is related to symbolic theology, which has as its object God in his dealings with us—his providence, his goodness. By contrast, love is an attachment to God in himself. Cf. *Song* 17 (PG 44:765C; Norris, 17).

[136]Ibid. (PG 44:765B; Norris, 17). [This threefold schema based upon the motivations of fear, hope, and love becomes ubiquitous in spiritual literature, most often associated with the figures of slave, servant, and son—motivated, respectively, by fear of punishment, hope for reward (i.e., a hired servant's wages), and love for the Father. Basil the Great describes these three spiritual dispositions in the introduction to his *Longer Rules* (PG 31:896B), which Abba Dorotheos explicitly borrows from him (*Discourse* 4.41). It later became ubiquitous in ascetical literature (e.g., St John Climacus, *The Ladder of Divine Ascent* 1.13, 8.27).—*Ed.*]

The General Characteristics of the Third Way

in the book, where he contrasts three categories of souls: the most perfect "are joined [προσκολλῶνται, *proskollōntai*] to [the Word] by a disposition shaped by erotic love [ἐρωτικῇ διαθέσει, *erōtikē diathesei*]."[137] They are contrasted with those who have only a rudimentary faith and with those who act through fear.

In various other texts this idea of a union in love is associated either with the vocabulary of the mysteries or the theme of darkness, both of which have seemed to us to be characteristic of the third way. For example, as for the mysteries, we find the following: "Having in this way purified the heart of its bent toward appearances"—this is the second way—"[Wisdom] then, in the Song of Songs, initiates the mind into the innermost divine sanctuary. What is described here is an account of a wedding, but what is intellectually discerned is the human soul's mingling with the Divine."[138] The link between "initiation into the mysteries" (μυσταγωγία, *mystogōgia*) and "mixing" or "mingling" (ἀνάκρασις, *anakrasis*) is very clear: the object of the mystical life is union with the divinity. As for the connection with darkness, an example can be found later in the book: "The Bride [i.e., the soul] who in her own mind has attained the highest of her hopes and has already, in her own judgment, been united with the One she desires should call her more perfect participation in the Good a 'bed' and should term the time of her going to bed 'night.' Now the word 'night' points to contemplation of things unseen [θεωρία ἀοράτων, *theōria tōn aoratōn*], just like Moses, who entered into the darkness in which God was."[139] This passage is invaluable, for it connects the theme of Exodus with that of the Song, and draws a parallel between contemplation of things unseen and union with God.

Thus the highest degree of the spiritual life is a life of love that produces union with God, a union that itself, however, contains several stages. To describe this life of love Gregory uses two words: *eros* and *agapē*. In his book *Eros och Agape*, Nygren claimed that the Church Fathers—Gregory of Nyssa in particular—had deformed the evangelical concept of *agapē* and had substituted for it the Platonic *eros*.[140] Thus, the very origins of mystical theology were in his view influenced by Platonism and the true evangelical doctrine distorted. This important question deserves closer study.

---

[137]*Cant.* 15 (PG 44:1112C; Norris, 491).
[138]*Cant.* 1 (PG 44:769D–772A; Norris 23–25).
[139]*Cant.* 6 (PG 44:892C; Norris, 193).
[140]See Anders Nygren, *Agape and Eros, Part I: A Study of the Christian Idea of Love, Part II: The History of the Christian Idea of Love*, trans. Philip S. Watson (New York: Harper & Row, 1969 [1st ed. Part I 1930, Part II 1936]), 430–46.—*Ed.*

We shall clarify the meaning Gregory gives to these two words, beginning with the concept of ἀγάπη (*agapē*). Though unknown to classical Greek,[141] the term is found in the Song of Songs to denote human love. This has given rise to the supposition that this may have been a local, Egyptian, use of the word, current at the time of the composition of the Septuagint. The New Testament, however, uses it specifically to refer to that new standpoint that forms the essence of the gospel message—the love of God for his creatures and the love of people among themselves. This is the meaning it normally has in Paul and John. With the occasional exception, it does not refer to the love of man for God. The response to divine *agapē* is, rather, faith (πίστις, *pistis*), which is a recognition and loving acceptance of the divine initiative. The essence of *agapē*, then, is that it is a free initiative that moves in a downwards direction, from a higher to a lower level. As Max Scheler has clearly shown, this dynamic is precisely opposite to the Platonic *eros*, which is an ascent of the lower to the higher. In this respect, *agapē* reveals something absolutely new, something unexpected, and demonstrated by the incarnation—the *katabasis* (κατάβασις) or "descent" of God, as the Fathers put it. Paganism totally disregarded this. For paganism, every descent is a fall. This is in fact something that most clearly distinguishes Christianity from a system such as that of the gnostics, for whom the descent of the Savior is itself a fall.

How, then, does Gregory's thinking fit into this context? His understanding of *agapē* can be seen in two important passages. The first is to be found in the dialogue *On the Soul and the Resurrection*. He begins by giving a very general definition: "This is love [*agapē*], the interior attachment [ἐνδιάθετος, *endiathetos*] to that which is pleasing [πρὸς τὸ καταθύμιον, *pros to katathymion*]."[142] An almost identical wording can be found in the second of these passages, which is from a later work—the *Homilies on Ecclesiastes*—though *agapē* is here replaced by the term φίλτρον (*philtron*): "The inner disposition toward what is desired is love [φίλτρον, *philtron*]."[143] It is directly contrasted with hatred (τὸ μῖσος, *to misos*), which is a disposition toward what is antipathetic (ἀηδές, *aēdes*).

---

[141]In prebiblical Greek, "The noun *agápē* occurs very seldom" (the earliest examples in Liddel, Scott, and Jones occur in the Septuagint and the New Testament); *Theological Dictionary of the New Testament Abridged in One Volume*, ed. Gerhard Kittel and Gerhard Friedrich, trans. Geoffrey W. Bromiley (Grand Rapids, MI: William B. Eerdmans Publishing Co., 1985), 8. Even so, the verb forms ἀγαπάω and ἀγαπάζω (*agapaō, agapazō*) can be found as early as Homer (e.g., *Odyssey* 21.224, 289), though with a weaker sense: to greet or to treat with affection, respectively.—*Ed.*

[142]*An. et res.* 6 (PG 46:93C; PPS 12:80).

[143]*Eccl.* 8 (PG 44:733B; Hall, 129).

The General Characteristics of the Third Way

At this point, we are not yet in the order of Christian love, but merely the philosophical definition of love. Moreover, in this understanding of the word, *agapē* is not determined by its object. It can be about good or evil: "The power of love [τῆς ἀγάπης, *tēs agapēs*] has turned away from the intelligible [τῶν νοητῶν, *ton noēton*], running riot [ὑλομανήσασα, *hylomanēsasa*][144] in the immoderate enjoyment of the sensual."[145] Likewise in the *Homilies on Ecclesiastes*: "The place we are drawn to [ῥέψωμεν, *repsōmen*] by affection is the one we adapt [οἰκειούμεθα, *oikeioumetha*] our souls to.... Whether the disposition [σχέσις, *schesis*] of the soul is toward good or evil, the object of affection [τὸ ἀγαπώμενον, *to agapēmenon*] infiltrates [κατακιρνᾶται, *katakirnatai*] the soul."[146]

What is noteworthy in these passages is the link that is established between agapē and union: the soul "becomes accustomed to" (οἰκειοῦται, *oikeioutai*), "mingles with" (κατακιρνᾶται, *katakirnatai*) what it loves. Now for Gregory this is the key point about *agapē* and explains why he uses it whenever he wishes to express the idea of union in the spiritual life. There are countless examples that illustrate this point. The following two must suffice: "If love is taken away, in what manner will we be joined [συναφθησόμεθα, *synaphthēsometha*] to the divine?"[147] This union becomes possible when the soul is purified of defilement, for only that which is pure can be united with what is pure: "So when the soul which has become simple and uniform [μονοειδής, *monoeidēs*] and an accurate image of God [θεοείκελος, *theoeikelos*] finds that truly simple and immaterial good, the one thing which is really lovable [ἀγαπητόν, *agapēton*] and desirable [ἐράσμιον, *erasmion*], it attaches itself[148] to it and combines with it through the impulse and

---

[144]With Krabinger, I read ὑλομανήσασα (*hylomanēsasa*) and not ὁλομανήσασα (*holomanēsasa*), as Migne's unintelligible reading would have it. [Cf. *S. Gregorii Episcopi Nysseni De anima et resurrectione cum sorore sua Macrina dialogus*, ed. J. G. Krabinger (Leipzig: Wuttig, 1837).] The word refers to the rank growth of vegetation when left to itself, and gives a very exact image of what is meant here. It is also found in the *Homilies on the Song of Songs*: "As its custom is, the Holy Scripture assigns the name 'wood' to that material life of the human race [τὸν ὑλώδη τῶν ἀνθρώπων βίον, *ton hylōdē tōn anthrōpōn bion*] that is bursting with [ὑλομανήσαντα, *hylomanēsanta*] the various sorts of passions." *Cant.* 4 (PG 44:841D; Norris, 129). [The words ὕλη and ὑλώδης (*hylē, hylōdēs*) can mean either "wood" and "wooded" or "matter" and "material," helping Gregory to make the connection between "the trees of the wood" (τοῖς ξύλοις τοῦ δρυμοῦ, *tois xylois tou drymou*; Song 2.3) and excessive attachment to the material world.—Ed.]

[145]*An. et res.* 3 (PG 46:65A; PPS 12:59).

[146]*Eccl.* 8 (PG 44:733B–C; Hall, 129). This entire passage contrasts these two loves (*philtron* and *agapē*), the former of which inclines toward the sensible, the latter toward spiritual goods.

[147]*An. et res.* 3 (PG 46:65A; PPS 12:59).

[148]See also *An. et res.* 6 (PG 46:93C; PPS 12:80), where Gregory writes of the "disposition of love [διάθεσις ἀγαπητική, *diathesis agapētikē*], as it becomes attached in its nature to the beautiful [φυσικῶς τῷ καλῷ προσφυομένη, *physikōs tō kalō prosphyomenē*]."

operation of love [διὰ τῆς ἀγαπητικῆς ἐνεργείας, *dia tēs agapētikēs energeias*]. It conforms itself to that which is always being grasped and found."[149]

Here are new words expressing this idea of union—συνάπτεσθαι (*synaptesthai*), for example. What is expressed here on the philosophical level is the same idea that, on the mystical level will be that of the Song of Songs: the soul that is purified of all stain and imperfection (by the Word) and is thereby deified can be united to God, who is purity itself. This is why union comes at the end of the process of purification: "[Wisdom], having in this way purified the heart of its bent toward appearances, then, in the Song of Songs, [teaches us about] the soul's mingling [ἀνάκρασις, *anakrasis*] with the Divine [πρὸς τό θεῖον, *pros to theon*]."[150] We should note the transforming character of this union, a transformation that continues without end.

Elsewhere it is in relation to the Eucharist that the unifying nature of *agapē* is emphasized:

> Whatever may be the nature of what is shared [μετεχόμενον, *metechomenon*], what shares in it [τό μετέχον, *to metechon*] must conform.... The virtue of Christ is a sweet smell, and the loving disposition [ἡ ἀγαπητικὴ σχέσις, *hē agapētikē schesis*] naturally [φυσικῶς, *physikōs*] brings about assimilation [τὴν ἀνάκρασιν, *tēn anakrasin*] to what is loved [τὸ ἀγαπώμενον, *to agapēmenon*], so whatever we choose in love [διὰ φιλίας ἐρώμεθα, *dia philias erōmetha*] we become, either the sweet smell of Christ or a foul stench (2 Cor 2.15). The one who loves the good will also be good himself, as the goodness generated in him changes into itself the one who receives it.
>
> The reason why the one who eternally is offers himself to us to eat, is that taking him into ourselves we may become that which he is.[151]

In this passage we again find the usual expressions, ἀνάκρασις (*anakrasis*), ἀγαπητικὴ σχέσις (*agapētikē schesis*). We should also note the "physical" character of the union that is described. But what is most interesting about this passage is that it brings us face to face with the way Gregory transposes the Platonist doctrine of participation. In particular, it is significant that participation for

---

[149] *n. et res.* 6 (PG 46:93C; PPS 12:80).

[150] *Cant.* 1 (PG 44:769D–772A; Norris, 23–25).

[151] *Eccl.* 8 (PG 44:737D–740A; Hall, 132). Elsewhere, he writes of Christ "mixing [κατακιρνάμενος, *katakirnamenos*] with the bodies of the faithful, so that, by union [ἕνωσις, *henōsis*] with the immortal, man might become a partaker [μέτοχος, *metochos*] of incorruption." Gregory, *Or. cat.* 37.12 (PPS 60:149).

The General Characteristics of the Third Way

Gregory does not preexist *agapē*, as it does Plato's *eros*. For Plato, the movement toward God is simply the return of the soul to the divine element (τὸ θεῖον, *to theion*) that is connatural (οἰκεῖον, *oikeion*) to it.[152] But we see that participation is the sharing of his divine life that God gives to the soul: loving God, we transform ourselves in him through the participation in his nature that he grants us. Love is not the consequence but the cause of the participation and the union. There is an essential difference here, one that we shall encounter again when we come to discuss the knowledge of God in the mirror of the soul.

This transformation will have no end. Being infinite, God always infinitely overflows the capacity of the soul. However, the soul can always grow in participation in the divine good. One of the aspects of *agapē* is this endless dilation: "For the participation [μετουσία, *metousia*] in the divine good is such that it makes anyone into whom it enters greater and more receptive. As it is taken up it increases the power and magnitude of the recipient [μετέχων, *metechōn*], so that the person who is nourished always grows and never ceases from growth, since the fountain of good things flows [εἰσρέον, *eisreon*] unfailingly."[153] This doctrine will be applied to the mystical life, which Gregory will define as one of perpetual progress: "Then when [the soul] has shared [μετασχοῦσαν, *metaschousan*], as far as is possible for her [ὅσον ἐχώρησε, *hoson echōrēse*] in the good things, [the Word] draws her [ἐφέλκεται *ephelketai*] toward participation in the transcendent Beauty just as though she had hitherto had no part [ἀμέτοχον, *ametochon*] in them at all."[154]

In this growth of love, there is one feature that stands out. We should not suppose that the communication of new good things fills some supposed gap. Rather is it the case that the soul, despite being at each moment satisfied and fulfilled, finds that each injection of grace dilates its capacity still further in the very act of filling it. There is thus the possibility of unrestricted development. This is what characterizes spiritual progress and also shows the purely gratuitous nature of the communication of these divine good things. In this respect, Gregory rightly observes that hope, which is about an absence, will pass, whereas love itself will not, for it contains no imperfection.

> But when the thing hoped for comes, all the others grow quiet while the operation of love remains. . . . So if the soul should ever reach this goal, it will

[152] *Virg.* 12 (PG 44:372C; Norris, 44).
[153] *An. et res.* 7 (PG 46:105B; PPS 12:87).
[154] *Cant.* 5 (PG 44:876B; Norris, 171).

have no need of the others, as it embraces the fullness of existing things and seems somehow alone to preserve in itself the impression of divine blessedness. For the life of the superior nature is love. . . . Since satiety does not cut off the attachment of love [ἀγαπητικὴ σχέσις, *agapētikē schesis*] to the beautiful, the divine life will always operate through love, the divine life that is beautiful by nature and from its nature is lovingly disposed [ἀγαπητικῶς ἔχει, *agapētikōs echei*] toward the beautiful. There is no limit to the operation of love, since the beautiful has no limit.[155]

Freed from its carnal bonds, the soul yields to the attraction of God, who pulls it to himself by a sort of gravitation, using its natural inclination, by a *pondus ad sursum*, "a weight [that pulls] upwards," as Augustine said.[156] This concept of a divine "attraction" that marks the primacy of grace over freedom is correlative to that of *agapē*, being, as it were, a response to it.[157] "Since, therefore, every nature tends to attract [ἑλκτική, *helktikē*] what is proper [οἰκεῖον, *oikeion*] to it, and the human is in some way proper to God, because it bears in itself the imitation of its Archetype, necessarily the soul is attracted to the Divine which is related to it (for what is proper to God must come safely to Him). But if the soul is light [κούφη, *kouphē*] and simple, with no bodily weight holding it down, its progress toward the One who attracts it becomes pleasant and easy."[158] Gregory contrasts this flight to the heights—so easy for the unburdened soul—with the distress of the soul that, on the one hand, is attracted by God but that, at the same time, is "fastened to the material condition with the nails of passionate attachment."[159]

All this enables us to understand what *agapē* means for Gregory. It is not the *caritas* of the Gospel. Nor is it, as Nygren would have it, the Platonic *eros* dressed up in a Christian name. It is love *qua* principle of unity between lover and beloved. In this sense, it corresponds exactly to what Gregory describes in

[155] *An. et res.* 6 (PG 46:96D–97A; PPS 12:80–81).

[156] Cf. St Augustine, *Confessions* 13. [The ancient idea of weight held that the elemental composition of a body determined its place in the universe, so that the heaviest bodies—those made up primarily of the element of earth—were drawn to the earth (and thus to the center of the geocentric cosmos), while those that contained more of the element of water were lighter and rested on the surface of the earth, likewise those made up of air were above the waters forming the atmosphere, and finally the celestial sphere of fire beyond the atmosphere contained that which was lightest, because it was composed of fire. Thus Augustine's "*Pondus meum amor meus*" (My weight is my love; *Confessions* 13.9) implies that those who love their heavenly homeland are, as it were, of a "heavenly" composition, and are thus drawn upward. This fits in well with the nostalgia for the angelic realm that Gregory everywhere evinces.—*Ed.*]

[157] See above, for the transforming action of Christ through the Eucharist.

[158] *An. et res.* 7 (PG 46:97B; PPS 12:83).

[159] Ibid. (PG 46:97C; PPS 12:83).

The General Characteristics of the Third Way

the third way of the spiritual life. He wishes to define the union of love between God and the soul in a non-intellectual manner, and the term *agapē* gives him the means to do so. One may say that in this way he gives the word an original meaning, following on from Origen.

The third way presupposes a soul that is already purified[160] and thus established in a certain community of life with God. In this respect, it contrasts with the first way, the way of purification. It entails the return of the soul to paradise and expands on what we have said about *parrhēsia*. The words that Gregory uses at the beginning of the *Homilies on the Song of Songs* are typical: the Song's theme is "participation [μετουσία, *metousia*] in the Godhead itself, since the divine Word in his own voice confers on the hearer a fellowship [κοινωνία, *koinonia*] with the undefiled Power."[161] This presupposes a certain connaturality, which is expressed by means of two sets of images. In the Song of Songs these are borrowed from the context of human love: the soul is the Bride of the Word. "The soul is in a certain manner led as a bride [νυμφοστολεῖται, *nymphostoleitai*] toward an incorporeal and spiritual and undefiled marriage [συζυγίαν, *syzygian*] with God."[162] "The virgin soul gives the name 'bed' [κλίνη, *klinē*] to communion [κοινωνίαν, *koinōnian*] with the Divine."[163] In *The Life of Moses*, we find a second image. Moses is described as "the friend of God" (φίλος θεοῦ, *philos theou*) [Ex 33.11], and this represents the highest level of perfection:

> What more trustworthy witness of the fact that Moses did attain the perfection which was possible would be found ... than the fact that he is named "friend of God" by God himself? ... This is true perfection: not to avoid a wicked life because like slaves we servilely fear punishment, nor to do good because we hope for rewards. ... On the contrary, disregarding all those things for which we hope and which have been reserved by promise, we regard falling from God's friendship [φιλίαν, *philian*] as the only thing dreadful and we consider becoming God's friend the only thing worthy of honor and desire [ἐράσμιον, *erasmion*].[164]

The nuances are different, but the concept of perfection is the same in both cases, consisting in a status of equality and intimacy.[165] We should point out

---

[160] *Virg.* 11 (PG 46:368B; FC 58:42).
[161] *Cant.* 3 (PG 44:808D; Norris, 79).
[162] *Cant.* 1 (PG 44:765A–B; Norris, 15).
[163] *Cant.* 4 (PG 44:836D; Norris, 121).
[164] *Vit. Moys.* 2.319–20 (PG 44:429B–D; Malherbe, 136–37).

that such equality with God does not belong to the soul by nature, as in Plato. In Gregory, the vocabulary of participation—κοινωνία (koinōnia), μετουσία (metousia)—is transposed from the realm of essence to that of grace. It is the Word who, in Baptism and then by successive graces, raises the soul up to this state of friendship where it regains *parrhēsia*, which corresponds to the higher forms of the spiritual life.[166] A profound transformation in the concepts is at work here. Nygren, in his evocative book, took insufficient note of this. He correctly saw that the Gregorian *agapē* was not the Pauline *agapē*, and that Paul's meaning was to be found, in Gregory, in the theme of the *katabasis* or descent of the Word.[167] But he did not determine with sufficient precision the original content of the term *agapē* as used by Gregory, and was too hasty in comparing it to the Platonic *eros*.

The way of love is the opposite of the way of knowledge. There is a singular correlation between it and the entry into the darkness, which, as we have already remarked, is one of the most noteworthy aspects of Gregory's mysticism. Indeed, it is this that establishes it in a distinct order, one that Origen had not clearly identified. For him the third way remained a matter of gnosis. With Gregory, this stage is surpassed: "The life of the superior nature is *agapē*, since the beautiful is in every respect lovable [ἀγαπητόν, *agapēton*] for those who know it, and the Divine knows Itself. But knowledge becomes love [ἡ δὲ γνῶσις ἀγάπη γίνεται, *hē dē gnōsis agapē ginetai*]."[168] Strictly speaking, it is a question here of God's love. But Gregory wants to show that this love is found in the perfect soul, and the above phrase expresses perfectly well this primacy of love over gnosis that in turn justifies the primacy of the mysticism of love over that of knowledge.

This irrational, ecstatic aspect of *agapē* is normally expressed by the term *eros*. In reality, however, the two are synonymous for Gregory. He uses them interchangeably, as can be seen in the following example: ἐρωτικὴ διάθεσις (*erōtike diathesis*, a disposition shaped by erotic love);[169] διάθεσις ἀγαπητική (*diathesis agapētikē*, the disposition of love).[170] Thus, they should not be contrasted with each other. *Eros* is simply used more rarely and represents a particular aspect

[165] On the use of the expression "friend of God" in Philo, to indicate the highest degree of perfection, see Völker, *Fortschritt und Vollendung*, 322.

[166] See Bas. (PG 46:800C; McCambley, 17) for comments on *agapē* as being "the highest good ... greater than all good things."

[167] See, for example, *Or. cat.* 15.1–3 (PG 45:48A–B; PPS 60:96–97).

[168] *An. et res.* 6 (PG 46:96C; PPS 12:81).

[169] *Cant.* 15 (PG 44:1112C; Norris, 491); *Vit. Moys.* 2.231 (PG 44:401D; Malherbe, 114).

The General Characteristics of the Third Way

of *agapē*. Before we consider what this specific nuance might be, let us note the interesting comment that Gregory makes at the beginning of the *Homilies on the Song of Songs*. It seems that he himself feels the need to justify his use of the word, which is not found in the Gospels and is charged with sensual resonances: "Therefore, since it is Wisdom who speaks, love her [ἀγάπησον, *agapēson*] as much as you are able, with your whole heart and strength; desire her as much as you can. To these words I am bold to add, be in love [ἐράσθητι, *erasthēti*], for this passion [πάθος, *pathos*] when directed to things incorporeal, is blameless and impassible, as Wisdom says in Proverbs when she bids us to be in love [τὸν ἔρωτα, *ton erōta*] with the divine Beauty."[171]

From this text we see that *eros* is a *pathos*. This implies in the first place a certain passivity, the idea of a dependency on something external to the soul. In the strict sense of the word, it is a dependency on something that is inferior to it. Here, however, it is a dependency on something superior—namely, God. And certain of the images that will be used to describe this *pathos*—such as wound—emphasize this idea of an alien intrusion, a "disturbance," something that wrests the soul out of itself.

Second, *eros*, like *pathos*, is beyond the *nous*, beyond reason. It entails a type of madness, in that it sweeps the soul away beyond itself, hurling it in pursuit of its Beloved. This is in fact the subject-matter of the Song of Songs, where we see the Bride, the figure of the soul, cast by love outside herself and all things, in search of the Beloved. What *eros* specifically signifies is this ecstatic aspect of love, its intensity. Gregory says as much in his own words: "She, then . . . who sees the unspeakable beauty of the Bridegroom with a pure eye and in this way is wounded by the incorporeal and fiery arrow of love [τοῦ ἔρωτος, *tou erōtos*; cf. Song 2.5], for *agapē* when intensified [ἡ ἐπιτεταμένη ἀγάπη, *hē epitamenē agapē*] is called love [ἔρως, *erōs*]."[172] Thus, *eros* is a specific aspect of *agapē*, its most intense form, its fervor. This is always the connotation it has in Gregory's usage. Moses, for example, is portrayed as an "ardent lover [σφοδρὸς ἐραστής, *sphodros erastēs*] of beauty"; his "soul . . . loves what is beautiful" (τῆς ψυχῆς διατεθείσης ἐρωτικῇ τινι διαθέσει πρὸς τὸ καλόν, *tēs psychēs diatetheisēs erōtikē tini diathesei pros to kalon*).[173] Associated with *eros* is not simply the idea of *pathos* (παθεῖν τὸ τοιοῦτο, *pathein to toiouto*) but also that of tension (διατείνομαι, *diateinomai*).

---

[170]*An. et res.* 6 (PG 46:93C; PPS 12:80).
[171]*Cant.* 1 (PG 44:772A; Norris, 25).
[172]*Cant.* 13 (PG 44:1048C; Norris, 403).

It is interesting to note that under the blow of this "passion," it seems to Moses "as if he had never partaken" (οὔπω μετεσχηχώς, *oupō meteschēchōs*) of God and wishes to see him "not according to his capacity to partake [μετέχειν, *metechein*], but according to God's true being."[174] *Agapē* enabled us to partake, but as if in a mirror; *eros* launches us beyond this, toward a relationship with God's "true being." It represents the pinnacle of *agapē*, a state of ecstasy in which the soul is impatient with the many veils that still separate it from God, and the ecstatic aspect that union with God always maintains.

In view of this, consideration of the concept of *eros* should normally take place at the culmination of any study of the mystical life, when dealing with its highest forms. Nevertheless, it was important to clarify its nature. As can be seen, it denotes less the privation of good things or an impetus toward that which is higher, as in Plato, than the supra-rational character and passive nature of love for God, of *agapē* in its highest form. Gregory will use other images to describe the soul's ascent—climbing, wings, a ladder. But of *eros* it is especially its passionate character that he chooses to focus on:

> Human nature can neither discover nor entertain anything greater than this for purposes of understanding. This is why the most intense [τὸ σφοδρότατον, *to sphodrotaton*] of pleasurable activities—I mean the passion of erotic love [ἐρωτικὸν πάθος, *erōtikon pathos*]—is set as a figure at the very fore of the guidance that the teachings give; so that by this we may learn that it is necessary for the soul, fixing itself steadily [ἐνατενίζουσαν, *enatenizousan*] on the inaccessible beauty of the divine nature, to love that beauty as much as the body has a bent for what is akin to it [συγγενές, *syngenes*] and to turn passion into impassibility, so that when every bodily disposition has been quelled, our mind within us may boil with love [ἐρωτικῶς, *erōtikos*], but only in the Spirit.[175]

Thus the significance of divine *eros* is this irresistible attraction, this gravitation, that attracts the purified soul to God, just as physical attraction draws bodies to each other. Fundamentally, then, it is an attraction of like for like that lifts the soul increasingly closer to God, as it becomes ever more like him.

* * *

---

[173] *Vit. Moys.* 2.231 (PG 44:401D; Malherbe, 114).
[174] *Vit. Moys.* 2.230 (PG 44:401D; Malherbe, 114).
[175] *Cant.* 1 (PG 44:773C–D; Norris, 29).

The General Characteristics of the Third Way

We can now summarize this doctrine of love. The soul that has reached spiritual maturity partakes of the divine life with a certain fullness. Since things of like kind (συγγενής, *syngenēs*; συναφής, *synaphēs*; οἰκεῖος, *oikeios*) are attracted to each other, the soul is drawn to God by an irresistible force; it thirsts to be united with him; it adheres to him (προσφύεται, *prosphuetai*),[176] cleaves to him (προσκολλεῖται, *proskolleitai*).[177] The expression of this attraction is love, which bears the general name of *agapē* but whose most ardent form is called *eros*. This love corresponds to a certain connaturality, without which it would not exist. This connaturality in turn presupposes a soul that is already to some extent deified and that has achieved the status of "fiancée" and "friend," which implies a certain equality with him. The Song of Songs describes the stages that precede the union—namely, the betrothal ceremony, when the fiancée adorns herself (νυμφοστολεῖται, *nymphostoleitai*) in preparation for the marriage.[178]

---

[176] *Cant.* 13 (PG 44:1045A; Norris, 399); *Cant.* 15 (PG 44:1088D; Norris, 459), ibid. (PG 44:1116D; Norris, 495).

[177] *Perf.* (PG 46:277D; FC 58:116); *Cant.* 15 (PG 44:1112C; Norris, 491); *Eccl.* 7 (PG 44:720A; Hall, 117).

[178] Cf. the image of a wedding preparation (γαμικὴ διασκευή, *gamikē diaskeuē*) in *Cant.* 1 (PG 44:772B; Norris, 25).

7

Mystical Experience

The illuminative way—which, as seen, is described in Ecclesiastes—convinces the soul of the vanity of all that is not God, and at the same time of its own utter inability to reach him by means of the natural powers of the intelligence.[1] This leads to the strange paradox of a mind that is commensurate with an object that is unreal but which, on the contrary, is bereft in the face of that which is supremely real. This impasse ejects the soul, as it were, from the normal ways of knowing into the darkness that symbolizes the soul's going out of itself.

It begins to understand that God cannot be treated as an object of knowledge, and can be known only to the extent that he freely manifests himself. It is a case of leaving behind all images and concepts and simply turning to God. Then he makes himself known. But this knowledge is of a kind that is absolutely irreducible to ordinary knowledge. It is the ineffable experience of a presence that comes ever nearer, and the place of this presence is the soul itself. Through his grace, then, God is present in the soul that turns to him. Mystical knowledge is the experience of this presence.

Such is the doctrine that Gregory expounds in his sixth homily on the Beatitudes. After demonstrating the powerlessness of the human mind to know God, he shows that the only way forward is indicated by the words Christ uttered when promising a vision of God to those who are pure in heart:

> The Lord does not say it is blessed to know something about God, but to have God present within oneself [ἐν ἑαυτῷ, *en heautō*]. . . . I do not think that if the eye of one's soul has been purified, he is promised a direct vision [θέαμα ἀντιπρόσωπον, *theama antiprosōpon*] of God; but perhaps this marvelous saying may suggest what the Word expresses more clearly when He says to others, "The Kingdom of God is within you" (Lk 17.21). By this we

---

[1] See *Eccl.* 7 (PG 44:728B–732D; Hall, 123f.); *Virg.* 9 (PG 46:361B–C; FC 58:35); *Beat.* 6 (PG 44:1264B–1265A; ACW 18:143–45); *Eun.* 2.89–95 (PG 45:941A–D; NPNF² 5:259).

245

should learn that if a man's heart has been purified from every creature and all unruly affections, he will see the Image of the Divine Nature in his own beauty.[2]

There can be no doubt as to the interpretation of this text. Gregory contrasts gnosis, which is impossible, with the union that introduces us to another order. This is affirmed more clearly still a little later in the text: "But since the promise of seeing God has a twofold meaning, on the one hand, that of knowing the Nature that is above the universe, on the other, that of being united [ἀνακραθῆναι, anakrathēnai] to Him through purity of life, we must say that the voice of the Saints declares the former mode of contemplation to be impossible [ἀμήχανον, amēchanon], whereas the second is promised to human nature in Our Lord's present teaching."[3] Here we find again the essential ideas that we have already seen: *amēchanon* is the word that characterized for the Preacher the limitations of the rational way of seeking to know God; whereas *anakrasis* denotes union, the way of love, which is that of the mystical life.

In the *Homilies on the Song of Songs*, we find the same contrast between conceptual knowledge, which is linked to the second way, and mystical knowledge, which is a possessing of God in oneself. Here is the text that Gregory comments on: "We shall make you golden earrings and beads of silver, while the King rests in his own room" (1.11–12).

> All teaching about the ineffable Nature amounts to likenesses of gold, not gold itself.... [F]or it does not manifest the form [εἶδος, *eidos*] of that which no one has seen or can see. Rather, it sketches darkly [σκιογράφει, *skiographei*], in a mirror and in an enigma, a reflection of what we seek that comes to birth in our souls on the basis of some conjecture. All speech, however, that refers to intuitions has the function of some indivisible mark, being unable to make clear [συνεπεκτείνεσθαι, *synepekteinesthai*] what the mind intends. Hence Paul says that the soul that is led by such intuitions to awareness of things that cannot be grasped must bring [εἰσοικίζειν, *eisoikizein*] the Nature that transcends all intellect within herself by faith alone [διὰ μόνης πίστεως, *dia monēs pisteōs*].[4]

---

[2] *Beat.* 6 (PG 44:1269C; ACW 18:148).
[3] Ibid. (PG 44:1273 B–C; ACW 18:151).
[4] *Cant.* 3 (PG 44:820C–821A; Norris, 95–97).

Mystical Experience

Thus the kind of knowledge that is conceptual (διὰ νοημάτων, *dia noēmatōn*) is only a first stage. The path to the deepest knowledge of God lies in another direction. Two essential traits characterize it, and together they define what is meant by mystical experience. First, it is knowledge of God present in the soul. This clearly has as a prerequisite the indwelling there of God—more precisely of the Word. It is an awareness of this presence. But this presence itself has as a prerequisite the purification of the soul. These, then, are the two principal elements of mystical, experiential knowledge according to Gregory. After examining them, we shall go on to study the doctrine of the spiritual senses and how, in connection with them, experiential knowledge develops.

The Mirror of the Soul

The key theme, then, of Gregory of Nyssa's mystical theology is that the soul acquires knowledge of God by returning to itself—since it is there that God's image is to be found—but also that the soul must first be purified, so as to restore the traits of this image. Here is how he expresses things in his *Sixth Homily on the Beatitudes*:

> For God imprinted on [your nature] the likeness of the glories of His own Nature. . . . But the evil that has been poured all around the nature bearing the Divine Image [θεοειδής, *theoeidēs*] has rendered useless to you this wonderful thing that lies hidden under vile coverings. If, therefore, you wash off by a good life the filth [ῥύπον, *rhypon*] that has been stuck on your heart like plaster, the Divine beauty will again shine forth in you. . . . For what is like to the Good is certainly itself good. Hence, if a man who is pure of heart sees himself, he sees in himself [ἐν ἑαυτῷ, *en heautō*] what he desires; and thus he becomes blessed, because when he looks at his own purity, he sees the archetype in the image.
>
> To give an example. Though men who see the sun in a mirror [κάτοπτρον, *katoptron*] do not gaze at the sky itself, yet they see the sun in the reflexion of the mirror no less than those who look at its very orb. So, he says, it is also with you. Even though you are too weak to perceive the Light Itself, yet, if you but return to the grace of the Image [ἡ χάρις τῆς εἰκόνος, *he charis tēs eikonos*] with which you were informed from the beginning, you will have all you seek in yourselves [ἐν ἑαυτοῖς, *en heautois*].[5]

---
[5] *Beat.* 6 (PG 44:1272A–C; ACW 18:148–49).

The essential point here is that of purity. It is something that Gregory returns to time and again: "If the eye of one's soul has been purified.... If a man's heart has been purified ... he will see the Image of the Divine Nature in his own beauty."⁶ It is an idea that is also found in Platonism, as the following citation makes clear: "And therefore while we live, it would seem that we shall be closest to knowledge in this way—if we consort with the body as little as possible, and do not commune with it, except in so far as we must, and do not infect ourselves with its nature, but remain pure from it."⁷ We encountered this issue earlier, toward the end of our examination of the first way, when seeking to define the nature of the purity that was its fruit. Here we are looking at things in a new light: precisely what *kind* of purity is the prerequisite for knowledge of God? The answer to this question will provide the key to a correct interpretation of our author's mysticism. Nowhere is his use of Platonic language so apparent. Thus if his thinking proves to be equally Platonic, we would be obliged to conclude that Gregory's mysticism is likewise entirely of the Platonic kind. We shall begin, then, by noting any similarities of expression and then examine the interpretation that should be given to the thinking that lies behind the words.

This process of purification is described in various ways. Sometimes the comparison is with mud that must be washed off. The image of a quagmire (βόρβορος, *borboros*) derives from Plato⁸ and is taken up by Plotinus, as in the following: "If a man has been immersed in filth or daubed with mud [βορβόρῳ, *borborō*], his native comeliness disappears and all that is seen is the foul stuff besmearing him; his ugly condition is due to alien matter [τὸ ἀλλότριον, *to allotrion*] that has encrusted him, and if he is to win back his grace it must be his business to scour and purify himself and make himself what he was."⁹ At other times Plotinus uses a comparison with rust: "What was one mass of rust [ἰοῦ, *iou*] from long neglect [the soul] has restored to purity.... Seen now unalloyed it is at once filled with admiration of its worth and knows that it has no need of any other glory than its own, triumphant if only it be allowed to remain purely to itself."¹⁰ A third image that he uses is that of a block of stone that must be rough-hewed so as to bring out the lineaments of the statue:

---

⁶Gregory, *Beat.* 6 (PG 44:1269C; ACW 18:148).
⁷Plato, *Phaedo* 67a.
⁸Ibid., 111e.
⁹ Plotinus, *Enneads* 1.6.5. See also ibid., 1.8.13; Plato, *Phaedo* 69c.
¹⁰Plotinus, *Enneads* 4.7.10.

> How are you to see into a virtuous soul and know its loveliness? Withdraw into yourself and look. And if you do not find yourself beautiful yet, act as does the creator of a statue that is to be made beautiful: he cuts away here, he smoothes there, he makes this line lighter, this other purer, until a lovely face has grown upon his work. So do you also: cut away all that is excessive [τὰ περιττά, *ta peritta*] ... bring light to all that is overcast, labour to make all one glow of beauty, and never cease chiseling your statue, until there shall shine out on you from it the godlike [θεῖον, *theion*] splendour of virtue.[11]

If we look now at Gregory's texts, we shall find that the lexical similarities are striking. Indeed they have often been noted.[12] For example, in the dialogue *On the Soul and the Resurrection*, Gregory writes as follows: "Therefore the soul will not receive any disadvantage in respect to participation in the good, if it should be freed from these impulses. It will go back to itself [πρὸς ἑαυτὴν πάλιν ἐπανελθοῦσα, *pros heautēn palin epanelthousa*] and see clearly what is in its nature, and through its own beauty it will look upon the archetype as if in a mirror and an image."[13] We find the same thought in the *Homilies on the Song of Songs*: "So the most secure watch over the good things within us is not to be ignorant of ourselves and for each to know what he is and to distinguish clearly between himself and the things around his edges, so that he may not end up keeping guard over what is alien rather than over himself."[14] The return of the soul to itself, the rediscovery of its true nature, the contemplation of the divine in this nature as in a mirror, provided that it gradually divests itself of the passions—all this interestingly reminds us of Plotinus. For, as seen, he too wrote of "returning to oneself," of an "alien element" (ἀλλότριον, *allotrion*) that has been added on, of the passions, and of "purification." As for the idea of "self-knowledge," this is simply the Socratic γνῶθι σεαυτόν (*gnōthi seauton*, know thyself) transposed to the domain of mysticism.

The means of this transformation, then, is the purification of the soul, without which it would not be able to unite with what is pure. This is the clear teaching contained in *Phaedo*. Gregory, for his part, writes as follows: "The only way for the soul to be attached [συναφθῆναι, *synaphthēnai*] to the incorruptible God is for it to make itself as pure as it can. In this way, reflecting as the mirror

---

[11] Plotinus, *Enneads* 1.6.9. See also 4.7.8.
[12] See Arnou, "*Platonisme des Pères*," col. 2375–88; Diekamp. *Die Gotteslehre*, 85ff.; von Ivánka, "*Vom Platonismus*," 185–190.
[13] *An. et res.* 6 (PG 46:89C; PPS 12:78).
[14] *Cant.* 2 (PG 44:804B; Norris, 71).

does, when it submits itself to the purity of God, it will be formed according to its participation in and reflection of the prototypal beauty."[15] The Platonic terminology is recognizable here: in particular, knowledge of like by like,[16] and purity. The thinking, too, seems close to that of Plato: to know God the soul must become pure. Purity is the way for the soul to return to its divine nature and to be united with God.

Gregory also makes use of the same Platonic metaphors. Like Plotinus, he compares this process of purification to the rough-hewing of a statue:

> First [the Word] separates [χωρίζειν, *chōrizein*] us, as it were, from the attached rock—I mean evil, of course—to which we have been attached by participation. Then it trims off the excesses [τὰ περιττά, *ta peritta*] of the material. After this it begins to form that which lies within in relation to the likeness of the aim. And thus it scrapes [ἐπιξύων, *epixyōn*] and polishes [λαμπρύνει, *lamprynei*] our understanding by means of more delicate teachings of ideas. Then, by means of the forms of virtues, it forms Christ in us, in accordance with whose image we existed in the beginning, and in accordance with which we again come to exist.[17]

We recognize the same lexis as used in the earlier quotation from the *Enneads*: the removing of what is superfluous (τὰ περιττά, *ta peritta*), scraping the surface of (ἐπιξύειν, *epixyein*) the mind, polishing it till it is shining, so that, in the words of Plotinus, the divine splendor of virtue (ἡ ἀγλαία θεοειδής τῆς ἀρετῆς, *hē aglaia theoeidēs tēs aretēs*) or, in Gregory's version, the image of virtue that is Christ (ἡ εἰκὼν τῆς ἀρετῆς ὁ Χριστός, *hē eikōn tēs aretēs ho christos*) shines (λαμπρύνειν λαμπρός, *lamprynein lampros*) in it. The main difference lies in Gregory's reference to the name of Christ, which gives a more precise definition to Plotinus' vague term θεοειδής (*theoeidēs*, godlike).

Let us look again at Gregory's sixth homily on the Beatitudes:

> If, therefore, you wash off by a good life the filth that has been stuck on your heart like plaster, the Divine Beauty [τὸ κάλλος, *to kallos*] will again shine forth in you. It is the same as happens in the case of iron. If freed from rust by a whetstone, that which but a moment ago was black will shine and

---

[15] *Virg.* 11 (PG 46:368B–D; FC 58:41).

[16] See Plato, *Timaeus* 45c. [The echo of this phraseology—ὅμοιον πρὸς ὅμιον (*homoion pros homoioun*, like by like)—is not found in the published English translation.—*Trans.*]

[17] *Inscr.* 2.11.134 (PG 44:544A–C; Heine, 164). [Note that the Word does the carving, while in Plotinus the soul carves itself: "Gregory . . . Christianized the illustration" (Heine, p. 163 n. 196).—*Ed.*]

glisten brightly in the sun. So it is also with the inner man, which the Lord calls the heart. When he has scraped off the rustlike [ἰώδη, *iōdē*] dirt which dank decay has caused to appear on his form, he will once more recover the likeness of the archetype and be good. For what is like to the Good is certainly itself good. Hence, if a man who is pure of heart sees himself, he sees in himself what he desires; and thus he becomes blessed, because when he looks at his own purity, he sees the archetype in the image.[18]

Plotinus too spoke of "the beauty [κάλλος, *kallos*] of the soul," of "the rust [ἰοῦ, *iou*] of the passions," of "the divine brilliance [αὐγή, *augē*]" that is seen once more. It is interesting to compare this passage with another (from Gregory's earliest work, *On Virginity*) in which we find the same expressions:

When the sequence of sin ruined the life of man . . . that godlike [θεοειδής, *theioeides*] beauty of the soul made in imitation of the prototype was darkened like some iron by the rust [ἰῷ, *iō*] of evil, and it no longer preserves the grace of its own natural form [ἡ χάρις τῆς εἰκόνος, *hē charis tēs eikonos*], but is changed into the sordidness of sin. Like man, this "great and honored being," as he was called by Scripture (Prov 20.6), falling [ἐκπεσών, *ekpesōn*] from his own worthiness like those who slip and fall into the mud [βορβόρῳ, *borborō*] and, having smeared themselves with mire [πηλῷ, *pēlō*], become unrecognizable even to their companions, so the one who falls into the mire of sin no longer is the image of the incorruptible God.[19]

In this passage we notice various expressions that also appear in the homily on the sixth Beatitude. But we see in it also a number of Plotinian features: the beauty of the soul, the rust (ἰόν, *ion*) by which it is obscured, the falling away from natural dignity (ἔκπτωσις, *ekptōsis*), and finally the coating of mud (τὸν πηλόν, *ton pēlon*) that covers the soul and renders it unrecognizable. The complex character of the passage is quite salient: on the one hand, there are expressions where we recognize the manifestation of sanctifying grace; on the other, an entire vocabulary that is strangely dependent upon Plotinus. And all this in Gregory's first treatise.

This complex mix of influences also appears in the rest of the passage: "So the one who falls into the mire no longer is the image of the incorruptible God

---

[18] *Beat.* 6 (PG 44:1272A-B; ACW 18:149). See also *De infantibus praemature abreptis* (*Infant.*) 2 (PG 46:164C; PPS 64:40–41).

[19] *Virg.* 12 (PG 46:372A-B; FC 58:44).

[ἀπώλεσε τὸ εἰκὼν εἶναι, *apōlese to eikōn einai*], and he is covered through sin with a corruptible and slimy form which reason advises him to reject. However, if purged by the water, so to speak, of his way of life, the earthly covering can be stripped off [ἀποκλυσάμενον, *apoklysamenon*], the beauty of the soul may reappear again. The rejection of what is alien [ἀλλότριον, *allotrion*] means a return to what is proper and natural to oneself, but this is not possible to achieve, unless one be created anew."[20]

Plotinian thought seems to be in evidence once more. There is the metaphor of mud again, this "alien" element. It was added (προσθήκη, *prosthēkē*), said Plotinus; it must be removed (ἀπόθεσις, *apothesis*), says Gregory. For this, the soul must be purified and washed clean. Then it "will return to its natural form," says Gregory; man "must make himself what he was," says Plotinus.[21] The similarity of lexis and thought between the *Enneads* and *On Virginity* is such that one is inevitably drawn to suppose a literal dependency.[22]

Moreover, the conclusions of the two passages seem to point to a Platonic allusion on the part of Gregory. Plotinus wrote: "It must be man's business [ἔργον, *ergon*] to scour and purify himself and make himself what he was." For his part, Gregory writes: "[To become again what it was, that is,] being like the divine is not our function [ἔργον, *ergon*], nor is it the product of human ability, but it is part of the generosity [μεγαλοδωρεᾶς, *megalodōreas*] of God who freely, at the birth of the first man, gave our nature a likeness to Himself."[23] Thus it would seem to be the case that Gregory takes up Plotinus' text, borrowing his images. But suddenly, at the end, he puts the emphasis on an irreducible difference: the likeness to God, the image, is no "business" or "function" (ἔργον, *ergon;* work) of ours; it is a grace. And this difference alone is sufficient to alter the meaning of all that has gone before.

Leaving this conclusion aside for the moment, however, let us return to the point with which we are principally concerned. Gregory's doctrine of the acquisition of the knowledge of God—that is, by the return of the soul to itself and its purification from any foreign element—does indeed closely resemble that of Plotinus, if one sticks to the letter of certain texts. As a result, some have concluded that Gregory is undeniably a Platonist. Are they correct in doing so?

---

[20] Ibid. (PG 46:372B–C; FC 58:44).
[21] Plotinus, *Enneads* 1.6.5. See also ibid., 4.8.8.
[22] *Virg.* 12 (PG 46:372A–C; FC 58:44); Plotinus, *Enneads* 1.6.5.
[23] *Virg.* 12 (PG 46:372C; FC 58:44).

Basically, the debate centers around the concept of purity and its relationship to the image of God in man. On the one hand, the soul begins by purifying itself, and, once purified, God appears to it. How does this happen? For the Neoplatonists this is easy to explain, as von Ivánka has pointed out: "If the soul is by essence divine . . . it will suffice for it to turn away from the external world, to return to its own essence by purifying itself of everything that is alien, and it will then find in itself the knowledge of God. This knowledge goes hand in hand with the knowledge the soul gains of its own true being. Both are on the same level."[24] The purified state of the soul suffices to restore in itself the splendor of the divine nature of which it partakes, and enables it to see God from then on.

But from a Christian point of view this line of thought is questionable. In what sense is the purified soul the mirror in which God is reflected? How does the return of the soul to itself restore the divine? What is this presence that follows on from the purification of the soul? All of this is unclear. The reason lies in the fact that, underlying the surface similarity of vocabulary, there is an entirely different conception of things. The divine likeness is not given to the soul in such a way that all that is required to recover it is a process of purification. Rather, it is given—along with purity itself—to the soul that turns to God. Here, the relationship between God's presence and purity is reversed. It is no longer purity that brings with it the presence of God, but the presence of God that brings purity. For purity and the presence of God are identical. Purity is the result of God's presence. Consequently, it is easy to understand that the soul that contemplates its own purity sees God in itself. For this purity *is* God.[25]

This entirely new perspective is found in such passages as the following: "Only you," Gregory writes of the soul, "came into existence as a copy of the Nature that transcends every intellect, a likeness of the incorruptible Beauty, an impress of the true Deity—a model of that true Light in the contemplation of which you become what it is, imitating that which shines within you by the ray that shines forth in response from your purity."[26] There are many other texts of this type, containing an understanding that is entirely different from the Plotinian point of view. In the latter, purity was the means by which the soul succeeded in restoring in itself the image of God that had been hidden under rust. Here the progression is not the same: the soul turns to God—and then God communicates his purity to it, which is the image itself and the divine likeness. Here is no

---

[24]Von Ivánka, "Die unmittelbare Gotteserkenntnis bei Augustin," 523.
[25]On all this, see the excellent comments by von Ivánka, "Vom Platonismus,"185f.
[26]*Cant.* 2 (PG 44:805D; Norris, 75). See also *Cant.* 3 (PG 44:809B; Norris, 81).

suggestion of a divinity intrinsic to the soul, but of a freedom that enables the soul to turn to God and to whom God then communicates his life.

The key metaphor used by Gregory to express this idea is that of the mirror. In the sense in which he understands it, this is a metaphor that is specific to him. The distinctive feature of a mirror is to be nothing in itself, but to configure itself (συσχηματίζεσθαι, *syschēmatizesthai*) to the objects toward which it is turned. Thus, it does not contain in itself the divine image, the *eikōn*, or grace. But it is capable of receiving it. The soul is not similar to God by nature but becomes so when it turns to him. Thus, it is in the act of love through which the soul turns to God that it comes to know him.[27] A turning around of the soul is indeed the precondition for knowledge of God, but it is a turning to God, and not to itself.

What we have here is a total transformation of Platonism, which we are able to witness in its very emergence and in the difficulties it encounters. It will enable an authentic Christian mysticism to become established. What is important is less the persistence of Platonic terms than the strenuous efforts to adapt Platonic forms so as to express a thought that is altogether different. Is it so surprising that certain expressions that are not entirely rethought should still remain? Von Ivánka expresses the point well: "It is true, as Bardenhewer has established, that insufficient attention has been paid to Gregory of Nyssa as a mystical writer. But it is unfair to add, as he does, that as a mystic he belongs in the line of Philo and the Neoplatonic tradition. Certainly, he continues this tradition. But it is wrong to maintain, on the one hand, that he is dependent on it and not to draw attention, on the other, to the new interpretation that all the Neoplatonic themes have acquired with him. It is true that Gregory himself was still developing this new interpretation and that one would not expect his writings to be entirely free of elements of the old approach. Certain atavistic expressions appear even in the *Homilies on the Song of Songs*."[28]

This clarification is correct in every detail. What we have is a new interpretation, Christian mysticism in the process of establishing itself—using Platonic elements, just as dogmatic theology will use Aristotelian elements. What we see in Gregory is a first working out of this interpretation thanks to the concurrence in him of philosopher and great mystic. Indeed, in the very passages where Platonic expressions can be detected, we also find, alongside them, the clearest of

---

[27] Man cannot by his nature be compared to God, but he can imitate God's works through his way of life. Cf. *Prof.* (PG 46:245D; FC 58:87).

[28] Von Ivánka, "Vom Platonismus," 192.

statements concerning the gratuitous, supernatural character of likeness to God and of purity. It is clear, then, that the expressions that cause problems—such as "a return of the soul to its natural form," "being purified of any alien element"—should be interpreted in a Christian sense and that their real content has nothing to do with Neoplatonism.

A more thorough study of such expressions confirms our first impression. The return of the soul to what it was, to its natural form—this has a totally different meaning in Gregory than in Plotinus. With the latter, it is a matter of the spiritual nature of the soul; with Gregory, it is a question of the original condition of man.[29] Now this original state is supernatural life, grace, God's image, such as we described at the beginning of this study. What has to be recovered is this lost grace. But "this is not possible to achieve, unless one be created anew. For, being like the divine is not our function, nor is it the product of human ability."[30] It is the same with purification. It is presented under the form of the traditional metaphors of mud to be removed, rust to be scraped off, as if one had to find a reality hidden underneath. But we should be distrustful of metaphors. The entire context of Gregory's thought, as we shall see even more clearly, shows that in reality this purity that we are to find again is in fact a gift that we must await from God, and that it coincides with grace itself. In this regard, one cannot agree with von Ivánka that there is an evolution in Gregory's thought from *On Virginity* to the sixth homily on the Beatitudes, in the sense that "the purity of the soul was there a means and a condition, whereas here it is the object of the vision."[31] It would be more accurate to say that in *On Virginity* the thinking is more awkwardly expressed. It is only on this point that there is progress.

And so we can ascribe to the expressions encountered during the course of this study their true meaning. Such expressions as the presence in the soul of the divine image (θεοειδὴς χαρακτήρ, *theoeidēs charactēr*), the deiform beauty, the grace of the image (ἡ χάρις τοῦ εἰκόνος, *hē charis tou eikonos*). This beauty is that which had been placed in the soul at the beginning, which sin had erased, and which we should recover. This grace is a mirror that reflects and communicates the divine nature. All these expressions clearly show that it is a question of the presence in the soul of supernatural life. As we have said, the word *eikōn*, though it sometimes denotes the very nature of the soul, also refers to the supernatural

---

[29]See *An. et res.* 6 (PG 46:89C; PPS 12:78), *Virg.* 12 (PG 46:372C; FC 58:44); *Beat.* 6 (PG 44:1272A; ACW 18:148).
[30]*Virg.* 12 (PG 46:372C; FC 58:44).
[31]Von Ivánka, "Vom Platonismus," 190.

life.³² Here it is a matter of the "image" that has been lost.³³ Therefore, it cannot be a question of its actual nature. Moreover, χάρις (*charis*, grace), though it is similar in meaning to κάλλος (*kallos*, beauty), also has the nuance of meaning "a free gift." Finally, θεοειδής (*theoeidēs*) strictly speaking denotes the "deiform" character of a soul that is divinized by grace.

Consequently, the most appropriate phrase that accurately describes the Platonic coloring of certain passages in Gregory seems to me to be von Ivánka's "atavistic expressions." In Gregory, there is indeed a core of Platonic images from which he cannot free himself and which govern the expression of what is a new doctrine and a personal creation of his. Sometimes he is enslaved by them, and they mask his thought. We shall look at this presently. Having thus identified these preliminary issues, we are in a better position to study what his thought actually is and to determine what is meant by the experience of God in the mirror of the soul, and to do so choosing texts that present no ambiguity whatsoever.

The soul is not divine by nature. It contains a reflection of God that is called freedom, but does not possess in itself the divine adornment of the virtues. This is a grace that it must receive. To become pure, it must turn to the source of purity. Then, transformed by grace and having become deiform, it has only to look at itself to see God shine in it as in a mirror. But the totally new meaning the concept of *katharos* takes on here is clear to see. It is not the mere elimination of alien elements and the return of the soul to itself, but an orientation of the soul toward the divine source, the divine life, which alone can communicate purity to it. It is not a matter of the soul achieving a state of solitude and isolation, but of its disengagement from the sensory world in order to turn to God.³⁴

We shall see how these ideas find expression in Gregory's texts. "If, then," he writes, "one should withdraw from those who seduce him to evil and by the use of his reason turn to the better, putting evil behind him, it is as if he places his own soul, like a mirror, face to face with the hope of good things, with the result that the images and impressions [τὰς εἰκόνας καὶ ἐμφάσεις, *tas eikonas kai emphaseis*] of virtue, as it is shown to him by God [θεόθεν, *theothen*], are imprinted on the purity of his soul."³⁵ And, conversely, for the soul, sin consists in "turning the back" to God: "For the mind, setting the idea of good like

---

³²See *Op. hom.* 16.4 (PG 44:180C; NPNF² 5:403).
³³See *Virg.* 12 (PG 46:372B; FC 58:44).
³⁴See von Ivánka, "Die unmittelbare Gotteserkenntnis bei Augustin," 526.
³⁵*Vit. Moys.* 2.47 (PG 44:340A-B; Malherbe, 65).

Mystical Experience

a mirror behind the back, turns off the incident rays of the effulgence of the good, and it receives into itself the impress of the shapelessness of matter."[36] And this—let us note this cosmic touch in passing—leads, in turn, to a disorder of nature, which is "the mirror of the mirror" (κάτοπτρον κατόπτρου, *katoptron katoptrou*).[37]

This is developed at greater length in the *Homilies on the Song of Songs*:

> Human nature has been endowed with free will [κατὰ γνωμήν, *kata gnōmēn*] and that toward which the inclination of its will [ῥοπή, *rhopē*] carries it, and therein it transforms itself into it. It is made in such a way that it is in its power to conform itself [συσχηματίζεσθαι, *syschēmatizesthai*] to that toward which it inclines. Also, it is quite rightly that the Word tells the soul that it has become beautiful: by distancing yourself from communion with evil, you have come near me. By coming near the inaccessible beauty, you too have become beautiful, reflecting my own form like a mirror. Human nature does indeed truly resemble a mirror; it assumes the form of what it will reflect [κατὰ τὰς ἐμφάσεις τῶν προαιρέσεων, *kata tas emphaseis tōn proaireseōn*]. When, having turned its back to sin, it has been purified by the Word [κεκαθαρμένη ὑπὸ τοῦ λόγου, *kekatharmenē hypo tou logou*], it receives in itself the disk of the sun, and it shines by the very light that appears in it. The Word can say to it: "You have already become beautiful by coming close to my light, making a participation in the beautiful your own by this drawing near" [προσεγγίσμενον, *prosengismenon*].[38]

The thinking here is quite clear. It is not a matter of the mere withdrawal of the soul, but of forsaking through an act of will all that is not God and of turning to him. The Word then purifies it; that is, as we shall see, he imparts his own light to it. This light is true purity, a positive purity, fruit of the presence of the Spirit in the soul and not of a separation from the external world. It is a partaking of the divine nature.[39] The soul sees in itself, as in a mirror, the divine nature, the reflected disk of the sun. There is no suggestion here of a natural identity of the soul with God, except in the sense that this orientation toward him that in turn attracts him to the soul, is the soul's natural vocation.

Other texts confirm this interpretation:

---

[36] *Op. hom.* 12.10 (PG 44:164A; NPNF² 5:398).
[37] *Op. hom.* 12.9 (PG 44:161D; NPNF² 5:398).
[38] *Cant.* 4 (PG 44:833A–B; Norris, 115).
[39] See *An. et res.* 6 (PG 46:89C; PPS 12:78).

> How after all is it possible for a beautiful image to appear in a mirror unless the mirror has received the impression [ἔμφασιν, *emphasin*] of a lovely form? Hence the mirror that is human nature does not become beautiful until it has drawn close to the Beautiful and been formed by the image [εἰκόνι, *eikoni*] of the divine Beauty. For just as human nature took the form of the serpent as long as it lay prostrate upon the earth and directed its gaze on him, in the same way, when it has risen up and shown itself to be face to face with the Good by turning its back upon evil, it is shaped in accordance with that which it looks upon—and what it looks upon is the archetypal Beauty. When, therefore, it has drawn close to the Light, it becomes light, and in this light the beautiful form of the dove is imaged—and the dove I am talking about is the one whose form makes known the presence [παρουσία, *parousia*] of the Holy Spirit.[40]

Here we have the final word on the transformation of the soul. It is the fruit of the presence of the Spirit; that is, a partaking of the divine life. It is striking that this was already Gregory's teaching in his very first work, *On Virginity*:

> How could anyone whose enthusiasm is directed toward the lowly rise to such heights? How could anyone fly up to heaven unless, equipped with heavenly wings, he be borne upwards because of his lofty way of life? Who is so removed from the mysteries of the Gospel, that he does not know that there is one vehicle [ὄχημα, *ochēma*] for the human soul for the journey to the heavens, and that is by likening itself to the cowering[41] dove whose wings the prophet David longed for (Ps 54.7). It is customary for Scripture to use this symbol in referring to the power of the Spirit.... So the mind of man... is purified through the power of the Spirit, becomes light-like [φωτοειδής, *photoeidēs*], and it is mixed with the true and lofty purity, and it glows and is filled with rays and becomes light, in accordance with the promise of the Lord who declared that the just will shine like the sun (Prov 4.18).[42]

The vocabulary here is more Platonic, as throughout this treatise. We recognize the wings, the vehicle, and the heavenly voyage of *Phaedrus*. But beneath the surface the thought is entirely Christian. It is the grace of the Spirit that alone

---

[40] *Cant.* 5 (PG 44:868C–869A; Norris, 163).
[41] [Callahan's curious translation—"cowering"—seems highly inappropriate, given the context. Migne's Greek reads καταπτάσης (*kataptasēs*), from the verb meaning "to fly down" or "descend"—terms that are much more neutral.—*Trans.*]
[42] *Virg.* 11 (PG 46:365B–368C; FC 58:40–41).

Mystical Experience

brings about the deification and transforms the soul into light. Aside from this, there is no way of obtaining the true goods. Gregory will say the same thing again in the *Homilies on St Stephen*.[43] When, in the next chapter, he uses the Plotinian image of the statue covered with mud, there can be no hesitation as to its interpretation. Is it not obvious that here, too, we should go beyond the literary disguise, the language common to the entire Hellenistic tradition, and seek under this veneer the entirely different realities it overlays?

For Gregory it is not only the soul but the eyes, too, that must be purified.[44] This purification must likewise be understood as an action of the Holy Spirit. It is the Spirit who gives the soul the eyes of the dove, without which it would remain blind to divine things: "Since [the soul] becomes wholly spiritual throughout (cf. Rom 8.13), not psychic or fleshly, it follows that the soul that has been delivered from bodily passion is attested as having in its eyes the shape of the dove—that is, the imprint of the spiritual life is beheld in the clear vision of the soul. Since, then, her purified eye has received the imprint of the dove, she is also capable of beholding the beauty of the Bridegroom. For now for the first time, the virgin gazes upon [ἀτενίζει, *atenizei*] the form of the Bridegroom."[45] Here we find the same equating of purity with the Holy Spirit. The transposition of the Platonist theme—even though its lexis (καθαρός, *katharos*; ἀτενίζει, *atenizei*) is still in evidence—is complete.

With this in mind, the various texts we have looked at become clearer. In particular, we are enabled to learn more about this vision of God in the mirror of the soul that Gregory speaks of. Diekamp classifies it as ordinary knowledge and sees mystical knowledge as beginning only with the theme of night.[46] But here we already are in this night. For it is a question of an experience of the presence

---

[43] See *Steph. I* (PG 46:717B; Greer, 61).
[44] See *Virg.* 11 (PG 46:368D; FC 58:42).
[45] *Cant.* 4 (PG 44:836A; Norris, 117).
[46] See also G. Horn, and H. von Bathasar, who cannot escape this criticism. The distinction between the two orders is clearly indicated in this passage from the third homily on the Song of Songs: "The divine nature transcends the mind's grasp. Our thought concerning it is a likeness or image of what we seek, for it does not manifest the form of that which no one has seen or can see. Rather, it sketches darkly, in a mirror and in an enigma, a reflection of what we seek that comes to birth in our souls on the basis of some conjecture [εἰκασμοῦ, *eikasmou*]. All speech, however, that refers to such intuitions has the function of some indivisible mark, being unable to make clear what the mind intends. Thus . . . the soul that is led by such intuitions to awareness [περινοία, *perinoia*] of things that cannot be grasped [ἀλήπτων, *alēptōn*] must bring the Nature that transcends all intellect within herself by faith alone." *Cant.* 3 (PG 44:821A-B; Norris, 97). Here one sees quite clearly the contrast between symbolic theology, which is the domain of the intellect, and mystical theology, which is knowledge based purely on the fact of a presence in the soul—that is, knowledge by an indwelling.

of God in the soul that cannot be perceived except through the eyes of faith, the eyes of the dove. Gregory's comment in his homily on the sixth Beatitude is thus fully explained: "The Lord does not say it is blessed to know something about God, but to have God present within oneself.... By this we should learn that if a man's heart has been purified from every creature and all unruly affections, he will see the Image of the Divine Nature in his own beauty."[47] It is a question of a presence and an awareness of this presence. We see now that this beauty is an emanation of the divine beauty. "You have within yourselves the standard by which to apprehend the Divine."[48] In fact, our knowledge of God is linked to our participation (μετουσία, *metousia*) in him, which means having the divine life in us. The greater the participation, the more we know God. "For the Godhead is purity, freedom from passion, and separation from all evil. If therefore these things be in you, God is indeed in you."[49] These things are the "luminous reflections of the Divine Nature, in which God is contemplated."[50]

The link that exists, then, between progress in purity—that is, in the divine life—and progress in the knowledge of God is clear. Purity is a sign of the presence of God in us, and through its progress, this presence becomes greater. It satisfies the soul yet at the same time stimulates its desire. By the "mirror" of God in the soul is meant the virtues that, weak at first like a faint whiff of fragrance, become the sign of his ever closer approach. This theme of the mirror leads to that of the spiritual senses, which is its development:

> If a person, having gathered every sweet-smelling flower or scent from the various blooms of virtue and having rendered his whole life a perfume by the fragrance of his daily doings, should become perfect in all respects, he does not have it in him to look intently upon the divine Word itself any more than upon the disc of the sun. Nevertheless, he sees the sun within himself as in a mirror. For the rays of that true and divine Virtue shine upon the purified life through the inward peace [ἀπάθεια, *apatheia*] that flows from them, and they make the Invisible visible for us and the Incomprehensible comprehensible, because they portray the Sun in the mirror that we are.[51]

---

[47] *Beat.* 6 (PG 44:1269C; ACW 18:148).
[48] Ibid. (PG 44:1272A; ACW 18: 148).
[49] Ibid. (PG 44:1272C; ACW 18: 149).
[50] Ibid. (PG 44:1272C; ACW 18: 150).
[51] *Cant.* 3 (PG 44:824C; Norris, 101).

Mystical Experience

We see how the great Platonic élan toward the interiority of the soul has been retained but transposed. On this point, his is a key role. Von Ivánka describes it this way:

> Gregory of Nyssa . . . is the first to have freed from their connection with the Platonic theory of the soul ideas that, through Pseudo-Dionysius, would go on to influence the entire Middle Ages, thus enabling them to become the foundation of a Christian mysticism. He was the first to recognize their mystical character. The doctrine that the human soul is divine arises from a mystical experience wrongly interpreted, in which all awareness of the distinction between subject and object, the soul and God, is lost. Yet it was on this that Plato and the Neoplatonists based their system. Gregory does us the service of being the first to separate the basic idea of the knowledge of God in the soul (and in a clearer fashion than Dionysius) from the Platonic doctrine of the soul, and thus to pass on what truth it did contain as a theory of mysticism to Christian doctrine.[52]

The Spiritual Senses

For man to be restored to his paradisal state, he must dispel the illusion of sensory pleasure and rediscover the taste of God. It is this experience of God—the most important aspect of life in paradise—that lies at the heart of the mystical life. Here the doctrine of the spiritual senses—through which we become capable of this taste—plays an essential role, and we shall see the importance it has for Gregory of Nyssa. The originality of Gregory's teaching on this point is that it is not simply the expression of the psychological experience of the *dulcedo Dei*, the sweetness of God. It is certainly this, but is also linked to his anthropology. In fact, for him it represents the true nature of man, that of the original Adam.

Here we broach a new paradisal theme: the tree of life. We know that this occupies a special place in Scripture since it appears in both Genesis (2.9 and 3.22) and Revelation (2.7 and 22.2, 14). Gregory's interpretation of the narrative in Genesis is clearly symbolic. The tree of life is itself a symbol of a spiritual reality, as he explains in chapters 19 and 20 of his treatise *On the Making of Man*. He has just stated that drinking and eating are linked to man's fallen condition and will no longer be necessary after the resurrection. One might object, he adds, that the resurrection cannot then constitute a return to an original state,

---

[52]Von Ivánka, "Vom Platonismus," 192–93.

since in the latter man did indeed need to feed himself. But Gregory goes on to counter this objection as follows: "I, however, when I hear the Holy Scripture, do not understand only bodily meat, or the pleasure of the flesh; but I recognize another kind of food also, having a certain analogy [ἀναλογίαν τινά, *analogian tina*] to that of the body, the enjoyment of which extends to the soul alone."[53] We note here the idea of a certain correspondence between the bodily and the spiritual order. We shall meet this again when we come to discuss the question of the spiritual senses in more detail. Gregory continues: "We ought, then, to conceive that the fruit in Eden was something worthy of God's planting (and Eden is interpreted to mean 'delight'), and not to doubt that man was hereby nourished: nor should we at all conceive, concerning the mode of life in Paradise, this transitory and perishable nutriment."[54]

What, then, does this tree of life signify? In answering this question, Gregory refers to another verse from Genesis: "Of every tree that is in the garden thou mayest freely eat" (Gen 2.16). By this one should understand, he says, "that very actual Good, which in truth is *every* good."[55] As regards the contrast between the tree of life and the tree of the knowledge of good and evil, he correctly observes that knowledge must here be understood as a disposition of the will, as experiential as opposed to something speculative. Gregory interprets this second, forbidden, tree as symbolizing sensory pleasures that appear to be good but are actually a source of evil. He makes the same contrast again in *On the Soul and the Resurrection*: "Human life was originally uniform. By uniform [μονοειδής, *monoeidēs*] I mean the life which exhibits the good only, unmixed with evil. This opinion is attested by God's first law, which gave to mankind unstinting participation in every one of the good things of paradise, excluding only that which had as its nature a mixture of opposites, evil combined with good."[56]

In the treatise *On Virginity*, where Gregory explains how the spiritual life is in essence a return to life in paradise, we find a passage of paramount importance that is significantly clarified by these comparisons: "Let us become what

---

[53] *Op. hom.* 19.1 (PG 44:196C; NPNF² 5:408). [For a recent treatment of the spiritual senses in Gregory, see Paul Gavrilyuk and Sarah Coakley, *The Spiritual Senses: Perceiving God in Western Christianity* (Cambridge University Press, 2012), 36–55.—*Ed.*]

[54] *Op. hom.* 19.2 (PG 44:196D; NPNF² 5:408). See also *Cant.* Prol. (PG 44:761B; Norris, 9): "Unless one perceives the truth in these matters through philosophy, what is being said [about the tree of life] will appear to the inattentive to be incoherent or mythical" (μυθῶδες καὶ ἀσύστατον, *mythōdes kai asystaton*).

[55] *Op. hom.* 19.4 (PG 44:197A; NPNF² 5:408).

[56] *An. et res.* 5 (PG 46:81B; PPS 12:70). See also *Inscr.* 1.8.90 (PG 44:473A; Heine, 113).

the first being was during the first period of his existence. But what was he? ... [N]ot yet judging the beautiful by taste and sight, but only enjoying the Lord. ... [Therefore, we] must disdain the deceptions of taste and sight ... partaking only of the pure and unmixed good."[57] This is the very goal of the spiritual life, beyond which there is nothing save ecstasy.

One sees the importance of this text. There was a time when man had no experience of the physical senses, and when his food was the divine goods. This "monoïdeic" concept will be developed by Diadochus of Photiki, who writes as follows:

> [The] perceptive faculty natural to our soul is single; indeed even the five bodily senses differ from each other only because of the body's varying needs. But this single faculty of perception is split because of the dislocation which, as a result of Adam's disobedience, takes place in the intellect through the modes in which the soul now operates. Thus one side of the soul is carried away by the passionate part in man, and we are then captivated by the good things of this life; but the other side of the soul frequently delights in the activity of the intellect and, as a result ... the intellect longs to pursue heavenly beauty. [58]

A return to the tree of life is possible, then, only by suspending our reliance on the bodily senses. This alone enables the awakening of the spiritual senses. We seem always to come back to the opposition between carnal, impassioned man and man as he was created, in the image. But here it is on the psychological plane of the spiritual life, as two realities whose existence each of us can experience for himself.

Having related this teaching to its paradisal origins, we can now study it in itself.

* * *

The doctrine of the spiritual senses is one of the essential components of Gregory of Nyssa's spiritual theology. For that matter, it is found in all the great writers on spirituality. We need only note some of the texts cited by Poulain[59] or Stolz.[60] One could also cite essential texts by St Augustine, St Bernard, St Bonaventure,

---

[57] *Virg.* 12, 13 (PG 46:374C, 376C; 45–46, 47).
[58] Diadochos of Photiki, *On Spiritual Knowledge and Discrimination* 29 (*Philokalia* 1:260–61).
[59] A. Poulain, *Des grâces d'oraison: Traité de théologie mystique* (Paris: Beauchesne, 1901), 93–117. [*The Graces of Interior Prayer*, trans. L. Smith (London: Kegan Paul, 1910), 88–113.]
[60] Stolz, *Théologie de la mystique*, 150ff. [*Spiritual Perfection*, 137ff.]

or St Teresa. However, this tradition perhaps represents a school that is not that of Dionysius the Areopagite, of Tauler, or of St John of the Cross. The first insists on the taste of God, the second on his inaccessibility. The importance of Gregory of Nyssa here is that with him both tendencies are represented. He is just as much the precursor of St Bernard—and before him of Diadochus—through his doctrine of the divine sweetness, as he is of John of the Cross—and before him of Dionysius—through his theology of darkness. Yet one should not exaggerate the contrast, for in fact the two trends represent the twin essential aspects of mysticism. On the one hand, it is darkness for the mind; but on the other hand, it involves an experiential knowledge of God that is precisely what the doctrine of the spiritual senses seeks to express.

The first systematic formulation of this doctrine is found in Origen,[61] who derives its elements from Scripture, where the metaphor of "divine sweetness" and the "taste" of God occupies an important place,[62] as does that of the "fragrance" of God.[63] It is a doctrine that is specifically biblical and Christian in nature. If we can detect the beginnings of it in Philo, this is because its sources are biblical. The only similarities are the ones Lohmeyer indicates,[64] and also the metaphor of touch (ἐπαφή, *epaphē*), that is used by Plotinus to denote the supra-rational experience of the divine.

Origen's specific contribution is that he grouped together these scattered elements and linked them to the five senses. The essential text is *Contra Celsum*, a fact that for us is all the more important since, as we shall establish, it is obviously Gregory's own source:

> Anyone who looks into the subject more deeply will say that there is, as the scripture calls it, a certain generic divine sense which only the man who is blessed finds on this earth. Thus Solomon says: "Thou shalt find a divine sense [αἴσθησιν, *aisthēsin*]" (Prov 2.5).[65] There are many forms of this sense: a sight which can see things superior to corporeal beings, the cherubim or seraphim being obvious instances, and a hearing which can receive impressions of sounds that have no objective existence in the air, and a taste which

---

[61]Rahner, "Le début d'une doctrine," 113–45.
[62]Ziegler, *Dulcedo Dei*, 13–58.
[63]Ibid., 7–12.
[64]E. J. Lohmeyer, *Vom göttlichen Wohlgeruch* (Heidelberg: Heidelberger Akademie der Wissenschaften: 1919): 7–25.
[65][Chadwick notes that this is not in the LXX, but it is in Clement of Alexandria (*Miscellanies* 1.27.2) and often in Origen.—*Trans.*]

feeds on living bread that has come down from heaven and gives life to the world (Jn 6.33). So also there is a sense of smell which smells spiritual things, as Paul speaks of "a sweet savour of Christ unto God" (2 Cor 2.15), and a sense of touch in accordance with which John says that he has handled with his hands "of the Word of Life" (1 Jn 1.1). The blessed prophets found this divine sense.[66]

A similar, if briefer, expression of this teaching is found in Origen's *De Principiis* (*On First Principles*): "[Solomon] knew that there were within us two kinds of sense: one kind of sense being mortal, corruptible, human, the other kind being immortal and intellectual, which here he calls 'divine.' "[67] With these texts in mind, let us now consider a passage in which Gregory presents the same doctrine:

> There is in us a dual activity of perception, the one bodily, the other more—just as the Word says somewhere in Proverbs, "You will find a divine mode of perception." For there is a certain analogy between the sense organs of the body and the operations of the soul. And it is this that we learn from the words before us. For both wine and milk are discerned by the sense of taste [γεύσει, *geusei*], but when they are intelligible things, the power of the soul that grasps them is a fully intellectual power. And a kiss comes about through the sense of touch for in a kiss lips touch each other. There is also, though, a "touch" [ἀφή, *aphē*] that belongs to the soul, one that makes contact with the Word and which is actuated by an incorporeal and intelligible touching, just as someone said, "Our hands have handled ... the Word of Life" (1 Jn 1.1). In the same way, too, the scent of the divine perfumes is not a scent in the nostrils but pertains to a certain intelligible and immaterial faculty that inhales the sweet smell of Christ by sucking in the Spirit.[68]

The points of contact between this text and Origen's are obvious. There is the distinction made between two types of senses, which reminds us of the comparison we observed earlier concerning the two types of food. Above all, there are the identical biblical citations: 1 John 1.1 and 2 Corinthians 2.15. The verse

---

[66]Origen, *Contra Celsum* 1.48 (PG 11:749A-B). Translation from Origen: *Contra Celsum*, trans. Henry Chadwick (Cambridge: Cambridge University Press, 1980, 1953), 44.

[67]Origen, *On First Principles*, 1.1.9 (PG 11:129C; Behr, 1:39. See other references in J. Daniélou, *Origène*, 299-301 [*Origen*, 307-309].

[68]Gregory, *Cant.* 1 (PG 44:780C; Norris, 35-37). A list of the spiritual senses in an eschatological context is found in *Mort.* 12 (PG 46:516C-D; PPS 64:17-18).

from Proverbs (2.5) deserves special attention. The Septuagint and the Vulgate translate the Hebrew *da'ath* as ἐπίγνωσις (*epignōsis*), and Aquila, Symmachus, and Theodotion opt for γνῶσις (*gnōsis*), both referring to "knowledge" of God. The translation given by Origen—αἴσθησις (*aisthēsis*, sense perception)—seems therefore to be a personal choice of his. It is from him that Gregory borrows it. We may compare this interpretation to the one seen earlier concerning the tree of the knowledge of good and evil, where Gregory saw in *gnōsis* a word whose connotation was more affective than intellectual—that is, referred not to a theoretical type of knowledge but to one comprising both participation and delight. And perhaps in this way, Origen and Gregory entered more deeply into the genius of the Hebrew language than the above, more literal, translators.

In the passage quoted, Gregory's imitation of Origen is quite literal. More frequently, when using the exegesis of his precursor, Gregory develops things in a way that suits his own concerns. We shall see shortly how such divergences appear. But let us quote one further passage where the filiation is clear. It is a discussion of the following verse from the Song: "As the apple among the trees of the wood, so is my beloved among the sons" (Song 2.3). "The Bridegroom," writes Origen, "is among the sons, therefore, as the apple tree is among the trees of the wood, in that He bears fruit that not only surpasses all other fruits in taste, but also in fragrance, and thus appeals equally to the soul in two senses, taste and smell. So does Wisdom furnish her table for us with a variety of riches: she not only sets thereon the bread of life, she also offers us the Flesh of the Word. And she not only mingles her wine in the bowl, she also supplies plenty of fragrant apples."[69]

Gregory takes this up and develops it as follows:

> [The apple tree] bears a fruit by which the perceptive faculties of the soul [τὰ τῆς ψυχῆς αἰσθητήρια, *ta tēs psychēs aisthētēria*] are touched with sweetness, it differs to a greater degree from the wood than the lily does from the thorns. The lily is pleasing in its appearance and its scent, but the delight afforded by the apple is shared, in a way suited to each, among three senses: it gladdens the eye by the splendor of its appearance; by its scent it gives pleasure to the sense of smell; and as food it provides sweetness to the organs of taste. . . . [Thus the Lord] is joy to our eyes when he comes as light, perfume to our sense of smell, and life to those who eat him.[70]

---

[69]Origen, *Commentary on the Song of Songs* 1.3.5 (PG 13:151C–152A; ACW 26:180–81).
[70]Gregory, *Cant.* 4 (PG 44:841D–844A; Norris, 129–31). Cf. ibid. (PG 44:848D; Norris, 137): "For taken as beautiful the apple is contemplated with desire, taken as perfume it gives pleasure to the sense

Mystical Experience

Here we find some of the traits that characterize the Gregorian interpretation of the spiritual senses: the use of the expression τὰ τῆς ψυχῆς αἰσθητήρια (*ta tēs psyches aisthētēria*, the faculties or senses of the soul), the order of sensations: sight, smell, taste; and finally, the importance of the Word as object of the spiritual senses. We shall return to all this.

The line of descent, then, from Origen to Gregory is well established. Rahner had already determined as much in his article on Origen. For our part, we shall be specifying more precisely the points where there is clear dependence, on the one hand, and those where Gregory is original. For the moment, let us examine in more detail the doctrine of the spiritual senses such as we find it in his writings. The first thing to note is the frequency of his references to them. Sometimes it is a case of a general expression, as when he speaks of "the faculties of [the] soul" (τὰ αἰσθητήρια τῆς ψυχῆς, *ta aisthētēria tēs psychēs*),[71] or of the "sense organs of [the] heart" (τὰ αἰσθητήρια τῆς καρδίας, *ta aisthētēria tēs kardias*),[72] an expression that comes from Jeremiah (4.19) in the translation of the Septuagint.[73] It is contrasted with τὰ αἰσθητήρια τῆς σαρκός (*ta aisthētēria tēs sarkos*, the sense organs of the flesh) in a text such as the following: "[The mind] listens to the singing of the heavens by transcending and being above the faculties of sense-perception that belong to our flesh."[74]

On other occasions, the different senses—mainly hearing and sight—are mentioned individually. Thus Gregory speaks of the "eye of Moses' soul" (ὁ ὀφθαλμὸς τῆς ψυχῆς, *ho ophthalmos tēs psychēs*),[75] or "the eyes of our soul" (ὄψις τῆς ψυχῆς, *opsis tēs psychēs*),[76] or of "the ear of the heart" (ἡ ἀκοὴ τῆς καρδίας, *hē akoē tēs kardias*).[77] Elsewhere we find mention of "a 'touch' that belongs to

---

of smell, taken as food it fattens the body and pleases the taste, taken as shade it cools the midday heat"; (*Cant*. 4; PG 44:844C–D; Norris, 131–33): "For the sense organs of the soul are truly touched with sweetness by the Word [γλυκαίνονται τῷ Λόγῳ, *glykainontai tō Logō*] when the apple tree's shadow protects us from the fiery blaze of temptations.... For the eye rests upon the splendor of its beauty, and the nostril breathes its fragrance in, and the body is nourished, and the mouth is touched with sweetness."

[71] *Inscr*. 2.13.188 (PG 44:565D; Heine, 182); *Cant*. 4 (PG 44:844A; Norris, 131); etc.

[72] *Cant*. 14 (PG 44:1076A; Norris, 439).

[73] See also τὰ νοητὰ αἰσθητήρια (*ta noēta aisthētēria*, noetic sensory or perceptual faculties). *Infant*. 12 (PG 46:180C; PPS 64:53).

[74] *Inscr*. 1.3.19 (PG 44:440D; Heine, 89).

[75] *Vit. Moys*. 2.189 (PG 44:388B; Malherbe, 103). See also *Inscr*. 1.8.76 (PG 44:465D; Heine, 109); *Cant*. Prol. (PG 44:756A; Norris, 3); *Infant*. 11 (PG 46:177D; PPS 64:51).

[76] *Vit. Moys*. 2.19 (PG 44:332C; Malherbe, 59).

[77] *Vit. Moys*. 2.169 (PG 44:380A; Malherbe, 96). [Malherbe and Ferguson translate τὴν ἀκοὴν τῆς καρδίας (*tēn akoēn tēs kardias*) as "hearing in his heart"; ἀκοή (*akoē*) is more frequently used for the faculty of hearing, rather than the bodily "ear."—*Ed*.]

the soul" (ἀφὴ τῆς ψυχῆς, *aphē tēs psychēs*).⁷⁸ Certain of these expressions are traditional. Thus "the eye of the soul" (ὁ ὀφθαλμὸς τῆς ψυχῆς, *ho ophthalmos tēs psychēs*) is found already in Philo⁷⁹ and in its more Semitic form—"the eye of the heart" (ὁ ὀφθαλμὸς τῆς καρδίας, *ho ophthalmos tēs kardias*) is found in St Paul (Eph 1.18). I have not come across the exact same forms of expression for sight or taste, but there are loosely similar equivalents. For example, "the scent of the divine perfumes is not a scent in the nostrils but pertains to a certain intelligible and immaterial faculty [δυνάμεως, *dynameōs*]."⁸⁰

The awakening of these spiritual senses corresponds to an already advanced stage of the spiritual life. To confirm this, Gregory, like Origen, refers to the verse in the Epistle to the Hebrews where Paul contrasts infants with the mature (τέλειοι, *teleioi*) who "have their senses exercised to discern both good and evil" (5.13–14). These verses are referred to by Gregory in the *Homilies on the Song of Songs*, but Paul's term αἰσθητήρια (*aisthētēria*, organs of sense) is replaced by the fuller expression τὰ αἰσθητήρια τῆς ψυχῆς (*ta aisthētēria tēs psychēs*, the perceptive faculties of the soul), which makes clearer that it is a question of senses that are spiritual.⁸¹ Elsewhere Gregory speaks of the "perfect . . . who have already experienced the purification of the faculties of their soul."⁸² Thus the blossoming of the spiritual senses is the fruit of purification, whose aim, as we have seen, is to liberate the soul from the sensory life, from the sense organs of the flesh, and to enable it to exercise again its divine faculties. This can already be found in Origen, as Rahner has shown: "Only the *perfect* possess the five spiritual senses. Consequently, only those who, in the active life, have attained *apatheia* will be able to use the spiritual senses."⁸³ These spiritual senses correspond to the third, and highest, degree of the spiritual life—*theōria*.

In this regard it is important to note again the link that exists between the mortification of the carnal senses and the blossoming of the spiritual ones. It is with good reason that Stolz deals with the spiritual senses in the chapter entitled "Of the Graces of the Cross." This link is already apparent in Origen, who writes: "Because [the Word] tastes so sweet and so delightful, all other flavours will

---

⁷⁸*Cant.* 1 (PG 44:780D; Norris, 37).
⁷⁹Philo, *The Special Laws* 3.1.6 (Yonge, 594).
⁸⁰Gregory, *Cant.* 1 (PG 44:780D; Norris, 37). See also "sense of smell" (ἡ ὀσφραντικὴ αἴσθησις, *hē osphrantikē aisthēsis*), *Cant.* 3 (PG 44:821C; Norris, 99).
⁸¹*Cant.* 14 (PG 44:1062D; Norris, 423).
⁸²Gregory, *Inscr.* 1.3.17 (PG 44:440A; Heine, 87).
⁸³Rahner, "Le début d'une doctrine," 132.

seem harsh and bitter."[84] It is an idea that one finds in a great number of spiritual writers. Alonso Rodriguez, for example, who said that to taste God, one should deprive oneself of all carnal pleasure, since spiritual joys are always linked to the mortification of the senses; and conversely that to one who has tasted spiritual joys, the pleasures of the flesh seem bitter or insipid.

This aspect is strongly emphasized by Gregory in his fourteenth homily on the Song, concerning the symbol of myrrh:

> [It] is disdain for the material life, which appears when everything that people work for in this life becomes inoperative and dead on account of their desire for transcendent goods.
>
> Now Paul pours just such myrrh as this . . . into the ears of the holy virgin named Thecla. By flowing into the soul, the myrrh reduces the outer man to death, extinguishing all thought and all carnal desire, so that for the one who has received it all the bodily senses are dead, only the Word lives in him. . . . In the same way did the great Peter give utterance once before Cornelius . . . and filled the souls of his auditors with myrrh; and they, as soon as they had received the word, were buried together with Christ by baptism, becoming dead to ordinary life.[85]

There are several noteworthy features in this text. The key idea is the death of the bodily senses, which is a prerequisite if the Word is to come and live in the soul. We have already encountered this in connection with the tree of life when we saw that, in order to find again the joy of paradise, one must first free oneself from the "illusions of sight and taste." It is worth noting that here—in line with a comparison that is frequently found in patristic literature—the Word takes the place of the tree of life. It is also worth reminding ourselves again how, with Gregory, the various levels of the spiritual life are interconnected. The experience described here—a cessation of the activity of the bodily senses and thus a mystical experience—is linked to the partaking of the death of Christ in Baptism. This is because for Gregory these lofty graces are but the flowering of baptismal grace. Baptism imparts to the Christian life a rhythm of death and resurrection that must be confirmed at every stage of its development.

Thus the doctrine of the spiritual senses is directly connected to Gregory's anthropology. We are to divest the outer man of the "garments of skin" in order

---

[84] Origen, *Commentary on the Song of Songs* 1.1.4 (PG 13:95C; ACW 26:78).
[85] Gregory, *Cant.* 14 (PG 44:1068A; Norris, 429–31).

to clothe the inner man, man in the image. We came across this contrast on the sacramental level with Baptism, which symbolically and inceptively works the death of the old man and the resurrection of the new. We found it on the level of ethics with the contrast between the passions that constitute the old man and the image constitutive of the new man. We encountered it with the problem of false or erroneous opinions, symbolized by the shoes of skin that Moses must remove so that he may approach the Burning Bush where "the One who is" lives. We find it now on the level of theology, with the contrast between the bodily senses and the spiritual ones. The "night" of the bodily senses is the prerequisite for the awakening of the spiritual ones.

In *The Life of Moses* it is this night of the senses that is symbolized by the crossing of the desert prior to the ascent of Sinai, "the mountain of theology." The soul has been purified of the passions by Baptism; it has been set free of its illusions through the illumination at the Burning Bush; now it advances deeper into the desert—that is, it deprives itself yet more of sensory enjoyment: "For to the one who has left behind the Egyptian pleasures which he served before crossing the sea, life removed from these pleasures seems at first difficult and disagreeable. But if the wood be thrown into the water . . . then the virtuous life . . . becomes sweeter and more pleasant than all the sweetness that tickles the senses with pleasure."[86]

Gregory eloquently describes the state in which the soul, deprived of Egyptian food but not yet having received food from heaven, sees no way out and finds itself in a sort of despair (ἀνελπιστία, *anelpistia*):

> Whenever someone flees Egypt and, after getting outside its borders, is terrified by the assaults of temptation, the guide [the cloud] produces unexpected salvation from on high. Whenever the enemy with his army surrounds the one being pursued, the guide is forced to make the sea passable for him.[87]

> And thus when they had no more food of the foreign food which they had laid by in Egypt, there flowed down from above food which was at the same time varied and uniform. . . . What then do we learn here? We learn by what purifications one should purify himself of Egypt and the foreign life so that he empties the sack of his soul of all evil nourishment prepared by

---

[86] *Vit. Moys.* 2.132 (PG 44:366B; Malherbe, 86).
[87] *Vit. Moys.* 2.120 (PG 44:361B; Malherbe, 82).

Mystical Experience

the Egyptians. In his way he receives in himself with his pure soul the food which comes down from above.[88]

The mystical character of the night of the senses is more evident still in those passages that deal with mystical sleep:

> There is no activity of seeing, or of hearing, or of smelling or tasting, or of touching in the season of sleep. What is more, it relaxes the body's tension ... and effects an insensibility to all evils.... Hence from our text we learn this: that she who makes the boast that "I sleep, but my heart lies awake" [Song 5.2] has risen higher than herself.
>
> For the truth is that insofar as only the intellect in itself is alive, without any distraction from the organs of sense perception, the bodily nature becomes inactive ... then the working of the heart is pure, and its discourse is focused on what is above it, untroubled and unaccompanied by the noise that stems from the stirrings of sense perception.
>
> For in the human constitution there is a double pleasure, one that is in the soul and is activated by impassibility and another that is occasioned in the body by passion, and whichever of the two our choosing shall elect is the one that prevails over the other. Thus if one focuses attention on sense perception and seeks for oneself the pleasure it grafts into the body, one's life is spent without tasting the divine gladness.[89]

The two levels of activity are here clearly differentiated and their incompatibility underlined. The exercise of the spiritual senses that allows one to taste "the divine gladness" is conditional on the sleep of the bodily senses.

What is true of contemplation is also true of apostolic activity. In fact, we know that Gregory does not separate the two but understands the contemplative graces to be charisms that empower those who have received them for the purpose of governing the Church, and for the ministry of the word. Now to be able to judge spiritually, they must be dead to the sensory life. Those who belong to the head of the Church, that is, "who bring glory to the church, must be superior to sense perceptions [κρείττους τῶν αἰσθήσιων, *kreittous tōn aisthēseōn*], concealing sense perception by wisdom, just as the proverb says: 'The wise will conceal sense perception' (Prov 10.14). Sight does not serve as their criterion of beauty, taste does not provide their assessment of goodness, their judgment

---
[88] *Vit. Moys.* 2.137–38 (PG 44:368B; Malherbe, 87).
[89] *Cant.* 10 (PG 44:992C–D; Norris, 327–29).

of virtue does not depend on smell or touch or any other organ of perception; on the contrary, all sense perception is done to death [πάσης αἰσθήσεως νεκρωθείσης, *pasēs aisthēseōs nekrōtheisēs*], and it is through the agency of the soul alone that they touch the good things and yearn for them as they are manifested in an intelligible form."[90]

It may be observed that in this passage, as well as in the preceding one, the activity of the soul is one, and contrasted with the five bodily senses. We might seem to be closer to Plotinus or Diadochus of Photiki than to Origen. However, this singleness is to be understood as being the general, overall expression of what the various individual spiritual senses describe in a more detailed way. Nevertheless, the emphasis is rightly put on its unifying character in contrast to the dispersion typical of the sensory life.[91] We may also note that these different passages refer to different states. The one that describes the sleep of the senses in contemplation, for example, seems to denote ecstasy properly speaking, with the effective suspension of the life of the senses, whereas the passage just translated indicates independence of spiritual judgment with respect to interference from the sensory life, not the non-exercise of the latter on its own proper level. But again, what we have here are various aspects and degrees of the same reality—and the value of Gregory's doctrine lies precisely in the connection he establishes between various psychological experiences, which enables us to organize them into some sort of system, the better to interpret them.

We must now begin a more detailed study of the various senses and the spiritual experiences that each of them symbolizes. The first question that arises concerns their order of appearance. Origen was the first to show that they do not all awaken at the same time, and that it is only in the perfect that all of them are active.[92] Their order of appearance and their respective place is something to which insufficient attention has so far been paid. Yet some consideration of it could serve to distinguish between various types of mystical temperament in the same way that we distinguish between different types of imagination—visual, auditory, and so forth. For example, it seems that in John of the Cross spiritual touch occupies an important place; in Augustine, taste and sight; in Gregory of Nyssa, the sense of smell. By this we mean no more than that a particular

---

[90]*Cant.* 15 (PG 44:1104B–C; Norris, 479).
[91]Manna, symbolic of spiritual nourishment, is "at the same time varied [ποικίλος, *poikilos*] and uniform [μονοειδής, *monoeides*]." *Vit. Moys.* 2.137 (PG 44:368B; Malherbe, 87).
[92]See Rahner, "Le début d'une doctrine," 132.

Mystical Experience

emphasis is put on one aspect of the mystical experience, though not to the exclusion of the others.

As regards Gregory, the first observation to be made concerns the nocturnal character of his mysticism—in contrast to that, for example, of Origen or Augustine, whose mysticism is solar. There is no assertion that recurs more frequently in Gregory than that of the divine invisibility. Thus for him sight does not take primacy over the other spiritual senses. Perception of God occurs in darkness. It involves first of all—and we shall come back to this—a perception of the divine fragrance, then a taste of God, and finally a mysterious comprehension, an obscure contact. Now, sight is the most intellectual of the senses; the vision of God is an experience of an order that is properly intellectual. It is significant that this is precisely what Gregory takes issue with. And this is perhaps the key lesson of his mysticism, one that will have a major impact and that makes of him, one may say, the founder of Christian mysticism. For him, there can be no vision of God but only an experience of his presence. God is grasped as a person, in an existential rapport that surpasses all understanding, in a relationship of love. This is what will subsequently become the very hallmark of mysticism. Dionysius the Areopagite will borrow this teaching from Gregory and, through Dionysius, John of the Cross will inherit of it.

It is not that Gregory disputes that there is such a thing as illumination (φωτισμός, *phōtismos*); simply that it is related to the first way. He is aware, of course, that its effects continue throughout the mystical life. In a very important passage of the *Homilies on the Song of Songs*, he points out that, although one might be surprised that God should appear first as light and then as darkness, it is precisely this that demonstrates that the soul is making progress. This is contested by Origen. For him, Moses, the man of the cloud, is still on the level of natural contemplation. And on this point Evagrius, too, will criticize Gregory.[93]

Thus the important revolution carried out by Gregory is to have overthrown the previous order and to have affirmed the priority of knowledge in darkness over knowledge from vision. In so doing, he defined the specific domain of mystical theology, professing the possibility—above and beyond all gnosis—of an ineffable, existential experience of God's presence. This amounted to affirming the primacy of love. Gregory's saying that "knowledge becomes love" (ἡ δὲ γνῶσις ἀγάπη γίνεται, *hē de gnōsis agapē ginetai*) admirably summarizes his

---

[93] Hausherr, "Ignorance infinie," 359.

contribution. This is the key affirmation of his doctrine and suffices to give it considerable importance. We shall return to this at length in the final part of our investigation. Having established this first point, we need now to contextualize the various senses and to determine the realities they encompass.

The motif of divine fragrance is already found in the Old Testament, especially in the Song of Songs. It is taken up by Origen and then by Gregory, especially in their commentaries on this text. It is also found in non-Christian literature, above all among the gnostics, which perhaps explains why it is enlarged upon in the first examples of popular Christian literature, such as the Acts of the Martyrs and the legends of the saints.[94] Often, it is mentioned in relation to the Holy Spirit.[95]

In Gregory, the most noticeable feature about perception of the divine fragrance is its connection with the virtues. As we have already seen, the virtues are both the fruit of human freedom and a flowing forth of the divine life. The divine fragrance, then, is the soul's perception of God as it partakes of him. In another form, this is the doctrine of the knowledge of God in the soul as if in a mirror. Here is how Gregory interprets the following verse from the Song, "the fragrance of your perfumed ointments is better than all spices" (Song 1.3): "The spices we take to be virtues, such as wisdom, temperance, justice, courage, prudence, and the like, and each different individual assumes a different scent as he is dabbed with them in accord with his own power and choice.... Nevertheless, none of these can be compared with that absolute virtue ... [which is] Wisdom herself and Justice itself and Truth herself and all things severally."[96]

The same idea is developed, and more closely linked to mystical experience, in a further passage:

> When [the soul] has approached the object of her desire more closely, but before his beauty is manifest to her eyes, she touches the one she seeks through her sense of smell [ἐφάπτεται διὰ τῆς ὀσφραντικῆς αἰσθήσως, *ephaptetai dia tēs osphrantikēs aisthēseōs*], as if by her power of smell she recognized the distinctive quality of some color, and she says that she recognizes [ἐπεγνωκέναι, *epegnōkenai*] his fragrance by means of the sweetness

---

[94] On this topic see Lohmeyer, *Vom göttlichen Wohlgeruch*; Ziegler, *Dulcedo Dei*, 60–67; W. Riedel, *Die Auslegung des Hohenliedes in der jüdische: Gemeinde und der griechischen Kirche* (Naumberg, 1898).

[95] As in *Cant.* 5 (PG 44:873B; Norris, 169). See H. J. Cadbury, "The Odor of the Spirit at Pentecost," *Journal of Biblical Literature* 47 (1928): 237–56.

[96] *Cant.* 1 (PG 44:781B; Norris, 39).

of a perfume whose name is spikenard—saying to the friends of the Bridegroom, "My spikenard gave off his scent." "For," she says, "just as you confer not the pure gold of the Godhead but, by way of concepts comprehensible to us, likenesses of gold and do not disclose what pertains to it in clear speech but furnish imitations of the Object of our search by means of the laconic tracings of the silver of rational speech, so too I, in the fragrance of my perfume, sense the sweetness of that very One himself."

The meaning that the statement seems to me to bear is as follows. It is an artful and balanced mixture of many different aromas—each with its proper sweetness—that produces this perfume, while of all those that are blended together it is one sweet-smelling herb called spikenard that lends its name to the entire preparation. Further, the purified sensibility [κεκαθαρμένη αἴσθησις, *kekatharmenē aisthēsis*], receives what has been put together into one fragrance out of all the special aromas as the very sweetness of the Bridegroom.

Hence we judge that the words of the text are teaching us this; namely, that that Reality, whatever it is in its essence, which transcends the entire structure and order of Being [τῶν ὄντων, *tōn ontōn*] is unapproachable [ἀπρόσιτον, *aprositon*] impalpable [ἀναφές, *anaphes*] and incomprehensible [ἄληπτον, *alēpton*] but that, for us, the sweetness that is blended within us by the purity of the virtues [διὰ τῆς τῶν ἀρετῶν καθαρότητος, *dia tēs tōn aretōn katharotētos*] takes its place because by its own purity it images that which is by nature the Undefiled—and by its goodness, the Good; and by its incorruptibility, the Incorruptible; and by its unchangeability, the Unchangeable; and by all the things within us that are rightly done in accordance with virtue, the true Virtue, concerning which the prophet Habbakuk says that it embraces all the heavens (cf. Hab 3.3). Therefore she who explains to the friends of the bridegroom, "My spikenard gives off his scent" seems to me to say, in her philosophic discourse, both these things and the following.

If a person, having gathered every sweet-smelling flower or scent from the various blooms of virtue and having rendered his whole life a perfume by the fragrance of his daily doings, should become perfect in all respects, he does not have it in him to look intently [ἀτενῶς ἐνιδεῖν, *atenōs enidein*] upon the divine Word itself any more than upon the disc of the sun. Nevertheless, he sees the sun within himself as in a mirror. For the rays of that true and divine Virtue shine upon the purified life through the inward peace [ἀπαθείας, *apatheias*] that flows from them, and they make the Invisible visible for us and the Incomprehensible comprehensible, because they portray the Sun in the mirror that we are.

Where this idea is concerned, it is one and the same thing to speak of rays of the sun or of emanations of virtue or of sweet aromatic scents. For no matter which of these we adopt to express the point of our text, all of them give rise to a single notion: that knowledge of the Good that transcends every intellect comes to us through the virtues, even as it is possible through some image to get a glimpse of the archetypal Beauty. So it was with the Bride Paul. He imitated the Bridegroom by his virtues and inscribed within himself the unapproachable beauty by means of their sweetness, and out of the fruits of the Spirit—love and joy and peace and the like—he blended this spikenard. Hence he said that he was "the aroma of Christ" (2 Cor 2.15), capturing within himself the scent of that transcendent and unapproachable Grace and providing himself for others to have a part in according to their ability.[97]

I have cited this important text in full, for it shows us that perception by the sense of smell is the first of all the spiritual perceptions; it precedes sight and also, as we shall see later, taste. It is compared to a touching—which emphasizes its experiential character—and to a color, as regards the sharpness of the discernment. It is thus a question of an absolutely specific type of perception, but one that is still far-off. It has as object the Word, not as he is in himself, but as he exists in the soul that is his image by reason of its virtues.[98] The nature of these virtues is specified by the use of those Pauline terms—joy, love, and peace—that describe the fruits of the Spirit and thus of those virtues that are supernatural. They allow us to interpret in the same sense the moral virtues that were symbolized by the spices. The word "grace"—χάρις (*charis*, freely bestowed favor)—also emphasizes this aspect.

It is also important to note that rays, aromas, and fragrances are all put on the same level, signifying the soul's participation in the divine life. Thus the first mystical perception essentially has as object the experiential awareness of the

---

[97] *Cant.* 3 (PG 44:821A–824D; Norris, 97–101). It is worth noting that Origen gives an entirely different interpretation of this text, seeing in it a symbol of the incarnation.

[98] On comparing virtues to fragrances, see *Cant.* 1 (PG 44:848C; Norris, 39) and, in particular, *Cant.* 5 (PG 44:872A; Norris, 167): "'You see,' he says, 'the meadow blooming because of the virtues; you see self-control, that is, the bright and fragrant lily; you see reverence, the red rose; you see the violet, the sweet smell of Christ.'"

Mystical Experience 277

life of grace in us, the supernatural life, which is an emanation of the divine life. This is precisely what is meant by mystical experience:

> God is present immediately and most intimately to the soul—namely, as the ultimate principle of the new supernatural equipment of grace. In exercising the supernatural virtues, the soul acts corresponding to its supernatural being. A reflection upon the proper vital principle of this activity can, in a manner analogous to the soul's knowledge of itself, lead to an experimental perception of God operating in the soul, that is, to an immediate mystical knowledge of God. . . . The knowledge of God as the mystics in general describe it rules out any vision. Immediate contact with God in His essence blinds the human knowing faculty. Thus the teaching of the mystics on the obscurity of mystical knowledge has a significance of its own.[99]

In this text we find all the features typical of our author. A direct vision of the divine essence is impossible for man. It would blind him. What is accessible, however, is the knowledge of God by means of the participation one has in him. To become aware of this, to reflect on it, is to experience an immediate presence of God in the soul. This is first of all an experience of the virtues themselves, which are, as it were, the aroma by which the presence is detected. For Gregory, this is the objective of the spiritual sense of smell—to perceive the supernatural virtues. One should not forget that in Greek the terms "participation" and "image" signify not merely an external resemblance, but an existential dependency, and thus to perceive the virtues, which are the aroma of God, is already truly to perceive God himself.[100]

It should be added that the supernatural virtues of the soul are not the only perceptible aromas of the good odor of God. There exist other ways of participating in the divine Being. One of these is of the same order as that of the soul: namely, the Church. In Gregory, the two are always linked to each other, for an authentic mystical experience is not possible except in the Church. Gregory compares the spikenard of the Song to that which Mary Magdalene poured out on the Lord's feet, commenting on the passage as follows: "Since, then, in the Song of Songs, the spikenard conveys to the Bride the scent of the bridegroom, while in the Gospel the sweetness that then filled the house becomes the ointment of

---

[99] Stolz, *Théologie de la mystique*, 173–75. [*Spiritual Perfection*, 158–59, 161].
[100] On the meaning of the word *eikōn* (image), see Festugière, "La divinisation du chrétien," 94f. On the idea of participation, see Maréchal, *Études sur la psychologie des mystiques*, vol. 2, 111.

the whole body of the church in the whole cosmos, this suggests that the two have something in common to the point of seeming to be the same."[101]

In Gregory, the "sight" of the soul is a metaphor that appertains to different domains. Sometimes it signifies the soul's orientation or intent, as when the verb βλέπειν (*blepein*) is used with the meaning "look to" rather than simply "look."[102] The soul that looks to God is compared to the eagle that fixes its eye on the sun. At other times the metaphor denotes the activity of the intelligence and is occasionally associated with the first, or illuminative, way.[103] In the light of death, for example, the soul is able to distinguish between good things and evil things, but this does not involve any direct experience. It is more a meditation on the great truths. What is more, in his key treatises—the *Homilies on the Song of Songs* and *The Life of Moses*—Gregory insists above all on the fact that there can be no "vision" of the divine essence.

Nevertheless, the metaphor of spiritual sight appears alongside that of the other senses to refer to a more or less analogous experience. As we have already observed on several occasions, it is often linked to the sense of smell. Thus "the lily is pleasing in its appearance and its scent," while the apple "gladdens the eye" and also "by its scent gives pleasure to the sense of smell, and . . . provides sweetness to the organs of taste."[104] The Bride approaches the object of her desire, "but before his beauty is manifest to her eyes, she touches the one she seeks through her sense of smell, as if by her power of smell she recognized the distinctive quality of some color";[105] to the spiritual sense "it is one and the same thing to speak of rays of the sun or . . . of sweet aromatic scents."[106] Here the virtues are no longer simply fragrances, but irradiations of the Word himself, and it is these that the eye of the soul, when purified, perceives in its reflection on itself.[107]

Such is the doctrine that Gregory outlines in his sixth homily on the Beatitudes concerning the saying, "Blessed are the pure of heart, for they shall see God."

> I do not think that if the eye of one's soul has been purified, he is promised a direct vision of God; but perhaps this marvelous saying may suggest what

[101] *Cant.* 3 (PG 44:825C; Norris, 103).
[102] *Inscr.* 1.8.76 (PG 44:465D; Heine, 109).
[103] *Inscr.* 1.6.44 (PG 44:453A; Heine, 98–99).
[104] *Cant.* 4 (PG 44:844A; Norris, 129).
[105] *Cant.* 3 (PG 44:821D; Norris, 97–99).
[106] *Cant.* 3 (PG 44:824C; Norris, 101). See also *Cant.* 15 (PG 44:1093A; Norris, 467).
[107] See *Perf.* (PG 46:261C; FC 58:103).

the Word expresses more clearly when He says to others, "The Kingdom of God is within you." (Lk 17.21) By this we should learn that if a man's heart has been purified from every creature and all unruly affections, he will see the Image of the Divine Nature in his own beauty. . . . To give an example. Though men who see the sun in a mirror do not gaze at the sky itself, yet they see the sun in the reflexion of the mirror no less than those who look at its very orb. So, He says, it is also with you. Even though you are too weak to perceive the Light itself, yet, if you but return to the grace of the Image with which you were informed from the beginning, you will have all you seek in yourselves. For the Godhead is purity, freedom from passion, and separation from all evil. If therefore these things be in you, God is indeed in you. Hence, if your thought is without any alloy of evil, free from passion, and alien from all stain, you are blessed because you are clear of sight. You are able to perceive what is invisible to those who are not purified, because you have been cleansed; the darkness caused by material entanglements has been removed from the eyes of your soul, *and so you see the blessed vision radiant in the pure heaven of your heart.*[108]

The Life of Moses describes a similar experience in connection with the Burning Bush: "It is upon us who continue in this quiet and peaceful course of life that the truth will shine, illuminating the eyes of our soul [τὰς ὄψεις τῆς ψυχῆς, *tas opseis tēs psyches*] with its own rays."[109] However, this last text does not refer to a mystical experience as such. The first text, by contrast, certainly does. It is the clearest description that Gregory gives us of the vision of God in the mirror of the purified soul. Significantly, it is given in a homily that is addressed not to monks but to the wider Christian public. For Gregory, in fact, it represents the first stage of the mystical life. God first appears as light, in contrast to the darkness of sin, but as the soul advances it will come to understand that this light is in fact dark only in comparison with the divine reality.[110]

I shall leave aside images borrowed from the sense of hearing, since these play a secondary role in our author[111]—by contrast, they are very important, for

---

[108] *Beat.* 6 (PG 44:1269C–1272B; ACW 18:148–50).
[109] *Vit. Moys.* 2.19 (PG 44:332C; Malherbe, 59).
[110] See *Cant.* 11 (PG 44:1000D; Norris, 339–41).
[111] See *Cant.* 5 (PG 44:860A–B; Norris, 151): the voice of the Bridegroom, like the perfume and the rays, are considered as giving only a conjecture (στοχασμός, *stochasmos*) not a knowledge that is certain. Likewise, the trumpets of Sinai, in *Vit. Moys.* 2.168–69 (PG 44:380A; Malherbe, 96). See also *Cant.* 6 (PG 44:889B; Norris, 189–91).

example, in Ambrose—and turn now to the spiritual sense that is most important for our investigation: the sense of taste. It is important for several reasons. First, because it indicates a mystical experience that is more profound. Second, because this sense occupies a special place in Gregory's mysticism. He is one of the mystics of "divine sweetness" and heralds Diadochus as well as St Bernard, while distancing himself from the more intellectual tradition of Origen, Evagrius, and Maximus. Indeed, from Dionysius too who, despite depending on him in so far as negative theology is concerned, breaks with him on this point, as Puech has correctly pointed out.[112]

The main terms we encounter are, first, general references to "taste" (γεῦσις, *geusis*) along with the corresponding verb γεύομαι (*geuomai*).[113] Next come the various expressions that denote sweetness, delectation, or delight: γλυκύς (*glykys*, sweet to the taste) and the verb καταγλυκαίνειν (*kataglykainein*, to sweeten);[114] τρυφή (*tryphē*, delight, a delicacy) and associated verbs; ἀπόλαυσις (*apolausis*, enjoyment).[115] When referring to spiritual pleasure, Gregory sometimes uses ἡδονή (*hēdonē*) but in general prefers εὐφροσύνη (*euphrosynē*): "By pleasure [ἡδονή, *hēdonē*] I mean that which is dear to the body, for the joy [εὐφροσύνη, *euphrosynē*] of the soul, which differs greatly, is remote from irrational and abject enjoyment."[116] Last, to this should be added expressions denoting specific food or drink. Regarding the mystical apple tree, for example, we have already observed that Gregory establishes a certain gradation between sight and fragrance, on the one hand—which are common to both the lily and the apple—and taste, which applies only to the latter. He returns later in the text to this idea, emphasizing in particular that the relation between a fragrance and taste is the same as that between the flower and the fruit. Fragrance is a promise, taste is a possession:

> There are two ways in which the grape gives pleasure: on the one hand, by its blossom, when it delights the senses with its smell [εὐοσμία, *euosmia*]; on the other, by its ripe fruit, when it serves, at one's will, either as food to give

[112] Puech, "La ténèbre mystique," 45.
[113] *Vit. Moys.* 2.153, 193, 269, 313 (PG 44:373A, 389B, 413B, 428B; Malherbe, 92, 104, 123, 134); *Inscr.* 1.5.41 (PG 44:452A; Heine, 97); *Eccl.* 8 (PG 44:740A; Hall, 132); *Beat.* 4 (PG 44:1248A; ACW 18:129).
[114] *Vit. Moys.* 2.132–33, 36–37 (PG 44:365B, 368A; Malherbe, 86, 87).
[115] *Cant.* 1 (PG 44:777B; Norris, 33). Gregory seems to have been the first—at least among the great mystics—to describe the mystical experience as *fruitio Dei* ("enjoyment of God"). See Scholz, *Fruitio Dei*, 201.
[116] *Inscr.* 1.2.14 (PG 44:437A; Heine, 86).

delight [κατατρυφᾶν, *katatryphan*] or by its wine to bring cheer at celebrations. In this case the Bride as yet bears the cluster in the form of a bloom, since she gives the name "blossom" to the vine's flower.

For the child who was born for us—Jesus, who within those who receive him grows in a variety of different ways in wisdom and stature and grace [Lk 2.52]—is not the same in all but indwells in a way that accords with the capacity of the one into whom he comes. He is manifested in a character that fits the ability of the one who takes him in, either as a babe or as making progress or as being perfected—and this accords with the nature of a grape cluster, which does not always have the same appearance on the vine but changes its character with time as it blossoms, takes on color, matures, ripens, and becomes wine. By its own fruit, then—which is not ripe enough to make wine but awaits 'the fullness of times' (cf. Gal 4.4) and yet is not meant to be merely a useless luxury—the vine affords a promise. For in anticipating good things it delights smell rather than taste and gives pleasure to the soul's senses with the fragrances [ἀτμοῖς, *atmois*] of hope; for to those who await it with eager patience there comes the trustworthy and unambiguous enjoyment of the grace that is hoped for. This, then, is the "cluster of grape blossoms," a cluster that gives promise of wine because it has not yet become wine but by its blossom—and hope is the blossom—gives assurance of the grace to come.[117]

This passage is of considerable interest on account of the way two themes merge: that of the spiritual senses and that of the progressive communication of the Word to the soul. This latter theme is found elsewhere in Gregory, with reference to manna: "This bread, then, that does not come from the earth is the Word. He changes his power in diverse ways to suit those who eat. He knows not only to be bread, but also to become milk and meat and greens and whatever else might be appropriate to and desired by the one who receives him. So teaches Paul the divine Apostle who spreads such a table as this for us—making his message strong meat for the more mature and greens for the weaker and milk for little children" (Cf. 1 Cor 3.2f).[118]

The beginnings of this doctrine are to be found in Scripture. The book of Wisdom (16.21) echoes Jewish traditions about the manna, which are also found

---

[117] *Cant.* 3 (PG 44:828C–829A; Norris, 107).
[118] *Vit. Moys.* 2.140 (PG 44:368C–D; Malherbe, 88). See also *Perf.* (PG 46:268A–B; FC 58:107).

in Philo.[119] There are also traditions, to which Origen refers, on the various manifestations of Jesus: "A tradition has come down to us according to which there were not only two forms in Christ, one by means of which all saw him, the other by means of which he was transfigured before his disciples on the mountain; but he also appeared to everyone according to what each had been worthy of."[120] De Lubac has shown how these traditions present strange analogies with certain Buddhist doctrines.[121] An echo of these transformations of Jesus can be found in Gregory: "Because he is present wherever he happens to be and contains everything in himself, he makes it deserving by receiving it. For not only was he a man among men but had united his own nature with that of the angels."[122]

But it is not the theological aspect of this tradition of transformations that is of interest to us here, but its spiritual transposition. It was Origen who compared it to the various tastes of the manna and the different degrees of spiritual food, to make of it a doctrine of the progressive manifestations of the Word to the soul. "Concerning the nature of the Word, just as the quality of food changes in a mother into milk suitable for the nature of her infant, or is prepared by a physician with the intention of restoring a sick man to health . . . so also God changes for men the power of the Word, whose nature it is to nourish the human soul, in accordance with [what is fitting for] each individual. To one he becomes 'the rational milk which is without guile,' as the Bible calls it (1 Pet 2.2); to another who is weaker he becomes like a 'herb' (Rom 14.2); while to another who is perfect, 'solid food' (Heb 5.12, 14) is given."[123]

This is the direct source of Gregory's own comments on the different tastes of manna, according to whether it is given to children, to the weak, or to the perfect. But this is still to repeat the general idea, borrowed from Origen, of the Logos as food for the soul.[124] In the *Homilies on the Song of Songs*, however, Gregory applies this idea more specifically to the mystical life and to the role of the spiritual senses. The mystical vine is Christ. He shows himself progressively, first as a child, then as an adolescent, and then as a man. The different spiritual

---

[119]According to Basil. See his *Letter* 190.3 (PG 32:700; NPNF² 8:658).

[120]Origen, *Commentary on the Gospel according to Matthew* (PG 13:1750B).

[121]H. de Lubac, "Textes alexandrins et bouddhiques," *Recherches de science religieuse* 27 (1937): 336–51.

[122]Gregory, *Ascens.* (PG 46:693A; McCambley, 4).

[123]Origen, *Contra Celsum* 4.18 (PG 11:1049C; Chadwick, 195). See also Daniélou, *Origène*, 254–58. [*Origen*, 257–62].

[124]See Lieske, "Zur Theologie der Christusmystik."

Mystical Experience

senses correspond to these successive manifestations. Jesus is first perceived as a perfume that hints at a presence, then becoming delectable food for the soul.

The same idea is found elsewhere in Gregory:

> Happy indeed are those gardens whose plants are attested to burgeon so with fruit that they are fit to be turned into every kind of delicacy to accommodate the desire for pleasure! For to one who delights in the sweet scent there comes myrrh with . . . fragrances by way of the mortification of earthly members, fashioning the pure and sweet-scented life that is blended out of the many different spices of virtue. Then for the one who is seeking more perfect nourishment, bread appears, and it is no longer eaten with "bitter herbs" (Ex 12.8) as the law commands—for the bitterness is a matter of the here and now—but with honey as its relish, whenever, in its own season, the fruit of virtue, touched with honey, conveys sweetness to the soul's senses [τὰ τῆς ψυχῆς αἰσθητήρια, *ta tēs psychēs aisthētēria*]—which is demonstrated by the bread that was manifested to the disciples after the Lord's resurrection (Jn 21.9–14). And for the one who drinks, the bowl is full of wine and milk. It is not a sponge soaked with vinegar and gall (cf. Mt 27.48), which is the sort of loving-cup that the Jews offered on a reed to the Benefactor.[125]

In this passage we should note the link established between myrrh, the mortification of the senses, and divine sweetness. The reference to honey as a symbol of divine sweetness is also significant.[126]

We shall return later to these texts and the information they provide as to the object of the mystical experience. Thus far, it has been sufficient to establish the order in which Gregory places the different senses, especially the connection between perfection and the taste of God, which represents a stage superior to the spiritual sense of smell. We must now develop this theme of the taste of God, which occupies such a large place in Gregory's writings. At the outset of the spiritual life, when the bodily senses were being robbed of their accustomed food and the spiritual senses were not yet awakened, virtue did indeed seem bitter. But gradually the bitterness changes into sweetness, as the following representative examples illustrate:

> For to the one who has left behind the Egyptian pleasures which he served before crossing the sea, life removed from these pleasures seems at first

[125] *Cant.* 10 (PG 44:988C–989A; Norris, 323).
[126] See *Cant.* 14 (PG 44:1084C; Norris, 451).

difficult and disagreeable. But if the wood be thrown into the water, that is, if one receives the mystery of the resurrection which had its beginning with the wood (you of course understand the 'cross' when you hear 'wood'), then the virtuous life, being sweetened [ἐφηδυνόμενος, *ephēdynomenos*] by the hope of things to come, becomes sweeter and more pleasant than all the sweetness [γλυκύσματος, *glykysmatos*] that tickles [γαργαλίζοντος, *gargalizontos*] the senses with pleasure.[127]

The image that recurs most frequently to express this gradual sweetening of the virtuous life is that of the pomegranate:

> That life imitates the nature of the pomegranate covered on the outside with a rough and course bark which is inedible, but the inside of which is pleasing to the eyes [ἡδύ ὀφθῆναι, *hēdy ophthēnai*] by the varied and regular manner in which the fruit is arranged, and still more pleasant to the taste and causing a delight [καταγλύκαινον, *kataglykainon*] for the senses. Thus the austere life, according to wisdom, is intolerable and disagreeable for the sensuality, but charged with good hopes for the day its fruit will be ripe. It is the divine apostle who has said: "For the moment, any discipline seems to bring not joy but sadness." And this is the impression a first contact with the pomegranate gives; but later, it carries "a fruit of peace": it is "the sweetness of the nourishment inside" [γλυκύτης τῶν ἔνδοθεν ἐδωδίμων, *glykytēs tōn endothen edōdimōn*].[128]

Other fruit trees, however, are also brought into service to express the same idea:

> Now it would be superfluous to explain one by one, in detail, the enigmas that prophecy sets out for us as touching these trees. Surely it is evident to all what the sweet fruit of the fig tree stands for. It matures as it is fed by the most bitter of saps, and at the beginning it is sour and inedible; but in the end it becomes a mellow fruit, affording sweetness to the soul's senses. . . . It is clear too how the date palm, hoarding its fruit up on high and never bringing it forth near the earth, makes it all but inaccessible to thieves, not

---

[127] *Vit. Moys.* 2.132 (PG 44:365B; Malherbe, 86). See also *Vit. Moys.* 2.136–37, 153, 316 (PG 44:368A, 373A, 428B; Malherbe, 87, 92, 136); *Inscr.* 1.5.41 (PG 44:452B; Heine, 97–98).

[128] *Vit. Moys.* 2.193 (PG 44:389B; Malherbe, 104). The image is used again in *Cant.* 9 (PG 44:969B–C; Norris, 293).

to mention the beauty of the vine, the happy scent of the cypress, and the sweetness of the myrtle.[129]

Let us summarize the expressions used to describe this spiritual taste. First, there are those that mention the act of tasting itself, such as "tasted the rock;" [130] "no longer tasted earthly food;"[131] "[t]he blood of Christ is sweet to those who taste it."[132] Then there are the various expressions that refer to sweetness: "He who ... was sweetened by the wood;"[133] "the inside [of the pomegranate] is a pleasant sight ... and it becomes even sweeter [καταγλύκαινον, kataglykainon] when it is tasted;"[134] "the sweetness of the nourishment inside."[135] There is also the idea of delight, of deliciousness (τρυφὴ, tryphē): "[He] delighted [ἐντρυφήσας, entryphēsas] in the apostolic springs."[136] "He preferred the delicacies of Wisdom to things that promise bodily enjoyment."[137] Last, there is joy (εὐφροσύνη, euphrosynē), an expression of spiritual pleasure: "godlike and sublime joy";[138] "virtue which brings joy to our soul."[139]

As for which food it is that delights the spiritual taste, apart from the fruits specified above, Gregory mainly uses the symbols of milk, bread, honey, and wine, on account of their biblical or sacramental associations. Milk and honey are, of course, the traditional symbol of the goods of the promised land. Moreover, a meal of milk and honey apparently formed part of certain ancient baptismal liturgies.[140] But, on the other hand, milk is essentially the food of children, and we have seen how Saint Paul used it symbolically in this sense. In Gregory, too, it usually symbolizes the spiritual nourishment of souls that are least advanced. Thus, commenting on the following verse from the Song, "How much more beautiful are your breasts than wine" (Song 4.10, LXX), he writes that the Lord, by calling the soul his sister and bride, "is explaining why her breasts have been changed for the better and become more perfect, breasts that no longer put

---

[129] *Cant.* 9 (PG 44:964A-B; Norris, 289)
[130] *Vit. Moys.* 2.269 (PG 44:413B; Malherbe, 123).
[131] *Vit. Moys.* 2.313 (PG 44:428B; Malherbe, 134).
[132] *Eccl.* 8 (PG 44:740A; Hall, 132).
[133] *Vit. Moys.* 2.136 (PG 44:368A; Malherbe, 87).
[134] *Vit. Moys.* 2.193 (PG 44:389B; Malherbe, 104).
[135] Ibid. (PG 44:389C; Malherbe, 104).
[136] *Vit. Moys.* 2.136 (PG 44:368A; Malherbe, 87).
[137] *Eccl.* 6 (PG 44:696D; Hall, 99). [Translation modified to reflect Daniélou's French.—*Trans.*]
[138] *Inscr.* 1.4.30 (PG 44:445C; Heine, 93).
[139] *Inscr.* 1.2.11 (PG 44:436C; Heine, 85).
[140] Ziegler, *Dulcedo Dei*, 72–76.

forth milk, the food of babes but gush forth pure wine, whose delights the tavern keeper's water has not diluted—for the delight of those who have made progress toward perfection."[141] Likewise, a little later in the treatise, we see "honey for the mature" contrasted with "milk for beginners."[142]

The symbol of bread relates above all to manna but, of course, also has eucharistic connotations. Gregory also combines it with honey as representing the perfect food in contrast to fruit, which is less nutritious.[143] As seen, honey is the symbol par excellence of divine sweetness. In this respect, it represents a higher form of spiritual taste.[144] It is wine, however, that represents the highest degree of spiritual sweetness: "In the more mature hearts of those who are no longer subject to the disturbances of youth but are capable of filling themselves from Wisdom's chalice and of drinking in her good things with their mouth, this wine occasions gladness [εὐφροσύνη, *euphrosynē*]."[145] The allusion to the mixing bowl, or chalice, of Wisdom—which has been a hallowed image of mystical language since Philo[146]—shows that here we are reaching the upper limits of what the spiritual senses can do and the threshold of a new stage of the mystical life—namely, ecstasy. In fact, it is this same symbol of wine that Gregory takes up again and develops in order to describe what he calls ecstatic inebriation,[147] as we shall see in due course when we consider this new theme.

Typically, then, Gregory tends to rank these various aspects of the taste of God, and the associated spiritual experiences, in ascending order.[148] With the different senses, it was a case of organizing them into a hierarchy; here it is the various aspects of one and the same sense. This all points to what is, in fact, the essential character of his mysticism—its progressive aspect. The different stages are not always specified in detail, the symbols are frequently polyvalent, but the essential theme of progress (προκοπή, *prokopē*) and successive ascents (ἀναβάσεις, *anabaseis*) always reappears.

This observation leads to another. Reading Gregory's texts on the spiritual sense of taste, one is struck by the fact that in a number of them taste is presented as a hope as much as an experience. We saw earlier that the divine fragrance

---

[141] Cant. 9 (PG 44:956A; Norris, 279).
[142] Ibid. (PG 44:960C; Norris, 285).
[143] See *Cant.* 10 (PG 44:988C; Norris, 323).
[144] See *Cant.* 9 (PG 44:960C-D; Norris, 285).
[145] Ibid. (PG 44:956D; Norris, 281).
[146] See Lewy, *Sobria ebrietas*, 17.
[147] See *Cant.* 10 (PG 44:990B; Norris, 325).
[148] See *Cant.* 9 (PG 44:967A-B; Norris, 295).

represented a promise more than a presence. Now we find this same idea again with reference to what did indeed seem to be a presence. At first sight, this would seem to weaken the value of these texts as witnesses to an experience—that is, an actual contact. Let us remind ourselves of some of these texts: "The virtuous life, being sweetened by the hope of things to come, becomes sweeter and more pleasant than all the sweetness that tickles the senses with pleasure."[149] Likewise, in connection with the pomegranate: "The philosophical life, although outwardly austere and unpleasant, is yet full of good hopes when it ripens."[150] There is also the passage commenting on the "winter-figs" (ὄλυνθοι, *olynthoi*):

> Therefore that which the fig tree puts forth in the form of a fruit prior to its sweet and perfect fruit is called "early fruit," and this itself is edible from time to time for those who like it. But it is not the fruit; it comes as the fruit's precursor. Someone who sees these summer figs, therefore, is still waiting for the real fruit, for the summer figs, which the fig tree is said to bring forth, are a sign of the edible figs to come.
>
> For since the Word is describing the spiritual springtime to the Bride, and since this season is a halfway house [μεθόριος, *methorios*] between two others—between wintry desolation and the summer's sharing in the harvest—for just that reason, while he openly proclaims the passing of evil things, he does not yet point to the full [τέλειοι, *teleioi*] fruits of virtue. These, however, he will dispense at the proper season, when the summer is come—and what "summer" means, you know well enough from the words of the Lord, which say: "The harvest is the consummation of the age." But now what he manifests is the hopes that come to blossom through the virtues, whose fruit, as the prophet says, is brought forth in due season (Ps 1.3).... [That is,] he stamps in our being an impress of the hoped-for happiness by means of a more honorable life—an impress not unlike the early figs.
>
> Interpret the blossoming vine in this way too. Its wine, rejoicing the heart, will one day fill up wisdom's chalice (cf. Prov 9.2–5) and ... be set before the fellowship of its drinkers, to be drawn at their pleasure for the sake of a good and sober drunkenness [νηφάλιος μέθη, *nēphalios methē*]. What I am referring to is the drunkenness that occasions that self-transcendence

---

[149] *Vit. Moys.* 2.132 (PG 44:365B; Malherbe, 86).
[150] *Vit. Moys.* 2.193 (PG 44:389B; Malherbe, 104).

by which people move out of the material sphere toward what is more divine.[151]

A feature common to all of these texts is the contrast between joys that are only hopes and a joy that is perfect. Nevertheless, this is not to deny the fact that an imperfect joy is still joy, and so does not diminish the value of the doctrine of the spiritual senses as a mystical experience. Yet such joy is but a foretaste of true joy. All the above texts affirm that this true joy will come "at the right time." But when is this time? It seems that there are two different ideas concerning this. The first identifies it with the bliss that awaits us in heaven. The banquet of bread and honey will follow the general resurrection. The harvesting of the fruits signifies the consummation of the age and the future beatitude. But the last text quoted above adds another idea, which is also important. It lets us glimpse the possibility of a participation in this beatitude starting here below, in the "ecstasy" symbolized by a state of "sober inebriation" in which the soul drinks from the mixing bowl of Wisdom.[152] Here we have a vocabulary that is properly ecstatic. We must remember that Gregory accepts, as being the highest stage of the spiritual life, but given to only a few, the fact of being "caught up to the third heaven" like St Paul (cf. 2 Cor 12.2–4) and thus of entering paradise already in this life.[153] The mystical life itself, then, comprises two distinct stages: one that involves the spiritual senses and which corresponds to the knowledge of God in the mirror of the soul, and, second, that of ecstasy which, to an extent that we shall have to determine, is similar to the face-to-face vision.

Another noteworthy point concerning the taste of spiritual bread and wine is the link that is established between divine sweetness and the Eucharist, and, consequently, between the Eucharist and the mystical life. Frequently in Gregory, as in Origen, images of eating and drinking are understood as referring to the spiritual reception of the Word in the soul. Nevertheless, at times their sacramental, eucharistic meaning is also implied. The expression "the mystery of the wine" (τὸ κατὰ τὸν οἶνον μυστήριον, *to kata ton oinon mystērion*)[154] is not conclusive, but there is another allusion that is quite clear:

---

[151]*Cant.* 5 (PG 44:872C–873B; Norris, 167–69).
[152]See J. Daniélou, "Les repas de la Bible et leur signification," *La Maison-Dieu: Cahiers de pastorale liturgique* 18 (1949): 28–32.
[153]*Vit. Moys.* 2.182 (PG 44:384A; Malherbe, 99–100).
[154] *Cant.* 4 (PG 44:845B; Norris, 133).

> With these words ... the Word sets forth to those nearby the mysteries of the Gospel: "You who are close to me, eat! And you, my brethren, drink and be drunken!" (Song 5.1) For to one who has known the mystical utterances of the Gospel, no difference will be discerned between the words of this text and the mystagogical instruction given to the disciples there. Just as is the case there (cf. Mt 26.26), so also here the Word says "Eat!" and "Drink!" As to the exhortation to drunkenness that the Word addresses to his brethren in our text, it may well seem to most people to contain something beyond what the Gospel says. But if one looks closely into the matter, this too will be found consonant with the content of the Gospels. For what the Word prescribes for his friends here, he there brought about by his deeds, since all drunkenness tends, in those who have been mastered by wine, to bring about a displacement [ἔκστασις, *ekstasis*] of discursive thought. Hence what he prescribes here came to pass when a change and displacement from worse to better accompany the food and drink. To be drunken in this manner is, as the prophecy says, for those who drink the fatness of God's house and water themselves at the stream of delight (cf. Ps 35.9).[155]

In this interesting text, to which we shall return when discussing ecstasy in more detail, the connection that is made between mystical ecstasy and eucharistic ecstasy is striking. We should note, however, that there is a certain ambiguity in the way the word ecstasy is used. It is understood first in its specifically mystical sense to indicate the going out of the mind from itself. But subsequently it has the more general meaning, such as is found in Origen, of our transformation into God by grace, especially through the effect of the sacraments, without any connotation of special psychological phenomena. In another passage, Gregory distinguishes between a double eating of the Word, the one being spiritual, the other sacramental: "If someone in examining this mystery should say that the Lord is rightly called 'spiritual food and drink,' he is not far from the truth. For His 'flesh is food indeed' and His 'blood is drink indeed.' [Jn 6.55] But, in connection with the thought just mentioned, there is participation in such nourishment for all, since the Logos who becomes food and drink is received and assimilated without distinction by those seeking Him. However, in connection with another idea, the participation in this food and drink is not careless or indiscriminate."[156]

---

[155]*Cant.* 10 (PG 44:989 B–C; Norris, 325).
[156]*Perf.* (PG 44:268B–C; FC 58:107–108). See also *Vit. Moys.* 2:138–39 (PG 44:368B–C; Malherbe, 87–88).

It is important to note the parallel that is drawn in these passages between the sacramental life and the mystical life. We have already pointed out the connection that exists between Baptism and the first stage of the ascent to God, the abandoning of the "garments of skin." We see now the same parallelism, as the spiritual life develops, between the bread of the Eucharist and divine sweetness. And last, the connection between the deification wrought by the eucharistic wine and the pinnacle of the mystical life—ecstatic inebriation. The mystical life is dependent upon the objective, sacramental action of Christ. This is the normal source of catholic mysticism, which is the transformation of the soul and body of the Christian into the soul and body of Christ. This understanding is characteristic of Greek mysticism, which knows nothing of the separation that came about in the West between the inner life and liturgical life. This remains a permanent feature of eastern theology, for which the inner life is totally immersed in the liturgical life.

To these key passages in which the idea of "sober intoxication" appears, we should add others in which we find one related theme or another. The mixing-bowl of Wisdom, for example, is mentioned on other occasions: "Virtue is the vineyard which provides wine for the bowl of wisdom through the intellectual grapes."[157] More interesting is the following: "One who plants [vines] in his own soul, and cultivates the wine which makes glad the heart (cf. Ps 103.15) . . . such a one will be most blessed in his husbandry, as he presses his own grapes into the cup of wisdom."[158] Here we again have the idea of the vine as virtue, and of wine as a symbol of spiritual joy.

But it is Gregory's *Homilies on the Song of Songs* that provide most examples. When Origen commented on the following verse from the Song—"Bring me into the house of wine" (Song 2.4)—he compared the house of wine to the dwelling place of Wisdom, and in so doing remained in a gnostic framework. Gregory's interpretation is different:

> And such is the vehemence of her thirst that the cup of Wisdom does not satisfy her (cf. Prov 2.9). Nor, for the slaking of her thirst, does she think that it is enough to pour the entire cup into her mouth. No, she seeks to be brought into the very house of wine, and to hold her mouth under the winevats themselves as they overflow with sweet wine (cf. Prov 3.10), and to see the grape cluster being pressed in the vats and the vine that puts forth

[157] *Inscr.* 1.8.102 (PG 44:477B; Heine, 116).
[158] *Eccl.* 3 (PG 44:661A; Hall, 69).

Mystical Experience

such a cluster and that Husbandman of the true vine whose work produces a cluster so sweet and thriving. . . . For these and the like reasons, the soul wants to come inside the house of wine, in which the mystery of the wine [μυστήριον οἴνου, *mystērion oinou*] is found.[159]

This is not yet a description of ecstasy, but rather of the divine sweetness. But several features are worthy of note. First, there is the soul's unquenchable thirst, which is one of the hallmarks of Gregory's mysticism. Second, the wine-grower who reddens his clothing in trampling grapes in his press symbolizes Christ in his passion. (Later, we shall discuss the connection that is made between the blood of the passion and the eucharistic wine that produces ecstasy.) Last, we should take note of the expression "the mystery of the wine." Earlier we saw Gregory writing: "For to one who has known the mystical [μυστικάς, *mystikas*] utterances of the Gospel, no difference will be discerned between the words of this text ['You who are close to me eat! And you, my brethren, drink and be drunken!'] and the mystagogical instruction given to the disciples [at the Last Supper]" (cf. Mt 26.26f).[160] In fact, the one term *mystērion* can refer both to the sacraments in particular and the mystical life in general, which helps to maintain a connection between the two. But this relationship can be interpreted in different ways, from being mere symbolism to the fullest realism. It is the latter position that is Gregory's.

The significance of wine as food for the perfect, which we saw in the *Sermon on the Ascension* and the fifth homily on the Song of Songs, is evident in another passage:

> For look how much the soul has increased now that she has known the sweet smell of the bridegroom in her own nard. . . . [S]he becomes mother of the cluster of divine fruit that blossoms—that is, blooms—before the passion, but after the passion pours forth wine. For the wine that "makes our heart glad" (cf. Ps 103.15) becomes and is called, after the economy of the passion, "blood of the grape."[161]

So then there are two ways in which the grape gives pleasure: on the one hand, by its blossom, when it delights the senses with its smell; on the

---

[159] *Cant.* 4 (PG 44:845A–B; Norris, 133).
[160] *Cant.* 10 (PG 44:990B; Norris, 325).
[161] Gregory links to this the words from Deuteronomy 32.14: "Of the blood of the grape thou drankest wine." On the comparison of the blood of Christ with the blood of the grape, see Clement of Alexandria, *The Instructor* 2.2.

other, by its ripe fruit, when it serves, at one's will, either as food to give delight [ἀπόλαυσις, *apolausis*] or by its wine to bring cheer [φαιδρύνεσθαι, *phaidrynesthai*] at celebrations [συμπόσια, *symposia*].[162]

Thus, Gregory continues, Jesus "adapts himself in a way that fits the ability of the one who takes him in . . . and this accords with the nature of a grape cluster, which does not always have the same appearance on the vine but changes its character with time as it blossoms, takes on color, matures, ripens, and becomes wine [πεπαινόμενοι, *pepainomenoi*]. . . . [Such a cluster] has not yet become wine but by its blossom (and hope is the blossom) gives assurance of the grace to come. . . . [Such] is that true Cluster who has manifested himself upon the poles of wood, whose blood becomes both drink and salvation to those who are being saved and are of good cheer."[163]

Here, wine is again a symbol of the blood of Christ. More important, however, is the fact that this text enables us to situate the concept of inebriation in the overall theology of the spiritual senses. It is the same cluster, Jesus, who is fragrance to begin with, and then a delight to the taste. But these are only promises of the wine, symbol of the highest good. This good is a joy (εὐφραινόμενος, *euphrainomenos*; φαιδρύνεσθαι, *phaidrynesthai*) that is superior to the sweetness given by the sharing of wine in banquets. Jesus as wine, giving joy, is the pinnacle of the spiritual life. But, as we have seen, this can be interpreted in two ways: either as referring to life eternal in the future, as Origen thought, or, in relation with the Eucharist, as a foretaste of it, which is what ecstasy is.

Or perhaps it is less a case of two interpretations than two levels. In Origen, wine is a symbol of joy in the normal sense. Gregory likewise speaks of wine that "brings gladness to its recipient."[164] But in Origen, this joy is identical to inebriation.[165] Gregory, by contrast, retains the idea of a joy that represents simply a more elevated stage of the spiritual life, while keeping the idea of ecstasy as well[166]—and it is specifically ecstasy that he means when he uses the term inebriation. But what Gregory shares with Origen is the link to John (15.1): "I am

---

[162]*Cant.* 3 (PG 44:828C–D; Norris, 105–107).

[163]Ibid. (PG 44:828D–829A; Norris, 107–109). The same idea of a vine suspended from wooden stakes suggesting Christ suspended on the wood of the cross can be found in *Vit. Moys.* 2.267–68 (PG 44:413A; Malherbe, 123).

[164]*Cant.* 15 (PG 44:1092D; Norris, 465).

[165]See Lewy, *Sobria ebrietas*, 118. Likewise in Philo.

[166]Lewy links *euphrosynē* to sober inebriation (*Sobria ebrietas*, 34ff.), but given the word's general meaning, one tends to favor Völker's view that "*Euphrosynē* has nothing to do with ecstatic experience" (*Fortschritt und Vollendung*, 325).

Mystical Experience   293

the true vine." In reality, Origen speaks above all of the joy of wine and associates it only on rare occasions with inebriation, whereas in Gregory these two aspects are clearly distinguished as symbolizing two distinct states.

We have seen "sober inebriation" contrasted more than once with physical inebriation, or with the inebriation associated with pagan wisdom. This is already found in Philo, where the concept is used precisely to contrast true Wisdom with the inebriation that occurred during the pagan mysteries, or their transposition to gnosticism.[167] This contrast is also found in Origen in connection with the following verse from the Song: "How much more beautiful are your breasts than wine" (Song 4.10, LXX): "The sons of Jonadab . . . refused to drink and take such wine," he writes, "that is to say, teachings poisonous and alien to the faith of God."[168] He sees in this wine the teaching of the prophets whose "wine," though good, is inferior to that given by the Bridegroom. In his commentary on the following verse from the Song (1.2), Gregory, on the contrary, confines himself to the first interpretation, agreeing with Philo: "[We learn] from the fact that the milk of the divine breasts is superior by comparison with the wine that brings us gladness (cf. Ps 103.15), that all human wisdom and knowledge of reality as well as every power of discernment and direct apprehension are incapable in a comparison, of matching the simpler fare of the divine teachings. For what flows from the breasts is milk, and milk is the food of babes. Wine, however, because of its vigor and warmth, becomes the enjoyment of the more mature. Nevertheless, that which is mature and perfect in non-Christian wisdom is a slighter thing than the most childish teaching of the divine Word."[169] Here we have an interesting development, where the allusion to pagan wisdom, represented by the wine, brings us very close to Philo's way of thinking: the "perfect" in gnosticism are inferior to beginners in grace. Here, wine is an image of perfection, with no allusion to ecstasy.

In a similar passage, it is on the contrary spiritual perfection that Gregory contrasts with its beginnings. "Hence the One who is calling her 'sister' and 'bride' is explaining why her breasts have been changed for the better and become more perfect, breasts that no longer put forth milk, the food of babes (cf. 1 Cor 3.1–2), but gush forth pure wine . . . and in the more mature hearts of those who are no longer subject to the disturbances of youth but are capable of filling themselves from Wisdom's chalice and of drinking in her good things with their

[167] See Lewy, *Sobria ebrietas*, 62.
[168] Origen, *Commentary on the Song of Songs* 1.1.2 (PG 13:89C; FC 26:68).
[169] Gregory, *Cant.* 1 (PG 44:781A; Norris, 37).

mouth, this wine occasions gladness."[170] The concepts are the same: perfection, characterized by joy, symbolized by wine, poured from the chalice of Wisdom. Wine and joy had already been linked by Philo and Origen. What is specific to Gregory is to have related this theme to the various ages of the spiritual life, equating wine with perfection and milk with childhood, thereby freeing it from the intellectualistic meaning it had in Origen.

With one last passage, we will have completed this survey of allusions to the chalice of Wisdom: "What we learn is this, that the Bridegroom does not lodge in a soul that lacks the virtues, and, further still, that if a person should become, in the sense required by the earlier text, a bowl of spice that produces fragrant ointments, such a person has become a mixing bowl of Wisdom's (cf. Prov 9.20) and receives within himself the divine and unadulterated wine that brings gladness to its recipient."[171] The metaphor is certainly in line with what we saw before: Jesus dwells in the soul that, through the virtues, has become God's image again. The wine that fills it like a cup symbolizes this presence that gives it joy. This is a continuation of the doctrine of the spiritual senses, indeed its summit. We see how this grouping of symbols is gradually organized so as to constitute the framework of a spiritual theology.

We can now assess the doctrine of the spiritual senses as Gregory of Nyssa presents it. We have seen that he borrowed the framework from Origen. Does it have the same content with him? "One should not," writes Rahner of Origen, "immediately set about seeking in his doctrine of the spiritual senses descriptions of mystical experience. Also, the manner in which he resolutely brushes aside all mention of ecstasy makes us doubt whether he himself had sufficient knowledge of the mystical states. . . . We must nevertheless admit that Origen applies this doctrine to a type of knowledge that in itself is of a mystical nature."[172] Indeed, with Origen's interpretation, the difficulty is to distinguish between what Rahner calls "Platonic enthusiasm"—that is, an intellectual experience expressed in a language borrowed from the mysteries according to the Alexandrian tradition—and mystical experience proper. Even though he excluded ecstasy, Origen may at least have known lower forms of mystical experience, such as provided by the spiritual senses. In this respect, Gregory's doctrine marks a significant step forward. For with him, the doctrine of the spiritual senses is clearly linked to the presence of Christ in the soul and to the supernatural life. Thus it is squarely

[170]*Cant.* 9 (PG 44:956A–C; Norris, 279–81).
[171]*Cant.* 15 (PG 44:1092D–1093A; Norris, 465).
[172]Rahner, "Le début d'une doctrine," 135.

situated in a domain which is not that of speculative knowledge but of holiness, with a real link to Christ.

It is noteworthy that for Gregory, unlike Origen, the practical, virtuous life and contemplation are not two successive ways, the latter being the goal of the former, but parallel ways along both of which one advances simultaneously. This is particularly in evidence in *The Life of Moses*.

It remains the case that, through the clear distinction he makes between the doctrine of the spiritual senses and speculation, Gregory has helped to keep this doctrine confined to the mystical domain, to which it is well suited, thanks to the characteristic of a direct, non-rational experience that the metaphor of the senses conveys. Moreover, unlike Origen, as we have seen, Gregory is acquainted with ecstasy. He sees it as being the strongest state in the mystical life and, as such, contrasts it with the spiritual senses, which are thus never allotted a more than appropriate place in his work.

As to the interpretation one should give to the spiritual senses, there are two opposing views. Poulain sees here the expression of an immediate contact between God and the soul: "During the union ... we are like a man placed beside one of his friends, in complete darkness and silence. He does not *see* him, therefore, he does not *hear* him; he only *feels* that he is there by the sense of touch, because he holds his hand in his own."[173] After quoting this text by Poulain, Stolz, on the other hand, goes on to dismiss this view:

> However much this latter assertion is to be accepted, the doctrine of the spiritual senses seems to have a different explanation theologically. It implies the redemption of sense-knowledge from the dulling effect consequent on original sin. Owing to the loss of original grace, sense-knowledge has to a certain extent been narrowed down to its proper object, whereas previously it played its part after its own fashion in the process of union between the spirit and God. The bliss of the spirit found an echo in it as well. In the paradisiac state the whole man rejoiced in intimate union with God. . . . By means of asceticism the Holy Ghost, the efficient cause of mystical contemplation, regains control also over the other faculties of man, and they for their part are made aware of their share in mystical union with God.[174]

---

[173] Poulain, *Des grâces d'oraison*, 101. [*Interior Prayer*, 95.]
[174] Stolz, *Théologie de la mystique*, 231. [*Spiritual Perfection*, 211.]

Stolz's interpretation has the merit of relating the doctrine of the spiritual senses to the return of the soul to life in paradise—and this is indeed one of Gregory's own fundamental concepts. But how is this paradisal life to be understood? Stolz gives it a physical meaning, and, consequently, insists on the participation in its goods of the *whole person, body and soul*. This is certainly not how Gregory sees things. For him, paradise is a symbol of man's ideal state. The various details—the tree of life and so forth—are to be interpreted spiritually. For him, the mystical life is a return to paradise in that it leads the soul to free itself from the life of the senses and to taste God alone once more. This "taste" should be interpreted as spiritual enjoyment; Gregory nowhere says that it has an impact on the sensibility. The idea of the sensibility's transfiguration may be acceptable in itself, but there is no basis for seeing it developed in his writings. We made a similar comment concerning the passions.

On the other hand, what can certainly be retained from Stolz's account is the fact of a continuity between the activity of the spiritual senses and the normal life of sanctifying grace. For Gregory, the experience of the sweetness of God, of the divine fragrance, is the normal fruit of the progress of the life of grace in us. It is the awareness of this life of grace. Thus, it does not presuppose some extraordinary mode of knowledge. In fact, as we have seen, the most significant characteristic of his teaching is the assertion that the divine essence can never be grasped by the soul. Moreover, questions of vocabulary are of little consequence here. For Gregory, the experience of the spiritual senses is accessible to any saintly soul, whether one calls this experience mystical or not. There is no privileged category of souls that might have an immediate experience of God. Such experience is, at any rate, radically inaccessible. Gregory never poses the widely discussed question of the possibility or otherwise of seeing the divine essence here below. For him, there can be no question of this. The example of Moses is precisely one that he relies on to contest this idea. As for the ecstasy of Saint Paul, he interprets this differently, as a mystical experience of a higher order, reserved for certain souls, but nevertheless not one that is entirely divorced from normal spiritual life. It is a "sober inebriation," following a "tasting" of God.

This is not to say that Gregory wishes to establish total discontinuity between the present and the future life. Rather, instead of accepting, as do certain authors, that there is continuity from the one to the other, in the sense that the mystical graces are already a vision of God, his point of view is the opposite. Namely, even

Mystical Experience   297

the life in heaven does not and cannot include a vision of the divine essence. Indeed, in keeping with his doctrine of participation, according to which one knows God to the extent that one is like him, perfect vision of the divine essence would mean total equality with God, which is a contradiction in terms. Beatitude consists precisely in a transformation into God that is never-ending and that is discovered to be continually new. Gregory's theology is remarkably coherent. Moreover, it is clear that his theological interpretation takes nothing away from the testimonies of the mystics, when they maintain that they sense or touch God.[175] Gregory was the first to claim as much. It is simply a question of clarifying the theological meaning of such experiences.

The Indwelling of the Word

Having described the activity of the spiritual senses and having attempted to situate them within the overall context of sacramental and spiritual life, we must now be more specific about their object. They represent the experience of a reality, but what is this reality? We observed earlier that this had to do with the life of grace in the soul. The virtues are fragrances or rays perceived by the spiritual senses of smell and sight. But these virtues are only a mirror, only an emanation, in which a personal presence is apprehended, but indirectly. This is still more evident in the case of those senses that indicate a deeper experience, particularly the sense of taste. What is tasted by the soul, what constitutes its food is a reality with which it is in direct, if obscure, contact. This reality is the incarnate Word. In fact, Gregory's mysticism is, as Lieske put it, essentially a *Christusmystik*. The object of the spiritual senses, then, is a progressive manifestation of Christ according to the extent that he lives in us.

We need only recall the symbols that Gregory uses in this context; they are almost always Christological. It is Christ who is the spikenard smelled by the Bride;[176] he is the stone that is transformed into water to be tasted;[177] he is the apple that delights all the senses;[178] he is the cluster of grapes that can serve either as food or as wine to slake one's thirst;[179] he is "the bread which came from heaven."[180] Gregory leaves us in no doubt that "there is also a 'touch' that

---

[175] See the texts gathered by Poulain, *Des Grâces d'Oraison*, 105–17. [*Interior Prayer*, 99–113.]
[176] See *Cant.* 3 (PG 44:824B; Norris, 99).
[177] See *Vit. Moys.* 2.135, 270 (PG 44:368A, 413B; Malherbe, 87, 123–24).
[178] See *Cant.* 4 (PG 44:844A; Norris, 129).
[179] See *Cant.* 3 (PG 44:828C; Norris, 107).
[180] *Vit. Moys.* 2.139 (PG 44:368C; Malherbe, 88). [See Jn 6.31–58.—*Ed.*]

belongs to the soul, one that makes contact with the Word;"[181] "[The Lord] is joy to our eyes when he comes as light, perfume to our sense of smell, and life to those who eat him."[182]

This leads us to a more precise clarification of the object of the spiritual senses, by relating it to its theological basis. The life of grace is essentially an emanation (ἀπόρροια, *aporroia*),[183] a participation (μετουσία, *metousia*; κοινωνία, *koinōnia*) in the life of Christ. This transformation of the soul into Jesus Christ is illustrated quite clearly in such passages as the following: "First [the Word] separates us, as it were, from the attached rock (I mean evil, of course) to which we have been attached by participation. Then it trims off the excesses of the material.[184] After this it begins to form that which lies within in relation to the likeness of the aim. And thus it scrapes and polishes our understanding by means of more delicate teachings of ideas. Then, by means of the forms of virtue, it forms [ἐμμορφοῖ, *emmorphoi*] Christ in us, in accordance with whose image we existed in the beginning, and in accordance with which we again come to exist."[185] The entire treatise *On Perfection*—which is not to be confused with *Concerning Perfection in Virtue*, the subtitle of *The Life of Moses*—is devoted to describing this imitation of Christ.

The soul's transformation of itself is at the same time Christ's work, too. In this respect, one should beware of making an error of interpretation. It is true that Gregory insists strongly on freedom. Thus, at the beginning of *The Life of Moses*, he presents the striving for perfection as being a freely undertaken work.[186] In describing the life of the soul, he uses the word virtue. All this might lead us to believe that we are in the realm of natural asceticism. Yet nothing could be farther from the truth. As we said earlier, for Gregory the virtues are the manifestations of sanctifying grace. And for him, freedom is the equivalent of grace. Progress in the spiritual life is a transformation into God in which the soul is unable to move from one stage to the next by its own powers. This is made clear in a passage such as the following:

---

[181]*Cant.* 1 (PG 44:780D; Norris, 37).
[182]*Cant.* 4 (PG 44:844A; Norris, 131).
[183]See *Cant.* 3 (PG 44:824C; Norris, 101).
[184]The same image is found in Plotinus, as seen earlier: "Act as does the creator of a statue that is to be made beautiful; he cuts away here, he smoothes there.... So do you also: cut away all that is excessive ... and never cease chiseling your statue, until there shall shine out on you from it the godlike splendour of virtue" (*Enneads* 1.6.9).
[185]*Inscr.* 2.11.134 (PG 44:544B; Heine, 164).
[186]For example, *Eccl.* 6 (PG 44:704A; Hall, 104).

Mystical Experience

> You see how in his generosity he does more than the Bride requested. The bride prayed that the plants in her garden, breathed through by the wind that blows from the south, might become wellsprings of fragrance and that the husbandman might be welcomed by the fruit of her fruit trees (plain as it is to everyone that though any sweet scent gives pleasure to the sense of smell, fruits are, from the point of view of the health of those who feed on them, less nutritious as nourishment than bread). But the husbandman came down to his garden and changed the nature of the fruit so that they became better and of more worth. Finding myrrh, he plucked it from the garden with fragrant spices of his own—for he is the source of anything lovely, in whatever subject it be found, as the prophetic words once sang (cf. Zech 9.17, LXX); and instead of fruit, he made the trees hang heavy with bread tinctured with his honey.... And their wine he draws off mixed with his milk. For "from him and through him and for him are all things" (Rom 11. 36).[187]

This transformation of the soul into Christ, brought about by him, is at the same time a coming of Christ into the soul. Gregory expresses this key point on numerous occasions. The idea is forcefully expressed already in his first work, *On Virginity*:

> For what happened corporeally in the case of the immaculate Mary, when the fullness of the divinity shone forth in Christ through her virginity, takes place also in every soul spiritually giving birth to Christ, although the Lord no longer effects a bodily presence [παρουσία, *parousia*]. For Scripture says, "We no longer know Christ according to the flesh" (2 Cor 5.16) but, as the Gospel says somewhere, He dwells with us [εἰσοικιζόμενος, *eisoikizomenos*] spiritually and the Father along with Him (cf. Jn 14.23).[188]

Thus "the child Jesus is born [in each of us]" but he "grows in a variety of different ways in wisdom and stature and grace [Lk 2.52] ... in a way that accords with the capacity of the one into whom he comes ... either as a babe or as making progress or as being perfected."[189]

---

[187] *Cant.* 10 (PG 44:988B–C; Norris, 323).
[188] *Virg.* 2 (PG 46:324B; FC 58:11).
[189] *Cant.* 3 (PG 44:828D; Norris, 107). On the theme of the birth of the Word in the soul in Origen, see Völker, *Das Volkommenheitsideal*, 98f. Hugo Rahner, "Die Gottesgeburt: Die Lehre der Kirchenväter von der Geburt Christi im Herzen des Gläubigen," *Zeitschrift für Katholische Theologie* 59.3 (1935): 333–418, at 340f.

It is a question of a presence in the innermost part of the soul. And here we see how expressions from the *Homilies on the Beatitudes* take on their full meaning: "to possess in oneself" (σχεῖν ἐν ἑαυτῷ, *schein en heautō*); the linking of blessedness with the quotation "the Kingdom of God is within you," a quotation also found in an analogous passage in *On Virginity*, which we shall discuss later;[190] the Pauline term "the inner man" (ἔνδον ἄνθρωπος, *endon anthrōpos*), which Scripture calls the heart (καρδία, *kardia*). One has only to enter into oneself to find this presence: "The goodness of God . . . is ever present in each individual, unknown and forgotten . . . but discovered again when we turn our attention back to it [ἐπιστρέφειν, *epistrephein*]."[191] "[The soul] will go back to itself [ἐπανελθοῦσα, *epanelthousa*] . . . and through its own beauty it will look upon the archetype as if in a mirror."[192]

Thus, it is Christ, present in the sanctuary of the soul, who is the principle of the fragrance of its virtues, through which it discerns his presence.[193] He is the hidden bundle of myrrh, whose perfume embalms the clothes:

> "As to me," she says, "the bundle that I hang from my neck upon the breast and by which I give my body a sweet smell is not one of the other perfumed herbs, but the Lord himself, become myrrh, lies in the bundle of my conscience, dwelling in my very heart." For the experts in these matters say that the location of the heart is between the breasts. The bride says that she keeps her receptacle there in the place where goodness is treasured up. But they also say that the heart is a source of the heat within us. From it warmth is shared out through the arteries to the whole body, and by its means the body's limbs become warm and alive, secretly heated by the heart's fire. When, then, she has accepted the sweet scent of the Lord within her ruling part [ἡγεμονικῷ, *hēgemonikō*] and has made of her heart a container for such incense, she accustoms all the several pursuits of her life, like the limbs of some body, to simmer with the Spirit that spreads from her heart, and no lawlessness chills the love of God in any member of her body.[194]

---

[190]See *Virg.* 12 (PG 46:372D; FC 58:44).
[191]Ibid. (PG 44:373A; FC 58:44).
[192]*An. et res.* 6 (PG 46:89C; PPS 12:78).
[193]For the indwelling of the Word in the soul, see *Cant.* 6, 12 (PG 44:893C, 1033C; Norris, 195–96, 385).
[194]*Cant.* 3 (PG 44:828A–B; Norris, 105).

Mystical Experience

Christ is present, then, in the soul that is in a state of grace. It is, in fact, he who is the principle of the virtues and gifts whose fragrance and taste delight the spiritual senses. "Thus, that these things may be wrought in us, their Maker must be begotten in us."[195] It is the virtues that reveal his presence, and it is indeed Jesus whom the spiritual senses perceive. Furthermore, although he is the principle of the virtues in the soul, at the same time their very presence attracts him all the more. And thus, progress in the virtues leads him to draw ever closer. It is the perception of this ever-closer presence that is indicated by the particular sequence of the spiritual senses:

> Who is there so blessed—or rather so raised above blessedness—that, when he looks upon his own fruit, what he sees in the very cluster of his own heart is the Lord of the vineyard? For look how much the soul has increased now that she has known the sweet smell of the Bridegroom in her own nard: she makes him the scent of myrrh and receives his scent into the receptacle of her heart, so that the Good may abide with her forever unexhausted; she becomes mother of the cluster of divine fruit that blossoms—that is, blooms—before the passion, but after the passion pours forth wine. For the wine that "makes our heart glad" becomes and is called, after the economy of the passion, "blood of the grape."[196]

Thus the soul "sees" the Lord of the vineyard in the grapes, after simply detecting his approach by their fragrance:

> The Bridegroom's vineyard in Gad, planted and growing in that place of abundance (that is, in the deep understanding [βαθεῖα διάνοια, *batheia dianoia*] that is watered by the divine teachings), bore this blossoming and blushing cluster in which she sees her own husbandman and vine-dresser. How happy such a garden is, whose fruit is made to be like the form of the Bridegroom! For since he is the true light and true life and true righteousness, as Wisdom says, and all such things, when a person becomes by his works these things that the Bridegroom is, he looks upon the cluster of his own conscience, and in it sees [βλέπει, *blepei*] the Bridegroom himself, and he mirrors the light of the Truth in his spotless and lightsome life.[197]

---

[195] *Eun.*3.1.55 (PG 44:585B; NPNF² 5:141).
[196] *Cant.* 3 (PG 44:828B–C; Norris, 105–107).
[197] Ibid. (PG 44:829B–C; Norris, 109).

Various terms are used in these texts to denote the place in the soul where the Word lives, such as καρδία (*kardia*, heart), ἡγεμονικόν (*hēgemonikon*, governing faculty), συνείδησις (*syneidēsis* conscience), and βαθεῖα διάνοια (*batheia dianoia*, the depths of the mind or thought). All indicate the deepest part of the soul and are the equivalent of terms used by all later mystics: "the ground" of the soul in Tauler, for example, or the "fine point" of St Francis of Sales. It is a question of a special presence of Christ—accompanied, moreover, by the other Persons [of the Trinity]—in the innermost depths of the soul.

We should clarify the use in the last passage of the term βλέπειν (*blepein*, to see). This could mislead us, if we were to understand it as indicating an intellectual vision. It is simply a matter of experiencing a presence. Its meaning can be correctly gauged by comparing it to a passage from the homily on the sixth Beatitude that deals precisely with the question of the vision of God in the "pure heart." "The Lord does not say it is blessed to know something about God, but to have God within oneself. . . . I do not think that if the eye of one's soul has been purified he is promised a direct vision of God."[198] Those who are pure in heart possess God within themselves, and by "vision" a certain awareness of this presence is meant.

Mystical experience is nothing other than a progressive awareness of the indwelling of the Word in the purified soul. For Gregory, this is the central mystery of the spiritual life. It is an aspect of the mystery of the incarnation, a specifically Christian reality, as Gregory explains in connection with the following verse from the Song: "'My kinsman has descended into his garden' (Song 6.2). [This signifies] his coming down [συγκατάβασις, *synkatabasis*] from unutterable majesty to the lowliness of our nature. From the enigma of the garden, on the other hand, we learn that we human beings are what the true Husbandman plants (for according to Paul's statement, we are his field)."[199] This garden is the inner space of souls adorned by the virtues—that is to say, by supernatural grace. "The Bridegroom does not lodge in a soul that lacks the virtues . . . [but] the Nature that contains whatever is and the Power that encompasses all things [ἡ περιεκτικὴ τῶν ὄντων δύναμις, *hē periektikē tōn ontōn dynamis*] takes as its place and its proper lodging the purity of those who receive it."[200]

These souls are the true Jerusalem where God abides:

---

[198] *Beat.* 6 (PG 44:1269C; ACW 18:148).
[199] *Cant.* 15 (PG 44:1092C; Norris, 465).
[200] Ibid. (PG 44:1093A; Norris, 465).

> The beauty of [the] soul is of the same order as goodwill (εὐδοκία, *eudokia*) exercised toward us by the Lord and Master.... [It] is manifested by the likening of the bride's comeliness to Jerusalem—the Jerusalem that is above, to be sure, the Jerusalem that is free and the mother of the free (cf. Gal 4.26), the city that we have learned from the words of the Lord and Master to belong to the Great King (cf. Mt 5.35); for the soul that contains [χωρήρασα, *chōrēsasa*] the Uncontained [ἀχώρητον, *achōrēton*], so that God dwells [ἐνοικεῖν, *enoikein*] and tarries [ἐμπεριπατεῖν, *emperipatein*] within her, has been beautified by the comeliness of the One who indwells her and becomes the heavenly Jerusalem because she has taken its beauty to herself.[201]

And thus the righteous soul is the true city of God, the heaven where he dwells, the true temple. Here we are at the very heart of mystical theology.

It is worth repeating that this presence of God in the soul is the fruit of grace. We have seen that God lives in the purity of the soul and it should by now be clear how we are to understand this purity, especially given its equivalence with the Pauline term πίστις (*pistis*, faith).

> For the horse [the soul] must first of all be adorned in every way [by the virtues] and then, in this state, receive the King as its rider. Whether he—the one who, according to the prophet, mounts himself on us horses and rides us for our salvation (cf. Hab 3.8)—renders the horse docile from above, or whether he comes to be within us as the one who at once indwells [ἐνοικῶν, *enoikōn*] and tarries [ἐμπεριπατῶν, *emperipatōn*] within us and makes his way through [διαδυόμενος, *diadyomenos*] to the depths of our soul, this makes no difference to the meaning.... [You] shall become a dwelling place and a servant by faith of the One who is coming to recline within you by dwelling within you.[202]

Various symbols help Gregory to express this indwelling:

> For there are many ways in which God comes within those who are worthy of him. He comes to be in each individual in a way that corresponds with that person's power and worthiness. One becomes God's "place," another his "house," another his "throne," another his "footstool." There is one who

---

[201] *Cant.* 15 (PG 44:1097C; FC 58:471).
[202] *Cant.* 3 (PG 44:820A–821B; Norris, 93–97). On the "circulation" of God in the soul, see Origen, *Homilies on Genesis* 1.13; *On Prayer* 23.4. Its origin is in Leviticus 26.12 and 2 Corinthians 6.16.

> even becomes his chariot or the docile steed that receives the good rider on its back and finishes its course in obedience to what seems good to the one who guides it.²⁰³ Accordingly, we now learn that there is also one who becomes his palanquin. . . .
>
> Hence the fact that one who bears God within is the palanquin of him who is enthroned within should be evident even before these words of ours; for he who, according to the holy Paul, is no longer living himself but has Christ living within him (cf. Gal 2.20) and gives proof of the Christ who speaks within him (cf. 2 Cor 13.13), this person is preeminently said to be, and becomes in truth, the palanquin of the One borne within him and carried by him.²⁰⁴

This entire doctrine of the Logos as present in the soul, and whose presence delights and nourishes it, is summarized in the following text from the homily on the fourth Beatitude:

> It seems to me that through the ideas of virtue and justice the Lord proposes Himself to the desire of his hearers. For he became for us wisdom from God, justification and redemption (1 Cor 1.30), but also Bread descending from heaven (Jn 6.33ff), and living water (Jn 4.10–11, 7.38). Somewhere in the Psalms David confesses his thirst for this when he offers this blessed malady to God and says: "My soul hath thirsted after the strong living God. When shall I come and appear before the face of God?" (Ps 41.3) This glory is true virtue, the good that is unmixed with evil, which comprises every concept concerned with goodness. This is God the Word Himself. . . and rightly have those who hunger for this justice of God been called blessed. For if, as the Psalmist says, a man has truly tasted the Lord; that is, if he has received God into himself, he is filled with Him for whom he has thirsted and hungered, as He promised who said: "[I and my Father] will come unto him and make our abode with him" (the Holy Spirit of course had already been dwelling there before). (Jn 14.23) I suppose the great Paul, too, who had tasted of these ineffable fruits from Paradise, was at the same time full of what he had tasted and always hungering for it. For he owns that he has been filled with what he desired when he says, "Christ liveth in me" (Gal 2.20); yet he is still hungry, for he always stretches forth [ἐπεκτείνεται, *epekteinetai*] to these

---

²⁰³On this image, see *Cant.* 3 (PG 44:813A; Norris, 85–87). The source is Origen, *Commentary on the Song of Songs* 1.2.6 (PG 13:130D; ACW 26:141).

²⁰⁴*Cant.* 7 (PG 44:909D–912A; Norris, 219).

things before him, saying: "Not that I have already attained, or am already made perfect" (Phil 3.12).[205]

But here a new idea emerges. Or, rather, a return to the key theme of the soul's continual progress—*epektasis*. This, the guiding thread of Gregory's thought, is applied now to the particular topic of the spiritual senses. Christ, living in the soul, is tasted by it. The soul is simultaneously sated and yet always hungry, as it transforms itself more and more into Christ. "It is the same with justice and every other virtue that goes with it. If what is eaten in the way of spiritual food be not ejected, it will by constant additions continually increase the stature of those partaking of it."[206] Thus the soul becomes ever more aware of the presence of Christ within itself, perceived through the grace that is a flowing forth of his own life. The three central themes—the tasting of God (Ps. 33.9), the indwelling of God in the soul (Jn 14. 23), and *epektasis* (Phil 3.13) are gathered together here into a single group.

The mystical life, then, is made up of a double relationship to the Word. It is first an experience, by means of the spiritual senses, of the presence of God in the soul and thus a withdrawing into the self, an *enstasy*. Second, it is a straining, a reaching out in love toward the Word as he is in himself—and this is *ecstasy*. It is the union of these two aspects that gives Gregory's mysticism its full meaning. It is at the same time both inwardness and outgoing love. "For what is higher than to be in the One who is the object of desire and to receive the object of desire within oneself?"[207] "[The] soul neither leaves off coming in nor ceases going out but is ever entering into what lies beyond by the progress she makes and always taking leave of what she has already apprehended. In just this way did that longed-for face of the Lord once pass by Moses and just so did the soul of the Lawgiver ever and again take leave of the situation she was in as she followed the Word that went on ahead of her."[208]

Of these two aspects, we have been considering the first. We shall now turn our attention to the second, as we examine the theme of ecstatic love.

---

[205] *Beat*. 4 (PG 44:1245D–1248B; ACW 18:128–29).
[206] *Beat*. 4 (PG 44:1248B; ACW 18:129).
[207] *Cant*. 6 (PG 44:892A; Norris, 191).
[208] *Cant*. 12 (PG 44:1025A; Norris, 375).

8

Ecstatic Love

As we have seen, the mystical life consists of two inseparably connected components—inwardness and transcendence, entering into the self (enstasy, *en-stasis*) and going out of the self (ecstasy, *ek-stasis*). The preceding chapter dealt with the former aspect, the indwelling of the Word in the soul. Mystical experience is the awareness the soul has of this; it is a "sense of presence." But at the same time as dwelling in the soul—depending on the degree of its participation in the divine life—the Word also transcends the soul. From another aspect, then, the soul is continually thrust out of itself in search of the Word. And the more it grows in the spiritual life, the more intense this movement also becomes. It is this going out of the self, this "mad love," that we must examine in this final chapter. Gregory uses a set of terms to describe it—ecstasy, inebriation, sleep, and wound. We shall look at each of them in turn.

This chapter is one of the most important in our investigation. It will introduce us to the most original aspect of Gregory's doctrine, one that makes of him, alongside St Paul and St Teresa, one of the great bards of mystical love. But we must be careful to clarify what is meant by this phrase. The terms which Gregory uses—ἔκστασις (*ekstasis*, ecstasy), μέθη (*methē*, inebriation), ὕπνος (*hypnos*, sleep), τραῦμα (*trauma*, wound), to which we may add γνόφος (*gnophos*, darkness) and eros, which we have already discussed—all convey the idea of something irrational, or a violent, passionate state in which man is as if wrested from himself. Now these psychological states can correspond to very different spiritual realities. In certain ancient cults—Dionysian or Orphic, for example—we see believers become objects of a type of possession by the god, who dispossesses them of themselves: *Mentemque priorem expulit*, "driving out her former mind," as Lucan writes of Apollo's possession of the Pythia, the Oracle of Delphi.[1]

We come across such cases of elation in all periods of Christianity. They had proliferated, for example, in Montanism in the second century. This resulted in

---

[1] Lucan, *Pharsalia* 5.167–68.

an extreme distrust by the orthodox Christians of the time of any psychological phenomenon that was out of the ordinary. We see evidence of this mistrust in Origen and Clement of Alexandria, who carefully try to avoid using the word *ekstasis*. The value of Gregory's testimony, on the other hand, lies in his affirmation that the most authentic spiritual life—including that of Origen and Clement themselves—normally does lead, at its summit, to states in which the presence of God, tasted by the soul, ends by wresting it away from itself at certain moments. Therefore there is such a thing as a good ecstasy, a good inebriation, and an eros that is holy. These are the very words that later mystics will use to describe their state. As Holl put it, "Gregory provided mystical theology with its vocabulary."[2] But at the same time, he does not free himself entirely from Origen's point of view. With the latter, the term *ekstasis* in no way denotes mystical ecstasy, but simply the transition from the sensory to the spiritual, an entering into the life of faith, as it can, at times, in Gregory. This use of the same word to mean different things is found with the other terms. Darkness, for example, is open to a dual interpretation. As we have seen, it can denote either a transition from the sensory to the spiritual, or the mystical life proper. The same is also true of eros, which sometimes refers simply to the ascending movement of the soul toward the intelligible world. This is the Platonic eros that corresponds to the second way. Yet, as we have already seen, sometimes it expresses the "madness" of love, of *agapē*, at the pinnacle of the mystical life.

Yet this very imprecision is significant in itself. It allows Gregory to specify things. It enables him to make it clear when he is referring, for example, to an ecstasy that is divine and that belongs to the realm of faith, being its summit. To do so, he is in the habit of adding an adjective to the terms used. Thus he does not speak of inebriation but of "sober inebriation," not of darkness but of "luminous darkness," not of sleep but of a "wakeful sleep," not of a wound but of a "blessed wound"—so many paradoxical expressions to describe a reality that is ineffable.

Moreover, the recurrence of the same themes at different levels of reality is itself deeply significant. It indicates that in the spiritual life this element of repetition is essential. In reality, one cannot speak of ecstasy, of darkness, or of wound in the singular. For Gregory, the spiritual life consists of successive ecstasies, darknesses, and wounds. Thus "ecstasy" denotes a permanent attitude, but has a different meaning at each level. It can refer, for example, to an

---

[2]Holl, *Amphilochios von Ikonium*, 205.

estrangement (ἀλλοτρίωσις, *allotriōsis*) from sin, a going out (ἔκβασις, *ekbasis*) from the sensible, or inebriation (μέθη, *methē*) in the mystical sense of the word. The soul must always go out of itself and discover, one day, that to relate in love to someone other than itself is the very law of its being. This perpetual going out of oneself is what Gregory calls *epektasis*, a concept that we shall study at the end of this chapter.

Going Out of Oneself

Etymologically, the word ἔκστασις (*ekstasis*) denotes a dis-placement.[3] In classical Greek, applied to man, it usually means an alienation of the mind, "madness."[4] It is often used in Holy Scripture, but with nuances that are difficult to determine. It denotes the "deep sleep" into which God plunges Adam, for example, at the time of the creation of Eve (Gen 2.21). It is also used for the "trance" that fell upon Abram just before God made his covenant with him (Gen 15.12). In Psalm 30.23 it indicates a state of "extreme fear," and in Psalm 115.2 "amazement." In the New Testament, it can refer to the astonishment caused by supernatural facts (Lk 5.26; Mk 5.42; Acts 3.10), but it also has the modern meaning of the word when used to describe the ecstasy or "trance" of St Peter (Acts 10.10).

There is an interesting classification of the different meanings of the word in Philo. He is commenting on the same verse from Genesis that refers to Adam's "trance" (Gen 15.12), and explains that there are four types of ecstasy:

> "And about the setting of the sun a trance fell upon Abraham, and, behold, fear with great darkness fell upon Him." Now there is one kind of trance which is a sort of frantic delirium [παράνοια, *paranoia*], causing infirmity of mind, either through old age, or melancholy, or some other similar cause. There is another kind which is excessive consternation, arising usually from things which happen suddenly and unexpectedly. Another kind is mere tranquility of the mind, arising when it is inclined by nature to be quiet: but that which is the best description of all is a divinely inspired and more vehement sort of enthusiasm [ἔνθεος κατοκωχή τε καὶ μανία, *entheos katokōchē te kai mania*], which the race of prophets is subject to.[5]

---

[3]The comments made at the beginning of this chapter are inspired by H.Ch. Puech's article, "Un livre récent sur la mystique d'Origène," *Revue d'histoire et de philosophie religieuses* 13 (1933): 508–36.
[4]Aristotle, *Categories* 8.10a.
[5]Philo, *Who is the Heir of Divine Things* 51.249 (Yonge, 297). Was Philo himself an ecstatic? That he was is the thesis of most critics: Lewy (*Sobria ebrietas*), Leisegang, Bousset, and Pascher (*Hē basilikē*

As an example of the first, Philo cites the following verse: "The Lord smite thee with insanity, and blindness, and astonishment of mind [ἐκστάσει διανοίας, *ekstasei dianoias*]" (Deut 28.28). For the second meaning, he refers to the moment when Isaac saw Esau approaching, believing that he had already blessed him: "And Isaac was amazed with very great amazement [ἔκστασιν μεγάλην, *ekstasin megalēn*]" (Gen 27.33). He also gives two examples where the corresponding verb is used. First, the reaction of the people as they arrive at Sinai: "And the people were exceedingly amazed [ἐξέστη, *exestē*]" (Ex 19.18). Then the reaction of Jacob on hearing that Joseph was still alive: "Jacob was amazed [ἐξέστη, *exestē*]" (Gen. 45.26). For the third meaning, Philo returns to the description of the ecstasy of Adam (Gen 15.12), and accompanies this with an interesting comment: "Here [he calls] the quietness [ἡσυχία, *hēsychia*] and tranquillity [ἠρεμία, *hēremia*] of mind a trance; for the slumber of the mind is the awaking of the outward sense: and, again, the awaking of the intellect [ἐγρήγορσις τῆς διανοίας, *egrēgorsis tēs dianoias*] is the reducing of the outward senses to a state of inactivity."[6] This notion of ecstasy-as-sleep occupies an important place, as we shall see, in both Plotinus and Gregory of Nyssa.

As for the fourth meaning, Philo refers again to the ecstasy of Abraham, seeing it as being a state of "enthusiasm" in the etymological meaning of the word:[7] "For the mind that is in us is removed from its place [ἐξοικίζεται, *exoikizetai*] at the arrival of the divine Spirit, but is again restored to its previous habitation when that Spirit departs, for it is contrary to holy law for what is mortal to dwell with what is immortal."[8] The prophet then becomes "a sounding instrument [ὄργανον, *organon*] of God's voice, being struck and moved to sound in an invisible manner [πληττόμενον ἀοράτως, *plēttomenon aoratōs*] by him."[9]

This last idea is related to a well-established ancient tradition, one that lies behind the belief in divination. It is found in the Dionysian rites, and in *Ion* Plato applies it famously to poetic inspiration. As we can see, Philo, for his part, applies it to prophecy. The prophet is inspired in the strong sense of the term;

---

hodos). Bréhier, in *Les idées philosophiques de Plotin*, is more hesitant. Only Völker (*Fortschritt und Vollendung*, 316–17) argues that he was not, seeing in his use of the vocabulary of ecstasy simply a literary procedure that had been current since Plato to express the highest form of knowledge.

[6] Philo, *Who is the Heir of Divine Things* 51.257 (Yonge, 298).
[7] The word is derived from the Greek ἐν (*en*, in) and θεός (*theos*, god).
[8] Philo, *Who is the Heir of Divine Things* 53.265 (Yonge, 299).
[9] Ibid. 52.259 (Yonge, 298). Gregory uses the following similar expression: "The Holy Spirit clings to the instrument of the prophet" (τὸ πνεῦμα τὸ Ἅγιον ἐμφυὲν τῷ ὀργάνῳ τοῦ προφήτου, *to pneuma to Agion emphyen tō organō tou prophētou*). *Inscr.* 2.10.129 (PG 44:541B; Heine, 162).

Ecstatic Love

that is to say, it really is God who acts in him and substitutes himself for him.[10] This doctrine spread to certain trends in early Christianity. One thinks of the utterance attributed to Montanus: "Lo, the man is as a lyre, and I fly over him as a pick. The man sleepeth, while I watch."[11] These excesses provoked a reaction among orthodox writers, as mentioned earlier, who became understandably distrustful of any form of "ecstasy."

Moving on to the third century, we encounter two authors whose treatment of ecstasy is of particular interest for our study—Plotinus and Origen. We know that Plotinus places ecstasy at the summit of the spiritual ascent. Porphyry tells us that Plotinus himself reached a state of ecstasy four times during his life. Ἔκστασις (*ekstasis*) is one of the words he uses to describe the supreme experience, union with the One. In a passage that interestingly contrasts with the third definition of Philo, he writes: "To an Intellectual-Principle Repose [νοῦ ἡσυχία, *nou hēsychia*] is not an abdication [ἔκστασις, *ekstasis*] from intellect."[12] By this he means that "knowledge of God and knowledge of self are the same."[13]

As for Origen, the question is far from being settled. Against the intellectualist interpretations of Dionysius and de Faye, Völker devoted several pages of his book to establishing the presence of an element of mystical ecstasy in his teaching.[14] Even so, the texts he mentions are not decisive. In one of these, the word *ekstasis* is translated by Rufinus as *contemplatio stuporis* (a contemplation of astonishment), which equates with Philo's second meaning. Another is simply a passage from Acts 10.10, referring to the "trance" of Peter. The most interesting text is from Origen's *Commentary on John*, where he writes of the mystical vine that it "completely rids it of human concerns and causes it to experience ecstasy and to be intoxicated with an intoxication which is not irrational but divine" (ἐξιστῶν ἀπὸ τῶν ἀνθρωπικῶν καὶ ἐνθουσιᾶν ποιῶν καὶ μεθύειν μέθην θείαν, *existōn apo tōn anthrōpikōn kai enthousian poiōn kai methyein methēn theian*).[15] The connection between the synonym ἐνθουσία (*enthousia*) and inebriation puts us in a more characteristic context. More recently, Rahner has spoken of

---

[10] On all this, see Lewy, *Sobria ebrietas*, 41–72.
[11] See P. Labriolle, "La polémique anti-montaniste contre la prophétie extatique," *Revue d'histoire et de littérature religieuses* 11 (1906): 97–145.
[12] Plotinus, *Enneads* 5.3.7.
[13] Plotin, *Ennéades*, vol. 5, ed. and trans. Emile Bréhier (Paris: Les Belles Lettres, 1931), note to 5.3.7.
[14] See Völker, *Fortschritt und Vollendung*, 134–44.
[15] Origen, *Commentary on John* 1.33 (PG 14:80A). Translation from *Origen: Commentary on the Gospel according to John. Books 1–10*, trans. R. E. Heine, Fathers of the Church 80 (Washington, DC: The Catholic University of America Press, 1989), 75.

the way in which Origen resolutely dismisses any form of ecstasy. In this, he is followed by Hausherr[16] and Viller.[17]

It seems that, in reality, there are two kinds of ecstasy, and we must distinguish between them. As Rahner writes, "Clearly, Origen takes issue with an *ekstasis* that would be 'a state of madness' (μανικὴ κατάστασις, *manikē katastasis*). The insistence with which he asserts that whoever is filled with the spirit must not be ecstatic, but entirely free and able to refuse the inspiration of the spirit, does not seem to fit the idea of a genuine divine ecstasy. It would seem to indicate that Origen was not thinking of an occurrence of this type at all. Elsewhere one finds in him the same rigid attitude toward Montanist mysticism."[18] But it does not seem that Origen had specifically admitted the possibility of true ecstasy.

The solution seems to be the one suggested by Puech.[19] In Origen there is a concept of ecstasy that is not that of Philo or the Montanists. Ecstasy for him is not a going out of oneself, but out of "all things human." It does indeed represent the summit of divine mysticism, but without depersonalization. It is a question of a going out of the body (*extra corpus*)—the phrase is found in Origen and St Paul also uses it in connection with his own rapture (2 Cor 12.3)—rather than out of the mind, or the self.

Of the various meanings so far encountered, which are the ones that we find in Gregory of Nyssa? To begin with, he sometimes uses *ekstasis* and related vocabulary in a profane sense. The term ἐξιστάναι (*existanai*) means to go beyond one's limits, in the physical or metaphysical sense. Thus in his *Homilies on the Song of Songs*, Gregory writes of the divine nature that it "stands unlimited in its goodness and is never alienated from [ἐξισταμένη, *existamenē*] itself because it is not open to participation in evil."[20] In this sense, the word is in competition with ἐκβαίνειν (*ekbainein*, go out of), which Plotinus prefers,[21] but which is also found in Gregory.

More interesting is the word's psychological meaning in non-religious contexts. Here it is generally associated with the idea of sleep, denoting the "going out of the self" that sleep symbolizes. Thus ἐκστάσεις (*ekstaseis*) is listed as being

---

[16]See I. Hausherr, "Les grands courants de la spiritualité orientale," *Orientalia Christiana Periodica* 1 (1935): 114–38, at 122f.

[17]See M. Viller, "Aux sources de la spirtualité de saint Maxime: les œuvres d'Évagre le Pontique," *Revue d'ascétique et de mystique* 11 (avril–juillet, 1930): 150–84; 239–68; 331–36; at 260.

[18]Rahner, "Le début d'une doctrine," 135.

[19]See Puech, "Un livre récent," 532.

[20]Gregory, *Cant.* 5 (PG 44:873D; Norris, 171).

[21]See Plotinus, *Enneads* 6.5.11. [The point of the reference is clearer in the Loeb edition (vol. 6, p. 355), which translates the verb as "exceed."—*Trans.*]

one of the problems of sleep, together with ἀλλοιώσεις (*alloiōseis*, changes), μεταβολαί (*metabolai*, changes) and λῆθαι (*lēthai*, oblivion, forgetting).[22] Likewise, in the *Homilies on the Song of Songs*, Gregory refers to the angels, "whom no force of the imagination [φαντασία, *phantasia*] alienates [ἐξίστησι, *existēsi*] from the truth."[23] Here the context is one that deals with the illusions that occur during sleep, figures of a mirage of the senses—and from which the angels are shielded. The connotation is clearly pejorative. We are reminded of Philo's comment concerning the third sense of the word *ekstasis*: "for the slumber of the mind is the awaking of the outward sense."[24] There is another passage in which *ekstasis* is linked to imagination. It is a description of an appearance of the risen Christ to the apostles, who believe they are "dreaming." We may take note of this, but should not assign too much importance to it, for the homily in which it occurs is apocryphal.[25]

We come to a positive meaning in a passage such as the following: "The psalm of ecstasy, which has been placed after the dedication and which has the following inscription, *unto the end, a psalm for David, in ecstasy*, is in agreement with our previous observations, which advise those things to be separated [ἐκστῆναι, *exstēnai*] whose combination is harmful."[26] This brings us a little closer to a mystical context, though here it is simply a question of turning from evil to good. And we cannot fail to observe a weakening of the concept's original meaning. *Ekstasis* here hardly differs from *ekbasis* (a way out). The psychological connotations have been erased, leaving only the material image of a "separation."

These various uses are of minor importance compared to those passages in which we find *ekstasis* being used to denote a mystical state properly speaking. One can divide them into two groups: first, those referring to persons from Scripture who have experienced such states, then others that all relate to the concept of "sober inebriation" (νηφάλιος μέθη, *nēphalios methē*), to which we shall return. In both, it is unquestionably a case of mystical events. We shall see that Gregory's interpretation of these states shows a return to the idea of ecstasy as a going out of the self, under the effect of an alien reality and having a non-rational

---

[22]See *In sanctum Pascha* (=*In Christi resurrectionem oratio III*) (*Sanct. Pasch.*) (PG 46:673B); English translation in *The Easter Sermons of Gregory of Nyssa*, ed. A. Spira and C. Klock (Cambridge, MA: Philadelphia Patristic Foundation, 1981), 18.
[23]*Cant.* 9 (PG 44:973C; Norris, 303).
[24]Philo, *Who is the Heir of Divine Things* 51.257 (Yonge, 298).
[25]See *In Christi resurrectionem: Oratio II* (PG 46:636A).
[26]*Inscr.* 2.6.65 (PG 44:509C–D; Heine, 140).

characteristic that points toward the *eros* of Pseudo-Dionysius and confirms that the danger of Montanism was no longer felt to be a threat.

In chronological order of composition, the first of these passages is from the treatise *On Virginity*. Gregory has just shown how much the divine reality is "beyond every good" (ἐπέκεινα παντὸς ἀγαθοῦ, *epekeina pantos agathou*). He continues as follows:

> The great David seems to me to have illustrated this impossibility [ἀμηχανίαν, *amēchanian*] well. When he was once lifted up [ὑψωθείς, *hypsōtheis*] in thought by the power of the Spirit, he was, as it were, divorced from himself [οἷον ἐκβὰς ἑαυτόν, *oion ekbas heauton*] and saw that incredible and incomprehensible beauty in a blessed ecstasy [ἐν μακαρίᾳ ἐκστάσει, *en makaria ekstasei*]. But he did see it as far as it is possible for a man to do so when he is released from [ἔξω γενόμενος, *exō genomenos*] the limitations of the flesh and comes to the contemplation of the incorporeal and intelligible through thought alone [διὰ μόνης διανοίας, *dia monēs dianoias*].[27] When he wanted to say something worthy of what he had seen, he sang out that song which all men sing: "Every man is a liar" (Ps 115.2).[28]

In the Septuagint, the full text of this verse 2 reads, "And I said in mine ecstasy, 'Every man is a liar'" (Ἐγὼ εἶπα ἐν τῇ ἐκστάσει μου· πᾶς ἄνθρωπός ἐστι ψεύστης, *egō eipa en tēs ekstasei mou: pas anthrōpos esti pseustēs*). Here the word *ekstasis* means distress or consternation, but Gregory interprets it in a mystical sense, relating it to a state of ecstasy on the part of David. He describes this as presupposing a lifting up of the thought (διάνοια, *dianoia*) by the Holy Spirit, a going out (ἐκβάς, *ekbas*) of himself, a blessed vision. But what is this going out of the self? Gregory specifies that it is not a loss of the mind—since the *dianoia*, the thinking faculty, is involved—but a going out "from the limitations of the flesh," and thus a leaving of the sensory life. The mind acts not simply on its normal level, but is raised up by grace. The object of the vision is the contemplation of incorporeal reality, which is always the object of mystical contemplation. Finally, this vision is the only one possible for man, from which we may conclude that, even in this extraordinary state, it is not a question of a total vision.

According to this text, then, ecstasy seems to comprise two aspects. On the one hand, there is a going out of the sensory. The mind (διάνοια, *dianoia*) at its

---

[27] A similar expression—νοήσει μόνῃ (*noēsei monē*, through the mind alone)—is found in Philo. See *On Dreams* 1.8.43 (Yonge, 369).

[28] *Virg.* 10 (PG 46:361A–B; FC 58:37).

Ecstatic Love

highest point, separated from everything sensory, contemplates the intelligible realities in an ineffable manner. Taking the terms by themselves, one could apply them equally well to the Plotinian understanding of ecstasy, which is also a going out of the sensory and a pure activity of the mind. But Gregory adds a second element: the *dianoia* is raised up by the Holy Spirit, and thus not only goes out of the sensory but also itself (ἔξω ἑαυτοῦ, *exo heautou*). But this is not to be understood in the Montanist sense, but rather as a raising of man above his nature.

We see here, in the very process of being formed, the main elements of an orthodox theology of ecstasy. We started, with Philo, from a Dionysian conception which entailed suppressing the νοῦς ἴδιος (*nous idios*, one's own mind). We then saw that Origen, in reaction, paid particular attention to upholding the part played by the mind, elevated above sensible reality. As a consequence his understanding of the concept was too intellectualistic, which explains the rationalistic interpretations of his thought.[29] Gregory, on the other hand, returns to the idea of a "going out of oneself,"[30] to the hypernoetic character of ecstasy. He restores to it the essential element of passivity. Yet it is not a substitution of the divine spirit for the human spirit, of the divine self for the human self, but rather, beyond the human *dianoia*, of a mysterious participation in the divine Spirit (πνεῦμα, *pneuma*)—that is to say, in the knowledge and the love with which God knows and loves himself.

It would seem that there is a comparison to be made here between the development of the theology of ecstasy and that of the incarnation. We know that Apollinarius, against whom Gregory wrote, did not accept that Christ had a human mind (νοῦς, *nous*). It seemed to him that attributing a mind to Christ other than that of the Word was to see in him two persons (δύο πρόσωπα, *dyo prosōpa*), which is what he reproached Gregory for doing. Gregory, on the contrary, shows that a clear distinction can be made between the *nous* and the *prosopon*, and that the Logos can indeed assume the humanity of Christ without expelling the *nous* from it. Mutatis mutandis, the same is true for ecstasy:

---

[29] See Lossky, "La théologie négative," 205.

[30] "Gregory's description of the stage at which one reaches the height of perfection is a landmark. In the wake of his non-Christian predecessor (Philo), Gregory dared to introduce an idea that had been rejected by the Christian Church since the Montanist heresy—namely, that one can only reach the summit by going out of oneself through ecstasy." Holl, *Amphilochius von Iconium*, 205. See also Lewy, *Sobria ebrietas*, 132–33. Holl notes that this idea is not found in Basil or Gregory of Nazianzus. An interesting verification of this is the fact that in his eulogy for Basil, even when comparing him to Paul caught up to the third heaven, Gregory concentrates on his brother's doctrine, not his mystical life.

the Spirit (πνεῦμα, *pneuma*) can inhabit the soul without expelling the *nous* from it. In both cases, it is a matter of deepening the concept of person. We should note, too, that Gregory prefers to use the term διάνοια (*dianoia*), which more effectively conveys the idea of the mind as a faculty, rather than the more ambiguous νοῦς (*nous*).

The above passage from *On Virginity*, however, emphasizes the detachment from the sensory and the activity of the *dianoia* more than the transcending of the *dianoia* by the *pneuma*. In this respect, it is still dependent on the intellectualism of Origen. In a later text, to which it seems no one so far has attributed the importance it merits—the *Homilies on Saint Stephen*—Gregory develops this aspect of the possession of the *nous* by the Holy Spirit: "For [Stephen], having left his nature [ἐκβὰς τὴν φύσιν, *ekbas tēn physin*] and before leaving [ἐκβῆναι, *ekbēnai*] his body, looked with pure eyes [καθαροῖς ὀφθαλμοῖς, *katharois ophthalmois*] at the heavenly gates opened to him and at what appeared within the inner sanctuary, the divine glory itself and the reflection of God's glory (cf. Acts 7.55–56; Heb 1.3). . . . Therefore, when Stephen had come to be outside human nature [ἔξω γεγονὼς τῆς ἀνθρωπίνης φύσεως, *exō gegonōs tēs anthrōpinēs physeōs*] and had been transformed to angelic grace, with the result that he astonished the bloodthirsty murderers when the form of his countenance was changed to the dignity of the angels (cf. Acts 6.15), he both saw what is unseen [εἶδε τὰ ἀθέατα, *eide ta atheata*] and proclaimed aloud the grace that appeared to him."[31] We note that it is a question of "going out of nature" or "human nature," and therefore certainly of transcendence properly speaking.

The continuation of the passage shows this more clearly: "How was it that Stephen saw the glory above heaven? Who was it that opened wide for him the gates of the heavens? Was it an achievement of human power? Was it one of the angels who caused that nature lying below to mount up on high? Not so. For the narrative about him does not say in this way that Stephen saw what he saw because he was great in power or because he had been filled with angelic help. What does it say instead? Stephen 'filled with the holy Spirit saw the glory of God and the Only Begotten Son of God' (cf. Acts 7.55)."[32] Consequently, our text takes on its full meaning. Stephen had exited nature and saw invisible things, just as, in his *Homilies on the Song of Songs*, Gregory describes the soul as having gone out of itself and contemplated invisible things. Why did he leave human nature?

---

[31]*Steph. I* (PG 46:713B–C; Greer, 59).
[32]Ibid. (46:716D–717A; Greer, 61).

Ecstatic Love

Because no one has ever seen God (cf. Jn 1.18; 1 Tim 6.16). "For Stephen did not look at the divine by relying on human nature and power, but it was after being mingled [ἀνακραθείς, anakratheis] with the grace of the Holy Spirit that he was exalted by him to the contemplation of God."[33] Stephen's ecstasy is a particular aspect, the highest degree, of this going out, this radical theological *ekbasis*, which results from the communication of the Holy Spirit to any Christian.

However, we must admit that in the passage just examined the actual word *ekstasis* is not found—only the equivalent terms ἐκβαίνειν (*ekbainein*) and ἔξω φύσεως εἶναι (*exō physeōs einai*). Nor is it found in those scriptural passages that describe this event in Stephen's life. It seems that Gregory uses *ekstasis* above all when commenting on passages where Scripture itself uses it. We saw that this was the case with the example of David. The same is true for Abraham, the epitome of ecstatics. Gregory's description of Abraham's ecstasy is one of his finest passages. It is also one that will help us to clarify the various elements that contribute to his theory of *ekstasis*, and to distinguish between the two meanings the word has in Gregory's usage. Used in a broader sense, it refers to the going out of the world of sense and human nature and the entry into the supernatural world. But it can also denote the psychological experience that corresponds to a particular aspect of this going forth—namely, *ekstasis* in the technical sense of the word.

> [Abraham] went out [ἐξῆλθε, *exēlthe*] by Divine command from his own country and kindred on a journey worthy of a prophet [ἀνδρὶ προφήτῃ, *andri prophētē*] eager for the knowledge of God. For no local migration seems to me to satisfy the idea of the blessings which it is signified that he found. For going out from himself [ἔξω γενόμενος ἑαυτοῦ, *exō genomenos heautou*] and from his country, by which I understand his earthly and carnal mind, and raising his thoughts as far as possible above the common boundaries of nature, and forsaking the soul's kinship with the senses, so that untroubled by any of the objects of sense his eyes might be opened to the things which are invisible [τῶν ἀοράτων, *tōn aoratōn*] ... [he knew] as much of God as it was possible for finite human capacity at its full stretch [ὑπερταθεῖσαν, *hypertatheisan*] to attain.[34]

---

[33] *Cant.*, 14 (PG 46:717B; ibid.).
[34] *Eun.* 2.85–86 (PG 45:940B; NPNF² 5:259).

Gregory then describes the different stages of this departure, according to a sequence that we will see in other texts of his, and which, beyond the world of sense, and then the intelligible world itself, leads to this total bareness that he elsewhere calls darkness. "[W]hen he had gone beyond every conjecture respecting the divine nature, having purged his reason of all such fancies, and arrived at a faith unalloyed and free from all prejudice, he made this a sure and manifest token of the knowledge of God, viz. the belief that He is greater and more sublime than any token by which He may be known. On this account, indeed, after the ecstasy [ἔκστασιν, *ekstasin*] which fell upon him, and after his sublime meditations, falling back on his human weakness, 'I am,' saith he, 'but dust and ashes,' that is to say, without voice or power to interpret that good which his mind had conceived."[35]

Here we find the two aspects of ecstasy brought together. On the one hand, Gregory retraces the metaphysical stages of this ascent through the various realms of being. But this going out of oneself, which in reality spans the entire domain of supernatural knowledge of God, represents only a specific psychological experience, ecstasy in the proper sense, in that special state that involves a suspension of the activity of the senses and of discursive knowledge—I do not say of all activity of the mind—and which, significantly, is the only place in the above passage where Gregory employs the word *ekstasis*, for the rest choosing the generic term ἔξοδος (*exodos*).[36] It is not only a transition from the lower to the higher, but truly a going out of oneself.

It is precisely this experience that Gregory describes above, using the same terms as Genesis: ἔκστασις ἐπέπεσε (*ekstasis epepese*), a "trance fell" upon Abraham. Here, then, it is a question of a sudden state that comes from outside, an *ekstasis* in the psychological sense. It is a transport of the mind into another world and whoever undergoes it will later need to "redescend" (κατακύψας, *katakypsas*), to return to ordinary experience. We should remember that this passage from Genesis is the one Philo gives as an example of the fourth kind of ecstasy. Gregory agrees with him that this is the highest form, seeing it as the sudden irruption of the divine Spirit into the human mind. They differ, however,

---

[35]*Eun.* 2.89–90 (PG 45:941A; NPNF² 5:259).

[36]The two concepts of ecstasy are clearly distinguished by Hausherr, *Ignorance infinie*, 356: "One runs the risk of confusing various doctrines, if one omits from the definition of ecstasy, that which constitutes its essential element: the going out of oneself, not by the unconsciousness of the suspension of the senses, but by a kind of projection, under the impulse of love, outside the laws of the intelligence itself. Cf. Pseudo-Dionysius: Ἑαυτοῦ καὶ πάντων ἔκστασις (*Heautou kai pantōn ekstasis*, a going out of oneself and everything), *The Mystical Theology* 1.1."

Ecstatic Love

in their interpretation. For Gregory, there is no loss of personality, but rather a transporting to the divine and a loss of bodily activity.

It seems, then, that one can claim that in this passage Gregory professes the reality of a specific mystical experience of going out of oneself, of alienation, and thus agrees with Philo. We also find the same assertion in Plotinus, though there is no trace of it in Origen. But this same psychological experience is interpreted differently by our three authors. For Plotinus, it entails a suppression of one's individuality and a fusion with the One; for Philo, it means expulsion of the νοῦς ἴδιος (*nous idios,* one's own mind) and possession (κατοχή, *katochē*) of the soul by the divine Spirit; for Gregory, on the other hand, it is a suspension of the natural life that leads to a blissful (μακαρία, *makaria*) contemplation of the divine reality. The great difference between Gregory and Origen is that the former recognizes a psychological *ekstasis,* an extraordinary phenomenon, which the latter dismisses because he lumps together its orthodox form and its Montanist or Dionysian imitations. A new set of texts, which we shall now consider, will confirm this conclusion.

These texts are the most important for our present purpose. In fact, the ones cited so far are passages in which Gregory is led coincidentally to allude to instances of ecstasy found in Scripture. On these occasions he simply clarifies the meaning of the word. But a study of ecstasy in itself is also to be found in his work—and precisely where we might expect it, in that treatise on the mystical life that is the *Homilies on the Song of Songs*. The theme appears in the fifth homily, to be taken up again at greater length in the sixth. In both passages it is linked to the concept of sober inebriation, which, in Philo, has mystical significance. Origen, in whom we can detect some vestiges of it, gives it a sacramental meaning, in keeping with his transposition of the doctrine of ecstasy—and he criticizes mystical interpretations of it. Gregory, by contrast, while keeping the sacramental connotations with which it has been enriched, restores to it a mystical significance. He inserts it into his overall framework, making of it the characteristic feature of one stage of the mystical life.

The first passage is useful in that it will allow us correctly to situate ecstasy on the mystical journey, by specifying its connection with the doctrine of the spiritual senses:

> Its wine, rejoicing the heart, will one day [τότε, *tote*] fill up wisdom's chalice (cf. Prov 9.2–5) and, as warranted by "the exalted summons" [ἐξ ὑψηλοῦ

κηρύγματος, *ex hypsēlou kērygmatos*], be set before the fellowship of its drinkers, to be drawn at their pleasure for the sake of a good and sober drunkenness [εἰς ἀγαθὴν καὶ νηφάλιον μέθην, *eis agathēn kai nēphalion methēn*]. What I am referring to is the drunkenness that occasions that self-transcendence by which people move out of the material sphere toward what is more divine [ἔκστασις ἐκ τῶν ὑλικῶν πρὸς τὸ θειότερον, *ekstasis ek tōn hylikōn pros to theioteron*]. So now the vine blossoms with its flower and from it gives out a fragrant scent, sweet and gentle, that is mingled with the Spirit that contains it.³⁷

From the last sentence we see that ecstasy represents a more advanced stage, compared with the fragrances that symbolize the first mystical perceptions of God's presence in the soul. Let us note, though, that these first perceptions are already the fruits of the Spirit. Consequently, it is not a question here of a radical "going out," a deification in the broader sense, but rather of one particular stage. Ecstasy will happen one day (τότε, *tote*). This last phrase reminds us of those passages in which Gregory speaks of it as occurring "at the proper time" (κατὰ καιρόν, *kata kairon*). This expression sometimes refers to eternal life. But it can also refer, as is the case here, to that anticipation of the eternal life, which is what ecstasy is. He "left his nature," as the first of the two *Homilies on Saint Stephen* put it, though not the body.³⁸

Two other features of this passage deserve mention. First, ecstasy is defined as a passing from earthly or material things to things divine. Here we are very close to Origen, who writes of the "true vine" that it "completely rids [one] of human concerns" and, as we saw, "causes [one] to experience ecstasy and to be intoxicated with an intoxication which is not irrational, but divine."³⁹ This is deification of the mind. Puech, citing this same passage, saw here the essential feature of Origen's understanding of ecstasy. It is a feature that Gregory maintains. It is interesting to note that the "intoxication" is specifically described as "not irrational," which is an obvious criticism of psychological theories of ecstasy.

Finally, we note that the call to ecstasy is the result of a call from on high, which again emphasizes its supernatural character. What is more, it results from a freely given, divine initiative, which comes at the appropriate time. This is something that highlights the passive aspect of ecstasy. The reference to

---

³⁷*Cant.* 5 (PG 44:873A–B; FC 58:169).
³⁸*Steph. I* (PG 46:713B–C; Greer, 59),
³⁹Origen, *Commentary on John* 1.30.

Ecstatic Love

an invitation from on high comes—as does the mixing bowl—from the Septuagint text of Proverbs 9.1–6, which is a description of the Banquet of Wisdom and is one of the passages most frequently cited in contexts dealing with ecstasy-as-inebriation.

Turning now to a second passage, we shall see that it is much more developed and more explicit.[40] It uses biblical examples that clearly illustrate ecstasies. It contains some of the examples given earlier. Gregory is commenting on the following verse from the Song: "You who are close to me, eat! And you, my brethren, drink and be drunken!" (Song 5.1). After connecting the words "eat" and "drink" to the Last Supper—which is in keeping with Origen's sacramental interpretation—he adds, "since all drunkenness tends, in those who have been mastered by wine, to bring about a displacement [*ekstasis*] of discursive thought [τῆς διανοίας, *tēs dianoias*]. Hence what he prescribes here came to pass then (at the Last Supper) because of that divine food and drink, and indeed always comes to pass when a change and displacement from worse to better accompany the food and drink."[41]

This is already very interesting for our purpose. If we understand it correctly, the two characteristic elements of ecstasy are brought together here. On the one hand, it is in essence "a transporting," "a going out" from what Gregory here calls the "worse"—which is a synonym for terrestrial or "human" (ἀνθρωπικός, *anthrōpikos*)—to pass to the "better"; that is, the divine.[42] The eucharistic wine symbolizes this ecstasy, the property of wine being to produce inebriation, which is also a going out of the self. And this is why the gesture of Christ, offering the eucharistic cup to the apostles, symbolizes what it brings about—namely, a transformation of the soul into God. This is an aspect of eucharistic symbolism where the concept of "sacrament"—that is, an efficacious sign—is realized perfectly. But at the same time the image of inebriation describes the psychological aspect of ecstasy; it implies that the mind is, as it were, overpowered (κεκρατημένη, *kekratēmenē*) and carried away out of natural life.[43] We will see in due course that it is indeed this kind of ecstasy that is involved here. But this enables us to perceive a new eucharistic relationship—not to deification in

---

[40]*Cant.* 10 (PG 44:989B–992B; Norris, 325–27).

[41]Ibid. (PG 44:989C; Norris, 325).

[42]Cf. "situating our thoughts in eternity instead of temporal concerns" (στήσας τοὺς λογισμοὺς ἀπὸ τῶν προσκαίρων πρὸς τὸ ἀΐδιον, *stēsas tous logismous apo tōn proskairōn pros to aidion*), *Ascens.* (PG 46:692B; McCambley, 3).

[43]See Lewy, *Sobria ebrietas*, 50f.

general, but to ecstasy in particular. This can be seen in the lives of the saints, where ecstasy is often associated with Communion. Here we have one of the oldest pieces of evidence, one which allows us to establish a special link between ecstasy and the Eucharist, and in general the sacramental character of Christian mysticism. This is something that later eastern mysticism will fully develop. One need only mention Diadochus of Photiki or Nicholas Cabasilas.

Gregory then goes on to enumerate some typical examples of ecstasy: "It is of this inebriation that David was inebriated the day, when having gone out of himself and having entered ecstasy [ἐν ἐκστάσει γενόμενος, *en ekstasei genomenos*], he saw the invisible beauty and uttered the famous phrase: 'Every man is a liar.'" [Ps 115.2] We have already encountered this ecstasy of David and the scriptural misinterpretation that is the basis for it. Let us note that a vision of invisible realities is mentioned here once again as a characteristic feature of *ekstasis*. David, as an ecstatic, reappears in the *Homily on the Ascension*: "Corporeal burdens do not oppress him . . ."—this is indeed a going forth from the body, a suspension of the senses—"and he has joined himself to the transcendent powers and reports their words to us"[44] This connection between the "going out" and a return to the sphere of the angels is interesting, for we have seen that this is one of the features of man's return to his original state. We saw earlier that ecstasy was a return to angelic grace (χάρις ἀγγελική, *charis angelikē*).

But let us continue our survey of the ecstatics presented to us in Scripture, turning now to Paul. "In the same way Paul as well, the younger Benjamin, was drunken [ἐμεθύσθη, *emethysthē*] when he entered into ecstasy and said, 'For if I am beside myself [ἐξέστημεν, *exestēmen*], it is for God' (since his ecstasy was directed upon God), 'and if I am in control of myself, it is for you' (2 Cor 5.13)—the people, to whom in his speech before Festus (cf. Acts 26.24–25), he showed that he was not out of his mind [μαινόμενος, *mainomenos*] but was speaking words of self-control and righteousness."[45] Gregory often repeats that Paul was an ecstatic. Paul's account of how he was caught up into paradise (2 Cor 12) is the most explicit text on ecstasy. It is strange, however, that this is not the text that Gregory quotes here. The first reference may well be related to ecstasy. In the second, Gregory seems implicitly to contrast a "sensible madness" (μανία σώφρων, *mania sōphrōn*) with the madness of which Festus accuses him. This oxymoron, analogous to "sober inebriation," is found in Hellenistic literature,

---
[44]*Ascens.* (PG 46:693A; McCambley, 4). [Translation modified to match Daniélou's version.—*Trans.*]

[45]*Cant.* 10 (PG 44:989D; Norris, 325).

both pagan and Christian. It has been studied by Lewy.⁴⁶ There are references to it in Plato.⁴⁷ It is also found in Clement of Alexandria, explicitly with reference to Paul: "But learn thou the more excellent way, which Paul shows for salvation. 'Love seeketh not her own,' (1 Cor 13.5) but is diffused on the brother. About him she is fluttered, about him she is soberly insane" (περὶ τοῦτον σωφρόνως μαίνεται, *peri touton sōphronōs mainetai*).⁴⁸

As for the epithet "new Benjamin," applied to Paul, it has quite a history. Verse 27 of Psalm 67 (in the Septuagint) reads: "There is Benjamin the younger in ecstasy" (ἐκστάσει, *ekstasei*). The original meaning had nothing to do with ecstasy, but the very presence of the word was sufficient to make of Benjamin an ecstatic. Paul, of course, belonged to the tribe of Benjamin. Consequently, it was entirely natural to see in the ecstatic Benjamin a figure of the ecstatic Paul, as Gregory himself explains: "By signs and symbols the prophecy foretells the distinctive features of the race of the disciples. The youngest among them is Benjamin, who is instructed in the mysteries by means of ecstasy [δι' ἐκστάσεως, *di' ekstaseōs*], even Paul, the divine apostle, from the seed of Abraham and the tribe of Benjamin."⁴⁹

Finally, it is Peter who completes the series of ecstatics referred to in Scripture:

> Think too of the blessed Peter in a drunken state of this sort, at once hungry and drunken. For before the corporeal food was set before him, when "he became hungry and wanted something to eat," the divine and sober drunkenness [ἡ θεία καὶ νηφάλιος μέθη, *hē theia kai nēphalios methē*] came upon him while his people "were preparing" a table, and it caused him to go out of himself [ἐξίσταται, *existatai*] and to see the evangelical "cloth . . . being let down upon the earth" from above "by its four corners." . . . Since then it is a drunkenness of this sort that is occasioned by the wine that the Lord sets before his companions—a drunkenness that causes the soul to move out of itself in the direction of things more divine—it is entirely right that his command is for those who have drawn near to him in virtue, and not those who have stood apart at a distance: "You who are close to me, eat! Drink and be drunken!"⁵⁰

⁴⁶See Lewy, *Sobria ebrietas*, 50f.
⁴⁷E.g., Plato, *Phaedrus* 244e.
⁴⁸Clement of Alexandria, *Who is the Rich Man That Shall Be Saved?* 38.1 (ANF 2:1257).
⁴⁹Gregory, *Inscr.* 2.14.212 (PG 44:577B; Heine, 190).
⁵⁰Gregory, *Cant.* 10 (PG 44:989D–992B; Norris, 325–27).

We recognize the allusions to the passage in Acts (10.10–16) where Peter's vision is reported, and which contains the very word *ekstasis*: "There came on him an ecstasy" (ἐγένετο ἐπ'αὐτὸν ἔκστασις, *egeneto ep' auton ekstasis*). I will return later to the characteristics of ecstatic inebriation as analyzed here. The fact remains that it is certainly a question of ecstasy in the strict sense. Furthermore, the various examples given above enable us from now on to determine without any possible ambiguity the meaning of the expression ἔκστασις πρὸς τὸ θειότερον (*ekstasis pros to theioteron*, ecstasy toward what is more divine), and thus its equivalents: πρὸς τὸ ἀΐδιον (*pros to aidion*, everlasting); πρὸς τὸ ἄμεινον (*pros to ameinon*, for the better). It is definitely a question of ecstasy in the modern sense of the word, something occurring suddenly, with suspension of the senses, and a vision. The language, then, is the same as that used by Origen, but the reality to which it refers is different. Without losing any of the theological richness that Origen had given the word *ekstasis*, Gregory restores to it its original mystical meaning.

Sober Drunkenness and Watchful Sleep

The expression "sober inebriation" (νηφάλιος μέθη, *nēphalios methē*) appears for the first time in Philo. It can be found in numerous texts.[51] It is part of a group of oxymorons used to describe the mystical life, such as "luminous darkness" (λαμπρὸς γνόφος, *lampros gnophos*), which we also come across in Gregory. Before Philo, the concept of an inebriation of the spirit is found in Dionysian circles, as well as in Plato. It had spread widely wherever Greek was used. It is found, for example, in the hermetic writings, from which trend Philo had borrowed it.[52]

But his use of the idea was original in two ways. First, he created the oxymoron by amalgamating two elements: the gnostic theme of divine intoxication (μέθη θεία, *methē theia*) and the idea of "soberness" (νῆψις, *nēpsis*), both of them in opposition to the gnostic concept of ignorance as a kind of intoxication. Second, he interpreted Jewish prophetic inspiration in terms of Hellenistic gnosis. Thus, for Philo, "sober inebriation" denotes true wisdom in contrast to pagan wisdom—particularly that associated with the Dionysian mysteries. "Inebriation" denotes union with God, which is a gift of the Spirit, whereas "soberness"

---

[51] See Philo, *On Drunkenness* 36.146f (Yonge, 219–20); *On Flight and Finding* 30.166 (Yonge, 336); *Allegorical Interpretations* 3.26.82 (Yonge, 59); *On the Life of Moses* 1.34.187 (Yonge, 476); and so forth.
[52] Lewy, *Sobria ebrietas*, 42.

Ecstatic Love

points to the spiritual character of this mystical condition, as contrasted with physical drunkenness.[53]

Other related themes include the vessel of wisdom (κρατὴρ τῆς σοφίας, *kratēr tēs sophias*) and the proclamation or invitation (κήρυγμα, *kērygma*). These gnostic elements had already been incorporated into Judaism prior to Philo. We referred earlier to the description of the Banquet of Wisdom found in Proverbs (9.2–5), and noted that the Greek text contains certain terms—*kratēr* and *kērygma*—that are not in the Hebrew. This occasions the following assessment from Lewy: "If we bear in mind that this passage is the oldest example of propaganda on behalf of Jewish wisdom, the hypothesis that the motif of the *kērygma* of the *kratēr*, the 'invitation to the *kratēr*,' was introduced to compete with that of the Greek mystery religions is in no way implausible."[54]

Thus Philo is merely continuing a procedure that first appeared at the time of the composition of the Septuagint. This is in an important point, for we find in Gregory the same themes grouped in the same way. He may have taken them directly from Philo, whom he had read. However, it is possible that there was an intermediary—namely, Origen.[55]

It is striking that the concept of "sober inebriation" does not appear in Clement of Alexandria. This is all the more remarkable since he depends heavily upon Philo. Yet, as Lewy says, it is precisely Philo's preeminent teaching on mysticism that he omits from his own writings. "His own gnosis is a matter of initiation (ἐποπτεία, *epopteia*) and contemplation (θεωρία, *theōria*); the ascent toward the highest mystical knowledge is accomplished without the help of mystical ecstasy."[56] Likewise Bigg: "There is not a trace [of ecstasy] in Clement. Though the father of all the mystics he is no mystic himself.... The instrument to which he looks for growth in knowledge is not trance, but the disciplined reason."[57] In fact, with Clement we have had two reasons for not finding any reference to the idea of mystical union. In the first place, in his day the fear of Montanism still persisted. Second, he is associated with the mysticism of illumination

---

[53]On all this, see Lewy, *Sobria ebrietas*, 3f.

[54]Ibid., 16.

[55]In Plotinus we read: "stripped of its wisdom [ἄφρων, *aphrōn*] in the intoxication [μεθυσθείς, *methystheis*] of the nectar, [the mind] comes to love; by this excess it is made simplex and is happy; and to be drunken is better for it than to be too staid [σεμνοτέρῳ, *semnoterō*] for these revels" (*Enneads* 6.7.35). Lewy shows that the image comes from the poetic language of the time in which "to become intoxicated on nectar" was a common expression. But it is to the Platonic use of the terms that we should return. Not only is there no oxymoron in the above extract from Plotinus, but inebriation is opposed to sobriety.

[56]Lewy, *Sobria ebrietas*, 111.

[57]Ch. Bigg, *The Christian Platonists of Alexandria* (Oxford: Clarendon Press, 1886), 98.

through contemplation, a trend that will be continued by Origen and Gregory of Nazianzus, but one that does not feature our oxymoron. This is why Gregory's originality as founder of mysticism properly speaking is so striking.

As mentioned, the theme of inebriation is found in Origen who, like Philo, contrasts it with ordinary drunkenness.[58] Yet the concept of "sober inebriation" is not found in so many words. The theme of inebriation, however, is definitely linked to the Banquet of Wisdom, which does point to a dependency upon Philo. At the same time, Origen enriches the theme by the use of new comparisons. In his *Commentary on John* 1.30,[59] he quotes Psalm 103.15: "Wine makes glad the heart of man." (Gregory quotes this too, using it to introduce the theme of ecstasy-as-joy.) In Origen's *Commentary on Matthew*,[60] it is Psalm 22.5 that is cited: "Thy cup is strong as the finest wine." Finally, Origen had commented before Gregory on those passages in the Song that refer to wine, interpreting them along the same lines.

We can now turn to Gregory's texts. The two most important passages are found in his *Homilies on the Song of Songs*. In the first, which we have already referred to, Gregory speaks of "the vine," whose wine, "rejoicing the heart, will one day fill up wisdom's chalice and, as warranted by 'the exalted summons,' be set before the fellowship of its drinkers, to be drawn at their pleasure for the sake of a good and sober drunkenness. What I am referring to is the drunkenness that occasions that self-transcendence by which people move out of the material sphere toward what is more divine."[61] Here, grouped together, are all the elements of this theme: sober inebriation (using Philo's exact phrase), the Banquet of Wisdom, the mixing bowl, and the invitation. The contrast between the two types of inebriation comes from Philo, whereas the allusion to Psalm 103 and the reference to the vine of the Song are from Origen.

The second passage from the Song connected with ecstasy also contains the phrase "a divine and sober inebriation." One of the adjectives is from Origen, the other from Philo. Gregory uses this phrase in conjunction with the following verse from the Song: "You who are close to me, eat! And you, my brethren, drink and be drunken!" (Song 5.1) and with Psalm 35.8: "They shall be drunk with the fatness of thy house, and thou shalt make them drink of the torrent of

---

[58]See p. 320 n. 37 above.
[59]See Origen, *Commentary on John* 1.31 (PG 14:77D; FC 80:74).
[60]Origen, *Commentary on Matthew* 85 (PG 13:1734B).
[61]Gregory, *Cant.* 5 (PG 44:873B; Norris, 169). The expression "sober inebriation" (νηφάλιος μέθη, *nēphalios methē*) also appears in *Cant.* 12 (PG 44:1032B; Norris, 383).

Ecstatic Love

thy delight." These combinations are new. He takes over the comparison with the eucharistic wine that was already in Origen: "For to one who has known the mystical utterances of the Gospel, no difference will be discerned between the words of this text and the mystagogical instruction given to the disciples there."[62]

However, on this last point, we can already make an observation that will enable us to situate Gregory in relation to Origen. For, in fact, the latter understands the eucharistic wine primarily in a spiritual sense, as the communication of the Logos to the soul. He makes no connection between sacramental reality and ecstasy. And this for two reasons: he deliberately overlooks sacramental realism, and does not acknowledge the fact of ecstasy. Gregory is opposed to him on both these points. Thus, despite the similar vocabulary we are in the presence of two quite different realities. For Origen, sober inebriation is a communication of gnosis by the Logos, a communication that will occur fully in eternity (to which he links the theme of inebriation)[63] and which, beginning here below, is a permanent state of deification. This is the theological ecstasy of which we have already spoken. Gregory's position is intentionally much more mystical.[64] For him, the "appropriate time" (τότε, *tote*), as we have seen, does not indicate eternity, but the present life. "Sober inebriation" is another name for psychological "ecstasy."

One last interesting feature of this text is the contrast Gregory creates between the fact that, in his ecstasy at Joppa, Peter was very hungry (πρόσπεινον, *prospeinon*) and at the same time drunk (μεθύοντα, *methyonta*). Thus, it seems clear that this inebriation is caused by something other than wine. And Gregory can thus conclude that it is a "sober inebriation." But Lewy correctly observes that the point Gregory highlights "is the contrast between this inebriation and that caused by wine—and thus that 'sober' does not denote a spiritual or bodily asceticism that serves to prepare the divine union, but simply a secular fast."[65]

There remains one last important text to consider, even though the word *ekstasis* is not found in it—the beginning of the *Sermon on the Ascension*.

---

[62]Gregory, *Cant.* 10 (PG 44:989B; Norris, 325).

[63]See Origen, *Homilies on Leviticus* 7.1 (PG 12:475B–477A). Translation from *Origen: Homilies on Leviticus 1–16*, trans. G. W. Barkley, Fathers of the Church 83 (Washington, DC: The Catholic University of America Press, 1990), 129–33.

[64]"When this delectation is ardent or of long duration, it produces a kind of spiritual intoxication that at times resembles a partial slumber" (Poulain, *Des grâces d'oraison*, 150 [*Interior Prayer*, 143]). Here we have the very order followed by Gregory: the spiritual senses, inebriation, and sleep.

[65]Lewy, *Sobria ebrietas*, 135.

Gregory retraces the stages of Christian initiation in the form of a commentary on Psalm 22. The "green pasture" represents catechesis; the "shadow of death," Baptism, which is "being buried with Christ"; the "prepared table" represents the Eucharist; and "the anointing with oil," confirmation. He continues as follows: "[The Spirit] offers wine to gladden the heart with that sober inebriation for the soul, situating our thoughts in eternity instead of temporal concerns.... [Such inebriation] extends our residence in God's house to length of days."[66]

This passage is one of the most characteristic. In it we find the customary groupings: "sober inebriation" is connected, as in Origen, to the eucharistic wine, the wine that makes glad the heart of man (Ps 103.15), the "thy cup is strong as the finest wine" (Ps 22.5). Inebriation, caused by the eucharistic wine, becomes the term of initiation. As Lewy correctly states, "According to Gregory, with the reception of the Holy Sacrament, eternal life begins. Its full blessedness awaits us in eternity but the savor of the eucharistic elements here below, in the moment of the ecstasy of communion, is a foretaste of it."[67] The concept of a transport to the divine world certainly comes from Origen, but not that of a momentary ecstasy nor the realistic character of the Eucharist.

At the end of the tenth and the beginning of the eleventh of his *Homilies on the Song of Songs*, after describing "sober inebriation," Gregory begins to describe the analogous concept of sleep. The two themes are linked explicitly: "Sleep naturally succeeds drunkenness" (ἀκολούθως διαδέχεται τὴν μέθην ὁ ὕπνος, *akolouthōs diadechetai tēn methēn ho hypnos*).[68] Thus, it is still a matter of ecstasy. This will not surprise us, if we recall how in Gregory's profane use of the terms "sleep" and "ecstasy" they were closely linked. But what is especially interesting here is that we see Gregory create a new oxymoron on the model of "sober inebriation"—namely, "watchful sleep." After examining the sources of this new theme, we shall consider the passages in which it occurs. They will provide us with new elements for our study of ecstasy.

There is a classical theme that compares the contrast between life according to the spirit and life according to the flesh to the difference between being awake and being asleep. Gregory develops this theme in an important passage at the beginning of the eleventh homily:

---

[66] *Ascens.* (PG 46:692B–C; McCambley, 3).
[67] Lewy, *Sobria ebrietas*, 136.
[68] *Cant.* 10 (PG 44:992C; Norris, 327).

One, and one of the weightiest, of the Lord's admonitions, by which the mind of the Word's disciples shakes off the materiality of their nature like so much dust [χοῦν, *choun*] and is elevated to a desire for things transcendent [ὑπερκειμένων, *hyperkeimenōn*], is this: that those who look toward the life above must be stronger than sleep [κρείττους τοῦ ὕπνου, *kreittous tou hypnou*] and ever wakeful in mind [ἐγρηγορέναι τῇ διανοίᾳ, *egrēgorenai tē dianoia*], fighting off the eyes' drowsiness as if it were some cheater of souls or plotter against the truth, chasing away somnolence [νυσταγμόν, *nystagmon*] from the eyes like a seducer of souls and the enemy of truth.

I refer to that drowsiness and that sleep that manufacture, for those who are sunk deep in life's deceits, dream images [τὰ ὀνειρώδη φαντάσματα, *ta oneirōdē phantasmata*] of high offices, treasures, lordships, self-conceit, bewitching pleasures [γοητεία τῶν ἡδονῶν, *goēteia tōn hēdonōn*], of lust for fame and luxury and vanity—and all things whatsoever that people without awareness chase after vainly in this life at the behest of some fantasy. These things, which flow away with time as it passes, have their being in seeming. They are not what they are esteemed to be, nor do they continue permanently to be thus esteemed....

In order, then, that our mind may be free of such fantasies, he orders that this heavy sleep [τὸν βαρὺν ὕπνον, *ton baryn hypnon*] be banished from the eyes of the soul, lest devotion to what is unreal cause us to bid farewell to true and substantive realities.... That is why he enjoins upon us the notion of wakefulness [ἐγρήγορσις, *egrēgorsis*] when he says, "Let your loins be girded and your lamps burning" (Lk 12.35).... It is apparent in any case what is conveyed by these enigmatic statements—namely, that the person who is girt about with self-control lives by the light of a purified conscience, with her life illumined by the lamp of candor; and when by these means truth becomes apparent, the soul of such a person abides untouched by sleep or by any deception [ἄυπνος καὶ ἀνεξαπάτητος, *aüpnos kai anexapatētos*] and does not dally with any of these misleading dreams [ἀτελῶν ὀνείρων, *atelōn oneirōn*].[69]

An initial reading of this text immediately shows that it relates not to the mystical life, but the illuminative life whose aim, as we have seen, is to make one understand the nothingness of all that is not God. We have already come across this theme of the illusion of the world of sense, and of the magic it exercises on

[69] *Cant.* 11 (PG 44:996A–D; Norris, 333–35).

the soul. In reality, it has no more consistency than a dream (ὄναρ, *onar*), for it exists only in our imagination. We should disentangle ourselves from this, dispel this sleep, and wake up (ἐγρηγορέναι, *egrēgorenai*) to the reality that is God.[70]

Here we touch on Gregory's method of composition. It is important to note this in passing, for it may well help us to avoid errors of interpretation. To a logically constructed framework are added vivid, dramatic rhetorical descriptions, the ἐκφράσεις (*ekphraseis*). This particular technique, which is that of the Second Sophistic, has been studied by Méridier.[71] Examples can be found in the works of St Augustine.[72] Here we clearly see how the technique is applied. The image of sleep (ὕπνος, *hypnos*), used first with reference to mystical sleep, leads to another theme. Such sequences sparked off by *verbal* association are common in Gregory.[73] They give his work its character, a musical imaginativeness presiding over the concatenation of incidental, secondary themes, without affecting the logical order of the essential themes.

The same theme appears in another passage from the *Homilies on the Song of Songs*. It deals with cinnamon, of which it is said that "if it is placed in the mouth of someone who is asleep, the sleeper is in no wise hindered from answering people who put questions but even in slumber remains present and returns sober [νηφαλέους, *nēphaleous*] and articulate answers to all queries." Gregory leaves aside the question of the scientific accuracy of this, pointing out that such concerns do not prevent one from drawing a spiritual lesson from the saying.

> For there is a kind of "cinnamon" to be found in the souls of those who have been trained and gifted with reflection. Suppose that a person who is either seething with desire or burning up with anger quenches the passions by articulate thinking. Or suppose that someone who exists in the sleep of this life [ἐν τῷ ὕπνῳ τοῦ βίου, *en tō hypnō tou biou*] but possesses in his mouth

---

[70]On the contrast between sleep as sin and being awake as virtue, cf. Gregory, *Contra fornicarios oratio* (*Fornic.*) (PG 46:493D–496A). English translation: *On Fornication*, R. McCambly, trans. http://www.lectio-divina.org/index.php/reflections/reflections-on-the-writings-of-gregory-of-nyssa, pp. 8–9. On the theme of the external life as a mirage, see Newman, according to Jean Guitton in his *Newman et Renan* (Paris: Aubier, 1938), 236: "Life is like a dream, as removed and different from our real existence as immortal spirits as a dream is from the state of being awake."

[71]See Méridier, *L'Influence de la Seconde Sophistique*, 139f.

[72]See Marrou, *Saint Augustin et la fin de la culture antique*, 375f.

[73]For example, the theme of divine fragrance is interpreted first in the sense that "the marvels discerned in each name and thought provide matter for our theological naming" (*Cant.* 1; PG 44:781D; Norris, 41)—which relates to symbolic theology—and then in the sense of the presence of God in the soul, as perceived by the virtues. This is part of mystical theology.

the sober "cinnamon" of articulate thought evinces, in a manner similar to that of the sleepless and wakeful [ἀύπνοις καὶ ἐγρηγορόσιν, aüpnois kai egrēgorosin] angels, unerring [ἀπλανῆ, aplanē] and sure understanding of the sense of what is said and so imitates, by the truth of what he says, the sleepless [ἄυπνον, aüpnon] nature of the angels, whom no force of the imagination alienates [ἐξίστησιν, existēsin] from truth—such a person might well be said to produce cinnamon through the mouth ... and to be purified by articulate thought from all the deceptive imaginings and confusions of this life.[74]

Here we encounter again several expressions seen in the preceding passages. The comparison with the angels—the "watchers" (ἐγρήγοροι, egrēgoroi) of Daniel and Enoch—is especially interesting. It had already been used by in Clement of Alexandria.[75] The physical nature of the angels, shielded as they are from the dreams of sleep and always awake and in the truth, is proposed as an example to man, so that he may turn away from the mirages of sin and the world so as to be anchored in God. The continuous vigilance of the angels symbolizes the escape from biological existence, subject as it is to the rhythm of sleep and waking, and which the soul should realize on the moral plane. Let us also note that the term ἀπλανής (aplanēs), combined with ἐγρηγορέναι (egrēgorenai), recalls that section of *The Apostolic Constitutions* where we come across the expressions "a mind watchful" (νοῦς ἐγρήγορος, nous egrēgoros) and "unerring knowledge" (γνῶσις ἀπλανής, gnōsis aplanēs) as indicating characteristics of perfection.[76]

Running through these passages is a theme that is found in all philosophic literature that has an a-cosmic tendency: the "mirage" of the outer world. It is a feature, for example, of Buddhist thought. More interestingly for us, it appears in Plotinus. Plato had already presented the sensible world as a "dream" and as "magic," but he makes no contrast between this dream and the spiritual life as watchfulness. This, however, is precisely what we find in Plotinus. The soul that wishes to free itself from the passions should remove the imaginings to which we lay ourselves open, in a way similar to someone "who wishes to throw off the shapes presented in dreams [τὰς τῶν ὀνειράτων φαντασίας, tas tōn oneiratōn phantasias], and to this end recalls to waking condition [ἐν ἐγρηγόρσει ποιοῖ, en egrēgorsei poioi] the mind that is breeding them.... Purification is the [soul's]

---

[74]*Cant.* 9 (PG 44:973A–C; Norris, 301–303).
[75]See Clement of Alexandria, *The Instructor* 2.9.
[76]*The Apostolic Constitutions* 7.45 (ANF 7:1047).

awakening from the baseless visions [ἔγερσις ἐκ τῶν ἀτόπων εἰδώλων, *egersis ek tōn atopōn eidolon*] which beset it."[77] The meaning of "awakening" is shown better still in the following passage: "If then this Act never came to be but is eternal—a waking without an awakener, an eternal wakening [ἐγρήγορσις, *egrēgorsis*] and a supra-Intellection—He is as He waked Himself to be. This awakening is before being [ἐπέκεινα τῆς οὐσίας, *epekeina tēs ousias*] and before mind [καὶ νοῦ, *kai nou*]."[78] Bréhier notes that this passage is full of expressions borrowed from religious language. Moreover, *egrēgorsis* is not itself a Platonic expression. What we have, then, is a concept of "watchfulness" borrowed from religious language and which, moreover, seems to denote an ecstatic state, a going out of nature. We are not far removed from Gregory's text.[79]

In fact, there exists a religious theme of "wakefulness" or "watchfulness." It is connected to the liturgical practice of "vigils." Such practices existed in the Hellenistic religious world and we know from Philo that the Jewish Therapeutae of Alexandria, for example, stayed up all night and only went their separate ways after a common meal, taken before the rising of the sun.[80] Furthermore, we are familiar with the Christian practice of holding vigils. These had assumed a symbolic meaning, denoting an awakening to the spiritual life. As the canticle reported by Paul (Eph 5.14) testifies:

> Ἔγειρε ὁ καθεύδων
> καὶ ἐπιφαύσει σοι ὁ Χριστός
> (*Egeire ho katheudōn
> kai epiphausei soi ho Christos*).
> Rise up, O sleeper,
> And Christ will shine on you.

Here we see the image of an awakening linked to that of an illumination. We are at the same time in the illuminative life, on the mystical level, and in the baptismal life on the sacramental level—the Eucharist and inebriation representing the higher stage.[81]

[77]Plotinus, *Enneads* 3.6.5.
[78]Ibid., 6.8.16.
[79]See Philo, *On Dreams* 2.23.160 (Yonge, 399).
[80]See Philo, *On the Contemplative Life* 11.89 (Yonge, 706).
[81]Cf. *The Apostolic Constitutions* 7.45 (ANF 7:477), "a mind watchful" (νοῦς ἐγρήγορος, *nous egrēgoros*). Clement of Alexandria, in *The Instructor* (2.9), says that those who keep vigil "make themselves like the angels, whom we call 'watchers.'" He also connects the practice to Baptism (enlightenment)—"he who has the light watches"; "he that is illuminated is awake toward God"—and with the

This theme of wakefulness as an ascetic practice is closely linked to soberness; abstinence from sleep and food are, in fact, two ascetic practices that are essential. They are mentioned in Philo[82] and also in the New Testament: "Let us watch and be sober" (1 Thess 5.6); "Be sober, be vigilant" (1 Pet 5.8). Soberness is, of course, one of the composing elements of the concept of sober inebriation, and in Philo inebriation is referred to in texts where it is simultaneously also a question of watchfulness and fasting, as the spiritual state that results from these practices. Such is the context of ideas within which Gregory's concept of "watchful sleep" is formed, based on Philo's notion of "sober inebriation."

Although the understanding of the spiritual life as "wakefulness" or "watchfulness" is a common theme in Hellenistic religious literature, Gregory's originality lies in explaining that this "wakefulness" is, in fact, itself a "sleep." That is, in its highest state, it expresses itself as a negation. As always, it is the apophatic aspect of the mystical life on which he insists. To refer to this ineffable experience, he typically has recourse to a series of oxymorons. Some are borrowed: "sober inebriation" and "luminous darkness" from Philo, the life/death from Paul. Others he himself created, as we have just seen with the example of "wakeful sleep" (ἐγρήγορσις ὕπνος, *egrēgorsis hypnos*). In *The Life of Moses* there is another example that we shall shortly consider: "immobile movement," where the opposites στάσις (*stasis*) and κίνησις (*kinēsis*) are brought together. This practice was fostered by the contemporary literary taste for oxymorons, but in Gregory's case these literary procedures are used to express experiences that are specifically spiritual.

The key text here is the one that ends the tenth of the *Homilies on the Song of Songs*: "Sleep naturally succeeds drunkenness. . . . This sleep, though, is a stranger and alien to the ordinary course of nature. For in the usual sort of sleep, the sleeper is not awake, nor does one who is waking sleep; rather, sleep and wakefulness both come to an end in each other. . . . In this text, however, one discerns in the Bride a novel and surprising [παράδοξος, *paradoxos*] mixture and coalescence of these opposites. For 'I sleep,' it says, 'but my heart lies awake.'"[83]

---

mystical life: "such dreams as are true . . . are the thoughts of a sober soul, undistracted . . . by the affections of the body" (ANF 2:552–53). See also Lewy, *Sobria ebrietas*, 34, and I. Schuster, *The Sacramentary (Liber Sacramentorum): Historical & Liturgical Notes on the Roman Missal* (London: Burns, Oates & Washbourne, 1924), 7.27.

[82]See Philo, *On Sobriety* [=*On the Prayers and Curses Uttered by Noah When He Became Sober*] 1.4–5 (Yonge, 227).

[83]Gregory, *Cant*. 10 (PG 44:992C; Norris, 327). See also M. de Gandillac, *La philosophie de Nicolas de Cues* (Paris: Aubier, 1941), 265–313.

From the beginning, Gregory distinguishes this sleep from ordinary sleep. But what is most important is its "paradoxical" character. Gregory sometimes uses the word παράδοξος (*paradoxos*). It expresses not only a surprising thing by accident, which one is not accustomed to come across, but one that is absolutely contrary to every possible experience, and that therefore places us on the supernatural level. Such paradoxes are expressed through a "coincidence of opposites," a contradiction in terms that presupposes that one has transcended the world of ordinary experience. It is important to note the appearance here of these paradoxical formulas to refer to the supernatural. It is well known how they will later spread from Pseudo-Dionysius to Nicholas of Cusa, from "luminous darkness" to *docta ignorantia*, "learned ignorance," the very title of Nicholas' definitive study of it.[84]

Let us return to *The Life of Moses* and the other example of a *coincidentia contrariorum*. "In another Scriptural passage the progress is a standing still, for it says, 'You must stand on the rock.' This is the most marvelous thing of all: how the same thing is both a standing still and a moving [στάσις καὶ κίνησις, *stasis kai kinesis*]. For he who ascends certainly does not stand still, and he who stands still does not move upwards. But here the ascent takes place by means of the standing."[85] The procedure is the same as for the coincidence of sleep and wakefulness. I admit that a certain self-satisfaction is involved, when a former rhetorician takes pleasure in emphasizing these examples of paradox. But by doing so he at least succeeds in better demonstrating their reality. Méridier's error is to have seen in these oxymorons mere literary techniques.[86]

Let us continue studying our text.

> Now what sense are we to make of this? Sleep is an image of death, for in death every perceptive activity of bodies is dissolved. There is no activity of seeing, or of hearing, or of smelling or tasting, or of touching in the season of sleep. What is more, it relaxes the body's tension and brings about forgetfulness of the person's thoughts. It puts fear to sleep and tames aggression and relaxes the intensity of bitterness and effects an insensibility to all evils, as long as it prevails over the body. Hence from our text we learn this: that

---

[84]See M. de Gandillac, *La philosophie de Nicolas de Cues*, 265–313.
[85]Gregory, *Vit. Moys.* 2.243 (PG 44:405C; Malherbe, 117).
[86]See Méridier, *L'Influence de la Seconde Sophistique*, 278–79. [Daniélou is himself something of a "former rhetorician." He gained his "aggrégation de grammaire" (Latin and Greek) at the relatively young age of 22 in 1927, two years before entering a Jesuit novitiate. The present book is his doctoral thesis (completed in 1943 and presented at the Sorbonne in 1944).—*Trans.*]

Ecstatic Love

she who makes the boast that "I sleep but my heart lies awake" has risen higher than herself.

For the truth is that insofar as only the intellect in itself is alive, without any distraction from the organs of sense perception, the bodily nature becomes inactive, as in slumber or profound sleep, and it is truly possible to say that through disuse [δι' ἀπραξίας, *di' apraxias*] the capacity to see all those shameful objects that regularly trouble childish eyes is put to sleep [κοιμᾶται, *kōimatai*]. ... When (the images and impressions of the other senses) are as it were bound in sleep by disuse, then the working of the heart is pure, and its discourse is focused on what is above it, untroubled and unaccompanied by the noise that stems from the stirrings of sense perception. ... Hence it is that the soul, when its only delight lies in contemplation of what is real, wakens to none of the pleasurable stirrings of the senses. It has put to sleep every corporeal notion, and wakened by the divine [διὰ θείας ἐγρηγόρσεως, *dia theias egrēgorseōs*], it embraces the revelation of God by pure and naked [γυμνῇ, *gymnē*] thought.

And may we too be judged worthy of this revelation, having accomplished by means of the aforesaid sleep the wakening of our soul in Jesus Christ our Lord.[87]

This is one of the most important texts for a description of the mystical life. In fact, it describes a mental contemplation (μόνος βιοτεύει, *monos bioteuei*) that includes the cessation (ἀπραξία *apraxia*) of activity of the bodily senses. Now, this is precisely what constitutes ecstasy. Here, one may recall Philo's definition of the third type of ecstasy: "Here calling the quietness and tranquillity [ἡσυχία, *hēsychia*] of mind a trance; for the slumber of the mind is the awaking of the outward sense [ὕπνος νοῦ ἐγρήγορσις αἰσθήσεως, *hypnos nou egrēgorsis aisthēseōs*]: and, again, the awaking of the intellect is the reducing of the outward senses to a state of inactivity."[88] Ecstasy is conceived of as a state of "quietude" (*hēsychia*) that goes so far as the inactivity (*apraxia*) of the senses. It is this that is denoted by the image of sleep.

The bringing together of sleep and death is an idea that comes from secular philosophy, as Gregory says elsewhere: "Hence some non-Christian philosophers have called sleep 'the brother of death.'"[89] In fact, we find this idea in

---

[87] *Cant.* 10 (PG 44:993A–C; Norris, 327–29).
[88] Philo, *Who is the Heir of Divine Things* 51.257 (Yonge, 298).
[89] *Sanct. Pasch.* 15 (PG 46:673A; PPS 64:103).

Cicero, and this is not the only point of convergence between the two authors.[90] But here this expression is of interest to us in the way it emphasizes the suspension of the activity of the senses. It is this element that Gregory emphasizes. It is a question, undoubtedly, of *egrēgorsis*, but of a wakefulness that goes so far as to suspend the activity of the senses. It then allows the mind to be totally absorbed in God. And therein resides this purity, this denuding (γυμνή, *gymnē*) that Gregory explains in terms that recall Plotinus. The bareness of the mind is the exercise of its activity when it is separated through ecstasy from any dealings with the body. It is then recollected in God (θεωρεῖ τὰ ἄνω, *theōrei ta anō*; lit. it beholds the things above). It enjoys complete rest (μένει, *menei*). These are the features that fit any prayer of quietness. But the emphasis put on *hypnos*, on *apraxia* adds the element of ecstasy to it. The divine joy that we have seen appear at the summit of the mysticism of the mirror becomes so powerful that it tears away the soul from the life of the body: inebriation marks this tearing away; sleep marks rather the state of rest that follows. Moreover, Gregory notes that sleep follows inebriation, not as a new state, but as a second aspect of the same state.

It is interesting to see that we find an analogous description with other mystics. Thus St Birgitta writes: "O my sweetest God, it is truly marvelous that you work with me; for when it pleases you, you bring my body into a spiritual sleep, and then you excite and raise up my soul to see and hear and feel spiritual things."[91] But even more precious, because it is linked to the origins of Christianity, is the testimony of the acts of the martyrdom of Saint Perpetua: "She [was] as if aroused from sleep, so deeply had she been in the Spirit and in an ecstasy."[92]

The Wound of Love

The various symbols of ecstatic love that we have considered so far—the going out of oneself, inebriation, sleep—all have as a common feature that they convey the "irrational" character of the higher forms of the spiritual life, in which the soul is wrested outside itself by the power of the divine attraction. In addition, they each express a particular aspect of these states. Ecstasy signifies the general

---

[90]See von Ivánka, "Die Quelle von Ciceros," 12. The idea goes back to Homer (*Iliad* 16.672). See also Methodius of Olympus, *On the Resurrection*, 1.52 (Bonwetsch, 309).

[91]Birgitta, *The Prophecies and Revelations of Saint Bridget [Birgitta] of Sweden* [4.77] (Altenmünster: Jazzybee Verlag, 2016), 416.

[92]*The Passion of the Holy Martyrs Perpetua and Felicity* 6.3 (ANF 3:705).

Ecstatic Love

idea of a going out of the self, inebriation emphasizes the superabundance of the joy that tears the soul away from itself, and sleep is a figure of its indifference to the external world, an indifference that can even result in an effective suspension of the senses. The image of a wound adds to this portrayal. On the one hand, it contains the same irrational element as the other images. In fact, it is related to *eros*, which for Gregory, as we said earlier, represents the highest form of divine love. Furthermore, it is linked to the supreme purifications of the soul, as it longs to cast off the last veils that separate it from God.

The applying of this image of a wound to the spiritual life is part of the wider transfer of images of secular love to divine love, which we saw taking place starting with Origen. Eros, Cupid, his quiver, his arrows, and the incurable wounds of secular love have all been sung by the poets. Even so, the Song of Songs (4.9) long ago enabled this symbol to be applied to the love of the soul for God. Soon Pseudo-Macarius would praise those who are "wounded by heavenly love."[93] In general, then, it is the irrational, passive character of the love of God that is denoted by this symbol. Unlike all the others we have looked at, in its mystical use it is related to a specifically Christian tradition.

It is a theme that appears repeatedly in Gregory's *Homilies on the Song of Songs*. It predominates in homilies twelve and thirteen, and it is these texts in particular that we shall study. It also appears, however, in an earlier passage that is worth noting, though one in which the image of the arrow serves to express a concept that is somewhat different. It marks less the soul going out of itself than the entry, the penetration, of the Word into the heart.[94] As such, it ought theoretically to have been discussed in the preceding chapter. Nonetheless, the commonality of the image allows us to cite it here. Once again, we shall see how much the twin ideas of "entering" and "leaving," whose union constitutes the mystical life, are associated in Gregory.

Gregory is commenting on the following verse: "I have been wounded by love" (Song 2.5).

---

[93] Pseudo-Macarius, *Homily* 5.6 (PG 34:501A), cited in Horn, "L'amour divin," 387. Translation from *Pseudo-Macarius: The Fifty Spiritual Homilies and The Great Letter*, George A. Maloney, trans., Classics of Western Spirituality (Mahwah, NJ: Paulist Press, 1992), 66. [The connection between Gregory of Nyssa and the Macarian corpus has long been debated, especially given the textual parallels between Gregory's *De instituto christiano* and the Macarian *Great Letter*: one clearly relies upon the other. See pp. xxvi–xxvii n. 43.—*Ed.*]

[94] In Origen, too, the arrow is an image of the Word. See *Commentary on John* 1.36 (PG 14:86B; FC 80:79).

> By these words she signifies the arrow that lies deep in her heart. But the archer who discharges the arrow is love (ἀγάπη, *agapē*). From Holy Scripture, however, we have learned that God is love (cf. 1 Jn 4.18,16), and he discharges his own chosen arrow (cf. Is 49.2)—the Only Begotten God—at those who are being saved, having smeared over the triple point of the barb with the Spirit of life (the barb is faith), so that, in the person in whom it is planted, it may introduce the archer together with the arrow, as the Lord says: "I and my Father will come and make our dwelling with him" (Jn 14.23). See, then, the soul that has been exalted through the divine ascents sees in herself the sweet arrow of love by which she is wounded and makes boast of such a blow by saying, "I have been wounded by love."
>
> O sweet and happy wound, by which life slips through to the inward parts . . . !⁹⁵

This text should be added to the list of those dealing with the indwelling of the Word in the soul. We should note that it is faith that opens the soul to divine love, and also that the soul sees the arrow (the Word) in itself. This further supports the view that mystical experience is essentially an awareness of the Word present in the soul through faith.⁹⁶

In the following passage, we find the same symbolism of the arrow as a figure of the "entry" of the Word into the soul, but with the related idea of suffering:

> That the wounds of love are things to be cherished we learn already from Proverbs, which says: "The wounds of a friend are desirable, but even the kisses of a foe are evils" (Prov 27.6). As to who the friend is whose wounds are more generous than the kisses of a foe, the answer is plain to anyone who is not ignorant of the mysteries of salvation. "Friend" signifies that true and unshakable One who has never stopped loving us even when we have been his foes. "Foe" indicates that savage and unreliable one who brings down to death those who have done him no ill. To the first humans, the prohibition of evil expressed in the commandment was a "wound" (for separation from what gives pleasure is reckoned to be a wound), while "kiss" meant incitement to what gives pleasure and appears good. Experience, however, has shown that from a friend things reckoned as wounds are more profitable and more to be desired than kisses from an enemy. . . .

---

⁹⁵*Cant.* 4 (PG 44:852A–B; Norris, 141).
⁹⁶See *Cant.* 13 (PG 44:1044B; Norris, 397–99): "It is possible . . . to see the pure Bridegroom, love's archer, and for each person's soul to say to him 'I am wounded by love.'"

Ecstatic Love

> The Bride, having returned her lover's love, discloses the arrow of love deeply lodged within her, that is to say, her fellowship with the Deity itself.
>
> For love is God, as we have said, come to inhabit the heart by the agency of the arrow of faith. And if it is right to set a name to this arrow, we repeat what we have learned from Paul, that this arrow is "faith working through love" (Gal 5.6).[97]

But with these passages we still are on the level of God's dwelling in the soul, of the divine life in us. However, the eleventh homily demonstrates a new aspect of the theme of the wound, one that corresponds to the level we are discussing now. It is a question of the passive purifications the soul must undergo in order to be united more intimately with God and to arrive at the highest forms of mystical union. These purifications are the "blessed wounds" that the soul ardently desires—regardless of the suffering it may feel—for they hasten the moment when it will be able to enjoy a more intimate union with God. These are among the features described most often by mystics, from John of the Cross to Catherine of Genoa. What is remarkable is that we should find them already discussed in our author, and with an experiential emphasis that leaves no room for doubting the mystical reality they embrace.

Following a procedure we have already met with in Gregory, he relates these to the general theme of which they are the supreme aspect: the mystery of death with Christ, which is the precondition for resurrection with him. We have already encountered this mystery twice. First, in its sacramental form, in our study of the material fact of our Baptism, death, and resurrection with Christ. We next met it in its ascetic form, in our study of voluntary mortification. Now we find it for a third time, in its mystical form, as passive purification. Thus what we have here is a point of view around which the entire spiritual life can be systemized—and which is specifically Pauline, which once again proves Gregory's dependency upon him. The sacramental life, the ascetic life, and the mystical life are seen to be unified, to be three aspects of the one mystery of death and resurrection with Christ.

At the beginning of the twelfth homily, commenting on the symbol of myrrh, Gregory traces this mystery in connection with the central theme of his mysticism, the indwelling of the Word in the soul:

---

[97] Ibid. (PG 44:1044B–D; Norris, 399). We may note the exegesis of the Pauline formula by Gregory. "Working" (ἐνεργουμένη, *energoumenē*) has a passive meaning. Charity is the love of God for man that in return provokes man's love ("faith") for God. There is no question of "works."

> "I rose up to open to my kinsman; my hands dropped myrrh, my fingers choice myrrh" (Song 5.5). Now there is only one way in which the living Word comes within us: I refer to the pure and incorporeal Bridegroom who makes the soul dwell with him by means of incorruptibility and holiness—namely, if one removes the veil of the flesh (cf. 2 Cor 3.16) by mortifying one's earthly members (cf. Col 3.5) and in this way opens to the Word the door through which he makes the soul his home. This is apparent not only from the divine teachings of the apostle but also from what the Bride says in this text. For, says she, "I rose up to open to my kinsman by making my hands founts of myrrh from which its spicy scent pours forth and by showing my fingers to be full of myrrh." For by these words she states the way in which the door is opened to the Bridegroom: "I have risen up by being buried with him through baptism into his death" (cf. Rom 6.4), for the resurrection does not become actual if it is not preceded by voluntary death.[98]

Here we have the themes of Baptism and voluntary mortification. We note, too, the image of the veil that protected the holy of holies in the temple and which, in the Letter to the Hebrews, is applied to the flesh of Christ. Here it denotes the flesh that prohibits entry into the sanctuary of the soul and thus the indwelling there of the Word. It is also linked to the parallel theme of the soul's access to the holy of holies, into which it should enter in search of the Word. These are all images of the mystical life and thus we see that asceticism here is of the order of mystical purification. This is more apparent in the following passage, where the theme of myrrh is taken up again:

> [Myrrh] is disdain for the material life, which appears when everything that people work for in this life becomes inoperative and dead on account of their desire for transcendent goods.
>
> Now Paul pours just such myrrh as this . . . into the ears of the holy virgin named Thecla . . . and she treated her outward self to death by quenching her every fleshly thought and desire. Once she had received the good teaching, her youthful folly was dead, as was her outward show of beauty, and dead were all her corporeal senses. All that was alive in her was the word, through which the whole cosmos died to her even as she, the virgin, died to the cosmos.[99]

---

[98] *Cant.* 12 (PG 44:1016 C–D; Norris, 363).
[99] *Cant.* 14 (PG 44:1068A; Norris, 429).

Ecstatic Love

The rest of the passage also alludes to Baptism, thereby maintaining the connection between these various themes. But the passages already quoted present only the first aspects of the mystery of death and resurrection. It is another set of symbols that enables us to discuss passive purifications per se—the veil that is removed and the blows that wound the soul. "The guards struck me, they wounded me, they took away my coat" (Song 5.6–7):

> How, then, does one who has been stripped of all covering still wear the veil that the guards now remove from her? But is it not the case that these words show how much progress upward she has made from that previous state? She who has removed that old tunic and been freed of all covering becomes so much purer than herself that by comparison with the purity that now becomes hers she does not seem to have taken off that clothing but again, even after that former stripping finds something on her to be taken off. Thus the ascent to the Divine shows that what she wears about her is coarser and heavier than what is forever being discovered.[100]

It can be seen that the spiritual life appears to consist of a series of divestings, and thus that here we have reached a new degree of purification.

What, then, is the significance of the wounds inflicted by the beatings that are linked to this tearing away of the veil? What is the meaning of the rod? Gregory mentions certain passages of Scripture in which beatings are understood in a positive sense.[101] He refers in particular to Psalm 22 (LXX), which we have already encountered and which is one of the texts always cited in connection with ecstasy, on account of the reference in it (v.5, LXX) to "thy cup is strong as the finest wine" (μεθύσκον, *methyskon*; lit. makes me drunk). In verse four, reference is made to the Lord's "rod and staff ... [which] have comforted [παρεκάλεσαν, *parekalesan*] me." "That is why," comments Gregory, "David said that the effect of a rod of this sort is not affliction but comfort."[102] And he links this wound to the other effects enumerated by the Psalm—"the oil that anoints his head and the unmixed wine in the cup, which works a sober drunkenness."[103]

We have already seen that this rod that consoles is connected to the Holy Spirit. Moreover, the fact of there being a wound indicates that it is not a matter

---

[100] *Cant.* 12 (PG 44:1029B; Norris, 381).
[101] See Prov, 23.13; Deut, 32.39.
[102] *Cant.* 12 (PG 44:1032B; Norris, 383).
[103] Ibid.

of a mere superficial touch, but that the soul is affected to the very depths by the supreme purifying action of the Spirit:

> And if she says that this came to her by way of a wound, what her words refer to is the mark left in the depth of her being by the divine rod; for it was not superficially that she felt the operation of the spiritual rod, so as to be ignorant of that the place where it struck her. No, the blow of which the Bride boasts marked her because of the wound it caused.
>
> And the meaning is this: that divine rod and comforting staff, by which a blow works healing, is the Spirit. . . . For Paul too, who bore the mark of such blows, similarly exulted in wounds of this sort when he said: "I bear on my body the marks of Christ" (Gal 6.17).[104]

The comparison with St Paul and the interpretation of the marks he bore as being spiritual purifications that inwardly conform the soul to Christ crucified is altogether remarkable. Moreover, this text is very interesting for the history of mysticism. The purification brought about by the Spirit is both painful and glorious,[105] the wounds are ones in which the Bride glorifies and which make new life well up in her: "She imitates the rock of which the prophet says: 'He smote the rock, and waters gushed out' (Ps 77.20). You see to what heights the Bride has ascended: she was struck just as the precipice was struck by Moses, in order that she too, like it, might gush forth, for those who are thirsty, the Word who poured water forth from his wound."[106]

Gregory clarifies the meaning of the purification brought about by the rod of the Spirit by comparing it to another kind of cleansing, one that is the very type of passive purification in Scripture—namely, the burning coal placed on the lips of the prophet to enable him to see the vision of the seraphim.

> Then no doubt someone will say that Isaiah's vision has something in common with the text at hand . . . one of the seraphim touched the mouth of the prophet with a fiery coal; and when this happened, not only were his lips purified but his hearing as well, for the reception of the Word. For just as in our text the Bride says that she was struck and wounded by the watchmen and that in this way she was stripped of the covering of her veil, so also in

---

[104]*Cant.* 12 (PG 44:1033C; Norris, 385).

[105]"When these sentiments of pleasure and suffering are of almost equal strength and are both very ardent, the resulting state takes the name of 'wound of love.'" Poulain, *Des grâces d'oraison*, 151 [*Interior Prayer*, 144].

[106]*Cant.* 12 (PG 44:1036B–C; Norris, 387).

Ecstatic Love

the case of Isaiah's vision, instead of the veil the "lintel of the door" was lifted so that he might have an unhindered vision of the shrine, while instead of watchmen the seraphim are mentioned, instead of the rod, a coal, and instead of a blow, the burning. What is more, the purpose is the same, both in the case of the Bride and in that of the prophet's soul—namely, purity.[107]

Many observations could be made concerning the doctrine contained in these passages. In finishing, however, we may group together the main characteristics by which Gregory describes these purifications. The first is that they are brought about by the Holy Spirit. It is the Spirit who is symbolized both by the rod of consolation and the burning coal. It is therefore a question of the activity of God in the soul, burning up its impurities. This removes from the soul the carnal veil that forms a screen between it and God. It is no longer a question of a moral but a physical purification—that is, of the inward transformation of the soul into God that takes place in the very depths of the soul where the wound was made. We find here the greatest degree of inwardness coinciding with the most characteristic passivity.

However, this is not Gregory's last word on the subject. To begin with, we understood the wound of love as symbolizing the penetration of the Word into the soul, and his indwelling there; then we saw that it signified the purification brought about the Holy Spirit in the innermost part of the soul. One other meaning remains to be mentioned: the wound of love made by God cannot be healed and compels the soul forever to seek him. In this sense, it can be linked to the theme of ecstasy:

> For the soul that goes out at his word, seeking the One who is not found . . . is, in a certain sense, struck and wounded by the hopelessness of what she seeks. . . . But the veil of her grief is removed when she learns that the true fruition of what she seeks is ever to make progress in seeking and never to halt on the upward path, since her fulfilled desire ever generates a further desire for what is beyond her. As, then, the veil of hopelessness is lifted and she sees the infinite and unlimited beauty of her Beloved, a beauty that for all the eternity of the ages is ever and again discovered to be greater, she is pulled by a yet more intense yearning [ἐν σφοδροτέρῳ τείνεται πόθῳ, *en sphodroterō teinetai pothō*] and . . . she discloses the state of her heart to her Beloved: how in the sting of faith she has received in herself God's chosen

[107] *Cant.* 12 (PG 44:1036D–1037A; Norris, 387–89).

arrow (cf. Isa 49.2) and has been struck in the heart by receiving love's shot in her vital part.[108]

Beyond any indwelling of God in the soul, beyond any purification, the desire for God wrests the soul away from itself. It understands that this ecstatic love is the highest degree it can reach, since it is a love for God as he is in himself. This insatiable desire is an end in itself: "The true sight of God consists in this, that the one who looks up to God never ceases in that desire."[109] For this is to love him as he is in himself. There we have the wound with which a seraph will one day wound the heart of Teresa of Avila.

But we are touching on one of Gregory's fundamental ideas, the most important, along with that of the indwelling of the Word in the soul—namely, the going forth of the soul out of itself. The entire spiritual life receives its full meaning in the light of this idea, which is referred to by the term *epektasis*. We shall now summarize our investigation, using this term as the focal point.

Epektasis

In the course of this study we have tried to reconstruct the various stages of the spiritual life according to Gregory of Nyssa. This has not been without its difficulties, since our author does not present his ideas in a systematic fashion but in a manner that is often puzzling. We hope, however, that we have not falsified the true nature of his thought. Moreover, in order to gain an exact picture of his work, one should not exaggerate the distinctness of the categories that we have tried to identify, but see them in the context of the general movement that carries all of Gregory's thought forward. In fact, what is most striking about his doctrine is the emphasis he places on the very momentum of the spiritual life rather than on the particular stages within it. We shall see that for him perfection lies in the very fact of progress itself, in the unending movement of the soul toward God. To express this idea, there is one verse from Scripture that recurs like a leitmotif. It is from St Paul's Letter to the Philippians (3.13): "Forgetting what lies behind and stretching forward [ἐπεκτεινόμενος, *epekteinomenos*] to what lies ahead."[110]

---

[108]*Cant.* 12 (PG 44:1037C; Norris, 389).
[109]*Vit. Moys.* 2.233 (PG 44:404D; Malherbe, 115).
[110]This idea had been discussed by Origen. See *Homilies on Numbers* 17.4; *On Prayer* 25.2 (PPS 26:170). It is also found in St Basil the Great, *Commentary on Isaiah* (PG 30:144D).

It is an idea that we have already come across but, in order to arrive at a summary of Gregory's understanding of spirituality, we shall now gather together the various scattered findings that we have discovered so far around this, its essential theme. We shall see how, from the outset, the aim is to awaken in the soul the desire for God. Then we shall observe how this desire increases in proportion to the soul's participation in the good things of the supernatural life. Finally, after a brief recapitulation of the stages detailed in this study, we shall see how Gregory portrays the soul at the term of the spiritual life as being consumed by an unquenchable thirst to be united with God. This is not to say that this desire ceases once the soul has attained beatitude, since it is related to divine transcendence itself and thus can never cease. Gregory understands the beatific vision in a dynamic sense, as being continually filled with wonder at the inexhaustible riches of the divine life.

At the beginning of our investigation, we saw how, using the three books attributed to Solomon, Gregory himself proposes a summary of the various stages of the spiritual life as a function of one's desire for God. The aim of Proverbs is to awaken this desire by showing the value of spiritual goods. This is what is meant by illumination, which is the principle of spiritual life and is symbolized by the vision of the Burning Bush in *The Life of Moses*. "Thus [Solomon] sets out to portray Wisdom . . . interpreting, in various ways and forms, the splendor of her unspeakable beauty, so that [one] may be roused to the participation of good things, not out of any fear or compulsion, but out of desire [πόθῳ, *pothō*] and yearning [ἐπιθυμίᾳ, *epithymia*]."[111] After this first stage comes Ecclesiastes, which aims to free the soul from attachment to the visible world. "When [Solomon] has again, with these and other words like them, set fire to that principle of desire that dwells in the interior self of one who is still youthful . . . [he] adds the philosophy contained in Ecclesiastes, disparag[ing] the human tendency to dwell on the appearance of things."[112] Finally, the soul is introduced into the sanctuaries of the Song of Songs, whose goal is the union of the soul with the divine.

It might seem that, once this union is accomplished, the soul's desire is fulfilled. Yet it is then that a new truth becomes apparent, one that is fundamental for Gregory: enjoyment of the divine goods only increases the soul's desire still more. This is at first something that the soul notices on a personal level—and

---

[111] *Cant.* 1 (PG 44:768B; Norris, 19).
[112] *Cant.* 1 (PG 44:769C; Norris, 23).

which, it seems, Gregory had himself experienced. But gradually a general law begins to emerge. The soul discovers that continual progress is of the very essence of the spiritual life and that, however paradoxical it may seem, perfection (τελειότης, *teleiotēs*) consists in unceasing progress (προκοπή, *prokopē*). We shall look at some of the texts in which Gregory articulates this central idea, and then consider its theological basis. It is a question, in fact, of the very expression of the transcendence of the divine essence, the preeminent form of negative theology.

Gregory explains this law in the first of his *Homilies on The Song of Songs*: "To turn toward ... that Good that alone is truly pleasant and desirable and lovable and whose enjoyment [ἀπόλαυσις, *apolausis*] is the ever-available opportunity [ἀφορμή, *aphormē*] of a yet nobler desiring because by participation [μετουσία, *metousia*] in good things it stretches and expands our longing [μείζονος ἐπιθυμίας, *meizonos epithymias*]."[113] Here we already have some of the ideas that we shall encounter in this analysis. This participation and union is progressive; to the extent that God communicates himself, he increases the soul's desire. Here, the enjoyment—far from producing satiety (κόρος, *koros*), as in sensory enjoyments—produces a greater thirst.

Gregory then illustrates the point by referring to such examples as Moses, Elijah, John, Peter, Paul, and the other apostles:

> And through the face-to-face converse accorded him by God—as the Scripture testifies (cf. Num 12.8)—he became more intensely desirous of such kisses after these theophanies, praying to see the Object of his yearning. ... In the same way, all of the others in whom the divine desire was deeply lodged never ceased from desire; everything that came to them from God for the enjoyment of the Object of yearning they made into the material and fuel [ὑπέκκαυμα, *hypekkauma*] for a more ardent [σφοδρότερος, *sphodroteros*] desire. And just as now the soul that is joined to God is not satiated [ἀκορέστως, *akorestōs*] by her enjoyment of him, so too the more abundantly she is filled up with his beauty, the more vehemently her longings abound.[114]

An essential characteristic of the union with God, then, is this feature of perpetual newness. Gregory mentions it here for the first time, but returns to it in

---

[113]*Cant.* 1 (PG 44:777B; Norris, 33).
[114]*Cant.* 1 (PG 44:777C-D; Norris, 33).

The Life of Moses, which was written at the same period. After being admitted to speak with God, Moses asks to see him, as if he had not yet seen him. "How," writes Gregory, "does someone who Scripture says saw God clearly in such divine appearances—'face to face [κατὰ στόμα, *kata stoma*], as a man speaks with his friend' (Ex 33.11)—require that God appear to him as though he who is always visible had not yet been seen, as though Moses had not yet attained what Scripture testifies he had indeed attained?"[115]

But exactly how can participation be the source of a yearning that becomes ever greater? We shall consider the answer Gregory gives later. For the moment, let us focus on Gregory's description of the way desire increases in proportion to the increase of participation and on the constant renewal that the spiritual life undergoes as a result. He returns to this in the *Homilies on the Song of Songs* in a passage of great beauty: "We see, then, that the Bride [the soul] is being led by the Word through the ascents [ἀνάβασις, *anabasis*] of virtue up to the heights, just as if she were climbing a ladder [κλῖμαξ, *klimax*]. The Word first of all sends in, through the prophetic windows and the law's lattices, the ray of the commandments and summons her to draw near to the light and to become beautiful once, in the light, she has been given the shape of the dove.[116] Then, when she has shared [μετασχοῦσα, *metaschousa*], as far as is possible for her, in the good things, he draws [ἐφέλκεται, *ephelketai*] her toward participation in the transcendent Beauty just as though she had hitherto had no part [ἀμέτοχον, *ametochon*] in them at all."[117]

Few passages put us more at the heart of Gregory's mysticism. First, there is the idea of the spiritual life as an ascent, the climbing of a ladder. As we have seen, these are classical images to describe the increase of desire.[118] At the beginning, it is a question simply of awakening such a desire. Then the soul is transformed into a dove and, having recovered its lost wings, ascends into the luminous ether and *circulates* in the heights (μετεωροπορεῖ, *meteōroporei*). All of these images describe participation in the divine life by the grace of the Holy Spirit. At this point, the soul might believe that it had reached the end of its ascent. But now the Word attracts it again to himself, revealing new splendors,

---

[115]*Vit. Moys.* 2.219 (PG 44:400A; Malherbe, 111–12).

[116]The person who is borne upward on the wings of the dove—the symbol customarily used by Scripture to refer to the power of the Spirit—will participate in the true light. Cf. *Virg.* 11 (PG 46:365C–D; FC 58:40).

[117]*Cant.* 5 (PG 44:876B; Norris, 171).

[118]The term *anabasis* is found in Plato, *Republic* 7 (515e).

compared to which what it had known hitherto appears now to be of little value, so much so that it has the feeling that it is only beginning.

Gregory continues as follows:

> The result is that it seems to her that desire increases in proportion to [κατὰ τὴν ἀναλογίαν, *kata tēn analogian*] her progress [τῆς προκοπῆς, *tēs prokopēs*] toward that Light which eternally shines out and at the same time that her ascent is just beginning, on account of the transcendence of the good things. That is why he says once again to the awakened soul, "Rise up," and to the soul that is coming, "Come!"
>
> For to one who has risen up in this manner there will never be wanting an up-rising without end; nor for one who runs to the Lord will opportunity for the divine race [θείῳ δρόμῳ, *theiō dromō*] be used up. For it is always necessary to rise up, and it is never right for those who are drawing near by their running to halt. For that reason, as often as he says "Rise up!" and "Come!" he confers the capacity for an ascent toward what is better.[119]

To the metaphors of an ascent and a ladder is added the third great image of spiritual progress: a race. But the overall message of this passage provides us with an initial explanation of the law of ever-increasing desire. It is important to note that here we are not on the level of the first way, where the soul is still separated from God and yearning for him. At that level, desire is a feeling of absence. Here, this is no longer the case. We are already in a life of union; the soul is participating in the Word, in so far as it is able. Thus, it would seem that it is sated. Moreover, from now on the initiative comes not from the soul itself, but from the Word.

And this is indeed how things stand: it is the Word that attracts (ἐφέλκεται, *ephelketai*) the soul, and it is the Word that gives it the strength to ascend. Everything now comes from him, both the call and the strength to respond. How can this be explained? Gregory already suggests an answer in this same passage. In communicating himself to the soul in each of his theophanies, his "births," the Word also augments the divine life of the soul, expanding its capacity. By filling it, and by the very fact that he fills it, he causes new desires to arise in it. Hence the soul is always simultaneously filled to satisfaction and yet thirsting: filled in so far as it really possesses the Word, thirsting in so far as it does not possess the entire Word. There is, then, a double disposition of interiority and exteriority, of

---

[119]*Cant.* 5 (PG 44:876B–C; Norris, 171–73).

Ecstatic Love

instasis and *ekstasis*, which is the characteristic feature of the mystical life. "God comes into the soul and correspondingly the soul is brought into God."[120]

We shall return to this reciprocity, to this perpetual dialectic between interiority and love, which is the specific character and the hallmark, as it were, of the mystical life. For the moment, let us simply seek to deepen our understanding of the law of the growth of desire in proportion to participation. It is explained at length in the dialogue *On the Soul and the Resurrection*:

> For the participation in the divine good is such that it makes anyone into whom it enters greater and more receptive [δεκτικότερον, *dektikoteron*]. As it is taken up it increases the power and magnitude of the recipient, so that the person who is nourished always grows and never ceases from growth. Since the fountain of good things flows unfailingly, the nature of the participants who use all the influx to add to their own magnitude (because nothing of what is received is superfluous or useless) becomes at the same time both more capable of attracting the better and more able to contain it. Each adds to the other: the one who is nourished gains greater power from the abundance of good things, and the nourishing supply rises in flood to match the increase of the one who is growing. Those whose growth is not cut off by any limit will surely continue to increase in this manner.[121]

The very style of this passage depicts this overflowing of life, this growth without loss, in which the soul that is attached to God constantly receives from him an increase of grace and yet becomes eager for more the more it is filled.[122] We should note here the idea that what characterizes the spiritual goods is that nothing is useless, as in bodily nourishment, but that they are changed entirely into the substance of the one who receives them. It follows that spiritual growth takes place more speedily than bodily growth. We may also notice certain remarkable expressions: the divine life flowing into the soul and dilating her capacity; the excess of divine life that always overflows (συμπλημμυρεῖν, *symplēmmyrein*) the soul. Souls are conceived of as being, as it were, infinitely expanding universes of grace. This is the image Gregory gives us of eternal life. The more all that hampers the ardor of love disappears, the more the soul, freed from its fetters, sinks into the infinite depths of the divinity, with an increasing fervor.

---

[120]*Cant.* 6 (PG 44:889D; Norris, 191).
[121]*An. et res.* 7 (PG 46:105B–C; PPS 12:87–88).
[122]This idea is briefly mentioned in Irenaeus, *Against Heresies* 4.11.2.

In fact, such is the image that Gregory proposes in *The Life of Moses*:

> Bodies, once they have received the initial thrust downward, are driven downward by themselves with greater speed without any additional help as long as the surface on which they move is steadily sloping and no resistance to their downward thrust is encountered. Similarly, the soul moves in the opposite direction. Once it is released from its earthly attachment, it becomes light and swift for its movement upward, soaring from below up to the heights.
>
> If nothing comes from above to hinder its upward thrust (for the nature of the Good attracts [ἔλκειν, *helkein*] to itself those who look to it), the soul rises ever higher and will always make its flight [πτῆσις, *ptēsis*] yet higher—by its desire of the heavenly things "straining [ἐπεκτεινομένη, *epekteinomenē*] ahead [ἔμπροσθεν, *emprosthen*] for what is still to come," as the Apostle says (Phil 3.14).
>
> Made to desire and not to abandon the transcendent height by the things already attained, it makes its way upward [τὴν ἐπὶ ἄνω φοράν, *tēn epi anō phoran*] without ceasing, ever through its prior accomplishments renewing its intensity for the flight. Activity directed toward virtue causes its capacity to grow through exertion; this kind of activity alone does not slacken its intensity by the effort, but increases it.
>
> For this reason, we also say that the great Moses, as he was becoming ever greater, at no time stopped in his ascent, nor did he set a limit for himself in his upward course. Once having set foot on the ladder which God set up (as Jacob says), he continually climbed to the step above [τῆς ὑπερκειμένης βαθμίδος, *tēs hyperkeimenēs bathmidos*] and never ceased to rise higher, because he always found a step higher than the one he had attained.[123]

Here we find grouped together several of the images that characterize the ascent of love. We have already come across the ladder with its steps, which will provide John Climacus with the title of his famous work. Here it is not used in conjunction with the ascent of a mountain or a race, but the ascending flight of a bird. The theme of the soul's wings is also closely related to the Platonic dialectic of love. But what is noteworthy is the insistence that any acquisition (καταλαμβανόμενος, *katalambanomenos*) is the starting point for new

---

[123] *Vit. Moys.* 2.224–27 (PG 44:400D–401B; Malherbe, 113–14).

progress.[124] Again we have the idea of participation enlarging the capacity, understood on another level. We also note the profound observation that spiritual activity is maintained through exercise, which completes the description Gregory gave earlier and in the same line of thinking. This entire passage directs us toward the perspective of a dizzying ascent, a limitless climb in which the soul, attracted by the irresistible force of the good, is perpetually carried away toward it by a gravitational pull toward the heights. This is the Augustinian *pondus ad sursum* ["a weight" that pulls "upward"].

"The soul," Gregory says in the passage just quoted, "rises ever higher ... 'straining ahead' [ἐπεκτεινομένη, *epekteinomenē*] for what is still to come.'" It is worth looking in more detail at this passage from Philippians (from which Gregory quotes), for it will explain certain aspects of his thought. "Not that I have already obtained [the prize]," writes Paul, "or am already perfect [τελειότητα, *teleiotēta*], but I press on to make it my own ... forgetting what lies behind and straining forward [ἐπεκτεινόμενος, *epekteinomenos*] to what lies ahead [τοῖς ἔμπροσθεν, *tois emprosthen*], I press on toward the goal" (Phil 3.12–14).

The imagery is clearly borrowed from the world of athletics. Paul compares himself to a runner stretching forward to the goal. This "stretching forward" is a theme that occupies a privileged place in Gregory's writings. It dominates the whole of *The Life of Moses* and returns like a leitmotif throughout the *Homilies on the Song of Songs*. It captures exactly the inner attitude that corresponds to the objective law of spiritual progress, which means that every gain will always be exceeded, every increase of grace being simply a starting point for new graces. The soul should never stop at what has already been acquired, but should always be stretching toward the future, in total dependence on divine generosity and without claiming anything for itself. And—supreme paradox—it is this progress itself which constitutes perfection.

Some examples of the way Gregory uses the verb ἐπεκτείνω (*epekteinō*) in general contexts may help us to determine its meaning. Thus ἐπεκτείνειν τὸν ὀφθαλμόν (*epekteinein ton ophthalmon*) means "to open wide one's eyes, to stare wide-eyed"; it connotes the effort of a gaze directed at a sensible object. More often it signifies the effort of the mind as it strives to apprehend an object that is invisible, in particular struggling to grasp the divine essence. "From the present

---

[124]On this theme of τέλος–ἀρχή (*telos–archē*) "limit/starting-point," see also *Cant.* 6 (PG 44:889B; Norris, 189): "The limit [τέλος, *telos*] that defines the things that have already been accomplished becomes the starting point [ἀρχή, *archē*] of [the soul's] being led to realities that transcend them [ὑπερκείμενα, *hyperkeimena*]." See also ibid. (PG 44:889D; Norris, 191).

instant, as from a centre and a 'point,' we extend thought in all directions, to the immensity of that Life."[125] Or it can refer to a soul reaching out toward the holiness of God: "How could it come about that human lowliness could be extended [ἐπεκτείνεσθαι, *epekteinesthai*] to the blessedness seen in God?"[126]

But most often the word is used in a quasi-technical sense with direct reference to the passage from St Paul. The *Homilies on the Song of Songs* offer us several striking examples that will allow us to review the same ideas as in the preceding paragraph, but grouped around the metaphor of a race.

> Now what awakens [the souls'] love is the sweet scent of the perfume, toward which, as they run [τρέχονται, *trechontai*] unceasingly, they stretch themselves out [ἐπεκτεινόμεναι, *epekteinomenai*] for what lies ahead, forgetting what lies behind. Hence it says: "We will run after you, toward the fragrance of your perfumed ointments." But it is those who do not yet possess the fullness of virtue and are still immature who promise that they will pursue the goal toward which the fragrance of the perfumes points them ... the more perfect soul, on the other hand, who has more eagerly been stretched out [ἐπεκταθεῖσα σφοδρότερον, *epektatheisa sphodroteron*] toward what lies ahead, already attains the goal for the sake of which the course is run.[127]

The metaphor of a race is invoked here quite naturally by the presence of the verse from the Song—"We will run after you" (1.4). The attraction exerted by God, on the other hand, is conveyed very effectively by the metaphor of fragrance. What we see here is the transposition into Christian language of what the dialogue *On the Soul and the Resurrection* expressed in a more philosophical manner.

> Contrariwise, that which is intelligible and immaterial, being released from [all] confines, escapes limit and is bounded by nothing.
>
> But again, the intelligible nature is also divided into two kinds. The first is uncreated and is that which brings intelligible realities into being. It is what it is eternally and is in every respect self-identical. Further, it is beyond any addition to, and incapable of any diminution of, the goods it possesses. The second, however, has been brought into existence by an act of creation. It looks eternally upon the First Cause [πρῶτον αἴτιον, *prōton aition*] of the

[125] *Eun.* 1.42.668 (PG 45:457A; NPNF² 5:97).
[126] *Prof.* (PG 46:245C; FC 58:86).
[127] *Cant.* 1 (PG 44:784D–785A; Norris, 43).

things that are and is preserved in every respect in the good by its participation in what transcends it. It is also, in a certain fashion, always being created [παντότε κτίζεται, *pantote ktizetai*] as it is changed for the better by being enhanced in goodness. For this reason, no end point can be conceived for it either, and its growth toward the better is not confined by any limit, but the good that is given at any particular time is always a starting point for something more and better, even though it already appears to be as great and as complete as possible. In its case too, then, the apostle's word is confirmed, because it stretches forward [ἐπεκτάσεως, *epektaseōs*][128] in forgetfulness of things that have already been accomplished (cf. Phil 3.13). For that good which is now and again discovered to be a better thing, not to say something surpassing, focuses the attention of those who have a share in it upon itself and does not permit [them] to look toward what is past, since it voids the recollection of inferior things by the enjoyment of those that are to be honored more highly.[129]

What is especially interesting about this passage is that it takes us to the heart of the doctrine of participation and connects *epektasis* to what is the very essence of the relationship between the Creator and creation. For Gregory, God and man are both part of the intelligible world. In itself, the soul is unlimited. In this respect, God and the soul are of the same order. But the essential difference is that God is infinite in act, whereas the soul is infinite in becoming. Its divinity comes from transforming itself into God. Hence one understands why progress should be a constitutive property of the soul. In fact, if it is "an infinity in the making," growth is necessary and essential for it. Without this, it would simply be finite—something that is a characteristic of the world of matter. Thus grace, this perpetual addition of new blessings, is precisely *epektasis*, which is what ensures that the soul is always turned toward what is beyond itself.

We can conclude that *epektasis* is the sine qua non of the soul. We see now that it is not something that concerns one particular stage in the spiritual life. We have discovered that this "tension," this stretching forward, is in fact the return of the soul to its true nature. Its essence lies in receiving itself from God at every instant, in being perpetually created, as Gregory admirably puts it. *Epektasis* is nothing less than the ratification by the free will of the soul's true condition, a recognition of what it is. Thus, if *epektasis* is the expression of the soul's deepest

---

[128]The substantive ἐπέκτασις (*epektasis*) in the mystical sense is found only here.
[129]*Cant.* 6 (PG 44:885D–888A; Norris, 185–87).

nature, we should not be surprised to see that Gregory affirms that it denotes a permanent attitude, one that is found throughout the spiritual life and that will persist in the next life.

Gregory says as much in the following passage:

> After his account to the Corinthians of his sublime vision (cf. 2 Cor 12.1–4)—in the course of which he also observed that he was uncertain of his own state at the time of his mystic initiation into paradise, whether he was body or thought—the grand apostle makes a solemn acknowledgment: "I do not consider that I have made it my own, but straining forward [ἐπεκτείνομαι, *epekteinomai*] to what lies ahead, I forget what has already been accomplished" (Phil 3.13). By this he shows that after that "third heaven" that he alone knew (for Moses told nothing about it in his cosmogony) and after the ineffable audition of the mysteries of paradise, he is still hastening toward something higher and never leaves off his ascent by setting the good he has already grasped as a limit to his desires.[130]
>
> In this way, as I see it, [Paul] teaches us, on the one hand, that what is ever and again discovered of that blessed Nature that is the Good is something great but, on the other hand, that what lies beyond what is grasped at any particular point is infinitely greater; and during the entire eternity of the ages [ἐν πάσῃ τῇ τῶν αἰώνων ἀϊδιότητι, *en pasē tē tōn aidiotēti*] this becomes the case for the person who participates in the Good.[131]

Here we have Gregory's last word on his doctrine, in its most dizzying form. It is no longer simply a question of the highest levels of the soul's ascent, for even these are only stages. We are beyond ecstasy, beyond the third heaven. Which is in fact why we had to end with this particular chapter. Yet Gregory goes much further still. Beyond death, it is the whole of eternity that he envisages. Moreover, he does not see this eternity as consisting in a state of static contemplation. Such an idea makes no sense in the context of his thought. The link between Creator and creature necessitates the maintaining of the relationship of grace and freedom, and thus progress in participation. The soul will forever be transforming itself into God throughout eternity without ever being able to become

---

[130] The same use of ἐπεκτεινόμενος (*epekteinomenos*), with respect to Paul's stretching out to the third heaven, is found in *Hex.* (PG 44:121A; McCambley, 21).

[131] *Cant.* 8 (PG 44:940D–941A; Norris, 257–59). See also *Cant.* 4 (PG 44:845A; Norris, 133); *Cant.* 12 (PG 44:1036A; Norris, 385).

his equal, but always discovering in him new splendors that fade before others that follow.

For, Gregory continues,

> The person who is pure in heart sees God (cf. Mt 5.8), ever grasping in the mind as much as he is able to take in, in proportion to [κατα ἀναλογίαν, *kata analogian*] his capacity. Nevertheless, the infinity and incomprehensibility of the Godhead remains beyond [ἐπέκεινα, *epekeina*] all direct apprehension.... So the great David—though "in the heart" he has traced out the glad "ascents" and always goes "from strength to strength" (Ps 83.6, 8)—cries out to God: "Thou, O Lord, art Most High forevermore" (Ps 90.8); and in my opinion what he means by his cry is this: "In the entire eternity of the unending age, the person who bends his course toward you is always becoming greater and higher than he is, making relative growth because of his 'ascent' through good things.... For that which is apprehended at any given time is in all respects greater than anything that has been apprehended previously, but it does not in and of itself set limits to the object of the search. On the contrary, for those who are in process of ascent, the outer limit of what has been discovered becomes the starting point of a search after more exalted things. Neither, moreover, does the one who is mounting up cease to promote one starting point into another [ἀρχὴν ἐξ ἀρχῆς, *archēn ex archēs*].[132]

We touch there upon the ultimate reason for this infinite growth. It is the absolute transcendence of the divine essence that is fundamentally inaccessible, so much so that for all eternity souls, like the stellar universes of modern physics, will with increasing force sink into the infinite depths of the divine darkness, without ever finding a boundary to these limitless spaces. But each progress is never more than a starting point, so much so that the soul always has the feeling that it is embarking on a beginning, that God is always an absolutely new reality, and that it lives in a state of amazement and of constantly renewed ecstatic astonishment. Gregory's most profound and moving words are reserved for these eternal "beginnings" that are the prize for those souls that endeavor to ascend.

It is of the utmost importance for the soul to realize this, and to awaken from the illusion that there is a stage at which it will be able to rest on its laurels, as it were. It must understand that this is inconsistent with the essence of the relationship between the soul and God, which is one of expectancy on the one

---

[132]*Cant.* 8 (PG 44:941A–C; Norris, 259–61).

hand and generosity on the other. For the soul, ceasing to be receptive would be to terminate this relationship of exchange with God, a relationship that is one of loving rapture:

> For the soul that goes out at his word, seeking the One who is not found and calling upon the One whom words cannot attain, is taught by the watchmen (the angels) that she is in love with the Unattainable and is directing herself toward the Incomprehensible. At their hands she is, in a certain sense, struck and wounded by the hopelessness [τῇ ἀνελπιστίᾳ, *tē anelpistia*], judging that her desire for the good is imperfect and falls short of its fruition. But the veil of her grief is removed when she learns that the true fruition of what she seeks is ever to make progress [προκόπτειν, *prokoptein*] in seeking and never to halt on the upward path, since her fulfilled [πληρουμένης, *plēroumenēs*] desire ever generates a further desire for what is beyond her. As, then, the veil of hopelessness is lifted and she sees the infinite and unlimited beauty of her Beloved, a beauty that for all the eternity of the ages is ever and again discovered to be greater, she is pulled [τείνεται, *teinetai*] by a yet more intense yearning [σφοδροτέρῳ πόθῳ, *sphodroterō pothō*], and . . . discloses the state of her heart to her Beloved.[133]

To describe this revelation of divine beauty that will continue throughout eternity, Gregory used a striking image—that of an ever-bubbling spring:

> You perceive how, for those who are making their way upwards toward God, the course they run has no end. . . . The words of the text, then, teach us this: that to those who are making progress toward what is better the word of the apostle always applies, the word that says, "If anyone seems to know something, he does not yet know as he ought to know" (1 Cor 8.2).
>
> For the soul has known him—to the extent that she has comprehended him—in what has already come to pass, but since that which is not yet comprehended is infinitely greater than that which has been comprehended, the Bridegroom is manifested to the soul frequently and promises the Bride by his voice that he will be revealed as one who has not yet been seen.
>
> In order that this idea may be the clearer to us, I shall set forth an image by way of illustration. Suppose that someone draws near to that fountain that the Scripture says welled up out of the earth at the beginning, and so

---

[133]*Cant.* 12 (PG 44:1037B–C; Norris, 389).

abundantly that it flooded the whole face of the earth (cf. Gen 2.6). The person who has drawn near to the fountain will marvel at that limitless supply of water that ever gushes out and flows from it, yet he would not say that he has seen all of the water. (For how can he see the water that is still concealed in earth's bosom? The fact is that even if he remains for a long time at the gushing spring, he is always just beginning to contemplate the water, for the water never stops in its everlasting flow nor does it ever cease beginning to gush forth.) In the same way, the person who looks toward that divine and infinite Beauty glimpses something that is always being discovered as more novel and more surprising [παραδοξότερον, *paradoxoteron*] than what has already been grasped, and for that reason she marvels at that which is always being manifested, but she never comes to a halt in her desire to see, since what she looks forward to is in every possible way more splendid and more divine than what she has seen.[134]

We see how it is possible for Gregory to use in a very precise sense the apparently paradoxical formulas in which he delights: "For it is not one thing to seek, and another to find, but the reward of seeking is the actual seeking. . . . For it is not at a fixed moment and an appointed time that it is good to seek the Lord, but never to cease from continual search."[135] "The Scripture teaches that a person who desires to see God catches sight of the One he seeks by always following after him and that the contemplation of God's face is an unceasing journey toward him that is brought to fulfillment by following behind the Word."[136] "Thus, what Moses yearned for is satisfied by the very things which leave his

---

[134] *Cant.* 11 (PG 44:1000A–B; Norris, 337–39).

[135] *Eccl.* 7 (PG 44:720C; Hall, 118).

[136] *Cant.* 12 (PG 44:1028A; Norris, 377). Perfection is a *sequela Verbi*, an expression whose origin is obviously Mark 11.11, although it has been influenced by similar philosophical expressions that have modified the original Messianic meaning. See the entry for ἀκολουθεῖν (*akolouthein*) in G. Kittel, *Theological Dictionary of the New Testament*, trans. G. W. Bromiley, (Grand Rapids, MI: Eerdmans, 1964), 1:213–14. For its use in a more metaphysical sense, see H. J. Schoeps, *Aus frühchristlicher Zeit* (Tübingen: Mohr, 1950), 295. Delatte notes that the expression ἕπεσθαι θεῷ (*hepesthai theō*, to follow God) is found among the Neopythagoreans to denote the ideal of perfection. See A. Delatte, *Études sur la littérature pythagoricienne* (Paris: Champion, 1915), 76. It is also found in Philo (Völker, *Fortschritt und Vollendung*, 327). Clement links it to the Pythagoreans (*Miscellanies* 2.15.70). It occurs in Origen (Völker, *Vollkommenheitsideal*, 216) and is also found in Gregory (*Vit. Moys.* 2.251; PG 44:408D; Malherbe, 119). It occurs in Philo (*On the Migration of Abraham* 23.127 [Yonge, 265]) and is also found in Ambrose (*On Abraham* 1.2.4), where the influence of Philo can be detected. It is possible, as Völker argues (*Fortschritt*, 27), that it is a spiritual transposition of the ἀκολούθως τῇ φύσει ζῆν (*akolouthōs tē physei zēn*, to live in accordance with nature) of Stoicism [see, e.g., Diogenes Laertius, *Lives of Eminent Philosophers* 7.1.88 (LCL 185:194–95)—*Ed.*]. In Marcus Aurelius (*Meditations* 7.31), one finds Ἀκολούθησον θεῷ (*Akolouthēson theō*, Follow God).

desire unsatisfied."[137] "This truly is the vision of God: never to be satisfied in the desire to see him."[138] "The true fruition of what [the soul] seeks is ever to make progress [τὸ ἀεὶ προκόπτειν, *to aei prokoptein*] in seeking."[139] Without doubt, we are here in the realm of paradox. But it is precisely the particularity of the mystical life that ordinary contrasts are transcended. We have already come across paradoxes more than once—luminous darkness, for example, or sober inebriation. Here we have the key to them.

And so we arrive at Gregory's theory of perfection, as explained in the opening pages of *The Life of Moses* and as justified by the entire work:

> The perfection of everything which can be measured by the senses is marked off by certain definite boundaries.... But in the case of virtue we have learned from the Apostle that its one limit of perfection is the fact that it has no limit. For that divine Apostle, great and lofty in understanding, ever running the course of virtue, never ceased "straining [ἐπεκτείνεσθαι *epekteinesthai*] toward those [things] that are still to come." ... Certainly, whoever pursues true virtue participates [μετέχει, *metechei*] in nothing other than God, because he is himself absolute virtue. Since, then, those who know what is good by nature desire participation in it, and since this good has no limit, the participant's desire itself necessarily has no stopping place but stretches out with the limitless [συμπαρατείνουσα, *symparateinousa*]. It is therefore undoubtedly impossible to attain perfection, since, as I have said, perfection is not marked off by limits.... [But] the perfection of human nature consists perhaps in its very growth in goodness.[140]

In the final analysis, the soul's spiritual status seems to us, then, to lie in the twofold nature of the relationship it enjoys with God—with, on the one hand, his essence that cannot be shared and, on the other, his energies[141] that are participable. Light and darkness, rest and movement, soberness and inebriation—these are less two successive moments than two complementary aspects. One (light and rest) corresponds to the reality of participation, the other to the infinite transcendence of the essence. The mystical state, in its ineffable

---

[137] *Vit. Moys.*, 2:235 (PG 44:404B).
[138] Ibid., 2:239 (PG 44:404D).
[139] *Cant.* 12 (PG 44:1037B; Norris, 389).
[140] *Vit. Moys.* 1.5, 7–8, 10 (PG 44:300C–301C; Malherbe, 30–31). See also *Perf.* (PG 46:285C; FC 58:121–22).
[141] [The term Daniélou actually uses here is δύναμις (*dynamis*, power).—*Trans.*]

Ecstatic Love

reality, is precisely the synthesis of these two apparently irreconcilable elements. The genius of Gregory is not to have sacrificed one to the other, not to have renounced the reality of participation (in the manner of the mystics of the void—an Eckhart, for example) nor to have minimized the element of transcendence, as Origen does. Hence the difficulty of categorizing him. He is at once the most demanding in the order of austerity and yet the most indulgent when it comes to "tasting God."

It is precisely this duality, which is at once a possessing and a going out, that Gregory seeks to describe by this strange term *epektasis*, which is found only in him. The very composition of the word suitably conveys this idea of duality. For on the one hand, it connotes possession (ἐπί, *epi*); there is a real acquisition of something and the presence of God in the soul. On the other hand, it signifies a going out (ἐκ, *ek*) of oneself and the infinite irreducibility of God to the soul. He constantly wrests the soul out of itself in an ecstasy of love. Through this, the opposition between *theōria* (contemplation) and *agapē* (love) is also overcome.

Gregory expressed this reality articulately in several essential passages. The problem is set out in precise terms in *The Life of Moses*: "Although lifted up through such lofty experiences, [Moses] is still unsatisfied in his desire for more. He still thirsts for that with which he constantly filled himself to capacity, and he asks to attain as if he had never partaken, beseeching God to appear to him, not according to his capacity to partake, but according to God's true being."[142] Moses wants to enjoy God not just "as far as he can be shared" (ὡς μέτεχειν δύναται, *hōs metechein dynatai*) but "as he is" (ὡς ἐκεῖνός ἐστι, *hōs ekeinos esti*). That is to say, his desire is directed not only at the energies that can be shared in, but also at the essence. What he does not see is that these two aspects are in reality the components of *epektasis*—that harmonizing of a real and growing participation in the energies and a simultaneous straining toward the infinity of the essence.

This is what God's answer to Moses signifies. "The divine voice granted what was requested in what was denied, showing in a few words an immeasurable

---

[142] *Vit. Moys.* 2.230 (PG 44:401C; Malherbe, 114). The text continues: "Hope always draws the soul from the beauty of what is seen to what is beyond, always kindles the desire for the hidden through what is constantly perceived. Therefore, the ardent lover [σφοδρός ἐραστής, *sphodros erastēs*] of beauty, although receiving what is always visible as an image of what he desires, yet longs to be filled with the very stamp [χαρακτήρ, *character*] of the archetype. And the bold request which goes up the mountains of desire asks this: to enjoy the Beauty not in mirrors and reflections [κατόπτροι καὶ ἐμφάσεις, *katoptroi kai emphaseis*], but face to face." Ibid. 2.231-32 (PG 44:401D; Malherbe, 114-15).

depth of thought. The munificence of God assented to the fulfillment of his desire, but did not promise any cessation or satiety of the desire."[143] Thus, the vision of God will be a real vision, a fulfilling of desire, and at the same time a satisfaction without satiety, a rest without immobility. We will consider shortly how Gregory describes this reality, but first we should note the reasons he gives for its complexity: "He would not have shown himself to his servant if the sight were such as to bring the desire of the beholder to an end, since the true sight of God consists in this, that the one who looks up to God never ceases in that desire."[144]

Why is this? Because the essence is intrinsically inaccessible. Consequently, to believe one has seen God's essence could only be an illusion—as was the case with Eunomius, who thought he would find it in the Ἀγέννητος (*Agennētos*, Unbegotten): "[Scripture] says: 'You cannot see my face, for man cannot see me and live.' Scripture does not indicate that this causes the death of those who look, for how would the face of life ever be the cause of death to those who approach it? On the contrary, the Divine is by its nature life-giving. Yet the characteristic of the divine nature is to transcend all characteristics. Therefore, he who thinks that God is something to be known does not have life, because he has turned from true Being to what he considers by sense perception to have being."[145]

This doctrine, which is the same as that proposed by apophatic theology, is found throughout Gregory's texts. We have already emphasized this, when discussing the second darkness. It is one of the two key elements of *epektasis*. Gregory draws the conclusions, as can be seen in the following passage: "It is not in the nature of what is unenclosed to be grasped. But every desire for the Good which is attracted to that ascent constantly expands as one progresses in pressing on to the Good. This truly is the vision of God: never to be satisfied in the desire to see him. But one must always, by looking at what he can see, rekindle his desire to see more. Thus, no limit would interrupt growth in the ascent to God, since no limit to the Good can be found nor is the increasing of desire for the Good brought to an end because it is satisfied."[146]

But this is only one aspect of *epektasis*; it is not just movement, but progress. Pure movement is proper to the material world, which is total dispersion. But

---

[143] *Vit. Moys.* 2.232 (PG 44:401D; Malherbe, 115).
[144] *Vit. Moys.* 2.233 (PG 44:404A; Malherbe, 115).
[145] *Vit. Moys.* 2.233–34 (PG 44:404A–B; Malherbe, 115).
[146] *Vit. Moys.* 2.238–39 (PG 44:404C; Malherbe, 116). See also *Cant.* 6 (PG 44:892A–B; Norris, 195); *Cant.* 12 (PG 44:1024C; Norris, 375).

Ecstatic Love

spiritual movement is a synthesis of change and continuity. It is a period of time in which the present is enriched with the past. Thus, it contains both an inner and an outer element. God is both present in the soul through the graces it has received and at the same time external to the soul in the sense that his essence remains infinitely transcendent. This is precisely what is meant by *epektasis*, which is the Christian name for progress and growth (προκοπή, *prokopē*), as *agapē* is that of *eros*.

In the soul there is an element of stability, of possession, which is the sharing it has in God—and, at the same time, an element of movement, which is necessitated by the infinite gap between what it possesses of God and what God is. Gregory expresses this fact in the following striking passage:

> Whereas, Moses, your desire for "what is still to come" (Phil 3.13) has expanded and you have not reached satisfaction in your progress and whereas you do not see any limit to the Good, but your yearning always looks for more, the place with me is so great that the one running in it is never able to cease from his progress.
>
> In another scriptural passage the progress is a standing still [στάσις, *stasis*], for it says, "You must stand on the rock." (Ex 33.21) This is the most marvelous thing of all: how the same thing is both a standing still [στάσις, *stasis*] and a moving [κίνησις, *kinēsis*]. For he who ascends certainly does not stand still, and he who stands still does not move upwards. But here the ascent takes place by means of the standing.[147]

Once again, the paradox is placed before us in all its acuteness, and *epektasis* is submitted to a more rigorous analysis. We are confronted with what has been a traditional problem since the Eleatics[148]—the problem of the existence

---

[147] *Vit. Moys.* 2.242–43 (PG 44:405B–C; Malherbe, 117).

[148] The Eleatics—Parmenides and Zeno of Elea and Melissus of Samos—were Presocratic Greek philosophers (5th century BC) who not only denied the possibility of spatial movement (e.g., Zeno's paradoxes) but also the reality of any change, becoming, or multiplicity. They were monists, holding that "all is one," and any apparent reality to the contrary—including space, time, and sensory experience—is illusory and false. Heraclitus of Ephesus (fl. *c.* 500 BC) held the opposite view—reality is change and becoming: all is in flux. Plato forged a synthesis: the world of our everyday experience is one of change, becoming, and flux, but the world of the forms is unchanging and eternal, and this constitutes the truer reality. This evokes the Eleatics, and greatly influenced subsequent Greek philosophy. St Gregory of Nyssa turns this all on its head: God is being himself (Ex 3.14) and beyond being, but he chooses to create the world, which comes into being and is "very good" (Gen 1.31). Thus becoming cannot be denigrated. "And since the only thing that is unalterable by nature is that which does not come into being through creation [i.e., God], but as many things as are brought into substantial being out of nonbeing by the uncreated nature, as soon as they begin to be as a result of change, always proceed by alteration, [and] if they should act

of movement. Gregory poses it here on the spiritual level, and maintains that real movement is spiritual movement, precisely because it contains an internal principle of unity that creates an overall continuity from the various individual moments of movement.

> I mean by this that the firmer and more immovable one remains in the Good, the more he progresses in the course of virtue. The man who in his reasonings is uncertain and liable to slip, since he has no firm grounding in the Good but is "tossed one way and another and carried along" (Eph 4.14), as the Apostle says, and is doubtful and wavers in his opinions concerning reality, would never attain to the height of virtue.
>
> He is like those who toil endlessly as they climb uphill in sand: even though they take long steps, their footing in the sand always slips downhill, so that, although there is much motion, no progress results from it. But if someone, as the Psalmist says, should pull his feet up from the mud of the pit and plant them upon the rock (Ps 39.3) (the rock is Christ [1 Cor 10.4] who is absolute virtue), then the more "steadfast and unmoveable" (1 Cor 15.58) (according to the advice of Paul) he becomes in the Good the faster he completes the course. It is like using the standing still (στάσει, stasei) as if it were a wing [πτερούμενος, pteroumenos] while the heart flies upward through its stability in the good.[149]

Here we have the most complete description of *epektasis*. It presupposes, on the one hand, a participation in the divine life, using the rock which is Christ as a support. This is expressed by means of various other images: it is the track on which the runner presses his foot in order to dash forward; it is the wing that enables the soul to support itself on the good things already acquired, so as to soar higher.[150] Thus, progress presupposes a prior acquisition, a consolidation

according to nature the alteration is always for the better for them." *Or. cat.* 8.18 (GNO III/4:35.16–23; PPS 60:89). Such change for the better, extended infinitely, is beatitude itself. *Epektasis* radically challenges Greek ontological assumptions in favor of a scripturally grounded affirmation of the goodness of created beings' transformation in Christ.—*Ed.*

[149] *Vit. Moys.* 2.243–44 (PG 44:405C–D; Malherbe, 117–18).

[150] The same idea is forcefully expressed by the metaphor of the ladder: "And so, too, all the other things which in the course of his reasoning [Abraham] was led to apprehend as he advanced ... using them all as supplies and appliances for his onward journey, ever making one discovery a stepping-stone to another, ever reaching forth to those things which were before ... and passing by all knowledge acquired by his own ability as falling short of that of which he was in quest." *Eun.* 2.89 (PG 45:941A; NPNF² 5:259). The attitude is the same, but here it is a question of the ascent, the stage that precedes the darkness. Hence the expression ἴδια δύναμις (*idia dynamis*, by his own ability). This confirms that *epektasis* is an analogical concept that is verified in different ways.

Ecstatic Love

in the good. Yet at the same time it assumes that there is no looking back, no stopping at the treasures already acquired, looking at itself, but rather a stretching forward to what is ahead, oriented to God and to all the riches it does not yet possess.

The various stages of the spiritual life are all as if gathered together—between participation in Christ, who is the principle of the divine life communicated at Baptism, and the transcendence of the divine essence that remains infinitely inaccessible. All of the metaphors we have encountered—the ladder, the ascent, the race, the wing—involve this double element of leaning on Christ while looking toward divine *essence*. The spiritual life is thus an endless transformation of the soul into Jesus Christ, evidenced by increasing fervor—since the thirst for God increases to the extent that one participates in him—and by ever greater stability as the soul continues to unify itself and to anchor itself in God. In short, the complex concept of *epektasis* proves to be a one-word summary of the whole of Gregory's mystical doctrine.

Gregory also used the image of a well, but a well of living waters, which strangely combines the notions of still water and running water: "And the most unbelievable thing of all is this: that of all the wells that contain a mass of water, only the Bride contains within herself water that is in transit, so as to possess a well's depth [βάθος, *bathos*], but at the same time a river's unceasing motion [διεξοδικόν, *diexodikon*]."[151] Like the stationary race, it is a paradoxical image that bewilders us, but which nonetheless expresses the mysterious life of the soul. It is this mysterious reality that Gregory, with the help of so many metaphors and approximations, has succeeded in formulating with unparalleled vividness and precision.

---

[151] *Cant.* 9 (PG 44:977C; Norris, 309). The term ἀεικίνητον (*aeikinēton*, ever-moving) is the one Plato uses to describe the nature of the soul. See *Phaedrus* 245c. This is the reading of most manuscripts and of Cicero, who translates it as *quod semper movetur*. However, on page lxxvii of his edition of *Phèdre* (Paris: Les Belles Lettres, 1933), Léon Robin gives reasons for preferring αὐτοκίνητος (*autokinētos*, self-moving), which is found in Oxyrhynchus papyrus 1016 (early 3rd century).

Conclusion

As we come to the end of this lengthy investigation, we are in a position to identify the main features of the spiritual doctrine that Gregory of Nyssa sets before us. Beneath an apparently sumptuous, "oriental" veneer of biblical and Platonic symbols, it seems to us, when all is said and done, to be one of great simplicity. Gregory himself gave the best image of it, using a symbol that he was particularly fond of: the pomegranate. It is an image that to an unusual degree combines exacting austerity with sweetness, the taste of God's sweetness. This same twofold characteristic typifies the mystery of the death and Resurrection of Christ, which is at the heart of Gregory's teaching. The entire spiritual life is, as it were, an extension of Baptism—a striving to cast off of the old man, beginning with the culpable passions and then progressing to the passive purifications of the mystical life—while at the same time being a putting on of Christ and being transformed in him.

In the course of this ascent—a process of casting off and putting on, as in the Hellenistic myths—two prominent features became apparent, which together constitute the essence of Gregory's doctrine. First, there is the indwelling in the righteous soul of the Word, and with him the entire Trinity. Gregory's mysticism is a mysticism of the Word; mystical experience is an awareness of this presence, it is the "sense of a presence." Second, there is the concept of perpetual progress that, Gregory affirms, is the law of the spiritual life. The soul should always turn away from the past and look to the future. It should live in a perpetual state of beginning, in the eternal newness of the faith. This is a mysticism of complete surrender to God and total confidence in him. It is at once very demanding and very joyful.

But to these features a final one should be added, one that is so intimately linked to the spiritual life that not to speak of it would falsify things altogether. Yet it receives no special development anywhere in Gregory's writings. It is one of the most curious, and at first sight most disconcerting, features of his spiritual treatises—namely, the constant transition that is made from the individual level to the corporate. In the Song, the Bride is constantly surrounded by a procession of young girls,[1] just as in *The Life of Moses* the Lawgiver is always surrounded by his people. In the closing pages of the latter work, after Moses has been led to the very summits of the mystical life, one is initially surprised to again come across episodes that relate to earlier stages of the ascent, to the ascetic life. However, this is because these concern not Moses himself, but rather the people that accompany him.

Thus, the ascent of the soul is never presented as a solitary affair; it ascends surrounded by an entourage of other souls. The graces of sanctification that it receives are not for itself alone, but to render it able to sanctify others. The mystical graces have an apostolic aim; in a sense, they are charismatic graces. To this apostolic aspect of the mystical life corresponds, conversely, the mystical aspect of the apostolic life. What I mean by this is that it is above all by sanctifying itself that the soul becomes a source of sanctification for others. And thus, far from separating the soul from others, sanctification is on the contrary precisely that which enables it to serve them. The picture Gregory paints is that of a soul entirely oriented toward God, and who can lift other souls up to him only because of this.

The type of life that Gregory has in mind is clear. It is, moreover, a reflection of his own—as well as that of Basil, his brother. It begins as being monastic and contemplative, then becomes episcopal and apostolic. But with Gregory, the emphasis is expressly placed on the contemplative life, which for him governs the whole of the apostolic life. It is this manner of life that he shows being achieved in *The Life of Moses*, in the *Eulogy for Basil the Great*, and in *The Life of Gregory the Wonderworker*. His great model is St Paul, whose influence is evident on every page of the *Homilies on the Song of Songs*. However, it is noteworthy that he also presents female examples. There are, for instance, intriguing analogies between the role of Macrina in the dialogue *On the Soul and the Resurrection* and that which he gives to the Bride in the Song. The homilies on the Song of Songs are themselves dedicated to the virgin Olympia.

Let us go over again the main features of this teaching. First, an apostle is filled with contemplative graces only so as to be able to communicate them to others. He is essentially an instrument, a channel, a mediator. We find this expressed in several notable passages. Thus Moses, for instance, is seen to be someone who

---

[1] E.g., *Cant.* 2 (PG 44:789B; Norris, 49). Cf. "The Bride herself, a lover of humanity [φιλάνθρωπος, *philanthropos*] . . . calls to the young women (who no doubt represent the souls of those who are being saved), saying, 'How long will you be shut up in the cavern of this life?'" *Cant.* 7 (PG 44:916A; Norris, 223–25).

transmits the prayer of the people to God, and the graces of God to the people. "He offers supplications to God on behalf of those who have been [removed from him through] sin. And he transmits the mercy of the supreme power to those who need mercy. We may learn from this that the more one has removed himself from things that are inferior and earthly, the more is he associated with that nature which transcends every mind. He imitates the deity by beneficence [εὐποιΐα, *eupoiia*], by doing that which is the distinctive characteristic of the divine nature [namely, to do good to those who are in need of beneficence]."[2]

This passage is of fundamental importance because it shows that the acme of holiness consists in imitating divine love. Indeed, nothing brings us closer to God than to imitate his love: "[The Bride/the soul] truly becomes close to the goodness of her Lord because she has drawn near to God by love of neighbor."[3] The mark of Moses' holiness lies in the fact that he intercedes for those who want to harm him but whom he does not love any the less: "It is shown in the fact that he is named the 'friend of God' by God Himself, and by preferring to perish with all the rest if the Divine One did not through his good will forgive their errors."[4]

This twofold characteristic—the contemplative and the apostolic—is found in all the saints. To describe it, Gregory uses striking images. St John the Evangelist, for example, is likened to a sponge (σπογγία, *spoggia*): "John, who rested on the Lord's bosom . . . and having brought his own heart, as if it were a sponge, up to the fount of life, was filled by an indescribable transmission with the mysteries lodged in the Lord's heart, and he offers to us . . . the things lodged within him by the fount of Goodness."[5] It is always in this way that the mediating role of the contemplative is presented: he derives the knowledge he communicates from being close to God. In another passage, where we find a curious combination of images from Scripture and the mystery religions, Gregory compares Philip to the torch bearer (δᾳδοῦχος, *dadouchos*) who would lead the new initiate: "And when he had drawn near to the true light, like some lamp he drew from it a share of its light; then he enlightened Nathanael by illuminating [δᾳδουχήσας, *dadouchēsas*] for him the mystery of true religion."[6]

---

[2] *Inscr.* 1.7.57 (PG 44:457B–C; Heine, 103). [Translation modified to match the Greek and Daniélou's French.—*Trans.*]
[3] *Cant.* 7 (PG 44:917B; Norris, 227).
[4] *Vit. Moys.* 2.319 (PG 44:429C; Malherbe, 137).
[5] *Cant.* 1 (PG 44:785C; Norris, 45).
[6] *Cant.* 15 (PG 44:1089A; Norris, 459–61).

To be able to fulfill this role of mediator one must first have come close to God, as we have said, which is why the contemplative life must precede the active life. Gregory disapproves of those who would begin to act before this preliminary sanctification: "What then does the history teach by this? That he who has not equipped himself by this kind of spiritual training to instruct the multitude must not presume to speak among the people."[7] This is why, at the beginning of his mission, Moses begins by withdrawing to the desert of Midian, to devote himself to profound meditation, being illumined by the Burning Bush. Thus the eremitic life is seen from a new angle: namely, as a preparation for the apostolic life. This mediating mission also presupposes a call, a divine choice:

> The instruments which ring out the Spirit's sound would be the Prophets and the Apostles.... The multitude was not capable of hearing the voice from above but relied on Moses to learn by himself the secrets and to teach the people whatever doctrine he might learn through instruction from above. This is also true of the arrangement in the Church: Not all thrust themselves toward the apprehension of the mysteries, but, choosing from among themselves someone who is able to hear things divine, they give ear gratefully to him, considering trustworthy whatever they might hear from someone initiated into the divine mysteries.... [B]ut this is not now heeded in many of the churches. For many, still in need of being purified... make an assault on the divine mountain.[8]

The role of the people in electing a mediator shows us that here Gregory is describing not just any spiritual person, but one who is also a consecrated man, whether priest or bishop. Indeed, it is typical of his apostolic doctrine that it is hierarchical, unlike that of Origen who contrasts the spiritual with the hierarchical. On the contrary, the type Gregory proposes is that of a holy priesthood that serves as normal intermediary between the Christian people and God. This is to be understood in a broad sense, for the ecclesiastical hierarchy he describes consists, alongside bishops and teachers, of monks and consecrated virgins: in short, all those who have a special vocation in the Church and are devoted to the service of God. Such is the hierarchy that is described in *The Life of Moses*: it includes the teachers, who are "the pillars of the Church," but also those who take care of the

---

[7] *Vit. Moys.* 2.55 (PG 44:341B; Malherbe, 66–67). [Cf. Gregory of Nazianzus, *Or.* 2.13, 16.—Ed.]
[8] *Vit. Moys.* 2.159–61 (PG 44:376B–C; Malherbe, 94). See also 2.279–80 (PG 44:416C; Malherbe, 125).

office of divine praise and who are symbolized by the incense, those who baptize, and finally those who dedicate themselves to the ascetic life.⁹

This mediating function, which is common to the entire church hierarchy, encompasses, as mentioned, two essential features. Turned toward God, the mediator represents the people to him, and also intercedes for them. This is the role of Moses as he prays on the mountain, while the people fight on the plain. On the other hand, when he turns to the people, he passes on to them the mysteries derived from contemplation. These are the curls covered in dewdrops, that is, drenched in the heavenly dew with which they were imbued in the divine night and which "rain upon the whole body of the Church the word of dark and hidden mysteries."¹⁰

These "curls" do not just symbolize the apostles. As can be seen from the following verse from the Song of Songs, Gregory also recognizes the way they communicate grace: "Your shoots [ἀποστολαί, *apostolai*] form a grove of pomegranate trees" (4.13). Holiness is a return to paradise, as we have said, just as it is an entry into the divine night. But even as the soul lets the drops of darkness filter into the Church, so also does it communicate the paradise it has rediscovered:

> [The Bride/the soul] not only becomes a locked garden that produces its own food, but she is also transformed into a fountain—and that sealed—and becomes water that the thirsty can drink.
>
> Nor does she stop even there. She has reached such a point in her growth and betterment that a paradise sprouts (for the reader who attends painstakingly to the sense of the Hebrew text reads "from your mouth [comes] a paradise of pomegranate trees" instead of "Your outsendings are [a paradise of pomegranates]," which is to say, "Your speech, which is sent forth through your mouth, is a garden of pomegranate trees." . . . Indeed the term "outsending" fits the underlying idea most aptly, for what is sent out [ἀποστολή, *apostolē*] makes its way from sender to recipient. . . . It was to those disciples who were "sent out" to proclaim the truth that the Word gave the name "apostles." But what is it that the mouth of the Bride sends forth? Plainly it is the word of faith, which, when it has reached its recipients, becomes a paradise planted in their hearts by the sense of hearing.¹¹

---

⁹*Vit. Moys.* 2.184–85 (PG 44:385A–C; Malherbe, 101–102).
¹⁰*Cant.* 13 (PG 44:1056D; Norris, 415).
¹¹*Cant.* 9 (PG 44:969A–B; Norris, 295–97). This passage poses a curious problem of exegesis, discussed by S. Euringer in his article "'Schöpferische Exegese' im Äthiopischen Hohenliede. Nachträge,"

The apostles are described as having lips that distil myrrh, but what is emphasized is less the communication of the word of truth as the transmission of holiness, symbolized by the myrrh that, as we have said, signifies mortification of the senses. "Now Paul pours just such myrrh as this, mingled with the pure lily of temperance, into the ears of the holy virgin named Thecla. With her soul she received the drops that poured out from the lily, and she treated her outward self to death by quenching her every fleshly thought and desire. . . . In the same way did the great Peter give utterance once before Cornelius to the radiant lilies of the message and filled the souls of his auditors with myrrh; and they, as soon as they had received the word, were buried together with Christ by baptism."[12] Myrrh is scorn for the world, communicated by the example and the words of the saints.

In this communication of holiness, the apostles must take care to adapt their teaching to the capacity of their audience. This is the teaching of St Paul, who advises giving solid food to the perfect, and milk to those who are still children. Gregory often returns to this idea: "[Paul] brought the divine drink forth within himself and through the 'sweet savor of Christ' [2 Cor 2.15] poured it out, like a perfumer blending for his hearers the varied blossoms of the virtues. Thus the message was found to be a spice suited to the need of the one who sought it."[13]

A particular aspect of this way of adapting things—and which is of special interest to us, since it is how Gregory himself justifies his entire method—is the manner of commenting on the Scriptures in such a way that makes them easily assimilated by the people. The apostles should be not only the "eyes" of the body of the Church, contemplating things divine, but they should be her "teeth;" that is, they should also grind the text of Scripture, in order to make it digestible: "Those who grind the divine mysteries up small by interpreting them [ἐξηγήσεως, *exēgēseōs*] more lucidly, so that this spiritual nourishment can the more easily be taken in the Church's body, these people carry out the work of teeth. They take the thick and compact bread of the Word into their own mouth and by an interpretation that divides it into small bits they supply it to the souls of its recipients in a more edible form."[14] He continues by giving two examples of this kind of spiritual exegesis borrowed from St Paul.

Biblica 20.1 (939): 27–37, at 31–32. [Norris also refers to this problem in notes 13 and 15 to Homily 9 (pp. 293, 297) in his edition of this text.—*Trans.*]
[12]*Cant.* 14 (PG 44:1068A; Norris, 429–31).
[13]*Cant.* 14 (PG 44:1065B; Norris, 427).
[14]*Cant.* 7 (PG 44:925B; Norris, 237).

These texts, to which several others could be added, are sufficiently compelling; there is no need to further belabor the point. Unquestionably, the whole of Gregory's work is animated by a fervent desire for God. But the soul is not selfish with regard to the spiritual gifts it receives; it longs to communicate them to others. And thus, this last detail allows us to complete the picture of the spiritual type portrayed by the Cappadocian monk-bishop. It is not that of a solitary, fleeing from mankind in order to ensure his personal tranquility. The central figures of his writings are surrounded by an entire people and are animated by a kind of perpetual ebb and flow between contemplation and apostleship. There is Basil, surrounded by the Christian people whose shepherd he is. There is Paul, ardently desiring to be freed from this mortal body and to be united with Christ, but who is also the founder of churches and the Apostle to the Gentiles. There is Moses who, on the mountain, was initiated into the mysteries of the divine life, but who is also the one who leads Israel out of the land of Egypt.

To sum up this task of initiation into divine Love that is Gregory's last word, we find that a single symbolic figure marks its successive stages. In *On the Soul and the Resurrection* it is Macrina, Gregory's sister, who plays this role, but she is the undisguised heir to the stranger of Mantinea, Plato's Diotima.[15] In the *Homilies on the Song of Songs*, it is the Shulamite, herself a symbol of the Church. Thus all the components of Gregory's thought are based on this one figure. Platonic *eros* culminates in evangelical *agapē*. The biblical Shulamite symbolizes the Christian virgin. Gathering all these eminent personages together, Gregory makes of them one unique type. At the most superficial level it seems to be Platonic; on a deeper level, however, we see that it is clothed in biblical garb. And yet beneath all such symbolic garments what emerges is the figure of the Christian apostle, sending out the cry of Wisdom to the passer-by: "Come, and drink deeply!"

---

[15] See Plato, *Symposium* 201d.

Abbreviations

ACW — Ancient Christian Writers: The Works of the Fathers in Translation. Edited by Johannes Quasten, Joseph C. Plumpe, et al. New York/Mawah, NJ: Paulist Press, 1946–

ANF — The Ante-Nicene Fathers. Translations of the Writings of the Fathers Down to A.D. 325. 10 volumes. Edited by Alexander Roberts and James Donaldson. Buffalo, NY: The Christian Literature Company, 1885–1896, and many reprints.

Brill Dictionary — *The Brill Dictionary of Gregory of Nyssa.* Edited by Lucas Francisco Mateo-Seco and Giulio Maspero and translated by Seth Cherney. Supplements to Vigiliae Christianae 99. Leiden and Boston: Brill, 2010.

FC — The Fathers of the Church: A New Translation. Edited by Ludwig Schopp, Roy Joseph Deferrari, Bernard M. Peebles, et al. Washington, DC: The Catholic University of America Press, 1947–

GNO — Gregorii Nysseni Opera. 10 volumes in 17 plus supplement. Edited by Werner Jaeger, Herman Langerbeck, Hadwiga Hörner, et al. Leiden: Brill, 1952–2014.

NPNF[1] — A Select Library of Nicene and Post-Nicene Fathers of the Christian Church. First Series. 14 volumes. Edited by Philip Schaff. Buffalo, NY: The Christian Literature Company, 1886–1900, and many reprints.

NPNF[2] — A Select Library of Nicene and Post-Nicene Fathers of the Christian Church. Second Series. 14 volumes. Edited by Philip Schaff. Buffalo, NY: The Christian Literature Company, 1886–1900, and many reprints.

PG	Patrologiae Cursus Completus, Series Graeca. 161 volumes. Edited by Jacques Paul Migne. Paris, 1857–1866.
PL	Patrologia Cursus Completus, Series Latina. 217 volumes. Edited by Jacques Paul Migne. Paris, 1844–1855.
PPS	PPS Popular Patristics Series. Edited by John Behr, Bogdan Bucur, Augustine Casiday, and Ignatius Green. Crestwood/Yonkers, NY: St Vladimir's Seminary Press, 1996–
SC	Sources chrétiennes. Edited by Henri de Lubac, Jean Daniélou, Claude Mondésert, et al. Paris: Les Éditions du Cerf, 1942–

Bibliography

d'Alès, A. "Les ailes de l'âme." *Ephemerides Theologicae Lovanienses* 10 (1933): 63–72.
Ambrose of Milan. *On Abraham*. Translated by Theodosia Tomkinson. Etna, CA: Center for Traditionalist Orthodox Studies, 2000.
_____. *On the Mysteries*. NPNF² 10:315–25.
_____. *On Paradise*. In *Saint Ambrose: Hexameron, Paradise, and Cain and Abel*. Translated by John J. Savage. The Fathers of the Church 42. New York: Fathers of the Church, Inc., 1961. Pages 285–356.
Anonymus in Ecclesiasten commentarius qui dicitur catena trium patrum. Edited by Santo Lucà. Corpus Christianorum, Series Graeca 11. Turnhout: Brepols, 1983.
The Apostolic Constitutions [= *Constitutions of the Holy Apostles*]. ANF 7:385–505.
Aristotle. *Nicomachean Ethics*. *The Complete Works of Aristotle: The Revised Oxford Translation*, volumes 1 and 2 [hereafter *Complete Works*]. Edited by Jonathan Barnes. Bollingen Series 71.2. Princeton University Press, 1984. Pages 2:1729–1867.
(Pseudo-)Aristotle, *De Mundo* [= *On the Universe*]. In *Complete Works* 1:626–40.
Arnou, R. "Platonisme des Pères." In *Dictionnaire de Théologie catholique*, Volume 12. Paris: Letouzey et Ané, 1935. Columns 2310ff.
Athanasius. *On the Incarnation*. Translated by John Behr. Popular Patristics Series 44a. Yonkers, NY: St Vladimir's Seminary Press, 2011.
Augustine. *Confessions*. Translated by Henry Chadwick. Oxford University Press, 1991.
_____. *Expositions of the Psalms, 51–72*. The Works of Saint Augustine, Part Three, volume 17. Edited by John E. Rotelle. Hyde Park, NY: New City Press, 2001.
_____. *On the Trinity*. NPNF¹ 3:17–228.
_____. *Two Books of Soliloquies*. NPNF¹ 7:537–60.
Azkoul, Michael. *St. Gregory of Nyssa and the Tradition of the Fathers*. Lewiston, NY: The Edwin Mellen Press, 1995.
Baghos, Mario. "Reconsidering Apokatastasis in St Gregory of Nyssa's *On the Soul and Resurrection* and the *Catechetical Oration*." In *Cappadocian Legacy: A Critical Appraisal*. Edited by Doru Costache and Philip Kariatlis. Sydney: St Andrew's Orthodox Press, 2013. Pages 395–440.

Balthasar, Hans Urs von. *Présence et pensée. Étude sur la philosophie religieuse de Grégoire de Nysse*. Paris: Beauchesne, 1942. English translation: *Presence and Thought: An Essay on the Religious Philosophy of Gregory of Nyssa*. Translated by Mark Sebanc. San Francisco: Ignatius Press, 1995.

Barnes, Michel R. "'Some Synchronic Moment': Gregory of Nyssa, Théologie Mystique and French Ressourcement." *Nova et Vetera* 18.2 (2020): 367–411.

Basil the Great. *Commentary on the Prophet Isaiah*. Translated by Nikolai A. Lipatov. Texts and Studies in the History of Theology 7. Mandelbachtal/Cambridge: edition cicero, 2001.

_____. *Homily 12: On the Beginning of Proverbs*. In *St Basil the Great. On Christian Doctrine and Practice*. Translated by Mark DelCogliano. Popular Patristics Series 47. Yonkers, NY: St Vladimir's Seminary Press, 2012. Pages 39–78.

_____. *The Longer Responses* [= *The Longer Rules*]. In *The Asketikon of St Basil the Great*. Translated by Anna M. Silvas. Oxford Early Christian Studies. Oxford: Oxford University Press, 2005. Pages 153–269.

_____. *On the Origin of Humanity: Discourse 1*. In *St Basil the Great: On the Human Condition*. Translated by Nonna Verna Harrison. Popular Patristics Series 30. Crestwood, NY: St Vladimir's Seminary Press, 2005. Pages 31–48.[1]

Bate, H. N. "Some Technical Terms of Greek Exegesis." *Journal of Theological Studies* 24 (Oct. 1922): 59–66.

Bernard of Clairvaux. *The Life and Works of Saint Bernard, Volume 4: Sermons on the Canticles*. Translation by Samuel J. Eales. London: John Hodges, 1896.

Bérulle, P. de. *Élévation sur Marie-Madeleine*. Saint Maximin: Éditions de la Vie spirituelle, 1922.

Bettencourt, S. *Doctrina ascetica Origenis*. Città del Vaticano : Libreria Vaticana, 1945.

Bidez, J. *La Vie de l'Empereur Julien*. Paris: Les Belles Lettres, 1930.

Bigg, Ch. *The Christian Platonists of Alexandria*. Oxford: Clarendon Press, 1886.

Birgitta [Bridget] of Sweden. *The Prophecies and Revelations of Saint Bridget of Sweden*. Altenmünster: Jazzybee Verlag, 2016.

Boersma, Hans. *Embodiment and Virtue in Gregory of Nyssa: An Anagogical Aproach*. Oxford: Oxford University Press, 2013.

_____. *Seeing God: The Beatific Vision in Christian Tradition*. Grand Rapids, MI: Eerdmans, 2018.

Bouyer, Louis. *L'Incarnation et l'Église-Corps du Christ dans la théologie de saint Athanase*. Paris: Éditions du Cerf, 1943.

---

[1] With regard to Nyssene authorship, Daniélou writes that "we must conclude that these two homilies are indeed inauthentic" (p. xxv) but later seems to quote the work as Gregory's (pp. 13, 41). For more recent scholarly opinion, which favors Basil's authorship, see p. xxv n. 39.

Bradshaw, David. *Aristotle East and West: Metaphysics and the Division of Christendom*. Cambridge: Cambridge University Press, 2004.

Bradshaw Paul F. and Johnson, Maxwell E. *The Origins of Feasts, Fasts and Seasons in Early Christianity*. Alcuin Club Collections 86. Collegeville, MN: Liturgical Press, 2011.

Bréhier, E. *Les idées philosophiques et religieuses de Philon d'Alexandrie*. Paris: A. Picard, 1908; Vrin, 1925 2nd revised edition.

Bremond, J. *Les Pères du désert*, volume 1. Paris: J. Gabalda, 1927.

The Brill Dictionary of Gregory of Nyssa. Edited by Lucas Francisco Mateo-Seco and Giulio Maspero. Translated by Seth Cherney. Supplements to Vigiliae Christianae 99. Leiden: Brill, 2010.

Cabasilas, Nicholas. *Explication de la divine liturgie*. Translated by S. Salaville. Sources chrétiennes 4. Paris: Éditions du Cerf, 1943. English translation: *A Commentary on the Divine Liturgy*. Translated by J. M. Hussey and P. A. McNulty. London: SPCK, 1960. Reprinted by St Vladimir's Seminary Press, 2002.

———. *The Life in Christ*. Translated Carmino J. De Catanzaro. Crestwood, NY: St Vladimir's Seminary Press, 1974.

Cabrol, F. and Leclercq, H. "Moïse." In *Dictionnaire d'Archéologie Chrétienne et de Liturgie*, Vol. 11. Paris: Letouzey et Ané, 1933. Columns 1655–56.

Cadbury, H. J. "The Odor of the Spirit at Pentecost." *Journal of Biblical Literature* 47 (1928): 237–56.

Carcopino, J. *Virgile et le mystère de la IVe Églogue*. Paris: L'Artisan du livre, 1930.

Carey, Phillip. *Augustine's Invention of the Inner Self: The Legacy of a Christian Platonist*. Oxford: Oxford University Press, 2003.

Cassian, John. *The Conferences*. NPNF² 11:291–545.

Cherniss, Harold Fredrik. *The Platonism of Gregory of Nyssa*. Berkeley, CA: University of California Press, 1930.

Cicero. *De Natura Deorum [On the Nature of the Gods]*. Translated by Francis Brooks. London: Methuen & Co., 1896.

Clement of Alexandria. *Exhortation to the Heathen [Protrepticus]*. ANF 2:171–206.

———. *The Instructor [Pædagogus]*. ANF 2:207–296

———. *The Stromata, or Miscellanies*. ANF 2:299–567.

———. *Who is the Rich Man That Shall Be Saved?* ANF 2:591–604.

Climacus, John. *The Ladder of Divine Ascent*, revised edition. Brookline, MA: Holy Transfiguration Monastery, 2012.

Cumont, Franz. *Les Religions orientales dans le paganisme romain*. Paris: Leroux, 1906. English translation: *The Oriental Religions in Roman Paganism*. Translated by Grant Showerman. Chicago: Open Court Publishing, 1911.

Cyril of Jerusalem. *Catechetical Lectures*. NPNF² 7:1–157.

Daniélou, Jean. "Apocatastase." In *L'Être et le Temps chez Grégoire de Nysse*. Leiden: Brill, 1970. Pages 205–26.

———. "L'Apocatastase chez saint Grégoire de Nysse." *Recherches de Science Religieuse* 30.3 (July 1940): 328–47.

———. *Bible et Liturgie*. Paris: Éditions du Cerf, 1951. In English translation: *The Bible and the Liturgy*. Notre Dame, IN: University of Notre Dame Press, 1956.

———. "Gregorio Nisseno." In *Enciclopedia Cattolica*, Volume 6. Vatican City, 1951. Columns 1096–1111.

———. "Notes sur trois textes eschatologiques de saint Grégoire de Nysse." *Recherches de Science Religieuse* 30.3 (July 1940): 348–56.

———. *Origène*. Paris: La Table Ronde, 1948. English translation: *Origen*. Translated by W. Mitchell. London and New York: Sheed and Ward, 1955.

———. "Les repas de la Bible et leur signification." *La Maison-Dieu: Cahiers de pastorale liturgique* 18 (1949): 28–32.

———. *Sacramentum futuri: Études sur les origines de la typologie biblique*. Paris: Beauchesne, 1950. English translation: *From Shadows to Reality: Studies in the Biblical Typology of the Fathers*. Translated by Dom Wulstan Hibberd. London: Burns and Oates, 1960.

Déchanet, Jean-Marie. *Aux sources de la spiritualité de Guillaume de Saint-Thierry*. Bruges: Beyaert, 1940.

Delatte, A. *Études sur la littérature pythagoricienne*. Paris: Champion, 1915.

Denis, J. F. *De la philosophie d'Origène*. Paris: Thorin, 1884.

Devreesse, R. "Les chaînes exégétiques grecques." In *Dictionnaire de la Bible, Supplément I*. Paris: Letouzey et Ané, 1928. Columns 1084–1233.

Diadochos of Photiki. *On Spiritual Knowledge and Discrimination: One Hundred Texts*. In *The Philokalia*, volume 1. Translated by G. E. H. Palmer, P. Sherrard and K. Ware. Faber and Faber: London, 1979.

Dictionnaire de spiritualité ascétique et mystique, doctrine et histoire, volume 1. Edited by Marcel Viller, Ferdinand Cavallera, and Joseph de Guibert. Paris: G. Beauchesne et ses fils, 1937

Didymus the Blind. *De Trinitate*. PG 39:269–1034.

Diekamp, F. *Die Gotteslehre des heiligen Gregor von Nyssa*. Münster: Aschendorff, 1896.

Diogenes Laertius. *Lives of Eminent Philosophers: Books 6–10*. Translated by R. D. Hicks. Cambridge, MA: Harvard University Press, 1925.

Dodd, C. H. *The Bible and The Greeks*. London: Hodder & Stoughton, 1935.

Dölger, F.-J. "Der Altarkuss." *Antike und Christentum* 2 (1930): 190–221.

———. "Der Durchzug durch das Rote Meer als Sinnbild der christlichen Taufe." *Antike und Christentum* 2 (1930): 63–69.

———. "Das Lösen der Schuhriemen in der Taufsymbolik des Klemens von Alexandrien." *Antike und Christentum* 5 (1936): 87–94.

———. "Das Schuh-Ausziehen in der altchristlichen Taufliturgie." *Antike und Christentum* 5 (1936): 95–108.

———. "Das Verbot des Barfussgehens und der kultisch reine Schuh der Täuflinge in der Oktav nach der Taufe." *Antike und Christentum* 5 (1936): 109–115.

Dorotheos of Gaza. *Discourses and Sayings*. Translated by Eric Wheeler, OSB. Cistercian Studies 33. Collegeville, MN: Liturgical Press, 1977.

Duncan, E. J. *Baptism in the Demonstrations of Aphraates the Persian Sage*. Washington, DC: Catholic University of America Press, 1941.

Eisler, R. *Orphisch-Dionysische Mysteriengedanken in der christlichen Antike*. Leipzig: Teubner, 1925.

Elm, Susanna. *Sons of Hellenism, Fathers of the Church: Emperor Julian, Gregory of Nazianzus, and the Vision of Rome*. Berkeley and Los Angeles: University of California Press, 2012.

Euringer, S. "'Schöpferische Exegese' im Äthiopischen Hohenliede. Nachträge." *Biblica* 20.1 (1939): 27–37.

Faye, E. de. *Clément d'Alexandrie*. Paris: E. Leroux, 1898.

Festugière, A.-J. *Le Dieu cosmique*. Paris: Lecoffre, 1949.

———. "La divinisation du Chrétien." *La Vie Spirituelle* 59, suppl. (1939): 90–99.

———. "Εἰς ἄνθρωπον ὑποφέρεσθαι." *Revue des Sciences Philosophiques et Théologiques* 20 (1931): 476–82.

———. *L'enfant d'Agrigente*. Paris: Éditions du Cerf, 1941.

———. *La sainteté*. Paris: Presses Universitaires de France, 1942.

Gandillac, M. de. *La philosophie de Nicolas de Cues*. Paris: Aubier, 1941.

Gavrilyuk, Paul and Sarah Coakley, editors. *The Spiritual Senses: Perceiving God in Western Christianity*. Cambridge University Press, 2012.

Geljon, Albert C. *Philonic Exegesis in Gregory of Nyssa's De Vita Moysis*. Providence, RI: Brown Judaic Studies, 2002.

Giet, S. "Saint Basile a-t-il donné une suite aux homélies de l'Hexaeméron?" *Recherches de Science Religieuse* 33 (1946): 317–359.

Gilson, Étienne. *La théologie mystique de saint Bernard*. Paris: Vrin, 1934. English translation: *The Mystical Theology of Saint Bernard*. Translated by A. H. C. Downes. London/New York: Sheed & Ward, 1940.

Golitzin, Abp Alexander. *Mystagogy: A Monastic Reading of Dionysius Areopagita*. Edited by Bogdan Bucur. Collegeville, MN: Liturgical Press, 2013.

Gregory the Great. *Dialogues*. Translated by Odo John Zimmerman. The Fathers of the Church 39. Washington, DC: The Catholic University of America, 1959.

Gregory of Nyssa. See Bibliography of St Gregory of Nyssa's Works in English. This volume, pages 389–402.

K. Gronau, *Poseidonius und die jüdisch-christliche Genesisexegese*. Leipzig: Teubner, 1914.

Guittton, Jean. *Newman et Renan*. Paris: Aubier, 1938.

Hausherr, I. "Les grands courants de la spiritualité orientale." *Orientalia Christiana Periodica* 1 (1935): 114–38.

———. "Ignorance infinie." *Orientalia Christiana Periodica* 2 (1936): 351–62.

Heinemann, I. *Posidonios' metaphysische Schriften*, volume 2. Breslau: Marcus, 1928.

Heinisch, P. *Der Einfluss Philos auf die älteste christliche Exegese*. Münster: Aschendorff, 1908.

Henry, Paul. *La vision d'Ostie*. Paris: Vrin, 1938.

Hilt, F. *Des hl. Gregors von Nyssa Lehre vom Menschen systematisch dargestellt*. Cologne, 1890.

Holl, Karl. *Amphilochius von Ikonium in seinem Verhältnis zu den grossen Kappadoziern*. Tübingen: Mohr, 1969.

Homer. *The Iliad: Books 13–24*. Translated by A. T. Murray. Loeb Classical Library 171. Cambridge, MA: Harvard University Press, 1985.

———. *The Odyssey: Books 13–24*. Translated by George E. Dimock. Revised by A. T. Murray. Loeb Classical Library 105. Cambridge, MA: Harvard University Press, 1919.

Horn, G. "L'amour divin. Note sur le mot 'Eros' dans Saint Grégoire de Nysse." *Revue d'Ascétique et de Mystique* 6 (1925): 378–89.

———. "Le 'miroir' et la 'nuée,' deux manières de voir Dieu d'après Saint Grégoire de Nysse." *Revue d'Ascétique et de Mystique* 8 (1927): 113–31.

Ignatius of Antioch. *Letter to the Ephesians*. In *The Letters*. Translated by Alistair Stewart. Popular Patristics Series 49. Yonkers, NY: St Vladimir's Seminary Press, 2013. Pages 27–41.

Innocent III. *De sacro altaris mysterio*. PL 217:775–916.

Irenaeus. *Against Heresies*. ANF 1:315–567.

———. *On the Apostolic Preaching* [= *Demonstration of the Apostolic Preaching*]. Translated by John Behr. Popular Patristics Series 17. Crestwood, NY: St Vladimir's Seminary Press, 1997.

Ivánka, Endre von. "Die Autorschaft der Homilien Εἰς τὸ Ποιήμεν ἄνθρωπον κατ' εἰκόνα ἡμετέραν καὶ ὁμοίωσιν." *Byzantinische Zeitschrift* 36.1 (January 1936): 46–57.

———. "Die Quelle von Ciceros *De natura deorum*, ii. 45–60. (Poseidonios bei Gregor von Nyssa)." *Archivum Philologicum* 59 (1935): 10–21.

Bibliography

———. "Die unmittelbare Gotteserkenntnis bei Augustin." *Scholastik* 13 (1938): 521–43.

———. "Vom Platonismus zur Theorie der Mystik (Zur Erkenntnislehre Gregors von Nyssa)." *Scholastik* 11 (1936): 163–95.

Jankélévitch, Vl. *La mauvaise conscience*. Paris: Alcan, 1933.

Julian the Apostate. [Apocryphal] *Epistula 180: Ad Sarapionem virum clarissimum*. In *Iuliani Imperatoris: Epistulae et Leges*. Edited by J. Bidez and F. Cumont. Paris: Les Belles Lettres, 1922. Pages 228–37. English translation: Apocryphal Letter 80: "To the most illustrious Serapion." In *The Works of the Emperor Julian*, volume 3. Edited and translated by W. C. Wright. London: Heinemann, 1923. Pages 266–83.

Justin Martyr. *Dialogue of Justin, Philosopher and Martyr, with Trypho, a Jew* [= *Dialogue with Trypho*]. ANF 1:194–270.

———. *The First Apology of Justin Martyr*. ANF 1:163–87.

Koch, Hugo. "Das mystische Schauen beim hl. Gregor von Nyssa." *Theologische Quartalschrift* 80 (1898): 397–420.

———. *Pseudo-Dionysius Areopagita in seinen Beziehungen zum Neuplatonismus und Mysterienwesen*. Mainz: Kirchheim, 1900.

Labriolle, P. "La polémique anti-montaniste contre la prophétie extatique." *Revue d'histoire et de littérature religieuses* 11 (1906): 97–145.

Lebreton, J. "La nuit obscure, d'après Jean de la Croix: Les sources et le caractère de sa doctrine." *Revue d'ascétique et de mystique* 9 (1928): 2–24.

Lewy, H. *Sobria ebrietas*. Giessen: Alfred Töppelmann, 1929.

Lieske, A. "Zur Theologie der Christusmystik bei Gregors von Nyssa." *Scholastik* 14 (1939): 485–514.

Lohmeyer, E. J. *Vom göttlichen Wohlgeruch*. Heidelberg: Heidelberger Akademie der Wissenschaften, 1919.

Lossky, Vladimir. "La théologie négative dans la doctrine de Denys l'Aréopagite." *Revue des Sciences Philosophiques et Théologiques* (April 1939): 204–221.

Lot-Borodine M. "La grâce déifiante des sacrements d'après Nicolas Cabasilas." *Revue des Sciences Philosophiques et Théologiques* 25 (1936): 229–30.

———. "Initiation à une mystique sacramentaire de l'Orient." *Revue des Sciences Philosophiques et Théologiques* 24 (1935): 664–75.

Loudovikos, Nikolaos. "Striving for Participation: Palamite Analogy as Dialogical Syn-energy and Thomist Analogy as Emanational Similitude." In *Divine Essence and Divine Energies: Ecumenical Reflections on the Presence of God in Eastern Orthodoxy*. Edited by C. Athanasopoulos and Christoph Schneider. Cambridge: James Clarke & Co, 2013. Pages 122–48.

Lubac, Henri de. "Textes alexandrins et bouddhiques." *Recherches de science religieuse* 27 (1937): 336–51.

Lucan. *Pharsalia*. Translated by Jane Wilson Joyce. Ithaca, NY: Cornell University Press, 1993.

Ludlow, Morwenna. *Gregory of Nyssa, Ancient and (Post)modern*. Oxford: Oxford University Press, 2007.

———. *Universal Salvation: Eschatology in the Thought of Gregory of Nyssa and Karl Rahner*. Oxford University Press, 2000.

(Pseudo-)Macarius. *The Fifty Spiritual Homilies and The Great Letter*. Translated by George A. Maloney. Classics of Western Spirituality. Mahwah, NJ: Paulist Press, 1992.

Marcus Aurelius. *The Meditations*. In *Marcus Aurelius*. Edited and translated by C. R. Haines. Loeb Classical Library 58. Cambridge, MA: Harvard University Press, 1916. Pages 1–345.

Maréchal, J. *Étude sur la psychologie des mystiques*, tome II. Bruxelles/Paris: L'Édition universelle/Desclée de Brouwer, 1937.

Marmion, C. *Le Christ, Idéal du moine*. Paris : Desclée de Brouwer, 1922. English translation: *Christ, The Ideal of the Monk*. Translated by A Nun of Tyburn Convent. London and Edinburgh: Sands & Company, 1926.

Marrou, H.-I. *Saint Augustin et la fin de la culture antique*, volume 1. Paris: Boccard, 1938.

Maximus the Confessor. *Four Hundred Texts on Love*. In *The Philokalia: The Complete Text*. Edited and translated by G. E. H. Palmer, Philip Sherrard, and Kallistos Ware. London: Faber & Faber, 1984. Pages 52–113.

Maximus of Tyre. *The Dissertations*, volume 1. Translated by T. Taylor. London, 1804.

de Mendieta, Emmanuel Amand. "Les deux homélies sur la creation de l'homme que les manuscripts attribuent à Basile de Césarée ou à Grégoire de Nysse: Le problème de leur redaction." In *Zetesis: Album amicorum door vrienden en collega's aangeboden aan Prof. Dr. E. de Strycker ter gelegenheid van zijn 65e verjaardag*. Antwerp and Utrecht: Nederlandsche Boekhandel, 1973. Pages 695–716.

Méridier, L. *L'influence de la seconde sophistique sur l'oeuvre de Grégoire de Nysse*. Paris: Hachette, 1906.

Merki, H. ὈΜΟΙΩΣΙΣ ΘΕΩ: *von der platonischen Angleichung an Gott zur Gottähnlichkeit bei Gregor von Nyssa*. Freiburg in der Schweiz: Éditions universitaires, 1952.

Methodius of Olympus. *From the Discourse on the Resurrection*. ANF 6:364–77.

———. *Methodius*. Edited by G. N. Bonwetsch. Die Griechischen Christlichen Schriftsteller 27. Leipzig: J. C. Hinrichs, 1917.

———. *The Banquet of the Ten Virgins; or Concerning Chastity* [= *Symposium*]. ANF 6:309–55.

Motia, Michael. "Dionysius and Gregory of Nyssa." In *The Oxford Handbook of Dionysius the Areopagite*. Edited Mark Edwards, Dimitrios Pallis, and Georgios Steiris. Oxford University Press, 2022. Pages 109–121.

Nygren, Anders. *Agape and Eros, Part I: A Study of the Christian Idea of Love, Part II: The History of the Christian Idea of Love*. Translated by Philip S. Watson. New York: Harper & Row, 1969 [1st edition of Part I, 1930; Part II, 1936].

Origen. *Commentary on the Gospel according to John: Books 1–10*. Translated by R. E. Heine. The Fathers of the Church 80. Washington, DC: The Catholic University of America Press, 1989.

———. *The Commentary of Origen on the Gospel of St Matthew*. Translated by Ronald E. Heine. Oxford Early Christian Texts. Oxford University Press, 2018.

———. *Contra Celsum*. Translated by Henry Chadwick. Cambridge University Press, 1980 [revised edition].

———. *Homilies on Exodus*. In *Homilies on Genesis and Exodus*. Translated by Ronald E. Heine. The Fathers of the Church Series 71. Washington, DC: The Catholic University of America Press, 1982. Pages 225–387.

———. *Homilies on Genesis*. FC 71:47–224.

———. *Homilies on Joshua*. Translated by Barbara J. Bruce. The Fathers of the Church Series 105. Washington, DC: The Catholic University of America Press, 2002.

———. *Homilies on Leviticus 1–16*. Translated by G. W. Barkley. The Fathers of the Church 83. Washington, DC: The Catholic University of America Press, 1990.

———. *Homilies on Numbers*. Translated by Thomas P. Scheck. Edited by Christopher A. Hall. Ancient Christian Texts. Downers Grove, IL: IVP Academic, 2009.

———. *Homilies on the Psalms. Codex Monacensis Graecus 314*. Translated by Joseph W. Trigg. The Fathers of the Church Series 141. Washington, DC: The Catholic University of America Press, 2021.

———. *Letter of Origen to Gregory*. In *St. Gregory Thaumaturgus: Life and Works*. Translated by Michael Slusser. Fathers of the Church 98. Washington, DC: The Catholic University of America Press, 1998. Pages 189–92.

———. *On Prayer*. In Tertullian, Cyprian, and Origen. *On the Lord's Prayer*. Translated by Alistair Stewart-Sykes. Popular Patristics Series 26. Crestwood, NY: St Vladimir's Seminary Press, 2004. Pages 111–214.

———. *The Song of Songs: Commentary and Homilies*. Translated by R. P. Lawson. Ancient Christian Writers 26. Westminster, MD: The Newman Press, 1957.

J. Pascher, J. *Hē basilikē hodos: Der Königsweg zu Wiedergeburt und Vergottung bei Philon von Alexandreia*. Paderborn: Schöningh, 1931.

The Passion of the Holy Martyrs Perpetua and Felicity. ANF 6:699–717.

Pera, C. "Denys le Mystique et la Theomachia." *Revue des Sciences Philosophiques et Théologiques* 25 (1936): 5–75.

Peterson, E. "Herkunft und Bedeutung der Monos pros monon-formel bei Plotin." *Philologus* 88 (1933): 30–41.

_____. "Zur Bedeutungsgeschichte von Παρρησία." In *Reinhold Seeberg Festschrift*, volume 2. Edited by W. Koepp. Leipzig: Scholl, 1929. Pages 283–97.

Philo of Alexandria. *On Abraham*. In *The Works of Philo: Complete and Unabridged, New Updated Version* [hereafter *Works of Philo*]. Translated by C. D. Yonge. Peabody, MA: Hendrickson Publishers, 1993. Pages 411–34.

_____. *Allegorical Interpretation* 1–3. In *Works of Philo*, 25–79.

_____. *The Cherubim*. In *Works of Philo*, 80–93.

_____. *On the Contemplative Life*. In *Works of Philo*, 698–706.

_____. *On the Creation*. In *Works of Philo*, 3–24.

_____. *On Dreams*. In *Works of Philo*, 365–410.

_____. *On Drunkenness*. In *Works of Philo*, 207–26.

_____. *On Flight and Finding*. In *Works of Philo*, 321–40.

_____. *On Husbandry*. In *Works of Philo*, 174–90.

_____. *On the Life of Moses* 2. In *Works of Philo*, 491–517.

_____. *On the Migration of Abraham*. In *Works of Philo*, 253–75.

_____. *On the Posterity of Cain and his Exile*. In *Works of Philo*, 132–51.

_____. *Questions and Answers on Exodus*. In *Philo: Supplement II. Questions on Exodus*. Translated by Ralph Marcus, Loeb Classical Library 401. Cambridge, MA: Harvard University Press, 1953.

_____. *On Rewards and Punishments*. In *Works of Philo*, 664–81.

_____. *On the Sacrifices of Abel and Cain* [= *On the Birth of Cain and Abel and the Sacrifices Offered by Him and by His Brother Cain*]. In *Works of Philo*, 94–112.

_____. *On Sobriety* [=*On the Prayers and Curses Uttered by Noah When He Became Sober*]. In *Works of Philo*, 227–33.

_____. *The Special Laws* 1. In *Works of Philo*, 534–67.

_____. *The Special Laws* 3. In *Works of Philo*, 594–615.

_____. *Who is the Heir of Divine Things*. In *Works of Philo*, 276–303.

Plato. *The Laws of Plato*. Translated by Thomas L. Pangle. University of Chicago Press,

_____. *Plato: Phaedo*. Translated by David Gallop. Oxford: Oxford University Press, 1993.

Bibliography   385

———. *Phèdre*. Edited and translated by Léon Robin. Oeuvres complètes, tome IV, 3ème partie. Paris: Les Belles Lettres, 1933.

———. *Plato: Phaedrus*. Translated by Robin Waterfield. Oxford: Oxford University Press, 2002.

———. *Plato: Republic*. Translated by Robin Waterfield. Oxford: Oxford University Press, 1993.

———. *Plato: Symposium*. Translated by Robin Waterfield. Oxford: Oxford University Press, 1994.

———. *Plato: Theaetetus*. Translated by John McDowell. Oxford: Oxford University Press, 1973, 2014.

Plested, Marcus. *The Macarian Legacy: The Place of Macarius-Symeon in the Eastern Christian Tradition*. Oxford University Press, 2004.

Plotinus. *Ennéades*, volume 5. Edited and translated by Emile Bréhier. Paris: Les Belles Lettres, 1931.

———. *Ennead VI.1–5*. Translated by A. H. Armstrong. Loeb Classical Library No. 445. Cambridge, MA: Harvard University Press, 1988.

———. *The Enneads*. Translated by Stephen MacKenna. Edited by John Dillon. Harmondsworth: Penguin Books, 1991.

Poimandres. In *Thrice Greatest Hermes: Studies in Hellenistic Theosophy and Gnosis*. Translated by G. R. S. Mead. London and Benares: The Theosophical Publishing Society, 1906. Pages 120–21 [Daniélou cites this as *Poimandres*, which in this translation is limited to pp. 1–20].

Porphyry. *On Abstinence*. In *Select Works of Porphyry; Containing His Four Books on Abstinence from Animal Food; His Treatise on the Homeric Cave of the Nymphs; and His Auxiliaries to the Perception of the Intelligible Natures*. Translated by Thomas Taylor. London: Thomas Rodd, 1823. Pages 1–170.

Poulain, A. *Des grâces d'oraison: Traité de théologie mystique*. Paris: Beauchesne, 1901. English translation: *The Graces of Interior Prayer*. Translated by L. Smith. London: Kegan Paul, 1910.

Prat, F. *La Théologie de saint Paul*, volume 2. Paris: Beauchesne, 1912. English translation: *The Theology of Saint Paul*, volume 2. Translated by John L. Stoddard. London: Burns, Oates and Washbourne, 1927.

Proclus. *Proclus: The Elements of Theology*. Edited and translated by E. R. Dodds. Oxford: Clarendon Press, 1933.

Prümm, K. "Mystērion bei Athanasius." *Zeitschrift für Katholische Theologie* 63 (1939): 350–59.

Puech, H.-Ch. "Der Begriff der Erlösung im Manichäismus." *Eranos-Jahrbuch* (1936): 183–286.

———. "Un livre récent sur la mystique d'Origène." *Revue d'histoire et de philosophie religieuses* 13 (1933): 508–36.

———. "Position spirituelle et signification de Plotin." *Bulletin de l'Asociation Guillaume Budé* 61 (Oct. 1938): 13–46.

———. "La ténèbre mystique chez le Pseudo-Denys l'Aréopagite et dans la tradition patristique." *Études Carmélitaines* 23 (1938): 33–53.

Pseudo-Melito. *De bestiis et cæteris animantibus* [= *Clavis* 9]. In *Spicilegium Solesmense complectens sanctorum patrum scriptorumque ecclesiasticorum anecdota hactenus opera*, volume 3. Edited by Dom. J. B. Pitra. Paris: F. Didot, 1855. Pages 1–101.

Radde-Gallwitz, Andrew. "Gregory of Nyssa on the Reciprocity of the Virtues." *Journal of Theological Studies* 58.2 (2007): 537–52.

Rahner, Hugo. "Die Gottesgeburt: Die Lehre der Kirchenväter von der Geburt Christi im Herzen des Gläubigen." *Zeitschrift für Katholische Theologie* 59.3 (1935): 333–418.

———. "Taufe und geistliches Leben bei Origenes." *Zeitschrift für Aszese und Mystik* 7 (1932): 205–22.

Rahner, K. "Le début d'une doctrine des cinq sens spirituels chez Origène." *Revue d'ascétique et de mystique* 13 (1932): 113–45.

Ramelli, Ilaria L. E. *The Christian Doctrine of Apokatastasis: A Critical Assessment from the New Testament to Eriugena*. Supplements to Vigiliae Christianae 120. Leiden: Brill, 2013.

Riedel, W. *Die Auslegung des Hohenliedes in der jüdischen Gemeinde und der griechischen Kirche*. Naumberg: 1898.

Rimbaud, A. *Une Saison en Enfer*. Bruxelles: Alliance Typographique (M.-J. Poot et Compagnie), 1873.

Sallustius. *Concerning the Gods and the Universe*. Translated by A. D. Nock. Cambridge: Cambridge University Press, 1926.

Schoeps, H. J. *Aus frühchristlicher Zeit*. Tübingen: Mohr, 1950.

Scholz, Heinrich. *Glaube und Unglaube in der Weltgeschichte: Ein Kommentar zu Augustins De civitate dei; Mit einem Exkurs: Fruitio Dei: Ein Beitrag zur Geschichte der Theologie und der Mystik*. Leipzig: J. C. Hinrichs'sche Buchhandlung, 1911.

Schuster, I. *The Sacramentary (Liber Sacramentorum): Historical & Liturgical Notes on the Roman Missal*. London: Burns, Oates & Washbourne, 1924.

The Shepherd of Hermas. In *The Apostolic Fathers: Greek Texts and English Translations*, third edition. Edited and translated by Michael W. Holmes. Grand Rapids, MI: Baker Academic, 2007. Pages 442–685.

Soury, G. *La démonologie de Plutarque*. Paris: Belles-Lettres, 1942.

Stiglmayr, J. "Die Schrift des hl. Gregor von Nyssa Über die Jungfräulichkeit." *Zeitschrift für Ascese und Mystik* 2 (1927): 334–59.
Stoicorum Veterum Fragmenta, volume 3. Edited by H. von Arnim. Stuttgart: Teubner, 1964 [1st ed. 1903].
Stolz, Anselm. *Theologie der Mystik*. Regensburg: Pustet, 1936. Translations: *The Doctrine of Spiritual Perfection*. Translated by Aidan Williams. St Louis, MO and London: Herder, 1938. *Théologie de la mystique*. Chevetogne: Bénédictins d'Amay, 1939.
Synesius of Cyrene. *On Imperial Rule*. In *The Essays and Hymns of Synesius of Cyrene, including the Address to the Emperor Arcadius and the Political Speeches*. Translated by Augustine Fitzgerald. London: Oxford University Press, 1930.
Talley, Thomas J. *The Origins of the Liturgical Year*. New York: Pueblo Publishing Company, 1986.
Teresa of Avila. *The Interior Castle*. Translated and edited by E. Allison Peers. London: Sheed & Ward, 1974.
Tertullian. *Against the Valentinians*. ANF 3:503–520.
———. *On Modesty*. ANF 4:74–101.
Theodore of Mopsuestia. *Les Homélies catéchétiques de Théodore de Mopsueste*. Translated by R. Tonneau. Studi e Testi 145. Vatican City: Biblioteca Apostolica Vaticana, 1949.
Theological Dictionary of the New Testament, volume 1. Edited by Gerhard Kittel. Translated by G. W. Bromiley. Grand Rapids, MI: Eerdmans, 1964.
Theological Dictionary of the New Testament Abridged in One Volume. Edited by Gerhard Kittel and Gerhard Friedrich. Translated by Geoffrey W. Bromiley. Grand Rapids, MI: William B. Eerdmans Publishing Co., 1985.
Tyrrell, George. *Christianity at the Crossroads*. New York: Longmans, Green and Co., 1909.
Viller, M. "Aux sources de la spiritualité de saint Maxime: les oeuvres d'Évagre le Pontique." *Revue d'ascétique et de mystique* 11 (avril–juillet, 1930): 150–84; 239–68; 331–36.
Völker, W. *Fortschritt und Vollendung bei Philo von Alexandrien*. Leipzig: Hinrichs Verlag, 1938.
———. *Das Vollkommenheitsideal des Origenes*. Tübingen: Mohr, 1931.
Willms, H. *Εἰκών: eine begriffsgeschichtliche Untersuchung zum Platonismus, I: Philon von Alexandreia*. Münster: Aschendorff, 1935.
Wilmart, A. "La Tradition de l'Hypotypose (PG 46:287A–305C) ou traité de l'ascèse attribué à Grégoire de Nysse." *Revue de l'Orient Chrétien* 21 (1918–1919): 412–21.
Ziegler, J. *Dulcedo Dei*. Münster: Aschendorff, 1937.

Bibliography of St Gregory of Nyssa's Works in English

This bibliography includes all the texts of the Nyssene corpus, listing their place in Migne's *Patrologia Graeca* and in the *Gregorii Nysseni Opera* series, along with major English translations (the most recent or the best translations are always listed, but many older translations are also included, especially when they are readily available and widely used, e.g., those found in volume 5 of the Nicene and Post-Nicene Fathers, second series). Texts are ordered alphabetically, according to the commonly used abbreviations of the Latin titles found in the GNO series, while under the heading of each work, the individual translations are ordered chronologically, beginning with the most recent translation.—*Ed.*

Abl. — Ad Ablabium, Quod non sint tres dei (PG 45:116–36; GNO III/1:37–57)
A Letter of Gregory, Bishop of Nyssa, to Ablabius, A Defense against the Notion that We Profess Three Gods. In *The Trinitarian Works of Gregory of Nyssa*. Translated by Brian Duvick. Popular Patristics Series [number to-be-determined]. Yonkers, NY: St Vladimir's Seminary Press, forthcoming.
Gregory of Nyssa: De Beatitudinibus IV, Ad Ablabium, *and* Adversus Macedonianos: *English and German Translations and Studies*. Edited by David J. McCollough, Igor Pochoshajew, and Oliver Erckens. Patrologia—Beiträge zum Studium der Kirchenväter 20. Bern, Switzerland: Peter Lang, 2008.
An Answer to Ablablius: That We Should Not Think of Saying There Are Three Gods. Translated by Cyril C. Richardson. In *Christology of the Later Fathers*. Edited by Edward R. Hardy and Cyril C. Richardson. The Library of Christian Classics, Volume 3. Louisville, KY: The Westminster Press, 1954. Pages 256–67.
To Ablabius: On "Not Three Gods." NPNF² 5:331–36.

An. et res. — De anima et resurrectione (PG 46:12–160; GNO III/3)
On the Soul and the Resurrection. Translated by Anna M. Silvas. In *Macrina the Younger, Philosopher of God*. Medieval Women: Texts and Contexts, Volume 22. Turnhout, Belgium: Brepols, 2008. Pages 171–246.
On the Soul and the Resurrection. Translated by Catharine P. Roth. Popular Patristics Series 12. Crestwood, NY: 1993.

On the Soul and the Resurrection. In *St. Gregory of Nyssa: Ascetical Works.* Translated by Virginia Woods Callahan. The Fathers of the Church 58. Washington, DC: The Catholic University of America Press, 1967. Pages 193–272.

On the Soul and the Resurrection. NPNF² 5:428–68.

Antirrh. — *Antirrheticus adversus Apollinarium* (PG 45:1124–1269; GNO III/1:131–233)

Refutation of the Views of Apolinarius. In *St. Gregory of Nyssa: Anti-Apollinarian Writings.* Translated by Robin Orton. The Fathers of the Church 131. Washington, DC: The Catholic University of America Press, 2015. Pages 91–258.

Against Apollinarius. Translated by Richard McCambley. https://www.lectio-divina.org/images/nyssa/Against%20Apollinarius.pdf.

Arium.[1] — *Adversos Arium et Sabellium, De Patre et Filio* (PG 45:1281–1301; GNO III/1:71–85)

A letter of Gregory, Bishop of Nyssa, against Arius and Sabellius. In *The Trinitarian Works of Gregory of Nyssa.* Translated by Brian Duvick. Popular Patristics Series [number to-be-determined]. Yonkers, NY: St Vladimir's Seminary Press, forthcoming.

Ascens. — *In ascensionem Christi Oratio* (PG 46:689–93; GNO IX:323–27)

On the Ascension of Our Lord Jesus Christ. In *Saint Gregory of Nyssa: Homilies on the Feasts of the Church.* Translated by Michael J. Petrin. Popular Patristics Series [number to-be-determined]. Yonkers, NY: St Vladimir's Seminary Press, forthcoming.

Homily on the Ascension. Translated by Richard McCambley. http://www.lectio-divina.org/index.php/reflections/reflections-on-the-writings-of-gregory-of-nyssa.

Bapt. — *De iis qui baptismum differunt* (PG 46:416–32; GNO X/2:355–70)

To Those Who Delay Baptism. In *Saint Gregory of Nyssa: Homilies on the Feasts of the Church.* Translated by Michael J. Petrin. Popular Patristics Series [number to-be-determined]. Yonkers, NY: St Vladimir's Seminary Press, forthcoming.

Bas. — *In Basilium fratrem* (PG 46:788–817; GNO X/1:109–134)

On His Brother Basil the Great. In *Saint Gregory of Nyssa: Homilies on the Feasts of the Church.* Translated by Michael J. Petrin. Popular Patristics Series [number to-be-determined]. Yonkers, NY: St Vladimir's Seminary Press, forthcoming.

A Eulogy for Basil the Great. Translated by Richard McCambly. http://www.lectio-divina.org/images/nyssa/Eulogy%20for%20Basil%20the%20Great.pdf.

---

[1]While Jaeger includes this in among the minor dogmatic works, its authenticity is now in doubt (Brill Dictionary, 84). Daniélou argued for its authenticity, but Hübner argues to the contrary (ibid., 85).

Encomium of Saint Gregory, Bishop of Nyssa, on His Brother Saint Basil, Archbishop of Cappadocian Caesarea: A Commentary, with a Revised Text, Introduction, and Translation. Translated and edited by Sister James Aloysius Stein. Patristic Studies 17. Washington, DC. The Catholic University of America, 1928.

Beat. — De beatitudinibus (PG 46:788–817; GNO VII/2:75–170)

Gregory of Nyssa: Homilies on the Beatitudes, An English Version with Commentary and Supporting Studies, Proceedings of the Eighth International Colloquium on Gregory of Nyssa (Paderborn, 14–18 Septempter 1998). Edited by Hubertus R. Drobner and Albert Viciano. Translated by Stuart George Hall. Leiden: Brill, 2000.

The Beatitudes. In *St. Gregory of Nyssa: The Lord's Prayer; The Beatitudes.* Translated by Hilda C. Graef. Ancient Christian Writers 18. Mahwah, NJ: Paulist Press, 1954. Pages 85–175.

Benef. — De beneficentia (= De pauperibus amandis oratio I) (PG 46:453–69; GNO IX:93–108)

On Almsgiving. In *On Christian Living.* Translated by Hannah Black. Popular Patristics Series [number to-be-determined]. Yonkers, NY: St Vladimir's Seminary Press, forthcoming.

On Good Works. Susan R. Holman. *The Hungry Are Dying: Beggars and Bishops in Roman Cappadocia.* Oxford University Press, 2001. Pages 193–99.

Concerning Almsgiving. Translated by Richard McCambley. http://www.lectio-divina.org/images/nyssa/On%Almsgiving.pdf.

Cant. — In Canticum canticorum (PG 44:756–1120; GNO VI)

Gregory of Nyssa: Homilies on the Song of Songs. Translated by Richard A. Norris, Jr. Atlanta, GA: Society of Biblical Literature, 2012.

Commentary on the Song of Songs. Translated by Richard McCambley. Brookline, MA: Hellenic College Press, 1987.

Cast. — Adversus eos qui castigationes aegre ferunt (PG 46:308–316; GNO X/2:321–32)

*This text is not yet translated into English.

Deit. Euag. — De deitate adversus Euagrium (= In suam ordinationem oratio) (PG 46:544–53; GNO IX:331–41)

Concerning His Own Ordination: To Euagrius, Concerning the Divinity. Translated by Richard McCambley. https://www.lectio-divina.org/images/nyssa/To%20Eugarius%20Concerning%20the%20Divinity.pdf.

Deit. Fil. — *De deitate Filii et Spiritus Sancti et in Abraham* (PG 46:553–76; GNO X/2:115–44)
On the Divinity of the Son and Holy Spirit and an Encomium of Abraham the Just. In *The Trinitarian Works of Gregory of Nyssa*. Translated by Brian Duvick. Popular Patristics Series [number to-be-determined]. Yonkers, NY: St Vladimir's Seminary Press, forthcoming.

Diem. lum. — *In diem luminum* (=*In baptismum Christi oratio*) (PG 46:577–600; GNO IX:221–42)
On the Day of Lights. In *Saint Gregory of Nyssa: Homilies on the Feasts of the Church*. Translated by Michael J. Petrin. Popular Patristics Series [number to-be-determined]. Yonkers, NY: St Vladimir's Seminary Press, forthcoming.
On the Baptism of Christ: A Sermon for the Day of the Lights. NPNF² 5:518–24.

Diem nat. — *In diem natalem* (PG 46:1128–49; GNO X/2:233–69)
On the Nativity of the Savior. In *Saint Gregory of Nyssa: Homilies on the Feasts of the Church*. Translated by Michael J. Petrin. Popular Patristics Series [number to-be-determined]. Yonkers, NY: St Vladimir's Seminary Press, forthcoming.
Oration on the Savior's Nativity. Translated by Andrew Radde-Gallwitz. In *The Cambridge Edition of Early Christian Writings, Volume 3: Christ: Through the Nestorian Controversy*. Edited by by Andrew Radde-Gallwitz and Mark DelCogliano. Cambridge University Press, 2022.

Diff. ess. hyp. — *Ad Petrum fratrem de differentia essentiae et hypostaseos* (= Basil's *Ep.* 38) (PG 32:325–40)
Letter 38: Gregory to His Brother Peter on the Difference between Substance and a Subsistent Entity. In *The Trinitarian Works of Gregory of Nyssa*. Translated by Brian Duvick. Popular Patristics Series [number to-be-determined]. Yonkers, NY: St Vladimir's Seminary Press, forthcoming.
To Peter His Own Brother on the Divine Ousia and Hypostasis. In *Gregory of Nyssa: The Letters—Introduction, Commentary, and Translation*. Translated and edited by Anna M. Silvas. Supplements to Vigiliae Christianae 83. Anna M. Silvas. Leiden: Brill, 2007. Pages 247–59.

Eccl. — *In Ecclesiasten homiliae* (PG 44:616–753; GNO V:277–442)
Homilies on Ecclesiastes. Translated by Richard McCambly. Edited by John Litteral. Ashland, KY: Litteral's Christian Library Publications, 2014.
Gregory of Nyssa: Homilies on Ecclesiastes, An English Version with Supporting Studies, Proceedings of the Seventh International Colloquium on Gregory of Nyssa (St Andrews, 5–10 September 1990). Edited by Stuart George Hall. Berlin: Walter de Gruyter, 1993.

Epist. — *Epistulae* (PG 46:1000–1100; cf. 32:1092–93, 1088; 45:237–44; GNO VIII/2)
Gregory of Nyssa: *The Letters—Introduction, Commentary, and Translation*. Translated end edited by Anna M. Silvas. Supplements to Vigiliae Christianae 83. Anna M. Silvas. Leiden: Brill, 2007.
[Select] Letters. NPNF² 5:524–48.

Epist. can. — *Epistula canonica ad Letoium episcopum* (PG 45:221–36; GNO III/5)
Canonical Letter to Letoius. Translated by Andrew Radde-Gallwitz. In *The Cambridge Edition of Early Christian Writings, Volume 2: Practice*. Edited by Ellen Muehlberger. Cambridge University Press, 2017. Pages 168–77.
Canonical Letter of the holy Gregory of Nyssa to Letoius among the saints, bishop of Melitene. In *Gregory of Nyssa: The Letters—Introduction, Commentary, and Translation*. Translated end edited by Anna M. Silvas. Supplements to Vigiliae Christianae 83. Anna M. Silvas. Leiden: Brill, 2007. Pages 211–25.

Eun. 1-2 — *Contra Eunomium libri, I et II* (=I et XII B) (PG 45:248–464, 909–1121; GNO I:22–225, 226–409)
Gregory of Nyssa: Contra Eunomium I: An English Translation with Supporting Studies. Translated by Stuart George Hall. Edited by Miguel Brugarolas. Supplements to Vigiliae Christianae 148. Leiden: Brill, 2018 [1st ed. 1988].
Gregory of Nyssa: Contra Eunomium II: An English Version with Supporting Studies, Proceedings of the 10th International Colloquium on Gregory of Nyssa (Olomouc, September 15-18, 2004). Translated by Stuart George Hall. Edited by Lenka Karfíková, Scot Douglass, and Johannes Zachhuber. Supplements to Vigiliae Christianae 82. Leiden: Brill, 2007.
Against Eunomius [Book I]. NPNF² 5:33–100.
Answer to Eunomius' Second Book NPNF² 5:250–314.

Eun. 3 — *Contra Eunomium libri, III* (=III–XII) (PG 45:572–908; GNO II:3–311)
Gregory of Nyssa: Contra Eunomium III: An English Translation with Commentary and Supporting Studies: Proceedings of the 12th International Colloquium on Gregory of Nyssa (Leuven, 14-17 September 2010). Translated by Stuart George Hall. Edited by Johan Leemans and Matthieu Cassin. Supplements to Vigiliae Christianae 124. Leiden: Brill, 2014.
Against Eunomius [Books III–XII]. NPNF² 5:135–248.

Eust. — *Ad Eustathium, De sancta Trinitate* (= Basil's *Ep.* 189) (PG 32:684–96; GNO III/1:3–16)

A letter of Gregory, Bishop of Nyssa, to Eustathius on the Holy Trinity. In *The Trinitarian Works of Gregory of Nyssa*. Translated by Brian Duvick. Popular Patristics Series [number to-be-determined]. Yonkers, NY: St Vladimir's Seminary Press, forthcoming.

To Eustathius the Physician on the Holy Trinity and against the Pneumatomachoi, that the Spirit is God. In *Gregory of Nyssa: The Letters—Introduction, Commentary, and Translation*. Translated end edited by Anna M. Silvas. Supplements to Vigiliae Christianae 83. Anna M. Silvas. Leiden: Brill, 2007. Pages 232–45.

Fat. — *Contra fatum* (PG 45:145–73; GNO III/2:31–63)

Against Fate. In *On Christian Living*. Translated by Hannah Black. Popular Patristics Series [number to-be-determined]. Yonkers, NY: St Vladimir's Seminary Press, forthcoming.

Casimir McCambley. "*Against Fate* by Gregory of Nyssa." *Greek Orthodox Theological Review* 37.1–2 (1992): 309–32.

Flacill. — *Oratio funebris in Flacillam imperatricem* (PG 46:877–92; GNO IX:475–90)

A Funeral Oration for the Empress Flaccilla. In *On Death and Eternal Life*. Translated by Brian Daley. Popular Patristics Series 64. Yonkers, NY: St Vladimir's Seminary Press, 2022. Pages 136–149.

A Funeral Oration for the Empress Flacilla. Translated by Richard McCambley. https://www.lectio-divina.org/images/nyssa/A%20Funeral%20Oration%20For%20The%20Empress%20Flacilla.pdf.

Fornic. — *Contra fornicarios oratio* (PG 46:489–96; GNO IX:211–17)

Discourse against Fornication. In *On Christian Living*. Translated by Hannah Black. Popular Patristics Series [number to-be-determined]. Yonkers, NY: St Vladimir's Seminary Press, forthcoming.

The Person Who Commits Impurity Sins Against His Own Body: A Homily. Translated by Richard McCambley. https://www.lectio-divina.org/images/nyssa/On%20Fornication.pdf.

Graec. — *Ad Graecos (Ex communibus notionibus)* (PG 45:176–85; GNO III/1:19–33)

How When We Say that there Are Three Persons in the Divinity We Do Not Mean that there Are Three Gods, A Letter of Gregory, Bishop of Nyssa, to the Greeks from the Common Notions. In *The Trinitarian Works of Gregory of Nyssa*. Translated by

Brian Duvick. Popular Patristics Series [number to-be-determined]. Yonkers, NY: St Vladimir's Seminary Press, forthcoming.

Hex. — *Apologia in Hexaemeron* (PG 44:61–124; GNO IV/1)
On the Six Days of Creation. Translated by Robin Orton. The Fathers of the Church: Shorter Works 1. Washington, DC: The Catholic University of America Press, 2021.
Hexaemeron. Translated by Richard McCambley. https://www.lectio-divina.org/images/nyssa/Hexaemeron.pdf.

Infant. — *De infantibus praemature abreptis* (PG 46:161–97; GNO III/2:67–97)
On Infants Taken Away Before Their Time. In *On Death and Eternal Life.* Translated by Brian Daley. Popular Patristics Series 64. Yonkers, NY: St Vladimir's Seminary Press, 2022. Pages 37–63.
On Infants' Early Deaths. NPNF² 5:372–81.

Inscr. — *In inscriptiones Psalmorum* (PG 44:432–608; GNO V:24–175)
On the Inscriptions of the Psalms. Translated by R. E. Heine. Oxford: Clarendon Press, 1995.
Commentary on the Inscriptions of the Psalms. Translated by Casimir McCambley. Brookline, MA: Hellenic College Press, 1995.

Inst. — *De instituto Christiano* (PG 46:288–305; GNO VIII/1:40–89)
On the Christian Mode of Life. In *St. Gregory of Nyssa: Ascetical Works.* Translated by Virginia Woods Callahan. The Fathers of the Church 58. Washington, DC: The Catholic University of America Press, 1967. Pages 123–58.
Artzer, James J. "The Goal of The True Ascetic Life According to God: A Translation with an Introduction and a Commentary." PhD Dissertation. Washington, DC: The Catholic University of America, 1956.

Lucif. res.[2] — *In luciferam sanctam domini resurrectionem* (=*In Christi resurrectionem oratio V*) (PG 46:684–80; GNO IX:315–19)
On the Light-Bringing and Holy Resurrection of the Lord. In *Saint Gregory of Nyssa: Homilies on the Feasts of the Church.* Translated by Michael J. Petrin. Popular Patristics Series [number to-be-determined]. Yonkers, NY: St Vladimir's Seminary Press, forthcoming.

---

[2]Scholars now generally reject this work as inauthentic, and often attribute it to Amphilochius of Iconium. See Brill Dictionary, 162 and 464; *Easter Sermons*, viii; PPS 64:xxxiii n. 9, 87.

Maced. — *Adversus Macedonianos, De Spiritu Sancto* (PG 45:1301-33; GNO III/1:89-115)

On the Holy Spirit against the Macedonian Spirit-Fighters. Translated by Andrew Radde-Gallwitz. In *The Cambridge Edition of Early Christian Writings, Volume 1: God*. Edited by Andrew Radde-Gallwitz. Cambridge University Press, 2017. Pages 270-93.

A Tract of Gregory, Bishop of Nyssa, on the Holy Spirit, against the Macedonian enemies of the Spirit. In *The Trinitarian Works of Gregory of Nyssa*. Translated by Brian Duvick. Popular Patristics Series [number to-be-determined]. Yonkers, NY: St Vladimir's Seminary Press, forthcoming.

On the Holy Spirit against Macedonius. NPNF[2] 5:315-25.

Macr. — *Vita s. Macrinae* (PG 46:960-1000; GNO VIII/1:370-414)

The Life of Macrina. Translated by Anna M. Silvas. In *Macrina the Younger, Philosopher of God*. Medieval Women: Texts and Contexts, Volume 22. Turnhout, Belgium: Brepols, 2008. Pages 109-148.

The Life of Saint Macrina. Translated by Kevin Corrigan. Eugene, OR: Wipf and Stock Publishers, 2001.

The Life of Saint Macrina. In *Handmaids of the Lord: Contemporary Descriptions of Feminine Asceticism in the First Six Christian Centuries*. Translated by Joan M. Petersen. Cistercian Studies Series 143. Kalamazoo, MI, 1996. Pages 51-86.

The Life of Saint Macrina. In *St. Gregory of Nyssa: Ascetical Works*. Translated by Virginia Woods Callahan. Fathers of the Church 58. Washington, DC: The Catholic University of America Press, 1967. Pages 159-91.

The Life of St. Macrina. Translated by W. K. Lowther Clarke. London: Society for Promoting Christian Knowledge, 1916.

Mart. Ia — *In XL Martyres* Ia (PG 46:749-56; GNO X/1:137-42)

In Praise of the Holy Forty Martyrs 1a. Translation by Rowan A. Greer. In Rowan A. Greer. *One Path for All: Gregory of Nyssa on the Christian Life and Human Destiny*. Eugene, OR: Cascade Books, 2015. Pages 71-75.

First homily on the Forty Martyrs of Sebaste (Ia and Ib). Translated by Johan Leemans. In Johan Leemans, Wendy Mayer, Pauline Allen, and Boudewign Dehandschutter. *'Let Us Die that We May Live': Greek Homilies on Christian Martyrs from Asia Minor, Palestine and Syria (c. AD 350-AD 450)*. New York: Routledge, 2003. Pages 91-97.

Mart. Ib — *In XL Martyres Ib* (PG 46:757–72; GNO X/1:145–56)

In Praise of the Holy Forty Martyrs 1a. Translation by Rowan A. Greer. In Rowan A. Greer. *One Path for All: Gregory of Nyssa on the Christian Life and Human Destiny.* Eugene, OR: Cascade Books, 2015. Pages 76—84.

First homily on the Forty Martyrs of Sebaste (Ia and Ib). Translated by Johan Leemans. In Johan Leemans, Wendy Mayer, Pauline Allen, and Boudewign Dehandschutter. *'Let Us Die that We May Live': Greek Homilies on Christian Martyrs from Asia Minor, Palestine and Syria (c. AD 350–AD 450).* New York: Routledge, 2003. Pages 91–99–110.

Mart. II — *In XL Martyres II* (PG 46:773–88; GNO X/1:159–69)

A Speech in Praise of the Forty Martyrs Delivered in the Martyrion. Translation by Rowan A. Greer. In Rowan A. Greer. *One Path for All: Gregory of Nyssa on the Christian Life and Human Destiny.* Eugene, OR: Cascade Books, 2015. Pages 85–93.

Melet. — *Oratio funebris in Meletium episcopum* (PG 46:852–64; GNO IX:441–57)

A Funeral Oration for Meletius, Bishop of Antioch. In *On Death and Eternal Life.* Translated by Brian Daley. Popular Patristics Series 64. Yonkers, NY: St Vladimir's Seminary Press, 2022. Pages 110–122.

A Funeral Oration for Meletius, Bishop of Antioch. Translated by Richard McCambley. https://www.lectio-divina.org/images/nyssa/Funeral%20Oration%20for%20Bishop%20Meletius.pdf.

Funeral Oration on Meletius. NPNF² 5:513–17.

Mort. — *De mortuis oratio* (PG 46:497–537; GNO IX:28–68)

A Discourse on the Dead. In *On Death and Eternal Life.* Translated by Brian Daley. Popular Patristics Series 64. Yonkers, NY: St Vladimir's Seminary Press, 2022. Pages 1–36.

In Regard to Those Fallen Asleep. Translation by Rowan A. Greer. In Rowan A. Greer. *One Path for All: Gregory of Nyssa on the Christian Life and Human Destiny.* Eugene, OR: Cascade Books, 2015. Pages 94–117.

Concerning Those Who Have Died. Translated by Richard McCambley. https://www.lectio-divina.org/images/nyssa/On%20Those%20Who%20Have%20Died.pdf.

Op. hom. — *De hominis opificio* (PG 44:125–256; GNO IV/2)

Gregory of Nyssa: On the Human Image of God [= On the Formation of the Human Being]. Edited and translated by John Behr. Oxford Early Christian Texts. Oxford University Press, 2023.

On the Making of Man. NPNF² 5:387–427.

Or. cat. — *Oratio catechetica magna* (PG 45:9–105; GNO III/4)
Catechetical Discourse: A Handbook for Catechists. Translated by Ignatius Green. Popular Patristics Series 60. Yonkers, NY: St Vladimir's Seminary Press, 2019.
An Address on Religious Instruction. Translated by Cyril C. Richardson. In *Christology of the Later Fathers.* Edited Edward R. Hardy and Cyril C. Richardson. The Library of Christian Classics, Volume 3. Louisville, KY: The Westminster Press, 1954. Pages 268–325.
The Catechetical Oration of St. Gregory of Nyssa. Translated by John Herbert Srawley. London: Society for Promoting Christian Knowledge, 1917.
The Great Catechism. NPNF² 5:471–509.

Or. dom. — *De oratione dominica* (PG 44:1120–93; GNO VII/2:1–74)
On the Our Father. Translated by Mark DelCogliano and Andrew Radde-Gallwitz. In *Gregory of Nyssa:* Homilies on the Our Father. *An English Translation with Commentary and Supporting Studies. Proceedings of the 14th International Colloquium on Gregory of Nyssa (Paris, 4–7 September 2018).* Edited by Matthieu Cassin, Hélène Grelier-Deneux, and Françoise Vinel. Pages 110–55.
The Lord's Prayer. In *St. Gregory of Nyssa: The Lord's Prayer; The Beatitudes.* Translated by Hilda C. Graef. Ancient Christian Writers 18. Mahwah, NJ: Paulist Press, 1954. Pages 21–84.

Pent. — *De Spiritu Sancto sive in Pentecosten* (PG 46:696–701; GNO X/2:285–92)
On Holy Pentecost. In *Saint Gregory of Nyssa: Homilies on the Feasts of the Church.* Translated by Michael J. Petrin. Popular Patristics Series [number to-be-determined]. Yonkers, NY: St Vladimir's Seminary Press, forthcoming.

Perf. — *De perfectione* (PG 46:252–85; GNO VIII/1:173–214)
On Perfection. In *On Christian Living.* Translated by Hannah Black. Popular Patristics Series [number to-be-determined]. Yonkers, NY: St Vladimir's Seminary Press, forthcoming.
Concerning Perfection. Translation by Rowan A. Greer. In Rowan A. Greer. *One Path for All: Gregory of Nyssa on the Christian Life and Human Destiny.* Eugene, OR: Cascade Books, 2015. Pages 24–44.
On Perfection. In *St. Gregory of Nyssa: Ascetical Works.* Translated by Virginia Woods Callahan. Fathers of the Church 58. Washington, DC: The Catholic University of America Press, 1967. Pages 91–122.
McCambley, Casimir. "Saint Gregory of Nyssa: *Peri Teleiotētos*—On Perfection." *Greek Orthodox Theological Review* 29.4 (1984): 349–79.

Prof. — *De professione Christiana* (PG 46:237–49; GNO VIII/1:129–42)
The Christian Profession. In *On Christian Living*. Translated by Hannah Black. Popular Patristics Series [number to-be-determined]. Yonkers, NY: St Vladimir's Seminary Press, forthcoming.
Concerning the Meaning of the Christian's Profession. Translation by Rowan A. Greer. In Rowan A. Greer. *One Path for All: Gregory of Nyssa on the Christian Life and Human Destiny*. Eugene, OR: Cascade Books, 2015. Pages 17–23.
On What It Means to Call Oneself a Christian. In *St. Gregory of Nyssa: Ascetical Works*. Translated by Virginia Woods Callahan. The Fathers of the Church 58. Washington, DC: The Catholic University of America Press, 1967. Pages 77–89.

Pulcher. — *Oratio consolatoria in Pulcheriam* (PG 46:864–77; GNO IX:461–72)
A Discourse of Consolation for Pulcheria. In *On Death and Eternal Life*. Translated by Brian Daley. Popular Patristics Series 64. Yonkers, NY: St Vladimir's Seminary Press, 2022. Pages 124–135.
A Homily of Consolation Concerning Pulcheria. Translated by Richard McCambley. https://www.lectio-divina.org/images/nyssa/A%20Homily%20Of%20Consolation%20Concerning%20Pulcheria.pdf.

Python. — *De Pythonissa* (PG 45:108–113; GNO III/2:101–108)
Letter to Theodosius concerning the Belly-Myther. In *The "Belly-Myther" of Endor: Interpretations of 1 Kingdoms 28 in the Early Church*. Translated by Rowan A. Greer and Margaret M. Mitchell. Atlanta, GA: Society of Biblical Literature, 2007. Pages 166–78.
Casimir McCambley. "Gregory of Nyssa: Letter Concerning the Sorceress to Bishop Theodoxios." *Greek Orthodox Theological Review* 35.2 (1990): 129–37.

Quat. uni. — *In illud: Quatenus uni ex his fecistis mihi fecistis (=De pauperibus amandism oratio II)* (PG 46:472–89; GNO IX:111–27)
"Inasmuch as you did it unto one of these, you did it unto me." In *On Christian Living*. Translated by Hannah Black. Popular Patristics Series [number to-be-determined]. Yonkers, NY: St Vladimir's Seminary Press, forthcoming.
On the Saying, "Whoever Has Done It to One of These Has Done It to Me." Susan R. Holman. *The Hungry Are Dying: Beggars and Bishops in Roman Cappadocia*. Oxford University Press, 2001. Pages 199–206.
As You Did It to One of These, You Did It to Me. Translated by Richard McCambley. http://www.lectio-divina.org/images/nyssa/On%Almsgiving.pdf.

Ref. Eun. — *Refutatio confessionis Eunomii (=lib. II)* (PG 45:465–572; GNO II:312–410)
Against Eunomius [Book II]. NPNF[2] 5:101–134.

Salut. Pasch. — *In sanctum et salutare Pascha (=In Christi resurrectionem oratio IV)* (PG 46:681–84; GNO IX:309–311)

On the Holy and Saving Pascha. In *Saint Gregory of Nyssa: Homilies on the Feasts of the Church*. Translated by Michael J. Petrin. Popular Patristics Series [number to-be-determined]. Yonkers, NY: St Vladimir's Seminary Press, forthcoming.

The Holy and Saving Pascha. Translated by Stuart George Hall. In *The Easter Sermons of Gregory of Nyssa: Translation and Commentary*. Edited by Andreas Spira and Christoph Klock. Patristic Monograph Series 9. Cambridge, MA: The Philadelphia Patristics Foundation, Ltd., 1981. Pages 51–53.

Sanct. Pasch. — *In sanctum Pascha (=In Christi resurrectionem oratio III)* (PG 46:652–81; GNO IX:245–70)

On the Holy Pascha. In *Saint Gregory of Nyssa: Homilies on the Feasts of the Church*. Translated by Michael J. Petrin. Popular Patristics Series [number to-be-determined]. Yonkers, NY: St Vladimir's Seminary Press, forthcoming.

An Oration on the Holy Pascha. In *On Death and Eternal Life*. Translated by Brian Daley. Popular Patristics Series 64. Yonkers, NY: St Vladimir's Seminary Press, 2022. Pages 87–109.

Discourse on the Holy Pascha. Translated by Stuart George Hall. In *The Easter Sermons of Gregory of Nyssa: Translation and Commentary*. Edited by Andreas Spira and Christoph Klock. Patristic Monograph Series 9. Cambridge, MA: The Philadelphia Patristics Foundation, Ltd., 1981. Pages 5–23.

Sext. ps. — *In sextum Psalmum* (PG 44:608–616; GNO V:187–93)

"Training for the Good Ascent: Gregory of Nyssa's *Homily on the Sixth Psalm*." Translated by Brian Daley. In Paul Blowers, Angela Russell Christman, David G. Hunter, and Robin Darling Young, editors. *In Dominico Eloquio, In Lordly Eloquence: Essays on Patristic Exegesis in Honor of Robert Louis Wilken*. Grand Rapids, MI: Eerdmans, 2002. Pages 211–17.

Casimir McCambley. "On the Sixth Psalm, Concerning the Octave by Saint Gregory of Nyssa." *Greek Orthodox Theological Review* 32.1 (1987): 39–50.

Simpl. — *Ad Simplicium, De fide* (PG 45:136–45; GNO III/1:61–67)

A letter from Gregory, Bishop of Nyssa, to Simplicius on Faith; Gregory to the Tribune Simplicius on the Father, Son, and Holy Spirit. In *The Trinitarian Works of Gregory of Nyssa*. Translated by Brian Duvick. Popular Patristics Series [number to-be-determined]. Yonkers, NY: St Vladimir's Seminary Press, forthcoming.

On the Faith: To Simplicius. NPNF[2] 5:337–39.

Steph. I — *In sanctum Stephanum I* (PG 46:701–721; GNO X/1:75–94)
On the Holy Protomartyr Stephen I. In *Saint Gregory of Nyssa: Homilies on the Feasts of the Church*. Translated by Michael J. Petrin. Popular Patristics Series [number to-be-determined]. Yonkers, NY: St Vladimir's Seminary Press, forthcoming.
In Praise of Stephen, Saint and Protomartyr I. Translation by Rowan A. Greer. In Rowan A. Greer. *One Path for All: Gregory of Nyssa on the Christian Life and Human Destiny*. Eugene, OR: Cascade Books, 2015. Pages 53–63.

Steph. II — *In sanctum Stephanum II* (PG 46:721–36; GNO X/1:97–105)
On the Holy Protomartyr Stephen II. In *Saint Gregory of Nyssa: Homilies on the Feasts of the Church*. Translated by Michael J. Petrin. Popular Patristics Series [number to-be-determined]. Yonkers, NY: St Vladimir's Seminary Press, forthcoming.
Another in Praise of Saint Stephen, the Protomartyr. Translation by Rowan A. Greer. In Rowan A. Greer. *One Path for All: Gregory of Nyssa on the Christian Life and Human Destiny*. Eugene, OR: Cascade Books, 2015. Pages 64–70.

Thaum. — *De vita Gregorii Thaumaturgi* (PG 46:893–957; GNO X/1:3–57)
Life of Gregory the Wonderworker. In *St. Gregory Thaumaturgus: Life and Works*. Translated by Michael Slusser. The Fathers of the Church 98. Washington, DC: The Catholic University of America Press, 1998. Pages 39–87.
The Life of Gregory the Wonderworker. Translation by Richard McCambley. https://www.lectio-divina.org/images/nyssa/Gregory%20the%20Wonderworker.pdf.

Theod. — *De sancto Theodoro* (PG 46:736–48; GNO X/1:61–71)
In Praise of Theodore, Holy and Great Martyr. Translation by Rowan A. Greer. In Rowan A. Greer. *One Path for All: Gregory of Nyssa on the Christian Life and Human Destiny*. Eugene, OR: Cascade Books, 2015. Pages 45–52.
A homily on Theodore the Recruit. Translated by Johan Leemans. In Johan Leemans, Wendy Mayer, Pauline Allen, and Boudewign Dehandschutter. *'Let Us Die that We May Live': Greek Homilies on Christian Martyrs from Asia Minor, Palestine and Syria (c. AD 350–AD 450)*. New York: Routledge, 2003. Pages 82–91.
In Praise of Blessed Theodore, the Great Martyr. Translation by Richard McCambley. https://www.lectio-divina.org/images/nyssa/In%20Praise%20of%20Blessed%20Theodore%20the%20Great%20Martyr.pdf.

Theoph. — *Ad Theophilum, Adversos Apollinaristas* (PG 45:1269–77; GNO III/1:119–28)
To Theophilus, Against the Apollinarians. In *St. Gregory of Nyssa: Anti-Apollinarian Writings*. Translated by Robin Orton. The Fathers of the Church 131. Washington, DC: The Catholic University of America Press, 2015. Pages 259–68.

Trid. spat. — *De tridui inter mortem et resurrectionem domini nostri Iesu Christi spatio (=In Christi resurrectionem oratio I)* (PG 46:600–628; GNO IX:273–306)

On the Three-Day Period Prior to the Resurrection of Our Lord Jesus Christ. In *Saint Gregory of Nyssa: Homilies on the Feasts of the Church*. Translated by Michael J. Petrin. Popular Patristics Series [number to-be-determined]. Yonkers, NY: St Vladimir's Seminary Press, forthcoming.

On the Three-Day Period. Translated by Stuart George Hall. In *The Easter Sermons of Gregory of Nyssa: Translation and Commentary*. Edited by Andreas Spira and Christoph Klock. Patristic Monograph Series 9. Cambridge, MA: The Philadelphia Patristics Foundation, Ltd., 1981. Pages 31–50.

Tunc et ipse — *In illud: Tunc et ipse Filius* (PG 44:1304–25; GNO III/2:3–28)

On the "Final Subjection" of Christ. In *On Death and Eternal Life*. Translated by Brian Daley. Popular Patristics Series 64. Yonkers, NY: St Vladimir's Seminary Press, 2022. Pages 65–85.

On "Then Also the Son Himself Will Be Subjected to the One Who Subjected All Things to Him." In Rowan A. Greer. *One Path for All: Gregory of Nyssa on the Christian Life and Human Destiny*. Eugene, OR: Cascade Books, 2015. Pages 118–32.

Casimir McCambley. "When (the Father) Will Subject All Things to (the Son), Then (the Son) Himself Will Be Subjected to Him (the Father) Who Subjects All Things to Him (the Son). A treatise on First Corinthians 15.28." *Greek Orthodox Theological Review* 28 (1983): 1–25.

Usur. — *Contra usurarios oratio* (PG 46:433–52; GNO IX:195–207)

Discourse against Usury. In *On Christian Living*. Translated by Hannah Black. Popular Patristics Series [number to-be-determined]. Yonkers, NY: St Vladimir's Seminary Press, forthcoming.

Casimir McCambley. "Against Those Who Practice Usury by Gregory of Nyssa." *Greek Orthodox Theological Review* 36.3–4 (1991): 287–302.

Virg. — *De virginitate* (PG 46:317–416; GNO VIII/1:247–343)

On Virginity. In *St. Gregory of Nyssa: Ascetical Works*. Translated by Virginia Woods Callahan. Fathers of the Church 58. Washington, DC: The Catholic University of America Press, 1967. Pages 1–75.

On Virginity. NPNF^2 5:343–71.

Vit. Moys. — *De vita Moysis* (PG 44:297–429; GNO VII/1)

Gregory of Nyssa: The Life of Moses. Translated by Abraham Malherbe and Everett Ferguson. Classics of Western Spirituality. Mahwah, NJ: Paulist Press, 1978.

General Index

Aaron, 96
Abraham, xxiv, 152, 157, 309, 310, 317, 318, 362
Adam, 32, 51, 113, 114, 263, 309, 310
Adversary, the (Satan), 92, 94, 95, 96
Adyton (sanctuary), 5, 123, 211–19, 222, 224, 227
Agapē: see Love as *agapē*
Altar, 22
Ambrose of Milan, 14, 19, 280, 357
Anachorēsis: see Withdrawal
Angels, xx, 77, 100, 170, 172–73, 178, 183–84, 185–97
Anger, 58, 59
Animals, symbolism of, 76–81, 87
Annesi, xxvi, 37
Apatheia: see Dispassion
Aphraates, 19
Apokatastasis: see Restoration
Apollinarius of Laodicea, xviii, 73
Aquilla, 266
Aquinas: see Thomas Aquinas
Archetype (*archetypon*), 42, 43, 300
Arianism, xvii, xviii
Aristotle, 65
Arius, xviii
Ascent (*anabasis*), 3, 164, 176, 286, 347
See also: Soar, to
Asceticism, 88, 90, 92–93
Athanasius, 229
Athenagoras, 99
Augustine of Hippo, 35, 36, 95, 165, 178–79, 238, 263, 272, 273, 330

Baptism, 3, 8, 11–25, 53, 86, 96, 111, 114, 202, 203, 206–7, 269, 340, 341
Basil of Caesarea, xvi, xxv, xxvii, 27, 37, 95, 315, 371
Beatitude (*makariotēs*), 49–51
Benjamin, 208, 323

Bernard of Clairvaux, xviii, 22, 40, 116–17, 118, 172, 232, 263, 264, 280
Bérulle, Pierre de, 24
Birgitta of Sweden, 336
Bonaventure, 263
Bride mysticism, 12–13, 17, 29, 100, 227, 301, 342–43
Buddhism, 131, 331
Bush, the Burning, xxii, 6, 15, 19–20, 22, 23, 270, 345, 368

Cabasilas, Nicholas, 7, 13, 25, 322
Caesarea of Cappadocia, 37
Cassian, John, 122
Chrysippus, 83
Church, 49
Cicero, 83, 336, 363
Citadel, image of, 83–84
Clement of Alexandria, 17, 54, 77, 97, 99, 166, 168, 169, 175, 212, 220, 222, 308, 323, 332
Cloud (*nephelē*), 6
Confession, 207
Contemplation (*theōria*), xix, xxi, xxii, 130, 167, 170, 171–72, 180–81, 183–85, 201, 203, 359
    mystical, 4, 5, 7, 11, 25, 27, 184, 194–95, 229, 232, 268
    natural, 4, 273
    of the spiritual meaning of biblical texts, 26, 167, 184
    of spiritual realities, 150–51, 164, 167–68, 169, 174
Cornelius, 370
Cosmology, 176–78
Culture, secular, 95

Daniel, 331

Darkness (*gnophos*), xx, xxii, 7, 163, 166, 221–32, 307, 308, 360
David, 208, 304, 314, 317, 322
Death
  and Baptism, 14–15
  and resurrection, 3, 202
Descartes, René, 117
Deification (*theous genesthai, theōsis*), xvii, 25, 80, 124, 204, 289, 321–22
  See also: Transformation
Deiform (*theoeidēs*), 250, 255, 256
Diadochus of Photiki, 13, 263, 264, 272, 280, 322
Didymus the Blind, 14
Diogenes Laertius, 357
Dionysius the Pseudo-Areopagite, xvi, xviii, 25, 97, 149, 184, 197, 205, 212, 222, 226, 261, 264, 273, 280, 311, 334
Diotima, 371
Discalceatio (removal of shoes), 15, 17, 19–20, 26
Dispassion (*apatheia*), xvii, xix, xxi, xxii, 4, 6, 11, 39, 40–41, 60, 61, 70, 73, 86, 87, 89, 90, 97–111, 112, 164, 172, 201, 203, 260

Ecstasy (*ekstasis*), xxi, 80, 204, 263, 289, 291, 292, 307–8, 309–24, 335–37, 348–49
Eckhart, Meister, 359
Eleatics, 361
Elijah, 346
Emanation (*aporroia*), 45, 100, 102, 155, 298
Emmelia, mother of Gregory of Nyssa, xvi
Enoch, 331
Enstasy (*enstasis*) 305, 307, 348–49
Epektasis (reaching forth, or continual progress), 230, 305, 309, 344–63
Epekteinesthai (to strain forward), 304, 350, 351, 352, 354, 358
Eriugena, Scotus, xviii
Erōs: see Love as *erōs*
Esau, 310
Essence, divine (*ousia*), 180, 201–2, 278
Ether, 178
Ethics (*ethikē*), 4, 6

Eucharist, 6–7, 96, 144, 206, 236, 288–89, 290, 292, 328, 332
Eunomianism, xviii
Eunomius of Cyzicus, 149
Evagrius of Pontus, xviii, 9, 97, 99, 100, 273, 280
Eve, 113, 309
Experience, mystical, 228, 245–47, 274, 277, 302

Faith (*pistis*), 234, 246, 303
Fall, 77, 88–89, 263
Fathers, Desert, 91, 95
Flight
  as *phygē*, 27
  as *ptēsis*, 350
  of "the alone to the alone," 28–29
Freedom, 117–18
  as *eleutheria*, 12, 13, 14, 84–85, 116
  as *parrhēsia*, xxiv, 44, 84, 111–25, 170
Friendship with God (*philia*), 120–21

Gazing on God, 106, 259
George of Pisidia, xvi
Gnosis: see Knowledge
Gnosticism, 166
God, presence of, 203, 204
  See also: Gazing on God
Grace (*charis*), 12, 13, 38, 204, 213, 255, 276, 298
Gregory of Nazianzus, xvi, 205, 315, 326
Gregory of Nyssa
  and acknowledgement of sources, 29
  on Baptism, 11–25
  and Platonism, xix, xx, xxi, 39, 44, 65, 162, 175–76, 252–55
  on sexuality and gender, xxvi, 46, 52
  on withdrawal from the world, 27
  works of: *Against Eunomius*, xxiv, xxvii, 72–73, 149, 152, 156, 158–59, 161–62, 164–65, 301, 317; *Catechetical Discourse*, 51, 71, 72, 88, 112; *Discourse on the Dead*, 57; *Eulogy for Basil*, xxvii, 27, 173, 366; *Funeral Oration for Meletius*, 53; *Homilies on the Beatitudes*, xxvi, 80, 103, 153–54, 213,

245–46, 250–51, 255, 260, 278–79; *Homilies on Ecclesiastes*, xxiii, xxiv, 7, 10, 101, 131, 134, 140–46, 210, 236; *Homilies on Saint Stephen*, 259, 316, 320; *Homilies on the Song of Songs*, xvi, xxiii, 4, 5, 9, 10, 12, 22, 24, 26, 29–30, 32–33, 34, 37–38, 102, 105, 107–8, 109, 129, 137, 151, 154–55, 156, 194–95, 209–10, 219, 221, 225, 229–30, 246, 249, 257, 258, 259, 260, 271, 273, 274–76, 280–81, 283, 284–85, 291–92, 300, 319–20, 326, 328–29, 330–31, 333, 337–39, 339–44, 346, 354–56, 366, 369, 371; *Homily on the Ascension*, 322, 327–28; *Letters*, xxvii; *Life of Gregory the Wonderworker*, xxvii, 27, 224, 366; *Life of Moses*, xvi, xxiii, xvii–xviii, 5–6, 10, 11, 15, 19, 21, 26, 34, 53, 61, 66, 68, 70, 73, 78, 79, 82, 88, 91, 94, 140, 149–50, 152, 165, 166, 167, 184, 185, 197, 209, 214, 222, 225, 226, 239, 270–71, 279, 283–84, 295, 334–35, 347, 350, 358, 359, 361–62, 366, 368; *Life of Saint Macrina*, 171–72; *On the Ascension of Christ*, 194; *On the Christian Mode of Life* (the *Hypotyposis*), xxvi; *On the Human Condition*, xxv; *On the Inscriptions of the Psalms*, xxiv, 10, 27, 67, 131–32, 133–34, 136, 179, 214, 220, 250; *On the Lord's Prayer*, xxiv, 28, 103, 122–23, 190, 211–12; *On the Making of Man* (the *Hexaemeron*), xxv, 68, 83, 117, 175, 176; *On Perfection*, xxvi, 81, 101, 298; *On the Six Days of Creation*, xxv; *On the Soul and Resurrection*, 53, 59, 64–65, 68, 69–70, 116, 234, 238, 249, 262, 349, 371; *On Virginity*, xvi, xxvi, 68, 90, 112–13, 145–46, 157–58, 251, 258, 262–63, 299, 314, 316; *On What It Means to Call Oneself a Christian*, xxvi
Gregory the Wonderworker (Thaumaturgus), xxvi, 27

Habbakuk, 105
Heart (*kardia*), 300, 302
Heaven, third, 177, 182, 229, 315

Hesiod, 76
Hoeschelius, David, xxviii

Iamblichus, 48
Ignatius of Antioch, 99
Ignorance (*agnoia*), 8
Illumination (*phōtismos*), 4, 10, 15, 20–1, 25, 273
Illusion, 135–40
Image (*eikōn*), 23, 31–32, 41–50, 102, 116, 118, 141, 145, 203, 223, 247–48, 255–56
Imitation, 102, 298
Immortality (*athanasia*), 45–46
Incarnation, 234
Incorruptibility (*aphtharsia*), 45–46, 50, 103–4
Inebriation, sober (*nēphalios methē*), 29, 222, 287, 290, 307, 313, 319, 320, 322, 323, 324–36
Innocent III, 22
Interiority, 203, 261
Isaac, 310
Isaiah, 76, 342–43

Jacob, 310
Jesus Christ, 18, 111, 123, 144, 281, 282, 292, 299, 315
John, Apostle, 346, 367
John of the Cross, 222, 223, 264, 272, 273
Joseph, 310
Joy, 288
Julian the Apostate, 48
Justice itself (*autodikaiosynē*), 105
Justin Martyr, 99

Kant, Immanuel, 142
Kierkegaard, Søren, 144
Kiss
  pleasurable, 338
  mystical, 8, 21, 22, 23, 24
"Know thyself" (*gnōthi seauton*), 34, 35
Knowledge (*gnōsis*), 131, 144, 149, 162–63, 166, 168
  apophatic, 165
  of God (*theognōsia*), 211, 219–21, 224
  mystical, 161, 163, 165, 232

symbolic, 161, 163
See also: Theology

Ladder, spiritual, 158, 347, 362
Life
    ascetic, 90, 91, 92–93, 111, 120
    mystical, 7, 9, 14, 91, 130, 144, 162, 204
    sacramental, 14
    the three ways of the spiritual, 130–31, 133, 146, 157, 245
    tree of, 262
Likeness (*homoiōsis*), 28, 41–42, 43, 105
Love
    as *agapē*, xviii, 9, 116, 144, 232–40, 241, 242, 243, 273, 359, 361, 371
    as *erōs*, xxiv, 116, 233, 238, 240–43, 308
    wound of, 336–44
Lucan (Marcus Annaeus Lucanus), 307

Macarius, Pseudo-, 337
Macedonians, xviii
Macrina the Elder, xvi
Macrina the Younger, xvi, 69, 179, 366, 371
Magic (*goēteia*), 138–39
Man
    the inner (*ho endon/esō anthrōpos*), 26, 37, 68, 300;
    as microcosm, 76
    the nature of, 55–57
Marcus Aurelius, 357
Marmion, Columba, 122
Marriage, 47
Mary Magdalene, 24, 197, 277
Maximus the Confessor, xviii, 280
Metamorphosis, 79, 81
Minotaur, 81
Monasticism, 27, 37, 203
Montanism, 307, 312, 319, 325
Montanus, 311
Mortality, 56
Moses, xx, xxii, 5, 19, 26, 27, 33, 37, 49, 75, 85–86, 91, 94, 95, 96, 98, 129, 162, 167, 208, 217, 221, 223, 224, 225, 267, 273, 296, 346, 354, 357–58, 359, 366–67, 368, 369, 371

Myrrh, symbol of, 269, 283, 300, 301, 340, 370
Mystagogy (*mystagōgia*), 9, 206, 210, 233
Mystery (*mystērion*), 205–11, 224, 291
Mysticism, Christian, 273, 290, 365

Nathanael, 367
Nature (*physis*), 41, 44, 101
Neoplatonism, 35, 36–37, 38, 261
Neo-ythagoreanism, 17
Nicholas of Cusa, 334
Night
    divine (*theia nyx*), 9, 228
    of the mind, 158, 159, 164
    of the senses, 158, 159
Nous (mind, or intellect), 33, 37, 61, 99, 201, 315–16

Observatory (*skopia*), 133–35, 164
Olympia, 366
Origen, xxii–xxiii, xxiv, 3–4, 11, 93, 94, 129, 130, 162, 163, 166, 168, 175, 182, 192, 219, 220, 232, 264–67, 272, 273, 274, 281, 289, 292–93, 294–95, 308, 311–12, 319, 320, 324, 325, 326–27, 337, 357, 368
Ousia: see Essence

Palamas, Gregory, xxiv, 154
Paradise
    as Garden of Eden, 114, 142, 262
    as heaven, 208, 209
Parrhēsia (freedom of speech, familiarity): see Freedom
Participation (*methexis, metousia*), 50, 102, 236–37, 240, 346, 347, 358
Passions (*pathē*), 16, 39–41, 57–86, 87, 202
    See also: Skin, garments of
Paul, Apostle, 18, 47, 49, 68, 71, 76, 101, 119, 176, 177, 182, 208–9, 229, 268, 269, 276, 281, 285, 304, 307, 312, 315, 322, 323, 332, 342, 344, 346, 354, 358, 362, 366, 370, 371
Perpetua, 336
Peter, Apostle, 206, 269, 309, 311, 323–24, 346, 370
Peter of Laodicaea, 17

General Index

Peter of Sebaste, xvi
Phaedrus, myth of the charioteer in, 65, 73, 75
Philip, Apostle, 367
Philo of Alexandria, xix, xx, 28, 42, 47, 53–54, 66, 75, 77, 175–76, 182, 205, 212, 222, 224, 264, 268, 282, 286, 309–11, 312, 315, 318–19, 324–25, 326, 332, 333, 357
Philosophy
    apophatic, 165
    in Gregory's understanding, 141–42, 165
    in the modern sense, 65
    in the monastic sense, 4, 35, 165
    practical, 167
Piety (*eusebeia*), 6
Plato, xix, 8, 22, 28, 59, 62–63, 65, 67, 68, 75, 84–85, 103, 105, 116, 131, 133, 151, 157, 162, 169, 174–75, 180, 181, 184, 186, 248, 249, 250, 261, 310, 331, 363
Platonism, xix, xx–xxi, 22, 39, 44, 47, 48, 60, 64, 73, 144, 151, 158, 165, 174, 175, 196, 233, 248
Plotinus, xix, xx, 27, 28, 29, 31, 33, 35, 36, 40, 54, 97, 98, 103, 105, 111, 138–39, 151, 158, 175, 176, 178, 182, 201, 205, 224, 248–49, 250, 251–52, 255, 264–65, 272, 310, 311, 319, 325, 331–32, 336
Pneuma (spirit), 99
    See also: Spirit, Holy
Pomegranate, symbolic image of, 93, 284
Porphyry, 311
Posidonius, 59, 64, 83
Prayer, 121–24, 170
Proclus, 54, 60–61
Progress (*prokopē*), 286, 346, 348, 361
Purification (*katharsis*), xx, xxi–xxii, 4, 40, 151, 172, 331–32
Purity (*katharotēs*), 43, 103–4, 253, 260

Religions, mystery, 205, 206
Resurrection, 47–48
Restoration (*apokatastasis*), 41, 49, 88, 115, 141, 195–96
Rufinus of Aquileia, 311
Revelation, 141

Sallustius, 173
Satan: see Adversary, the
Senses, spiritual, 261–97
Septuagint, 266, 314
Sexuality, 46–47, 52, 61
Shame (*aischynē*), 113–15
Sight, spiritual sense of, 273, 278–79
Sin, 74, 202
Sinai, Mount, 270, 310
Skin, garments of (*dermatinoi chitōnes*), 16, 17, 18, 39, 44, 51–57, 71, 72, 87, 112, 118, 145, 269–70
Slavery (*douleia*), 118–20
Sleep, 333–34, 335–36
Smell, spiritual sense of, 274–77
Soar, to (*meteōroporein*), xxi, 171, 174, 176, 347
Solitude (*idiazein, hēsychia*), 30–31, 33, 35, 37
    See also Monasticism
Solomon, 345
Sophistic, Second, 330
Soul, 8, 30
    beauty of, 251
    as mirror, 247, 253, 254, 256–58, 259, 260
    original unity of, 32
    powers of, 58, 61
    progress of, 70
    structure of, 66, 71
    See also: Interiority
Spinoza, Benedict de, xx
Spirit, Holy, 6, 8, 110, 202, 274, 341–42, 343
Stephen, protomartyr, 316–17
Stoicism, 63–64, 65, 98, 110, 116, 155, 157, 357
Symmachus, 266
Synergism, 13
Synesius of Cyrene, 61–62, 68

Taste, spiritual sense of, 280–88
Tauler, Joannes, 264
Temptation, 91
Teresa of Avila, 217, 263, 307, 344
Thecla, 370
Theodotion, 266
Theognōsia: see Knowledge of God
Theology
    apophatic, 149, 163

mystical, 25, 106, 151, 202, 219
   subject matter of, 151
   symbolic, 146, 147–49, 163, 164, 165
Therapeutae, 332
Theurgy, 205
Thomas Aquinas, 154
Transcendence, 316
Transformation, 298–99
Truth itself (*autoalētheia*), 105
Tyranny, 82, 84, 86

Ulysses, 80
Union, 235
   as *anakrasis*, xxii, xxiv, 5, 7, 12, 144, 236, 246
   as *henōsis*, 12, 25

Virginity (*parthenia*), 47–48, 61, 89, 90
Virtue (*aretē*), 105–11
Vision, beatific, 180

Ways, the three: see Life, the three ways of the spiritual
Will, free (*proairesis, to autexousion*), 60, 115–16
Wine, symbolism of, 285–86, 290–92, 293–94, 341
Wisdom itself (*autosophia*), 105
Withdrawal (*anachorēsis*), 6, 10, 11, 16, 26, 37, 203

Index of Modern Authors

d'Alès, A. 174
Amand de Mendieta, E., xxv
Arnou, R., xxi, 249
Athanasopoulos, C., xxiv
Azkoul, M., 196

Baghos, M., 196
Bardenhewer, O., xxv, 254
Bardy, G., 98
Barkley, G. W., 327
Bate, H. N., 167
Behr, J., xxvi, 56, 169, 265
Bettencourt, S., 94
Bidez, J., 48, 188
Bigg, C., 325
Boersma, H., xxvi
Bonwetsch, G. N., 51, 52, 53, 139, 168, 176
Botte, B., 19
Boulding, M., 179
Bousset, W., 309
Bouyer, L., 46
Bradshaw, D., 154
Bradshaw, P. F., 193
Bréhier, E., 91, 98, 310, 311, 332
Bremond, J., 95
Bromiley, G. W., 234, 357
Brooks, F., 83
Bucur, B., 25
Burrus, V., xxvi

Cabrol, F., 20
Callahan, V. W., xxi, xxvi, xxvii, 92, 258
Carcopino, J., 178
Carey, P., 179
Chadwick, H., 179, 264, 265
Cherniss, H. F., 39, 64, 175
Clark, E., xxvi
Cumont, F., 54, 188

Daley, B., 34
Daniélou, J., xvii, xxviii, 14, 15, 57, 172, 189, 194, 195, 196, 265, 282, 288, 334
De Catanzaro, C. J., xvii
Déchanet, J.-M., xix
Delatte, A., 357
DelCogliano, M., 4, 186
Denis, J. F., 175
Devreesse, R., 146
Diekamp, F., xv, 232, 249, 259
Dodd, C. H., 107
Dodds, E. R., 54
Dölger, F.-J., 15, 17, 22
Downes, A. H. C., xix
Duncan, E. J., 19

Eales, S. J., 40
Edwards, M., xviii
Eisler, R., 81
Elm, S., 95
Euringer, S., 369

Faye, E. de, 99, 168, 169, 311
Ferguson, E., xxiii, 6
Festugière, A.-J., xxi, 85, 97, 98, 105, 176, 205, 277
Fitzgerald, A., 62
Forbes, G. H., xxvii
Friedrich, G., 234

Gallop, D., 151
Gandillac, M. de, 333, 334
Giet, S., xxv, 95
Gilson, É., xix, 90, 116
Golitzin, A., 25
Graef, H. C., xxv, 24
Green, I., 11, 197
Greer, R. A., 120, 121
Gronau, K., 59, 65

Guitton, J., 330

Hall, S. G., xxiii et passim
Harrison, N. V., xxv, 13
Hart, M., xxvi
Hausherr, I., xvii, 273, 311
Heine, R. E., xxiv et passim
Heinemann, I., 83
Heinisch, P., 75
Henry, P., 179
Hibberd, W., 15
Hilt, F., 87
Holl, K., xxv, xxvii, 308, 315
Horn, G., xv, 223, 259
Hussey, J. M., 185

Jaeger, W., xxvi, xxvii
Jankélévitch, V., 139

Johnson, M. E., 193

Kittel, G., 234, 357
Klock, C., 313
Koch, H., xv, 205, 212, 223
Krabinger, J. G., 235

Labriolle, P., 311
Lawson, R. P., 4
Lebreton, J., 223
Leclercq, H., 20
Leisegang, J., 309
Lieske, A., xv, 12, 282, 297
Lewy, H., xv, 25, 286, 292, 293, 309, 311, 321, 323, 324, 325, 327, 328, 333
Lohmeyer, E. J., 264, 274
Lossky, V., 149, 154, 230–31, 315
Lot-Borodine, M., 20, 25, 44, 154
Loudovikos, N., xxiv
Lubac, H. de, 282
Lucà, S., 146
Ludlow, M., 195

McCambley, R., xxvii et passim
McDowell, J., 28
MacKenna, S., 28, 158
McNulty, P. A., 185

Malherbe, A., xxiii et passim
Marcus, R., 66
Maréchal, J., xv, 50, 231–32, 277
Marrou, H.-I., 95, 330
Maspero, G., 196
Mateo-Seco, L. F., 196
Mead, G. R. S., 16
Méridier, L., 171, 330, 334
Merki, H., 42
Mitchell, W., 57
Motia, M., xviii

Newman, J. H., 330
Nock, A. D., 29, 91, 142, 173
Norris, R. A., xxiii et passim
Nygren, A., 233, 238

Orton, R., xxv, 45, 73

Pallis, D., xviii
Palmer, G. E. H., 32
Paschali, G., xxvii
Pascher, J., 212, 309
Peers, E. A., 217
Pera, C., xviii
Peterson, E., 28, 111
Plested, M., xxvii
Poulain, A., 263, 295, 297, 327, 342
Prat, F., 187
Prümm, K., 205
Puech, H.-Ch., xv, xvii, xviii, 5, 139, 166, 218, 222, 223, 229, 231, 280, 309, 320

Radde-Gallwitz, A., 110, 186, 192
Rahner, H., 13, 299
Rahner, K., 4, 131, 148, 264, 267, 268, 272, 294
Ramelli, I. L. E., 196
Riedel, W., 274
Rimbaud, A., 197
Rodriguez, A., 269
Rotelle, J. E., 179

Salaville, S., 184
Schneider, C., xxiv
Schoeps, H. J., 357

Index of Modern Authors

Scholz, H., 280
Schuster, I., 333
Sebanc, M., xvii
Sherrard, P., 32
Showerman, G., 54
Silvas, A. M., 37
Slusser, M., xxvi, xvii, 26
Smets, A., xxv
Smith, L., 263
Soury, G., 96
Spira, A., 313
Srawley, J. H., 19
Steiris, G., xviii
Stewart-Sykes, A., 32
Stiglmayr, J., xv, 47
Stoddard, J. L., 187
Stolz, A., 76–77, 89, 122, 172, 178, 263, 268, 277, 295–96

Talley, T. J., 193
Taylor, T., 54, 62
Thompson, T., 19
Tonneau, R., 19

Van Esbroeck, M., xxv
Völker, W., xvi, 11, 168, 172, 175, 222, 240, 292, 299, 310, 311, 357
Von Arnim, H., 63
Von Balthasar, H. U., xvii, 182–84, 195, 259
Von Ivánka, E., xv, xxv, 36, 59, 83, 143, 181, 249, 253, 254, 255, 256, 261

Ware, K., 32
Waterfield, R., 8, 158
Watson, P. S., 233
Williams, A., 76
Williams, R., xxvi, 62
Willms, H., 42
Wilmart, A., xxvi
Wright, W. C., 188

Yonge, C. D., 16 *et passim*

Ziegler, J., xv, 264, 285
Zimmerman, O. J., 172

Index of Greek Words

ἀγάπη (*agapē*), xviii, 9, 43, 116, 121, 143, 144, 232, 233–41, 273
ἀγέννητος (*agennētos*), xviii
ἀγνοία (*agnoia*), 8
ἀγνωσία (*agnōsia*), 231
ἄδυτον (*adyton*), 5, 123, 211–19, 222, 224, 227
ἀθανασία (*athanasia*), 45–46
αἴσθησις (*aisthēsis*), 165, 204, 264, 266, 272, 273, 274, 275
αἰσθητήριον (*aisthētērion*), 283
ἀλλότριον (*allotrion*), 46, 248, 249, 252
ἀλλοτρίωσις (*allotriōsis*), 11, 309
ἀνάβασις (*anabasis*), 164, 347
ἀνακραθῆναι (*anakrathēnai*), 246, 317
ἀνάκρασις (*anakrasis*), xxiv, 4, 5, 7, 12, 14, 144, 233, 246
ἀναχώρησις (*anachōrēsis*), 5, 6, 11, 16, 26, 37, 203
ἄνθρωπος, ὁ ἔσω (or ἔνδον) (*anthrōpos, ho esō or endon*), 68, 300
ἀνυπόδητος (*anypodētos*), 19
ἀνυπόστατος (*anypostatos*), 135–36, 145
ἀόρατον (*aoraton*), 7
ἀπάθεια (*apatheia*), xvii, xxi, xxii, 6, 8, 11, 16, 33, 39, 40, 41, 43, 45, 70, 73–74, 87, 89, 97–104, 105, 107, 108–9, 110, 111, 112, 113, 120, 130, 164, 172, 203, 260
ἀπαθής (*apathēs*), xix, 45, 72, 98, 112
ἀπάτη (*apatē*), 134, 142
ἀποκατάστασις (*apokatastasis*), 41, 49, 88, 141
ἀπόρροια (*aporroia*), 45, 100, 102, 155, 298
ἀπόστασις (*apostasis*), 11
ἀποστῆναι (*apostēnai*), 7, 8
ἀρετή (*aretē*), 85, 89, 97, 105, 108–9, 275
ἀρχέτυπον (*archetypon*), 42, 43
ἀταραξία (*ataraxia*), 98, 99, 100

ἀτενίζειν, ἀτενῶς ἐνιδεῖν, ἐνατενείζειν (*atenizein, atenōs enidein, enatenizein*), 33, 35, 106, 259, 275
αὐτεξούσιος, τὸ αὐτεξούσιον (*autexousios, to autexousion*), 116, 117, 119
αὐτεξουσιότης (*autexousiotēs*), 117
ἀφαίρεσις (*aphairesis*), 60
ἀφθαρσία (*aphtharsia*), 45, 103, 104, 108
ἄφθαρτος (*aphthartos*), 50

βλέπειν (*blepein*), 301, 302

γεῦσις (*geusis*), 280
γνόφος (*gnophos*), xx, 5, 7, 147, 223–26, 307, 324
γνῶναι (*gnōnai*), 34
γνῶσις (*gnōsis*), 131, 144, 145, 151, 161, 165, 168, 232, 240, 266, 273
γοητεία (*goēteia*), 138

διάνοια (*dianoia*), 44, 67, 165, 302, 314–15, 316
δόξα (*doxa*), 16, 150, 151
δουλεία (*douleia*), 118, 119–20

ἐγκώμια (*enkōmia*), xxvii
ἐθική (*ethikē*), 4, 6
εἰκών (*eikōn*), 23, 31, 41, 42, 48, 69, 107, 141, 145, 247, 254, 255–56
ἐκβαίνειν (*ekbainein*), 152, 153, 312, 314
ἔκστασις (*ekstasis*), xvii, xxi, 14, 80, 307–14, 320, 322, 323, 324
ἐλευθερία (*eleutheria*), 116, 120, 125
ἐνοίκησις (*enoikēsis*), 227
ἕνωσις (*henōsis*), 12, 25
ἐξιστάναι (*existanai*), 312
ἔξοδος (*exodos*), 318
ἐπέκτασις (*epektasis*), 230, 305, 353, 359

ἐπεκτείνεσθαι (*epekteinesthai*), 304, 350, 351, 352, 354, 358
ἐπιθυμία (*epithymia*), 58, 61, 66
ἐπίνοιαι (*epinoiai*), 149, 156
ἐποπτική (*epoptikē*), 131
ἔρως (*erōs*), 116, 240–43
εὔδρομον (*eudromon*), 8
εὐφροσύνη (*euphrosynē*), 285, 286
εὐσέβεια (*eusebeia*), 6

ἡγεμονικόν (*hēgemonikon*), 27, 300, 302
ἡσυχία (*hēsychia*), 27, 33, 98, 310, 311

θεογνωσία (*theognōsia*), 5, 151, 219–21, 224
θεοειδής (*theoeidēs*), 31–32, 38, 63, 247, 250, 255, 256
θεωρία (*theōria*), xvii, xix, xxi, xxii, 5, 7, 11, 25, 26, 130, 131, 148, 150, 167–70, 172, 176, 177, 180, 181, 183, 184–85, 191–92, 197, 201, 203, 232, 233, 325
θεωρική (*theōrikē*), 4, 131, 163
θέωσις (*theōsis*), 25, 80
θυμός (*thymos*), 58, 59, 61, 66

ἰδιάζειν (*idiazein*), 26, 30
ἴλιγγος (*ilingos*), 142
ἱμάτια φωτεινά (*himatia phōteina*), 111
ἰσάγγελος (*isangelos*), 100, 187
ἱστορία (*historia*), 26

καθαρός (*katharos*), 256, 259
καθάρσιος (*katharsios*), 23
κάθαρσις (*katharsis*), xx, 4, 14, 38, 40, 151
καθαρότης (*katharotēs*), 43, 45, 100, 103, 104
κάλλος (*kallos*), 250–51, 256
κατανόησις (*katanoēsis*), 165, 166, 168
καταφρόνησις (*kataphronēsis*), 38, 135
κοινωνία (*koinōnia*), 12, 239, 240
κοινωνοί (*koinōnoi*), 123

λογισμοί (*logismoi*), 83
λόγος (*logos*), 38, 43, 44, 63

μακαριότης (*makariotēs*), 51, 55, 104
μέθεξις (*methexis*), 50

μέθη νηφάλιος (*methē nēphalios*), 29, 287, 313, 320, 323, 324
μεθόριος (*methorios*), 171, 176, 179
μετέχειν (*metechein*), 21, 50, 242, 347, 359
μετεωροπορεῖν (*meteōroporein*), xxi, 171, 174, 176, 347
μετεωροπόρος (*meteōroporos*), 171
μετουσία (*metousia*), 229, 239, 240, 260
μετριοπάθεια (*metriopatheia*), 98
μῆλον (*mēlon*), 8
μονοειδής (*monoeidēs*), 31, 32, 36, 61, 195
μόνος, μόνος μόνῳ, μόνος πρὸς μόνον (*monos, monos monō, monos pros monon*), 27, 28–9, 30, 37
μυσταγωγεῖν (*mystagōgein*), 5, 209, 210
μυσταγωγία (*mystagōgia*), 9, 233
μυστήριον (*mystērion*), 96, 205–11, 224, 288, 291
μυστικός, μυστικώτατος (*mystikos, mystikōtatos*), xvi, 8, 20, 25, 210

νεκρότης (*nekrotēs*), 14
νεφέλη (*nephelē*), 5, 14, 147
νῆψις (*nēpsis*), 324
νοητός (*noētos*), 157, 158, 167, 168, 169, 176, 180, 181, 182, 196
νοῦς (*nous*), 37, 43, 44, 63, 71, 118, 201, 241, 315–16, 319
νύξ, θεία (*nyx, theia*), 7, 9, 228

οἰκονομία (*oikonomia*), 12
ὁμοιοῦσθαι (*homoiousthai*), 105, 109
ὁμοίωσις (*homoiōsis*), 28, 41–42, 43, 104
ὁρμαί (*hormai*), 65
οὐσία (*ousia*), xviii, 106, 161, 201

πάθος, πάθη (*pathos, pathē*), 16, 39, 55, 59, 71–72, 73, 82, 87, 90, 111, 138, 241
παράνοια (*paranoia*), 309
παρθενία (*parthenia*), 47
παρρησία (*parrhēsia*), xxiv, 44, 84, 90, 111–25, 170, 240
πίστις (*pistis*), 165, 246, 303
πνεῦμα (*pneuma*), 38, 44, 71, 118
πρακτική (*praktikē*), 25
πρᾶξις (*praxis*), 167

Index of Greek Words

προαίρεσις (*proairesis*), 60, 115–16, 257
προκοπή (*prokopē*), 286, 346, 348, 361
προκόπτειν (*prokoptein*), 356, 358
προσευχή (*proseuchē*), 121, 123, 124
προσεχέστερος (*prosechesteros*), 5, 130

σκοπιά (*skopia*), 133, 134, 164
σκότος (*skotos*), 5
συγγένεια (*syngeneia*), 101, 123
συναφθῆναι (*synaphthēnai*), 249
συνεργός (*synergos*), 13
σχέσις (*schesis*), 129, 143

ὑπερουράνιος (*hyperouranios*), 217
ὑποκείμενον (*hypokeimenon*), 49
ὑπόστασις (*hypostasis*), 137

φαινόμενον (*phainomenon*), 6, 7, 8, 129, 139, 147, 148, 155, 158

φαντασία (*phantasia*), 9, 138, 165
φάντασμα (*phantasma*), 138
φίλημα, μυστικόν (*philēma, mystikon*), 7, 20, 21
φιλανθρωπία (*philanthrōpia*), 145
φιλία (*philia*), 120, 121, 143
φυγή (*phygē*), 28
φυσική (*physikē*), 4, 130–31
φύσις (*physis*), 48, 59, 145
φῶς (*phōs*), 5, 7, 20
φωτισμός (*phōtismos*), 4, 14, 15, 20, 25, 273
φωτοειδής (*phōtoeidēs*), 16, 52, 258

χαρακτήρ (*charactēr*), 109
χάρις (*charis*), 276, 322
χιτῶνες (*chitōnes*)
    δερμάτινοι (*dermatinoi*), 16, 17, 54, 55
    ἀφθαρσίας (*aphtharsias*), 53
ψυχή (*psychē*), 44

www.ingramcontent.com/pod-product-compliance
Lightning Source LLC
Chambersburg PA
CBHW051623230426
43669CB00013B/2156